Rajendra Prasad (1884–1963) was the first President of the Republic of India. An Independence activist and a prominent Gandhian, Rajendra Prasad was a close associate of Gandhi's from the time of the Champaran Satyagraha in 1916. Prasad was elected president of the Indian National Congress in 1934, and again in 1939. He served as president of the Constituent Assembly which drafted India's Constitution over 1948 and 1949. On 26 January 1950, Rajendra Prasad was sworn in as the first President of India. He remained in the post for twelve years, before resigning in 1962. He was also honoured with the Bharat Ratna that year.

BY THE SAME AUTHOR

Autobiography

INDIA
DIVIDED

RAJENDRA PRASAD

PENGUIN BOOKS

PENGUIN BOOKS

USA | Canada | UK | Ireland | Australia
New Zealand | India | South Africa | China

Penguin Books is part of the Penguin Random House group of companies
whose addresses can be found at global.penguinrandomhouse.com

Published by Penguin Random House India Pvt. Ltd
7th Floor, Infinity Tower C, DLF Cyber City,
Gurgaon 122 002, Haryana, India

Penguin
Random House
India

First published in 1946
Published by Penguin Books India 2010

ISBN 9780143414155

Typeset in Sabon by InoSoft Systems, Noida
Printed at Replika Press Pvt. Ltd, India

www.penguin.co.in

CONTENTS

LIST OF TABLES

The question of partition of India into Muslim and Hindu zones has assumed importance since the All-India Muslim League passed a resolution in its favour at Lahore in March 1940. Much has been written on it and a literature has grown round it. But I believe there is room for another book which tries to discuss the question in all its aspects. In *India Divided* I have made an attempt to collect in a compact form information and material likely to help the reader in forming an opinion of his own. I have expressed my own opinion on the basis of the material so collected but I believe I have placed the material apart from any conclusions I have drawn therefrom and it is open to the reader to ignore my conclusions and draw his own inferences, if he can.

The book is divided into six parts. Part I deals with the theory of Hindus and Muslims of India being two nations. While showing that the theory is as unsupported by history and facts of everyday life, as by the opinion of distinguished and representative Musalmans, it points out that even if it be assumed that the Musalmans are a separate nation, the solution of the Hindu–Muslim problem in India should, on the basis of experience of other countries and on the strength of the latest and most authoritative writers of international repute on the subject, be sought in the formation of a multinational State in which a powerful political union guarantees cultural autonomy to different national groups; and not in the creation of national States which will not only leave the problem of national minorities unsolved but will also create more new problems relating to questions— financial, economic, industrial and political, and military defence and strategy—than it will solve.

Part II discusses at length how the Hindu–Muslim problem has arisen and grown to its present proportions and how with the lengthening of the base of the communal triangle, the angle of difference between the communities has become wider and wider.

Part III gives the summary of a number of schemes of partition which have appeared.

Part IV points out the vagueness and ambiguity of the Lahore Resolution of the All-India Muslim League and the difficulty which faces anyone trying to consider it on its merits. It analyses the Resolution and, giving their natural meaning to the words used in the Resolution, it fixes the boundaries of Pakistan.

Part V deals with the resources of the Muslim States and shows how the scheme of partition is impracticable.

Part VI gives various proposals put forward by persons or bodies for solving the Hindu–Muslim problem.

Parts I, III, IV, V and VI of the book were written in the Bankipur jail and during intervals of comparatively good health. They, therefore, naturally bear the inevitable marks of work done under some limitations. Since my release I have been able to find time to write Part II—but none to revise the portion written previously. The difficulty of getting books in jail was removed to a considerable extent by the kindness of Dr Sachchidananda Sinha who freely allowed books to be lent out of the Sinha Library and of Sir Rajiva Ranjan Prasad Sinha, President of the Bihar Legislative Council, who lent some books from the Library of the Bihar Legislature. Shri Shanti Kumar Morarji of Bombay supplied me with a number of books and some statistics. My thanks are due to all these gentlemen. I am thankful to Shri K.T. Shah of Bombay and Professor Balkrishna of the Birla College, Pilani, for some valuable suggestions and to the Birla College for a free use of its library. Typed copy of the portion written in jail was prepared there and my thanks are due to Shri M. John, Secretary, Tata Workers' Union, Jamshedpur, for making the typed copy, and to Shris S.H. Razi, M.D. Madan and M.K. Ghosh for comparing the typed copy. I am grateful to the Government of Bihar for permitting Shri John to prepare the typed copy. Shri M.K. Ghosh of the Tata Research Laboratory, Jamshedpur, kindly checked the figures and prepared the graphs and I owe him a debt of thanks. My thanks are due also to Shri Mathura Prasad and to Shri Chakradhar Sharan for help of various kinds in preparing Part II and for seeing the book through the press.

I have acknowledged my indebtedness wherever I have taken any statement or quotation from others.

Sadaqat Ashram,   Rajendra Prasad
Dighaghat, Patna,
15 December 1945

PART I

THE TWO NATIONS THEORY

ONE

~

TWO NATIONS—BASIS OF PAKISTAN

The proposal to divide India into separate Muslim and non-Muslim zones, each such zone being constituted into an independent sovereign state, is based on the theory that Hindus and Musalmans constitute two separate nations. 'Musalmans are a nation,' said Mr M.A. Jinnah in his presidential address at the Lahore session of the Muslim League, which adopted a resolution favouring such division, 'according to any definition of a nation, and they must have their homelands, their territory and their state.'[1] 'It is extremely difficult to appreciate why our Hindu friends fail to understand the real nature of Islam and Hinduism. They are not religions in the strict sense of the word, but are, in fact, different and distinct social orders, and it is a dream that the Hindus and Muslims can ever evolve a common nationality, and this misconception of one Indian Nation has gone far beyond the limits and is the cause of most of our troubles and will lead India to destruction if we fail to revise our notions in time. The Hindus and Muslims belong to two different religious philosophies, social customs, literatures. They neither intermarry nor interdine together, and, indeed, they belong to two different civilizations which are based mainly on conflicting ideas and conceptions. Their aspects on life and of life are different. It is quite clear that Hindus and Musalmans derive their inspiration from different sources of history. They have different epics, different heroes, and different episodes. Very often the hero of one is a foe of the other and, likewise, their victories and defeats overlap. To yoke together two such nations under a single state, one as a numerical minority and the other as a majority, must lead to growing discontent and final destruction of any fabric that may be so built up for the government of such a state.'[2]

[1] *Recent Speeches and Writings of Mr Jinnah*, p. 155.
[2] Ibid., p. 153.

'A Punjabi' who has written a book named *Confederacy of India* has based his thesis on the same theory: 'From our previous discussions we find that the Hindus and Muslims are two absolutely different entities. Their civilizations are pronouncedly individualistic, and although they may have influenced each other, yet they cannot suffer absorption into each other. Their habits and customs, social systems, moral codes, religious, political and cultural ideas, traditions, languages, literature, art and outlook on life are absolutely different from, nay hostile to, one another. These heterogeneous essentials of their respective lives are not the elements which go to the formation of a single nation. They always create mutual distrust and misunderstanding. The basic differences between the communities, the memories of their past and present rivalries, and the wrongs they registered against each other during the last one thousand years form an unbridgeable gulf between them. As we have already observed the only thing common between them for the last few centuries has been the common yoke of a foreign rule. As soon as the cord which binds them in a common allegiance to a foreign state snaps, they will disintegrate and their mutual differences, which are not felt at present as acutely as they should, will show themselves more glaringly.'[3]

Professors Syed Zafrul Hasan and Mohamad Afzal Husain Qadri of Aligarh, who have written a pamphlet in which they have worked out a scheme of division of India, are not less emphatic than 'A Punjabi'. They say: 'Its [of the Government of India Act of 1935] fundamental fault is that it does not recognize the undeniable fact that the Muslims of India are a nation distinct from Hindus, vitally opposed to the latter in their outlook and aspirations and incapable of being merged into any other so-called nation, Hindu or non-Hindu.' Again: 'We are convinced that we, the Muslims of India, must insist persistently and strenuously on—among other things—that the Muslims of India are a nation by themselves. They have a distinct national entity wholly different from the Hindus and other non-Muslim groups. Indeed, they are more different from the Hindus than the Südeten Germans were from the Czechs.'

El Hamza has written a book *Pakistan—A Nation* for the purpose of showing (1) that India is not one country but several

---

[3] 'A Punjabi', *Confederacy of India*, pp. 150–51.

countries, with widely different human environments, and (2) that the diversity of race and culture of its inhabitants is so great that they cannot be regarded as one nation (in the modern political sense of the word 'nation') but must be considered as belonging to several nations.[4] In showing these differences he has become rapturous, idyllic:' Hinduism is of the monsoon as Islam is of the desert.'[5] 'Probably the individuality of the North-West is indicated by no other single fact in so striking a manner as by the distribution of camels over India.'[6] 'Our associations with the camel in different directions of thought—geographical, historical and philosophic—are so multitudinous that the history of an epoch in the evolution of civilization can be read in their light. The camel may be taken as the symbol of that great transformation in the historical process which, proceeding from south-western Asia as a spontaneous race-urge, took in its sweep all the known world. Living several hundred years after, we see the brilliant colours of Arab greatness in distant and blurred magnificence; and throughout this pageant of centuries the caravans of conquest move on camels' backs against a background of Simoom-blown sands. The days of Arab greatness are past, but the camel is still the associate of man in a world distinct in its arid vastness and the essential uniformity of religion and culture of its inhabitants. The land of the camel is still the land of scimitars and tambourines, mosques and muezzins, and domes and minarets.'[7] Only, the writer does not appear to appreciate the incongruity of argument based on the camel and such-like things for separation of the north-western region, which has its camels in common with Arabia no less than with another part of India like Rajputana, which is not 'the land of scimitars and tambourines, mosques and muezzins and domes and minarets'. If this argument were to prevail, there should be no ground for the separation of the eastern zone which is tropical in its fauna and flora, its green fields and prolonged and terrific monsoon. Nor should there be any Muslims in the other tropical countries like the Malaya Peninsula.

[4] Pakistan—A Nation, El. Hamza, p. 7.
[5] Ibid., p. 45.
[6] Ibid., p. 70.
[7] Hamza, *Pakistan*, p. 72.

The weakness of the argument in favour of a north-western Pakistan based on the topographical diversity and such-like things has not been missed by Mr F.K. Khan Durrani who in his book *The Meaning of Pakistan* holds that 'All Muslims, whether they live in Pakistan or Hindustan, constitute one nation, and we of Pakistan must always treat our co-religionists in Hindustan as flesh of our flesh and blood of our blood.'[8]

Dealing with the argument of El Hamza he writes: 'The author of *Pakistan—A Nation* bases his whole argument on the geographical peculiarities that distinguish the north-western provinces, the Punjab, Kashmir, the NWFP, Sind and Baluchistan, from the rest of India. Some provinces get heavier rains than do the others. The staple food of some provinces is wheat; of others rice. Vegetation in the lands of the monsoon is rank and lush; in others it is scanty. The flora and fauna of the provinces differ considerably. The dry lands of the North-West are the natural home of the camel, while the wet lands of the South and Assam and Bengal produce the unwieldy elephant. The dry lands of the North-West have given birth to a racial type which in many respects is different from the softer and darker types met with elsewhere. In a large country like India, inhabited as it is by peoples of many races, enclosed within many degrees of latitude and longitude, and exposed to a variety of influences of sea, mountain and desert, such diversities of peoples and produce are natural and unavoidable, and to the politics of Muslim India they are wholly irrelevant; for were we to follow this line of argument, we of the North-West will have of necessity to wash our hands of the larger portion of the Muslim population of India who live in lands other than those of Pakistan, dress differently and eat food which is not exactly the same as ours. We would have to treat them as aliens, with whom we can have no community of life or interests, a proposition which no Muslim of Pakistan would care to maintain even for a minute, which in fact every Muslim of the Punjab would dismiss forthwith as thinkable.'[9]

To prove the thesis, others—notably Dr B.R. Ambedkar in his book *Thoughts on Pakistan*—have taken pains to collect together passages from books on history to show how Muslim invaders and

[8] F.K. Khan Durrani *The Meaning of Pakistan*, p. viii.
[9] Durrani, *The Meaning of Pakistan*, pp. 1–2.

rulers of India desecrated and destroyed thousands of Hindu temples and broke into pieces images installed in them and converted them into mosques or removed their building materials like posts and pillars to be used in the construction of Muslim mosques in other places; how they offered to Hindus who came under their sway the alternative of the sword or the Quran and how thousands of Hindus were tortured or slaughtered on their refusal to accept the Muslim faith. The inference that is drawn is that the Hindus have not forgotten and cannot forget these atrocities and they have indelible marks burnt on their memory which cannot be obliterated. It is further asserted that Hindu–Muslim riots due to some minor cause—such as music before a mosque or the sacrifice of a cow—give further point to the argument that the old hostility persists, and common subjection to the British, and a strong rule by the latter have not succeeded in bringing about a reconciliation between the two communities.

Now, it is somewhat difficult to understand this line of argument for carving out portions of India to be placed under Muslim rule, which after all, is the subject of those who advocate such division of India into Hindu and Muslim zones.

Is it suggested that Islam sanctioned and encouraged those acts of sacrilege and vandalism—sacrilege from the point of view of the non-Muslim and vandalism from the point of view of art? If it sanctioned and justified those acts, then can it be said that it has ceased to sanction and encourage such acts? What evidence is there that there has been a change in the attitude of Islam in these respects? If they were acts of barbarity done by ambitious men professing Islam who took cover under Islam in pursuit of their aim, which had nothing to do with the faith of the Prophet of Arabia; what chance or expectation is there that people professing Islam will not arise in the future with similar ambitions and will not utilize the power that they will enjoy in the same way? Is it suggested that Muslim rule should be established in the segregated portions so that the same atrocities may be committed and perpetuated on those non-Muslims who may have the misfortune to be left there? If that is so, then none should expect a non-Muslim to be a party to any such scheme.

If all that is not the teaching of Islam and is in fact opposed to its fundamental tenets of peace and tolerance, is it desirable to rake up old history and place those instances before the Muslims and non-Muslims today? Can it be done without reviving bitter memories, which had better be forgotten for the good of all—for the sake of Muslims as a shameful chapter in the history of Musalmans who defiled their faith by such acts in the name of Islam when it did not sanction or justify them and when they committed them for their own aggrandizement and not for the propagation of Islam, which depended and depends upon purer and nobler methods for its propagation; and for the sake of non-Muslims so that the nightmare of a religion, which can perpetrate such atrocities for its propagation, may be lifted and the era of goodwill and reconciliation may continue and prosper?

If what is sought to be made out by such quotations is even partially accepted by Muslims and non-Muslims as a part of Muslim rule, then Muslims have to acquire the right to perpetrate and perpetuate them by the same methods by which those who perpetrated them in the past acquired the power to do so. The same sources which furnish these instances and quotations will also show that the Muslims of those days never got that right or power by agreement or consent of their non-Muslim contemporaries. If the passage of centuries and all that has happened in the world during these centuries and world conditions of today have not brought about any change in the attitude of Muslims of India towards the non-Muslims of India and vice versa, why should it be expected that the non-Muslims should change in this one respect and agree to the perpetration of wrongs and atrocities, which are condemned by all civilized persons all the world over, including the Muslims of India? Either such acts are a part of Islamic law and faith or they are not. If they are, no non-Muslim can agree to anything which gives the least opening for their repetition by the establishment of an 'ideal Islamic state with the ultimate ideal of a world revolution on purely Islamic lines'[10]—an Islamic state which on the assumptions made above is *ex hypothesi* out to repeat its history as disclosed in such quotations. If they are not, no useful purpose is served by reviving their memory. They can only further exacerbate the feelings of non-Muslims, and whether one approves of a division or not, further exacerbation of feelings can hardly be the object of any one. If it is intended to show that Hindus and Muslims cannot on account of such dealings in the

[10] A Punjabi, *Confederacy of India*, pp. 269–70.

past agree to live together and must therefore agree to separate, it is worthwhile remembering that just the opposite effect may be produced. The Hindus may not agree for this very reason to leave millions of their co-religionists in the Muslim area for a repetition of the same deeds against them. Such citations and quotations have thus no value or use in considering the question in a practical way.

Now, the object or utility of such quotations apart, it does not require much industry or acumen to cull together such passages from dry-as-dust books written in the distant past or modern times. Books on history until recently dealt commonly and very largely only with kings and conquerors, their doings and misdoings, their wars and victories, the magnificence of their courts and the intrigues of their palaces. Not much attention was paid by the writers of these books to the common man, who was content to lead his humdrum life in a quiet and peaceful manner, earning his livelihood by the sweat of his brow either in the field with his plough and spade, or in his home with his spinning wheel and loom or adze and chisel or sickle and hammer or needle and thread, and a host of other instruments used in cottages in small industries. The lives and doings of priests and pious men, of savants and sages, of learned men and social reformers, poets and philosophers, painters and musicians, have not been given the importance they deserve in the life history of a people. The writers of such books have been not a little influenced by a false notion that the religious zeal of a Muslim king or conqueror could be proved only by such deeds against *kafirs* and they owed a duty to these kings and conquerors—whose courtiers they used to be in most cases—and to Islam, to record such incidents with circumstantial details to serve as examples to other rulers to follow and to the conquered people to be frightened by. One need not discount the incidents that are related as exaggerated or false. Only, one must remember that such incidents were not the only incidents worth recording; and if an equally detailed account of other incidents showing how Hindus and Muslims lived together sharing one another's sorrows and joys for hundreds of years, how the saints and sadhus of each influenced and moulded the customs and rites, the lives and environment of the other, how the rites and festivities observed in many Muslim houses in connection with births and marriages tally with those observed in Hindu homes, how the same rites and customs differ among Muslims living in different provinces of India as much as they differ among the Hindus, how it was Muslim saints to whom the credit for conversion of large numbers of Hindus should go more than to the fire and sword of the Muslim conquerors and kings, the space occupied by such accounts would be infinitely more than that taken up by the accounts of the oppression and tyranny of the Muslim kings and conquerors. The number of pages taken in writing such a history would bear the same proportion to the pages occupied by the books from which quotations are made and on which textbooks on history are based, as the common people of the country bear to the number of kings and their courtiers, their generals and governors, their harems and their palaces. It bears the same proportion as the days of peaceful life and deeds of goodwill and charity, fellow-feeling and tolerance bear to those of strife and conflict, of riots and hooliganism, of murder, arson and loot committed by members of the one community against those of the other. And yet even today the space occupied in newspapers by the latter is out of all proportion as compared with that of the former; and if one were to write a history after 500 years, based on such newspaper reports or to quote only these reports, one could easily prove on their basis that there was hardly a day of peace in India even during the prevalence of the Pax Britannica. For comparative lack of appropriate material it is, therefore, not easy to write a complete and comprehensive book dealing with social and cultural movements, their deep and abiding effects on the life, and their intangible and invisible moulding of the make-up, of the people concerned.

TWO

NATIONALITY AND STATE

Since the demand for the establishment of separate and independent Muslim states in the north-west and east of India is based on the theory that Muslims constitute a separate nation—separate from the Hindus and all others who inhabit the geographical entity we call India, it is necessary to understand clearly what is meant by a nation. The fact of geographical unity of India cannot be denied, for the simple reason that the geography cannot be altered by man. Indeed Mr FK. Khan Durrani says distinctly. 'I agree on the contrary, with Dr Beni Prasad, that "there is no country marked out by the sea and the mountains so clearly to be a single whole as India." From the Suleman Range to the hills of Assam and from the Himalayas to the sea, in spite of all its variety of races, climes and topographical details, India is one geographical unity.'[1]

What then is a nation? What constitutes a nation? The question has been posed and answered by the supporters of the scheme for Partition, and learned authors have been quoted in support of the answer given. Mr Durrani, who has dealt with the point at great length, comes to some conclusions worthwhile recording:

'(I)   Though geographically India is one unity, its people are not, and in the making of states and nations it is the people that count and not geography . . . The living spirit of man cannot be enslaved, in the words of Renan, "by the course of rivers or the direction of mountain ranges". "The land," says Renan, "provides a substratum, the field of battle and work; man provides the soul: man is everything in the formation of that sacred thing which is called a people. Nothing of material nature suffices for it . . .'

[1]   F.K. Khan Durrani, *The Meaning of Pakistan* p. 2.

(2)   In fact, race too, like geography is not a determining factor
        either for or against the formation of nations . . .

(3)   Hindu leaders have been propagating the idea for two
        decades that religion should not be mixed with politics,
        and that a united nation should be formed on the basis
        of politics alone. Now is it possible to create a nation on
        the basis of politics alone? Political philosophers think
        that purely political ties do not suffice to create a nation'.[2]
        He quotes Lord Bryce and Professor Sidgwick in support
        of his thesis. Sidgwick writes: 'A political society is in
        an unsatisfactory and comparatively unstable condition
        when its members have no consciousness of any bond
        of unity among them except their obedience to the same
        government. Such a society is lacking in the cohesive force
        required to resist the disorganizing shocks and jars which
        foreign wars and discontents are likely to cause from time
        to time. Accordingly, we recognize that it is desirable that
        the members of a state should be united by the further
        bonds vaguely implied in the term "Nation".[3] Further,
        Sidgwick writes: 'What is really essential to the modern
        conception of a state which is also a Nation is merely that
        the persons composing it should have, generally speaking, a
        consciousness of belonging to one another, of being members
        of one body, over and above what they derive from the fact
        of being under one government, so that, if their government
        were destroyed by war or revolution, they would still tend
        to hold firmly together. When they have this consciousness,
        we regard them as forming a "Nation", whatever else
        they lack.'[4] Again, Lord Bryce defines nationality as 'an
        aggregate of men drawn together and linked together by
        certain sentiments', and says: 'The chief among these are
        Racial sentiment and Religious sentiment, but there is also
        that sense of community which is created by the use of a
        common language, the possession of a common literature,
        the recollection of common achievements or sufferings in
        the past, the existence of common customs and habits of

[2] Durrani, *The Meaning of Pakistan*, pp. 4–6.
[3] Ibid., p. 7.
[4] Ibid., p. 9.

thought, common ideals and aspirations. Sometimes all these linking sentiments are present and hold the members of the aggregate together; sometimes one or more may be absent. The more of these links that exist in any given case, the stronger is the sentiment of unity. In each case, the test is not merely how many links there are, but how strong each particular link is.'[5] After quoting some others, Mr Durrani comes to the conclusion that 'nationality is in fact a matter of consciousness only, a mere psychological condition,'[6] and in this he is supported by Dr Ambedkar whom he quotes: 'It is a feeling of consciousness of a kind which on the one hand binds together those who have it so strongly that it overrides all differences arising out of economic conflicts or social gradations, and, on the other severs them from those who are not of their kind.'[7]

The final conclusion of Mr Durrani, therefore, is:

'(4)   There is absolutely no group-consciousness or consciousness of kind between the Hindus and the Muslims. They cannot sit together at the same dining table; they cannot intermarry. The food of one is abomination to the other. The Hindu gets even polluted by the Musalman's touch. There are no social contacts between them to make possible the birth of a common group-consciousness. It is, indeed, psychologically impossible for the two groups to combine to form a single united whole.'[8]

Now this conception of nationality is comparatively speaking a modern and recent conception which has been developed during the last two or at the most three centuries or so. While the elements mentioned by Lord Bryce or Professor Sidgwick are found more or less in all these groups, which are regarded as constituting a nation, it is not correct to take each item by itself and see whether, and to what extent, it is present in any particular group and determine therefrom whether that particular group can be called a nation. It is the resultant of the totality of these various elements

[5]   Durrani, *The Meaning of Pakistan*, p. 8.
[6]   Ibid., p. 11.
[7]   Ibid., p. 12.
[8]   Ibid., p. 13.

acting and reacting upon one another, and the historical setting in which they have so acted and reacted that determines nationality. As Stalin has pointed out, 'a nation is primarily a community, a definite community of people which is not necessarily racial or tribal'. It is not also a casual or ephemeral conglomeration but a 'stable community of people'. A common language is one of the characteristic features of a nation. And so is also a common territory another characteristic feature of a nation. Community of economic life— economic cohesion—is one more characteristic feature. Apart from these a nation has its own specific spiritual complexion, its own psychological make-up—or what is otherwise called national character—which manifests itself in a distinctive culture. 'A nation' according to Stalin 'is a historically evolved, stable community of language, territory, economic life, and psychological make-up manifested in a community of culture.'[9]

We must also draw a distinction between a State and a nation. They are not always conterminous and we have had in the past and have got in the present living examples of multinational States or States comprising more than one nation. Thus the English and the French in Canada, although belonging to two different national groups, constitute one state. The English and the Boers of South Africa, after a bloody war/by agreement constituted one State. In the United States of America, people belonging to many nationalities have settled down as members of one State. The Soviet Republic of Russia comprises many nationalities which enjoy administrative autonomy and have the right to secede from the Union guaranteed by the Constitution. The administrative autonomy of the constituent republics now extends as far as the maintenance of their own armed forces and the right to enter into direct relations with foreign States, conclude agreements with them, and exchange diplomatic and consular representatives. The Swiss furnish the classical illustration of peoples bearing national affinity to three nations by whom they are surrounded—the French, the German and the Italian—and yet constituting one single State. 'It is more accurate to say that the word nationality can refer to either one of two sentiments,' says C. A. Macartney,[10] 'which in their origin and their essence are absolutely distinct, although in

[9] J. Stalin, *Marxism and the Question of Nationalities*, p. 6.
[10] C.A. Macartney, *National States and National Minorities*.

practice the one commonly identifies itself with the other. It is unfortunate that the accident of historical development in England has tended to make them in fact almost identical in that country, and the English language, reflecting the slovenly realism of its users, makes do with one term for the two. Nevertheless, nationality, meaning the feeling of appurtenance to a *nation,* is fundamentally different from nationality in the sense of membership of a State. They spring from different causes; and it is perfectly possible for them to be directed towards different objects.

'The former, which may for convenience be called the sense of personal nationality, is founded on characteristics which are personal, often inherited, and usually objective. These characteristics exist in the individual quite independently of the locality in which he may be domiciled, whether the majority of the inhabitants share them or no, and independently of the political regime under which he may live, whether this be in the hands of persons possessing the same characteristics or no. The body of persons possessing these characteristics constitutes the nation.[11] The characteristics on which this consciousness is based vary greatly, but broadly speaking, they are covered by the *trinity of the Minority Treaties: race, language and religion.* In themselves, it must be repeated, they are absolutely devoid of political significance. A German of Austria, Czechoslovakia/Brazil, or Honolulu is every bit as much a German as is a citizen of Berlin.

'Entirely different in its basis and true purpose is the State. The State is the organ by means of which the common affairs of a number of people are administered and (usually) protected; the people who collectively compose the State being, unfortunately, known in England by the same name "nation" as is also applied to the quite different natural unit discussed above. The extent to which their affairs are regarded as being of common concern, and thus falling within the competence of the State to regulate, varies enormously, not only from age to age but also from country to country. In some cases it goes hardly beyond defence; in others it covers most aspects of life beyond purely private relationships. It is, however, worth remarking that those cultural attributes which go to make up the idea of personal nationality are among the very last to which most States have turned their attention and that

[11] Ibid., p. 6.

even today they are largely considered as being no matter for State
control . . . On the other hand, most of the duties performed by
the State are entirely unrelated to questions of personal nationality.
The defence of the common home, the maintenance of public
order, the prevention and punishment of crime, the construction of
communications, the preservation of the public wealth, the equal
imposition and collection of taxes, are matters of equal concern
to every inhabitant of the State, whether he acknowledges Christ
or Mahomet, whether his mother-tongue be English, Welsh or
Yiddish. All must contribute towards these political and social
activities which are the true functions of the State, and all alike
benefit from them.'[12]

Thus while personal nationality is an important factor in the
formation of a State, it is not always the sole or even the dominant
factor. On the other hand, while it may be conceded that purely
political ties do not suffice to create a nation, it cannot be denied
that they do constitute an important factor. If a group is subject
to external pressure, then that 'pressure from without', in the
words of Julian Huxley, 'is probably the largest single factor in
the process of national evolution.' So it has happened in India—
but of this later.

The question of national States has been subjected to intensive
study since the end of the First World War and much literature has
grown round it. This study has been pursued after the publication
in 1934 of C.A. Macartney's authoritative book from which I have
quoted at length in the preceding pages. The result of all this study
has been to confirm the conclusions he arrived at, namely, that
a distinction should be made between personal nationality and
political nationality, that a State need not be conterminous with a
nationality, that in fact the attempt to establish national States has
ended in failure and created new problems, that the experience of
national States and their treatment of national minorities within
them has not been happy or encouraging, that the guarantee even
of the League of Nations for enforcing the Minority Treaties against
national States has proved, in many cases, ineffective and futile,
that the solution of the question of minorities does not lie in the
direction of establishing national States, which is impossible of
attainment on account of the impossibility of getting a completely

[12] Macartney, *National States* . . ., pp. 11–12.

homogeneous State eliminating all heterogeneous minorities and
that the solution should be sought in a multinational State, which
allows freedom for all national minorities to develop their special
personal nationality.

Friedmann points out that nationalism and the modern State are
two forces neither identical nor necessarily parallel or allied.[13] His
conclusion is: 'What this brief survey has attempted to demonstrate
is the inherent self-contradiction of the ideal of the sovereign State
based on national self-determination, and the impossibility of a
satisfactory solution as long as the sovereign national state remains
the ultimate standard of value. It seems that all serious students
of the problem agree on this point. After a searching study of the
problem, Macartney commends, on the basis of the experience
of Soviet Russia and Great Britain, the multinational State.'[14] He
quotes with approval from *The Future of Nations* by Professor
Carr, p. 49: 'The existence of a more or less homogeneous racial
or linguistic group bound together by a common tradition and the
cultivation of a common culture must cease to provide a prima
facie case for the setting up or maintenance of an independent
political unit,'[15] and from *Europe, Russia and the Future* by D.H.
Cole, p. 14: 'But nationalities can no longer in this twentieth
century provide a basis for the State.'[16]

His further conclusion is that the national State, particularly
if it happens to be a small State, is impossible under the present
technical and mechanical development in the world. It is impossible
for such a State to defend itself against aggression, even if it is able
to provide more or less adequately for the necessities of life within
its borders. 'But modern defence implies much more than that. It
implies the comprehensiveness of resources and reserves in men and
materials, which has greatly accentuated the inequality between big
powers and small national States.[17] He summarizes his conclusion
thus: 'The analysis has revealed that the predominant trend of the
political, economic and social forces of today leads away from
the national State . . . The alliance between Nationalism and the

[13] W. Friedmann, *The Crisis of the National State* (1943), p. 9.
[14] Ibid., p. 40.
[15] Ibid., p. 133.
[16] Ibid., p. 9.
[17] Ibid., p. 140.

State reaches a crisis when both Nationalism and the modern State begin to overreach themselves . . . An alternative solution of the dilemma of national self-determination is the national State in which a powerful political union guarantees cultural autonomy to different national groups, but demands the sacrifice of political, military and economic sovereignty.'[18]

Mr A. Cobban's study on national self-determination was issued in 1945 under the auspices of the Royal Institute of International Affairs. His conclusions are the same as those of Macartney and Friedmann quoted above, as the following extract from his book will show: 'The nation as a political unit, or State, is a utilitarian organization, framed by political ingenuity for the achievement of political, with which may be included economic, ends. Politics is the realm of expediency, and the measure of its success is the degree to which the material bases of the good life—law and order, peace and economic welfare—are realized. The nation as a cultural conception, on the contrary, is normally regarded as a good thing in itself, a basic fact, an inescapable datum of human life. It belongs to the realm of the activity of the human spirit, its achievements are in the field of art and literature, philosophy and religion . . . The distinctness of the ends proposed for the two developments which both, unfortunately, are described by the same word nation, is fundamental. That this is not merely a theoretical differentiation can easily be shown.'[19] He cites the example of the French and British Canadians having a common political nationality without abandoning their personal nationality and of the various States of Spanish America that have the same cultural background but are divided into a number of separate political states. 'Many other illustrations of the failure of cultural and political nationality to coincide might be found, and where the attempt has been made in modern times, to force them both into the same mould, the result has usually been disaster.'[20]

He further points out that nationality as a criterion of statehood furnishes only a variable standard inasmuch as nationality varies from period to period, from country to country and even from individual to individual. It also implies homogeneity in the

[18] Friedmann, *The Crisis of the National State*, pp. 163–64.
[19] A. Cobban, *National Self-determination*, p. 60.
[20] Ibid., p. 60.

population of the State which is patently not true, as the world cannot be divided into homogeneous divisions of the human race. His final conclusion is: 'In the Old World where a *tabula rasa* cannot be made of the pre-existing complex of cultural nations and political states, there is an evident necessity of abandoning the belief that the Nation-State is the one and only model for a sound political community. The multinational State must re-enter the political canon from which, as Actoli many years ago declared, it should never have been expelled . . . The history of the recent past, as well as of the last century is far from teaching the necessary identity of the political state and the nation in any other sense. We found ourselves indeed forced to the conclusion that in most cases they cannot possibly be made to coincide . . . The attempt to make the culturally united Nation-State the one and only basis of legitimate political organization has proved untenable in practice. It was never tenable in theory.'[21]

The confusion that has arisen between the two distinct entities, nation and State, is due to the setting up of national self-determination as an absolute dogma according to which every cultural group *ipso facto* is entitled to claim a separate independent State for itself. But it cannot be denied that there can be no such absolute principle and that national self-determination is just as limited as the freedom allowed to an individual in a society by various considerations.

'In short,' asks Cobban, 'are there not geographical, historical, economic, and political considerations which rule out national self-determination in the form of the sovereign State for many of the smaller nationalities of the world? Even if the majority of members of a nation desire political independence, circumstances may prohibit it, and the mere desire, of however many people, will not alter them. In the words of Burke "If we cry like children for the moon, like children we must cry on."'[22]

I may add that all these considerations prohibit any partition of India, particularly because it is impossible to draw any boundary line separating the partitioned states without leaving at least as large a minority in the partitioned Muslim states as the Muslims constitute in the whole of India. The economic and military

[21] Cobban, National self-determination, pp. 62–63.
[22] Ibid., p. 74.

conditions of India dictate its continuance as a large political State and forbid its break-up into smaller independent national units. Secession is a work of destruction and can be justified not as the first but as the last step in an extreme case when all else has failed. Even if that condition has been reached in India—and no group except the Muslim League has asserted anything approaching such an extreme proposition—separation of any particular area will not solve the problem as there will be no less than 200 or 300 lakhs of Muslims left in Hindu India and no less than 479 or 196 lakhs of non-Muslims left in the Muslim states according as areas with non-Muslim majorities are included in or excluded from the Muslim state as shown later on. We must, therefore, think of a solution which is in keeping with modern thought, which does not cut across the history of centuries, which does not fly in the face of geography, which does not make the defence of the country infinitely more difficult if not impossible in the present-day conditions of the world, which does not place a burden on the separated states that they will not be able to bear, which does not condemn in its result the common man in the new states to a life of misery and squalor for an indefinite period, which does not create the problem of irredentism alike in the Muslim and the Hindu states, and which has not been conceived in frenzy and does not prepare the ground for perpetual conflict.

~

THREE

MUSLIMS—A SEPARATE NATION

To prove the case for Partition it is not enough to show that Hindus and Musalmans do not constitute a nation. It must further be shown that the Musalmans constitute a nation and need a separate State. Mr Durrani is explicit in his views: 'The ancient Hindus were not a nation. They were only a people, a mere herd.

'The Muslims of India were none better. Islam, indeed, became a state in the lifetime of its Founder himself. It has a well-defined political philosophy: I should say Islam is a political philosophy . . . I do not at all mean that the Islamic State is a theocracy . . . The Islamic State is a democracy, for whose maintenance every individual Muslim is responsible. *La Islam ilia be Jamaet-hu—* "There is no Islam without an organized society," says Omar the Great. Unfortunately, the Islamic State did not endure long enough. The Omayyads and the Abbasids destroyed it and turned it into *mulk* or autocratic, despotic, hereditary monarchy . . . It was under these two autocracies that two more elements entered into the Muslim society to vitiate and corrupt its political life, namely, theology and Sufism . . . These two things combined to pervert the Muslim's conscience and changed Islam from an ethico-political philosophy into a sort of "religion", a something which political slogan-mongers call private relation between the individual and his God . . . At the time the Muslims conquered India the divorce of religion and politics had become the accepted creed of the Muslims throughout the world. The men who conquered India were not the national army of a Muslim State but paid mercenaries of an imperial despot. The State they established in India was not a national Muslim State, but held, maintained and exploited in the interests of an autocrat and his satellites. The Muslim Empire in India was Muslim only in the sense that the man who wore the crown professed to be a Muslim. Through the whole length of their rule in India Muslims never developed the sense of nationhood . . .

So we had two peoples, Hindus and Muslims, living side by side in equal servitude to an imperial despotism, and both devoid of any national feeling or national ambition.

'Much has been written on the irreconcilability of the religious conceptions, beliefs and practices of the Hindus and Muslims . . . Yet, in spite of them all, there is something in their respective faiths which enabled the two peoples to live amicably together for many centuries, and which, if what they have learnt and suffered under British Rule could be washed out of their minds and the same old religious mentality could be recreated in them which inspired their fore-fathers of a century ago, would enable them again to live amicably together as *good* neighbours and citizens of the same State. That something is the spirit of tolerance inculcated in both religions . . . If these relations between the two communities had continued uninterrupted, in due time a nation, united in mind and soul, would have been born on the soil of India. Can those days ever possibly come back?[1]

'So, in spite of their centuries of close association and sympathetic intercourse the Hindus and the Muslims remained separate. The two streams could not mix. They were two nationalities, so utterly different indeed that if at any time the sentiment, which the political philosopher calls national consciousness, were to awaken in them and become dynamic, they could not but react differently; they could not but grow into two separate nations. For nationalism or nationhood is nothing but the consciousness of separate nationality become dynamic. This is what has happened to the Hindus and the Muslims.'[2] 'The two peoples have become self-conscious nations, and not until they readjust their relations in the light of this new consciousness will there be any peace between them.'[3]

Mr Durrani then proceeds to inquire how this consummation has taken place and comes to the conclusion that, 'in a word, it was one of the direct results of the British policy of discrimination and favouring one community at the expense of the other.'

'The nationalism of the Hindus and the Musalmans has been of slow growth and no definite date can be assigned as to when it ripened definitely. It showed itself at first in the form of economic rivalry, especially with respect to Government employment,

[1] F.K. Khan Durrani, *The Meaning of Pakistan*, pp. 34–44.
[2] Ibid., p. 47.
[3] Ibid., p. 48.

which later turned into political rivalry and finally into national animosity.'[4]

   Among the many things which helped to depress and ruin the Musalmans under the British, he mentions:

(1)   the ruin of industry and commerce in Bengal;
(2)   the Permanent Settlement of Bengal by which the lower Hindu revenue collectors were made landlords and the higher Muslim revenue officers were thrown on the rubbish-heap and replaced by European officers;
(3)   the resumption of rent-free grants upon which the Muslim system of education depended, causing its decay;
(4)   with their educational system ruined, the Muslims could not but lose their place in government services leading to a Hindu monopoly of official preferment, which monopoly has been maintained by low trickery and petty intrigues —these communal inequalities in the services forming a large part of India's politics and contributing in no small degree to the embitterment of communal relations.

Side by side there has been a growth of aggressiveness on the part of the Hindus and of distrust and political rivalry between the two communities, particularly in Bengal and in northern India as witnessed by:

(i)   the spirit underlying the song of Bandemataram;
(ii) the estrangement which followed immediately after the Mutiny of 1857 started by the Hindus and the Muslims throwing in their lot with them, and which being quelled, the Hindus turned traitor to their erstwhile comrades in arms and became informers, the whole wrath of the government thus falling upon the Muslims, thousands perishing in the massacres that followed the suppression, their properties confiscated and their orphaned children handed over to the Christian missionaries;
(iii) the Hindu agitation started in 1867 by leading Hindus of Benares that Urdu, which had grown up to be the common language, should be replaced by Brij-bhasha and the Arabic characters by Devnagri characters with the result that 'for

[4] Durrani, *The Meaning of Pakistan*, p. 67.

three quarters of a century the Hindus have been trying to unlearn Urdu and replace it by Hindi, until Mr Gandhi, who bespeaks the Hindu mind in such matters more faithfully than any other, says unashamedly that 'all those words must be expunged from Hindustani, which remind the Hindus of the Muslims having once ruled over the country—and naturally also of their presence in it;' [5]

(iv)   the interest of Hindus in their historical past which supplied the 'one very important element whose absence had prevented the race from becoming a nation'—although this interest grew out of the system of education introduced by the British prescribing textbooks of history written by British civilians or Christian missionaries and 'purposely so designed as to instil poison and create hatred and enmity in the hearts of the Hindus against Muslims;'

(v)   'the anti-cow-killing movement started by that Mahratta fanatic Bal Gangadhar Tilak, founder of a new Sivaji cult', and 'a Congress leader of the front rank'. [6]

'These were the various factors which determined the policies of Sir Syed Ahmad Khan and led him to counsel his co-religionists to keep aloof from the Congress,' and in this he was not a little influenced by 'the attitude of the Hindu press of Bengal which painted the Muslims as rebels and urged that on this account they should be kept out of government services.' [7]

Thus from 1857 onwards the Hindus and the Muslims never felt as one people and 'Sir Syed Ahmad Khan warned the government as well as the public that representative institutions were suited only to those countries which had homogeneous populations but that in India, whose population was extremely heterogeneous, parliamentary institutions could not be introduced without grave socio-political risks.' [8] But when it became known that popular councils were going to be established in 1906, a deputation of Muslims asked for and got separate representation for the Muslim community.

[5] Ibid, p. 68.
[6] Ibid., p. 74.
[7] Ibid., p. 70.
[8] Durrani, *The Meaning of Pakistan*, p. 70.

'Absence of separate electorates would certainly not have created a united homogeneous nation. It would have simply resulted in the dominance of the Hindus over the Muslims.'[9]

Although Hindu revivalism had preceded political awakening, till 1906–07, the Hindus had not developed the Gandhian ideology of supercommunal nationalism and everybody was frankly a Hindu or Muslim, and communalism had not yet become a term of abuse, and the Hindus and Musalmans could afford to deal with their rivals with courtesy, tolerance and sympathetic understanding. This was reflected in both the Hindu Sabha, which was founded first in the Punjab in 1907 and later became an all-India organization, and in the All-India Muslim League which was formed in December 1906.

'The Muslim policy under Sir Syed Ahmad Khan's leadership, dictated by sheer fear of British oppression, had been one of loyalty and abject flattery. This policy was inherited by what is called the Aligarh School as a matter of tradition, though the conditions that inspired it had ceased to exist.[10] The Muslim loyalty received jolts from:

(i)   Italy's invasion of Tripoli in 1911 and the British government's share in it;

(ii) repeal of the Partition of Bengal in December, 1911;

(iii) the attack on Turkey by the Balkan States in the autumn of 1912 with the full moral support of Britain;

(iv) the massacre of Muslims at Cawnpore (Kanpur) for their opposition to a road-building scheme; and all this effected a fundamental change in the outlook of the Muslim League which declared the attainment of responsible self-government as its political goal and thus brought it in line with the Congress. The two organizations began to hold their annual sessions at the same place, until in 1916 they concluded the famous Lucknow Pact which was incorporated in the Government of India Act, 1919. The Pact did less than justice to the Muslim community but is of far-reaching importance in its implications in that 'by that Pact the Congress acknowledged the fact that the Hindus and the Muslims were two separate nations, and

[9] Ibid., p. 79.
[10] Ibid., p. 83.

that while the Congress itself was the representative of
the Hindus, the Muslim League represented the Muslim
community,' from which position the Congress has now
resiled, claiming to represent the whole of India.[11]

The First World War was the outcome of an exaggerated sense of
nationalism and only made the sentiment fiercer and inoculated with
it peoples who had been hitherto free from the virus. It 'created a
passionate desire among the peoples of India to be free from the
foreign yoke and it was this fierce passion for freedom that made
Hindu–Muslim unity possible in 1919–22.'[12] 'But Mr Gandhi and
his co-workers let themselves be carried away by the charming
spectacle of territorial nationalism.' 'The Congress Pandits declared
that religion must not be allowed to intrude into politics,' and
'the Congress sought to build a united Indian nation on the basis
of geography, politics and economics. In fact it presumed that the
nation was already in existence. The presumption was palpably
false; the bases were wrong and the edifice of nationalism which the
Congress had sought to build crashed in less than three years . . .
The Mahatma went to jail and the show of Hindu–Muslim unity
broke up. Swami Shraddhanand and Pandit Madan Mohan
Malaviya came out of jails and launched an open and unashamed
propaganda against the Muslims. The All-India Hindu Mahasabha
was reorganized in 1923 . . . The policy enunciated in 1907 and
1915 of looking after the Hindu interests without prejudice to
the interests of other communities was thenceforward abandoned
and a new ideology was evolved, namely, that India was the Holy
Land of the Hindus, that the Hindus were a nation in their own
right in which Muslims, Christians and Parsis had no place, and
that the political goal of the Hindus was Hindu Raj.'[13] In 1925,
a piece of Hindu writing called *Mere Vichar* by the late Lala
Hardyal, which he called his political testament, reached India
and was published throughout the country by the Hindu press.
Mr Durrani quotes some passages from it on the authority of
Mr Indra Prakash who has quoted them in his book *Where We
Differ* and of Dr Ambedkar who quotes them in his *Thoughts on
Pakistan*. I may just summarize them in the words of the original.

[11] Ibid., pp. 84–85.
[12] Durrani, *The Meaning of Pakistan*, p. 90.
[13] Ibid., pp. 91–93.

The State should belong to the Hindus and the Mohammedans may live there. But the State cannot be a Muslim State nor can it be a jointly Hindu–Muslim administered State . . . To attain Swaraj we [Hindus] do not need the Muslim assistance nor is it our desire to establish a Joint Rule . . . The future of the Hindu race of Hindustan and the Punjab rests on these four pillars:

(i)   Hindu Sanghatan,
(ii)   Hindu Raj,
(iii) Shuddhi of Muslims, and
(iv)   the conquest and Shuddhi of Afghanistan and the frontiers.[14]
       This has been the ideology that has governed the policy of the Hindu Mahasabha from 1923 to this day and in support Mr Durrani quotes at great length from the statements of Mr Savarkar as saying that 'India cannot be assumed today to be a Unitarian and homogeneous nation; but on the contrary, there are two nations in the main, the Hindus and the Muslims in India.' Mr Durrani proceeds: 'Mr Savarkar's thesis is wholly in accord with facts of history and with political theory, and it is not possible to quarrel with it. The quarrel arises when he becomes inconsistent with his own thesis. The political scientist will say that when two communities have developed the consciousness of being separate nations, as the Hindus and the Muslims have in this country, it is time that in order to avoid inner tensions, civil wars and the like, they parted company and established separate national governments of their own. That is also the contention of the All-India Muslim League. Mr Savarkar, however, having once repudiated the territorial basis of nationhood with considerable acumen, falls back on the geographical motif and claims the whole of India as a heritage of the Hindu nation by calling it the Holy Land of the Hindus. He therefore visualizes a single government for the whole of India dominated by the Hindus in which the Muslims will have a subordinate and subservient position. In other words the Hindus will be the ruling race; the Muslims a subject people.'[15]

[14] Speech of Mr V.D. Savarkar at the Ahmedabad session of the Hindu Mahasabha in 1937, quoted in Durrani, *The Making of Pakistan*, p. 102.
[15] Durrani, *The Making of Pakistan*, p. 105.

The Indian National Congress is in no better position. 'The birth of the Congress was a culmination of Hindu revivalist movement. In fact, it marked the birth of the Hindu nation. It is true a few Muslims were also associated with the Congress in the earlier days of its history. But it never lost the character, except for a very brief period, of being a Hindu organization, and bears its birthmark on its face, if anything more markedly, to this day.'[16] This was frankly admitted by the Congress when it entered into the Lucknow Pact in 1916. The brief period was the period of the non-cooperation movement under the leadership of Mr Gandhi and the Ali Brothers. But the movement was a colossal failure and the Musalmans lost heavily in the process. Even during that period there were fissures visible under the facade of Hindu–Muslim unity. 'Mr Gandhi has a deep insight into the workings of the Hindu mind . . . He has never had the courage to flout Hindu public opinion even when he knew that the latter was wrong. He is too clearheaded to have any respect for the common Hindu superstitions, such as cow-worship. But to humour the Hindu public he has had to declare more than once that Swaraj was not worth having if it did not protect the cow from slaughter.'[17]

After the reorganization of the Hindu Mahasabha in 1923 a three-fold programme was launched for the realization of its aim of establishing a Hindu Raj. 'Though the Muslims are in minority they have always enjoyed a prestige for their military prowess, and Hindus, in spite of their huge numbers, have been but sheep before them.'[18] The Hindu Mahasabha, when it adopted its new ideology in 1923, struck upon a novel plan for creating the spirit of aggressiveness among the Hindus and killing the fear that the name of the Musalman inspired in the Hindu's breast. It started a series of well-planned riots through the length and breadth of the country, staging small battle-fields in the streets of cities where the Hindu could learn how to face the Muslim in the game of bloodshed . . . So long as the Hindu retained a wholesome fear of the Musalman there could be no riots. The riots were the course of training by which the Hindus were to be militarized.'[19] Pandit Malaviya was the person chiefly responsible for organizing them,

[16] Ibid., p. 109.
[17] Ibid., pp. 110–11.
[18] Ibid., p. 113.
[19] Durrani, *The Making of Pakistan*, p. 114.

as a reference to his itineraries published in newspapers of those years will show, 'Pandit Malaviya's visit to a town being followed a few weeks later by a bloody riot in the town. When Mr Gandhi came out of jail in February 1924 he found the country in the grip of Pandit Malaviya's gangster politics, but had not the courage to face the situation . . . the Mahatma did nothing to quench the fires and left the evil genius of Malaviya to direct the political life of Hindu India for five long years (1923–27).'[20] The Hindus wanted to boycott the Simon Commission and desired that the boycott should be a united Hindu–Muslim affair. 'Accordingly, as is their wont, Hindu leaders met in secret and decided to call off the anti-Muslim campaign of terrorization and the riots came to an abrupt end.'[21] 'Mr Gandhi kept mum and did not raise his little finger to check the gory drama that was being played all over India by Pandit Malaviya, Lala Lajpat Rai and other Mahasabhaites, and when he did emerge from retirement towards the close of 1928, he did so not as an all-India leader of both the Hindus and the Muslims as he had been before his incarceration and retirement but as a leader of the Hindu community alone. With the Mahatma's conversion to the Malaviyan ideology of Hindu nationalism and Hindu Raj, Pandit Malaviya himself left the stage and gradually sank back into private life. Since then Mr Gandhi has been a leader of the Hindu community only, which he has confessed on several, occasions and the Congress has been in its policies and almost completely in its membership a purely Hindu national organization.'[22] There is exchange of workers between the Mahasabha and the Congress. The AICC threw out a resolution at Bombay in 1938 which would have prevented members of the Congress becoming members of the Mahasabha and vice versa 'though the ban against the Muslim League remained strictly in force'.[23] 'From 1924 to 1928 was his period of incubation at the end of which he [Mr Gandhi] emerged as a leader of the Hindu community pure and simple,' and launched his civil disobedience movement from which the Muslims as a community held completely aloof. Before he left for the Round Table Conference in 1931 an effort was made to bring the two communities to some agreement

[20] Ibid., pp. 115–16.
[21] Ibid., p. 116.
[22] Ibid., p. 117.
[23] Ibid., p. 118.

but Mr Gandhi torpedoed the effort and required that Muslims should come with a unanimous demand, knowing that the handful of so-called nationalist Muslims whom he carried in his pocket would not agree.[24]

'After the 1935 Constitution the Muslim League resolved to co-operate with the Congress in working the new Constitution and Mr Jinnah expected in view of the sameness of the professed creeds of the League and the Congress that the latter would not oppose the League in the elections . . . But the Congress threw the gauntlet, set up candidates against the League and Pandit Jawaharlal Nehru, the Congress President, replied that there were only two parties in the country—the Congress and the British Government.' The Congress success was overwhelming in the 1937 elections but it was confined mainly to Hindu constituencies. Out of the 482 Muslim seats, the Congress ventured to contest only fifty-eight of which it lost thirty-two. On account of the success their heads got swollen beyond all proportions and they began to demand that the Muslim League should be wound up or at least should cease to function as a political organization. The Muslim mass contact movement was launched and Muslims were asked to enter the Congress as individuals, leaving their communal labels behind. The appeal was addressed to Muslims alone and Hindus could be members at once of the Congress and the Hindu Mahasabha.[25] The Congress refused to form governments in the provinces where it had a majority 'except on the condition that a guarantee were given them that the Governors would not exercise the special powers vested in them under the constitution for the protection of minorities and other special interests.'[26] In view of impending war clouds to purchase peace the government surrendered, gave the guarantee demanded by the Congress and betrayed the Muslims once again. 'The Congress on entering office declared firstly that it was under no obligation to take Muslims into the Cabinets. Accordingly, the Orissa Cabinet had no Muslim member and occasion was soon found to rid the CP Cabinet of its Muslim minister. Secondly, the Congress declared that it would take Muslims into its Cabinets provided they resigned from their parties and signed the Congress pledge.'[27]

[24] Durrani, *The Making of Pakistan*, p. 120.
[25] Ibid., pp. 123–24.
[26] Ibid., p. 126.
[27] Ibid., pp. 127–28.

'But the fact stands that the Congress rule was extremely unjust and oppressive to the Muslims . . . The Hindus of the provinces in which they are in majority felt and began to behave as if Hindu Raj had come . . . The Congress ministries issued orders that the Congress flag should be flown on all public buildings and schools . . . They ordered or permitted the singing of Bandemataram, the symbol of the restoration of Hindu sovereignty and hatred of the Muslims, on all public occasions. Even some Assemblies in the Congress-governed provinces began their proceedings with the Bandemataram song.'[28] 'The campaign of mass terrorization of Muslims and planned riots which Pandit Malaviya had carried on so vigorously in 1923–27 was revived, the details of which may be found in the two volumes of the Sharif Report, Mr Fazlul Huq's statement and K.S. Abdul Rahman Khan's Report.[29]

The technique adopted by the Congress governments to protect Hindu offenders consisted of:

(i)   encouraging subordinate officials to bring about a compromise whereby Muslims agreed to give up their right of cow-slaughter and apologized, and

(ii) allowing the police to delay investigation so that culprits might go scot-free in the absence of evidence. Magistrates were transferred and punitive police posted in Muslim quarters.

Mr Durrani then proceeds to quote at great length from the judgement of the High Court acquitting the accused in the Chandur Biswa case in which some Muslims had been sentenced to death and some to transportation for life for the murder of a Hindu. The Sessions Judge by the way was an Englishman. Mr Durrani's comment is: 'Had the Premier of the CP some sense of shame, he would have committed suicide or at least retired from public life for good. Mr Yusuf Sharif was dismissed for releasing a prisoner who had served almost the whole of his sentence. But the Congress did not call Pandit Shukla [the Premier] to account for this abominable conspiracy against the lives of citizens . . . Mr Gandhi, the Congress dictator and Pandit Shukla's patron, is eternally chattering about truth and non-violence and his inner voice. I am sure God Almighty never speaks to such hypocrites

[28] Durrani, *The Making of Pakistan*, pp. 129–30.
[29] Ibid., p. 131.

and Mr Gandhi's inner voice must be somebody else's. In any case with such instances of justice and good government before them, the Muslims of India can never agree to being put in a position of subjection to the Hindus.'[30]

He goes on to recount further the atrocities of the Congress governments: 'The Muslims were forbidden at places to call the "Azan" or kill cows for their food. Their mosques and graveyards were desecrated without hope of redress. But the most subtle and thoroughgoing plan to de-Muslimize the Muslims, to destroy their cultural and social unity . . . was the Wardha scheme of education which was to be imposed compulsorily upon all alike under the future Congress Government of India and a foretaste of which was administered in the CP in the shape of the Vidya Mandir Scheme.'[31] After all this, the resignation of the Congress governments naturally came as a great relief to the Muslims. Then followed the individual civil disobedience movement and the Cripps offer, the terms of which were generous, with only one fly in the ointment—the provision of the possibility of the secession of Muslim India and the establishment of an independent Muslim State which the Congress could not swallow.

The 'open rebellion' resolution of the AICC of 8 August 1942 'was an open invitation to Japan, whose armies were waiting on the other side of the border, to cross over and occupy the country. Viewed thus, the August resolution was an act of blackest treachery to India, but especially to the Muslims who have no such affinity with Japan as Hindus claim to have.'[32] 'For once in his long Viceroyalty Lord Linlithgow's Government acted promptly and effectively, and Mr Gandhi's melodrama was blanketed in the first act. Muslim India was once again saved from the mercies of Hindu Raj.'[33]

'Though Islam is but an ethico-political philosophy, the Indian Muslims have been as a whole poor political thinkers. But the world in which they were placed would not leave them alone, and the "total" war which the Hindus had declared against them shook them profoundly. In 1937 we find them shaken and amazed. In 1938 we find signs of growing recognition among the Muslims

[30] Ibid., pp. 134–35.
[31] Ibid., 135–36.
[32] Durrani, *The Making of Pakistan*, pp. 139–40.
[33] Ibid., p. 141.

that there was no place for them in a common Hindu–Muslim nationality, and towards the close of the year voices began to be audible all over India that there were two nations in India, that the Muslims were a nation in their own right,'[34] and therefore the Pakistan resolution of the All-India Muslim League in its Lahore session in March 1940 'was but an expression and adoption by the League of what had already been their political faith.'[35] It was thus in 1938 that according to Mr Durrani the Muslims of India realized the consciousness of being a separate nation and set their hearts on Pakistan 'which has put the Muslim imagination afire. They see strange, undreamed of, limitless possibilities in it. They imagine Pakistan to be a state in which men shall be free from oppression, injustice and exploitation, and free from selfish greed, covetousness, and fear of poverty . . . in which, though, or rather because, it will be an Islamic state, there will be no distinction of Muslim and non-Muslim among its citizens in the matter of civic rights and economic benefits . . . They call it *Hukumat-i-Ilahi* or the Kingdom of God which some people in their ignorance have translated into theocracy. But the Islamic state is not a theocracy . . . The Islamic state is a democracy, whose citizens feel and have the right to declare—"We are the state."'[36]

I have quoted at such great length from Mr Durrani not because I accept his statements or conclusion—many of them are so obviously ridiculous and outrageously false—but because he gives in a systematic manner how the two nations theory has taken shape and because he claims that he was one of the earliest to have published a definite 'thesis of the Hindus and the Muslims being not merely two communities but two nations, that they being two nations, a pact could not bring forth a single united nation out of them and that the natural and rational solution of the Hindu–Muslim problem was that one community should either absorb or extinguish the other community or otherwise render it harmless . . . Being a member of the Muslim nation, naturally I contended that Muslims should strive to reconquer India for Islam and make that their political goal. I am still of the same mind, for I believe the ultimate political salvation of India lies in Islam only.'[37]

[34] Ibid., pp. 153–54.
[35] Ibid., p. 157.
[36] Ibid., pp. 158–59.
[37] Durrani, *The Making of Pakistan*, p. 146.

FOUR

~

NATIONAL AND MULTINATIONAL

What we are more immediately concerned with is, whether, assuming for the sake of argument the main thesis that since 1938 the Musalmans of India have realized the consciousness of being a separate nation, the creation of separate Hindu and Muslim States will serve the problem and place the minorities in the two kinds of national States in a better position. In this connection it is profitable to study the history of the West and learn, if possible, a lesson from what has happened there in the recent past. It is well known that at the end of the First World War, a number of new States were created out of the wreckage of the Central European Empires. An attempt was made as far as possible to create homogeneous States. In the result many nationalities which had been minorities before the war found themselves as majorities in the new States which were named after them, and members belonging to the former majority in the old dismembered States, along with others, became minorities in the new States. As it was apprehended that on account of ill-treatment of minorities, the peace of the world might be disturbed, the treatment of minorities came to be regarded as a matter of international concern and most of the new States were required to enter into treaties for the protection of the minorities within them. These treaties are known as 'the Minority Treaties' and the League of Nations became their guarantor.

The object of Partition is to have separate Muslim and Hindu States—just as national States were created after the First World War in Europe—so that both Muslims and Hindus may have an opportunity in their respective States to develop their cultural, spiritual, economic and political life in accordance with their own genius and shape their own future destiny. There is no need to quarrel with this object—if it can be attained. The Hindu and Muslim populations are so spread and intermingled with each other that it is impossible to have a homogeneous State of either the Hindus or the Muslims in any part of the country without a considerable minority of the other community in it. Hindu and Muslim States created especially and openly on the basis of the religion of the majority of their inhabitants are bound to become what are called national States of Hindus and of Muslims; and having been so created, it would be impossible for them to escape the inevitable psychology and philosophy that dominate a national State. In the words of Macartney, 'so long as the majority nations which have assumed command of the different States [in India it will be Muslims in the Muslim States and the Hindus in the Hindu State] persist in their theoretically absurd and practically unattainable endeavour to make of those States the exclusive instruments of their own national ideals and aspirations, so long will the minorities be placed in a position which no system of international protection can render tolerable.'[1] A national State and national minorities are incompatible. There are two ways of dealing with the problem: one is to get rid of the minority—it may be done, either

(a)   by adjusting the boundaries of the State so as to eliminate the minority; or

(b)   by exchange of population.[2] The other is to change the basis of the State and make it an unnational or multinational State.

[1]   C.A. Macartney, *National States and National Minorities*, (1934) p. 421.
[2]   Dr Ambedkar who has supported the creation of Pakistan says: 'The best solution of the communal problem is not to have two communities facing each other, one a majority and the other a minority, welded in the steel-frame of a single government' and if this cannot be attained by redrawing the boundaries of the provinces excluding the portions with non-Muslim majorities from Pakistan and by exchange of populations, then the scheme of Pakistan does not eradicate the evils which lie at the heart of the communal question. And he therefore suggests both the redrawing of the boundaries and the exchange of populations both of which he considers practicable so far as Pakistan is concerned. But for Hindustan, he too has no method of making it a homogeneous Hindu state without a Muslim minority of considerable size. He has to be content with pointing out that the extent of the problem will be greatly reduced and the Hindus should find it on the whole advantageous to have the problem

The Hindus and Muslims are spread over the whole of India
in such a way and have got so intermingled with one another
in the population of the country that it is impossible to cut out
any portion and convert it into a State which will not have a
considerable minority left. This is admitted by all and therefore
the suggestion is not for a purely Muslim State but for States with
Hindu and Muslim majorities each having a minority belonging to
the other community. Homogeneity by any division of the country
is thus impossible.

Can homogeneity be attained by exchange of population? No
one except Dr S.A. Latif and Dr Ambedkar has suggested it. Mr
Jinnah said in his presidential address at the Lahore session of the
League in March 1940, that 'exchange of population, however, on
the physical division of India as far as practicable will have to be
considered.'[3] Others have considered it impracticable on account
of the magnitude of the numbers involved and the consequent
cost and inconvenience as also of the strong attachment to their
lands of the inhabitants—both Hindus and Muslims—who will
have to be shifted. In this connection the experience of minorities
in Europe may be noted:

The voluntary exchange and compulsory exchange of populations
were both tried under the Peace Treaties. Macartney says that 'the

so reduced.—vide Dr B.R. Ambedkar see *Pakistan or the Partition
of India*, Chapter. VI, sections 2 and 3, pp. 95–107.

Now so far as redrawing boundaries is concerned, I have considered
at length what the boundaries can be on a fair interpretation of the
League resolution, but Mr Jinnah at the time of the conversations with
Mahatma Gandhi in 1944 is reported to have insisted on the present
provincial boundaries. As regards exchange of population it is enough
to state that with boundaries suggested by Dr Ambedkar, the number
of non-Muslims to be transferred from the Muslim states in the north-
western and eastern zones will be more than 61 lakhs and 1 crore
34 lakhs respectively. I do not know where Dr Ambedkar gets that
'exchange of population in Turkey, Greece and Bulgaria' involved 'the
transfer of some 20 million people from one habitat to another.' The
figure of the entire population of the three states given by Macartney is
a little over 25 millions. The minorities of all kinds in the three *states*
numbered just over 3 $\frac{1}{2}$ millions. Macartney also mentions that the
Commission appointed to deal with exchange between Bulgaria and
Greece had to deal with only 154,691 persons and similarly the number
of persons dealt with between Greece and Turkey came to 545,551.
[3] *Speeches and Writings of Mr Jinnah*, third edition, p. 158.

genuine voluntary emigrants were thus few indeed' and that 'the genuine voluntary and reciprocal emigration which the Convention was designed to effect never occurred at all except on a minute scale.'[4] There is no reason to think that the case will be otherwise in India. A compulsory exchange was, however, carried through between Greece and Turkey. Summarizing his conclusion, Macartney says: 'Such experience as we possess of the exchange of population as a means of solving the minorities' problem is not, therefore, calculated to encourage a repetition of the experiment. It may be argued that conditions in Turkey and the Balkans after the War were quite abnormal, and that neither the physical hardships nor the financial losses would recur under more settled conditions. The answer is that the method is *ex hypothesi* a drastic one. If conditions are settled and the relations between minorities and majorities happy, exchange is unnecessary, and an appeal for voluntary exchange will meet with no result. A compulsory exchange, against the wills of the individuals concerned, is admittedly a barbarous act; but experience has shown that a voluntary exchange simply does not take place, except under conditions which amount, in reality, to compulsion. It seems, therefore, that the operation is inseparable from hardships; the only question is whether these are to be inflicted in hot or in cold blood.'[5]

Macartney, therefore, comes to the conclusion that 'all attempts to solve the minority problem by getting rid of the minority have thus proved thoroughly discouraging . . . It seems, therefore, that states of mixed population must reconcile themselves to the continued pressure of their minorities . . . The troubles of our day arise out of the modern conception of the national state; out of the identification of the political ideals of all the inhabitants of the state with the national-cultural ideals of the majority in it. If once this confusion between the two things which are fundamentally different can be abandoned, there is no reason why the members of a score of different nationalities should not live together in perfect harmony in the same state, and not even the smallest of them need suffer from the moral degradation which today attends the lot of the national minority. Even today there are certain states in Europe which have refrained from the attempt to constitute

---

[4] Macartney, *National States* . . ., pp. 440–41.
[5] Ibid., pp. 448–49.

themselves as national states, and in which, in consequence, no true minority problem exists.'[6] And he mentions the example of the Soviet Union. He has cast a glance at the problem in India also. 'It may, however, be suggested that not only the British rulers in India, but also the native population of India itself, would lose nothing by considering the history of the minorities struggle in Europe. In the Indian situation today there are two quite distinct conflicts. There is the conflict of the native against the Englishman, and that of the Hindu against the Mahomedan (not to mention the endless complications of the minor races). Since the English in India are not so much a dominant, indigenous race as the representatives of a foreign administrative authority, the former struggle resembles fairly closely that waged by the Magyars against the House of Habsburg; and the support given to British rule by the Mahomedans of India recalls the alliance so often made between the Habsburgs and the Germans and Croats of Hungary. And just as the conflict between the Magyars and the "Nationalities" in Hungary did not reach its climax until the Habsburgs had practically abdicated their right to intervene in Hungary's internal affairs, so the presence of the English in India is postponing the true clash between the native races. As India acquires more real self-government, so that clash will come to resemble more closely sundry of the internal conflicts which have rent the states of Eastern Europe . . . One may pray that those who read the history will have the wisdom to learn the lessons.'[7] One such lesson he has mentioned earlier in the book, which we in India will do well to bear in mind. When open conflict broke out between the Magyars and the Habsburgs, the Croats and almost all the other minorities sided with the Crown and the Magyars were overcome. Hungary came to be ruled from Vienna by a centralized and Germanizing bureaucracy giving satisfaction neither to the Magyar nor to the Slavonik ambition. This evoked from a witty Magyar the comment to a Croat friend that 'you have got as reward what we have got as punishment.'[8]

Instead, therefore, of seeking a solution of the Indian problem in the creation of national States of Hindus and Musalmans, in

[6] Macartney, *National States* . . ., p. 450.
[7] Ibid., pp. 480–81.
[8] Ibid., p. 118.

each of which there will remain a considerable minority of the
other community, is it not better to allow India to continue as an
unnational State that she is and has been? The desire expressed by
the League to have separate national States of Musalmans is not
even six years old, and, as we shall see, cuts across the history
of more than as many hundred years. The object therefore should
be not the creation of national States but the strengthening of the
unnational State in India, removing from it all those aspects and
features which detract from its unnational character.

I cannot do better than conclude this discussion with a quotation
from Lord Acton (who has been quoted by the protagonists of
the two nations theory) with which Macartney ends his book:[9] 'If
we take the establishment of liberty for the realization of duties
to be the end of civil society, we must conclude that those states
are substantially the most perfect which include various distinct
nationalities without oppressing them. Those in which no mixture
of races has occurred are imperfect; and those in which its efforts
have disappeared are decrepit. A state which is incompetent to
satisfy different races condemns itself; a state which labours to
neutralize, to absorb, or to expel them, destroys its own vitality;
a state which does not include them is destitute of the chief basis
of self-government.'

[9] Macartney, *National States* . . ., p. 501.

~

FIVE

THE PICTURE FROM ANOTHER ANGLE

We have seen much in the foregoing pages that tends to show that Hindus and Muslims are separate and the twain shall never meet. But there is another angle from which the picture can be viewed. Let us turn to it for a while.

'Very many human activities, aspirations, and emotions have contributed, either naturally or artificially to build up the great synthesis that we term a "nation"; language, religion, art, law, even food, gesture, table-manners, clothing, and sport—all play their part,' says Julian Huxley.[1] Again, 'The special form of group sentiment that we call "nationality", when submitted to analysis, thus proves to be based on something much broader but less definable than physical kinship. The occupation of a country within definite geographical boundaries, climatic conditions inducing a definite mode of life, traditions that gradually come to be shared in common, social institutions and organizations, common religious practices, even common trades or occupations—these are among the innumerable factors which have contributed in greater or less degree to the formation of national sentiment. Of very great importance is common language, strengthened by belief in a fictitious "blood tie". But among all the sentiments that nurture feelings of group unity, greater even than the imaginary tie of physical or even of historic relationship, is the reaction against outside interference. That, more than anything else, has fostered the development of group-consciousness. Pressure from without is probably the largest single factor in the process of national evolution.'[2]

Let us take some of the more important of these elements and see how they have influenced the Hindus and Muslims of India.

[1] Julian Huxley, *Race in Europe*, p. 3.
[2] Huxley, *Race in Europe*, p. 15.

I. RELIGION

Let me begin with Religion. It is true that the Hindus and Musalmans of India follow different religions and that their social life derives from these religions. It is also true that some of the religious rites and customs differ very materially and to all outward appearance are irreconcilable. But in some of the most fundamental things the differences among them are no greater than they are among followers of faiths going under one comprehensive name and who are admittedly living peacefully and amicably as members of one nation. The austere simplicity of the inside of a Muslim mosque with only prayer mats and water pots contrasts with the decorated images and paraphernalia of worship of the inside of a Hindu temple no more than the inside of a Protestant or Presbyterian Church, with nothing but seats for the worshippers and a pulpit for the preacher contrasts with the magnificent decoration and image and painting and candle and what not of the Roman Catholic Church. Even among Musalmans, the orthodox Sunni looks upon the pomp and paraphernalia of the Moharram celebrations—the *tazias* and *taboots*, the *separs* and the *alams*, the *paiks* and *bahishti*—of the Shiyas with something akin to the horror with which he looks upon the procession of the image of Durga of the Hindus. And yet no one has claimed that the Protestants and Catholics of England do not constitute a nation or that the Sunnis and Shiyas are two different nations. Among the Hindus also there are sects that are as critical of temples and images and of many of the rites and ceremonies of others also called Hindus.

Apart from outward signs and symbols, rites and ceremonies, forms and exercises of religion and worship, people have known philosophers of both faiths who have dived deep into the mysteries of life and death and life after death, and who have proclaimed the same faith in the Oneness of God, the immortality of the Soul, the ephemeral character of all material things, and the eternal value of things spiritual. The Vedantic philosophy of the Hindus and the Sufism of the Muslims, whether or not they have derived inspiration from each other or from a common source in the ultimate experience of the human soul in its quest after the eternal verity, have tended to converge towards a single point. A person learned in both the lores like Dr Bhagwan Das can easily cull together parallel passages from the standard works of both religions.

'The third foreign source of Muslim mysticism was Indian. It has been pointed out in an earlier chapter that India and the Persian Gulf had a close commercial intercourse; with trade, undoubtedly ideas were exchanged. It stands to reason that if things of material use like Indian steel and swords, and Indian gold and precious stones, and if things of artistic value like the painted arch and the bulbous dome, reached Persia and Iraq, Indian philosophical ideas should have travelled there too. Many Indians held posts in the financial department at Basra under the early Umayyads; the Caliph Muawiya is reported to have planted a colony of them in Syria, especially at Antioch and Hajjaj, and to have established them in Kashgar. The black-eyed and olive-complexioned Hindus were brushing their shoulders against those of the Muslims in the cities of the Caliphate. The eastern dominions of the empire, that is, Khorasan, Afghanistan, Sistan and Baluchistan were Buddhist or Hindu before they were converted.' Balkh had a large monastery (*vihara*) whose superintendent was known as the Baramak. His descendants became the Barmakide Vizirs of the Abbaside Caliphs.

'Then the Arabs familiarized themselves from early times with Indian literature and sciences. They translated Buddhist works in the second century of the Hijra: for instance, *Kitabal-Bud* and *Bilawhar wa Budasif,* treatises on astronomy and medicine called *Sindhind* (Siddhanta) and *Shushrud* (Susruta) and *Srak* (Charaka); story books like *Kalilah Damnah* (Panchatantra) and *Kitab Sindabad;* ethical books of Shanaq (Chanakya) and Bidpa (Hitopadesa); and treatises on logic and military science.

'They were exceedingly keen on informing themselves of the customs, manners, sciences and religions of the people with whom they came into contact. Al-Kindi wrote a book on Indian religions, Sulaiman and Masudi collected information in their travels which they used in their writings. Al-Nadim, Al-Ashari, Al-Biruni Shah-rastani and many others devoted chapters in their books to describe and discuss Indian religions and philosophic systems.

'The legend of Buddha entered into Muslim literature as the type of the saintly man, and Muslim hagiologists assimilated the stories of Ibn Adham to the Buddhist legend. Indian ascetics travelling in pairs and staying not more than two nights at one place were directly known to the Muslim adepts, who took from them their four-fold vows—of cleanliness, purity, truth and poverty— and the use of the rosary. What wonder then that the conception of Nirvana, the discipline of the eight-fold path, the practice of *jog* and the acquaintance of miraculous powers were appropriated in Islam under the names of Tana, Tariqa or Saluk, Moraqabah and Karamat or Mujiza.'[3]

'But the man who produced the greatest stir in the world by the boldness of his doctrines was Husain-bin-Mansoor Hallaj . . . He travelled about in many lands, among them India, and thrice visited Mecca. At last his activities became so obnoxious that he was arrested in AD 922.'[4] Kabir, Dadu, Nanak and other Indian saints used the language of Muslim Sufism.

Mansoor's theories were later worked up in the systems of Ibn-al-Arabi and Abdul Karim Jili and in the poetry of Ibn-al Farid and Abri Said Ibn Abulkhair and their influence spread to far off countries including India.

'Jili was acquainted with Hindu religion, for among the ten principal sects he noted the Brahima (Brahman). About them he says that they worship God in His absolute aspect, without reference to prophet or apostle. The scriptures of the Brahmina according to him were revealed to them not by God but by Abraham (Brahma); they contained five books, the fifth on account of its profundity was unknown to most of the Brahmans but those who read it invariably became Muslims. Apparently Jili's fifth book is the Vedanta whose monistic philosophy in the eyes of Jili made it indistinguishable from Islam.'[5] 'The Muslim mystic who sets out upon the path of union (*wasl*) of absorption (*fana*) always needs a spiritual guide, "for if a man has no teacher his Imam is Satan." The guide or the preceptor (Pir or Shaikh) is the priest round which the whole machinery of Sufi monachism moves . . . The disciple is advised to keep his Murshid constantly in mind, to become eventually absorbed in him through constant meditation and contemplation of him, to see him in all men and in all things, and to annihilate his self in the Murshid. From this state of self-absorption in the

---

[3] Dr Bhagwan Das quoted in Tarachand's *Influence of Islam on Indian Culture*, pp. 67–70.

[4] Tarachand, *Influence of Islam* . . ., pp. 69–70.

[5] Ibid., pp. 77–78.

Murshid the master leads him on through several stages at last
to absorption in the Deity. Muhammad taught surrender to God
(Islam), Sufism surrender to the teacher who is the representative
of God upon earth.'[6]

Haji Waris Ali Shah was a Sufi saint in northern India. His
tomb is at Dewa Sharif in Barabanki district (UP). His disciples
add 'Warisi' to their names and are said to be most numerous. He
has summarized the Sufi teachings in a few Persian verses which
may be quoted here as illustrative:

> Mun hameen go-em ke pir-e-man khudast,
> Pesh-e munkir een sakhun guftan khatast;
> Ek swalay meen kunum ai marduman,
> Pas jawab oora dehund ai mominan
> Hezum under nar choon shud sokhta
> Rishta under jame shud choon dokhta
> Pas wara hezam bagoem ya ke nar
> Rishta ra jama bagoem ya ka tar
> Choon key pir-e-mun fana fillah shud
> Ruft bashriyat hama Allah shud
> Pas be paye oo kunum hardam sajood,
> Waqf kardam dar rahush jan o wajood;
> Ashqi az jumle alam bartar ast
> Zan ke e.en millat Khudai akbar ast.

Translated as follows:

I say Pir is my God. To say this before a *munkir* (non-believer)
is a mistake. O man, I ask one question. O believers, answer it.
When fuel gets burnt in fire, when thread gets woven into cloth,
then should I call it fuel or fire, then should I call the thread cloth
or thread? So when my Pir got absorbed in God, the human being
disappeared—all became God. I therefore bow to his feet every
moment and have dedicated my life and being to his path. Love
is superior to all the world inasmuch as it is the *millat* (*bhakti*)
of God the Great.

Hindu scripture abounds in references to the necessity of a Guru
or preceptor who is to guide the disciple through the difficult and
rigorous discipline he has to go through, and without such a Guru

[6] Ibid., p. 81.

progress is practically impossible. In fact 'the Guru is Brahma, the Guru is Vishnu, the Guru is Maheshwar, the Guru is Para-Brahma Himself and to that Guru I bow' is a common everyday prayer. It is the duty and ambition of every Hindu to have a Guru and to be initiated by him.

'In the Pantha (way, sect) of Kabir, the Guru holds the same position as in any other Sufi order. If it is true of the Sufis that "among them the worship of God is the same as the worship of man" it is equally applicable here, for says Kabir:

'Consider the Guru as Govinda (God).' Nay more—

'If Hari becomes angry still there is some chance, but if the Guru is angry then there is no chance whatever.' And as among Sufi orders so in Kabir-Pantha,

'The real meditation (*dhyana, dhiker*) is of the Guru's form, the real worship is of the Guru's feet. The real boat is the Guru's word, which in essence and feeling is true 'and 'in the three worlds and nine regions none is greater than the Guru.'[7]

'Like all Sufis Nanak taught that in the soul's journey towards God it was necessary to be guided by a Guru. In his system the preceptor occupies the same position as in that of Kabir.'[8]

The names of Kabir and Nanak will thus spring to the mind of every Hindu of northern India as those of persons who were deeply influenced by Islam and the Hindu Vedanta alike. The Sakhis of Kabirdas and his devotional songs are repeated by innumerable Hindus and sung at the time of prayers morning and evening in countless Hindu homes.

'Thus did Kabir turn the attention of India to a religion of the universal path; a road was laid out on which both could tread together. No Hindu or Muslim could take exception to such a religion. This was the constructive part of Kabir's mission. But it had a destructive side also. It was impossible to build a new road without clearing away the jungle which obstructed the ancient foot-paths. Kabir therefore attacked with fearless indignation and in trenchant language the whole apparatus of externalia which obscured the truth or separated the Indian communities from one another. He spared neither the Hindu nor the Musalman.

'He asked the Hindus to give up what every reformer since the days of Buddha had insisted upon—ceremonial, sacrifice, lust for

[7] Tarachand, *Influence of Islam . . .*, p. 158.
[8] Ibid., p. 176.

magical powers, lip worship, repetition of formulae, pilgrimages, fasts, worship of idols, gods and goddesses, Brahmin supremacy, caste differences, prejudices concerning touchability and food . . . He asks the Musalmans to give up their exclusiveness, their blind trust in one Prophet and his book, their externalism in the performance of rites—pilgrimage to Mecca, fasts, and regulated prayers, their worship of saints (*aulia* and *pirs*) and prophets (*paighambar*).

'He asks both Hindus and Muslims to have reverence for all living creatures and to abstain from bloodshed. He asks them both to give up pride whether of birth or of position, to give up extremes of asceticism and worldliness and to consider life as a dedication . . . He repeats again and again that Hindus and Muslims are one, they worship the same God, they are children of the same Father, and they are made of the same blood.'[9]

Everyone knows that the entire teaching of Guru Nanak is nothing but a synthesis of the fundamental principles of both the religions. 'The mission of Nanak was the unification of the Hindu and the Musalman. He realized that in order to heal the wounds of society it was essential to end the conflict of religions.'[10] 'Nanak shows little mercy to himself and he is naturally not very tender when he deals with others. With a mind definite, clear-cut and keenly alive to the sharp distinctions between good and evil, he condemns with Semitic vehemence the superstitions and formalism of Hinduism and Islam.'[11] Kabir was a Muslim and Nanak a Hindu by birth and yet they are both the products of that fusion which was going on despite the continuance of all outward separation and isolationism.

It was not only in the realm of philosophic and religious thought that this rapprochement proceeded. In actual practice any number of instances may be found of Muslim kings endowing temples and '*maths*' and granting jagirs to pious Hindus and Pandits learned in the Hindu lore. It would be a useful service if some scholar could bring together in a compact form a list of the numerous endowments and grants made by Muslim kings to Hindu temples and religious shrines such as has been done of those desecrated and destroyed by them.

'If there had been no cultural co-operation as a rule, why were *sanads* granted by the Muslim rulers to Hindu seats of worship

[9] Tarachand, *Influence of Islam*, pp. 163–65.
[10] Ibid., p. 168.
[11] Ibid., p. 172.

and learning and vice versa? Students of the history of south India must have come across innumerable instances of such grants, made to Brahmins by the Adil Shahi, Kutub Shahi and Asaf Shahi dynasties. Likewise such endowments were made to Muslim places of worship by Maratha rulers even after the political strife with Delhi Emperors.'[12] I may mention two instances in Bihar. The nucleus of the large zamindari of the mahant of Bodh Gaya whose yearly income runs into lakhs was a grant by Mohammad Shah of Delhi, who by a firman granted the village of Mustipur Taradih to Mahant Lal Gir who was the fourth in succession from the founder. Similarly the great zamindari—perhaps the greatest zamindari in India—of Darbhanga owes its origin to a grant by the Mughal Emperor Akbar to the ancestor of the present Brahmin Maharajadhiraj, for his learning and piety. 'To encourage education among his Hindu subjects he [Sher Shah] granted them wakfs and allowed them a free hand in their management. For this liberal policy he was liked by his subjects of all castes and creeds.'[13]

A few other instances supplied to me by Dr Syed Mahmud may be mentioned here:

Sultan Zainulabdin of Kashmir used often to visit Amarnath and Sharda Devi's temple, and had houses built there for the comfort of pilgrims.

The Pathans of Najibabad ruled over Hardwar about 1780. The Nawab built big houses for the comfort of Hindu pilgrims which are still in existence and in possession of Hindus.

In 1588, Guru Arjun Dev dug a tank at Amritsar and in the same year proposed to build the temple there for worship. They got the foundation of Harmandir laid by a Musalman of piety named Mian-Peer alias Bala Peer.
—From *The History of the Darbar of Amritsar*, by Sirdar Udham Singh

Munshi Sujan Rai of Batala, the famous historian of the time of Alamgir, mentions in his *Khulastul-Tawarikh*, a village called Depalival, which is near Kalanur and where the tomb of Shah Shamshuddin Daryayi is situated. This tomb is visited by a large number of people. He writes: 'Both Hindus and Musalmans have a great faith in Shah Shamshuddin. But a Hindu named Deepali

[12] Atulananda Chakravarti, *Call It Politics?* p. 44.
[13] Ishwari Prasad, *History of Muslim Rule in India*, p. 339.

has proved superior to both Hindus and Musalmans in his faith.
After Shah Daryayi's death, Deepali was appointed the first
trustee and keeper of the tomb with unanimous consent of both
Hindus and Musalmans although he was not a Musalman by
religion . . .Some years ago the Musalmans tried to get the Hindu
keepers dismissed, so much so that religious reasons were urged
for this. But the Alamgiri Hukumat did not allow the agitation
to succeed. At the time of writing this book in the third year of
Alamgir's rule the Hindus are the keepers of this tomb.'

Even today in Hyderabad (Deccan) a Brahmin family continues
to be the mutwalli of the dargah of a famous buzurg (pious man).
The Nizam has granted a big jagir to this dargah and the public
also make offerings. Musalmans tried to get the Hindu Mutwalli
dismissed but the Nizam did not allow this.

Even today there is a grant on behalf of the Nizam to the temple
of Sitaram in the town of Hyderabad and to another temple at
Mahor (Adilabad), the annual income from which comes to fifty
or sixty thousand. The jagir granted by the Nizam to the Gurdwara
of Sikhs at Nander has an annual income of twenty thousand.

Some sanads in Persian for a grant may be quoted. One is dated
1167 Hijri and was granted by Ahmad Shah Bahadur Ghazi:

'Be it known to the Zamindars and cultivators of Kasba Achnera
in the district of Akbarabad that seventeen bighas of *muafi-land*
(land free from rent) are granted "Punyarth"' (as a religious act)
to Sheetal Dass Bairagi, for the expenses of *bhog* and *naived* of
Shri Thakurji, so that with the income from the said land, the said
Bairagi may meet the expenses and perform the rites of Shri Thakurji.

'Be it known to the Choudhri of the Bazar of Achnera that
he should give twenty *bhar* (measures) of grain to Shri Thakurji.
The aforesaid Bairagi should not be deprived of it. Dated 3rd
Ramzan, 1139, Fasli.'

Another is from Shahabuddin Khan granting a jagir for the
expenses of the famous temple of Ganesh at Chinchwad.

Qaulnama

In the name of Moraya Gossain of Chinchwad appertaining to
Pergannah Poona, about whom Khan-e-Hikmat Nishan Nahar Khan
has informed that he wants *Qaul* (binding words) of grant. So it
is given in writing that he should dwell with his own people and

connections in this village and strive to make the lands prosperous and productive. May no hardship or injury befall him through the will of Allah the Great. The date of *Qauliyatnama* for this purpose is the 12th of Zeqad 1326 Hijri.

There are two firmans of similar grants in Allahabad. One of these is in favour of the priests of the famous temple of Maheshwar Nath. It was granted by Aurangzeb.

Aurangzeb made grants to Girdhar, son of Jagjiwan of Sakin Mouza Basti (resident of village Basti) in the district of Benares, Jadu Mishra, resident of Maheshpur Pergannah Haveli, and to Pandit Balbhadra Mishra, who were all priests.

Aurangzeb made a grant of a monetary allowance of a hundred rupees to Mishra Kalyandas for the temple of Tutlamaee in Multan which is still in existence—vide Settlement Report of the District of Multan by Hukmchand, Extra Assistant Commissioner.

Sultan Mohammad Murad Bakhsh in 1153 Hijri made a grant that four seers of ghee be given every day from the stores of Ujjain so that the temple of Mahakal may be illuminated every night.

It may be stated in a general way that many of the Muslim kings and rulers were great patrons of learning and encouraged the study not only of Persian and Arabic but also of Sanskrit and Indian literature and sciences. It is not possible even to summarize all that they did for the promotion of learning in India. 'Under the imperial patronage several Sanskrit books dealing with diverse subjects were translated into Persian and Arabic. Besides, there were scores of Muslim chiefs who themselves studied Sanskrit and patronized it without stint. Many of them translated Sanskrit works into Persian in order to put the treasures of Hindu lore within the reach of the Muslim world and encouraged others in this direction. Often Sanskrit works were included in the courses of study for Hindu students. In short, Sanskrit was encouraged in every possible way.'[14] Dr James H. Cousins, writing about education in Muslim India says: 'Muslim Kings and Princes themselves became students and included Hindu culture in their intellectual interests. Muslim literary education intermingled as freely with Hindu literatures as Moghal painting with Rajput painting. Hindu

[14] S.M. Jaffar, *Education in Muslim India*, p. 15.

classics were translated into Persian and as a consequence Persian
culture influenced Hindu culture.'[15]

The Hindus are seen even now assembling in as large numbers
as Muslims at the dargah or tomb of a Muslim saint or on the
occasion of Urs fairs from all over India at a place like Ajmer
Shareef and from within the province of Bihar at Bihar Shareef,
Maner Shareef and Phulwari Shareef. Many Hindus have actually
a sort of relationship with Muslim divines akin to that of guru
and chela, or preceptor and disciple.

The participation by masses of Hindus in the Muslim celebrations
of Moharram is well known all over northern India. There used
to be a time not long ago when perhaps the number of Hindus
joining them exceeded that of the Muslims for the simple reason
that the former are more numerous than the latter. It was not only
in the processions that the Hindus joined. They actually observed
Moharram as Muslims did in their homes as days of mourning and
prayer when no festivities could be indulged in and no auspicious
act, such as a marriage or entry into a new house could be
celebrated. Many Hindus had their own *tazia*s and *separs,* and
Hindu boys fully became *paik*s and *bahishti*s donning the green
dress and badge *(badhi*s as they are called in Bihar) and carrying
the water *mashak*. Hindu *akhara*s vied with Muslim *akhara*s in
displaying their feats with sword and scimitar, *gadka* and lathi
and a host of other instruments. Better still, very often, perhaps
oftener than not, these *akhara*s were not the exclusive *akhara*s of
either Hindus or Muslims but joint *akhara*s of both.

There used to be no objection to the very noisy music of the
Moharram processions even when they passed by mosques, and
there used to be no breaking of heads and worse as so often
happens now-a-days on account of Hindu music before mosques.
It is a curious thing that in most cases the music accompanying
Hindu processions that are objected to by Muslims in some places
is played mostly by professional Muslim musicians. Similarly, the
cow whose sacrifice on the Bakr Id day by a Muslim is so often
the cause of a flare-up among Hindus (who tolerate her slaughter
from day to day for meat and hide in almost every town of any
importance and particularly in cantonments) has very often been
the property of a Hindu who has sold her to a Muslim for money,
well knowing the use to which she would be put by the purchaser.
On the other hand, we have instances of Muslim rulers from

---

[15] Ibid, p. 15, quoted from *Eastern Times* dated 7 June 1935.

Babar downwards laying stress on the desirability of respecting the Hindu feeling by not slaughtering cows, if not actually prohibiting cow-slaughter altogether, and there are innumerable respectable Muslim families among whom beef is never used out of regard for the feelings of Hindu neighbours. 'On the occasion of Id it appears the cow was not sacrificed, for we are told: "On that day [Id] everyone who is able will sacrifice a goat in his house, and keep the day as a great festival."'[16]

It is worthwhile reproducing the secret will of Zahiruddin Mohammed Badshah Ghazi (Babar) to Prince Nasiruddin Muhammad Humayun:

'Oh Son! the Kingdom of India is full of different religions. Praised be God that He bestowed upon thee its sovereignty. It is incumbent on thee to wipe all religious prejudices off the tablet of thy heart, administer justice according to the ways of every religion. Avoid especially the sacrifice of the cow by which thou canst capture the hearts of the people of India and subjects of this country may be bound up with royal obligations.

'Do not ruin the temples and shrines of any community which is obeying the laws of government. Administer justice in such a manner that the King be pleased with the subjects and the subjects with the King. The cause of Islam can be promoted more by the sword of obligation than by the sword of tyranny.

'Overlook the dissensions of the Shias and the Sunnis, else the weakness of Islam is manifest.

'And let the subjects of different beliefs harmonize in conformity with the four elements (of which the human body is harmoniously composed) so that the body of the Kingdom may be free from different dissensions. The memoirs of Timur, the master of conjunctions, (the fortunate,) should always be before thine eyes so that thou mayest become experienced in the affairs of administration. First Jamaidiulawal 935 A.H.'[17]

Some instances of tolerance by Muslims may also be mentioned here, given to me by Dr Syed Mahmud:

The famous Portuguese historian Fari Souza writes in his *Dakkhan-Ki-Halat:* 'Hindus and Musalmans served one another

---

[16] Ishwari Prasad, "*A Short History of Muslim Rule in India*, p. 738, quoting Pelsaert, p. 74.

[17] Translation of the will of Babar, a copy of which used to be in possession of the late Dr Balkrishna, Principal, Rajaram College, Kolhapur; published in *The Searchlight*, dated 30 May 1926.

and Muslim kings used to appoint Hindus to high posts and confer on them high ranks.' In other words, there was no discrimination against Hindus, and they used to perform their religious rites and ceremonies without hindrance. The Musalmans used to show great consideration for the religious feelings of the Hindus.

Sir Alfred Lyall writes in *Asiatic Studies,* p. 289: 'But so far were they [Muslim rulers] from converting India, that among the Mohammadans themselves, their own faith never acquired an entire, exclusive monopoly of the high officers of administration.'

Aurangzeb recommended to Shah Jahan and his ministers many able Hindus for appointment. For example, when there was a vacancy in the post of Diwani of Ellichpur, he strongly recommended a Rajput officer named Ramkaran but for some reasons Shah Jahan did not accept the recommendation. Aurangzeb wrote a second time that a better man could not be found. *(Ruqaat-Alamgiri,* Vol. I, p. 114.) Many instances of such recommendations may be found in *Ruqaat-Alamgiri,* and *Adab-e-Alamgiri.*

It is generally believed that Aurangzeb forcibly converted Hindus to Islam. But a curious incident may be described here which shows his attitude. Shah Jahan had imprisoned the Raja Indraman of Wandhera for his repeated acts of disobedience of orders. When Aurangzeb was appointed Subedar of the Deccan he strongly recommended his release to Shah Jahan. But Shah Jahan was so displeased with Indraman that he turned down Aurangzeb's recommendation and wrote to him that Indraman had repeatedly caused him displeasure, but he might be set free if he became a Musalman. Aurangzeb strongly protested against this and wrote to Shah Jahan that this condition could not be acted upon and was impolitic and short-sighted, and that if he was to be released, he should be released on conditions offered by him. Aurangzeb's letter to Shafaullah Khan, the Prime Minister, on this subject is to be found in the *Adab-e-Alamgiri.*

II. SOCIAL LIFE

The influence exerted by the Hindu on Muslim social life and custom and vice versa was no less remarkable. This can be illustrated easily by reference to the rites and ceremonies connected with the three most important and significant incidents in human life—birth, marriage and death. I shall mention here some common or similar rites and customs observed by middle-class Hindus and Musalmans in Bihar.

It is a common custom that at the time of the birth of a child, particularly if it happens to be a male child, songs are sung which are known locally as *sohar*. Women from neighbouring houses assemble and join the singing and other festivities At the door of the room of confinement, fire is kept burning and a piece of iron and a thorny plant of the cactus class known as *muthiasij* and certain other articles are kept to keep out evil spirits. On the sixth day after the birth the mother and baby are washed and this ceremony is known as *chhathi* or sixth-day ceremony and the mother, taking the baby in her arms, looks at the sky and counts the stars. There are other ceremonies on the twentieth and fiftieth day known as *bistouri* and *chheella* respectively. During the period of confinement up to the sixth day, in particular, the mother is considered to be impure and is not permitted to touch food to be taken by others. Both the idea of spirits haunting houses and of untouchability of food are foreign to orthodox Islam and so also is the idea of baths on fixed days after the birth of a child—but they are prevalent and acted upon in practice in Muslim households.

Removing the hair with which a baby is born from its head is another rite of some importance both among Hindus and Musalmans. It is known as *mundan* among Hindus and as *aqiqa* among Musalmans. It may have some religious significance but the similarity of rites is remarkable.

In Islam, marriage is a contract in the legal sense of the term. The bridegroom and the bride agree to live together as husband and wife and like other contracts, the agreement has to be attested by witnesses and requires consideration to be passed. It is also dissoluble but like other contracts the dissolution is subject to payment of damages. The damages are ascertained and are fixed at the time of the marriage, that is, of the contract itself, the payment of which is deferred till the dissolution of the marriage. The more essential part of the marriage ceremony is a very short business and consists practically of agreement by the parties concerned in the presence of witnesses and takes but a few minutes. This is the *nikah* proper and may be separated from the festivities which are known as *shadi*. In Hinduism, marriage is a sacrament and is accordingly indissoluble in theory. The vow that is taken is a religious vow and is witnessed not only by human beings but also by the sun and the moon, fire and the earth, water and stone—the symbols of existence that last till the separate human soul is merged in the Eternal at the end of a cycle. The ceremony when duly performed takes a long time. It would thus seem that the two differ fundamentally from each other. But as a matter of practice, while the fundamental ceremonies are observed by both the Hindus and Muslims according to their religious precepts, the other rites which are not essential have become assimilated to one another to a considerable extent. The pomp and procession, they feasts and festivities, the songs sung by women, the presents, the practical jokes and playful practices are all alike. Islam forbids all pomp; Hinduism neither enjoins nor forbids it; but in both communities today one sees things happening on the occasion of marriage which are hardly distinguishable.

A detailed description may be of some interest.

The rites and ceremonies and festivities connected with marriage which are prevalent among Musalmans in Bihar have been greatly influenced by similar rites, ceremonies and festivities common among Hindus. As stated above, *nikah* is the essential ceremony for a Muslim marriage. It is often made coincident with what is known as *shadi,* which is the festivity part of it. But it is sometimes separated from the *shadi,* which takes place at a different time and place. At the time of *shadi* the bridegroom's party, which varies in splendour, pomp and paraphernalia with the wealth and social status of the bridegroom's family, goes to the house of the bride and is lodged ordinarily not in the house of the bride's father but in another house and often in tents. For some days prior to the arrival of the party some rites are performed at the houses of the bridegroom and the bride. One rite is known as *rat jaga* when the women keep awake at night and prepare a kind of pudding. On another day the ceremony of *mandwa* is performed when a sort of tent or canopy is fixed in the courtyard of the inner apartments on tall bamboos. On a third day the rite of *kandoori* is performed when food is cooked, and distributed in the name of dead persons. This food can be taken only by Syed women. On a fixed day the party or *barat* starts and reaches the bride's home. For some days before the marriage, the bride has to observe what is known as *mayun* or *manja* when she has to keep indoors and so no one except some selected women of the family can see her during the period. She is anointed with *ubtan* (a preparation of turmeric and some other things) every day, and she comes out only on the day of marriage.

Among the Hindus the *mandwa* or *mandap* is made on an auspicious day one or two days before the marriage, which is performed in the *mandap*. There is a particular religious ceremony whereby dead ancestors are invited to witness and bless the marriage and to take the new couple within their fold of kinsmen. The girl is anointed with turmeric which is considered a very important ceremony and the saying goes that this ceremony of anointing with turmeric cannot be performed twice on a girl, that is to say, there cannot be a second marriage of a girl, if one husband dies. She is kept secluded for a number of days before the marriage when she may not see anyone and what with the anointment and what with the abstinence from bathing on those days she looks emaciated and dirty; just a day or two before the marriage she has to take a bath with ceremony. Feeding Brahmins on every important occasion is a common thing among all Hindus throughout India. The *barat* or marriage processions of Hindus and Muslims are indistinguishable in their pomp—a great parade of elephants, horses and now-a-days, motor cars, and if at night, with lights of all kinds, music, and so on. Both among Hindus and Musalmans, the bridegroom's party is usually accommodated at another house or in tents, chiefly because the bride's father is unable to find accommodation in his own house for such large crowds that constitute it.

Among Hindus in Bihar the procession goes to the house of the bride where the bridegroom is received by the women of the bride's family who sprinkle a little water and scatter rice over the bridegroom, put the *tilak* on his forehead, and wave a light in front of him. The father of the bride also receives him with ceremony and makes some present. The other guests are received and offered drinks and light refreshments. The whole party then proceeds to its lodgings. This is known as *parichawan*. Soon after, the bride's party, accompanied by some women with water and eatables, approach the bridegroom's party at the latter's lodgings and invites them formally to dinner. Presents are made to the bridegroom's elders. This is known as *dhurchak*.

A little later the bridegroom's party proceeds to the bride's house when the bride is seated in the *mandap* and the elder brother of the bridegroom presents to her clothes and ornaments, and sweets and scents carried in a specially made basket which looks like a temple with a broad base and a tapering top. This is the only occasion when an elder brother of the bridegroom is supposed or expected to see or touch the bride. This is known as *kanyanirikshan* (seeing the bride). Next is the ceremony of marriage proper. The bridegroom and bride are brought together in the *mandap*—the bride with clothes and ornaments presented by the bridegroom's party, and the bridegroom with the clothes presented by the bride's party and after worship of God, the parents of the bride make a formal gift of the girl to the bridegroom with due ceremony. Some of the near relations of the parties are present. In Bihar, on account of strictness of the *purdah*, men of the bridegroom's party except the priest and such other persons as have to officiate and participate in the ceremonies, are not allowed to attend this ceremony, as the ladies of the bride's family are present. All who join the party are supposed to be witnesses and the ceremonies include invocations to God and the sun, the moon, fire, water, earth and stone, and so on to witness and bless the union, and a repetition by the bridegroom and bride of certain *mantra*s promising to be true and faithful to each other. The pair then goes round the fire and the ceremony is completed with the bridegroom besmearing the forehead of the bride with vermilion. This is known as *sindurdan* or gift of vermilion. This vermilion mark is the sign of the woman's good fortune and she puts it on so long as her husband is alive.

Among the Musalmans, after the arrival of the bridegroom's party there is a ceremony of what is known as *bari* when people of the bridegroom's party proceed from their lodgings to the bride's house, with clothes, oil, sweets, fruits, and other items, accompanied by music. In front is carried what is known as *sohagpura* which is a kind of basket with a broad base and a tapering top containing spices, fruits, sweets, coloured yarn, rice, etc., exactly like that of the Hindus. When these presents have been received by the bride's people they in their turn present clothes, etc., known *askhilat* for the bridegroom. He wears the clothes so presented. The *nikah* or essential marriage ceremony if it has not taken place already is performed at this time. The bridegroom puts sandal-paste on the head of the bride as vermilion in the case of Hindus and the ceremony is known as *mangbhari*. At this time pieces of poetry suitable to the occasion are repeated and songs are sung. The Hindus also on the occasion of the *dhurchak* and *kanyanirikshan* have the custom of repeating verses and discussions among the younger folk and learned Pandits, in earnest as also in fun. On each and every occasion, both among Hindus and Musalmans, the women folk sing suitable songs, which are similar in tune and substance.

The marriage party generally departs from the bride's house after a day's stay. On the second day the bridegroom is taken to the *mandap* and some ceremonies in which the women participate are performed. These have no religious significance but are customary and vary from place to place. Among the Hindus the boy is anointed with *ubtan* to which he consents only if a present is made to him. In the evening the women take him to the bride's room and perform what is known as the *kohbar* ceremony. Before the party departs the ceremony of *muhdekhi* (seeing the face) is held when the bridegroom and bride are seated together and the bridegroom's relations are supposed to see the girl's face and to make presents. And lastly there is the *bidai*, or farewell ceremony. In between, the bridegroom's party is fed by the bride's party. Among Musalmans also, the bridegroom is taken to the *mandwa* and the ceremony of *runumai* (face-seeing) is held when the husband and wife see each other's face in a mirror. At the time of the departure of the bridegroom and bride for the former's house, presents are made to the bridegroom both among Hindus and Musalmans, which are mostly articles of household utility and may include clothes, beddings, utensils and conveyance like a *palki* in which the bride is taken. Among Hindus, a cow is often presented and those who can afford it present a horse or an elephant and now-a-days, a motor car.

Among Musalmans the bride on arrival is not taken straight to the bridegroom's house but is stopped at some place like a *dargah* where the women of the bridegroom's family come with water and twigs of mango and perform some rites. On arrival at the house of the bridegroom, the husband of the bridegroom's sister stops the conveyance and does not allow it to enter the house before a present is made to him. Among the Hindus also the sister's husband is offered a present for a similar symbolic obstruction, and the boy and the girl are taken round to places of worship like a temple or *Kaliasthan*.

There is thus a close similarity in the ceremonies and rites of both Hindus and Musalmans, and this in spite of the fact that Islam does not prescribe any of them and some of them may appear to orthodox and puritanical Musalmans to be even opposed to its tenets.

Hinduism as generally understood does not permit dissolution of marriage not only in life, but even after death, and hence there can be no remarriage for a widow. Islam does nothing of this sort and indeed remarriage of a widow has the high authority of the Prophet himself who married widows. Yet Hindu customs and environment have cast such great influence on Muslims that in northern India at any rate, remarriage of a widow though not prohibited, either socially or as a matter of religion, is not looked upon with favour in respectable Muslim families.

The essential funeral ceremonies are also performed by the Hindus and Musalmans as prescribed by their respective religions. Among Musalmans before the burial, prayers are offered; later again prayers are offered and food distributed to the poor on the third or fourth and again on the tenth and fortieth day for the benefit of the departed soul. I do not know if these observances on fixed days after death are prescribed by Islam but there is no doubt that they look very much like those of the Hindus on prescribed days—the second, the seventh, the tenth and the twelfth or thirteenth or thirtieth day, when they also, after offering water and *pinda* (oblation), to the departed soul feed the poor and distribute alms.

Even the caste system has not left the Indian Musalmans untouched and unaffected. The Syed, the Shaikh, the Pathan, the Malik, the Momin, the Mansoor, the Rayeen; the Qasab, the Raki, the Hajjam, the Dhobi and a host of other caste names may be mentioned to show the division among Musalmans. Some of these are the result of the profession followed, while others are based on birth and heredity. As in the case of widow marriage, while marriages of members of one with those of another are not prohibited socially or as a matter of religion, they often, if not in very many cases, take place within the group to which both parties belong. But more than marriage, one can almost feel while moving and living intimately among them that these groups have developed to a considerable extent the exclusiveness and that indefinable consciousness of separateness from other groups which is so characteristic of castes among Hindus. One need only mention the Muslim Bhangi who has no higher status in Muslim society than a Hindu untouchable of that class among Hindus. Not that Islam sanctions any of these things. It is the influence of the environment, which the Muslims of India have not been able to withstand.

It is necessary in this connection also to mention that large communities among Musalmans who have been converted to Islam from among Hindus have carried with them, and still maintain, many of their Hindu usages and customs even after a long lapse of time since their conversion. One need only mention that the Malkana Rajputs, an unsuccessful effort for whose conversion back to Hinduism made about twenty years ago led to so much bad blood, still observe and maintain many old rites and ceremonies which they used to observe as Hindus. Doubtless there are other groups who have similarly not given up their old customs.

It is also a well-known fact that many large groups of Muslims retained till recently even the laws of inheritance which they used to have before their conversion to Islam, in spite of the fact that Islam lays down its own laws. The Khojas and the Cutchi Memons and Boharas are rich Muslim communities in Sindh, Gujarat and Bombay. They have trade and business not only in other parts of India but also in many foreign countries like South and East Africa, Arabia, Persia and Malaya. Many of them till 1937 retained not only many Hindu customs but also the Hindu law of inheritance. Similarly, Baluchis and some Punjabi Musalmans have had their own customary law. The Moplahs are governed by the Marumak-kathayam law. It was only in 1937 that an Act was passed whereby Shariat was made applicable to Musalmans—any custom or usage not incorporated in a statute to the contrary notwithstanding.

Hindus have undoubtedly always refused to dine with Musalmans. But all Hindus do not dine with one another. This taboo has existed and exists even today not only between Hindus and Musalmans but also between different castes and even sub-castes among Hindus themselves. Thus a Brahmin does not dine with a Rajput, and a Rajput does not dine with a Baniya or Kayastha. Even among Brahmins, a Sakadwipi Brahmin does not dine with a Sarjoopari or a Dakshini Brahmin with a Bengali or Maithili Brahmin and vice versa. Sarjoopari Brahmins do not dine with one another unless they are related, nor does a Srivastava Kayastha dine with an Ambastha or Kama Kayastha. If a non-Hindu wishes to go into details of these taboos he will find himself absolutely and completely bewildered in their mazes. Not only is there a distinction between caste and caste and the sub-castes of a caste, but taboo extends to various kinds of food and the way it is cooked. In Bihar, bread if fried in ghee may be eaten, even if touched by a man of another caste, but not if it is baked on fire; it is not so in Bengal. Some vegetables cooked without salt may be eaten but not if salt is mixed. These distinctions differ also from province to province, from caste to caste, and from article to article. No one who has not been born and brought up in the system can know, much less understands, these taboos or the principles, if any, on which they are based. It is therefore not surprising if, say, a Kayastha hardly ever feels hurt or humiliated if, say, a Rajput refuses to take food touched by him and vice versa. They all take it as a matter of course and feel no sense of humiliation or inferiority. Even the so-called untouchables until recently accepted their fate without bitterness and malice. What I have said above applies to the ordinary mass of Hindus and is not true of those who have received modern education or come under the influence of caste conferences and reform movements like that of the Brahmo Samaj or Arya Samaj or the levelling influence of Mahatma Gandhi. These educated or reformed Hindus have in many cases dropped and given up in their own lives many of these taboos, and many who still stick to them in practice, give no intellectual appreciation or support to them.

The Musalmans who have come in close contact with the Hindus and their society with its caste system have not failed sympathetically to understand these taboos and have not in actual practice resented them, as they know that they imply no inferiority, but are only just a custom which has come down and has been accepted as such by the Hindus. They have therefore freely joined Hindu festivities in connection with marriages, child-births, and so on when invited, and have invited Hindus on similar occasions to their own houses and families. Food has not stood in the way of free and cordial social relationship. The Hindu has provided food to his Muslim guests, observing his own caste rule, and the Muslim has fed and entertained his Hindu guests without in any way interfering with their caste prejudices. Here again, what I have said applies to the ordinary unsophisticated Musalman and not to all educated and modern Muslims. What I have stated above is not in justification of the caste system or in extenuation of its evils. I have only stated facts as they have been; but times have changed and with them views and attitudes too. While therefore it is highly desirable to remove and abolish as many of these distinctions and differences as possible and that as soon as possible, especially when an ever increasing number of persons both among the Hindus and Musalmans have begun to resent them, it is not right to attach too much importance to them as factors standing in the way of conciliation, goodwill and fellow-feeling between the two communities, whether in the past or at present.

In a village where both Hindus and Musalmans live—and that is the case in innumerable villages both in provinces where the Muslim population preponderates and in provinces where Hindus form a majority of the population—it is a common experience to see a real and genuine friendship and neighbourliness established and a Hindu as unabashedly calls a Muslim neighbour as *bhai* or *chacha* or *kaka* as a Muslim does a Hindu neighbour. Indeed there are many names which are common to members of both communities, particularly among the lower strata of society, and Hindu names have been adopted or retained by Muslims and Muslim names have been taken many Hindus. This is true not only of the surnames and titles which imply distinction of posts and professions but also of the real and particular names of individuals. Not only men but also villages, towns, tanks—in fact everything which can bear a name—has a Hindu or a Muslim name or a name which is half Hindu and half Muslim, irrespective of the fact whether they are inhabited or owned by Hindus or Muslims or as is more frequently the case, by both.

The old village life is being gradually disrupted and broken up. Being born and bred up in a village in Bihar and not having cut myself off from village moorings, I make bold to describe the general life there as it existed not long ago when I was a youth and which has not disappeared even now. Every village was more or less a self-contained unit in many respects. It had its own land which was cultivated by the village people, its own pasture land and its own complement of workers and artisans and people of various grades and professions. Thus in a typical village one would find peasants and labourers, zamindars and Brahmins, and

in many places both Hindus and Musalmans. Each village had
its carpenter and blacksmith, barber and washerman, potter and
bangle-seller *(churihar)*, grain-parcher and oil-presser. There were
also the *mehtar* or *bhangi* (sweeper) and *chamar* and *dome*. Each
of these had his utility in the social and economic life of the village
and was in most cases paid in kind at the time of harvest by each
peasant. Most of them had a part to play on ceremonial occasions
such as child-birth, marriage, death, for which he got some special
reward or perquisite according to the status and financial position
of the person to whom he rendered service. Now, some of these
might be Musalmans, but nevertheless they rendered the same
service as their Hindu compatriots and were remunerated in the
same way. The barber, for example, is a very important person
in connection with many ceremonies among Hindus. Thus in the
ceremony of *chura-karan* (first shaving of the head) which goes
mostly with the ceremony of giving the sacred thread to a boy
among Hindus of higher castes, he is a principal performer. On the
occasion of marriage and, in fact, practically in all ceremonies he
has some part or other to play. In connection with funeral rites,
again, shaving is an important item among Hindus of all castes
and the barber is naturally in demand and does a lot of other
things in connection with the offering of oblations and *pinda* at
the time of *shraddha*. There are many villages where there is no
Hindu barber. The Muslim barber does all the things that a Hindu
barber does except offering eatables and water. The Hindu does
not object to accepting his services as being against his religion
or custom, nor does the Muslim barber object to rendering his
services which in many instances are more or less of a religious
nature and thus may be repugnant to the strict tenets of Islam.
Wearing of bangles is regarded as an indispensable requisite for
every Hindu woman whose husband is alive. Those who supply
bangles at the time of marriage and other auspicious occasions
when they are required to be changed, as also for ordinary everyday
use, are invariably Muslims whose women folk have access for
this purpose to the ladies of even well-to-do Hindu families who
observe strict *purdah*. Similarly the washerman or the *bhangi*
may be a Hindu or Muslim and does his ordinary work as also
his special part on ceremonial occasions irrespective of the fact
whether he is a Hindu or Muslim. Another caste is that of *malis*
who are expert gardeners and rear flowers. Their function is to

supply flowers not only for ceremonial purposes but also for all religious functions and for daily worship. The *mali*, too, does this service irrespective of the fact whether he is a Hindu or Musalman. The Hindu does not object to receiving flowers from a Muslim *mali* for offering them to his God, nor does the Muslim *mali* object to supplying flowers intended for being offered to an idol in a temple or in connection with any other religious ceremony. All this has been going on for hundreds of years and must have been the product of intimate contact between the members of the two communities.

Dress

Dress is influenced more than anything else by the climatic conditions of the place where the wearers live. It is therefore not surprising that dress in India differs from province to province and to a considerable extent according to the means of the wearers. Among the lower strata of society and the poorer people, there not much difference and similarly, among the people more or less at the top of the social ladder there is not much difference. The difference in fact is more between the rich and well-to-do on the one hand and the poor on the other. No foreigner could ordinarily notice a difference between the Indian costume of a Pandit Motilal Nehru, Sir Tej Bahadur Sapru, Dr Sachchidananda Sinha, or Pandit Jawaharlal Nehru or Kumar Ganganad Sinha, President of the Bihar Provincial Hindu Mahasabha, and that of Nawab Muhammad Ismail or Chaudhri Khaliquzzaman, shining lights in the Muslim League, or Sir Ali Imam, or for that matter, of Qaed-e-Azam Jinnah. Similarly, he would not find a distinction between the dress of Sardar Sardul Singh Caveeshar or Sardar Marigal Singh who are Sikhs and of Maulana Zafar Ali or Maulana Abul Kalam Azad expect for the head dress of the Sikhs. If he went to a village in Bihar or Bengal or the Punjab or the UP where the Muslim *kisan* is busy cultivating his field, he would not find him wearing a dress which would distinguish him from his Hindu compatriot engaged in the same occupation. I take no notice of the fez-cap, which is not Indian, and is only a recent introduction and donned by some Muslims, particularly among the educated classes in some places in imitation of Turkey which has now given it up.

Pyjamas are worn by Muslims more largely than by Hindus and may thus be considered as peculiar to them in some places but the number of Hindus wearing pyjamas is not small, and the pyjama is not worn by the vast majority of Musalmans. The *dhoti* whose very name is derived from Sanskrit and is a peculiarly Hindu dress is actually worn in one form or another by the vast majority of Muslims of India, as any one who has seen villages and come in contact with the masses of Musalmans both in towns and villages—but more largely in villages—can easily testify.

The assimilation of articles of personal adornment has passed even into the *zenana,* in spite of the *purdah.* Many ornaments worn by women are common to both Hindus and Musalmans and many of them have their names derived either from a Hindu or Muslim source and continue to bear those names irrespective of the fact that they are worn by Hindu or Muslim women. Similarly the sari is the most common dress of women all over India. It is worn by both Hindu and Muslim women, and where pyjamas are worn by women as in parts of the north-western region, they are worn not only by Muslim women but by Sikh and Hindu women as well. In the hills, pyjamas are commonly worn by all on account of the severe cold of the locality.

Purdah

One social institution which will strike every foreign visitor to India is the institution of *purdah*, or *gosha* as it is called in some places. It is purely an Islamic institution, although in India it has developed its own technique independently. I am told that according to Islamic Shariat, women are not prohibited from going out of their homes, only they must cover their faces like other parts of their bodies with a veil or *burqa*. In India, they generally are not permitted to go out of their houses. This is possible only in the case of those who can afford to keep within doors. The poorer people who cannot afford it have perforce to go out for various kinds of business.

The ancient Hindu custom does not recognize or encourage *purdah* at all. In fact, Sanskrit literature is full of references to women who freely came out and joined their husbands in all their undertakings in which women could participate. The modern custom of observing *purdah* is entirely borrowed from Musalmans and is enforced with the greatest rigour in places which have come most under Muslim influence. It is not prevalent in the south where Muslim influence did not penetrate to the extent it did in the north, except among some of the classes which imitated the Muslim rulers. Today, reform for abolishing purdah makes easier headway among Hindus than among Musalmans, because it has some sort of sanction in Islam which it lacks in Hinduism.

It will thus appear from the above discussion that there has been considerable influence exerted by the two communities on each other and they came to live together in peace and harmony in spite of their religious differences which undoubtedly had shaped their social institutions also separately and in different moulds. It is nevertheless true that the two never coalesced and neither was able to absorb the other completely. It was not to be expected that this would happen. The mere fact that Islam was a religion which had its origin in a foreign land and had a complete code for governing and regulating the life of its adherents based on a different background would make it difficult, if not impossible, for it to be absorbed by Hinduism or to absorb Hinduism in itself. Hindu literature, philosophy and religion are highly developed and command the reverence and adherence of millions of people. Hinduism has absorbed all protestant sects which rose and grew on the Indian soil in course of time. Professor Rhys Davids writing about the relation of Hinduism with Buddhism says that 'Hinduism permits the most complete freedom of thought and expression which the world has yet witnessed.'[18] This has come down from the earliest days of the Vedas and the Upanishads and explains the development of various schools of thought and philosophy. There is, therefore, no formula of faith which a Hindu must accept. But Hinduism insists upon certain rules of personal and social conduct which have varied from time to time and from place to place to suit exigencies and contingencies. There is, therefore, extensive room for social reform among Hindus and it is this elasticity which has helped the Hindu society not only to adapt itself to changing circumstances but also to assimilate a host of others who did not have the same sort of philosophical and religious background of long standing. In absorbing its own protestant sects it was helped not a little by this social adaptability and freedom of thought

[18] Rhys Davids, *Buddhist India*, p. 258.

which did not hesitate to apotheosize even the founders of these
protestant sects as was the case with Buddhism. Buddha was
accepted as one of the *Avatars,* although one can quote passages
from books denouncing the Buddha, which was symptomatic of
the conflict that was going on during the period of assimilation.
And today Buddhism—that is, its philosophy and code of morals
and conduct—has been so completely absorbed in Hinduism
that there is practically no Buddhist left in the land of the birth
of Buddhism. Buddhism was an offshoot of Hinduism and the
whole background of its philosophy is Hindu in conception and
expression. It was therefore easily absorbed in Hinduism in India,
but flourished as a separate religion in other countries where there
was no such opportunity for either its absorbing or being absorbed
by any other religion or philosophy. It is, therefore, not surprising
that with such a background, Hinduism did not and could not
absorb or get absorbed in Islam. But the fact that the two lived
and flourished side by side has, I believe, been for the good of
both and I do not think it is doing service to either to rake up
old and forgotten incidents and episodes in their long history of
association for proving their separateness or, what amounts to the
same thing, for creating rivalries and bad blood among them. It is
more profitable and certainly much more honourable to recognize
the fact that both have lived together for hundreds of years mostly
on terms of amity and goodwill and, what is more important,
that there is no escape for either from this association in future.

I cannot do better than close this section with quotations
from two Professors of History—one a Hindu, Dr Tarachand
whom we have quoted frequently, and the other a Muslim, Mr
Salahuddin Khodabaksh, Professor of Law and Islamic History,
Calcutta University.

Writes Dr Tarachand:

'It is hardly possible to exaggerate the extent of Muslim influence
over Indian life in all departments. But nowhere else is it shown
so vividly and as picturesquely as in customs, in intimate details
of domestic life, in music, in the fashions of dress, in the ways
of cooking, in the ceremonial of marriage, in the celebration of
festivals and fairs, and in the courtly institutions and etiquette
of Maratha, Rajput and Sikh Princes. In the days of Babar, the
Hindu and Muslim lived and thought so much alike that he was
forced to notice their peculiar "Hindustani way"; his successors

so gloriously adorned and so marvellously enriched this legacy that India might well be proud today of the heritage which they in their turn have left behind.'[19]

Mr Salahuddin Khodabaksh writes:

'We are constantly told that Mohammedans are a distinct people, as unlike the Hindus as the Semitic is unlike the Aryan; that there are differences penetrating to the very root of life; differences of habit, temperament, social customs, racial type; that these differences are so vital and so enormous that fusion between the two is a hopeless impossibility, an impracticable dream. Now I am not at all sure that this argument is sound. Admitting that the Mohammedans came to India as foreign conquerors as utterly different to the Hindus as the British are different to us both, we cannot forget that for many centuries they have lived side by side, freely mixing with the people of the land, naturally influencing each other, taking Indian women as their wives, adopting local customs and local usages: in fine, permeated and pervaded through and through by local characteristics and local peculiarities. The most infallible proof of this we find in the marriage ceremonies, which are entirely Hindu ceremonies, in the customs of the women folk, such as the use of the vermilion mark, the symbol and token of wedded life, the restrictions imposed upon the dress and diet of widows, the disapproval, nay, condemnation, of widow marriages—and indeed in a thousand little practices behind the zenana. All this indicates somewhat more than mere superficial connection between the two communities which mainly divide the Indian population. A yet clearer proof is the unity of language, and the similarity of dress. Moreover, say what you will, a large number, in fact the largest portion of the Mohammedan population, are Hindu converts to Islam. It rests upon no unwarranted assumption, but upon well-ascertained facts, that Hinduism and Mohammedanism have acted and reacted upon each other, influencing social institutions, colouring religious thoughts with their mutual, typical and religious hues; these being conspicuous illustrations of the union of the two streams of Hinduism and Islam which, since Muslim conquest, have flowed side by side in India.'[20]

Is all this beautiful warp and woof which has been woven into the most delicate and exquisite fabric of our social life by

[19] Tarachand, *Influence of Islam on Indian Culture*, pp. 141–42.
[20] Quoted by Dr Sachchidananda Sinha in his *Some Eminent Bihar Contemporaries*, pp. 185–86.

unintended action or conscious effort of innumerable men and
women—Hindu and Muslim—in the course of centuries to be torn
to pieces by the cruel and undiscerning hand of unununderstanding
politics?

III. LANGUAGE

The language that is spoken and understood in northern India
now, by whatever name we may call it, has undoubtedly been
greatly influenced by, if it is not the product of, the joint efforts
of Hindus and Musalmans. Its origin is surely to be sought in the
Sanskrit language and its offshoots, Prakrit and Pali, which became
current after Sanskrit had ceased to be the spoken language of
the masses. The language of the Muslim invaders and conquerors
differed according to the tribe to which they belonged, influenced
and affected as that language was by Arabic and more largely by
Persian. During the period of Muslim rule, Persian became the
court language and was largely studied by the higher classes of the
Hindus also, particularly such of them as came in close contact
with the state and the ruling people. But it never became, as it
could never have become, the language of the masses. As the bulk
of Musalmans of India were Indians by birth, the Persian language
was never the language of the vast majority of Musalmans even
of those days. A language which could be used as the medium of
intercourse between the foreign Muslim rulers and both Hindus and
Musalmans—was therefore a necessity. Both joined in developing
it and as early as the days of Amir Khusro, it had become so far
advanced as to be used by him for his verses, which are popular
even to this day. The protagonists of both Urdu and Hindi as
understood today, admit the contribution of both Hindus and
Musalmans to the growth of the literatures of both—if they
are treated as separate languages. As Hindus looked to Sanskrit
literature for religious inspiration and the Muslims to Arabic and
Persian, it was only natural and to be expected that they would
import words derived from the one or the other, leaving the
structure of the language intact. That structure, which is the real
framework of a language, is still common to both forms of the
language known as Hindi and Urdu. The difference mainly is in
respect of a portion of the vocabulary only. It is therefore that
in northern India there is one language that is understood and

spoken by both Hindus and Musalmans, although educated people in writing it use more or less words of Sanskrit and Persian or Arabic according to the education and training they have received. It is unfortunate that a controversy has been raised even in regard to what can and ought to be justly claimed as a common heritage of both Hindus and Musalmans.

The protagonists of Hindi cannot forget or ignore the very valuable contribution made by Musalmans to the growth of that language and its literature right from the days of Amir Khusro to the present day. One has only to turn to a selection of poems written by Musalmans from time to time contained in one of the volumes of *Kabita Kaumudi* compiled by Pandit Ramnaresh Tripathi. There we find that not only is the language employed by the Muslim poets what writers of Hindi claim to be Hindi but there are also devotional songs, the very theme of which is Hinduistic. It is well known that Sita Ram and Radha Krishna furnish themes for the bulk of the literature of the Hindus. A small volume comprised in the series of five volumes published by the Gita Press of Gorakhpore contains devotional hymns composed by Musalmans only, and no devotee can fail to be elated and inspired by them. The *doha*s of Rahiman are household property all over northern India like the *sawaiyya*s of Giridhar for their wit and wisdom. Kabir has already been mentioned as the devotee philosopher who brought down the lofty teachings and philosophy of the Upanishads and Vedanta from their high pedestal to the level of understanding of the common man and the village—dragged them out of the secluded cloisters and forest and mountain ashramas of yogis, and introduced them into the huts and hamlets of the peasants. What Tulsidas did in northern India and Mahaprabhu Chaitanya in Bengal and Orissa for popularizing the cult of Bhakti, Kabir did in northern India for popularizing Yoga and the Vedanta.

Similarly, who can deny the contribution made to Urdu literature by Hindus and who can say that Hindus even today do not constitute a very considerable proportion of the people interested in and devoted to Urdu language and literature? It is thus not only against facts of history but also a denial of facts of everyday life and occurrence to make the question of language a bone of contention between Hindus and Muslims.

But it was not only Hindi or Urdu that owed a debt to Muslim rulers for their growth and development. Other provincial languages

were also helped and owed not a little to the encouragement given
by Muslim rulers. 'In the north Hindi, in the west Marathi, and in
the east Bengali developed into literary languages, and Hindus and
Musalmans share in the glory of their achievements. Above all, a
new linguistic synthesis takes place: the Muslim gives up his Turkish
and Persian and adopts the speech of the Hindu. He modifies it like
his architecture and painting to his needs and thus evolves a new
literary medium—the Urdu. Again, both Musalmans and Hindus
adopt it as their own and a curious phenomenon occurs, Hindi
Bhasha is employed for one kind of literary expression, the Urdu
for another; and thus whenever the creative impulse of the Muslim
or the Hindu runs in one channel he uses Hindi and when it drives
him into the other he uses Urdu . . . Muslim influence upon Hindi
as such was deep and is seen in its vocabulary, grammar, metaphor,
prosody and style; and what is true of Hindi is true of Marathi
and Bengali and more so of Punjabi and Sindhi.'[21]

'The efforts of the rulers of Bengal were not confined to the
promotion of Mohammedan learning alone, for they also directed
their fostering care for the advancement of letters into a new channel
which is of particular interest to the Bengali-speaking people. It may
seem to them an anomaly that their language should owe its elevation
to a literary status not to themselves but to the Mohammedans . . .
It was the epics—the *Ramayana* and the *Mahabharata*—that first
attracted the notice of the Mohammedan rulers of Bengal at
whose instance they were translated into Bengali, the language
of their domicile. The first Bengali rendering of the *Mahabharata*
was ordered by Nazir Shah of Bengal (AD 1282–1385) who was
a great patron of the vernacular of the province and whom the
great poet Vidyapati has immortalized by dedicating to him one
of his songs . . . It is doubtful whether a Muslim ruler of Bengal
or the Hindu Raja Kans Narayan appointed Kirtibas to translate
the *Ramayana* into Bengali. Even if the latter story be true it is
undoubted that Muslim precedents influenced the action of the
Raja . . . Emperor Husain Shah was a great patron of Bengali.
Haldhar Basu was appointed by him to translate the *Bhagwat
Purana* into Bengali . . . Paragal Khan, a general of Husain Shah
and Paragal's son Chhuti Khan, have made themselves immortal by

[21] Tarachand, *In Influence of Islam*, pp. 139–40.

associating their names with the Bengali translation of a portion of the Mahabharat.'[22]

The question of language has to be considered from another point of view. So far as the two nations theory is concerned, it does not at all help the protagonists of Partition. Language differs from area to area and not from community to community. Thus Bengali is the language of both Hindus and Musalmans of Bengal. So is Gujarati of Gujarat and Punjabi of the Punjab and Hindi or Urdu (or Hindustani or by whatever other name one chooses to call it) of northern India, including the whole area from the borders of the Punjab to the borders of Bengal on the one side and from the foot of the Himalayas to the borders of the Marathi-speaking and Telugu-speaking provinces in central and southern India. These languages differ from the south Indian languages like Telugu, Tamil, Kanarese and Malayalam and have their own local variations and dialects which are used by the common folk. There is no division of the population in any part of India which coincides both in respect of language and religion. The distribution of languages is territorial and not communal or religious. If the common language of both Musalmans and non-Musalmans—among whom the vast majority is Musalman—in the north-eastern zone of India is Bengali, if the common language of Hindus, Sikhs and Muslims of the Punjab is alike Punjabi, there is no language which is common to all the people comprised in the four or five divisions of the North-West which are sought to be included in the north-western zone. Punjabi is at least as different from Pushto or Sindhi or Baluchi as Hindi is from Bengali, and as Pushto is from Sindhi or Kashmiri. It is thus clear that if the question of nationality has to be determined on the basis of language, then the Bengalis, whether Muslim or Hindu, have to go together as they have one common language and equally clearly the Punjabi, the Sindhi, the Pathan and the Baluchi cannot go together as forming one nation as their languages differ from one another as much as they differ from Bengali.

The religious literature of Hindus and Muslims derives its inspiration from Sanskrit and Arabic respectively, which are their fountain-heads. A Bengali-speaking Hindu draws that inspiration from Sanskrit just as the Tamil-speaking or Sindhi-speaking Hindu

---

[22] N.N. Law, *Promotion of Learning in India during Muhammadan Rule*, pp. 107–10.

does. Similarly a Punjabi-speaking Musalman turns to the same fountain-head of Arabic as does the Musalman of the south or the east. While thus Hindus and Musalmans have different sources for their religious inspiration and ideals, sources which are not the common or spoken language of the people of any part of this country, they have both a common language of speech and intercourse whose literature in some parts is quite rich and extensive, irrespective of their religious faith, although this common language differs from province to province or territorially.

If Hindi and Urdu are different languages, the one of the Hindus and the other of the Muslims, and if after the Partition of India into Hindu and Muslim zones, each zone is free to develop itself on the lines considered best by itself subject to provision of safeguards for the protection of the rights of the minorities including their language, what large and inspiring future can Urdu have, since it will not be the language of the people of any Muslim zone and will have either to be forced or at least supported and nurtured as an exotic in the north-western and eastern zones (of neither of which it is the spoken language) and will only be protected as the language of a minority in the central zone where non-Muslims (who *ex hypothesi* have a different language) predominate?

If also they are really two separate languages, let them be developed on their own independent lines, leaving a common language, which is loaded neither with pure Sanskrit nor pure Arabic and Persian words, to grow and prosper as a national language for the whole country.

IV. ART

Among arts the most important are architecture, sculpture, painting, music and dancing. Each of these had, like Sanskrit and some provincial literatures, attained high development in India before the arrival of the Musalmans. It was, therefore, not to be expected that they would be absorbed by corresponding Muslim arts and this is just what happened. They assimilated whatever was suitable and assimilable and like the language of northern India, developed a sort of new synthesis and in fact, in some respects, greatly influenced Islamic culture.

Architecture

Indian architecture of the Muslim period differs considerably from that of the Hindu or Buddhistic period in Indian history. But it cannot be said to be altogether an exotic brought from outside and planted in a foreign environment. It is hard to imagine that Hindu architects and skilled artisans had absolutely no hand in the building of the Taj or that Muslim workers had nothing to do with the building of Hindu temples erected during the Muslim period. In northern India today, it is very largely Muslim masons and workmen who are employed in building not only houses of Hindus but also their temples. Experts and specialists in architecture have pointed out the special features representing a combination of Hindu and Muslim art in some of the most famous pieces of architecture of the Muslim period.

The buildings erected by the Musalmans for religious, civil or military purposes were not purely Muslim-Syrio-Egyptian. Persian or Central Asian, nor were the Hindu buildings, temples or palaces or cenotaphs purely Hindu. The simple severity of the Muslim architecture was toned down, and the plastic exuberance of the Hindu was restrained. The craftsmanship, ornamental richness and general design remained largely Hindu; the actuated form, plain domes, smooth-faced walls, and spacious interiors were Muslim super impositions. The artistic quality of the buildings erected since the thirteenth century, whether by Hindus or by Muslims, is the same, although differences are introduced by considerations of purpose and use, and styles are varied according to differences of local traditions and regional peculiarities.

'In all the Indian–Mohammedan styles of Furgusson's academic classification—at Delhi, Ajmer, Agra, Gaur, Malwa, Gujrat, Jaunpur and Bijapur—whether the local rulers were Arab Pathan, Turk, Persian, Mongol or Indian, the form and construction of the domes of mosques and tombs and palaces as well as the Hindu symbols which crown them, the *mihrabs,* made to simulate Hindu shrines; the arches Hinduized often in construction, in form nearly always: the symbolism which underlies the decorative and structural designs—all these tell us plainly that to the Indian builders the sect of the Prophet of Mecca was only one of the many which made up the synthesis of Hinduism; they could be good Mohammedans but yet remain Hindus.'[23] Havell has so brilliantly sustained this thesis in his work on Indian art that it is hardly necessary to expatiate upon it.[24] The influence of the style spread in the eighteenth century to all parts of India. Even far-off Nepal did not escape the contagion.[25] The palaces, cenotaphs and temples of the nineteenth century, whether built in the west at Jamnagar, or the east at Calcutta or in the Punjab by the Sikhs or in Central India by the Jains are all in the same style of the Hindu–Muslim architecture.[26] And not only did this Hindu–Muslim style become dominant in the monumental art of India but it also acquired the same hold over all utilitarian architecture—houses, streets landings and bathing places (ghats).[27] The residential house of a Hindu does not differ in construction and plan from that of a Muslim, although there are considerable differences due to climate between the houses of one province and another.

Sculpture

Sculpture is an art which was highly developed in India on account of the importance and prevalence of images and idols for Hindu temples. Idols and images and their worship are condemned by Islam and it was, therefore, not developed in Islamic countries and has had practically no effect on Indian sculpture, although 'following the example of Persian Kings, the Muslim Rulers of India, especially the Great Moghals, sought the aid of the sculptor's (quite as much as of the painter's) art for the beautification of their buildings, palaces and pleasances.'[28]

Painting

Painting of human figures and music, especially instrumental music and dancing, are also not encouraged by Islam if they are not tabooed. It is in painting and music that a most far-reaching assimilation between Hindu and Muslim arts has taken place,

[23] Havell, *Indian Architecture*, p. 101.
[24] Tarachand, *Influence of Islam*, pp. 243–44.
[25] Ibid., p. 256.
[26] p. 256.
[27] Ibid., p. 251.
[28] S.M. Jaffer, *Cultural Aspects of Muslim Rule in India*, p. 110.

and that notwithstanding Islam's attitude of indifference, if not of positive discouragement to them. The art of painting did not receive the attention and encouragement which other arts did at the hands of the early Muslim kings of India. This was mainly because it was tabooed in the early days of Islam on account of its close association with idolatry. It was only occasionally that the Muslim kings and nobles broke away from the general convention and practised this art, but in view of the fact that a large number of Hindus, among whom painting had long been popular, had embraced Islam but had not given up their old habits and hobbies altogether it may reasonably be conceded that the art was not neglected by the then Muslims of India quite as much as it is believed to have been. A large majority of the new Muslims and their descendants must have resorted to it, and the Muslims who came from outside and had imbibed Persian ideas and inspiration must also have pursued this art though not quite so zealously and with the same object as their contemporary Hindus did. Thus it appears that while the rulers were indifferent, if not actually averse to it, the people in general cultivated it to a great extent.

'The Mughals, however, stood on a different footing. They had their own ideas about art, which they loved and patronized in all its forms and phases. Babar brought with him all the choicest specimens of painting which he was able to obtain from the library of his ancestors—the Timurids—who were noted for their love of and proficiency in the art of painting. These specimens were treasured by the Mughal Emperors of India as their most precious and proud possessions.'[29]

'Pre-Muslim Indian paintings—Hindu, Jain, or Buddhist—have a character of their own. The vision of reality which inspires them and gives significance to their form is their own. They are the aesthetic expression of a culture which grew out of the synthesis of the racial experience, a synthesis which implies a balance between opposing tendencies—joy and sorrow, pleasure and pain, success and failure, worldliness and other-worldliness, attachment to life and renunciation of life, domination by sense and control of sense, ambition, activity and passion, and satisfaction, passivity and calm serenity . . . The frescoes of Ajanta are almost the only surviving remains of the Indian art as it was practised in the ancient period . . .

[29] Ibid., pp. 125–26.

Scholars have discovered references to the art in the pre-Christian literature, for instance, in the Vinaya Pitaka and in later Hindu poetry, *Mahabharata*, *Ramayana*, *Sakuntala* and so forth. There are actual fragments of paintings belonging to great antiquity existing in various caves, but the only adequate remains which truly reflect the character of the art which at one time was spread widely all over India and was extremely prolific in its output, are found at Ajanta. The paintings adorn the ceilings and walls of the temples excavated out of living rock . . . They were excavated during .the first six centuries of the Christian era . . . The wealth of kings and merchant princes must have been poured out in order to create the works in which both ambition and piety were satisfied.'[30]

'When Babar conquered India the star of Bihzad was in its zenith, his style was the standard of perfection; naturally the connoisseurs of art, Babar and his companions, and afterwards on the return of Humayun from his enforced exile from Persia to India, the Chaghtai nobles set Bihzad before Indian painters as the master in whose footstep they should follow, and whose paintings they should copy. Bihzad and his school thus became the exemplars of Indian painters and the elements of the Timuride School were engrafted upon the traditions of Ajanta. The character of this art is its intense individualism. This art is not interested in masses and crowds; it has hardly any direct interest in composition. It sees things limned in clear light and in definite outline, It looks at every detail of the individual figure and takes infinite pains with it, it feels the urge of life with tremendous force and it communicates this passionate energy to what it delineates.'[31] 'As in the case of Ajanta so here the line is the medium of expression. Yet what a vast difference between the character of the two lines! . . . The elements which combine to make these paintings are very different from those found in the work of Ajanta.'[32] The meeting of those two art consciousnesses under the fostering care of the Mughal emperors was productive of a new style. Upon the plasticity of Ajanta were imposed the new laws of symmetry, proportion and spacing from Samarqand and Herat. To the old pomp new splendours were added, and to the old free and easy naiveté of

[30] Tarachand, *Influence of Islam*, pp. 258–59.
[31] Ibid., pp. 265–60.
[32] Ibid., p. 268.

life a new sense of courtly correctness and rigid etiquette. In the result a certain amount of the energy and dynamic of both the Hindu and Muslim were sacrificed, and a stiff dignity was acquired, but along with it a marvellous richness of colour and subtlety of line. The evolution of the new style was rapid. Probably Babar introduced the models of the Timuride School to the Hindu and Muslim artists of India at Agra . . . It is interesting to find even in this early school—called the school of Humayun by Clarke—an unmistakable Indian feeling . . . The later artists of Akbar must have been trained in this school, probably under the four Muslim masters mentioned by Abul Fazl—Furrukh Qalmak, Abdus Samad of Shiraz, Mir Syyid Ali of Tabriz and Miskin. The pupils who were Hindus were in all likelihood painters who had acquired proficiency in traditional methods and were possessed of sufficient repute to be summoned to the Imperial Court. They had only to transfer their talents to the services of their new masters and paint the pictures that pleased them. This explains why so early in Akbar's reign the new Hindu–Muslim school made its appearance fully developed. The names of Daswant, Basawan, Keso Lal, Mukund, Madho, Jagannath, Mahes, Khem Karan, Tara, Senwalah, Hari-bans and Ram are recorded in the *Ain-i-Akbari*. Many other Hindu names 'appear on the paintings of the period . . . Among the illustrations of the manuscripts now preserved in the Khuda Bakhsh Library at Bankipur occur the names of Tulsi, Surjan, Surdas, Isar, Sankar, Ram Asr, Banwali, Nand, Nanha, Jagjivan, Dharmadas, Narayan, Chatarman, Suraj, Deojiva, Saran, Ganga Singh, Paras, Dhanna, Bhim, etc. In some cases the place from which the artists came is denoted and it is interesting to find only Gwalior, Gujarat and Kashmir mentioned. These then were pre-eminently centres of Hindu culture during the early medieval period, and the fact that the painters of Akbar came from these places confirms the tradition that the Hindu art continued to flourish after Ajanta; it also clearly establishes the contention that the Mughal art was not altogether an offshoot of Central Asian and Persian styles, but a development of the ancient art under new impulses.'[33]

'Of this Hindu–Muslim style, related on the one hand with the mural art of Ajanta, and with the true miniature painting of Samarqand and Herat on the other, there were many offshoots

[33] Tarachand, *Influence of Islam*, pp. 268–71.

differing in their character as they approached the one or the
other pole of this style. The Rajput and Pahadi styles of Jaipur,
Kangra and the Hindu states of the Himalayan hills had a greater
inclination towards the ancient Hindu; the Qalams of the Deccan,
Lucknow, Kashmir, Patna gravitated more towards the Muslim; the
Sikh Qalam was somewhere between them. They are all, however,
sub-styles derived from the parent stock which is the style of the
Court at Delhi or Agra.'[34]

Mr P.C. Manuk of Patna who is the proud possessor of a most
valuable collection of Indian paintings and is himself no mean
connoisseur, in a paper on Pictorial Art of India, after dealing
with the development of the art of painting in the Mughal period,
says, 'To the orthodox Mohammedan the depicting of the human
figure or anything that had life was declared *"haram"* or sinful
by the edicts of his religion—the old Mosaic law "Thou shalt
not make unto thyself any graven image" carried to its extreme
interpretation. True, under the enlightened Shah Abbas of Persia
and the liberal early Mughals, the followers of Mahomed broke
away from these edicts, but wonderful as their productions are
in the delight they give to the eye and senses, they rarely appeal
to the soul; No such prohibition stood in the way of their Hindu
disciples and colleagues to whom their Gods and Goddesses
were very real beings, assuming traditional shapes and forms
and this may be the reason why the Hindu artist was more able
to appeal by his productions to the soul of man, which is after
all the supreme test of high art. It must be remembered that Art
and Religion have been closely connected for long ages and most
of the masterpieces of the European Renaissance depict religious
subjects or quasi-religious subjects culled from the mythology of
Ancient Greece and Rome.'[35]

Music

Modern Indian music owes not a little to Islamic influence and
inspiration and although it was a highly developed science and
art in India and was not encouraged by orthodox Islam it is a
structure of Hindu and Muslim contribution—with a base which

[34] Ibid., p. 272.
[35] *The Searchlight*, Patna, Anniversary Number, 1926, p. 15.

is Hindu and with decorations and fringes which are the result of a synthesis. If a history of the origin and development of the very numerous musical instruments were to be written, I doubt not that many of them will be found to owe their present form and perfection to joint efforts of both Hindus and Muslims, the contribution of Muslims being very considerable in many cases and even exclusive in some. Similarly, the modern *rag*s and *ragini*s have also been developed in course of time with considerable contributions by Muslim artists.

'In the early days of Islam music suffered in the same way as painting, not so much on the same ground but probably because it tended to dominate the human mind so much as to render it incapable of thinking of anything else . . . It was perhaps on account of its too powerful attractions that music was discouraged in the beginning. Despite this discouragement, however, human nature proved too strong and the art began to be cultivated in the same way and with the same if not greater zeal as painting. The contact of Islam with Iran, where music was most popular, and the influence of Sufis (Muslim mystics) who believed in the efficacy of music as a means of elevating the soul and as an aid to spiritual progress, brought about a great change in the attitude of Musalmans towards this art and went a long way in wiping off the stigma attached to it. The position was further simplified when Musalmans settled down in India and found music occupying a high place in the scheme of Hindu social and religious life. The result was that though divine service in mosques continued to be performed on orthodox lines, without aid of music, either vocal or instrumental, the art became so popular that musicians began to loom large on almost all festive occasions. The Sufi's fondness for music brought into vogue, the practice of holding semi-religious congregations where songs of divine love called Qawwalis were sung by professional singers called Qawwals.'[36] 'Music in short was most popular in Muslim India—more than we are led to believe. One reason for its popularity may be found in the fact that a vast majority of Indian Muslims were originally Hindus or offspring of Hindus, who were too fond of it to give it up after embracing Islam, with the result that the art imperceptibly permeated Muslim ranks and became widely popular. It may

[36] Jaffar, *Cultural Aspects* . . ., pp. 155–56.

also be noted here that music, like other fine arts, opened a new channel of intercourse between the Hindus and Muslims of India. The process of co-operation and intermutation began right from the advent of Muslims in India and it was distinctly manifest how the two communities borrowed from each other the precious stores they possessed and thus enriched each other.'[37]

'The sister art of music obtained also a great encouragement from the Emperor and reached a high excellence in his reign. There were numerous musicians at his court—Hindus, Iranis, Turanis, Kashmiris, both men and women . . . The world renowned singer Mian Tansen, a Hindu convert to Islam whose tomb at Gwalior has become a place of pilgrimage to the Indian musicians, was a court singer of Akbar. There flourished at the time the great singer Haridas, the master of Tansen and Ramdas, the second Tansen who hailed from Lucknow and received, it is said, on one occasion a present of a lakh of rupees from Khan-i-Khanan . . . At the time of Akbar the art of music reached its noonday splendour. The vocal music with its various *rag*s and *ragini*s many of which have now been forgotten for want of cultivation received a good deal of attention, while instrumental music with its various musical instruments was equally cared for. In the domain of music it is very perceptible how the Hindus and the Muhammadans were borrowing from one another, each community enriching the other with the precious store it possessed. This process of intermixture was not new in the time of Akbar but dated from a long time back. The history of Indian music after the advent of the Muhammadans unfolds a chapter of co-operation and intercourse between the two communities socially and politically. *Khayal,* for instance, which is associated with the name of Sultan Husain Sharqui of Jaunpur as its inventor has become an important limb of Hindu music, while *Dhrupad* has engrafted itself on Muhammadan music; the state of Indian music in former times no less than its present eclectic condition testifies a good deal to this intermixture taking place through centuries . . . It was not merely the Emperor or the chiefs of the Provinces who turned their attention to this fine art but the nobles also entertained themselves and their families by this means of diversion.'[38] 'Shah Jahan was a great patron of Music

[37] Ibid., pp. 164–65.
[38] Law, *Promotion of Learning* . . ., pp. 155–58.

and, it seems, could himself sing well. His two great singers were Ramdas and Mahapattar.'[39]

If a complete list of the best living exponents of the art were made there would doubtless figure on it Musalmans whose number would, perhaps, be larger than their proportion in the total population and perhaps also larger than that conceded to Musalmans for representation in Legislatures. A casual visit to any respectable music conference which has been convened by people who know something of the art and the living artists in India will give to the sceptic the most convincing proof of the amalgam, which may in one word be called Indian culture, as represented by Indian music as distinguished from any communal or parochial music, if this last at all exists in any part of India.

Summarizing the effort of intercourse between Hindus and Muslims, Mr S.M. Jaffar writes in his book *Some Cultural Aspects of Muslim Rule in India*:

'The Musalmans who came into India made it their permanent abode and naturalized in it. For them it was impossible to live in the land of the Hindus in a state of perennial hostility. Living together led to mutual intercourse and mutual understanding. In course of time the force of circumstances compelled them to find out a via media whereby to live together as friendly neighbours. They evolved out a new language out of the warp and woof of Persian and Sanskrit and the current of common culture, Hindu–Muslim, abandoned its ancient beds and began to flow through this new channel, Urdu. The culture that was thus evolved was neither purely Muslim nor exclusively Hindu but a happy union of both. The Muslim Kings and Chiefs encouraged Hindu arts and literature, sciences and philosophy, and opened the doors of their schools and seminaries to all and sundry without any restrictions of rank, race, or religion. Like Saints and Sages they, too, in their own spheres tried to bring about an approximation between the Hindus and Muslims. The result was an almost complete reconciliation of the two. It need not occasion surprise, therefore, if the Hindus offered sweets at Muslim shrines, consulted the Quran as an oracle, kept its copies to ward off evil influence, and celebrated Muslim feasts and the Musalmans responded with similar acts . . . Since a vast majority of Indian Muslims were drawn from the masses of the

[39] Ibid., p. 183.

Hindus, their social position and culture did not change all at once, though they undoubtedly improved in many ways. They had changed their religion no doubt but they still retained their ancient customs and practices, habits and hobbies. The change of religion did not change their environments and atmosphere which were permeated through and through with social isolation, superstitious ideas and caste restrictions. The result was the Indo-Muslim society which incorporated a number of Hindu social features.'[40]

Culture is a most complex thing and its contents are as difficult to define as those of a nation. Yet one born and brought up in a particular culture cannot fail to distinguish it from any other. And even within the same cultural zone or group there may be sub-zones or sub-groups and yet belong to and form part of the same culture.

Any culture which represents the result of a combination of varying and even conflicting social, religious and other forces that go to create a culture cannot fail to have such sub-groups or sub-zones. That does not negate the existence of the over-all culture which belongs to all the sub-groups or sub-zones any more than that of the sub-groups or sub-zones themselves. Whenever we have to compare one culture with another, the right method would be to compare the over-all culture of one group or zone with that of another and not to compare the sub-groups or sub-zones as among themselves. They, of course, differ among themselves and still have many things in common which distinguish them from any other culture. The Hindus, Muslims, Christians, Parsis, Sikhs of India differ as among themselves in many respects and yet they all have something in common which distinguishes them from a foreigner, say a European. To anyone who doubts this proposition, the position of Indians in British colonies, Protectorates and dominions ought to furnish a complete and unrebuttable refutation of the claim that Hindus and Muslims of India represent two altogether different cultures. To the South African or Australian or Canadian European or to the European in Kenya the Indian, irrespective of the fact whether he is a Hindu or Musalman or Sikh or Parsi or Christian, is the same person who has to be kept in his place and not allowed to defile European culture or lower its standard

[40] Jaffer, *Cultural Aspects* . . ., pp. 206–07.

of living. Not only is that the case with the Indian who belongs to a subject race and can therefore be dealt with as an inferior person. Even the Chinese who are an independent people, and the Japanese, who until the Second World War were regarded with the greatest consideration, if not respect, could not escape similar treatment at the hands of these custodians of European culture and standard of living in both the hemispheres. That discrimination has been based on difference in culture of Asia and Europe. It is thus clear that in spite of all differences and distinctions that exist between Hindus and Muslims, it is idle to deny that both have laboured and lived to develop a joint culture which is the Indian culture and which at once distinguishes an Indian from any foreigner coming from the West or the East, whether from other continents and countries of the Old World or the New World. With the long history of association and joint enterprises in works of war no less than in those of peace, it could not in the very nature of things be otherwise. If two independent saplings of mango have been joined together—or if one sapling has been grafted on a branch of another tree—the result is an improved variety of the fruit that the tree bears. It is wrong and cruel to tear them asunder, and what is even more important to bear in mind, it is not easy either to do so after such a long lapse of time in the course of which the new tree has weathered many a storm and gained strength and cohesion in the process. If the attempt succeeds, it can do so at the expense of both, making each weaker and more exposed to danger and attack from all sides.

V. ONE COUNTRY

There is a great variety in climate and physical contours of the country in India which extends from the cold snow-clad mountains of the Himalayan Range in the north to a point almost near the equator in the south. We have also a large inland space which is altogether cut off from the sea, while we have a coastline of some four thousand miles. We have the deserts of Rajputana and Sind and the evergreen plains of Bengal and Assam. We have an immense record of annual rainfall both in the north-eastern province of Assam and in the south-western spurs of the Western Ghats; and against this we have practically no regular rainfall worth the name in the deserts of Rajputana and Sind and some parts of the

Ceded Districts of Andhra. We have also extremes of cold and heat at some places inland, particularly in the Punjab and NWFP and no winter or summer properly so called on the sea-coast in the southern portions of the peninsula. As in so many other matters, this variety and difference in climatic and topographical conditions does not coincide with any division of the population on religious or communal lines. The cold and arid north-west and the wet, tempestuous and evergreen east and north-east differ from each other in every climatic and topographical respect,-but they have both a very large Muslim population which enables a demand for division of India on communal basis to be made.

All this variety in climate and topography has had its effect on the development of the people inhabiting the different parts, on their dress and the kind of houses in which they live, on many of the social customs, and on their life generally. But in spite of these differences, India is one whole country designed by nature to be separated from other adjoining countries by almost insurmountable natural barriers like high mountains and seas. Every invader, conqueror and emperor of India, whether during the Hindu period or Musalman rule, has accordingly attempted with varying success to extend his empire to the whole of this country. It has been the ambition of every ruler to bring the whole of it under his suzerainty if not under his direct rule. There has been a certain region in the north-western corner which has always been a sort of no-man's land, changing its rulers, now being under an Indian ruler and now under an outsider or non-Indian. The British government has only followed the age-old practice of the Hindu *chakravartis* and Muslim emperors in gaining suzerainty over the whole of this country. There have been kingdoms just as there are provinces now, which sometimes quarrelled with one another. But there is no evidence that anyone living in or ruling one of those kingdoms regarded himself as anything but an Indian and his part of the country as anything but a part of India as distinguished from, say, China or Persia or Turkistan or Arabia or even perhaps Burma. On the other hand every Hindu who performs his *sandhya* has to repeat a *sloka* in the *sankalpa* in which he pictures the country as a whole and imagines the waters of the Sindhu, the Ganga, and the Cauvery to be mingled together in the water of his small water pot. And this has gone on not only during the period of Hindu rule when occasionally a chakravarti claimed suzerainty over the whole country but also during the period when there were different kings ruling in different parts of the country, when Muslim emperors ruled at Delhi and when small Muslim kingdoms were established in different parts of the country. It is repeated even today when British suzerainty spreads over the whole peninsula. There are four places of pilgrimage which are known as the four *Dhams,* a visit to which is said to earn the greatest virtue for a Hindu. They are: Rameshwaram in the southern tip of the peninsula, Badrik-ashrama deep in the Himalayas at a height of some 15,000 feet, Jagannath Puri on the east coast in Orissa, and Dwarka on the western sea-coast in Kathiawar. It cannot be denied that irrespective of who ruled and what were the administrative or political divisions of the country, the Hindus have never conceived of India as comprising anything less than what we regard as India today. The Muslim and British rulers have simply accepted the Hindu traditional delimitation of the country.

On the other hand, until the two nations theory was proclaimed the other day, the Musalmans also never treated or thought of any part of present-day India as anything but a part and parcel of India. No Muslim conqueror of India ever thought of annexing any part of India to the foreign country from which he came. Whoever was able settled down in India and tried to bring the portions of India which did not accept his suzerainty under his sway. The fact that on the border there was a fringe which fell on the one or the other side of the natural boundary line does not in any way affect the validity and correctness of the above statement.

Not only as rulers but even during the period of British rule, Musalmans of British India no less than those of the Indian states never until the other day treated or claimed any part of the soil of India as anything but a part of India. I do not know if even the Muslim League claims that the north-western and eastern zones which it desires to have constituted into independent states are outside India or as being anything but parts of India. So far as I am aware, Mr C. Rahmat Ali, who is the Founder President of the Pakistan National Movement, is the only person who has openly proclaimed that 'to accept the territorial unity of "India" is to fasten the tyrannical yoke of "Indianism" on the "Millat",' and has called upon his co-religionists 'to live to sever all ties with "India" and to save the "Millat" from "Indianism" and to serve

"Pax-Islamica".'[41] He falls foul of the All-India Muslim League for its name—'for its very name bears the stamp of "Indianism" and so belies our struggle against "Indianism". It breeds the spirit of "Indianism" and thus betrays our Millat to "Indianism". Let us not minimize the effect and importance of names. They are the distinguishing marks; and, as such, establish the identities of their bearers. More than that, they are the moral symbols; and as symbols, the sources of inspiration . . . The mistake has certainly cost us dear. It has compromised our nationality, labelled us as "Indian". I say this, not because there is anything wrong with the word "Indian" which, in itself, is as respectable as any other name; but because we are not "Indian", and therefore, for us to style ourselves or our institutions as "Indian", is nothing but an act of renegation.'[42] Mr Rahmat Ali after the realization of this fact gave the 'five north-western strongholds 'of Islam the name of Pakistan in 1933 and in 1937 to Bengal-Assam the name of Bang-i-Islam and to Hyderabad-Deccan the name of Usmanistan, the three regions which he regards as the three *Milli* strongholds arbitrarily included in the binational sub-continent of 'India'.[43] So it is only since 1933 that India has begun to be treated as a sub-continent comprising different countries by Mr Rahmat Ali and the Pakistan National Movement. I do not know if there is any other organization or individual of note who has followed his lead in this respect up to now. Divisions for administrative purposes may be made but I do not know if countries have been or can be created by men in this way. Whenever an attempt has been made in Europe to cut up a country, the result has been a legacy of hate and bitterness resulting in sanguinary wars, including the global one that has just been devastating the world. That ought to furnish us a lesson and serve us as a warning.

VI. ONE HISTORY

The invasions of India by Muslims started with the landing of Mohammad Bin Kasim on the shores of Sind in the ninth century

[41] 'The Miliat of Islam and the Menace of "Indianism"'—being a letter addressed by C. Rahmat Ali to the Supreme Council of the Pakistan National Movement, p. 7.
[42] Ibid, p. 15.
[43] Ibid., pp. 1 and 16.

AD and went on till the eighteenth century when Ahmad Shah Abdali made his last assault. It is doubtful if any one of these invasions extending over about eight or nine hundred years was a purely religious invasion undertaken by religious fanatics or enthusiasts for spreading Islam. Like all conquests, they were actuated by temporal and material motives rather than by religious zeal. The earliest ones were naturally resisted by the Hindus who alone then inhabited the country, and took the shape of conflicts between the Hindus and Musalmans. But from early times the ambition of these invaders was to settle down in India, and from the time of Shahabuddin Ghori in the eleventh century downwards Musalman invaders whether they were Pathans, Tartars, Turks, Mughals or Afghans who came from outside India, assumed suzerainty over parts of India and in course of time extended the area of their suzerainty. As their kingdom extended it became difficult, if not impossible, to rule the whole of it from Delhi, their capital seat, and they had to appoint governors in the more distant parts. These governors were not slow to take advantage of any weakening of the Centre and to establish themselves as independent kings in the provinces to which they had been posted. We thus have two kinds of war in the long history of Muslim rule in India. There were wars by the Muslim kings to extend their kingdom, and in the earlier period they were naturally against Hindus who still ruled in the parts sought to be conquered and annexed to Delhi. But it was not long before independent Muslim kingdoms had grown up and many of the wars which the Muslim emperors of Delhi had to wage and many of the expeditions which they had to lead were not against Hindu kings but against Muslim kings who had established themselves, or against their own governors who had revolted. In these wars and expeditions Hindus fought on both sides. All the Muslim invaders who came from the north-west after the Ghoris had to and in fact did invade a Muslim kingdom in India and had to and did fight and defeat a Muslim ruler who had established himself on the throne at Delhi. The invasions of Timur and Nadir Shah were not against Hindu kings but against Muslim kings of Delhi and were resisted by them. Babar had to fight and defeat not a Hindu king of Delhi but Ibrahim Lodi, a Muslim king, at the battle of Panipat, before he could establish the Mughal empire. When Babar fought Rana Sanga of Mewar, the latter was assisted not only by Rajputs but also by Hassan

Khan of Mewat and Sultan Mahmud Lodi, a son of Sikandar Lodi, who had been acknowledged king of Delhi by Sanga and it was after defeating this combined force of Rajputs and Musalmans at the battle of Kanwah in 1527 that his empire became established. Humayun, the son of Babar, lost the empire for a time to Sher Shah, a Muslim Pathan, and when it was recovered after Sher Shah's death, Akbar after him had to fight Muslim rulers for strengthening the foundations of that empire. Much of the time and energy of the Mughal emperors from Akbar right down to Aurangzeb was taken up in suppressing the revolts of Muslim Governors of provinces or in conquering independent Muslim kingdoms. It is well known how Aurangzeb spent many years in the south conquering the Kingdoms of Bijapur and Golkonda and that he died there. Many of these expeditions and wars were led on behalf of the emperors at Delhi by Hindu generals like Man Singh and Bhagwandas in the time of Akbar and by Jaswant Singh and Jay Singh in the time of Aurangzeb, conquering and suppressing not only Muslim rulers and governors but also Hindus who were ruling at the time in parts of the country. It is thus clear that the wars and expeditions of India and in India during the long period of Muslim rule were actuated by the same temporal and mundane motives which have actuated all wars and conquests at all times—personal ambition, dynastic rivalries and a desire to extend and consolidate an empire, and acquire the honour and glory which conquest and empire are supposed to confer.

The history of India for 600 years, beginning with the thirteenth century when Qutbuddin Aibak established the Sultanate in 1206 down to the end of the eighteenth century when the British power had succeeded in firmly establishing itself, is therefore not a history of continuous conflict and wars between Hindus on the one side and Muslims on the other. This is not the place nor is there space here to show that during this long period there were more conflicts between Muslims and Muslims in India than between Muslims and Hindus. Only a bird's eye view may be attempted.

The period may be divided into two parts, the first covering the period when the sultans reigned at Delhi and the second the period of the Mughal rule. The first saw not only the establishment of Muslim rule in India and its expansion covering practically the whole length and breadth of the country from the foot of the Himalayas down, to Rameshwaram and from the western frontier to the east coast of Orissa and Bengal, but also the establishment and growth of a number of small independent or semi-independent kingdoms under Muslim rulers. There were also changes of ruling, dynasties at Delhi. The sultans of Delhi were most of the time busy not only conquering portions of India from Hindus but also suppressing the rebellions of their own subordinates, sometimes trying to reconquer what the latter had converted into independent kingdoms and sometimes trying to defend their own position on the throne. Between 1193 and 1526 there sat on the throne of Delhi no less than thirty-five sultans belonging to no less than five dynasties. Each of these dynasties professed Islam and each was replaced in its turn by another Muslim dynasty. Of the thirty-five monarchs who sat on the throne no less than nineteen or a majority were killed or assassinated not by Hindus but by Musalmans.

Among the independent or semi-independent kingdoms which grew up may be mentioned—Bengal, Jaunpur, Gujarat, Malwa, Khandesh, and the Bahmani kingdom which was split up into five kingdoms of Berar, Ahmadnagar, Bijapur, Golkonda and Bidar. Each of these kingdoms had an independent history of its own—a history of wars with other neighbouring Muslim kingdoms and with the king of Delhi, if occasionally also with Hindu Rajas who still held sway in parts of the country.

The Indian Muslim rulers had also to meet attacks on India by Musalmans who came time after time from the North-West, so much so that from the time of Allauddin onwards frontier fortifications with special arrangements for meeting invasions from that side had to be maintained.

After Babar had defeated Ibrahim Lodi at Panipat in 1526 and laid the foundation of the Mughal Empire, the throne of Delhi was no bed of roses for his successors. His son Humayun had to fight his own brother Kamran, who not content with Kabul and Qandahar captured Lahore and brought the whole of' the Punjab under his sway. Humayun had also to fight his other brothers, Hindal and Mirza Askari. Hindal was killed in a fight; Kamran was taken prisoner and deprived of his eyesight. Askari was captured but allowed to proceed to Mecca.

Humayun had to be constantly fighting to retain his position in upper India. He had to lead a fight against Bahadur Shah of Gujarat but was unable to hold Gujarat 'on account of the revolt

of Sher Khan, Afghan chief of Bihar—to whom he ultimately lost
the throne of Delhi—and was a fugitive outside India seeking the
help of the Shah of Persia.

Sher Shah was followed on the throne by his son Salim Shah;
who, unable to control the Afghan nobles, had to imprison or put
to death several of them. The Governor of the Punjab rebelled but
was defeated, and fled to Kashmir where he was killed.

Salim Shah was succeeded by his son Firoz Khan who was soon
murdered by his maternal uncle, Mubariz Khan, who ascended
the throne under the title of Muhammad Shah. His affairs were
managed by a Hindu named Hemu. Rebellions of nobles broke
out and Delhi and Agra were seized by Ibrahim Sur who was
defeated by Sikandar Sur. Humayun who had been waiting for an
opportunity, taking advantage of the chaotic condition of Hindustan
advanced with an army and defeated Sikandar Sur at Sirhind, got
back his throne in 1555 and died soon after.

Akbar succeeded Humayun. His younger brother, Muhammad
Hakim, remained in possession of Kabul which was nominally
regarded as a dependency of Hindustan. Akbar was young and
under the guardianship of Bairam Khan. His first serious danger
came from the Surs whose Hindu minister Hemu had marched on
Delhi and inflicted a defeat on the Mughal General Farid Beg who
was put to death by Bairam Khan for his incompetence. Hemu,
after his victory, assumed the title of Vikramaditya and made a
bid for the empire but was defeated at Panipat and taken prisoner
and put to death by Bairam Khan. Sikandar Sur thereafter also
surrendered and the sovereignty of the Sur dynasty came to an
end in 1556.

Akbar became impatient of the tutelage of Bairam Khan and
in this he was encouraged by his mother Hamida Begum and
Maham Ankah, his foster-mother, and her son Adham Khan. Akbar
dismissed Bairam Khan in 1560 who submitted and started for
Mecca. Suspecting that he might rebel, Akbar sent a force under
Pir Muhammad to hasten his departure. Being thus annoyed he
rebelled and proceeded towards the Punjab, followed by Akbar
himself. He ultimately submitted and in recognition of his past
services was allowed by Akbar to proceed again to Mecca. On the
way he was murdered by a private enemy at Patan in Gujarat.

Akbar's generals Pir Muhammad and Adham Khan conquered
Malwa from the Muslim king of that place with much cruelty.

Akbar had to suppress the rebellions:

(1)   of Abdullah Khan Uzbeg who had superseded Pir Muhammad in Malwa,
(2)   of Khan Zaman who had revolted in Jaunpore and
(3)   of his brother Mirza Hakim who, encouraged by Uzbegs, claimed the throne. Akbar inarched towards the Punjab and Hakim beat a hasty retreat. Khan Zaman was defeated in battle and, killed and his brother captured and beheaded. Other rebels were severely dealt with.

Akbar completed the conquest of Gujarat from Muzaffar Shah in 1573 and annexed it to his empire. This was an important epoch in Akbar's history.

Bengal was held by Afghan chiefs in the time of Sher Shah, but in 1564 Sulaiman Khan of Bihar occupied Gaur and became the ruler of the two provinces. After his death Bayazid, his son, succeeded him but he was murdered by his ministers who placed his younger brother Daud on the throne. Daud incurred the emperor's wrath by seizing the fort of Zamania. Akbar sent Munim Khan, his general, and also himself marched against him and Daud was finally defeated and killed in battle in 1576. Bengal and Bihar became parts of the empire. Orissa was annexed later in 1592.

Muzaffar Khan Turbati was made Governor of Bengal. His harsh measures and injustice in assessment of revenue incensed the local chiefs. Taking advantage of the unpopularity of Akbar's religious policy of universal tolerance, *Sulh-i-Kul*, resented by the ulema who, under the Qazi of Jaunpore, issued a *fatwah* declaring it lawful to take up arms against the emperor, the Qaqshals, an important Chagtai tribe under Baba Khan, advanced upon Gaur. Todarmal, a Hindu, was sent by Akbar to restore order. Muzaffar Khan was killed and the whole of Bengal and Bihar fell into the hands of the rebel Qaqshals. Ultimately, however, the rebellion was suppressed.

Hakim again invaded the Punjab but was defeated by Akbar. After his death in 1585 Kabul was annexed to Delhi and the government of the country entrusted to Raja Man Singh, a Hindu. The tribes on the frontier were also suppressed. The Muslim king of Kashmir was forced to submit and Kashmir annexed to the empire, and so was Sind from its ruler Mirza Jani. Qandahar was annexed in 1595.

Having made himself master of the whole of Hindustan, and, the Afghan regions beyond the Hindukush, Akbar turned towards the Deccan. He annexed the kingdom of Ahmadnagar in 1600 after overcoming its gallant defense by Chand Bibi, the sister of Burhan Nizam Shah. He then attacked Burhanpur and took Asirgarh from Miran Bahadur, the ruler of Khandesh in 1601.

When Akbar left for the Deccan he placed his son Salim in charge of the capital, with instructions to commence operations against Mewar with Man Singh and Shah Quli Khan. But the prince rebelled and declared his independence. Akbar returned from the south. Salim set up an independent kingdom at Allahabad but subsequently begged pardon of Akbar and a reconciliation was effected. A conspiracy was, however, made by the nobles to deprive Salim of his succession and to put his eldest son Khusru on the throne. But it failed and on Akbar's death in 1605 Salim became emperor as Jahangir.

Jahangir had first to meet and suppress the conspiracy in favour of his own son Khusru who escaped from Agra and with the help of many nobles raised a revolt. He was defeated, arrested and brought in chains before the emperor. He was imprisoned and his followers were punished with severity. His charming manners made him again a centre of intrigue and a plot was laid to murder the emperor and to proclaim him emperor. The plot was discovered, Khusru was blinded and kept a solitary prisoner in a dungeon for years. In 1616 he was entrusted to the custody of his mortal enemy Asaf Khan who made him over to his rival brother Shah Jahan, who had him murdered in 1622. After his death his father relented and he was given a second burial at Allahabad in what is still known as Khusru Bagh. Shah Jahan had as his rival and opponent another person—Shahriyar, who was son-in-law of Nur Jahan. Shah Jahan too revolted against his father and remained in that condition from 1622 till about the death of his father. After spending several years with varying fortunes he ultimately surrendered and had to send his sons, Dara and Aurangzeb, as hostages to the court. Jahangir had also to suppress the rebellion of Afghans in Bengal and of his own nobles like Mahabat Khan who once made him and Nur Jahan prisoners. Jahangir's two important actions against Hindus were the conquest of Kangra in 1620 and the forced submission of Mewar which had resisted the

Mughal empire since the days of Akbar. The empire lost Qandahar, which was captured by the Persians after a siege.

On Jahangir's death, Shahriyar made a bid for the throne but failed. He was imprisoned and blinded and Shah Jahan became the emperor after sending his rivals to the other world with the help of his father-in-law Asaf Khan who had the princes of the royal family butchered ruthlessly. Many ladies committed suicide. Shah Jahan's original name was Prince Khurram. He had got the title of Shah Jahan from his father for his campaign against the Muslim kingdoms of the Deccan. On coming to the throne in 1628, Shah Jahan had to meet the rebellion of the Bundela chief which was suppressed. In 1629 he had to meet the rebellion of Khan Jahan Lodi, Governor of the Deccan, who was finally defeated. His head was cut off and a hundred of his followers suffered the same fate.

Akbar had conquered Khandesh (1599) and Ahmadnagar (1600) and annexed them to the empire but Ahmadnagar had never been effectively brought under his control. During Jahangir's reign no substantial progress had been made on account of the resistance of Malik Ambar. Shah Jahan's triumph had proved short-lived and the sultans of the Deccan were not subdued. The kingdom of Ahmadnagar finally came to an end in 1633. Bijapur and Golkonda remained unconquered. On account of the help which Bijapur had given to Ahmadnagar and also because Shahji had set up a Nizam Shahi boy as king of Ahmadnagar, the emperor's wrath was roused. He sent generals to chastise them and forced the king of Golkonda to make his submission. Bijapur also acknowledged the suzerainty of the emperor. After this Aurangzeb was appointed Viceroy of the Deccan. The peace was, however, only short-lived and action was again taken some years later. Bidar was captured. Bijapuris were defeated at Gulbarga and the fort of Kalyani captured after a siege in 1658. Apart from political reasons the two southern kings were Shias and that was another reason for the Sunni emperor to seek to suppress them.

Qandahar had been seized by the Persians during the time of Jahangir. Repeated attempts were made during the time of Shah Jahan to recover it. It was recovered in 1639, as Ali Mardan Khan, the Persian Governor, being suspected by his own Shah and fearing foul play at his hands, sent word to the emperor of Delhi whose forces marched and easily acquired possession of it. The Persians did not give it up and recaptured it in 1649. Several expeditions were led on behalf of the emperor of Delhi and Qandahar was besieged but Delhi ultimately failed after having spent twelve crores on the enterprise.

Shah Jahan attempted the conquest of Balkh and Badakhshah. Prince Murad was sent with a large force and, taking advantage of a dispute between Naz Muhammad Khan, ruler of Bokhara, and his rebellious son, he entered Balkh without opposition in 1646, Naz Muhammad having fled. Murad, however, left for Hindustan and a second expedition had to be organized under Aurangzeb. At first there was no pitched battle but ultimately the Uzbegs fled from the field when the Mughals and Rajputs opened fire and Aurangzeb entered Balkh in triumph and placed it under the command of the Rajput chief, Madhu Singh Hada. Aurangzeb proceeded further but had to face much difficulty and had at last to yield. On his way back, his army suffered much and the Rajputs who had been left behind died without food and shelter. The enterprise failed dismally and cost nearly four crores.

Shah Jahan fell ill in September 1657 and this led to rumours of his death, causing public disquietude and leading to a war of succession. It is well known how Aurangzeb waded to his father's throne through the blood of his own brothers—Dara, Shuja and Murad. It has also been mentioned already how he had to carry on prolonged wars against Bijapur and Golkonda which were ultimately conquered and annexed after an eventful career of over 250 years.

If in his wars Aurangzeb employed Hindu generals, his Hindu rival 'Sivaji also had in his employ quite a number of Muslim military officers. Some of them held important positions, like the Generals Siddi Hullal and Nur Khan. In Sivaji's Navy there were at least three Muslim Admirals—Siddi Sambal, Siddi Misri and Daulat Khan.'[44]

I have strayed into this rather long historical discussion not to show that the Muslim rulers of India did nothing more than fight amongst themselves. They in fact did a great deal more. They consolidated an empire which reached the height of glory. They encouraged arts and were instrumental in the long run in evolving what may be called a national State of India—as States were in

[44] Mehta and Patwardhan, *The Communal Triangle*, p. 18.

those days. I have mentioned these instances only to show that Muslims fought Muslims more than they fought Hindus and that it is a wrong and one-sided view of history to imagine, as has been done by some persons, that during the long period of over six hundred years they were constantly engaged in wars against the Hindus whom they were oppressing all the time, leaving a legacy of hate and bitterness, the effects of which have not been and cannot be obliterated or forgotten.

In more recent times, Indian soldiers in the British army have been sent out of the country to fight wars for the British Empire in China, in Malaya, in Burma on the East, and in Arabia, in Persia, in Afghanistan, in Egypt, in Turkey, in Cyrenaica, in Tripoli and even in Europe on the West. Musalman soldiers have fought and helped in the destruction of the empire of Turkey. The fact that some of the powers and countries against which they fought were also Musalman has not stood in their way. There is nothing surprising in all this. The history of Islam outside India is replete with instances in which Muslims have fought Muslims, and one Muslim country or king has fought, defeated and conquered another Muslim country or king.

The Prophet had enjoined Muslims not to kill Muslims, and on some occasions in his lifetime when a person, even in the course of a battle declared himself to be a Muslim, and the question was raised whether such a person who professed to be a Musalman but about whose honesty of profession doubts were entertained should be killed or spared in battle, he directed that once the man declared himself converted, he should not be killed and his life should be spared. But soon after his passing away the injunction appears to have been forgotten even by those who had had the privilege of direct association with the Prophet himself or with those who had had such association with him. Hazrat Usman, who was not only the third Caliph but very closely related to the Prophet, having married two of his daughters, was killed by Musalmans who had rebelled against him. The fourth Caliph Hazrat Ali, who was a cousin as also another son-in-law of the Prophet, had to fight a battle with Hazrat Ayesha, a widow of the Prophet and also shared the fate of Hazrat Usman—was murdered by Musalmans. The sons of Hazrat Ali were also killed by Musalmans who supported the claim of the Omayyad Yezid to the Caliphate. If such was the case within a few years of the

Prophet's death and with those who had been amongst the earliest of Muslims—Hazrat Ali was the first youth to accept Islam at the hands of the Prophet himself—and his lifelong associates, it is easy to understand that the later Muslims could also fight other Muslims.

In the later wars between Muslims, certainly, if not even in these early ones, Islam as a religion or its propagation and protection played no more part than it did in the numerous wars and expeditions against or in India. After conquest and consolidation of his power, every conqueror, king, or emperor carried on the administration as he considered best and safest in the circumstances of the country and the people among whom his lot was cast. Islam undoubtedly influenced the administration and the lives of the people—both the rulers and the ruled. But that is something very different from saying that the propagation or protection of Islam was the object of any of these temporal rulers either in India or outside. In India particularly, Musalman rulers, and indeed all Muslims generally, formed what may be described as small islands which had grown and were constantly growing in size and extent by accretion. The number of foreigners who came as invaders or conquerors and settled down in India was indeed small compared with that of non-Muslims. The present-day Muslim population is composed very largely—in fact overwhelmingly—of Indians who adopted Islam as their religion and the descendants of such converted persons who must have been Hindus.

When we find so much of confidence, fellow feeling and joint action in matters military, it is only reasonable to expect that there would be even more of it in civil administration and in the ordinary life of the people at large, and this expectation is well founded in facts furnished by history.

'The employment of the Hindus was a necessity of their rule. Mahmud of Ghazni had a numerous body of Hindu troops who fought for him in Central Asia and his Hindu commander, Tilak, suppressed the rebellion of his Muslim general, Niyaltgin. When Qutub-uddin Aibak decided to stay in Hindustan, he had no other choice but to retain the Hindu staff which was familiar with the civil administration, for without it all government including the collection of revenue would have fallen into utter chaos. The Muslims did not bring with them from beyond the Indian frontiers artisans, accountants and clerks. Their buildings were erected by

Hindus who adapted their ancient rules to newer conditions, their coins were struck by Hindu goldsmiths, and their accounts were kept by Hindu officers. Brahmin legalists advised the king on the administration of Hindu law and Brahmin astronomers helped in the performances of their general functions.'[45] 'One noteworthy fact of the reign of Ibrahim Adil Shah I (AD 1534–57) was that public accounts began to be kept in Hindi instead of in Persian and many Brahmins were appointed in charge of the accounts so that they soon acquired a great influence in the government. In the reign of Yusuf Adil Shah the Hindus had also been admitted to the exercise of considerable powers in his revenue department.'[46]

Sultan Muhammad Tughlak 'had many Hindus in his employ. One of the highest officers of his Finance Department was a Hindu by name Ratan. Akbar's celebrated Finance and Revenue Minister, Raja Todar Mal, introduced far-reaching changes in administration and was reckoned among the highest dignitaries of the State. Aurangzeb's Finance Minister, Ragh Nath, was also a Hindu.'[47]

Even today in Indian States, Hindus and Musalmans are appointed to the highest posts irrespective of their religion. It is enough to cite the instances of Maharaja Sir Kishen Prasad of Hyderabad and Mirza Sir Mohammad Ismail of Mysore and now of Jaipur.

The Revolt of 1857 against the British was a joint enterprise of Hindus and Muslims who had both rallied round Bahadur Shah, the titular emperor of Delhi. Had it succeeded, it would have re-established and consolidated the Empire of Bahadur Shah, as surely as its failure resulted in his imprisonment and exile and the destruction of the great house of the Mughals as emperors of India.

During the years immediately following the Revolt of 1857 Muslims came in for a great deal of repression at the hands of the British government. The ulema particularly never wholeheartedly submitted to the rule of the British. With their long, historical background, the reaction of the Musalmans against outside interference of the British was great. Such 'pressure from without

---

[45] Tarachand, *Influence of Islam on Indian Culture*, pp. 136–37.
[46] N.N. Law, *Promotion of Learning in India during Muhammedan Rule*, p. 93.
[47] Mehta and Patwardhan, The Communal Triangle, p. 19.

is probably the largest single factor in the process of national evolution' in the words of Julian Huxley quoted above;[48] and no wonder all these have combined in forging an Indian nation. Musalmans no less than Hindus were emphatic in asserting the existence of this Indian nation, albeit with distinct religions of which two were the most important as being followed by the largest numbers of the population. Sir Syed Ahmad Khan, who is credited with having kept large bodies of Musalmans from joining the Congress, held this belief in his earlier days. He regarded the Hindus and Muslims as the two eyes of a maiden, and you could not injure one without injuring the other. It is unnecessary to cite quotations from the speeches and writings of Musalmans who have been associated with the Indian National Congress.

I shall close this discussion of the two nations theory with some quotations from distinguished Musalmans of India. First and foremost I shall give two passages from the speeches of Sir Syed Ahmad Khan and end with citations from two living distinguished Muslims of our day. In a speech delivered at a gathering at Gurdaspur in 1885, Sir Syed spoke as follows:

'From the oldest times the word Nation is applied to the inhabitants of one country, though they differ in some peculiarities which are characteristic of their own. Hindu and Muhammadan brethren, do you people any country other than Hindusthan? Do you not inhabit the same land? Are you not burnt and buried in the same soil? Do you not tread the same ground, and live upon the same soil? Remember that the words "Hindu" and "Muhammadan" are only meant for religious distinction, otherwise all persons, whether Hindu, Muhammadan, or Christian, who reside in this country belong to one and the same nation. Then all these different sects can only be described as one nation; they must each and all unite for the good of the country which is common to all.'

On another occasion he spoke about the same thing at Lahore:

'In the word Nation I include both Hindus and Muhammadans because that is the only meaning which I can attach to it. With me it is not so much worth considering what their religious faith is, because we do not see anything of it. What we do see is that we inhabit the same land, are subject to the rule

---

[48] Julian Huxley, *Race in Europe*, p. 3.

of the same government, the fountains of benefits for all are the same and the pangs of famine also we suffer equally. These are the different grounds upon which I call both these races which inhabit India by one word, i.e. Hindu of meaning to say that they are inhabitants of Hindusthan. While in the Legislative Council, I was always anxious for the prosperity of this nation.' (*Indian Nation Builders—Sir Syed Ahmad Khan,* pp. 41–42).[49]

In his Foreword to Atulananda Chakravarti's *Hindus and Musalmans of India,* Sir Shafaat Ahmad Khan, no mean historian, after a bird's-eye view of social and cultural development of India during the ages, has come to the following conclusion:

'In almost every sphere of our national activity, there was greater solidarity and rapport between the two communities than is generally supposed. The history of Indian culture shows continuous reciprocity of feeling and solidarity of sentiment between the masses no less than the classes of the two communities and the classics of Indian languages give us a more complete embodiment of the national spirit than can be shown by any other nation in Asia. This understanding which purified the tastes and instincts of the aristocracy and the populace, has penetrated and refined the whole nation. Whatever our political differences may be—and I shall be the last to minimize them—the fact remains that in the temper of their intellect, their traditions of life, their habits, and the circle of their thought, there is a powerful tradition of unity, which has been forged in the fires and chills of nearly a thousand years of a chequered period, and is indestructible and immortal.'[50] What is needed, to quote Sir Shafaat once again, is that 'the myopia which sees social phenomenon as merely political phenomenon, and regards the ailments of a national body as political disorder must be corrected by the intensive study of Hindu–Muslim culture and a deeper understanding of the forces which have moulded Indian thought and aspirations in our splendid past.'[51]

Sir Sultan Ahmad is no less emphatic in his opinion: 'The Hindu–Muslim differences of today threaten to undo the historic fellowship between the two communities that, beginning under the

[49] Quoted in *Pakistan Examined, Rezaul Karim,* p. 117.
[50] Atulananda Chakravarti, *Hindus and Musalntans of India,* pp. xix–xx.
[51] Ibid., p. xvi.

Moghuls, has existed for centuries. It is seldom realized that to disunite Hindustan would be to work against the one constructive factor of the history of Muslim rule in this country. The Indians of today certainly possess far more knowledge than their ancestors, but the picture of their ideas is dwarfed by the large canvas on which is imprinted the Aryan-Saracenic conception of unity. Indian leaders and thinkers of a remoter age sought to establish harmony between the two religions. Prince Dara Shekoh compared them to two confluent rivers, *Majma-ul-Bahrein;* Kabir and Nanak tried to fuse them together and imported into their prayers the names of both "Allah the Bountiful and Ram". The Hindu and Muslim masters were inspired to bring into existence common arts and crafts that touched the souls and satisfied the utilitarian needs of both Hindus and Muslims. Common notions of joy and beauty were evolved. The Indian of today is out to destroy the edifice built for him by the hand of history. Unable to appreciate that history, he gives it a bad name.

'It is strange that Hindu–Muslim unity should be going to pieces in spite of the existence of so many common points between the Hindus and Muslims. It should have been our duty to use these points for broadening the basis of unity. A common cultural heritage in music and literature, painting and architecture, was not the only treasure bequeathed to us; a common political destiny too was evolved as the Hindu and the Muslim fought together in many a battle. In social life, again, the traditions and practices of the two communities were interwoven one with the other. Common ways of life were already in evidence even as early as the days of the Emperor Babar, who facetiously described them as the "Hindustani ways", in which both Hindu and Muslim traits were found freely mixed up. Then came the Urdu language, beginning as the language of the camp. Even in religion, in those days the most cherished of all things, the two influenced each other. The Muslim gave a new turn and a new tinge to the religion of the mass of Hindus; his own in turn took on an Indian complexion. This change was noted by his ultramontane co-religionists.

'The Muslim in India became the son of the soil. This course was irrevocably decided for him when Qutbuddin separated the Sultanate of Delhi from the Ghaznivite Empire. That a Muslim king should not discriminate against any section of his subjects was an injunction, clear and definite, for he was enjoined to "regard all sects of religion with the single eye of favour, and not bemother some and bestep-mother others". It is interesting to trace the growth of the love for India as the mother country as we compare Babar's *Memoirs* and Abul Fazl's *Ain-i-Akbari,* The founder of the Empire complains—"Hindustan is a country that has few pleasures to recommend it." But gone was this newcomer's attitude by the time that Akbar came to the throne, whose historian is carried away by the "beauties of Hindustan" and apologizes for a digression which proceeded from "the love of my native country".[52]

[52] Sir Sultan Ahmad, *A Treaty between India and the United Kingdom,* pp. 60–61.

PART II

THE COMMUNAL TRIANGLE

~

SIX

INTRODUCTORY

We have seen how during the long period of Muslim connection
with India, persistent efforts had been made alike by the Muslim
rulers, artists, *faqirs* and others to assimilate as much as possible
of the Hindu culture. This had been reciprocated to a remarkable
extent by the Hindus on their side. Although the two had not
coalesced and become one, the points of contact and common
interest had increasingly grown and what may be called a
Hindustani culture had developed in course of time. In politics
this was bound to create a nation in the modern sense of the term
and this happened particularly after the establishment of British
rule in India to which both the Hindus and Muslims became
subject. We have quoted authoritative Muslim opinion to show
that Musalmans, no less than Hindus, treated both Hindus and
Muslims as constituting a nation. At the same time we know
that the All-India Muslim League and its spokesmen are equally
emphatic today in declaring that they, the Muslims, constitute a
nation separate from the Hindus. What can be the explanation
of this phenomenon? An answer to this question requires an
examination of some historical facts.

The attitude of the Muslim conquerors had, on the whole, been
one of toleration, and in spite of the fanatical zeal manifested by
some of them at times, it may be safely asserted that there had
been a continuous attempt from the earliest days to deal with
the Hindus fairly. One early instance may be quoted. When the
people of Brahmanabad, which had been conquered by Mahommad
bin Qasim, implored him to grant them freedom of worship, he
referred the matter to Hajjaj, the Governor of Iraq who sent him
the following reply: 'As they [the Hindus] have made submission
and have agreed to pay taxes to the Khalifa, nothing more can
be properly required from them. They have been taken under our
protection and we cannot in any way stretch our hands upon their
lives or property. Permission is given them to worship their gods.

Nobody must be forbidden or prevented from following his own religion. They may live in their houses in whatever manner they like.'[1] This was in keeping with the teachings of the Prophet and the principle which governed the conduct of the early Caliphs who treated in this way non-Muslims who had submitted and agreed to pay *jeziya*.

The rulers were not slow to take an independent line of their own, irrespective of what the Muslim divines might consider necessary or proper, thus making the State independent of religion. Allauddin Khilji, whose empire embraced the whole of the north and south of India, was opposed to interference of the ulema in matters of state and laid down that the law was to depend upon the will of the monarch and had nothing to do with the law of the Prophet. He upheld the royal prerogative of punishment and justified the mutilation of dishonest and corrupt officers, though the Qazi declared it contrary to common law. He explained to the Qazi his doctrine of kingship in significant words: 'To prevent rebellion in which thousands perish I issue such orders as I consider to be for the good of the State and benefit of the people. Men are heedless, disrespectful and disobey my commands. I am then compelled to be severe to bring them into obedience. I do not know whether this is lawful or unlawful; whatever I think to be for the good of the State or suitable for the emergency, that I decree; and as for what may happen to me on the approaching day of judgement, that I know not.'[2] This is what benevolent autocrats have always claimed and shows complete separation between the functions of the monarch as the ruler of peoples following different religions and customs, and as the follower of a particular faith.

The testamentary injunction of Babar already quoted at length was followed by the Mughal emperors, resulting in the expansion of their empire. Departure from it created conditions which ultimately led to its disruption. Foreigners also notice the consideration shown to Hindu sentiment. 'On the occasion of Id it appears the cow was not sacrificed, for we are told, "On that day [Id] everyone who is able will sacrifice a goat in his house and keep the day as a great festival."'[3] No wonder that the communities lived side by

---

[1] Ishwari Prasad, *A Short History of Muslim Rule in India*, p. 46.
[2] Ishwari Prasad, *A Short History . . .*, p. 126.
[3] Ibid., p. 698, quoting Pelsaert, p. 74.

side amicably, although they never coalesced and never became merged one in the other.

Mr F.K. Khan Durrani has summarized the position and I cannot do better than quote a pretty long extract here:

'The ancient Hindus were not a nation. They were only a people, a mere herd.

'The Muslims of India were none better. Islam, indeed, became a State in the lifetime of its Founder himself. It has a well-defined political philosophy. I shall say Islam is a political philosophy . . . The Islamic State is a democracy for whose maintenance every individual Muslim is responsible—"*La Islam ilia be Jamaet-hu:* There is no Islam without any organized society," says Omar the Great. Unfortunately, the Islamic State did not endure long enough. The Omayyads and the Abbasids destroyed it and turned it into *mulk* or autocratic, despotic, hereditary monarchy.[4]

'At the time the Muslims conquered India, the divorce of religion and politics had become the accepted creed of the Muslims throughout the world. The men who conquered India were not the national army of a Muslim State but paid mercenaries of an imperial despot. The State they established in India was not a national Muslim State, but held, maintained and exploited in the interests of an autocrat and his satellites. The Muslim Empire in India was Muslim only in the sense that the man who wore the crown professed to be a Muslim. Through the whole length of their rule in India Muslims never developed the sense of nationhood. Imperial policy from beginning to end was inimical to the growth of that sense . . .[5]

'So we had two peoples, Hindus and Muslims, living side by side in equal servitude to an imperial despotism, and both devoid of national feeling or national ambitions . . .

'Much has been written on the irreconcilability of the religious conceptions, beliefs and practices of the Hindus and the Muslims . . . Yet in spite of them all, there is something in their respective faiths, which enabled the two peoples to live amicably together for many centuries and which, if what they have learnt and suffered under British rule could be washed out of their minds and the same old religious mentality could be recreated

[4] F.K. Khan Durrani, *The Meaning of Pakistan*, pp. 34–35.
[5] Durrani, *The Meaning of Pakistan*, pp. 35–36.

in them which inspired their forefathers of a century ago, would enable them again to live amicably together as good neighbours and citizens of the same State. That something is the spirit of tolerance inculcated in both religions.'[6]

Now *Divide et Impera*—Divide and Rule—is a maxim hoary with age and has been adopted by all conquerors in all countries and in all ages, Once the validity of foreign rule is admitted, no special blame attaches to the foreign ruler for having recourse to it. The British cannot, therefore, be blamed if they have not risen superior to other foreign conquerors and have followed the advice given by Mountstuart Elphinstone: '*Divide et Impera* was the old Roman motto and it should be ours.' It is the sanctimonious pose that whatever they do in India is actuated by lofty idealism and unadulterated altruism that irritates. The present seemingly irreconcilable differences between the Hindus and Muslims are in no small measure the result of a deliberate application of the policy of divide and rule. It started in the days of the East India Company when the British were just establishing themselves as rulers of India and can be easily seen working in the latest statements made by the ex-Secretary of State for India, Mr L.S. Amery, and other high placed Britishers connected with the Government of India. This is what makes so difficult the recreation of that old mentality which 'would enable Hindus and Muslims to live amicably together as good neighbours and citizens of the same State.'

The communal question in India is thus not a question between the Hindus and Musalmans who can solve it as they like, if they will. There is a third party, and in some respects a most important party, that is, the British government. We have thus what has been very expressively termed a communal triangle, with Hindus and Muslims, as its two sides and the British government as the base. As this base has grown in size it has simultaneously widened the angle of difference between the two sides.

[6] Ibid., pp. 36–37.

~

SEVEN

'DIVIDE AND RULE' AND THE EAST INDIA COMPANY

While the East India Company was engaged in carving out an empire in India in the disturbed times of mutual strife and conflict among those who had set themselves up as independent rulers in the declining days of the Mughal empire, the fundamental policy of the Governors appointed on behalf of the Company in India was to take advantage of such conflicts and strife and to see to it that Indians did not combine against the British. It was one of the objectives of the Company's officers to prevent a combination between the Marathas, the Nizam and the Nawab of Carnatac, and later between Hyderabad and Tipoo Sultan. 'It is true,' says W.M. Torrens, 'to use the words of Malcolm, that "Hindustan could never have been subdued but by the help of her own children." At first it was Nizam against Arcot and Arcot against Nizam, then Mahratta against Muslim, and Afghan against Hindu.'[1] The differences among the Marathas themselves were in no small measure the result of British intrigue at the Maratha court. 'In Mahratta history there are two central figures round which are to be traced the rise and decline of the Mahratta Empire. The valour and genius of Shivaji laid the foundation of the Empire; the imprudence and intrigue of Raghunath Rao precipitated its fall.'[2]

'Mr Mostyn,' writes Grant Duff, 'was sent to Poona by the Bombay Government for the purpose of using every endeavour by fomenting domestic dissensions or otherwise to prevent the Mahrattas from joining Hyder Ali or the Nizam.'[3] He helped Raghoba who became a tool in his hands. He made him wage war with the Nizam and Hyder Ali without gaining any advantage for the Maratha

[1] W.M. Torrens, *Empire in Asia*, p. 19.
[2] B.D. Basu, *Rise of Christian Power in India*, p. 209.
[3] Grant Duff, *History of the Mahrattas*, p. 340.

empire. Nana Farnavis soon discovered that Raghoba was merely a tool in the hands of the Bombay government and that the end of the Maratha empire would not be far off if Raghoba continued to hold the Peshwaship. Raghoba, finding that Nana Farnavis and other ministers were opposed to him, fled to Gujarat and sought the assistance of the President and Council of Bombay who were only too willing to render him assistance so that the Maratha empire might be weakened and they might get advantages for the East India Company on the west coast, and particularly the cession of the islands and peninsula of Salsette and Bassein.

'In this policy no distinction was made between Hindus and Mussalmans on religious basis, and Mussalmans were set up against Mussalmans as much as against Hindus, just as Hindus were set up against Hindus as much as against Mussalmans. The, result aimed at was to defeat and suppress each with the help of the others who in their turn were similarly treated. An illustration of this is furnished by the treatment given to the Rohillas during the time of Warren Hastings. The Rohillas occupied a territory on the border of the territory of the Vizier of Oudh. They were locally ruled by their own chiefs and magistrates, but they enjoyed more than ordinary freedom and consequently more prosperity than many other communities. The Rohillas, like the Swiss, sedulously cultivated the arts of peace. Their territory lay between Oudh and the recent conquest of the Mahrattas and when the Mahrattas menaced the Vizier's territory and offered advantageous terms to the Rohillas for allowing them passage through their country, they refused the terms and thus exposed themselves to the ravages of Maratha inroads because they had a treaty of mutual alliance with the Vizier which had been entered into at the express instance of the English and under their solemn guarantee. When once the Mahrattas had been repelled there was secret conspiracy between the Vizier and the Governor-General for annexing the territory of the Rohillas. Hastings induced the Vizier to employ the subsidiary force within his dominions professedly to defend him against foreign enemies but to be officered and commanded exclusively by the Company. In return the Vizier was to pay a stipulated sum which was a source of profit and revenue to the Company. It was with a view to increase of their profit that the sale of Rohilkhand was agreed to . . . A secret treaty was, therefore, entered into between the Subedar and the Governor-General whereby the Company engaged, whenever a suitable pretence should be found or made, in consideration of a sum of 40 lakhs of rupees and payment of all expenses to be incurred on the business, in concert with the troops of Oudh to crush the Rohillas and to add their country to the dominions of the Vizier.'[4] Various pretences were, of course, found and Rohilkhand was invaded and after brave resistance the Rohillas were defeated. 'Seldom, if ever, have what are called the rights of victory been more inhumanly abused. "Every man who bore the name of Rohilla was either put to death or forced to seek safety in exile." But this did not exceed the stipulation of the treaty; for by Hastings's own letter it appears that in its provisions there was the specific agreement that, if necessary "the Rohillas should be exterminated." The language is his own.'[5] In the result, says Torrens, Hastings pocketed twenty thousand pounds as a private present for signing the treaty and the public treasury was replenished to the extent of four hundred thousand pounds.

The turn of Nawab Vizier soon came. More money was needed. The Nawab pleaded poverty. 'Negotiations took place which resulted in the memorable device for replenishing the exchequer of Calcutta without exhausting that of Lucknow. "It was," says Lord Macaulay, "simply this, that the Governor-General and the Nawab Vizier should join to rob a third party, and the third party whom they determined to rob was the parent of one of the robbers."[6] The persons to be robbed were the mother and widow of the late Vizier who were supposed to have vast treasures and the spoil was reckoned at 1,200,000 pounds.

Hastings had set the precedent of 'hiring out to the Princes of Hindustan, permanent bodies of British troops under the designation of subsidiary forces, and thereby was a means established of sapping the authority and independence of every one of them. Hastings avows that in establishing such a force in Oudh, he designed to weaken the native Government and reduce it to dependency; and how soon his accomplice found that he had sold himself with his prey, subsequent events clearly set forth.'[7]

It is unnecessary to cite further instances of the working of the British policy of setting one Indian ruler against another

[4] Adapted from Torrens, *Empire in Asia*, pp. 100–01.
[5] Torrens, *Empire in Asia*, p. 102.
[6] Ibid., p. 116.
[7] Ibid., p. 101.

~

EIGHT

THE WAHABI MOVEMENT

Although Musalmans had lost their position as a great political power in the country, they were still not looked upon with favour. There arose also among them men fired with religious zeal for reform. They attributed their fall from political power to their fall from the ideals of Islam and exhorted them to go back to the early teachings of Islam and get rid of many customs and rites which had grown up in course of time but which were not strictly speaking sanctioned by Islam. One of the early reformers was Maulvi Shariatullah of Bahadurpur in the district of Faridpur in Bengal who had spent some twenty years in Arabia and after his return, had established in the first decade of the nineteenth century a sect known as 'Fraizi'. His son, Dudhu Mian, succeeded him and established his headquarters at Bahadurpur and carried on his movement amongst the peasants not only for religious reform but also for protecting them against the oppression of the zamindars.

Some years later, a movement was started by Syed Ahmad of Rai Bareili which had its branches all over India and played a great part in the first half of the nineteenth century. He was born in Rai Bareili and received his education in Delhi and acquired a great fame not only for his learning but also for his piety. Many of the learned ulema of the time accepted him as their leader and he carried on a great agitation against social evils like drinking and prostitution. He sent his disciples and agents to distant places like Hyderabad and places further south and to Bengal. He became, the centre of *jehad* against the Sikhs of the Punjab, who, it is said, ill-treated the Musalmans, prevented them from fulfilling their religious obligations and desecrated their places of worship. He, therefore, declared their state as *Darul-Harb* and decided to lead *jehad* against them. Although the Marathas had also established their rule, they had not interfered with the religion of the Musalmans—had allowed them to perform their

religious duties and even allowed Muslim Qazis to function, and
the Musalmans regarded their state as also that of the Rajputs
as *Darul-Ishlam* and not *Darul-Harb*. Syed Ahmad Brelvi made
preparations for *jehad* against the Sikhs and his disciples spread
all over the country to collect men and money for it. He himself
had some experience of fighting and took the lead of the army
so collected. The British authorities were kept informed of the
preparations but did not interfere, as the preparations were directed
against the Sikhs whose power was tolerated but looked upon
with disfavour by them. Sir Syed Ahmad Khan wrote about these
preparations as follows:

'In those days Musalmans used publicly to ask Muslim masses to
carry on *jehad* against the Sikhs. Thousands of armed Musalmans
and a large incalculable store of war materials were collected
for *jehad* against Sikhs. But when the Commissioner and the
magistrate were informed of it, they brought it to the notice of
the Government. The Government clearly wrote to them not to
interfere. When a Mahajan of Delhi misappropriated some money
of the *jehadis,* William Fraser, Commissioner of Delhi, gave a decree
for it which was realized and sent to the Frontier.'[1] 'There is no
doubt,' says Muhammad Jafar Saheb in *Sawanat Ahmadia,* p. 139,
that 'if the Sarkar [British Government] were against Syed Saheb,
then no help could reach Syed Saheb from Hindustan. But the
British Government in those days heartily desired that the power
of the Sikhs should be diminished.'[2] In the result, Syed Ahmad led
an army through Sind and the Bolan Pass into Afghanistan and
then attacked the Punjab through the Khyber Pass in 1824 and
continued his war with varying success until he captured Peshawar
in 1830. Sultan Mohammad Khan, who was the Governor on behalf
of the Sikhs, swore allegiance to him and was continued in his
post. Maulvi Mazhar Ali was appointed Qazi. He thus succeeded
in securing religious freedom to the people of the Frontier tracts.
But there were old feuds between Sultan Mohammad Khan and
Qazi Mazhar Ali. After Syed Ahmad had left Peshawar, Sultan
Mohammad got Qazi Mazhar Ali murdered in an open durbar. In

---

[1] Translation of an extract from an article of Sir Syed Ahmad Khan
   published in the *Institute Gazette* of 8 September 1871. Quoted by
   M. Tufail Ahmad in *Musalmanon Ka Roshan Mustaqbal*, p. 102.
[2] Ibid., p. 103.

conspiracy with local leaders he also got persons who had been appointed collectors by Syed Saheb murdered. This so much upset Syed Saheb that he left the Frontier towards the end of 1830 with a number of his followers and was ultimately killed in a battle in 1831 at the age of forty-five.

Although his army dispersed after his death, the *jehadi*s had established their headquarters at Sittana in the Swat valley in the Frontier, from where they continued their fight with the help they received from Hindustan. The British government connived at this until the Punjab was conquered, as will appear from the following quotations from Sir William Hunter's *Indian Mussulmans:* 'They perpetrated endless depredations and massacres upon their Hindu neighbours before we annexed the Punjab, annually recruiting their camp with Mahommadan zealots from the British districts. We took no precaution to prevent our subjects flocking to a fanatical colony which spent its fury on the Sikhs—an uncertain coalition of tribes, sometimes our friends and sometimes our enemies. An English gentleman who had large indigo factories in our north-western Provinces, tells me that it was customary for all pious Musalmans in his employ to lay aside a fixed share of their wages for the Sittana Encampment. The more daring spirits went to serve for longer or shorter periods under the fanatic leaders. As his Hindu overseers now and then begged for a holiday for the annual celebration of their fathers' obsequies, so the Mahommadan bailiffs were wont between 1830 and 1846 to allege their religious duty of joining the crescentaders as a ground for a few months' leave.'[3] 'Upon our annexation of the Punjab', continues Sir William Hunter, 'the fanatic fury, which had formerly spent itself upon the Sikhs, was transferred to their successors. Hindus and English were alike Infidels in the eyes of the Sittana Host, and as such were to be exterminated by the sword. The disorders which we had connived at, or at least viewed with indifference, upon the Sikh Frontier, now descended as a bitter inheritance to ourselves.'[4] Their followers were found preaching sedition in different parts of the country so far apart as Rajshahi in Bengal, Patna in Bihar, and the Punjab Frontier. 'Throughout the whole period the fanatics kept the border tribes in a state of chronic

[3] W.W. Hunter, *Indian Mussalmans*, p. 20, quoted in Tufail Ahmad, Musalmanon, p. 110.

[4] Ibid., pp. 21–22, quoted in Ahmad, *Musalmanon Ka Roshan.*

hostility to the British Power. A single fact will speak volumes. Between 1850 and 1857 the Frontier disorders forced us to send out sixteen distinct expeditions, aggregating 33,000 Regular Troops; and between 1857 and 1863 the number rose to twenty separate expeditions aggregating 60,000 Regular Troops, besides Irregular Auxiliaries and Police.'[5]

It is unnecessary to go into further details of the doings of the *mujahids* beyond stating that the disciples of Syed Ahmad Brelvi continued helping the *jehadis*. Two of the principal disciples, the brothers Maulvi Wilayat Ali and Maulvi Enayat Ali, belonged to Patna. After the conquest of the Punjab, the British compelled the Indian *mujahids* to return to Hindustan and Maulvi Wilayat Ali came back to Patna with his followers. He had to give an undertaking that he would not go to the Frontier for some years, after the expiry of which he and his brother sold their property and undertook *hijrat* to Sittana and thus started a movement for *hijrat* which lasted for a pretty long time and received an impetus after the rebellion of 1857. When the British started their forward policy in the Frontier in 1864, it became necessary that all connection between the Frontier people and the people of India should be cut off and during 1864 and 1870, five cases of rebellion were instituted against Indians among whom some of the most important accused were of the Patna family and from amongst their disciples. The charge against them was that they had continued correspondence with their relations on the Frontier and had helped them with money. Some of them were given death sentences which were reduced to transportation for life. It may be noted that these persons had done nothing more or worse than what the British government had not only connived at since 1824 but actually encouraged by realizing *hundis* on behalf of the *mujahids* and remitting the same to them on the Frontier. This movement started by Syed Ahmad Brelvi and carried on after his death by his followers and disciples has been given the name of the Wahabi movement. Among their teachings about social and religious reform, the Wahabis also preached the great doctrine of *jehad*. India, having come under the rule of the Christian British, became *Darul-Harb* against which *jehad* was obligatory. 'Throughout the whole literature of the sect this obligation shines

---

[5] Ibid., p. 24, quoted in Ahmad, *Musalmanon Ka Rashan*.

forth as the first duty of regenerate man.'[6] If *jehad* was impossible, then *hijrat* was the alternative.

The situation created by the Wahabi movement was met by two-fold action of the government. On the one hand, the great state trials broke up the organization of the Wahabis, and on the other, counter-propaganda against their teaching was started and *fatwas* against *jehad* were obtained and circulated. Sir William Hunter says: 'It has always seemed to me an inexpressibly painful incident of our position in India that the best men are not on our side . . . And it is no small thing that this chronic hostility has lately been removed from the category of imperative obligation.'[7]

The whole episode is illustrative of the policy of 'divide and rule'. So long as the Sikhs were a thorn in the side of the British, the Musalmans were encouraged to carry *jehad* against them. Once the Sikhs had been defeated and the Punjab conquered, the *jehadis* were declared rebels, against the British and convicted and sentenced to transportation for life and their entire organization broken up.

[6] Hunter, *Indian Mussalmans*, pp. 64–65.
[7] Ibid., p. 144.

NINE

THE EARLIER DAYS OF SIR SYED AHMAD KHAN

The revolt of 1857 was the result of causes which had been operating and accumulating for a pretty long time. It is not necessary to go into its causes or follow its course here. One thing is certain. Both Hindus and Musalmans joined it and both rallied round the emperor of Delhi. Both suffered heavily. But the attitude of the British had been more hostile to the Musalmans from whom they had conquered a great part of the country. Lord Ellenborough had written in 1848: 'It seems to me most unwise when we are sure of the hostility of one-tenth, not to secure the enthusiastic support of the nine-tenths who are faithful. I cannot close my eyes to the belief that this race [Muslims] is fundamentally hostile to us and therefore our true policy is to conciliate the Hindus.'[1] The policy had not been quite successful as the Hindus no less than the Muslims had enthusiastically joined the revolt of 1857; but the rulers had not evidently lost faith in it in spite of their experience, as the following extracts will show:

'Besides the charge brought by Lord Ellenborough against Lord Canning, the European inhabitants of Calcutta sent in a petition to the proper authorities demanding the recall of Lord Canning. The charge brought against Lord Canning by them was that he did not support the anti-Muslim cry raised by the European community in India after the Sepoy Mutiny.' The protest went home and had its effect and as Sir William Hunter wrote: 'After the mutiny the British turned upon the Musalmans as their real enemies.' The heavy hand of reprisal ruined many families which had enjoyed both pelf and power. A deliberate policy of depressing them was followed in all departments of government. Musalmans had held the highest posts not only in the civil administration of the country but had been even more prominently associated with the army. Two causes combined to deprive them of their predominance in the

[1] Quoted by Atulananda Chakravarti in *Call It Politics?*, p. 35.

former. There was the policy of the British government working against them. It was reinforced by the attitude of the Musalmans themselves, who after their sad experiences sulked in their tents and for some time did not take advantage of English education which had been introduced and without which government employment had progressively become more and more difficult to obtain.

A change in the government policy came about 1870 particularly after the publication of Sir W. Hunter's book referred to above. He concludes his book as follows:

'The foregoing chapters establish the two great facts of a standing rebel camp on the frontier and a chronic conspiracy within the Empire. The English Government can hold no parley with traitors in arms. Those who appeal to the sword must perish by the sword . . . But while firm towards disaffection we are bound to see that no just cause exists for discontent . . . This, however, it can do only by removing the chronic sense of wrong which has grown in the hearts of the Musalmans under British rule.'[2]

He then .goes on to recount at great length how the Musalmans, especially in Bengal, had been suppressed under the British government, how they had been .deprived of power and position, and how they had been impoverished, how their education had been starved, how their educational endowments had been despoiled. He pleads for justice to them and specially for a system of education which would suit them better, and concludes: 'We should thus at length have the Mohammedan youth educated on our own plan. Without interfering in any way with their religion, and in the very process of enabling them to learn their religious duties, we should render that religion perhaps less sincere, but certainly less fanatic. The rising generation of Mohammedans would tread the steps which have conducted the Hindus, not long ago the most bigoted nation on earth, into their present state of easy tolerance.'[3] This was the precursor of a change in the government policy. The encouragement given to the Aligarh Educational Scheme resulted from this policy. The British Principals of the Aligarh College drew inspiration, and the college, full material benefit from it.

The Indian Army of the British before the revolt of 1857 had been a cosmopolitan army in which Hindus and Musalmans, Sikhs

[2] W.W. Hunter, *Indian Mussalmans*, p. 147.
[3] Hunter, *Indian Mussalmans*, p. 214.

and Poorbiahs were mixed up. Its common effort in 1857, which
had resulted from a growing sense of national unity against the
foreign rulers opened their eyes and the subsequent policy was
directed towards breaking up this solidarity. Sir John Lawrence
wrote: 'Among the defects of the pre-mutiny army, unquestionably
the worst, and one that operated most fatally against us, was the
brotherhood and homogeneity of the Bengal Army and for this
purpose the remedy is counterpoise of the Europeans, and secondly
of the native races.'[4]

The result was a reorganization of the army based on tribal,
sectarian and caste distinctions so arranged that the groups retained
their tribal or communal loyalties and balanced the characteristics
and influences of one another. As the Bengal army, which was
composed largely of men from what are Bihar and the UP of the
present day, had taken a prominent part in the Revolt of 1857
and as the newly conquered Punjab had come to the rescue of the
British, the former were progressively eliminated and the latter made
more and more predominant in the composition of the army, as
the following Table—giving the percentages of men from different
parts of India in the army quoted by Dr Ambedkar from articles
by Mr Chowdhry in the *Modern Review*—will show:

TABLE I

Percentages of Men from Different Parts of India in the Army

Year	NW India Punjab, NW Frontier and Kashmir	Nepal, Garhwal and Kumaon	NE India, UP and Bihar	S. India	Burma
1856	Less than 10	Negligible	Not less than 90	–	Nil
1858	47	6	47	–	–
1883	48	17	35	–	–
1893	53	24	23	–	–
1905	47	15	22	16	–
1919	46	14.8	25.5	1.2	1.7
1930	58.5	22	II	5.5	3

[4] Quoted by Mehta and Patwardhan in *The Communal Triangle*,
   p. 54.

We are now told that there are certain classes which are martial and there are others that are not martial. The races and communities in the north-west of India are regarded as the martial races while those of the UP and Bihar are not so classed. It is forgotten that it was the army composed largely of the latter that had conquered for the British the Punjab and the NWFP and that they were demartialized as a result of the deliberate policy pursued since 1858. The immediate effect of the policy after 1857 was to exclude very largely the people of the UP and Bihar from the army, bringing in their place the Sikhs, the Gurkhas and the Garhwalis.

Sir Syed Ahmad Khan had himself suffered at the hands of the rebels in 1857 and had helped the British against them. He was much affected by the ruin which overtook the Musalmans. He also saw that they were excluded from employment on account of their lack of English education. He was a nationalist and a believer in the Hindus and Musalmans constituting one nation which he called the Hindu nation on account of both being inhabitants of Hindustan. He, therefore, in his earlier days spoke and wrote like a nationalist and was regarded as a national leader by both Hindus and Musalmans. He was, however, rightly keen about improving the lot of Musalmans and particularly about providing educational facilities for them. He had helped in founding schools at places where he was posted during the period of his service and some of these are still in existence. He also believed that British rule was for the good of the people of India and whatever defects and shortcomings there were in it had to be brought to the notice of the rulers to get them remedied or removed. In this he was at one with other political leaders of the time, including those who helped in founding the Indian National Congress with whom he shared his political aspirations. He held that there should be no distinction between Europeans and Indians on the ground either of race or colour in the matter of government employment, social intercourse, and political or constitutional rights. He accordingly supported the Ilbert Bill as a member of the Viceroy's Council and on the occasion of the durbar at Agra walked out from it as in the seating arrangement the chairs for Europeans were placed on the platform and those for Indians down below. He established the Scientific Society of which Hindus, Musalmans and Europeans became members and in which papers were read. He wrote in *Tahzibul Akhlaq* as follows:

'No nation can acquire honour and respect so long as it does not attain equality with the ruling race and does not participate in the Government of its own country. Other nations can have no respect for Musalmans and Hindus for their holding the position of clerks or other similar petty posts. Rather, that Government also cannot be looked upon with respect which does not give to its subjects due respect. Respect will be commanded only when my countrymen will be holding positions equal to those of the ruling race. The Government have in sincerity, good faith and justice given the right to their subjects in every country to attain such position of equality. But for Indians there are many difficulties and obstacles. We must work with determination and perseverance and should not keep back on account of the fear of any trouble befalling us.'[5]

In 1853, when the Local Self-Government Bill was before the Council, he suggested that, as there were people following different religions and rites and customs in India, it was necessary that some places on the boards should be filled by nomination and it was decided that one-third of the seats should be so filled, so that people who represented the interests of particular classes but who were not elected could be nominated by the government to remove this deficiency. It is noteworthy that he did not demand that seats should be reserved for Musalmans or that there should be separate electorates for them. Indeed he could not have made this demand when he held that Hindus and Musalmans constituted one nation, as the following extracts from his writings will show:

'The word nation (qaum) applies to people who inhabit a country . . . Remember that Hindu and Musalman are religious words; otherwise, Hindus, Musalmans and even Christians who inhabit this country—all constitute, on this account, one nation. When all these groups are one nation, then whatever benefits the country, which is the country of all of them, should benefit all . . . Now the time is gone when only on account of difference in religion the inhabitants of a country should be regarded as of two different nations.'[6]

---

[5] Translation of quotation given by M. Tufail Ahmad in *Musalmanon Ka Roshan Mustaqbal*, pp. 281–82.

[6] Tufail Ahmad, *Musalmanon Ka Roshan Mustaqbal*, p. 283, quoted from *Majmua-i-Lectures Sir Syed Ahmad*, p. 167.

On another occasion he said: 'Just as the Aryan people are called Hindus, even so are also Musalmans Hindus, that is to say, inhabitants of Hindustan.'[7]

Addressing the Hindus of the Punjab he said: 'The word Hindu that you have used for yourselves is in my opinion not correct, because that is not in my view the name of a religion. Rather every inhabitant of Hindustan can call himself a Hindu. I am therefore sorry that you do not regard me as a Hindu although I too am an inhabitant of Hindustan.'[8]

No wonder that Hindus, no less than the Musalmans, regarded him as their leader. No wonder that in 1884 he organized a meeting for Surendranath Bannerji to address about simultaneous examinations for the Civil Service and himself presided over it. No wonder that he was a great admirer of the Bengalis who were the torch-bearers in the national movement.

It is an interesting and intriguing question how such a personage, holding such views, could only a few years later advise the Musalmans to keep away from the national movement which found its expression in the Indian National Congress founded in 1885 with the help of a European member of the Civil Service, Mr A.O. Hume. The answer is to be found in the influence which the English Principals of the Aligarh Mohammedan Anglo-Oriental College came to acquire, and the history of Muslim politics of the following fifteen or twenty years is a history of the activity of these shrewd Englishmen who managed to create the gulf, which with some interruptions has gone on widening ever since.

---

[7] Ibid., p. 283, quoted from *Sir Syed ke Akhri Mozamin*, p. 55.
[8] Ibid., p. 283, quoted from *Safarnama Punjab—Sir Syed Ahmad*, p. 139.

~

TEN

THE BRITISH PRINCIPALS OF THE ALIGARH COLLEGE AND ALIGARH POLITICS

As stated above, Sir Syed Ahmad was very keen about the English education of Musalmans and he founded in 1875 a school which developed into the Mohammedan Anglo-Oriental College and later into the Muslim University of Aligarh. One Mr Beck became its Principal in 1883 and continued in that position till his death in 1899. He came in right good time. English education, which had spread among Hindus, had brought with it ideas of freedom and democracy which were finding vocal expression. Nationalism had been growing apace. The British realized that to counteract this growing nationalism, the time had arrived to draw under their protecting wings the Muslims who had so far been looked upon with disfavour. Mr Beck carried this policy through with missionary zeal. Mr Beck assiduously tried to wean Sir Syed 'away from nationalism, to transfer his political attachment from the British liberals to the conservatives and to evoke in him enthusiasm for a rapprochement between the Muslims and the Government. He was singularly successful in his objective.'[1] One of the first things he did was to secure editorial control of the *Institute Gazette*, which was being conducted for years by Sir Syed. Unlike European professors who had been in the College before him, Mr Beck used to mix very freely with the Muslim students and became very popular among them. Other English professors took their cue from him and helped in starting various organizations and activities within the college. On account of their influence the district officers 'also began to associate themselves with the activities and sports of the college, so much so that in 1888 Sir Auckland Colvin, the Lieutenant-Governor of the province, compared the students of the college with those of the public schools and universities of

[1] Mehta and Patwardhan, *The Communal Triangle*, p. 58.

England. Sir Syed Ahmad Khan was a great admirer of the English way of living and tried to introduce a standard of living among the students, which was regarded by several of his co-workers and supporters as too high and too expensive for a comparatively poor country. But this very fact, coupled with the influence the British Principal and professors had with the government and the change in the government policy, helped in securing government posts and employment for the students of the Aligarh College. All this could not fail to have its effect on Sir Syed Ahmad.

The policy of the *Institute Gazette* under the editorial control of Mr Beck, but still under the nominal editorship of Sir Syed Ahmad, underwent a change. Sir Syed was in those days a great admirer of Bengalis. 'Till then there was a great impression on Sir Syed about the bona fides of Bengalis. He thought that on account of them there had been great improvement in education, and ideas of freedom and patriotism had spread in the country. He used to say that they were the head and crown of all the communities of India and he was proud of them.'[2] 'Mr Beck began to write in the *Institute Gazette* editorial articles against the Bengalis and their movement which were attributed to Sir Syed, and the Bengalis began to criticize Sir Syed. In this way an open conflict began with the Bengalis.'[3] It was at this juncture, when Mr Beck had succeeded in creating an atmosphere against the Bengalis, that the first session of the Indian National Congress was held in Bombay in December 1885 under the presidency of Mr W.C. Bonnerji, a Bengali.

There was nothing in the objects of the Congress to which objection could be taken by an Indian. The resolutions passed at the first Congress demanded the election of the Secretary of State's Council, an increase in the number of elected members in the Provincial Legislative Councils, establishment of such Councils in the Punjab and UP, simultaneous Civil Service examinations in India and England, that there should be no increase in the military expenditure and that there should be no annexation of Upper Burma. The two resolutions regarding simultaneous examinations for Civil Service and the extension of Legislative Councils dealt with matters which had been discussed by Sir Surendranath Bannerji in

[2] Tufail Ahmad, *Musalmanon Ka Roshan*, p. 291.
[3] Ibid., p. 292.

his speech at a public meeting at Aligarh in 1884 which had been organized and presided over by Sir Syed Ahmad himself. These subjects had evoked opposition from Anglo-Indian newspapers to which Mr Beck contributed articles. Sir Syed Ahmad did not say anything at the time but in December 1886 at the time of establishment of the Muhammedan Educational Congress, which later came to be known as the Muslim Educational Conference, he said that he did not agree with those who thought that the Musalmans would make progress by taking up discussion of political matters and that he rather thought that education was the only means for their progress.

The second session of the Congress was held in Calcutta in December 1886 under the presidentship of Mr Dadabhai Naoroji and it passed resolutions demanding trial by jury, separation of judicial and executive functions and enrolment of volunteers for defence purposes. None of the resolutions passed at the first two sessions of the Congress contained anything which was opposed to Muslim interests. Sir Syed himself had supported simultaneous examinations for Civil Service. The demand for separation of executive and judicial functions was in keeping with the practice followed during the Muslim rule in which there had been such separation in force. The two functions had been combined during the time of the Company and after a period of separation again combined in 1858 after the Mutiny. The demand for the increase of the elective element in Legislative Councils and their establishment in the provinces where they did not exist had also received his support in earlier days, although in 1883 he had expressed his difference about the method of election. So there was no reason why Sir Syed Ahmad should oppose the Congress. But some officials looked upon the Congress movement as a revolutionary movement and he could not help being influenced by the idea which was impressed upon him, particularly by Mr Beck, that the education of Musalmans had not yet reached a stage when they could be trusted to confine themselves to constitutional agitation and that if they were roused they might once again express their discontent in the way they had done in 1857; and he was fully convinced that their participation in political agitation would be to their detriment. Mr A.O. Hume wrote an open letter to Sir Syed Ahmad which was published in the *Institute Gazette* of 12 December 1887 with Sir Syed's reply.

The third session of the Congress was held in Madras in December 1887 and was presided over by Mr Badruddin Tyabji and attended by a large number of Muslims. The higher officials of the government had not yet adopted a hostile attitude and the Governor of Madras gave a party to the delegates of the Congress. The resolutions of the Congress demanded the appointment of Indians to commissioned posts in the army, the establishment of a Military College in India, the amendment of the Arms Act, exemption of incomes of less than a thousand a year from the Income Tax and encouragement of technical education. The Muhammedan Educational Congress was held at Lucknow about the same time as the Congress and it was at a public meeting held after this session that Sir Syed Ahmad delivered his first speech against the Congress. It is surprising how Sir Syed Ahmad, who had always insisted on equality between Indians and Englishmen, could go so far as to insist that members of Legislatures should not be appointed by election because it might bring in men from the common ranks who are unfit to be addressed as 'My honourable colleague' by the Viceroy and who could not be allowed to sit at the same table with dukes, earls and other noblemen at social dinners or in assemblies, although they might have attained BA and MA degrees and were otherwise quite capable. The government, therefore, could not be blamed for nominating *raises* (aristocrats) to the Councils. He opposed simultaneous examinations for Civil Service on the ground that although as a result of examinations in England anyone, whether he belonged to an aristocratic family or happened to be the son, say, of a tailor could enter the service, but as here in India this fact was not known, the people submitted to their rule; but the aristocratic people of India would never agree to be ruled by lower classes among their own people with whose origin they were acquainted.

Mr Badruddin Tyabji wrote to Sir Syed Ahmad that if the Muslim delegates were opposed to any matter being considered by the Congress then it would not be taken up. Sir Syed Ahmad replied that because the Congress was a political body there was no political question which would not be opposed to the interest of the Musalmans. We thus see that Mr Beck had completely succeeded in misguiding and converting Sir Syed Ahmad. No wonder that Sir Theodore Morrison asserts in his history of the Aligarh College that as a result of Sir Syed's speech the

Musalmans altogether left the Congress and began to oppose the introduction of representative institutions in India. In March 1888, Sir Auckland Colvin visited the Aligarh College and in his reply to an address, extolled the institution and its students as no one had done before. In the following April Sir Syed Ahmad delivered his second speech against the Congress at Meerut. The Congress was to be held at Allahabad in the following December 1888, and Sir Auckland Colvin and his government did their best to prevent the session but it was held in spite of them. Lord Dufferin who had encouraged Mr A.O. Hume to establish the Congress had by this time become opposed to it.

A movement had been started about this time for cow-protection of which advantage was taken by pro-government Musalmans and they held a meeting at Allahabad in which they passed resolutions not only against cow-protection but also against Muslim participation in the Congress. Some persons issued a *fatwa* against Musalmans joining the Congress. Against this, Maulvi Abdul Qadir Ludhianwi obtained and got published *fatwas* under the signatures of ulema of Ludhiana, Jullundar, Hoshiarpur, Kapurthala, Amritsar, Chapra, Gujarat, Jaunpur, Ferozpur, Kasur, Muzaffarnagar, Delhi, Rampur, Bareilly, Moradabad and even Madina Manauara and Baghdad Sharif. Many of those who had signed these *fatwas* were famous ulema and divines of the time. The *fatwas* stated that in worldly matters it was allowable for Muslims to work in combination with the Hindus in the Congress. We thus see that while on the one hand there was the great personality of Sir Syed Ahmad opposed to the Congress, on the other hand the Musalmans of Bombay and Madras under the leadership of Messrs Tyabji, Ali Mahommad Bhimji and Rahmatullah Sayani were in favour of it and noted ulema sanctioned Muslim participation in it.

In August 1888 was established the United Indian Patriotic Association at Aligarh in which both Hindus and Musalmans joined. The objects of the Association were:

(1)   to inform the members of Parliament and the people of England through newspapers and tracts that all the communities of India, the aristocracy and the Princes were not with the Congress and to contradict its statements;

(2)   to keep the Parliament and the people of England informed about the opinions of Hindu and Muslim organizations which were opposed to the Congress; and

(3)   to help in the maintenance of law and order and the strengthening of the British rule in India and to wean away people from the Congress. This whole scheme was the result of Mr Beck's efforts and he and Sir Syed were put in charge of it. A branch of the Association was opened in England at the house of Mr Morrison who subsequently became the Principal of Aligarh College after Mr Beck's death. It was decided to appoint princes as patrons of the Association. Many of the big Hindu and Musalman landlords and some Europeans joined the Association. Raja Sheoprasad proposed in the Taluqdar Association of Oudh that an Indian Loyal Association should be established and that the Patriotic Association should become a branch of it. He also proposed that the government should be requested to stop speeches and writings in Indian languages which were likely to create trouble and revolt. The object was that the Congress should be suppressed. In spite of all this opposition of the government, the United Indian Patriotic Association and men like Raja Sheoprasad, the Allahabad session of the Congress was attended by 1248 delegates as against 607 who had attended the previous session; and it was pointed out by the Muslim delegates that the increase in their attendance was directly the result of the opposition of the leaders of Aligarh. It is worth noting that the Congress session at Allahabad against which so much opposition had been engineered passed resolutions supporting temperance, demanding increased expenditure on education, extension of Permanent Settlement, and opposing the Salt Tax.

In 1889, Mr Bradlaugh introduced a Bill in Parliament with the object of establishing democratic institutions in India. Mr Beck prepared a memorandum against it, in which it was stated that democratic institutions were unsuited to India because there were different communities inhabiting it. He obtained a large number of signatures on the memorandum through the instrumentality of the students of the Aligarh College who were sent out in batches. One such group went to Delhi under the leadership of Mr Beck himself. 'He himself sat at the door of Jama-e-masjid and the students under his instructions secured signatures from those going in for prayers by representing that the Hindus wanted to stop cow-slaughter and this was the petition to be sent to the government against this move. This statement is made by Walait Hussain Saheb in the Conference Gazette of Aligarh. However, having secured 20,735 signatures in this way in Delhi alone this marvellous petition was sent to be presented to the Parliament in England in 1890.'[4]

The United Indian Patriotic Association continued to oppose the Congress in the name of Musalmans for some years but in 1893, a new organization under the name of Mohammedan Anglo-Oriental Defence Association of Upper India was founded. The objects of the Association were:

(a)   to place the opinions of Musalmans before Englishmen and the Government of India and to protect their political rights]

(b)   to prevent political agitation from spreading among the Musalmans;

(c)   to adopt all such means as would be helpful in strengthening the British rule and maintaining law and order and creating sense of loyalty among the people. It would appear that the Patriotic Association was a joint organization of Hindus and Muslims. Mr Beck could not tolerate their joint action even in strengthening the British rule and he, therefore, got the Defence Association established in which Musalmans were separated from other Indian communities but joined the reactionary Englishmen and even gave it the name of a 'Defence Association'. This name was borrowed from the Anglo-Indian Defence Association which had been established against Lord Ripon in 1883 but which had ceased to exist after completing its work. Mr Beck became its Secretary.

In his opening speech at the first session of the Association he pointed out that although, the Patriotic Association had secured signatures against Mr Bradlaugh's Bill, it suffered from two serious defects. It was a joint organization of Hindus and Musalmans and had many other organizations affiliated to it. In the second place it used to hold public meetings and thus create public agitation.

---

[4] Tufail Ahmad, *Musalmanon Ka Roshan*, pp. 311–12.

The Defence Association would be an association of Musalmans from which Hindus were excluded and it would not hold public meetings or create agitation; nor would it affiliate institutions. It would have a Council and the entire work of the Association should be entrusted to the Council and should not be left in the hands of the general members. It is worth while quoting a significant passage from this opening speech of Mr Beck. 'For the last few years there are two kinds of agitation which have been gaining strength in the country—one is the National Congress and the other is the movement against cow-slaughter. Of these the first is entirely opposed to Englishmen and the second movement is against the Musalmans. The object of the National Congress is that the political power of the English Government should be transferred to some groups amongst the Hindus, the ruling race should be weakened, the people should be given arms, the army should be weakened and the cost on it be reduced. The Musalmans can have no sympathy with these objects. The object of the movement of cow-slaughter is to prevent Musalmans from cow-sacrifice and to prevent both Englishmen and Musalmans from slaughtering cows for food. To prevent cow-slaughter they boycott their opponents to starve them into submission. This has resulted in bloody riots in Bombay, Azamgarh, etc. The Musalmans and Englishmen have become the targets of these two movements. It is therefore necessary that Musalmans and Englishmen should unite in opposing them and that the establishment of democratic political institutions should be opposed as they are not suited to this country. We must, therefore, carry on propaganda in favour of true loyalty and unity of action.'[5]

We have already seen how Mr Beck had sent up a representation against Mr Bradlaugh's Bill with some 50,000 signatures. He got another representation sent with Muslim signatures against simultaneous examinations for Civil Service. When news was received that the request contained in the representation had been accepted, the Defence Association passed a thanksgiving resolution, adding that to hold simultaneous examinations would be detrimental to the stability of British rule in India, that the government would be weakened, and that there would be difficulty

[5] Tufail Ahmad, *Musalmanon Ka Roshan*, p. 315.

in protecting life and property on which the moral and material prosperity of India depends.

Mr Beck also engineered opposition to appointments being made in India by competitive examinations and suggested that the Musalmans should rather depend on their loyalty to the British government to secure appointments. The Defence Association carried on propaganda in England also where Mr Beck himself delivered a lecture in 1895. The thesis of this lecture was that Anglo-Muslim unity was possible but Hindu–Muslim unity was not possible and that parliamentary institutions were entirely unsuited to India. If they were established, the Musalmans being the minority, would be overpowered by the Hindus who are in a majority. In this lecture he sometimes patted the Muslims on the back and sometimes threatened them with dire consequences if they did not behave and followed the policy of the Hindus.

The British government at that time was thinking of pushing on its forward policy on the Frontier and wanted to increase the military expenditure which was opposed by the Congress. Mr Beck in his annual report of the Defence Association, 1896, emphasized that for the stability of the government it was necessary that the army and the navy should be strengthened and Sir Syed Ahmad himself placed a resolution to the effect that the Association was opposed to any decrease in the military expenditure. 'In proposing this resolution he said that in his opinion the number of English soldiers was very small and that he had impressed upon Lord Dufferin on one occasion that the army was insufficient for the defence of the Frontier.[6] As against this the Congress passed resolutions opposing the forward policy of the government on the Frontier and suggesting that a friendly policy towards the Frontier people should be followed and the heavy expenditure on the Swat valley should be stopped. It is worth noting that the Congress was opposing the forward policy which was responsible for the death and destruction of the Frontier people who were all Musalmans, while the Mohammedan Defence Association was demanding increased expenditure and a larger army for that purpose.

All this could not fail to cause a searching of hearts amongst many Muslims who found themselves torn between loyalty to Sir Syed on the one hand and loyalty to the true interests of

---

[6] Tufail Ahmad, *Musalmanon Ka Roshan*, p. 330.

Musalmans on the other, as appears from what Nawab Waqar-ul-mulk wrote a few years later, in 1907. 'Seeing all this, those who had the interest of the community at heart became anxious and consultations began to take place. Ultimately some of the trustees in spite of the power, prestige and greatness of Sir Syed Ahmad, whose peer will not be found for a long time, came to the conclusion that they should keep in view only the interest of the community and set aside any consideration which they had for the great Leader. It was decided to publish a series of articles in *Paisa Ikhbar* of Lahore. These articles were not to be anonymous but were to have the signature of men like Nawab Mohsin-ul-Mulk, Shamshul-Ulema Maulvi Khwaja Altaf Husain Hali, and my humble self was also to be a signatory. The first of the series was written by me and was sent to Nawab Mohsin-ul-Mulk Bahadur and Shamshul-Ulema Maulvi Hali Saheb, who were probably living at Aligarh during those days, for their signatures. Suddenly news of the death of the Leader reached me and I immediately wired to Nawab Mohsin-ul-Mulk to return the articles because after his death we had no other thought except of his goodness and matchless qualities. As the idea of writing that series of articles was given up at that time and no complaints could any longer be harboured, I am making these facts known today only for the good of the College.'[7]

After Sir Syed's death in 1898 Mr Beck continued his policy but he too died in the following year, 1899.

In the words of Sir Arthur Strachey, Chief Justice of Allahabad High Court, he was one of those Englishmen who were engaged in different parts of the world in building up the empire and he died like a soldier during his duty.

Mr Theodore Morrison became the Principal of the college after Mr Beck. It will be recalled that it was at Mr Morrison's house in England that a branch of the Patriotic Association had been formed and it was natural that he should take Mr Beck's place not only as the Principal of the Aligarh College but also as his representative in politics. Certain events happened which helped the work of alienating the Musalmans from the Hindus in which the English Principals of the Aligarh College were engaged. In April 1900, the government of the United Provinces issued a resolution

[7] Extract from *Waqar-i-Hayat*, p. 420, quoted by Tufail Ahmad, *Musalmanon Ka Roshan*, p. 334.

which led to the Urdu–Nagri agitation in the province; the Hindus
supported the government move for permitting the use of the Nagri
script in courts and the Musalmans opposed it. For many years
the Hindus had been agitating for the use of Nagri script but on
account of the opposition of Sir Syed they were unsuccessful. In
1900 an epidemic of plague appeared in the province and the
government adopted measures of segregation which led to riots in
some towns in which both Hindus and Musalmans joined. One
such riot took place in Cawnpore on 1 April 1900 and caused
trouble and anxiety to the government and within a fortnight of
this incident the resolution sanctioning the use of Nagri script in
courts and offices of the government came out. The result was
a conflict between Hindus and Musalmans. A meeting of protest
was held at Aligarh in May 1900 under the presidentship of the
Nawab of Chhatari. Nawab Mohsin-ul-mulk delivered a strong
speech, and a resolution requesting the government to withdraw
the resolution was passed. This brought upon the President the
displeasure of the government and he resigned his presidentship.
Then Nawab Mohsin-ul-mulk became the President and delivered
some speeches about it. The Lieutenant-Governor himself visited
Aligarh, saw the trustees of the college and told them that Nawab
Mohsin-ul-mulk must choose between remaining the President of the
Urdu Conference and working as the Secretary of the college. He
could not carry on political agitation while continuing as Secretary
of the college. In view of the importance of the college work he
had to give up the Presidentship of the Urdu Conference under
pressure of the trustees. The work of the Patriotic Association and
the Mohammedan Defence Association was to oppose the Congress
and to oppose the introduction of parliamentary institutions into
India, simultaneous examinations for the Civil Service, reduction of
military expenditure, abolition of the Salt Tax, amendment of the
Arms Act, and soon. But all this was not considered as political
work and not only the Secretary of the college Sir Syed Ahmad
Khan but also its Principal, Mr Beck had been permitted and
even encouraged by the government to carry it on. But Nawab
Mohsin-ul-mulk was not permitted to continue as President of the
Urdu Conference because it was considered political work. The
reason is obvious. The former suited the government, the latter
did not. Mr Morrison saw that the agitation against the Nagri
script among the Musalmans could be suppressed with difficulty

and he, therefore, advised them that it was not desirable to have any political organization at all. He pointed out to them the harmful effect of democratic institutions and wrote in a letter published in the *Institute Gazette* in 1901 that 'democratic rule would reduce the minority to the position of hewers of wood and drawers of water.' He also opined that it was not desirable to have a separate organization of Musalmans, as the big men of the community for fear of government displeasure would not join it, and this would create differences amongst the Musalmans themselves. He, therefore, concluded: 'In my opinion a political organization instead of being beneficial would be injurious to the interests of Musalmans, because during the last twenty or twenty-five years the government has been showing concession to them. If like the Congress they also started an organization and demanded their right and the Parliament were to appoint a Commission the Musalmans would not derive as much benefit from it as they would if they were to leave their fate in the hands of Sir Anthony Macdonell.'[9] He also pointed out that government officials used to show preference to Musalmans which would cease if they also made political demands. He, therefore, suggested that Musalmans should have only a Council with an office manned by able men and equipped with political literature, to advise members of legislatures. His further advice was that the Musalmans should pay more attention to economic than to political questions.

The proposal was never implemented because funds could not be raised and all political movement amongst the Musalmans was, in the words of Maulvi Tufail Ahmad, buried under the ground for the time being.

Although the government was opposed to the Secretary of the college participating in the Nagri–Urdu controversy because of its political nature, they did not hesitate to use the college and its students for political purposes. In those days Russia and England were rival powers courting the goodwill of Persia. In 1902 Lord Curzon considered it desirable to have some boys from Persia educated at the Aligarh College. Mr Morrison proposed that a deputation from the college should be sent to Persia. When Nawab Mohsin-ul-mulk objected to the cost of the deputation being paid out of the college funds, Mr Morrison forced his hands and he had

[8] Tufail Ahmad, *Musalmanon Ka Roshan*, p. 349.
[9] Ibid., p. 350.

ELEVEN

~

THE ORIGIN OF SEPARATE ELECTORATES

Bengal was the earliest province to come under the rule of the East India Company and English education made its first appearance in that province. The Bengali Hindus were quick to take advantage of it. The Musalmans, in pursuance of the policy then in vogue, were deliberately kept back by the government. The Hindus not only filled government posts in all departments but also produced great reformers, great lawyers, medical practitioners, scientists, public speakers, writers and men who had drunk deep from fountain of English literature and had acquired a great admiration for British institutions, particularly the British Constitution. It was not to be expected that such a community could long remain satisfied with posts in the lower rungs of the government service ladder. Many showed a growing desire for the introduction of progressive institutions on the British model. They contributed to a very great extent to the awakening amongst the educated classes of the country as a whole and were in no small measure responsible also for the establishment of the Indian National Congress, over the first session of which a Bengali, Mr W.C. Bonnerji, presided. They had naturally won the esteem and admiration of all men of progressive thought, and, as has been stated above, Sir Syed Ahmad Khan was one of them. But for the very same reason they became suspect in the eyes of British officials, who did not conceal either their contempt or their fear of them. They had by their ability and devotion to duty earned the admiration of Sir Anthony Macdonell, who was then the Lieutenant-Governor of Bengal, for their work as Municipal Commissioners of the Municipality of Calcutta. Lord Curzon with his masterful personality was not to be expected to tolerate the rising influence of the Bengalis. One of his first acts was, therefore, to attack the Municipality of Calcutta, by reducing the number of elected members. There was to be an official Chairman and thus the Municipality came under the controlling power of the government. This attack on the premier city, which was the centre and source of nationalism in northern and eastern India at least, if not in the whole country, was naturally resented. This incensed Lord Curzon still more and in December 1903 he adumbrated a scheme for cutting out the Chittagong and Dacca divisions from Bengal and tacking them to Assam. There was great agitation against it. Even Nawab Salimullah Khan of Dacca regarded it as a 'beastly arrangement'. Lord Curzon came into further conflict with the public opinion of India on account of his address at the Convocation of the Calcutta University in which he said that Orientals had no regard for truth. There were protests against this speech. These constant protests further enraged Lord Curzon. He went to Dacca and in a public meeting he told the Musalmans that his object in partitioning Bengal was not only to reduce the burden on the Lieutenant-Governor, who had in his charge such a big area as was then comprised within the province of Bengal, but also to create a Muslim province in which they would have a preponderating voice. Many Musalmans were taken in by this. Nawab Salimullah of Dacca, who had been opposed to the plan of partition, became one of its ardent supporters, although his brother, Khwaja Atiqullah, continued his opposition to it. It is said by Mr Gurumukh Nihal Singh that the support of Nawab Salimullah of Dacca was won by advancing a loan of about 100,000 pounds at a low rate of interest, soon after the partition.[1] In face of the unanimous opposition of the Hindus and a great many Musalmans led by Mr A. Rasool and Khwaja Atiqullah, the province was partitioned. 'The object of the measure,' in the words of Sir Henry Cotton, was 'to shatter the unity and to disintegrate the feeling of solidarity which are established in the Province. It was no administrative reason that lay at the root of this scheme. It was a part and parcel of Lord Curzon's policy to enfeeble the growing powers and to destroy the political tendencies of a patriotic spirit.' In the words of the *Statesman* the object was 'to foster in Eastern Bengal the growth' of Mohammedan power, which, it is hoped, will have the effect of keeping in check the rapidly growing strength of the Hindu community.'[2]

[1] Gurumukh Nihal Singh, *Landmarks in Indian Constitutional and National Development*, p. 319.
[2] From *India in Transition* quoted by Mehta and Patwardhan in *Communal Triangle*, p. 64.

Lord Curzon left India the legacy of a very bitter controversy over the partition question in which not only Bengalis but people from other parts of the country also joined. It very often happens that plans made by men of little minds go awry. And so it was in India. What was intended to suppress political life served as a great inspiration. The anti-partition agitation roused the country as a whole as nothing else had done since 1857.

When Lord Minto became Viceroy in November 1905 after Lord Curzon's retirement, he was face to face with a very tense situation and within a few months of his taking office he wrote to Mr John Morley: 'As to Congress . . . we must recognize them and be friends with the best of them, yet I am afraid there is much that is absolutely disloyal in the movement and that there is danger for the future . . . I have been thinking a good deal lately of a possible counterpoise to Congress aims. I think we may find a solution in a Council of Princes or in an elaboration of that idea: a Privy Council not only of native Rulers, but a few other big men, to meet say once a year for a week or a fortnight at Delhi for instance. Subjects for discussion and procedure would have to be very carefully thought out, but we should get different ideas from those of Congress, emanating from men already possessing great interest in the good government of India . . .'[3]

Mr Morley wrote on 6 June following, to Lord Minto: 'Everybody warns us that a new spirit is growing and spreading over India: Lawrence, Chirol, Sydney Low, all sing the same song: "You cannot go on governing in the same spirit; you have got to deal with the Congress party and Congress principles, whatever you may think of them. Be sure that before long the Mohammedans will throw in their lot with the Congressmen against you" and so on and so forth.'[4]

The idea of establishing a Council of Princes to act as a counterpoise to the Congress and generally to every national upsurge did not fructify at the time. But another and a more effective method was found. Lord Minto soon began to elaborate, in consultation with his Council, a plan for reforms which he hoped would satisfy at least the moderate elements in India. In this connection while on the one side the scheme was being elaborated, on the other an

[3] Lady Minto, *India Minto and Morley*, pp. 28–9.
[4] Minto, *India* . . ., p. 30.

attempt was made to wean away the Muslims from the politics of
the country. Maulvi Syed Tufail Ahmad Mangalori writes: 'On the
30 July 1906 Haji Mahommad Ismail Khan Sahib, Rais Aligarh,
who was at Nainital and had access to officials, sent a draft of
representation to Nawab Mohsin-ul-mulk Bahadur, Honorary
Secretary of the College, that the Musalmans should also demand
their rights. And generally speaking the educated Musalmans turned
their attention to this. In those days Mr Archbold, the Principal
of the College, was at Simla on account of the long vacation
and used to meet the high officials there. He had a talk with the
Private Secretary of the Viceroy about a proposed deputation.
The letter which Mr Archbold wrote on the 10th August 1906,
after the talk, to the late Nawab Mohsin-ul-mulk was printed and
distributed to the members of the deputation. It appears from a
summary of this letter which is given below how the Principals
of the Aligarh College used to guide the details of the political
policy of the Musalmans and how they occupied the position
of a resident of the Government at Aligarh. Every word of this
summary deserves careful study:

'"Colonel Dunlop Smith [Private Secretary to the Viceroy]
now writes to me that the Viceroy is prepared to receive the
deputation of Musalmans and intimates me that a formal petition
be submitted for it. In this connection the following matters require
consideration.

'"The first question is that of sending the petition. To my mind
it would be enough that some leaders of Musalmans, even though
they may not have been elected, should put their signatures to
it. The second is the question as to who the members of the
deputation should be. They should be representatives of all the
provinces. The third question is of the contents of the address. In
this connection my opinion is that in the address loyalty should be
expressed, that thanks should be offered that in accordance with
the settled policy steps are going to be taken in the direction of
self-government according to which the door will be opened for
Indians to offices. But apprehension should be expressed that by
introducing election injury will be done to Musalman minority
and hope should be expressed that in introducing the system of
nomination or granting representation on religious basis the opinion
of Musalmans will be given due weight. The opinion should also

be given that in a country like India it is necessary that weight should be attached to the views of zamindars.

"'My personal opinion is that the wisest thing for Musalmans to do would be that they support the system of nomination because the time for introducing election has not yet come. Besides it will be very difficult for them if the system of election is introduced to secure their proper share.

"'But in all these matters I want to remain behind the screen and this move should come from you. You are aware how anxious I am for the good of the Musalmans and I would, therefore, render all help with the greatest pleasure. I can prepare and draft the address for you. If it be prepared in Bombay then I can revise it because I know the art of drawing up petitions in good language. But Nawabsaheb, please remember that if within a short time any great and effective action has to be taken then you should act quickly.'"[5]

Nawab Mohsin-ul-mulk accordingly, in the words of Lady Minto, 'engineered'[6] the Mohammedan deputation. The address was prepared and the deputation under the leadership of His Highness the Agha Khan waited on the Viceroy on 1 October 1906. Lady Minto writes in her journal of that date:

'This has been a very eventful day: as some one said to me, "an epoch in Indian history". We are aware of the feeling of unrest that exists throughout India, and the dissatisfaction that prevails amongst people of all classes and creeds. The Mohammedan population which numbers 62 millions, who have always been intensely loyal, resent not having proper representation and consider themselves slighted in many ways, preference having been given to the Hindus. The agitators have been most anxious to foster this feeling and have naturally done their utmost to secure the co-operation of this vast community. The younger generation were wavering, inclined to throw in their lot with advanced agitators of the Congress, and a howl went up that the loyal Mohammedans were not to be supported, and that the agitators were to obtain their demands through agitation. The Mohammedans decided, before taking action, that they would bring an address before the Viceroy, mentioning their grievances. The meeting was fixed

[5] Tufail Ahmad, *Mushalmanon Ka Roshan*, pp. 360–1.
[6] Minto, *India . . .*, p. 56.

for today and about 70 delegates from all parts of India have
arrived. The ceremony took place this morning in the Ball-room.
The girls and I went in by a side door to hear the proceedings
while Minto advanced up the room with his staff and took his
seat on the dais. The Agha Khan is the spiritual head of the Khoja
Moslem community. He claims to be descended from Ali and is
their Ruler by divine right, but without territory. The Prince was
selected to read the very long but excellent Address stating all their
grievances and aspirations. Minto then read his answer which he
had thought out most carefully—"You need not ask my pardon for
telling me that representative institutions of the European type are
entirely new to the people of India' or that their introduction here
requires the most earnest thought and care. I should be very far
from welcoming all the political machinery of the Western world
among the hereditary traditions and instincts of Eastern races . . .
Your address, as I understand it, is a claim that, in any system of
representation, whether it affects a Municipality, a District Board, or
Legislative Council, in which it is proposed to introduce or increase
an electoral organization, the Mohamedan community should be
represented as a community. You point out that in many cases
electoral bodies, as now constituted, cannot be expected to return
a Mohammedan candidate, and that if by chance they did so, it
could only be at the sacrifice of such candidate's views, to those
of a majority opposed to his own community, whom he would in
no way represent, and you justly claim that your position should
be estimated not merely on your numerical strength but in respect
to the political importance of your community and the service it
has rendered to the Empire. I am entirely in accord with you . . .
I am as firmly convinced as I believe you to be, that any electoral
representation in India would be doomed to mischievous failure
which aimed at granting a personal enfranchisement, regardless
of the beliefs and traditions of the communities composing the
population of this continent.""[7]

On the same day Lady Minto further writes in her journal:
'This evening I have received the following letter from an official:
"I must send your Excellency a line to say that a very very big
thing has happened today. A work of statesmanship that will affect
India and Indian history for many a long year. It is nothing less

[7] Minto, *India* . . ., pp. 45–7.

than the pulling back of 62 millions of people from joining the ranks of the seditious opposition."' Very much the same view was taken at Whitehall. Mr Morley, after receiving an account of the proceedings wrote: 'Morley to Minto—"October 26—All that you tell me of your Mohammedans is full of interest, and I only regret that I could not have moved about unseen at your garden party. The whole thing has been as good as it could be, and it stamps your position and personal authority decisively. Among other good effects of your deliverance is this, that it has completely deranged the plan and tactics of the critical faction here, that is to say it has prevented them from any longer representing the Indian Government as the ordinary case of bureaucracy versus the people. I hope that even my stoutest Radical friends will now see that the problem is not quite so simple as this."'[8]

Buchan, Lord Minto's biographer, says: 'The speech undoubtedly prevented the ranks of sedition being swollen by Moslem recruits, an inestimable advantage on the day of trouble which is dawning,'[9] and he describes it as a Charter of Islamic Rights.

Maulvi Tufail Ahmad writes that things had been so arranged that the deputation should receive a good press in England. The deputation was to wait on the Viceroy on 1 October 1906 and in the London *Times* appeared on the same day a long article in which the wisdom of Musalmans was extolled. It was said that the Musalmans were never enamoured of representative councils on the European model, that there was no nation in India as in England and that there were various religions and so on. Other papers also wrote similar articles. 'It appears from these articles, how the English press looked upon Indians being one nation with a sense of shock and heart-burning and how pleased they were to see it broken into pieces and how proud they felt in setting the Indians against one another on the basis of religion and of creating lasting hostility between them.'[10] It took time for the scheme to be worked out and a lot of correspondence passed between the Viceroy and the Secretary of State and ultimately, as a result, separate electorates for Musalmans were established.

[8]   Minto, India . . ., pp. 47–48.
[9]   Buchan, *Lord Minto*, p. 244, quoted by Gurumukh Nihal Singh, *Landmarks* . . .
[10] Tufail Ahmad, *Mushalmanon Ka Roshan*, p. 363.

~

TWELVE

THE MUSLIM LEAGUE FOUNDED AND THE LUCKNOW PACT

The All-India Muslim League was established in the wake, of the Muslim deputation to the Viceroy. On 9 November 1906 Nawab Salimullah issued a circular in which he suggested that an organization to be known as the All-India Muslim Conference should be established and ultimately in the following December, a conference was held at Dacca attended by representatives and leaders from all over India. Nawab Waqar-ul-Mulk presided and the All-India Muslim League was established. Nawab Waqar-ul-Mulk was appointed the Secretary and Nawab Mohsin-ul-Mulk the Joint Secretary, but unfortunately the latter passed away soon after. One of the resolutions supported the partition of Bengal and opposed the boycott movement. The establishment of the League was welcomed by the *Times* of London. It is curious to note that the Hindu Mahasabha was also established in the same year. Mr Ramsay Macdonald in *The Awakening of India* wrote about the part played by officialdom as follows: 'The Mahommedan leaders are inspired by certain Anglo-Indian officials, and these officials have pulled wires at Simla and in London and of malice aforethought sowed discord between Hindu and Mahommedan communities by showing the Muslims special favour.'[1] The result of separate electorates has been not only to create a gulf but also to widen it progressively.

The Muslim League began to meet in annual sessions and pass resolutions in support of the partition of Bengal and separate electorates to be introduced not only for the Legislative Councils but also in the local bodies and demand representation of Muslims not only in the services but also in the Privy Council. His Highness the Agha Khan presided over the session of the League held in January 1910 at Delhi and expressed satisfaction over

[1] Quoted by Mehta and Patwardhan, *The Communal Triangle*, p. 66.

the Reforms which had been introduced and sounded a warning that there should be no opposition to them lest the government should withdraw them. An incident occurred which throws a flood of light on the government policy. It will be recalled that in the time of Sir Anthony Macdonell, Nawab Mohsin-ul-Mulk, who was the Secretary of the Aligarh College, was pulled up by the Lieutenant-Governor for taking a prominent part in the Urdu–Nagri controversy and had to give up his presidentship of the organization known as *Anjuman-i-Himayat Urdu* on the ground that the Secretary of the college should not be associated with a political organization. The Lieutenant-Governor went so far as to order the title of Nawab, which had been conferred upon him by the Nizam, should not be used in government correspondence. The government, however, did not object to his engineering the Muslim deputation and to his becoming the Joint Secretary of the All-India Muslim League while he continued to be the Secretary of the college. Nawab Waqar-ul-Mulk, who presided over the conference at Dacca where the League was established, and was appointed its General Secretary, became the Secretary of the college after the death of Nawab Mohsin-ul-Mulk. He continued to participate in the Muslim League, the head office of which was established at Aligarh and remained there till 1910. Some difference arose between Nawab Waqar-ul-Mulk and the English Principal of the College. The Governor sided with the Principal. There was public agitation among the Musalmans in support of the stand taken by Nawab Waqar-ul-Mulk. The Lieutenant-Governor was forced to withdraw his orders but he was not to be beaten. He had his revenge. The head office of the Muslim League was shifted by His Highness the Agha Khan, who was its President, from Aligarh to Lucknow in the hope that the League would get out of the influence of Aligarh. The unexpected result of this move, however, was that the policy of the League got out of the control of the Principals of the college.

The announcement of the annulment of the partition of Bengal by the King at the Delhi Durbar in December 1911, came as a rude shock to many Musalmans and was so heart-breaking for Nawab Salimullah that after presiding over the session of the League, which was held in Calcutta in March 1912, he announced his withdrawal from all public activities and died shortly afterwards.

Other events were happening which had considerable influence
on the Musalmans. Maulvi Shibli Naumani had the reputation of
being among the most learned Musalmans of the time and has
written the standard work in Urdu on the life of the Prophet as
also a life of Sir Syed Ahmad Khan. He was the founder of the
Academy at Azamgarh which has been publishing works of great
historical value under the guidance of Maulana Sulaiman Nadvi
after his death. He had been a life-long co-worker of Sir Syed
Ahmad but had towards the latter part of his life, begun to doubt
the wisdom of his policy and attitude towards the Congress. He
had been drawing the attention of the Musalmans to the more
fundamental question of India's freedom and advising them not
to be content with the role of being mere critics of the Congress.
In the course of an article published in the *Muslim Gazette* of
Lucknow dated 9 October 1917, he said, after discussing the
politics and the policy of the Muslim League: 'A tree is judged
by the fruit it gives. If our politics had been serious politics they
would have evoked a zest for struggle and a readiness to suffer
and sacrifice for an ideal.'[2]

Other events were happening which influenced the Muslim mind
considerably. 'The working of the reformed councils was beginning
to demonstrate the community of interest between the different
communities and the essential unity of all Indians. And above all
the nationalist movements in distant countries, specially in Turkey
and Persia, were infusing a more national spirit in the minds of
the Muslim youth in the country . . . The policy followed by
Great Britain towards Turkey during the Tripoli and Balkan wars
showed the British in their true colours and demonstrated to Indian
Musalmans the hollowness and insincerity of British professions
of friendship. On the other hand Moslem hearts were touched by
expressions of brotherly sympathy in the Indian nationalist press
for them in their grief over the treatment meted out to Turkey
by the European nations.'[3] In 1912 Dr M.A. Ansari organized
and led a medical mission to Turkey. Maulana Zafarali, editor
of the *Zamindar,* went himself to present a purse to the Vizier
at Constantinople which had been raised for the Turkish Red
Crescent. Maulana Abul Kalam Azad started the *Al-Hilal* which

---

[2] Tufail Ahmad, *Musalmanon Ka Roshan*, p. 389; and Mehta and
Patwardhan, *The Communal Triangle*, p. 30.

[3] Gurumukh Nihal Singh, *Landmarks in Constitutional and National
Development*, pp. 490–91.

by its inspiring style of writing no less than by its high ideals of nationalism, freedom and sacrifice made an appeal unsurpassed by any other paper in Urdu. Maulana Mohammad Ali was conducting the *Comrade* in English and the *Hamdard* in Urdu which helped to swell the mighty current in favour of nationalism. The League could not remain unaffected and its constitution was amended at its session at Lucknow in March 1913 presided over by Sir Ibrahim Rahimtullah. The object of the League was defined among other matters to be the attainment under the aegis of the British Crown of a system of self-government suitable to India, through constitutional means by bringing about, amongst others, a steady reform of the existing system of administration, by promoting national unity, by fostering public spirit among the people of India, and by co-operating with other communities for the said purpose. The object of the League was thus brought in line with that of the Indian National Congress and paved the way for communal unity and common action which followed soon.

In August 1914, the First World War commenced. There was excitement amongst Indians and some people, amongst whom Musalmans were prominent, planned daring schemes for an independent Republic of India. Sheikhul-Hind Maulana Mahmudul Hassan with his colleagues Maulana Hussain Ahmed Nadvi and Maulvi Aziz Gul was arrested and interned at Malta. Maulanas Mohammad Ali, Shaukat Ali, Azad and Hasrat Mohani were all interned for their sympathy with Turkey which had joined the war against the Allies and for their outspoken nationalism. In December 1915, the League and the Congress both held their sessions at Bombay. Many Congress leaders including Pandit Madan Mohan Malaviya, Shrimati Sarojini Naidu and Mahatma Gandhi attended the League session. His Highness the Agha Khan resigned as permanent President of the League. The League appointed a Committee to prepare a scheme for India in consultation with the Congress. At Lucknow, the League and the Congress again held their annual sessions at the same place and time. In the year which had intervened between the Bombay and Lucknow sessions the Committee had prepared the scheme. The Congress was strengthened by the bridging of the breach between the moderates and progressives which had occurred nine years before at Surat and so it was attended not only by the moderate leaders like Sir Surendranath Bannerji and Pandit Madan Mohan

Malaviya but also by Lokamanya Tilak. An agreement was arrived at between the Congress and the League which accepted separate electorates for Musalmans and allowed them representation much in excess of their proportion of population in the provinces except in the Punjab and Bengal. It further provided that no Bill or any clause thereof nor any resolution introduced by a non-official member affecting one or the other community in the Legislative Council concerned shall be proceeded with if three-fourths of the members of the community in the particular Council, Imperial or Provincial, opposed the Bill, any clause thereof, or the Resolution. Apart from this pact between the Congress and the League the plan elaborated a scheme of reforms and it was demanded that a definite step should be taken towards self-government by granting the reforms contained in the scheme and that in the reconstruction of the empire of India should be lifted from the position of a dependency to that of an equal partner within the empire with the self-governing dominions. Mr M.A. Jinnah was the President of the session of the League and, on the Congress side, all the leaders including Lokamanya Tilak approved of the pact. Other resolutions were on the same lines as those of the Congress and it seemed that a concordat between the Congress and the League was established.

The Muslim League thus became an ardent supporter of the political programme which the Congress had adopted. The new spirit was seen in the following session which elected Maulana Mohammad Ali, who was then in internment, as its President. Like the previous two sessions this session was also held at the same time and place as the Congress in December 1917, in Calcutta. Mahatma Gandhi and Shrimati Naidu attended the League session and participated in the proceedings of the League by supporting a resolution demanding the release of the Ali Brothers.

By the time the next session of the League met in December 1918, in Delhi where the Congress also held its session, much had happened in the country and in the world. Mr Montagu had visited India and in conjunction with Lord Chelmsford, the Viceroy, prepared his report about reforms in pursuance of the declaration of British policy made in August 1917. The war had ended in favour of the Allies and against Germany and Turkey. The defeat of Turkey had brought into prominence certain problems which affected the Musalmans of India. While the war was going on, British spokesmen had given assurances that Turkey would be fairly treated after the war and nothing would be done which would adversely affect the Muslim Holy Places in Arabia and Mesopotamia. Although it was not yet quite clear what the terms to be imposed on Turkey would be, the Musalmans were agitated over the incidents which had occurred in Arabia under British instigation, resulting in the Arabs asserting their independence of Turkey. Other incidents like the suppression of riots with a strong hand at Cawnpore (Kanpur) and the proscription of the speech of Dr M.A. Ansari as Chairman of the Reception Committee of the Delhi session of the League, had served only to exacerbate Muslim feelings. The ulema re-appeared on the political stage of Indian Musalmans and began to take a leading part in their political movement. The League demanded the application of self-determination to India.

The peace proposals falsified the promises held out to Indian Musalmans about the Khalifa, his territories and his power. The Holy Places of Islam appeared to come under the control of non-Muslims as a result of weakening of the Khilafat. The Khilafat movement in India was a movement of protest against the Allies, particularly the British, and in support of the Khalifa. The Hindus under the guidance of Mahatma Gandhi lent their whole-hearted support to the Khilafat movement. The anti-Turkish policy of the British government alarmed even Mr Montagu, the Secretary of State for India; and Lord Reading, the Viceroy, in a telegram urged the evacuation of Constantinople, the suzerainty of the Sultan over the Holy Places and the restoration of Ottoman Thrace and Smyrna. The publication of this telegram at a time when negotiations were going on resulted in the resignation of Mr Montagu. The feeling in India became more and more embittered and with a view to concentrating attention on the subject, the Central Khilafat Committee was formed, with branches all over the country. The ulema under the leadership of Maulana Mahmudul Hassan Sheikhul-Hind established Jamait-ul-Ulema-i-Hind. Deputations were sent to England to impress upon the authorities the strength of Indian Muslim sentiment in favour of the Khilafat and to plead that nothing should be done to bring about its dismemberment or to weaken its position as a power for the protection of the Holy Places of Islam. The failure of the deputation and the progress of the peace negotiations, making it abundantly clear that the Allies were not to be deterred by the Muslim sentiment from their determination to impose a harsh treaty on Turkey even against pledges given, made a countrywide upheaval inevitable. The Khilafat Conference and the Jamait-ul-Ulema-i-Hind hereafter became the most active and influential organizations of the Musalmans and continued leading them for some years. The League used to have its session side by side with the session of the Congress and these organizations used to be presided over by the most progressive nationalists amongst the Muslims like Hakim Ajmal Khan, Dr M.A. Ansari, Maulana Hasrat Mohani and the Ali Brothers.

The Khilafat agitation coincided in time with the agitation against the government for enacting what were known as the Rowlatt Bills. It is not necessary to go into the details of these measures which roused such fierce opposition throughout the country amongst all communities. In a word, they were the result of recommendations of the Sedition Committee presided over by Sir Sydney Rowlatt and intended to perpetuate in a modified form some of the obnoxious provisions of the Defence of India Act, which was to cease to operate after the war. The agitation against these Bills roused the country as a whole as nothing else had done and there were riots in the Punjab, the Bombay Presidency, Delhi

and some other places. The hand of repression fell heavily and
what has come to be known as the Jallianwalla Bagh tragedy was
enacted at Amritsar followed by a regime of martial law in the
Punjab. The misdeeds committed during the martial law regime
came to the knowledge of the public only some time after they
had been perpetrated and particularly in course of the enquiry
which the government had ordered, by a Committee presided
over by Lord Hunter. The Congress also held a separate enquiry.
When the reports of these two Committees were published there
was great indignation throughout the country. This, coupled
with the Muslim resentment over the Khilafat question, brought
about joint action between the Congress on the one hand and the
Muslim organizations on the other. A common line of action was
decided upon and non-violent non-co-operation became the joint
programme. The Jamait-ul-Ulema issued the *fatwa* which was signed
by 925 eminent Muslim divines and sanctioned the programme of
non-violent non-cooperation. Many of the ulema were lodged in
jails. The feeling was so strong that a large number of Musalmans
took to *Hijrat* and suffered indescribable miseries.

The Congress at a special session held in Calcutta in September
1920 adopted the resolution in favour of non-violent non-
cooperation which was confirmed at the annual session at Nagpur
in the following December. The year 1921 was a year of intense
activity and unprecedented cooperation between all communities
and joint political action for securing Swaraj and redress for
the Punjab and Khilafat wrongs. Thousands of men and women
belonging to all communities were imprisoned even before a scheme
of civil disobedience and non-payment of taxes was adopted.
Maulanas Mohammad Ali and Shaukat Ali, Hussain Ahmad,
Abul Kalam Azad, Deshbandhu Das, Pandit Motilal Nehru, Lala
Lajpat Rai and other prominent leaders and a very large number
of Congress and Khilafat members and workers were imprisoned
towards the closing months of the year. But the annual sessions of
all these organizations were held amidst scenes of unprecedented
enthusiasm-at Ahmedabad. A programme of non-payment of taxes
and civil disobedience was adopted. But before it could be launched
there were serious riots at Chauri Chaura and the programme
was called off. The arrest and sentence of Mahatma Gandhi for
six years followed and the movement then came to a standstill.
Attempts were made to re-organize it but proved ineffectual.

The session of the Muslim League held at Ahmedabad in December 1921 was the last session which was held at the same place and time as the Congress. Although Maulana Hasrat Mohani was its President, the League as a body showed that it was unable to keep pace either with the Congress or the Khilafat Committee or the Jamait-ul-Ulema. It did not adopt any resolution in favour of civil disobedience as was done by the other bodies. For seven years it had gone on parallel lines with the Congress, and changed its constitution; but when civil disobedience was adopted it ceased to have annual sessions with the Congress, the Khilafat Committee and the Jamait-ul-Ulema.

Maulvi Syed Tufail Ahmad writes: 'Now the question is, why did the Muslim League fall behind its contemporary organization? The answer to the question is contained in the writings of Maulana Shibli the substance of which is as follows: "The first foundation stone of the League was the Simla deputation and whatever constitution may be given to it in the future the spirit of the Simla deputation will continue in it. The first brick of the foundation of the League was wrongly laid, and whatever structure is raised on such a foundation is bound to fall out of the line. The politics of the League is only this—whatever rights and places are won by the Hindus, the share of the Musalmans in them must be fixed. This is not real politics. Real politics is concerned with the demand of the people as against the government and in this respect politics is as powerful as religion. On account of the lack of this strength a member of the Muslim League cannot be prepared to suffer any injury and does not find in himself any high determination or courage."'[1]

The flame of enthusiasm could not remain at white heat for an indefinitely long period and after the withdrawal of civil disobedience and Mahatma Gandhi's imprisonment there was weakening and frustration. The Muslim League suffered more than any other organization and its session at Lucknow in 1923 had to be abandoned for want of a quorum. The subsequent sessions of 1924, 1925 and 1926 showed that the difference between the League and the Congress was growing wider.

When the relations between the Hindus and Musalmans were of the best in 1921, when at the time of the Bakr-Id of that year

---

[1] Tufail Ahmad, *Musalmanon Ka Roshan*, p. 410.

Musalmans of their own accord gave up the sacrifice of cows in many places, and when the participation of Hindus in the Khilafat agitation appeared to have firmly established Hindu–Muslim unity, certain incidents happened which created a rift in the lute. The Khilafat agitation was very strong in the Malabar district where there is a large population of Muslims who are known as Moplahs. The Hindus of the place joined the Khilafat agitation as Hindus had done everywhere. The lesson of non-violence had not been imbibed even to the extent it had been in other places. The agitation took a violent turn. Maulana Mohammad Ali was proceeding to Malabar. If he had been permitted to reach the district, he would undoubtedly have controlled the situation. But the government had him arrested on the way and also prevented other leaders from going there. The masses went out of control and as always happens in such cases government repression was severe and unsparing. Although some of the Hindu leaders were given as stiff sentences as any Moplah, there were reports that the Moplahs perpetrated atrocities against the Hindus whom they suspected of having gone over to the government side or at least not being on their side. Forcible conversions to Islam were alleged. All this created bitterness amongst the Hindus, even in northern India, who were influenced by reports of incidents which were undoubtedly exaggerated. But the situation remained under control so long as the leaders and particularly Mahatma Gandhi were out of prison. Swami Shraddhanand, who was one of the leaders of the non-cooperation movement and who had won the confidence and esteem of the Musalmans by his bold and courageous action to such an extent that they invited him to deliver an address at the Jama Masjid of Delhi, was deeply stirred. After his release he started the Shuddhi movement.

The Shuddhi movement of Swami Shraddhanand has come in for a great deal of criticism both from the nationalists and Musalmans. Whatever one may have to say about its opportuneness at that particular moment, it is difficult to understand how Christians and Musalmans can object to it on merits. They are constantly engaged in their proselytizing mission and in converting Hindus to their own faiths. If the Hindus on their side also start converting non-Hindus to their faith, it is no business of non-Hindus to object—especially if they are themselves engaged in the work of conversion. The Hindus must have the same right of propagating their faith as others have. But men are not always guided by logic or by a sense of justice and fairness. And there was much bitterness among Musalmans against the Shuddhi movement and against Swami Shraddhanand personally, as a result of which he fell a victim to a Muslim assassin some time later. Musalmans on their side started the Tabligh and Tanzim movements.

Towards the latter part of 1922, there occurred serious riots in Multan in which Hindu places of worship were desecrated, many Hindus were killed and many Hindu houses were looted and burnt. This was the first of a large number of communal riots which continued for several years and which occurred in almost all parts of the country. Congress and Khilafat workers and all nationalists, whether Hindu or Muslim, felt much disturbed and did their best to stem the tide but found themselves helpless. There can be no doubt that there were forces working behind the scenes. Some protagonists of Pakistan have attributed all these riots to the excesses of the Hindus. Some have gone so far as to suggest that they were actually organized by Hindu leaders, if for nothing else, at least as an exercise and training for the Hindus to stand up against the Musalmans before whom they had always behaved as mere sheep. This explanation over-simplifies the problem and is obviously made to serve as a link in the argument in favour of Pakistan. It has no foundation in fact. If the history of the communal riots, say during the last thirty years or so, is studied without prejudice, it will be found that these riots show a knack of appearing at critical moments in the political history of the country. We had them occurring whenever the demand for transfer of power from British to Indian hands has become insistent and strong, and whenever the two major communities of India have shown unity of purpose and action. We have seen that there was a concordat between the Congress and the League in December 1916, followed by an intensive agitation for Home Rule in 1917. Towards the latter part of 1917, there occurred serious riots in the district of Shahabad in Bihar in which Musalmans suffered heavily at the hands of the Hindus and the Hindus in their turn suffered even more heavily at the hands of the government. In the following year, 1918, there were equally serious riots at Katarpur in the United Provinces with similar results. The Khilafat and the Punjab wrongs had brought about an almost complete unity between the two communities between 1919 and 1922. Hindu–Muslim riots re-appeared in 1922 and continued for some years.

When Mahatma Gandhi was released in 1924 before serving out his sentence of six years fully on account of his very serious illness, he was deeply touched by the orgy of riots which were having their toll of death and destruction all round and he undertook, as is his wont, a fast of twenty-one days. The object was to appeal to the hearts of the Hindus and Musalmans to arrest the progressive deterioration in the communal situation by putting a stop to this fratricidal conflict. A conference of representatives of all communities and leading men from all over the country was hurriedly convened by Maulana Mohammad Ali who was the President of the Congress at the time. It was successful in so far as it was able to pass a set of just and fair resolutions defining the rights and obligations of religious communities and suggesting a course of conduct in situations which led to conflicts. It was hoped that this would ease the situation and if its decisions had been given the publicity they deserved and acted upon with sincerity, there is no doubt the situation would have been brought under control. It is no use blaming any particular community for being entirely and alone in the wrong. The fact is that communal riots in many cases have a political background, although apparently they are caused by religious fanaticism. When once a riot has occurred, it leaves a legacy of bitterness and suspicion behind and itself becomes the cause of further trouble. The atmosphere gets so vitiated that it becomes difficult even for otherwise steady and level-headed men to keep their equilibrium and to probe into the causes and the incidents and to adopt measures of conciliation. So devastating is the aftermath of these riots that even an attempt to bring about reconciliation is often misunderstood and misinterpreted. It is obvious to anyone who applies his mind to the question that it serves no useful purpose to prolong a bitter controversy about a riot or to keep the memory of its incidents green. The effect of protracted investigation by the police and courts, which sometimes lasts for years, is to keep up and maintain the tension, because not only the parties but also the witnesses are divided on communal lines and people are not wanting who come forward as champions of their respective communities. Yet attempt at conciliation by private efforts and involving withdrawal of prosecutions has been condemned as tactics for saving the miscreants. The fact very often is that many of the miscreants, particularly those who are responsible for creating the tense atmosphere and preparing the ground by rousing passions which result in these riots, are clever enough to escape unharmed in the riots, and unmolested by the police and the courts. It is only the simple, unsophisticated masses who get involved in these prosecutions and who, having acted in the heat of the moment, are soon able to steady themselves and to repent of what has happened. There is nothing wrong morally or otherwise in trying to save such men, specially when it serves also the purpose of removing the tension and re-establishing fellow feeling and goodwill all round. And yet it has been seriously suggested that this is one of the tactics employed by Hindus to save themselves. It need hardly be pointed out that those who suggest and take such conciliatory steps do not plead for the members of any one particular community but urge the cause of both and in cases arising out of such communal riots very often there are counter cases in which members of both communities are accused and a settlement accrues to the benefit of them all. It has been found, as is apparent from reports of enquiry into the causes of some of these riots, that a firm handling of the situation by the government would not only prevent these riots but also check their progress if they have actually begun. There were serious riots in Bombay resulting in the death of eighty-nine Hindus and fifty-four Mohammedans, one European and one Parsi and injury to 643 persons. An enquiry was held and the Riots Enquiry Committee wrote: 'We are of opinion that there is a considerable force in the contention that the Commissioner of Police should have proposed the calling out of the Military somewhat earlier than he did. At any rate the experience of the recent riot shows that it is desirable to call out a strong force of the Military and to take other drastic measures at an early stage . . .'

There were serious riots in Cawnpore in 1931. 'The report of the Commission of Enquiry into the causes of Cawnpore riots says: "There is a general feeling," said a witness before me, "that the local authorities did not choose to take immediate and stringent measures because they were displeased with businessmen for helping the Congress activities, and they wanted to show that without the help of the authorities they cannot protect their life and properties." This attitude of the Police during the riots was reprehensible and inexcusable. Every class of witness agreed in this one respect—that Police showed indifference and inactivity in dealing with various incidents in the riot. These witnesses include European businessmen, Moslems and Hindus of all shades of opinion, military officers, the Secretary of the Upper India Chamber of Commerce, representatives of the Indian Christian Community and even Indian officials. It is impossible to ignore such unanimity of evidence . . . There is no doubt in our mind that during the first three days of the riot the Police did not show that activity in the discharge of their duties which was expected of them . . . A number of witnesses have cited instances of serious crimes being committed within view of the Police without their active interest being aroused . . . We are told by a number of witnesses and the District Magistrate has said so in his evidence that complaints about the indifference and inactivity of the Police were made at the time. It is to be regretted that no serious notice was taken of these complaints.'[2]

[2] K.B. Krishnan, *The Problem of Minorities*, pp. 272–73.

FOURTEEN

THE BASE OF THE TRIANGLE LENGTHENS

Just before the Congress session of Gauhati in December, 1926, Swami Shraddhanand was murdered in cold blood on his sick bed in his house in Delhi by a Muslim fanatic, who had sought an interview with him. This naturally sent a thrill of horror all through the country and it was felt that further efforts should be made for settling the political as well as the social and religious differences between the Hindus and Musalmans. It may be noted here that on the introduction of the Montagu–Chelmsford Reforms of 1920, the Indian National Congress and the Khilafat Committee boycotted the Legislative Councils and took no part in the elections of 1920. After the virtual withdrawal of the civil disobedience movement in 1922 differences arose amongst the leaders of both the organizations and as a result the boycott was lifted and Congressmen and Khilafat workers participated in the elections which were held towards the end of 1923 and in subsequent elections. The Congress was functioning in the matter of its work in the Legislatures through the agency of the Swaraj Party which had been established. The Swaraj Party was not in favour of working the reforms but of non-cooperating with the government through the Legislatures. Congress members, therefore, put forward resolutions in the Central Legislature demanding a revision of the Constitution and also rejected the Finance Bill, forcing the hands of the Governor-General to get supplies, not with the sanction of the Legislature but by the use of extraordinary powers. Many of the Muslim members of the Legislature who did not belong to the Congress joined the Congressmen in this action. It is thus clear that while there was this tension in the country there was a certain amount of cooperation between the Hindu and Muslim members of the Central Legislature.

The British government had resolutely resisted all proposals for any advance in constitutional matters. But it was felt that the government could not continue its resistance long and no advance was possible without some sort of communal settlement. The Gauhati Congress, therefore, authorized its Working Committee to take immediate steps in consultation with Hindu and Musalman leaders to devise measures for removal of the present deplorable differences between the Hindus and Musalmans. Some informal conferences with Hindu and Muslim leaders and members of the Central Legislature were held by the Congress President Shri Shrinivas Iyengar. Towards the end of March 1927 some prominent Muslim leaders met together in Delhi and put forward what came to be known as the Muslim proposals. They expressed their preparedness to agree to joint electorates for Provincial and the Central Legislatures, provided

(a)   Sind was made into a separate province;
(b)   the North-West Frontier Province and Baluchistan were treated on the same footing as the other provinces;
(c)   in the Punjab and Bengal the proportion of Muslim representation was in accordance with their population;
(d)   and in the Central Legislature it was not less than one-third of the total. At two meetings held in the following May and October the All-India Congress Committee passed resolutions substantially accepting the Muslim proposals and also laying down certain rules dealing with the religious and social aspects of the question. The next annual session of the Congress was held in Madras and it passed a resolution on the lines laid down earlier in the year by the All-India Congress Committee. By another resolution it authorized the Working Committee to confer with similar Committees to be appointed by other organizations in the country and to draft a Swaraj Constitution for India on the basis of a Declaration of Rights and to place the same for consideration and approval before a special Convention of the All-India Congress Committee, the leaders and representatives of the other organizations, and the elected members of Provincial and the Central Legislatures. The Muslim League met in Calcutta in the same week and passed a Resolution authorizing its Council to appoint a Sub-Committee to confer with the Working Committee of the Congress and other organizations for drafting a Constitution for India and to

take part in the National Convention as suggested by the Congress. It reiterated the points of the Muslim proposals mentioned above, emphasizing that separate electorates could be abandoned by the Musalmans only in case the other demands mentioned were fulfilled. The Resolution further incorporated the Madras Congress settlement regarding liberty of conscience, religious legislation, the cow and music questions, and conversion. It may be noted here that a split had occurred in the All-India Muslim League, one section holding the session in Calcutta and the other at Lahore under the presidentship of Sir Mian Muhammad Shafi. It was the Calcutta session which passed the above resolution under the presidentship of Maulvi Mohammad Yaqub. Mr M.A. Jinnah was its leading light and guiding spirit.

It is worthwhile recording here some facts which had brought about this rapprochement between the Congress and a section of the League on the one hand and the split in the League itself on the other. It has been stated above that the government had opposed all proposals for constitutional advance. Lord Birkenhead was the Secretary of State at the time. On 10 December 1925, he wrote to the Viceroy, Lord Reading, about advancing the date of the appointment of the Statutory Commission provided for in the Government of India Act, 1920, for reporting on the working of the Reforms at the end of ten years at the latest from the time of commencement. He wrote as follows:

'I should, therefore, like to receive your advice, if at any time you discern an opportunity for making this [the Statutory Commission] a useful bargaining counter or for further disintegrating the Swarajist Party . . . If such acceleration affords you any bargaining value, use it to the full, and with the knowledge that you will be supported by the Government.'[1]

His hands were, however, forced by the situation in England in 1927. 'Forecast of the coming general election at home was ominous. A Labour Government was in sight. He could not afford to "run the slightest risk that the nomination of 1928 Commission should be in the hands of our successors . . . Colonel Wedgewood and his friends" . . . That would upset his plan for

[1.] *Birkenhead—The Last Phase*, Vol. II, p. 25 quoted by K.B. Krishnan in his *Problem of Minorities*, p. 307.

"further disintegrating the Swarajist Party.""[2] He announced the appointment of the Statutory Commission in November 1927. The Commission was to consist of seven members, including Sir John Simon as Chairman. There was to be no Indian member on it. The Central Legislature was to be invited to appoint a Joint Select Committee which would place its views before the Commission for examination. The exclusion of Indians from the Commission altogether was treated by Indians as an insult and a humiliation, and a boycott of the Commission was decided upon not only by the Congress but also by a large group of Muslims outside the Congress and the Khilafat Committee and even by the liberals who were believed to hold very moderate views on matters political and who alone of all political groups in the country had tried to work the Montagu–Chelmsford Reforms when the Congress had boycotted them. The split in the All-India Muslim League had occurred on the question of cooperation with the Simon Commission and the question of separate electorates. Lord Birkenhead was fully conscious of the value of antagonism between the different groups in India and 'as Secretary of State for India he communicated his advice to the Viceroy, Lord Reading: "The more it is made obvious that these antagonisms are profound, and affect immense and irreconcilable sections of the population, the more conspicuously is the fact illustrated that we, and we alone, can play the part of composer."'[3] When the Commission was boycotted in India he wrote again to the Viceroy 'Lord Irwin: 'We have always relied on the non-boycotting Moslems, on the depressed community, on the business interests, and on many others, to break down the attitude of boycott. You and Simon must be the judges whether or not it is expedient in these directions to try to make a breach in the wall of antagonism, even in the course of the present visit.'[4]

He wrote again to the Viceroy, a few days later in February 1928: 'I should advise Simon to see at all stages important people who are not boycotting the Commission, particularly Moslems and the depressed classes. I should widely advertise all his interviews with representative Moslems. The whole policy is now obvious. It

[2] Birkenhead, *The Last Phase*, Vol. II, pp. 250–1, quoted by Atulanand Chakravarti in his *Call It Politics?* p. 58.

[3] Ibid., pp. 245–6, quoted in *Call It Politics* p. 57.

[4] Ibid., p. 254, quoted in Call It Politics.

is to terrify the immense Hindu population by the apprehension
that the Commission having been got hold of by the Moslems,
may present a report altogether destructive of the Hindu position,
thereby securing a solid Moslem support and leaving Jinnah high
and dry.'[5]

No wonder Sir Mohammad Shafi organized a separate meeting
of the League in Lahore while Mr Jinnah was left 'high and dry'
to guide the lawful League which met in Calcutta in December
1927 at the same time as the Shafi League in Lahore.

The joint action of the Congress, the All-India Muslim League
and the other organizations in the beginning of 1928 in drafting a
Constitution for India was thus the result of the humiliation heaped
on Indians by the appointment of the Simon Commission and a
challenge thrown out by Lord Birkenhead to India to produce a
Constitution acceptable to all. The All Parties Conference which met
in pursuance of the above resolutions proceeded with the work of
constitution-framing and after doing a substantial part of it left it
to a Committee of which Pandit Motilal Nehru was the Chairman.
The Committee prepared a report which came to be known as
the Nehru Committee Report. It was discussed and adopted with
modifications at a meeting of the All Parties Conference at Lucknow
and was ultimately placed before an All Parties Convention held
in Calcutta in the last week of December 1928. Other forces had
been working in the meantime and differences had arisen with the
representatives of the All-India Muslim League. These differences
boiled down to only three points, namely:

(1)   That the Muslim representation in the Central Legislature
      should not be less than one-third;
(2)   That in the event of adult suffrage not being granted as
      proposed in the Nehru Report, the Punjab and Bengal should
      have seats on a population basis and no more, subject to
      re-examination after ten years;
(3)   That residuary powers should vest in the provinces and
      not in the Centre. These were placed in the form of a
      resolution by Mr Jinnah before the Convention. They were
      discussed at great length in a Committee meeting appointed
      for the purpose sitting till the small hours of the morning

[5] Ibid., p. 255, quoted by Krishnan, *Problem of Minorities*, p. 308.

but no agreement was reached and they were rejected by the Convention, The League thereafter practically withdrew from the Convention, and its session which was being held in Calcutta about the same time was adjourned to meet later to consider the position.

The other wing of the League, which had held its session at Lahore in the previous year, was not sitting idle. It had at that session rejected the Congress Resolution passed at its Madras session and appointed a Committee to devise a constitutional scheme and to collaborate with other organizations in framing a Constitution on the principle adopted at the Lahore session for presenting the same before the Statutory Commission. It also passed a resolution authorizing the President to convene a Round Table Conference of Muslims with a view to uniting the different elements amongst them. A Muslim All Parties Conference was accordingly convened to meet in Delhi on 31st December 1928; H.H. the Agha Khan, who had led the Muslim deputation in 1906 to Lord Minto, was invited to preside and he responded to the invitation. The proceedings of the All Parties Convention in Calcutta had embittered some Musalmans, and some of them among whom the most prominent were Maulana Mohammad Ali and Maulvi Shafi Daudi attended the Conference. The All-India Muslim League in Calcutta had refused to accept the invitation to the Muslim All Parties Conference. The Conference passed a resolution to the following effect:

(a) The only form of government suitable to Indian conditions is a federal system with complete autonomy and residuary powers vested in the constituent states, the central government having control only over such matters of common interest as may be specially entrusted to it by the constitution;

(b) No Bill, resolution, motion, or amendment regarding inter-communal matters should be moved, discussed, or passed by any Legislature, central or provincial, if three-fourths majority of the members of the community affected thereby opposed it;

(c) The Musalmans should have their representatives in the Legislature and other statutory self-governing bodies through their own separate electorates, of which they should not

be deprived without their own consent; they should have
their due share in the Central and Provincial Cabinets; their
majorities in the Legislative Councils in provinces where
they were in a majority in the population should not be
affected and in Provinces where they were in a minority,
they should in no case have a representation less than that
enjoyed by them under the existing law; their representation
in the Central Legislature should be thirty-three and one-
third per cent;

(d)   Sind should be created into separate province; and
(e)   The North-West Frontier Province and Baluchistan should
      have the same constitutional reforms as other provinces;
      they should have adequate representation in the services:
      there should be adequate safeguards for the protection of
      Muslim culture and for the promotion of Muslim education,
      language, religion, personal law, charitable institutions, and
      for a due share in grants-in-aid.

The resolution emphatically declared that no Constitution by
whomsoever proposed or devised would be acceptable to Indian
Musalmans unless it conformed with the principles of this
Resolution.

An attempt was made by Mr Jinnah to bring about a
reconciliation between the two groups in the Muslim League and
the Muslim All Parties Conference. Mr Jinnah, after consulting
leading men, prepared a draft resolution on the basis of which a
settlement could be made. It was in this draft resolution that he
formulated his Fourteen Points as necessary for safeguarding the
rights and interests of Musalmans. These Fourteen Points may
be summarized:

1.   The form of the future Constitution should be federal, with
     the residuary powers vested in the provinces.
2.   A uniform measure of autonomy for provinces.
3.   Ali Legislatures and other elected bodies should be
     constituted on the definite principle of adequate and effective
     representation of minorities in every province without
     reducing the majority in any province to a minority or
     even equality.
4.   In the Central Legislature, Muslim representation shall not
     be less than one-third.

5. Representation of communal groups to be by separate electorates provided that it shall be open to any community at any time to abandon its separate electorate in favour of joint electorate.

6. Any territorial redistribution not in any way to affect the Muslim majority in the Punjab, Bengal and the NWF Province.

7. Full liberty of belief, worship, and observance, propaganda, association and education shall be guaranteed to all communities.

8. No Bill or Resolution or any part thereof shall be passed in any Legislature or any other elected body if three-fourths of the members of any community in that body opposed it as being injurious to the interests of that community.

9. Sind to be separated from the Bombay Presidency.

10. Reforms to be introduced in the Frontier Province and Baluchistan as in other provinces.

11. Adequate share for Musalmans to be provided in the Constitution in all services, subject to requirements of efficiency.

12. Adequate safeguards for the protection and promotion of Muslim culture, education, language, religion, personal laws, and charitable institutions and for their due share in the grants-in-aid.

13. No Cabinet either Central or Provincial to be formed without at least one-third of the ministers being Muslims.

14. No change of the Constitution by the Central Legislature except with the concurrence of the states constituting the Indian Federation.

It may be noted that in the League of which Mr Jinnah was the President, nationalist Muslims had a predominant voice. The Shafi League was sticking to its Lahore Resolution and had practically become a part of the Muslim All Parties Conference. Mr Jinnah's draft resolution formulating the fourteen points became the demand of the Muslims outside the nationalist group. These fourteen points have an importance of their own as they were adopted practically in their entirety by Mr Macdonald's Communal decision or Award. The difference between the nationalist Muslims and the Muslim All Parties Conference was on the question of the acceptance of the Nehru Report, the former holding that the Report should be accepted.

The Calcutta Congress in December 1928 had resolved that in case the British government did not accept the Nehru Report, which provided that India should have the status of a Dominion within a year by the 31 December 1929, the Congress would give up the Report and insist on independence. The year 1929 saw a great awakening in the country. On 31 October 1929 the Viceroy, Lord Irwin, who had in the meantime visited England for consultation, made an announcement that when the Simon Commission had submitted their Report, the British government would invite representatives of different parties and interests in British India and Indian States to meet in a Round Table Conference for discussion of the Indian problem. The announcement further declared: 'I am authorized to state clearly that in their judgement it is implicit in the declaration of 1917 that the natural issue of the Indian constitutional progress as there contemplated is the attainment of Dominion Status.' As this part of the declaration left in doubt whether the Conference was to meet to frame a scheme of Dominion Constitution for India, clarification of the point was sought by a Leaders' Conference which met at Delhi to consider the announcement. Mahatma Gandhi, Pandit Motilal Nehru, President Patel, Sir Tej Bahadur Sapru and Mr Jinnah met the Viceroy on 23 December on the eve of the Lahore session of the Indian National Congress, in this connection. The Viceroy was not prepared to give the assurance that the purpose of the Conference was to draft a scheme for Dominion Status. The Congress in pursuance of the Resolution passed at its session in Calcutta declared that the word Swaraj in Article 1 of the Congress Constitution shall mean Complete Independence and that the entire scheme of the Nehru Committee's Report had lapsed. It authorized the All-India Congress Committee to launch a programme of civil disobedience including non-payment of taxes. The civil disobedience movement was started in the following March and continued for one year. The Simon Commission Report was submitted about the middle of 1930 and the First Round Table Conference was convened in the following autumn and met in London. The Congress was not represented. The Round Table Conference comprised representatives from British India among whom were Musalmans, and from the Indian States. It decided in favour of a Federal Constitution for

India comprising provinces of British India as well as such States or groups of such States as elected to join it. It decided in favour of the creation of Sind as a separate province and introduction of Reforms in the North-West Frontier Province. Opinion on the question of joint or separate electorates was expressed and appeared to be in favour of maintaining separate electorates and not abolishing them without the consent of the parties enjoying them. The powers to be exercised by the Federal Government and the units were considered in detail and allocated to them in separate lists but the question of the residuary powers was not fully decided nor was any decision taken on the quantum of Muslim representation in the Federal Legislature.

'After the First Round Table Conference a truce was made between Lord Irwin for the Government of India, and Mahatma Gandhi on behalf of the Congress, which opened the way for the Congress to join the Second Round Table Conference which was to meet in the autumn of 1931. Just about this time serious Hindu–Muslim riots occurred in Benares, Cawnpore and other places. The chief difference between the Nationalist Muslims who had become organized as the Muslim Nationalist Conference and the Muslim All Parties Conference—which had practically absorbed, so far as the programme was concerned, the All-India Muslim League and the Khilafat Conference—was on the question of the electorates, the former favouring joint electorates, and the latter insisting on separate electorates. The Muslim Nationalist Conference held its session under the Presidentship of Sir Ali Imam at Lucknow in April 1931 at which he declared that although he himself belonged at one time to the school of political thought that laid great stress on separate electorates and was in fact a member of the deputation that waited on Lord Minto, he had after careful study come definitely to the conclusion that separate electorate was not only a negation of Indian nationalism but also positively harmful to Muslims themselves. The Conference passed a resolution that in the Constitution there should be a declaration of Fundamental Rights guaranteeing protection of culture, language and personal laws, and other rights, that it should be a Federal Constitution vesting residuary powers in the federating units, that appointment to the Services should be made by a Public services Commission according to a minimum standard of efficiency without depriving any community of a fair share in the services and that Sind should be constituted into a separate province and the North-West Frontier and Baluchistan should have the same form of government as the other provinces. As regards the measure and method of representation in the Federal and the Provincial Legislatures, the resolution laid down that there should be universal adult franchise, joint electorates and reservation of seats on a population basis for minorities of less than 30 per cent with a right to contest additional seats. Every attempt was made to bring about a settlement between the Muslim All Parties Conference and the Muslim Nationalist Conference but it ultimately failed. A joint conference was to be held at Simla for considering the various proposals for compromise on 22 June 1931. With regard to it Dr M.A. Ansari made a public statement that 'on arrival here we found that the Simla atmosphere was very inauspicious for any compromise. Our apprehensions have, alas, turned out to be only too true. The unfortunate Simla surroundings and influences, by now too well known to the public to require specific mention, proved too strong for the forces working for unity, and all efforts to find a formula that would unite the two parties were set at naught.'[6]

Mahatma Gandhi was deputed on behalf of the Congress as its sole delegate to the Second Round Table Conference. The British government had nominated Indians from British India, including many Musalmans but rejected Mahatma Gandhi's suggestion to invite Dr Ansari. One of the Committees appointed by the Round Table Conference was the Minorities Committee to which was entrusted the task of dealing with the question of minorities. The Committee failed to come to any agreed solution and the Second Round Table Conference was concluded without any final decision on the point and consequently also on many other points. No Indian was surprised at the failure. There were forces working behind the scenes which made any such settlement impossible. Mr Edward Thompson writes: 'During the Round Table Conference there was rather an obvious understanding and alliance between the more intransigent Moslems and certain particularly undemocratic British political circles. That alliance is constantly asserted in India to be the real block to progress. I believe I could prove that this is largely true. And there is no question that in former times we frankly practised the "divide and rule" method in India. From Warren

6 Annual Register for 1931, p. 305.

Hastings' time onwards, men made no bones of the pleasure the Hindu–Muslim conflict gave them; even such men as Elphinstone and Malcolm and Metcalfe admitted its value to the British.'[7]

Mr Ramsay Macdonald, the Prime Minister, in winding up the proceedings of the Second Round Table Conference announced that the British government held to the principle of a responsible Federal Government subject to certain reservations and safeguards through a period of transition, that the Governors' provinces of the future were to be responsibly governed units enjoying the greatest possible measure of freedom from outside interference and dictation in carrying out their own policies in their own sphere, that the North-West Frontier Province should be constituted a Governor's province of the same status as other Governor's provinces, and that Sind should be constituted a separate province if satisfactory means of financing it could be found. About the communal problem, he said that the communal deadlock constituted a formidable obstacle in the way of progress but that His Majesty's Government 'are determined that even this disability should not be permitted to be bar to progress. This would mean that His Majesty's Government would have to settle for you, not only your of representation but also to decide as wisely and justly as possible, what checks and balances the Constitution is to contain, to protect the minorities from unrestricted and tyrannical use of the democratic principle expressing itself solely through the majority power.'[8]

After this declaration the Communal Award was the natural outcome, and it was given in August 1932. The scope of this scheme was purposely confined to the arrangements to be made for the representation of the British Indian communities in the Provincial Legislatures, consideration of representation to the Legislature of the centre being deferred for the time being, as it involved the question of representation of Indian States which needed further discussion. The hope was expressed that once a pronouncement had been made upon the basic questions of the method and proportions of representation, the communities themselves might find it possible to arrive at a *modus vivendi* on the communal problems. If, before the new Government of India Act had passed into law, the government were satisfied that the communities concerned were mutually agreed upon an alternative

[7] Edward Thompson, *Enlist India for Freedom*, p. 50.
[8] Annual Register, Vol. II, 1931, p. 446.

scheme they would be prepared to recommend to Parliament that
the alternative should be substituted for the provision outlined in
the Communal Award. By the Award, Mohammedans, Europeans
and Sikhs were given the right to elect their representatives through
separate communal electorates. Seats were reserved for Mahrattas
in certain selected general constituencies in Bombay. The depressed
classes were given seats which were to be filled by elections from
special constituencies in which they alone could vote. They would
also be entitled to vote in the general constituency. Indian Christians
were also allotted seats, to be filled by voters voting in separate
communal electorates and so also Anglo-Indians. A number of seats
were allotted specially to women, which were divided between
the various communities. Then there were special seats allotted
to Labour to be filled from Labour constituencies. Special seats
were given to commerce and industry, mining and planting, to be
filled by Chambers of Commerce and other associations. Similarly,
seats allotted to landholders were to be filled by landholders'
constituencies. It will thus be seen that the principle of dividing
the population into communal groups which had been adopted in
the Morley–Minto Reforms had been considerably extended, even
beyond what had been done by the Montagu–Chelmsford Reforms.
'The electorate in 1919 was broken up into ten parts; now it is
fragmented into seventeen unequal bits. Separate electorates were
thrust, against their wishes, on women and Indian Christians.
The Hindu Community was further weakened by giving separate
representation to the scheduled classes. Divisions on the basis of
religion, occupation and service were made. Every possible cross
division was introduced.'[9]

The distribution of seats among the various communities
was no less remarkable. In all discussions about the communal
problem Bengal and the Punjab presented difficulties. In both these
provinces the Musalmans are in a majority; but the majority is
a small one—about 55 per cent. In both these provinces it was
demanded on behalf of the Musalmans that there should be both
separate electorates and reservation of seats for them although
they happened to be in a majority. In Bengal the position was
complicated by the desire of the British government to give a very
heavy weightage to the Europeans, while in the Punjab the non-

[9] Mehta and Patwardhan, *The Communal Triangle*, p. 72.

Mohammedans were divided into Hindus and Sikhs. The Sikhs insisted that, if there were to be separate electorates and reservation of seats, they as an important minority community should be given weightage as Musalmans had got in other provinces where they were in a minority. The Communal Award maintained with a small variation the proportion of seats given to Musalmans by the Montagu–Chelmsford Reforms in all the provinces except Bengal and the Punjab. In Bengal the Hindus were in the minority of 44.8 per cent of the total population. They were given only 80 out of 250 seats, that is, only 32 per cent of the total. The Mussalmans who were 54.8 per cent of the population were given 119 seats, that is, 47.6 per cent of the total. The Europeans who were .01 per cent of the population were given 25 seats, that is, 10 per cent of the total number of seats. It will thus appear that the Musalmans who were in a majority were reduced to a minority in the representation and the Hindus who were in a minority were deprived even of their due proportion—in order to give a very heavy weightage of 1,00,000 per cent to the Europeans. What is noteworthy is that although the representation of both Muslims and Hindus was reduced, the cut was greater in the Hindu representation. In other words, unlike other provinces, weightage was given to the smallest community not out of the majority community alone but out of another minority that was required not only to give up any weightage, which it might feel entitled to as a minority, but also to make a greater sacrifice proportionately than the majority community. In the Punjab also, to give weightage to the Sikhs, the Hindus were required to give up a portion of their representation, although they were in a minority and would be entitled to weightage according to ordinary canons of fairness and justice. It may also be noted that in both these provinces the Award reduced the Muslim representation to such an extent as to make it a minority of the total, although they still constituted the largest group in the Legislative Assembly and had those seats reserved for them to be filled through separate electorates. 'No wonder the Award was assailed with great vehemence by the Hindus who were required to make sacrifices in the provinces where they were in a majority and also in the provinces where they were in a minority, and in Bengal the sacrifice that was imposed on them was proportionately much greater—nearly double—than that required of the majority community. The

government anticipated opposition and the communiqué issued
by the Government of India in this connection said: 'In so far as
each party to the dispute has put forward demands for greater
representation than the other could agree to, it is inevitable that
the terms of the settlement should fall short of what they require.
Indeed, the more equitable the settlement is, the more likely is it
to prove disappointing to all concerned in it. But since the British
Government is entirely disinterested, and fin making the Award is
doing its utmost to solve the most difficult problem in the best
interest of all, it hopes that Indians will accept it in the spirit it
is made, and will honestly try to make it work. Finally it may be
mentioned that the Secretary of State has promised that if, before
the new Government of India Act is passed, the various Indian
Communities can reach a general settlement of their own which
differs from his, he will willingly accept it.'

The British government is 'entirely disinterested' forsooth! It
was this disinterestedness which induced it to penalize the Hindus
everywhere, to cut down their representation even though they
were in a minority in Bengal and cut it down to a greater extent
than it did in the case of the Muslims, and that for the purpose
of giving weightage to Europeans—of 1,00,000 per cent! This
disinterestedness in them induced them to refuse to the Sikhs the
quantity of weightage in the Punjab which they had granted to
Musalmans in other provinces and to allow not only separate
electorates but also a reservation of seats for the Musalmans
even where they were in a majority. Having created conditions
which made any communal settlement impossible, the government
promised willingly to accept any alternative settlement which the
communities could reach amongst themselves!

As between British India and the States, the Act of 1935 is
generous to the Princes at the cost of British India. The population
of the States is only 23 per cent of the population of India, but
their rulers are given 33 per cent of the voting power in the
Lower and 40 per cent in the Upper House of the Federation. It
should be remembered that the power of sending representatives
to the Federal Legislature is not given to the people of the States
but to their rulers. Thus has been preserved for the Federation
the system of nomination through the States to the extent of 33
per cent of the Lower House. It is difficult to conceive of a more

ingenious method of taking away with the one hand what has been apparently given by the other.

An effort was, however, made for a communal settlement in India even after this Award and it was almost accomplished when the British government once more intervened and made it impossible of accomplishment as the following narrative of events will show. The Communal Award was announced on 16 August 1932. After Mahatma Gandhi's fast and an amendment of the Award affecting the depressed classes in pursuance of the Poona Pact, negotiations were started between Pandit Malaviya and Maulana Shaukat Ali for working out a substitute for the Communal Award. The preliminary talks appeared promising. Maulana Shaukat Ali appealed to the Viceroy to release Mahatma Gandhi, or at least to afford facilities for interviews with him to help in the negotiations on 6 October 1932. On 7 October 1932 a statement was issued on behalf of the President of the Muslim All-Parties Conference to the effect that it was highly inopportune to re-open the question of separate versus joint electorates and that the Muslim community was not prepared to give up this safeguard but it would be prepared to consider definite proposals comprehending all the vital issues involved if initiated by the majority community. The statement was issued from Simla. On 9 October, the Viceroy's Private Secretary replied to Maulana Shaukat Ali's telegram: 'The first step will be for you to assure yourself that in the action you contemplate you have the support of the Muslim community in general. In this connection attention is invited to the statement issued to the Press on 11 October by the President of the Muslim All-Parties Conference and others.'[10] It hardly requires to be pointed out that the telegram of Maulana Shaukat Ali of 6 October was not answered by the Private Secretary of the Viceroy till the statement on behalf of the Muslim All-Parties Conference had had time to be published on the 6th and was actually referred to in the reply sent on the 9th. When on 26 October Maulana Shaukat Ali reiterated his request and asked the Viceroy to use his influence with all concerned so that there could be a peace that would benefit all, the reply promptly given on 27 October was that so long as Mr Gandhi did not definitely dissociate himself from civil

[10] Mitra's Annual Register, 1932, Vol. II, pp. 281–82.

disobedience his request could not be acceded to. A subsequent request for interviews with Gandhiji only elicited the reply that the letter of 27 October was intended to convey that interviews also could not be granted.

Undeterred by the attitude of the government, an All Parties Muslim Conference was convened on 16 October at Lucknow and unanimously passed a resolution welcoming the suggestion of Pandit Madan Mohan Malaviya for the appointment 'of a Committee of the Conference to meet representatives of Hindus and Sikhs and actually a Committee was appointed to negotiate an agreed solution of the Communal Problem. The Unity Conference began its sittings at Allahabad on 3 November 1932. It was attended by sixty-three Hindus, twelve Sikhs, thirty-nine Muslims and eight Indian Christians. The Conference appointed a Committee for bringing about an agreement and to report to the Conference. This Committee sat from day to day and passed a number of resolutions dealing with most of the points about which differences did or could arise. Even on the much-vexed question of Bengal and the Punjab, an agreement was reached so far as the Hindus and the Muslims were concerned, the Hindus agreeing to reservation of 51 per cent of the seats to Musalmans to be filled by joint electorates. A formula was evolved which satisfied all parties on the question as to whether residuary powers should vest in the Centre or in the federating units. Another formula accepted joint electorates but made it incumbent on candidates to secure at least 30 per cent of the votes polled of their own community, failing which the candidates securing the highest number of votes of their community were to be returned. There was an agreement also on the question of Muslim representation in the Central Legislature which was fixed at 32 per cent. Both parties had yielded on some points while they had gained on others.

There was one point, however, on which agreement between Hindus and Musalmans alone would not suffice and that was the huge weightage given to the Europeans in Bengal. Under the agreement arrived at, the Hindu and Muslim representatives would take up between themselves 95.7 per cent of the seats and thus the Europeans could not get the 10 per cent of the seats that had been given to them. It was, therefore, decided that both the Hindus and the Muslims should discuss the question with the Europeans in Calcutta and the Conference was accordingly adjourned after finishing its session in Allahabad.

It will be recalled that the Communal Award had left the question of Muslim representation in the Central Legislature over for subsequent decision and had made the separation of Sind subject to satisfactory means of financing it being found. While Pandit Malaviya was on his way to Calcutta along with Muslim representatives to have a talk with the Europeans about their weightage, the newspapers published the news that Sir Samuel Hoare had forestalled him by announcing that His Majesty's Government had decided to allot $33^{1}/_{3}$ per cent of British Indian seats in the Central Legislature to Muslims, and not only to constitute Sind into a separate province but also to provide it with adequate finances as subvention from the Central Government. Thus the fruits of the labour of the Unity Conference which had sat for weeks and after great efforts had succeeded in reaching an agreement on all points as between Hindus, Muslims, Sikhs, Christians and other Indian communities were cruelly dashed to pieces by the very timely announcement of Sir Samuel Hoare. It was not to be expected that any agreement could be reached between all parties when it was clear that some group or other could always be found to object to any agreement, however just, and when the British government was prepared to offer better terms than any that an agreed settlement could secure, for a group willing to accept the highest bid.

~

THE ANGLE OF DIFFERENCE WIDENS

We have seen that the Communal Award had allowed separate electorates and reservation of seats to the depressed classes also. The provision was modified after the Poona Pact which was brought about by Mahatma Gandhi's fast and by which the depressed classes got a very much larger number of seats than were allowed by the Communal Award reserved for them to be filled by a special procedure of election. This was in accordance with the promise made at the time of giving the Award that its provisions were liable to be replaced by an agreement that might be reached between the parties concerned before the new Constitution was enacted. The hope and attempt of the Allahabad Unity Conference was to get the Award relating to Musalmans substituted by an agreement between the Muslims on the one side and other communities on the other. We have seen how it was successfully torpedoed by Sir Samuel Hoare just when it was about to succeed. This, however, did not succeed in silencing the opposition of the Hindus and Sikhs. The opposition went on gathering volume and strength while the Reform proposals went through their interminable course. The British government had stated that they would not allow want of agreement on the part of the communities to block the Reforms and for this reason they announced the Award in August 1932. But it took them three years to get the Bill passed, which happened in the month of June 1935. The Congress had in the meantime gone through another ordeal of suffering and when it was in a position to express its opinion freely it refused, because of the conflict of views between the Hindus and Musalmans, either to accept or reject the Award at its session held at Bombay in October 1934. A few weeks later, elections to the Central Assembly were held and the Congress attitude of neutrality about the Award was naturally one of the points against which attack was directed. The Congress was successful in most of the provinces but in Bengal the members elected, though accepting the Congress programme on other points, were free to take their own line on the question of the Award. Bitter controversy against the Award and the policy of the British government had borne fruit in the shape of an apple of discord. An attempt was made again early in 1935 for arriving at an agreed settlement between the President of the Congress and the President of the Muslim League but it proved unsuccessful.

The Government of India Act was passed in June 1935, and elections under the new Act were held in the winter of 1936–37. The All-India Muslim League at its session held in April 1936 at Bombay passed a resolution recording its emphatic protest against forcing a Constitution on the people of India and declaring its opinion that the Provincial Scheme of the Constitution be utilized for what if was worth in spite of its most objectionable features, which rendered real control and responsibility of ministry and Legislature nugatory; and that the All-India Federal Scheme was most reactionary, retrograde, injurious and fatal to the vital interest of British India vis-à-vis Indian states, and was calculated to thwart and delay indefinitely the realization of India's most cherished goal of complete responsible government and was entirely unworkable in the interests of India. It will be noticed that the Federal Scheme was condemned because it was calculated to thwart and delay indefinitely the realization of India's most cherished goal of complete responsible government, and because it was unworkable in the interests of India and not because by conceding a Federal Constitution, or in any other way, it injured the interests of Musalmans as such. The League appointed a Parliamentary Board which issued an election manifesto on "which the elections were fought. It stated: 'The main principles on which we expect our representatives in various Legislatures to work will be

(1)   that the present Provincial Constitution and the proposed Central Constitution should be replaced immediately by democratic full self-government;

(2)   and that in the meantime, representatives of the Muslim League in the various Legislatures will utilize the Legislatures in order to extract the maximum benefit out of the Constitution for the uplift of the people in the various spheres of national life. The Muslim League party must

be formed as a corollary so long as separate electorates exist, but there will be free cooperation with any group or groups whose aims and ideals are approximately the same as those of the League party. The programme which was laid down in the manifesto contained only two clauses which refer to Musalmans in particular:

(a) to protect the religious rights of Musalmans, and
(b) to devise measures for the amelioration of the general condition of the Musalmans; the rest referred to matters which were common to all irrespective of religious faith, for example repeal of repressive laws, rejection of measures detrimental to the interests of India and fundamental liberties of the people and leading to economic exploitation of the country, reduction of the cost of administration and the army, allocation of funds for nation-building departments, development of industries, regulation of currency and exchange in the interest of the country, uplift of the rural population, etc. At the elections the Muslim League either did not set up candidates in all the provinces for the Muslim seats or did not win them. The Congress, on its side, set up candidates for most of the Non-Mohammedan General constituency seats but only a few candidates for the Muslim seats. The result of the elections was as follows:

TABLE II

Result of General Elections, 1937

Provinces	Total no. of seats	No. of seats won by Congress	Total no. of Muslim seats	No. of seats won by League	No. of seats won by other Muslim groups
Madras	215	159	28	11	17
Bombay	175	86	29	20	9
Bengal	250	54	117	40	77
UP	228	134	64	27	37
Punjab	175	18	84	1	83
Bihar	152	98	39	-	39
CP	112	70	14	-	14
NWFP	50	19	36	-	36
Assam	108	33	34	9	25
Orissa	60	36	4	-	4
Sind	60	7	36	-	36
Total	1585	714	485	108	377

It will be noticed that the Congress had a majority in five of the provinces. In Bombay and the North-West Frontier Province, people returned on Independent tickets joined it and gave it a majority and so it was in a position to form ministries of its own. The Muslim League did not have a majority of its own even in the provinces where the population comprises a majority of Muslims—Bengal, the Punjab, the North-West Frontier Province and Sind, in none of which it had even a majority of Muslim seats. So it could not form a League Ministry anywhere without the help of other groups of Muslims or non-Muslims. It did not win any seat at all in four of the provinces and in the Punjab it won only one seat. When the time came for forming ministries the Congress refused to do so unless the leader of the Congress Party in the Legislatures is satisfied and is able to state publicly that the Governor will not use his special powers of interference or set aside the advice of ministers in regard to constitutional activities. As the Governors did not give the necessary assurances the Congress Party did not accept office. The assurances for which the Congress asked were in respect of the special responsibilities of the Governor, that is to say, matters in respect of which the Governor could act in his discretion without consulting his ministers and matters in which he could exercise his individual judgement after consulting his ministers. 'The cumulative effect of the list of special responsibilities justifies the statement of Sir Samuel Hoare that it covers the entire field of administration, the prevention of any grave menace to the peace and tranquillity of the Province, the safeguarding of the legitimate interests of the minorities, the safeguarding of the rights and legitimate interests, whatever that may mean, of the members of the Public Services and their dependants, the prevention in the sphere of executive action, of discrimination against Britishers and British concerns, the peace and good government of partially excluded areas, the protection of the rights of States and the Rulers, and the execution of orders or direction of the Governor-General in his discretion.'[1]

It will be noted that safeguarding of the legitimate interest of the minorities is only one out of so many other matters which cover the entire field of administration; and 'minorities' included Britishers in India along with so many other minorities of the

[1] Chintamani and Masani, *India's Constitution at Work*, pp. 91–92.

country apart from the Muslims. Yet Lord Zetland, the Secretary
of State for India, when declaring that the demand for assurance
could not be met without an amendment of the Constitution,
illustrated this point by drawing attention to the situation which
would arise if the Congress ministry acted against the interests of
a minority. He said: 'A reduction in the number of schools for
a minority community by a ministry would be clearly within the
Congress formula, for it would be legal and could not be described
as other than a constitutional activity. So the Governor would no
longer be free to protect the minority. It was precisely because
it was realized that such an action would be possible within the
Constitution that Parliament had inserted the safeguards.'[2] The
object of the reference to a minority community was obvious and
had its full effect.

The Congress wanted this assurance not for its ministries alone
and the parties in majorities in other provinces could well have
joined the Congress in pressing for this assurance and thus made
it possible for the administration to free itself to some extent from
the possibility of interference by the Governor in the constitutional
activities of the ministers. But they did not, and formed their
ministries without any such assurance. The Congress waited. The
discussion which followed made it clear that interference with the
constitutional activities of the Congress ministries would not be at
any rate easy or frequent. It is one of those curious experiences
of politics in which what has been called the irrational plays such
an important part. This demand for assurance, although claimed
for all popular ministries, has been described as a demand which
would benefit the Congress ministries alone. The Secretary of State
insinuated that the Congress ministries might use their powers
against a minority, and that has been accepted by the Muslim
League as the only object for which the assurance was needed.
The League has gone further. Its protagonists have said that the
assurance was wanted to enable the Congress ministries to use
their powers against the Muslim minority for oppressing it. The
entire field of administration minus this small corner in respect of
which the asssurance was demanded has been left out of account
altogether by the propagandists on behalf of the League. In actual
fact, however, there were occasions where the Congress ministries

[2] Ibid., p. 106.

forced the hands of Governors to act according to their advice by resignation or threat of resignation, but no single occasion arose where the rights of a minority were sought to be in any way affected by any action of any Congress ministry where the Governor's hands were forced.

Later on in July 1937, the Congress decided to form ministries as a result of the discussions which had taken place in the meantime. The question then arose whether it should form coalition ministries with the Muslim League. Any such coalition was out of the question in provinces where the League had no member at all—Bihar, Orissa and the Central Province. In the United Provinces and Bombay, an effort was made which, however, did not bear fruit. The Congress had gone to the Assemblies with a definite programme and in furtherance of a definite policy; and it could not, without being false to the electorate, admit into the ministry persons who did not accept that policy and that programme. The programme, too, was not such as could be objected to on communal grounds, although there might be classes comprising all religious groups and communities who might raise objections to certain items in it. It was therefore not a communal programme on which differences could arise with the Muslims as such. It was a political and economic programme and Musalmans who accepted that programme did not cease to be Musalmans for that reason. The Congress naturally preferred such Musalmans to those who did not accept its programme. The Congress decided to stick to the well-known and well-understood constitutional principle of having homogeneous Ministries composed of its own members among whom Musalmans were, of course, included. It accordingly chose Muslim ministers from among those who were members of the Congress Party. This was the head and front of the offence of the Congress. The hint given by Lord Zetland has been used for propaganda purpose to the fullest extent.

'In the matter of appointments to the Ministries the Musalmans as such, and the other minorities had more than their proportionate share. Of the 71 Ministers of the eleven Provinces, 26 were Muslims, 10 of the other minority communities and 35 Hindus; of the 35 Ministers in the "Hindu Congress Provinces", 6 were Muslims and 5 of the other minority communities. Some, time later the Congress formed coalition Ministries in two more Provinces, the North-West Frontier Province and Assam. That increased

the number of Muslim Ministers still further. In the North-West
Frontier Province three out of the four Ministers including the
Prime Minister, Dr Khan Saheb, were Muslims, while in Assam
there were three Muslim and five non-Muslim Ministers. These
figures easily disprove the sweeping and fantastic assertions made
by the League apologists.'[3]

The Congress took office about the middle of July 1937, and had
hardly been in office for eight months when on 20 March 1938,
the Council of the All-India Muslim League passed a resolution
to the effect that whereas numerous complaints had reached the
central office of the hardship, ill-treatment and injustice that were
meted out to the Muslims in various Congress government provinces
and particularly to those who were workers and members of the
Muslim League, the Council resolves that a special Confidante
be appointed consisting of the [following] members to collect all
information, to make all necessary enquiries and to take such
steps as may be considered proper and to submit its report to the
Council from time to time. The Committee, which was presided
over by the Raja of Pirpur submitted its report on 15 November
1938. It is not possible here to go into the details of the complaints
mentioned in the Pirpur Report. It may be mentioned that after
its publication the Congress ministries made enquiries into the
allegations and issued communiqués giving detailed replies. Some
of them were discussed also in their respective Legislatures. The
charges have never been put to the test of impartial investigation.
Mr Fazlul Huq, who was then a leading member of the League,
threw out a challenge to Pandit Jawaharlal Nehru and Pandit Nehru
agreed to go round with Mr Huq, as the latter had suggested, to
ascertain the truth but Mr Huq did not fulfil the engagement. In
October 1939, the writer of this book, who happened to be at
that time the President of the Congress, wrote to Mr Jinnah to
have the complaints investigated by an impartial authority and
suggested the name of Sir Maurice Gwyer, the Chief Justice of
the Federal Court, for the purpose. Mr Jinnah, however, refused
to accept this suggestion. He wrote in reply: 'The matter is now
under His Excellency's [Viceroy's] consideration and he is the proper
authority to take such action and adopt such measures as would

[3] Mehta and Patwardhan, *The Communal Triangle*, p. 114.

meet our requirements and restore complete sense of security in those Provinces where the Congress Ministries are in charge of the administration.' Neither His Excellency the Viceroy nor any of the Governors of the provinces where Congress ministries functioned, nor Lord Zetland, who remained the Secretary of State for India during the whole period the Congress ministries functioned, ever raised any question of Congress atrocities against Musalmans or against any other minorities. We are not aware that the Viceroy took any action on the representation of Mr Jinnah to which he referred in his reply quoted above, nor are we aware that Mr Jinnah himself pursued the matter any further with the Viceroy. Later, Mr Jinnah came out with a demand for a Royal Commission to enquire into the charges but that was not acceptable to the Government and the matter was left there. The Congress Prime Ministers, before their resignation, were asked by the Congress Parliamentary Board to invite the Governors of the provinces to point out any policy or act of their ministries which adversely affected the minorities and particularly the Muslim minority. In not a single case was any Governor able to point out an instance. Indeed after retirement Sir Harry Haig, the Governor of the United Provinces, who did not suffer from any evil reputation of having a soft corner for the Congress, testified to the scrupulous care of the Congress ministries to deal fairly and justly with the Musalmans. The so-called atrocities, therefore, have remained mere allegations of a complainant which have never been tested and put to the proof. They have, nevertheless, been a principal plank of the League programme and utilized for propaganda purposes.

I might just mention some of the prominent points in the charges. The Bandemataram song was regarded as one of the causes of conflict between the two major communities. It may be mentioned that the song was composed in the eighties of the last century and has remained popular since the early years of the present century not only in Bengal but even in other provinces. It has been sung, in Congress and other assemblies almost regularly since then. Mr Jinnah himself was a prominent member of the Congress for at least fifteen years when it used to be sung there and never found anything objectionable in it from the Muslim point of view. It was sung in innumerable gatherings in the days of the Khilafat agitation when Congress had the support of Muslims in its fight as never before or since, but it was never objected to in those

days. Yet it was made one of the major grievances and causes
of conflict after the Congress ministries were established and is
mentioned as the very first in the Pirpur Report. The Congress
Working Committee, however, to meet all possible objections and
to remove all possible misunderstanding directed that only the
first two stanzas of it should be sung. The possible objection on
what may be called the religious aspect of it was thus removed.
It was said, however, that the Musalmans could not forget the
background of the story in which the song occurs. It may be
safely asserted that not one in a thousand outside Bengal knew
anything about the story until it became necessary to requisition
it as a justification for objecting to the song.

The second item is the tri-colour flag. This flag came into
prominence during the days when the Congress was being supported
by the Musalmans during the Khilafat agitation. It was accepted
as a national flag by the Hindus and Musalmans in those days.
Like the Bandemataram song it had drawn against itself the wrath
of the British government, which regarded both the song and the
flag as revolutionary symbols and tried to suppress them. It had,
therefore, won the distinction of having been defended by many
Hindus and Muslims who had suffered imprisonment, lathi charges,
or even death, in its defence. Musalmans as such had never raised
any objection until the Congress ministries came into office. It
may be added that it is not the Hindu flag.

Another item of the Congress programme that is regarded as an
attack on the Muslims is mass contact. The Congress has, at least
for the last twenty-five years, become a mass movement—as the
various Satyagraha movements have proved. At its call, masses have
come forward to suffer for the sake of freedom. It is unnecessary
to go into any details of these movements. Musalmans joined
these movements and suffered. It is difficult to understand how it
becomes an offence on the part of the Congress if it tries to reach
the Muslim masses also, unless it be assumed that the Muslim
League alone has the right to speak to a Muslim in India and
nobody else—Hindu, Muslim or other—can approach them and
speak to them about political, economic or any other matter of
general interest. In every free country, every individual or group
has or ought to have the freedom to place before the people his
or its own ideals and programme of action; and it is to be hoped
that even in Pakistan this right will not be denied to its citizens.

The Congress, and for that matter any other body—national or communal, religious or social, political or economic—cannot give up this right and the hue and cry against it betrays a lack of appreciation of the right of free speech and free association. The communal separate electorates have divided the communities on religious and communal lines; their effect has been to emphasize the communal and religious differences. This has been recognized even by Musalmans and a split in the League itself occurred on the question Mr Jinnah leading the group opposed to separate electorates. But others did not accept his lead and he had to give in. If the Congress still holds to the opinion that communal electorates are bad in principle and mischievous in operation, how can any one blame it? And yet, what is now demanded is that not only should separate electorates be continued and the voters prevented from voting for men of another community, and the candidates from seeking and receiving the suffrage of people belonging to another faith, but that non-official organizations should not have any contact with the Muslims at all. It is a demand which not only extends the mischief of separate electorates to activities not connected with elections, but makes it impossible for Musalmans to come in contact with people of any other community. The situation has only to be visualized to be rejected outright.

Another item which has come in for a great deal of criticism on the part of the League is the Wardha Scheme of Basic Education. The fundamental principle of that scheme is that education should be imparted not through books so much as through crafts. Psychologists and educationists in the West have adopted this method and it has been accepted basically by the Sargent Scheme. The committee which worked it out at Wardha was presided over by Dr Zakir Hussain, an educationist of no mean repute. He was assisted in this work by Khwaja G. Sayyedain who was at one time connected with the Aligarh University and later became the Director of Public Instruction, Kashmir. It is difficult to understand how a scheme which has been prepared by two distinguished Muslim educationists can be part of a programme hatched by Hindus to injure Muslim interests. Its only fault is that it was Mahatma Gandhi who placed the idea before the public and was responsible for convening the Conference which prepared it. This scheme has been given practical shape and is being worked out in Jamia Millia of Delhi under the direct guidance of Dr

Zakir Hussain. I am not sure if it has been tried so successfully anywhere else in the country and yet it is one of the items in the Congress atrocities.

I may mention here that special objection was taken to what came to be known as the Vidya Mandir Scheme of the Central Province. A conference of Muslim members of the Legislative Assembly of the province was convened by the Prime Minister on 7 February 1939, and was attended by Nawabzada Liaqat Ali Khan, the Secretary of the All-India Muslim League, on invitation. The Vidya Mandir scheme was explained by the Prime Minister, who emphasized that it was intended to remove illiteracy in the rural areas, irrespective of caste and creed, and that it rested on endowments of land and money by private donors. A private association was registered for this purpose and the government was to give financial assistance to the association to supplement its own resources. He said that he would welcome the formation by the Muslims of a similar separate association if they so desired; The Nawabzada said that the Muslims would call the association Madinatul-ilm and the scheme, Madinatul-ilm Scheme. The Prime Minister promised the same help to this association and scheme as to the other. The complaints, not only about the Vidya Mandir scheme but all others, were gone into in detail and settled to the satisfaction of the Muslim members of the Provincial Assembly and the Secretary of the All-India Muslim League in an atmosphere of cordiality. The terms of settlement were signed by the Prime Minister and Nawabzada Liaqat Ali Khan, and the Satyagraha started by some Muslims was in consequence withdrawn and so also were the prosecutions arising out of it. On 19 February 1939, the government issued a communiqué on the subject. The Vidya Mandir Scheme, however, continued to furnish an item to the catalogue of atrocities of the Congress. When Mr Fazlui Huq revived it, the gentleman's agreement signed by the Nawabzada and Pandit Shukla, the Prime Minister, was published by the government in December 1939 with the consent of the Nawabzada, more than a month after the Congress ministry had resigned and can be read in the *Hitavada* of Nagpur dated 22 December 1939.

Another important item against the Congress ministries is that there were Hindu–Muslim riots. Unfortunately, these riots do occur in the country and they did so before the Congress ministries were constituted and also after they had ceased to function. It cannot also be denied that they have become more wide spread and progressively more frequent since separate electorates were introduced with the Morley–Minto Reforms. It is not possible to deal with particular cases and such of them as went to the courts must have been dealt with by them. Mr Durrani has, however, laid special stress on one case which happened in Berar and has quoted some remarks from the judgement of the High Court on the basis of which he has called upon the then Prime Minister of the province 'to commit suicide or to retire from public life'. Certain facts in connection with the case may, therefore, be mentioned. A prominent Hindu was murdered and some others were injured. The investigation of the case was held under the supervision of a European DIG of Police, Mr B.G. Taylor. The trial was held not in the district where the incident occurred but at Nagpur at the request of the accused. The Sessions Judge who tried the case was a European member of the Indian Civil Service, Mr M.N. Clark. He was evidently an experienced judge as he was soon after raised to the High Court Bench at Nagpur. The trial was held after the Congress ministry had resigned and the judgement of the Sessions court and also of the High Court were delivered months after the resignation of the Congress ministry. It is an everyday affair in courts that the judgement of a judge is upset by the judgement of an appellate court and so it happened in this case. There is one thing which has been made much of against the Prime Minister. He delivered a speech which is said to have prejudiced the investigation of the case. It must be remembered that it was made on an adjournment motion in the Assembly and purported to give 'the facts of the case as reported'. The debate was raised only three days after the incident and before the matter had been taken cognizance of by any court. The Prime Minister had, on account of reports of serious communal tension, visited the place of occurrence and had taken care to take with him three Muslim members of the Assembly, one of whom was K.S. Abdur Rahman Khan, the Secretary of the Provincial Muslim League. He had also addressed a public meeting at Khamgaon. The complaint against him was that in the debate he described the crime while the matter was still under investigation as a carefully planned murder ruthlessly carried out. In the debate, Muslim members also described—the offence as murder and condemned it in very strong terms. As regards the conduct of the Prime Minister, K.S.

Abdur Rahman Khan, in the course of that very debate, spoke appreciatively in the following words: 'I was so pleased to hear the Hon'ble Premier in Khamgaon. I only wish my friends had only followed him in the noble sentiment he has expressed and the lead he has given.'[4] As the High Court had made adverse remarks against the conduct of the investigation of the case, the government appointed Mr Justice A.S.R. Macklin, a judge of the Bombay High Court, to examine the conduct of the police investigation into the case and the preparation of the case for trial in the courts, and to report what persons were responsible for the defects and irregularities, if any. It appears that allegations of ill-treatment of the Musalmans were made and Mr Justice Macklin says that the government of the Central Province at once interested itself in the allegation of ill-treatment and immediately ordered an enquiry which was held by Mr Hill, the District Magistrate, and the allegations were found by him to be without foundation. Mr Justice Macklin was satisfied that the complaints of ill-treatment were not true. He also found that the police were not responsible for bringing up false evidence in the case and absolved the police from all blame in this respect. Administration would become impossible if a Prime Minister was to be held responsible for every prosecution that succeeds in the first court, but is reversed by the appellate court. There is no suggestion that the Sessions Judge was open to be influenced by the Prime Minister, specially when the trial took place after the Prime Minister had resigned and had become a mere citizen.

The Hindi–Urdu controversy has been brought in as another instance of Congress atrocities. This is an old controversy and still continues. There is nothing that the Congress ministries did to aggravate it so far as the Musalmans were concerned. In fact, whatever they did was for bringing about a reconciliation. But before anything effective could be accomplished they resigned.

The subsequent history of the communal problem from 1937 up to date is one of repeated attempts on the part of the Congress to have a settlement and of mounting demands by the Muslim League, now supported indirectly by the British government and now discouraged, thus keeping the country on tenterhooks. We have seen how the atrocity scare has been developed. In 1938

[4] CP Legislative Assembly Proceedings, 1939, pp. 307–08.

efforts were made by Mahatma Gandhi and by Shri Subhas Chandra Bose, the then President of the Congress, to get from the League an idea of what would satisfy it so that the Congress and the country might consider the demands and meet them if possible. This was necessary because the Fourteen Points of Mr Jinnah had been practically conceded by the British government and incorporated in the Constitution Act of 1935. The negotiations between Mr Jinnah and the then President of the Congress (author of this book) early in 1935, took place before the Act had been passed and proceeded on the basis of joint electorates. After the Act had been passed and not only separate electorates but other points had been conceded, it was hardly to be expected that the League would agree to give up separate electorates or concede any of the other points. In spite of all the safeguards that the League had demanded and obtained, in spite of the fact that Muslim ministries were functioning in the Muslim majority provinces, such as the Punjab, Sind, North-West Frontier Province, Bengal, and off and on in Assam, the League came to the conclusion that the Muslims were being oppressed and that all the safeguards and above all the promise of the British government to safeguard their interests through the special and reserve powers of the Governor had proved ineffective and unreliable. Either the conclusion was a correct conclusion or a false imaginary complex of fear and distrust. If it was the former, then even separation from India of the provinces with Muslim majorities and the establishment of independent states in them would not provide any safeguards for the Muslims of those provinces, where the Muslims were in a minority as we shall see later. But if the latter, there is no remedy except time, which may wear off the distrust. The League has, however, gone on adding to its demands and making any settlement impossible. The prolonged correspondence and negotiations between Mahatma Gandhi, Shri Subhas Chandra Bose and Pandit Jawaharlal Nehru on the one hand and Mr M.A. Jinnah on the other did not proceed beyond the stage of scrutinizing the credentials of the negotiating parties to arrive at a settlement. Mr Jinnah insisted that the League should be recognized as the one and single body that represents the entire Muslim community and that the Congress should speak on behalf of the Hindus. The Congress was unable to concede any of these points and indeed it could not. The negotiations did not succeed even in getting a formulation of the demands of the Muslim League.

It cannot be forgotten that there are other Muslim organizations in the country and they do not admit the claim of the League. I may mention the nationalist Muslims organized under different names from time to time: the Ahrars who have shown grit and undergone sacrifices; the Jamait-ul-Ulema who have consistently fought and suffered in the cause of national freedom and possess an influence of their own which is derived from their position as divines and representatives of Muslim learning; the Shias who have a separate Conference of their own and have demanded separate safeguards for their rights even as against the League—and that in spite of the fact that Mr Jinnah and some other leading members of the League are also Shias; the Momins who constitute a very large proportion, if not a majority, of the Muslims, who are organized in a separate Jamait of their own, and who have openly and repeatedly repudiated the Muslim League claim; the Nationalists of Baluchistan, organized as Khuddam-e-Watan (servants of the mother country); the Khudai-Khidmatgars of the North-West Frontier Province; the Krishak Praja Party of Bengal; and last, though not least, the Khaksars led by Allama Mashraqi who do not see eye to eye with the League on many questions. The strength of these parties is variously estimated, their supporters claiming majority among the Musalmans, the Leaguers to the contrary.

The Congress could not concede that it was a Hindu organization—that would be denying its own past, falsifying its history, and betraying its future. It has claimed to represent Indians of all faiths and communities insofar as the urge for political and economic independence is concerned. It does not represent the Hindus as such insofar as Hindus may have any separate interest vis-à-vis Musalmans and other communal or religious groups. It could not, therefore, accept the position of a communal organization of the Hindus alone. In not admitting the League's point of view, the Congress only stated facts. It was nevertheless prepared to explore avenues of settlement of the communal question with the Muslim League but that did not satisfy Mr Jinnah and the negotiations were barred *in limine*.

To support the above contention a few citations will suffice. Writing to Mahatma Gandhi on 3 March 1938, Mr Jinnah said: 'We have reached a stage when no doubt should be left. You recognize the All-India Muslim League as the one authoritative and representative organization of Musalmans in India, and on the other hand, you represent the Congress and other Hindus throughout the country. It is on that basis we can proceed further and devise a machinery of approach.'[5] In course of negotiations with Shri Subhas Chandra Bose, Mr Jinnah suggested a formula in the following words: 'The All-India Muslim League, as the authoritative organization of the Indian Muslims and the Congress as the authoritative representative organization of the solid body of Hindu opinion have hereby agreed to the following terms by way of pact between the two major communities as a settlement of the Hindu–Muslim question.' This was, after further consideration, altered by him as follows:

'The Congress and the All-India Muslim League, as the authoritative and representative organization of the Musalmans of India, have hereby agreed to the following terms of a Hindu–Muslim settlement by way of a pact.' The Executive Committee of the All-India Muslim League passed a resolution to the effect that 'it is not possible for the All-India Muslim League to treat and negotiate with the Congress the question of Hindu–Muslim settlement except on the basis that the Muslim League is the authoritative and representative organization of the Musalmans of India.' Mr Jinnah, writing to Shri Subhas Chandra Bose on 2 August 1938, went further and said: 'The Council wishes to point out that it considered undesirable the inclusion of Musalmans on the Committee that might be appointed by the Congress because it would meet to solve and settle the Hindu–Muslim question.' When Sir Tej Bahadur Sapru suggested to Mr Jinnah in February 1941 that he and Mahatma Gandhi should meet for settling the Hindu–Muslim differences, Mr Jinnah wrote to him in reply on 19 February 1941: 'I have always been ready and willing to see Mr Gandhi or any other Hindu leader on behalf of the Hindu community and do all I can to help the solution of the Hindu–Muslim problem.'

That this demand was a new one is apparent from the fact that it had never been made before. The conversations which led to the Lucknow Pact went on without assigning the status of the authoritative and representative organization of the Muslims to

[5] *Unity Talks*, p. 28.

the League and a similar status of being the authoritative and representative organization of the solid body of Hindu opinion to the Congress. In the conversations the then President of the Congress had with Mr Jinnah in 1935, the question was never raised and indeed Mr Jinnah was not prepared to have an agreement with the Congress without its endorsement by Pandit Malaviya on behalf of the Hindu Mahasabha and as a matter of fact, the negotiations fell through because the Congress President could not undertake to secure such endorsement by the Hindu Mahasabha.

Further, as stated above, the League not only insisted upon the recognition of its own status and assuring the status of a Hindu organization to the Congress but also wanted to determine who should constitute the Congress delegation for any Conference for settling the Hindu–Muslim question with its representatives, as is apparent from the passage quoted above. When Mahatma Gandhi wanted to have Maulana Abul Kalam Azad with him in his talks with Mr Jinnah the latter declined.

Pandit Jawaharlal Nehru made many attempts in the course of conversations and long correspondence with Mr Jinnah to ascertain the points which the Muslim League considered required discussion and settlement, but he failed. In reply to an earnest appeal made by him to enlighten him on the points requiring discussion and settlement, Mr Jinnah said in his letter dated 17 March 1938: 'Perhaps you have heard of the 14 points' and he referred to an article in the *Statesman* dated 12 July 1937 under the heading 'Through Muslim Eyes' and an article in the *New Times* dated March 1938 mentioning and showing the various suggestions which would have to be considered. When Pandit Jawaharlal Nehru in his letter dated 6 April 1938 analysed the points mentioned therein and explained the Congress viewpoint with regard to them Mr Jinnah turned round and in his letter dated 12 April 1938 said: 'You have formulated certain points in your letter which you fasten upon me to begin with, as my proposals.' And naturally no one was any the wiser about the points which the League would have the Congress consider.

When the war broke out in September 1939, another attempt was made by Mahatma Gandhi and Pandit Jawaharlal Nehru but without any effect, and Pandit Nehru in despair was compelled to write on the 16 December 1939: 'Unfortunately we never seem to reach even the proper discussion of these problems as various hurdles and obstructions in the shape of conditions precedent come in our way . . . As these hurdles continue and others are added to them I am compelled to think that the real difficulty is the difference in the political outlook and objectives.'

The League and its President, while unwilling to formulate the points of difference for discussion with the Congress, were not equally undisposed towards disclosing some of them to the Viceroy from time to time. The British government too, on its side, was not unwilling to take advantage of the differences that existed—for which purpose it was necessary to help the League to strengthen, its position in the country. It will be recalled that it was the Muslim All-Parties Conference which had insisted upon a Federal Scheme for India. But by the time the Act of 1935 had devised such a scheme, the League and particularly Mr Jinnah, had undergone a complete change in their outlook and the Federal part of the Constitution had become the chief target of their attack. The Viceroy announced on 11 September, 1939, that preparations in connection with the introduction of Federation would remain in suspense during the pendency of the wan. The Working Committee of the All-India Muslim League passed a resolution appreciating the suspension and expressing a wish that the Federal Scheme should be abandoned completely, urging the British government to revise the entire problem of India's future Constitution *de novo* and asked 'for an assurance that no declaration regarding the question of constitutional advance for India should be made without the consent and approval of the All-India Muslim League nor any Constitution be framed and finally adopted by His Majesty's Government and the British Parliament without such consent and approval.'

Lord Linlithgow replied on 23 December 1939, that 'His Majesty's Government are not under any misapprehension as to the importance of the contentment of the Muslim community to the stability and success of any constitutional development in India. You need therefore have no fear that the weight which your community's position in India necessarily gives their views will be underrated.' Mr Jinnah had an interview on 6 February 1940 with the Viceroy and the government communiqué issued after the meeting stated: 'His Excellency assured Mr Jinnah that His Majesty's Government were fully alive to the necessity for safeguarding the legitimate interest of all minorities and that he need be under no apprehension that the importance of those subjects will be lost sight of.' This, however, did not satisfy the Muslim League and explaining the view of the Working Committee of the League after quoting the passage mentioned above, Mr Jinnah wrote to the Viceroy in his letter dated 23 February 1940:' I regret to say this does not meet the point raised by the Muslim League, because it still leaves the position of 90 millions in India only in the region of consultation and counsel and vests the final decision in the hands of Great Britain to determine the fate and future of British India. We regret that we cannot accept this position.' He insisted upon a definite assurance that 'no commitment will be made with regard to the future Constitution of India or any interim settlement with any other party without our approval or consent.' The British government made another attempt through the Viceroy and the Secretary of State made a statement in the House of Lords on 1 April 1940, which the Viceroy communicated to Mr Jinnah in another letter. It was as follows: 'The undertaking given by His Majesty's Government to examine the constitutional field in consultation with the representatives of all parties and interests in India connoted not dictation but negotiation. Admittedly a substantial measure of agreement amongst the communities in India is essential, if the vision of United India which has inspired the labours of so many Indians and Englishmen is to become a reality; for I cannot believe that any Government or Parliament in this country would attempt to impose by force upon, for example, 80 million Muslim subjects of His Majesty in India a form of constitution under which they would not live peacefully and contentedly.' The Working Committee of the League was not satisfied with this further clarification. Mr Jinnah had another interview with the Viceroy on 25 June 1940 and submitted a note to him of the points which he had discussed with him, in his letter dated 1 July 1940. That note contained the following points:

1.   That no pronouncement or statement should be made by His Majesty's Government which would in any way militate against the basic and fundamental principles laid down by the Lahore resolution about the division of India and creating Muslim states in the north-west and eastern zones.

2.   That His Majesty's Government must give definite and

categorical assurance to the Musalmans of India that no interim or final scheme of Constitution could be adopted by the British government without the previous approval and consent of Muslim India.

3.   That intensification of war efforts, and mobilization of Indian resources can only be achieved provided the British government are ready and willing to associate the Muslim leadership as equal partners in the government both at the Centre and in all the provinces. In other words, Muslim India's leadership must be fully trusted as equals and have equal share in the authority and control of governments, central and provincial.

4.   Provisionally and during the period of the war, the following steps should be taken:

a   The Executive Council of the Viceroy should be enlarged within the framework of the present Constitution, it being understood that the Muslim representation must be equal to that of the Hindus if the Congress comes in, otherwise the Muslims should have the majority of the additional members as the main burden and the responsibility will be borne by the Musalmans in that case;

b   A War Council should be established of not less than fifteen members including the Viceroy as its President. The representation of Muslim India on it must be equal to that of the Hindus if the Congress comes in, otherwise they should have the majority;

c   Finally, the representatives of the Musalmans on the proposed War Council and the Executive Council of the Governor-General and the additional Advisers of the Governors should be chosen by the Muslim League.

The Viceroy could not fail to appreciate that the demand was really for transfer of power to the Muslim League and in his reply dated 6 July 1940 he said that while he readily accepted the importance of securing adequate representation of Muslim interests there was no question of 'responsibility' falling in greater or less degree on any particular section. 'Responsibility,' he said, 'will be that of the Governor-General in Council as a whole. Again it will be clear that under existing law and practice it must remain in the Secretary of State in consultation with the Governor-General, to decide upon such names as he may submit to His Majesty the King for inclusion in the Governor-General's Council and such persons 'cannot be the nominees of political parties, however important.' He said further: 'I ought, I think, to make it clear that it would be constitutionally impossible for the choice of Muslim gentlemen to be appointed to my expanded Executive Council or as non-official advisers to rest with the Muslim League. But in the contingency envisaged you need not fear that any suggestion you may put forward would not receive full consideration.'

On 7 of August 1940, the Viceroy issued a statement declaring the government's policy. After referring to the government's previous declarations relating to the examination of the entire Act of 1935 in any review of the Constitution of India, he said that the government could not contemplate the transfer of their responsibilities for the peace and welfare of India to any system of government whose authority is directly denied by large and powerful elements in India's national life, nor could they be parties to the coercion of such elements into submission to such a government. He promised on behalf of the government the setting up, after the conclusion of the war, of a body, representative of the principal elements in India's national life to devise the framework of a new Constitution. He also announced the government's intention to invite a certain number of representative Indians to join the Governor-General's Executive Council and to establish a War Advisory Council. Mr Amery in the course of the discussion of the Viceroy's offer in the House of Commons underlined the differences in India. He said: 'The constitutional deadlock in India is not so much between His Majesty's Government and a consentient Indian opposition as between the main elements of India's own national life. It can, therefore, only be resolved not by the relatively easy method of a bilateral agreement between His Majesty's Government and representatives of India but by the much more difficult method of a multilateral agreement in which His Majesty's Government is only one of the parties concerned.' Among the other parties he mentioned the Muslims, the Scheduled Castes, and the Indian Princes. At the same time he also said that India is a self-contained and distinctive region of the world and that it can boast of an ancient civilization and of a long history common to all its people. We thus see the third side of the triangle gradually but nonetheless steadily expanding. On the one hand, while democratic principles are given lip-homage the 'elements in the national life of India' are patted on the back or on the face as it suits the occasion. Substantial measure of agreement for any constitutional advance is insisted upon and the deadlock is described to be not between India and Britain but between different groups or interests of Indians themselves. When the Muslim League demands previous approval and consent to any constitutional measure and the sole right to nominate the Muslim representatives to various bodies, the first demand is evaded by a general declaration and the second by a more specific refusal. When it demands separation of the north-west and north-east zones, India is reminded that it is a self-contained and distinctive region of the world and has an ancient civilization and a long history common to all its people. The Working Committee of the League considered the Viceroy's declaration, so far as it related to the future Constitution, to be satisfactory, but the specific offer regarding the expansion of the Executive Council as most unsatisfactory. The Viceroy's offer to appoint two members to the Executive Council out of a panel of four to be submitted by the League did not commend itself to them nor did a similar offer regarding the Advisory Council. Fresh negotiations did not carry matters further and Mr Jinnah came out with a statement on 29 September 1940 before a meeting of the Council of the All-India Muslim League that the British government appeared to have no intention to part with power and that they were trifling with 90 million Muslims who were a nation. Thus the effort to have what Mr Jinnah called a war contract between the government and the Muslim League failed for the time being.

Later in the year, the Congress started what is called the individual civil disobedience movement for vindicating the right of free speech. It was obvious that the movement had nothing to do with the Musalmans or the League and the right for which it was started would accrue to the benefit as much of the Musalmans as of anybody else. Yet the Muslim League treated it as directed against the Muslims. The Council of the All-India Muslim League adopted a resolution stating that they 'have no doubt as to the real motive and object of Mr Gandhi in launching and; pursuing vigorously his movement of Satyagraha' and drew 'the attention of the British government that if any concession to the Congress is made which adversely affects or militates against the Muslim demand it will be resisted by the Muslim League with all the power it can command and the Muslim League desires to place it on record that if the situation demands it would not hesitate to intervene and play such part in this struggle as may be necessary for the protection of the rights and interests of the Musalmans of this country.'

The following session of the Muslim League was held in Madras in April 1941 and the Constitution of the League was so amended as to embody the attainment of Pakistan in the creed.

The next stage in the process of bargain between the British government and the Muslim League was what has been called the Cripps offer. In March 1942 Sir Stafford Cripps, a member of the War Cabinet of Britain, came to India with a declaration of the government's policy and proposal. It contemplated the creation of a new Indian Union which should form a Dominion equal in status to the other Dominions of the Crown. It laid down the procedure for the framing of a new Constitution for India and His Majesty's Government undertook to accept and implement the constitution, subject to the rights of any province in British India that was not prepared to accept the new Constitution, to retain its constitutional position, provision being made for its subsequent accession if it so decided. Further, His Majesty's Government would be prepared to agree upon a new constitution for the non-acceding provinces, giving them the same status as to the Indian Union. The declaration further contained an invitation to Indian leaders to participate in the counsels of the country, retaining the control and direction of the defence of India in the hands of the Government of India.

The declaration thus conceded the right of secession to any province of British India from the All-India Union and practically accepted the demand of the Muslim League for the creation of Muslim States independent of the Indian Union. The Congress Working Committee did not reject the offer, as it could have done, on the ground that it contemplated a break-up of the Indian unity. On the other hand it made it clear that it 'cannot think in terms of compelling the people in any territorial unit to remain in an Indian Union against their declared and established will but pointed out that any break-up of that unity would be injurious to all concerned.' It rejected the offer on the other ground that the offer kept the defence out of the sphere of responsibility and reduced it to a farce and nullity. The Muslim League Working Committee, however, waited until the decision of the Congress Working Committee rejecting the offer had become known, and then passed a resolution that the proposals in the present form were not acceptable. It expressed gratification at the fact that the possibility of Pakistan was recognized by implication and expressed its conviction that it was neither just nor possible in the interests of peace and happiness of the two peoples to compel them to constitute one Indian Union composed of the two principal nations—Hindus and Muslims—which appeared to be the main object of the declaration, the creation of more than one Union being relegated only to the realm of remote possibility and purely illusory. It also objected to the machinery for the creation of the Constitution-making body as being a fundamental departure from the right of the Musalmans to elect their representatives with separate electorates. It even objected to the procedure for obtaining the verdict of a province for or against accession. It laid down that the plebiscite in the provinces in which the Musalmans are in a majority should be not of the whole adult population but of the Musalmans alone. Otherwise it would be denying them the inherent right to self-determination. It thus becomes clear that when the British government has conceded the right of a province to keep out of the Indian Union and lays down that this should be decided by the Legislative Assembly by a majority of 60 per cent and in case such majority is not available, then on a demand being made by the minority, by a plebiscite of the male adult population, the League insists that the vote of the Assembly cannot be a true criterion of ascertaining the real opinion of the Musalmans of those provinces. It insists that the plebiscite should be confined to the Musalmans alone, and the minorities—even though they may happen to be something in the neighbourhood of 45 per cent as is the case in Bengal and the Punjab—should be ignored altogether and should have no voice at all in deciding a vital question involving the breaking-up of the unity of India and cutting the minorities off from the rest of their countrymen with whom they have been associated from time immemorial.

The Cripps Mission having failed, the All-India Congress Committee at its meeting held in Bombay on 7 and 8 August 1942, passed its memorable resolution, which has come to be known as the 'Quit India' resolution. On the eve of the meeting, as on various previous occasions, declarations had been made on behalf of the Congress that it did not want power for itself but for the people of India and that it would be content if the Muslim League took office with real power. But when the Working Committee of the Muslim League met from 16 to 20 August 1942, it passed a resolution which contained the following:

'It is the considered opinion of the Working Committee that this movement directed not only to coerce the British government into handing over power to a Hindu oligarchy and thus disabling themselves from carrying out the moral obligations and pledges given to the Musalmans and other sections of the peoples of India from time to time but also to force the Musalmans to submit and surrender to the Congress terms and dictation . . .' After making an offer to the British government that the League was prepared to take up responsibilities on a footing of equality provided its demands were met, the Working Committee of the League called upon the Musalmans to abstain from any participation in the movement initiated by the Congress. Thereafter the movement was regarded as one directed against the Muslims and League propagandists insisted on the withdrawal of the August Resolution of the All-India Congress Committee before the release of Congressmen from prison and before any negotiations with the Congress for settling the deadlock could be initiated. They have persisted in their charge that the Congress was in league with Japan even after the British government has repudiated such charges.

Mahatma Gandhi's prolonged conversations with Mr Jinnah in September 1944 proved unfruitful and did not succeed even in eliciting from Mr Jinnah a complete picture of his Pakistan with its boundaries demarcated, Constitution foreshadowed and safeguards for the minorities in it defined.

The Wavell proposals for a provisional interim settlement without any prejudice to the future Constitution which would be devised after the war were made in June 1945. One of the fundamentals of the proposals was that there should be parity of representation in the Viceroy's Executive Council between Hindus other than the Scheduled Castes and the Musalmans. Thus what the League had been insisting upon, that is, equality of representation in the provisional government with the Hindus was conceded. The Muslim League and Mr Jinnah have since 1937 taken the minorities of India under their special protection and care and while pressing their own demands, have never failed to impress upon all concerned that the Hindu majority and particularly the Congress, which had been 'the authoritative and representative organization of the solid body of Hindu opinion', were out to 'oppress and suppress the minorities'. They have treated the depressed classes as apart from the Hindus and as a minority requiring their protection. The British government has been anxious to keep the League on the right side as the only counterpoise to the growing strength of the masses of India represented by the Congress and has gone on making concession after concession to satisfy the ever-expanding demands of the League, and this last offer of a parity between the Muslims and the Hindus other than the Scheduled Castes was in keeping with their policy of appeasement. But as on previous occasions it failed to appease and Mr Jinnah's insistence that he should nominate all the Muslim members to the Council and no one else, brought about a failure of Lord Wavell's offer who, however, took upon himself the 'responsibility 'for such failure, as in truth it was. But another curious development came out as a result of the Simla failure. It brought about the emergence of a further demand from the Muslim League which in effect amounts to a claim that the Muslim League should have a parity not only as against the Hindus other than the Scheduled Castes but also against them and all others including all other minorities combined. Mr Jinnah said at a Press conference after the Simla Conference on 14 July 1945: 'Next in the proposed Executive we would be reduced to a minority of one-third. All the other minorities such as the Scheduled Castes, Sikhs and Christians have the same goal as the Congress. They have their grievances as minorities, but their goal and ideology is and cannot be different from or otherwise than that of a united India. Ethnically and culturally they are very closely knitted to the Hindu society. I am not against full justice being done to all the minorities. They should be fully safeguarded and protected as such, wherever they may be. But in the actual working and practice invariably their votes will be against us and there is no safeguard for us except the Viceroy's veto, which, it is well known to any constitutionalist, cannot be exercised lightly as everyday business against majority decisions with regard to the policy and the principles that will have to be laid down and measures adopted both administrative and legislative.' It is clear,

~

SIXTEEN

SUMMARY OF PART II

We have gone at considerable length into the history of the communal problem with particular reference to the Muslim question and the part the British government has played in it. We may here summarize the long discussion by dividing it into several parts.

First we have the period when the East India Company was acquiring power and was establishing the British rule in India. Its policy was frankly based on the age-old maxim of divide and rule and consisted in taking the side of one Indian Prince against another and preventing their combining against the foreign Company. By the end of the first quarter of the nineteenth century, almost all the independent Indian Princes had been either subjugated or brought under alliance and the Mughal emperor had become a powerless puppet at Delhi. Those that remained were soon liquidated.

The next period witnesses many annexations on one pretext or another and the firm establishment of the Company's rule. There was discontent, deep and widespread, against foreign rule. Musalmans felt keenly not only the loss of power and prestige but also of material prosperity. A movement for reform was started but it took the form of a *jehad* against the Sikhs who were then ruling in the Punjab. The British government connived at the *jehad* if it did not actually encourage it, so long as the Sikhs were an independent power on the north-west of British territory; but after the conquest of the Punjab from the Sikhs the movement was suppressed with a heavy hand.

Discontent, which had been smouldering, burst out in 1857 in the form of a rebellion in which Hindus and Muslims both joined and rallied round the old emperor at Delhi. The rebellion failed and the Mughal empire was brought to an end and the sovereignty of India passed to the Queen of England. The rebellion was followed by severe measures from which Musalmans suffered greatly. It took a few years for the country to recover from the repression that had followed the rebellion.

Hindus had taken advantage of English education which had been introduced but the Musalmans had sulked and thus lagged behind. Sir Syed Ahmad Khan started the movement for the educational uplift of Musalmans and established the Aligarh College. On the political side, the Indian National Congress came into existence in 1885 and furnished a platform for all English-educated Indians from all provinces to meet and discuss questions of public importance and offer suggestions to the government for removing grievances. One Mr Beck became the Principal of the Aligarh College and took charge not only of the students but practically also of Muslim politics. Sir Syed Ahmad Khan under his influence advised the Musalmans to keep aloof from the Congress. Many Musalmans, however, continued their association with the Congress but the influence of the Aligarh College continued to be exercised in favour of alliance with conservative elements in England and reliance on officials here for the advancement of the Musalmans. The Patriotic Association and the Mohammedan Defence Association were established and worked under the inspiration and guidance of Mr Beck and Mr (afterwards Sir) Theodore Morrison, Principals of the Aligarh College.

In the first decade of the twentieth century, Lord Curzon partitioned Bengal ostensibly for creating a province with a majority of Muslim population. This led to a bitter agitation and created, as was expected, bad blood between the Hindus and Musalmans of Bengal although there were many Musalmans of note who were opposed to the partition. Lord Minto became the Viceroy of India after Lord Curzon's retirement and he, in collaboration with Lord Morley, the Secretary of State for India, worked out a measure of reform. In anticipation of the proposals of reform, a deputation of Muslims was organized under the advice of Mr Archbold, the then Principal of the Aligarh College, who had been in touch with the Private Secretary of the Viceroy. In response to the deputation of the Muslims led by the Agha Khan, the Viceroy recognized the special claims of the Musalmans and gave them representation in the Legislative Council through separate electorates. In British circles both here and in England this was regarded as a great service by the Viceroy as it was nothing less than keeping back the Musalmans from joining the ranks of the seditionists. Thus the seed was sown which has now grown into a tree with deep roots and widespread branches, to the great detriment of India and the lasting benefit of Britain which has succeeded in thus blocking the way to Indian Independence.

Not only did the Congress accept separate electorates, though reluctantly but offered to the Muslims, in those provinces where they were in a minority, representation much in excess of their proportion in the population. The Lucknow Pact was entered into between the Indian National Congress and the All-India Muslim League in December 1916 and a joint demand was put before the British government comprising two parts, one dealing with separate electorates and representation of Musalmans in Legislatures and the other with political demands of a mild nature for a share in the government of the country to be enjoyed by its people. The British government declared itself in favour of the progressive realization of self-government by the people of India. In the actual working put of the reform proposals associated with the names of Mr Montagu, the Secretary of State, and Lord Chelmsford, the Viceroy of India, the separate electorates part of the demand was accepted in its entirety but the political part was ignored and substituted by what came to be known as dyarchy in the provinces.

Events in Europe and India continued to bring about a great awakening amongst Indians of all castes and creeds. The Punjab tragedy and the Khilafat wrongs brought the Hindus, Musalmans and others together in a mass upheaval and the Congress, the Khilafat Committee, the Jamait-ul-Ulema and other organizations worked together with a common programme and were, in the words of Lord Lloyd, within an ace of succeeding. The Viceroy was 'puzzled and perplexed'. After many of the most prominent Hindu and Muslim leaders had been clapped in jail and the movement of civil disobedience withdrawn as a result of violence by mobs against the police, Hindu–Muslim riots arose and continued to deface the country for many years. The inspiring scenes of fraternal cooperation and collaboration gave place to fratricidal feuds and conflicts. The programme of non-violent non-cooperation, which had been jointly adopted and acted upon by the Congress and Muslim organizations, weakened and lapsed.

After the Gauhati Congress, an effort was made to bring about a solution of what had already become the Hindu–Muslim problem. Early in 1927, there was an exchange of thought between Hindu and Muslim leaders and some prominent Muslim leaders formulated what came to be known as 'Muslim Proposals'. There were four points in it. Thoughtful Indians had realized the mischief of separate electorates and the Muslim proposals contemplated their abolition, provided the four points mentioned in them were conceded, namely:

(i)   creation of Sind into a province;
(ii)   introduction of reforms in the North-West Frontier Province and Baluchistan as in other provinces;
(iii)   representation of Musalmans in Legislative Councils of Bengal and the Punjab in proportion to their population; and
(iv)   their representation in the Central Legislature to be not less than one-third of the total.

As a result of consideration and further consultation, a settlement between the Congress and the League looked very much like being achieved when the Madras session of the Congress was held in December 1927.

The Reforms introduced in 1920 had been boycotted by the Congress and the Muslim organizations and had satisfied no party in the country but had been worked by moderate elements. A demand had been insistently made for their revision and persistently refused by the British government until towards the end of 1927 it decided to appoint a Statutory Commission to report on their working. This Commission had no Indian on it and naturally caused resentment which was shared alike by Congressmen, Muslim Leaguers, Liberals and others. The Congress and the Liberals decided to boycott the Commission. There was a split in the Muslim League on the question of the boycott of the Commission and the abolition of separate electorates. In pursuance of a resolution passed by the Congress at Madras, a committee in collaboration with other groups and committees framed a scheme, of constitutional reforms for India and its report, known as the Nehru Committee Report was placed before an All-India Convention of all parties in Calcutta. Some amendments to the proposals in the report were moved on behalf of the League demanding that the Muslim representation in the Central Legislature should not be less than one-third, that in case of adult franchise not being granted, Bengal and the Punjab should have seats on population basis and the residuary powers should vest in the Centre. These not being accepted, the League withdrew. The Muslim All-Parties Conference came into existence and in course of time, the two wings of the League became merged in it and the Fourteen Points of Mr Jinnah became the Muslim demand.

Two of the principal items in the Muslim demand were that the form of the Constitution of India should be federal and that the Legislatures and other elected bodies should be constituted on the definite principle of adequate and effective representation of minorities in every province without reducing the majority in any province to a minority or even equality. The First Round Table Conference accepted the federation. The Minorities Committee of the Round Table Conference having failed to achieve agreement, Mr Macdonald gave what has come to be known as the Communal Award in which he practically conceded most of the other items of the Fourteen Points, reserving the question of Muslim representation in the Centre for future decision and making the creation of Sind into a separate province, subject to its being financially able to maintain the administration. The award is unjust to the Hindus and Sikhs. It maintained the weightage given to Musalman representation in the Legislatures in provinces where Musalmans are in a minority. Instead of giving weightage to Hindus in Bengal it gave them only 32 per cent of the seats when they constituted 44.8 per cent of the population—in order to be able to give the very high weightage of 10 per cent of the seats to Europeans when they were only 0.01 per cent of the population. It cut down the representation of the Musalmans also but the cut in the case of the Hindus was greater than that of Musalmans. In the Punjab too, the Hindus instead of getting weightage as a minority, had their representation cut down to give some weightage to the Sikhs. The Sikhs also failed to get the weightage that Musalmans got in other provinces. The Award was naturally opposed by Hindus and Sikhs but was incorporated in the Act of 1935. Attempts to find a substitute for it by the Unity Conference of Allahabad were sabotaged by the British government and the agreement reached was nullified.

After the Act of 1935 was passed, the Muslim League took a somersault and became the most determined opponent of the Federal Scheme which it, along with the Muslim All-Parties Conference, had persistently demanded and which had been conceded by the British government and embodied in the Act of 1935. At the election that followed under the Act of 1935 the League was unable to secure any seats in four provinces and a majority of even Muslim seats in the provinces where Muslims are in a majority in the population. It could not therefore form any ministry in any province without combining with other groups and the Congress was unable to have a coalition with it in other provinces, in some of which it had no representatives at all and in none, except one, of which it had a majority even of Muslim seats. This enraged the League against the Congress and it became bitterly hostile to it. Hardly had the Congress ministries been in the saddle when it came out with its list of acts of tyranny and oppression committed by the Congress ministries against Musalmans. It may be pointed out that not one of the Governors with whom rested the responsibility of protecting minorities did once, even when invited by the Congress ministries, point to any injustice done by them to Musalmans and they indeed eulogized their administration both while they were in power and after they had resigned. An effort by the Congress to have the charges investigated by an independent and impartial person like the Chief Justice of India was rejected by Mr Jinnah. Efforts by the Congress to discuss and settle, if possible, the points of difference between it and the League were barred *in limine* by the League demand that the Congress should recognize the League as the sole representative of the Muslims of India, thus throwing overboard not only the Musalmans who were in the Congress but also other Muslim organizations, and that the Congress should treat itself as the representative of the Hindus. On the start of the Second World War the Congress ministries resigned and the Muslim League celebrated the event by observing a day of deliverance. The British government, while rejecting the Congress demand for clarification of the war aims as applicable to India and a promise of independence after the war and establishment of national government during the war, suspended the federal part of the Act of 1935 in response to the League demand and declared that no constitutional proposals would be furthered which did not command the approval and consent of important elements in the national life of India, including among them the Princes, the Musalmans, the Scheduled Castes, etc. Not content with this the League adopted the resolution for Pakistan at its Lahore session in March 1940, and made its attainment a part of its creed at the following annual session at Madras.

Till then the League, as all other Muslim organizations, had been content to regard the Muslims as a minority community in India whose interests needed to be safeguarded. Various suggestions for safeguarding them, beginning with separate electorates and weightage in representation and ending with the Fourteen Points, were made, and adopted from time to time by the British government. One of the most important of these proposals was that the Government of India should be of the federal type and this too, was accepted. All this did not satisfy the League and it decided to have independent Muslim states in the north-western and eastern zones of India where Muslims were in a majority. In the course of the negotiations which took place during the Second World War between the League and the British government, the League demanded (i) that Pakistan should be conceded and that in any case nothing should be said or done in the interim which would prejudice it when the constitutional problem was finally settled, (ii) that in the interim expansion of the Viceroy's Executive Council, the Muslim representation should be equal to that of the Hindus in case Congress representatives were taken but that the Muslims should be in a majority if the Congress did not join, and (iii) that the Muslim members should be nominees of the Muslim League and no others. The Muslim League posed as the champion and protector of rights of other minorities against the tyranny of Hindus and the Congress. It treated the Scheduled Castes as separate from the Hindus and as a minority. The British government practically accepted the first demand by conceding to provinces the right of secession from the Indian Union. It did not accept in so many words the second demand, but conceded it in action by appointing an equal number of Hindus and Musalmans on the Executive Council. Curiously enough, the Hindu Mahasabha acquiesced in this position, allowing its representatives to join the Executive Council. The British government did not accept the third demand and preserved intact its right to appoint whomsoever it liked. The Congress was insistent that the independence of India should be assured and that there should be a present transfer of power to Indians in all matters except in regard to the actual conduct of the war. The British government's rejection of these demands led to the All-India Congress Committee resolution passed

at Bombay on 8 August 1942 sanctioning civil disobedience, the
sudden arrest of Congress leaders and the events that followed
it. The Muslim League treated the August resolution as being
directed against the Muslims and insisted on its withdrawal. The
British government, however, came forward with fresh proposals
known as the Wavell proposals and released the members of the
Congress Working Committee to enable them to consider the
proposals. Lord Wavell convened a Conference to which were
invited leaders of the Congress and the League and the leaders of
parties in the Central Legislature and Prime Ministers of Provinces.
In the proposals, a fundamental item was that in the Executive
Council there would be parity of representation between Muslims
and Hindus exclusive of the Scheduled Castes. As stated above,
this parity has been in action since 1941 but was now accepted
by the British government as an essential part of the proposals.
The Conference failed. The Muslim League insisted that only
its nominees and no others should be appointed as the Muslim
representatives on the Council. Mr Jinnah was dissatisfied further
because in the proposed Executive the Muslims would be reduced
to a minority of one-third inasmuch as 'all the other minorities such
as the Scheduled Castes, Sikhs and Christians have the same goal
as the Congress 'and 'in the actual working and practice invariably
their votes will be against us [Muslims] and there is no safeguard
for us except the Viceroy's veto which, it is well known to any
constitutionalist, cannot be lightly exercised.' When parity between
Hindus and Musalmans is acted upon in practice and conceded
in terms, Mr Jinnah would insist on parity between Musalmans
on the one hand and the Hindus who are the majority and all
other minorities put together on the other. Indeed, even such a
parity may not provide a sufficient safeguard and a majority of
Muslims may become the next demand.

We have thus since 1930 three stages in the evolution of the
Muslim League demands and British concessions. In the first stage,
federation and effective and adequate representation in legislatures
for minorities are insisted upon. Since in some provinces Musalmans
are in a majority and other communities constitute minorities, and
the latter may demand the same weightage as is given to Muslims
in Muslim-minority provinces, effective and adequate representation
of minorities is limited by the proviso that in no case should a
majority be reduced to a minority or even to equality in any

province. The British government accepts federation. It conceded heavy weightage to Muslims in provinces where they are in a minority. It refuses such weightage to Hindus in Bengal and in the Punjab where they are in a minority and in Bengal it gives them less representation than their proportion in the population and indeed imposes upon them a larger cut than on Muslims for providing extra representation to Europeans.

In the second stage the League rejects Federation as soon as it is conceded by the British government and embodied in the Act of 1935, and demands creation of independent Muslim States in the north-western and eastern zones of India. It gives up its insistence on the proviso that in no case should a majority be reduced to a minority or even equality, when that applies to the non-Muslim majority and demands that there should be equality between the Hindu majority and the Muslim minority, if the Congress cooperates, but if the Congress does not cooperate, then the Hindu majority should be reduced to a minority and the Muslim minority given a majority. The British government suspends the federation and promises that no constitutional scheme would be accepted which did not secure the approval of Muslims. It accepts equality of representation between Hindus and Muslims in practice.

In the third stage, the British government accepts parity between Hindu and Muslim representation as an essential part of its proposals. The League rejects the government proposals because it is not allowed to nominate all the Muslim representatives and further points out that the majority community of the Hindus and all other minorities like the Scheduled Castes, Sikhs and Christians will always act together and the Muslims would be in a minority and unable to safeguard their interests. The interests of the Muslim minority cannot be safeguarded unless that minority is given a majority in the Executive as against not only the Hindu majority but as against the Hindu majority and all other minorities combined together.

In this race between Muslim League demands and British government concessions the League is always ahead of the British government by a few lengths, and the Hindu majority and all other minorities cannot have even an entry. No wonder the base of the communal triangle lengthens and the angle of communal differences widens.

PART III

SCHEMES OF PARTITION

We have considered at some length the thesis that Hindus and Musalmans constitute two separate nations and we have seen how during the long period of Muslim rule in India, a culture which was neither exclusively Hindu nor exclusively Muslim but a Hindu–Muslim culture—a Hindustani way—was developing as a result of conscious effort on the part of both Muslims and Hindus and of the reaction of economic, political, social and religious factors, which were operating all through the period. We have also seen that the two nations theory has been improvised only during the last few years to support the proposal for division of India into Muslim and non-Muslim states. There is, however, no denying the fact that the All-India Muslim League has resolved more than once since 1940 to achieve this division, and the All-India Muslim League does represent a great many Musalmans. It is therefore necessary to consider the proposal on its merits, apart from the argument by which it is supported. A great deal has been spoken and written for and against the proposal. On both sides passionate pleading has been indulged in and not a little sentimentalism brought into play. Sentiment has its value and should not be lightly cast off. Nor can it be nonchalantly brushed aside. But it can certainly be checked and regulated in the light of hard realities and facts which have a knack of asserting themselves at most critical moments and upsetting many a plan that has ignored them. I propose, therefore, to place some facts for the consideration of all those who are interested in the problem, whether as supporters or opponents. But before proceeding to do that, I may summarize the various proposals for the division of India into independent States or for the redistribution of her various component provinces and States on a cultural basis and for cultural purposes. It is necessary to do so as the All-India Muslim League has not yet published any detailed plan and has contented itself with laying down some general principles on which the proposed division should be based. Many plans were published before the All-India Muslim League passed its first resolution on the subject at its annual session at Lahore in March 1940; but the League, instead of adopting any of them or formulating a separate plan of its own, thought fit to resolve only on principles, leaving the plan to be worked out later. It has not published any plan up to this moment, although five years have elapsed since the general principles were enunciated. Anyone wishing to consider the' League proposal on its merits is thus put at a disadvantage and has to consider the various plans published from time to time by individuals or by groups who do not and cannot claim any authority on behalf of the League. It may also be pointed out at this stage, as will be seen from the discussion that follows, that none of the schemes so far published coincides with, or can be legitimately said to fulfil, the basic principles which the League has laid down in its resolution. It is nevertheless useful to summarize these schemes and to point out in what respect they fail to satisfy the tests laid down by the League.

The schemes which have been published from time to time fall into two categories:

(i)   Schemes for creation of independent Muslim and non-Muslim States, and

(ii)   Schemes for re-distribution of provinces and States from a cultural point of view and for cultural purposes. The main and fundamental difference between the two sets of schemes lies in the fact that those included in the first category contemplate completely independent Muslim and non-Muslim States, each having its own arrangement for defence, foreign policy and development, and definitely discarding any central authority having even limited power on the different parts; those in the second class while conceding considerable autonomy to each part contemplate a Central or federal authority with some power, however limited, over the whole country.

~

SEVENTEEN

A SCHEME FOR A 'CONFEDERACY OF INDIA'

This is a scheme by 'A Punjabi' published in a book bearing that name and is worked out in some detail. According to this scheme, the present subcontinent of India can be split up into various countries on the following lines and reassembled in a Confederacy of India:

(i) *The Indus Regions' Federation* with the Punjab (minus its eastern Hindu tracts comprising the Ambala division, Kangra district and Una and Garhshankar tahsils of the Hoshiarpur district), Sind, the North-West Frontier Province, Baluchistan, Bahawalpur, Amb, Dir, Swat, Chitral, Khairpur, Kalat, Las Bela, Kapurthala, and Malerkotla as its federal units. The author has calculated that this federation of the Indus region, which he proposes to name as 'Indus-stan 'will comprise an area of 3,98,838 sq. miles with a population of about 3,30,00,000, of whom about 82 per cent will be Muslims, about 6 per cent Sikhs, and about 8 per cent Hindus.

(ii) *The Hindu India Federation* with the United Provinces, the Central Province, Bihar with some portions of Bengal, Orissa, Assam, Madras, Bombay and the Indian States, other than Rajasthan and Deccan states included in the Deccan States' Federation, as its federal units. He has not worked out the area and population of these units except the Bengal Federation but they will be as follows:

Area	..	..	7,42,173 sq. miles
Population	..	..	21,60,41,541
Percentage of Hindus		..	83.72
Percentage of Muslims	..	11.0	

(iii) *The Rajasthan Federation* with the various states of Rajputana and Central India as its federal units. The area and population will be as follows:

Area	..	..	..	180,656 sq. miles
Population	..	..	..	1,78,58,502
Percentage of Hindus	..	86.39		
Percentage of Muslims	..	8.09		

(iv) *The Deccan States' Federation* comprising the Hyderabad, Mysore, and Bastar States. Their area and population are as follows:

Area	..	..	..	1,25,086 sq. miles
Population	..	..	..	2,15,18,171
Percentage of Hindus	..	85.82		
Percentage of Muslims	..	8.09		

(v) *The Bengal Federation*—The prominent Muslim tracts of Eastern Bengal and Goalpara and Sylhet districts of Assam as its provincial units and Tripura and other States lying within the provincial unit or cut off by its territories from Hindu India as its States' units. The area and population of this federation will be as follows:

Area	..	..	..	70,000 sq. miles
Population	..	..	..	3,10,00,00
Muslim	..	..	..	2,05,00,000 or 66.1 per cent
Hindu	..	..	..	1,01,00,000 or 32.6 per cent

'A Punjabi' admits that not being familiar with the conditions prevailing in this area, his suggestion is subject to adjustments which local Muslims may consider necessary. His figures, too, do not appear to be quite accurate, although they roughly represent the percentages. The districts of Bengal which he includes in this federation are Dinajpur, Rangpur, Malda, Bogra, Rajshahi, Murshidabad, Pabna, Mymensingh, Nadia, Jessore, Faridpur, Dacca, Tippera, Noakhali, Bakarganj, Khulna and Chittagong.

Thus of the five federations into which India would be divided according to this scheme, two will be Muslim federations with Muslim majorities and the remaining three will be Hindu federations in which the population will be overwhelmingly Hindu. It is noteworthy, however, that in the Indusstan Federation there will be a Hindu population of 8 per cent and Sikh population of 6 per cent—or a non-Muslim minority population of 14 per cent; while in the Bengal Federation the Hindus will be no less than 32.6 per cent. In the three Hindu federations the Muslims who will be the minority will form 11, 8.09 and 8.9 per cent.

The five federations will be assembled in a Confederacy. 'In a confederation of India on the lines chalked out above each federation joining it can have a governor-general with governors of its provincial units under him, responsible to the central confederal authority in relation to the confederal subjects and matters relating to the rights and obligations of the Crown in respect of the Indian states within the federation. The confederal authority can be vested in the Viceroy assisted by a confederal assembly consisting of members drawn from the various Indian Federations. The number of such members to be drawn from a federation can be fixed according to its importance judged from the point of view of its significance to the confederacy as regards its geographical situation in the sub-continent, population, area, economic position, etc. Foreign relations, defence, matters relating to water-supply from the common natural sources, and rights and obligations of the Crown in relation to the Indian states (which may join any of the British provinces' Federations), can be entrusted to their governor-generals who will be responsible to the Viceroy. The various federations joining the confederacy can either directly contribute towards the revenues of the confederacy or assign some portions of their revenues from some specific heads towards its expenses.'[1] 'Under no circumstances should the Muslims of North-West consent to assign customs as a source of the confederal revenues.' The author is at pains to point out two things. In the first place this quinquepartite confederation 'does not mean breaking up the geographical unity of the Indian sub-continent by tearing it up into pieces and assigning them to the communities on a population and cultural basis. It simply means internal partition effected between the various members of a joint family without breaking their ritually bond of relationship. Consequently, separation means assigning different parts of the sub-continent to different communities on cultural basis and their reunion in a confederacy.'[2] In the second place—'we should also make it clear to those Muslim separationists who want separation in order to link their destinies with states outside the Indian sub-continent, that in demanding separation we should not be inspired by any such extra-territorial ideals, ambitions, or affinity. We should be

[1] *Confederacy of India*, by 'A Punjabi', pp. 12–13.
[2] Ibid., p. 15.

separationists-cum-federationists, and, if the Hindus disagree with
the idea of a confederacy of a Hindu India and a Muslim India,
then we should be simply separationists, demanding secession of
our regions from Hindu India without any link between them . . .
The foreign element amongst us is quite negligible and we are as
much sons of the soil as the Hindus are. Ultimately our destiny lies
within India and not out of it. And it is for this reason that we have
abstained from using the word "Pakistan" and have instead used
the word "Indus-stan" to denote the North-West Muslim block.'[3]
But that this is not going to remain the final objective is apparent
from the following in the last pages of the book: 'It is necessary to
make it clear that the separation of our regions from Hindu India
is not an end in itself, but only a means for the achievement of
an ideal Islamic state. The proposed separation will undoubtedly
lead to our emancipation from the economic slavery of the Hindus.
But as our object is the establishment of an ideal Islamic state,
it also denotes complete independence. After independence has
been achieved, it would be impossible for us to maintain for long
in an un-Islamic world, our ideal of an Islamic state. As such,
we shall have to advocate a world revolution on Islamic lines.
Consequently our ultimate ideal is a world revolution on purely
Islamic lines. Separation, emanciption from the economic slavery
of the Hindus, and freedom from the constitutional slavery of the
British, are only some of the means for the achievement of our
ultimate ideal of a world revolution on completely Islamic lines.'[4]
The author does not like exchange of population and says: 'We
would prefer separation of the predominant Muslim regions from
Hindu India without any exchange of population. Indus Regions
minus the Ambala division and other Hindu tracts of the Punjab
in the North-West and Chittagong, Dacca and Rajshahi Divisions
of Bengal with the Districts of Goalpara and Sylhet of Assam in
the East can be easily separated from India and constituted into
two separate states. In this sense, separation will help 2,57,14,657
Muslims of the Indus Regions and about 2,30,00,000 of Bengal and
Assam to escape Hindu domination, while 2,89,63,343 Muslims
will remain in Hindu provinces.'[5] In other words, about 63 per
cent of the Muslims will, to use the author's expression, 'escape

[3] 'A Punjabi', *Confederacy of India*, p. 17.

[4] Ibid., pp. 269–70.

[5] Ibid., p. 204.

Hindu domination' and just more than 37 per cent will remain under that domination.

This scheme differs fundamentally from the Muslim League proposal in that it contemplates a confederacy. There will be a confederal or central authority which will deal with confederal subjects including 'foreign relations, defence and matters relating to water-supply from the common natural sources and rights and obligations of the Crown in relation to the Indian states.'[6] According to the scheme the Muslim regions will not be completely independent states, with full control finally of defence, foreign affairs, communications, customs and such other matters as may be necessary. In its essence it is a scheme not for creating completely independent Muslim States and non-Muslim States but one for redistribution of the various parts of the country into five zones, each of which will have several subordinate zones. The subordinate zones will be more or less autonomous and will constitute federations. Those federations will be assembled into a confederacy of the whole country.

The Muslim League resolution says nothing, as will be seen later, about Indian states; but this scheme includes all the states and places them under one federation or another.

It frankly does not contemplate independence of India or any part of it from the British empire and bases itself on the continuance of the offices of the Governor-General, the Viceroy and the Governors.

It tries roughly to satisfy the test of the Muslim League resolution that 'the area in which the Muslims are numerically in a majority as in the north-western and Eastern Zones—with such territorial readjustments as may be necessary', should be grouped to constitute independent states. In doing so it excludes certain areas from the Punjab and some from Bengal in which Muslims are in a minority, but in working this out it is not quite correct, as some other areas also should be excluded from the Muslim State on the same basis. For example, the whole of the Jullundar division ought to be excluded from the Indus-stan Federation as Muslims are in a minority in each of the districts of that division, the Hindus and the Sikhs forming a majority. If we take the three principal communities separately district by district of

[6] Ibid., p. 13.

that division, the Hindus form an overwhelming majority in the
districts of Kangra and Hoshiarpur. There are more Sikhs than
Muslims in the district of Ludhiana. In the districts of Jullundar
and Ferozepur alone, the Muslims are more than the Hindus
and Sikhs taken singly, but less than the Hindus and Sikhs taken
jointly. In the Amritsar District of the Lahore division also the
Hindus and Sikhs jointly constitute a majority, the Muslims being
in a minority, the proportion of non-Muslims to Muslims being
approximately 54 to 46. In the Bengal Federation also, he is not
justified in including the district of Goalpara where the Muslims
are in a minority as against the non-Muslims. As the separation
is to be for creating Muslim units, there is no reason why any
area in which Muslims are in a minority as compared with non-
Muslims should be included in the Muslim unit.

Apart from other criticisms to which all schemes of separation
are open and which will be dealt with later, the scheme of 'A
Punjabi' lends itself to certain comments which are peculiar to
itself. The five federations into which the country is to be divided
do not appear to be based on any intelligible principle except that
a majority of the inhabitants of the two Muslim federations are
Musalmans. The Hindu federation comprises no fewer than six
regions separated each from others by other federations intervening.
It spreads from the Himalayas to Cape Comorin and from the
north-eastern corner of India bordering on China and Burma to
the Arabian Sea. Several corridors have to be provided to connect
one portion with another. Several tracts are torn from their natural
surroundings and tacked onto others from which they are separated
by long distances. Within this vast area all the languages; that are
spoken in the whole of India except Sindi, Baluchi and Pushto will
be found to be spoken. Similarly, the inhabitants of this area will
be found to follow each and every religion of the country, only
their numbers and proportions will be different. It will contain
portions of British India and Indian States. If this can form one
federation with more than two crores of Muslims and all the
other differences and diversities within it, there is no reason why
the whole of India cannot form one federation. If the Rajputana
and Central India Agency States form one federation, there is no
reason why Bastar, which naturally by language belongs to the
Chhattisgarh or Orissa States, should be torn from them and
attached to the Hyderabad federation. Similarly, there is no reason

why Travancore and Cochin, which are more or less contiguous to Mysore, should be attached to the Hindu federation and torn away from the Deccan States' Federation. Within the Hyderabad State, three languages are spoken by the inhabitants—Marathi, Telugu and Kanarese—apart from Urdu which is the language of the Ruler. The addition of Mysore and Cochin and Travancore will add only one more language to the Federation, viz. Malayalam which is spoken in Cochin and Travancore, the language of Mysore being Kanarese.

There was an outline of a scheme suggested by Mr M.R.T. published in the *Eastern Times* which is reproduced in *India's Problem of her Future Constitution*. As it follows more or less closely the scheme of division suggested by 'A Punjabi', it is not given here separately.

EIGHTEEN

THE ALIGARH PROFESSORS' SCHEME

The second scheme is that proposed by Professors Syed Zafrul Hasan and Mohammed Afzal Husain Qadri of Aligarh. It is to divide India into several wholly independent and sovereign states as follows:

(i)   *Pakistan* comprising the Punjab, NWFP, Sind, Baluchistan, and the states of Kashmir and Jammu, Mandi, Chamba, Sakit, Sumin, Kapurthala, Malerkotla, Chitral, Dir, Kalat, Loharu, Bilaspur, Simla-Hill states, Bahawalpur, etc. Population 3,92,74,244—Muslims 2,36,97,538—60.3 per cent

(ii) *Bengal* (excluding Howrah and Midnapur districts), Purnea district (Bihar), Sylhet division (Assam). Population 5,25,79,232—Muslims 3,01,18,184—57.0 per cent

(iii) *Hindustan* comprising the rest of India and Indian States (excluding Hyderabad, Pakistan, Bengal and the States included therein). Population 21,60,00,000—Muslims 2,09,60,000—9.7 per cent

(iv) *Hyderabad* comprising Hyderabad, Berar and Karnatak (Madras and Orissa). Population 2,90,65,098—Muslims 21,44,010—7.5 per cent

(v)   *Delhi Province* including Delhi, Meerut division, Rohilkhund division and the district of Aligarh (Agra division) Population 1,26,60,000—Muslims 35,20,000—28 per cent

(vi) *Malabar Province* consisting of Malabar and adjoining areas, that is, Malabar and South Kanara. Population 49,00,000—Muslims 14,40,000—27 per cent

Further, all the towns of India with a population of 50,000 or more shall have the status of a borough or free city, with a large measure of autonomy. These will have a Muslim population of

13,88,698. The Muslims in the rural areas of Hindustan must be persuaded not to remain scattered in negligible minorities as they do at present but to aggregate in villages with a preponderant Muslim population.

The aforesaid three States of Pakistan, Bengal and Hindustan should enter into a defensive and offensive alliance on the following basis:

(i)   Mutual recognition and reciprocity.

(ii)   That Pakistan and Bengal be recognized as the homeland of Muslims and Hindustan as the homeland of Hindus, to which they can migrate respectively, if and when they want to do so.

(iii)   In Hindustan, the Muslims are to be recognized as a nation in minority and part of a larger nation inhabiting Pakistan and Bengal.

(iv)   The Muslim minority in Hindustan and non-Muslim minority in Pakistan and Bengal will have (a) representation according to population and (b) separate electorates and representation at every stage, together with effective safeguards guaranteed by all the three states. Separate representation according to population may be granted to all considerable minorities in the three States, such as Sikhs, non-caste Hindus.

(v)   An accredited Muslim political organization will be the sole official representative body of the Muslims in Hindustan.

Each of the three independent States of Pakistan, Hindustan and Bengal will have separate treaties of alliance with Great Britain and separate Crown representatives, if any. They will have a joint court of arbitration to settle any dispute that may arise between themselves or between them and the Crown.

Hyderabad commands a position which is exclusively its own. It is recognized as an ally by the British government. In truth it is a sovereign State by treaties. Berar and Karnatak were taken from it by the British for administrative reasons and so they must be restored. Hyderabad with its restored territories should be recognized expressly as a sovereign State, at least as sovereign as Nepal. With Karnatak restored, it will have a sea-coast and will naturally become the southern wing of Muslim India.

The scheme is open to most of the objections to which Punjabi's scheme is open and in many respects in an aggravated form. It does not even attempt to fulfil the Muslim League test of including only areas with Muslim majorities within the Muslim States, thus including the division of Ambala with a clear and overwhelming Hindu majority as also the division of Jullundar with an equally clear non-Muslim majority, in Pakistan. In the eastern zone it includes districts of Bengal which have a Hindu majority and of Assam with clear non-Muslim majorities. It includes even the district of Purnea of Bihar, which has a large Hindu majority.

It creates Hyderabad with Berar and Karnatak added to it as a sovereign Muslim State. It is not clear why it should be treated as a Muslim country when the population is so overwhelmingly Hindu—the Muslims being only 10.4 per cent of the population. If the fact that the ruler is a Muslim is the decisive and only point for making it a Muslim country, there is no reason why Kashmir, which has a Hindu ruler, should be tacked to Pakistan.

It seeks to intensify the division by creating so many separate and independent 'free cities' all over India. Since the authors have compared Hindus and Muslims to Czechs and Südeten Germans, one may compare these cities to Danzig and one can only hope that it is not intended that history should repeat itself and India see a war for the conquest of the Czechs (the Hindus) and of Hindustan (Czecho-Slovakia) on the pretext of the Indian Czechs'—the Hindus'—ill-treatment of the Indian Südetens—the Muslims, and to free the so-called free cities—the Danzigs of India.

The authors contemplate mutual recognition and reciprocity as between Hindu and Muslim States. When defining the bases of 'defensive and offensive alliance' between them, they claim that in Hindustan the Muslims are to be recognized as a nation in minority and part of a larger nation, but they make no mention of a similar right to be given to Hindus living in Pakistan and Bengal. Again, they claim that an accredited Muslim political organization will be the sole official representative body of the Muslims in Hindustan but give no such right to the Hindus and other minorities in Pakistan and Bengal to have an accredited political organization of their own to be their sole official representative.

In short, it is a scheme for creating separate independent Muslim states based on only one intelligible principle which runs through the whole scheme—heads you lose, tails we win.

~

NINETEEN

C. RAHMAT ALI'S SCHEME

The third scheme is the one contained in a pamphlet by Chaudhry Rahmat Ali entitled *The Millat of Islam and the Menace of 'Indianism'*. It was written in 1940. The writer is the Founder-President of the Pakistan National Movement, which he started in 1933. Originally, it was confined to the formulation of a demand for Pakistan, that is, for separation of the five constituent parts which give to the whole zone the name of Pakistan—Punjab, Afghania (North-West Frontier Province of which the inhabitants are mainly Afghans), Kashmir, Sind and Baluchistan. In 1940 he felt that the reception which had been given to his scheme 'encourages us not only to continue our labours in that sphere but also to initiate the second part of the programme, the part pertaining to Bengal and to Usmanistan (Hyderabad-Deccan).'[1] 'For in all human certainty, if once we agree to remain within "India", we 'shall, for ever, rot in subjection to "Indianism" which is solemnly canonized into a new cult by its clever devotees—the Indian nationalists, cringingly accepted by its miserable creatures, the Muslim careerists and cruelly supported by its self-seeking patrons the British Imperialists.'[2] He finds fault with the All-India Muslim League for its name—the All-India Muslim League, who, at long last now claim for the Millat nationality distinct from the "Indians" but still cling to "India" and call her their "common motherland".[3] 'To accept the territorial unity of "India" is to fasten the tyrannical yoke of "Indianism" on the Millat.'[4] '"Let them be conclusive and abandon "India". That is, live to sever all ties with "India", to save the Millat from "Indianism" and to save "Pax

---

[1] Chaudhry Rahmat Ali, *The Millat of Islam and the Menace of Indianism*, p. 1.
[2] Ibid., p. 4
[3] Ibid., p. 6.
[4] Ibid., pp. 11,12.

Islamica".'⁵ The author insists upon sovereign States of Pakistan, of Bengal and of Usmanistan. Assam is only a hinterland attached to Bengal and this area is to be known as Bang-i-Islam. 'It is advisable to state the pivotal fact that we derive our right to Usmanistan from those canons of International Law from which other nations deduce their claims to their domains, that this right includes her *de jure* sovereignty which is solemnly acknowledged in the treaties originally entered into between the British Government and the Ala Hazrat of Usmanistan, the "Faithful Ally"; and that this State is unique in the sub-continent in that no other state enjoys it, in the same sense and to the same extent, as does Usmanistan.' 'When that is done, we must—and we will— build on solid and secure foundations of Pakistan, Bengal and Usmanistan, three independent nations which will be larger, bigger, and more powerful than any that ever existed in history.'⁶ 'If we really wish to rid ourselves of "Indianism", to re-establish our nationhood as distinct from "India" and to link our national domains to one another as South Asiatic countries, we must scrap, the All-India Muslim League as such and create instead an alliance of the nations of Pakistan, Bengal and Usmanistan.

'For this alone would set the final seal on our separation from "India", inspire the Millat and impress the world as nothing else would. That done we would have stood the test and made the choice, we would have achieved the supreme unity of purpose, plan and effort in our strongholds and given a new birth to our sacred cause in South Asia. And then inspired by the solemn conviction in our historic mission and united under the "crescent and stars" we would carry through our fight to final victory.'⁷

The author is thus a most uncompromising protagonist of the two nations theory, or rather of Muslim States wherever they can be established. Such details as the areas to be included in them and the rights, if any, of non-Muslims living in them and of Muslims living in 'India' do not appear to him to be deserving of discussion, when he wrote this pamphlet. He is inspired by a prophetic vision and is not disturbed by such petty considerations. If Muslim States are once established, all will be right; if they are not established, nothing can be right.

⁵ Ibid., p. 14.
⁶ Rahmat Ali, *The Millat of Islam*, p. 15.
⁷ Ibid., p. 16.

Mr Rahmat Ali was not satisfied with his scheme for the establishment of Pakistan, Bangistan and Usmanistan. He inaugurated in 1942 what he calls Parts III, IV, VI and VII of the Pak Plan—'The Seven Commandments of Destiny for the Seventh Continent of Dinia' are contained in the pamphlet under the caption of *The Millat and The Mission*. They are:

(i)   Avoid minorityism.
(ii)   Avow nationalism.
(iii) Acquire proportional territory.
(iv)   Consolidate the individual nations.
(v)   Co-ordinate them under the 'Pak Commonwealth of Nations'.
(vi)   Convert 'India' into 'Dinia'.
(vii) Organize 'Dinia' and its dependencies into 'Pakasia'.

(i)   *Avoid Minorityism*—'The commandment means that we must not leave our minorities in Hindu lands, even if the British and the Hindus offer them the so-called constitutional safeguards!'

(ii)   *Avow Nationalism*—'This commandment is complementary to the previous one and means that-we must assert and demand recognition of the distinct national status of our. minorities in the Hindu majority regions of Dinia and its dependencies and reciprocally offer to give similar status to the Hindu and Sikh minorities in Pakistan, Bangistan and Usmanistan! The commandment is inspired by the truth that nationhood is to people what majority or manhood is to individuals . . . It is true that until 1940 there were colossal difficulties in the way of making such a demand for our minorities, but now they have been removed by the Sikh claim to separate national status in Pakistan. So we must make the most creative use of the claim and, on the principle of proportional territory, offer to meet it—as met it can be—in the area of the three Sikh States of Patiala, Nabha and Jhind, on the absolute condition that our demand for similar status for our minorities in the seven Hindu majority regions of Dinia and its dependencies (Siddiqistan, Faruqistan, Haideristan, Muinistan and Maplistan, Safiistan and Nasaristan) is met simultaneously by the supporters of

the Sikhs, i.e. the British and the Hindus who, by holding
out a threat of Sikh claim, have throughout the past eighty-
five; years tried to stifle our aspirations.'[8]

(iii)   *Acquire proportional territory* to create Siddiqistan,
         Faruqistan, Haideristan, Muinistan, Maplistan, Safistan
         and Nasaristan. This commandment means 'that we should
         acquire our share of the territories of the continent of Dinia
         and its dependencies and convert it into countries for our
         nation . . . for instance, in the Hindooistan (United Provinces
         of Agra and Oudh) our minority forms about 15 per cent
         of the population and we are therefore entitled to 15 per
         cent of her area. That is about 17,000 square miles, which
         we must acquire and convert into Haideristan . . . In the
         same way, the proportional area for our minorities in the
         Central Provinces, Bundelkhand and Malwa, Behar and
         Orissa, Rajasthan, the Bombay Presidency and South India,
         Western Ceylon and Eastern Ceylon must be claimed and
         converted into our new national countries of Siddiqistan,
         Faruqistan, Muinistan, Maplistan, Safiistan and Nasaristan
         respectively.'[9]

(iv)   *Consolidate the individual nations.* The commandment
         means 'that as it is dangerous to leave dispersed our
         minorities in the Hindu majority regions of Dinia and in
         Ceylon, we must unify and consolidate them as nations
         in the countries that will comprise the proportional areas
         acquired under the previous commandment.'[10]

(v)   *Co-ordinate the nations under a Pak Commonwealth of
         Nations.* This commandment means 'that we must bring
         together in an international organization at least our ten
         countries'—the -istans which the author has visualized as
         constituting Dinia.

(vi)   *Convert the subcontinent of India into Dinia.* This
         commandment means 'that we must "Liberate the soul and
         soil" of /"India" from the domination of "Indianism" into
         the domain of "Dinianism" and thereby restore her to her
         original and rightful position in the world. So we must

[8] Rahmat Ali, *The Millat and the Mission*, pp. 12–13.
[9] Ibid., pp. 13–14.
[10] Ibid., p. 16.

rededicate ourselves to our age-old ideal, and as a token
of rededication, concentrate on three fundamentals. First
we must write "finis" to the most deceptive fiction in the
world that "India" is the sphere of "Indianism", second,
we must record the most significant truth in the world,
that "India" is the domain of "Dinianism". And, third,
we must proclaim the most solid fact to the world that
the subcontinent of India is the continent of "Dinia".'[11]

(vii) *Organize the continent of Dinia and Usmanistan
dependencies into the orbit of Pakasia.*

Mr Chaudhry Rahmat Ali would not only create the three
independent States of Pakistan, Bangistan, and Usmanistan but
would also have seven Muslim nations settled in the Hindu region
in their own territory which would be proportionate to their
population and all these would constitute the Pak Commonwealth.
Even the name of India should disappear and the subcontinent
should be converted into a continent called 'Dinia' which comprises
the same letters as 'India' and the Pak Commonwealth will then
come into the orbit of Pakasia.

Mr Rahmat Ali, being the originator of the idea of Pakistan
and its name and having been first to put forward the claim for
independent Muslim States as a protest against the betrayal by
the Muslim delegates to the Round Table Conference of the cause
of the Millat by accepting a Federal Constitution, he claims that
the Muslim League has been partly converted to his views. Who
knows that in course of time the other parts of his scheme already
published and yet to be published will also be not accepted by the
League and thus Indians must be prepared to look forward for
the day when the very name India will have disappeared and, the
Millat being established all over, the continent will have acquired
the name of Dinia.

---

[11] Rahmat Ali, *The Millat and the Mission*, p. 18.

TWENTY

DR S.A. LATIF'S SCHEME

Dr S.A. Latif is the author of another scheme, which he has elaborated in his book *The Muslim Problem in India*. It is not a separatist move involving endless complications but claims to be a scheme for the unification of India on natural lines and is, therefore, entirely Indian in outlook. It seeks to have a federation of culturally homogeneous states for India to form a nation of at least the type of Canada where two different races work together for a common country, while living in separate zones of their own. It claims to be a scheme for unity and not for disruption.[1]

According to this scheme, 'India may be divided into four cultural zones for the Muslims where homogeneity may be introduced, and at least eleven for the Hindus. The Indian States interspersed all over the country may be distributed between the different zones in accordance with their natural affinities. Each such zone will form a homogeneous state with a highly decentralized form of government within, wherever more than a unit should compose the zone, but fitting along with similar states into an all-India Federation.'[2]

Muslim Cultural Zones:

(i) *North-West Block* consisting of Sind, Baluchistan, the Punjab, NWFP and the Indian States of Khairpur and Bahawalpur converted into a single autonomous State on the basis of federal relationship between the six units, thereby allowing over 25 millions of Muslims a free home of their own.

(ii) *North-East Block* comprising eastern Bengal which will include Calcutta and Assam of over 30 million Muslims who may be assigned a free political existence.

[1] S.A. Latif, *Muslim Problem in India*, pp. 28–38.
[2] Ibid., p. 30.

(iii)   *Delhi–Lucknow Block*. In between the two above-mentioned
        blocks, the Muslims are unevenly distributed. Those of
        this area living close to each of the two blocks should be
        attracted for naturalization to the one nearer to them. The
        rest, the great bulk, belonging at present to the United
        Provinces and Bihar numbering about 12 millions may be
        concentrated in a block extending in a line from the eastern
        border of Patiala to Lucknow rounding up Rampur and
        including Agra, Delhi, Cawnpore and Lucknow but leaving
        out great Hindu religious centres like Benares, Hardwar,
        Allahabad and Mathura.

(iv)   *The Deccan Block* comprising Hyderabad, Berar and a
        strip of territory restored in the south running through the
        districts of Kurnool, Cuddappah, Chittoor, North Arcot
        and Chingleput down to the city of Madras providing an
        opening to the sea. The Muslims of the Peninsula—the
        Central Province, the whole of the Bombay and Madras
        Presidencies, Mysore, Cochin and Travancore will be
        gathered in this block. The surplus population of Muslims
        from the north-east and Delhi–Lucknow blocks may also be
        settled in this. Besides the above four blocks the Muslims
        living in Rajputana, Gujarat, Malwa and Western India
        States will need to be concentrated in the territories of
        the Muslim States of Bhopal, Tonk, Junagadh, Jaora and
        others and in the nearby constituted free city of Ajmer, on
        the basis of the exchange of population.

Hindu, Cultural Zones:
 (i)   *Portions of Bengal* extended into a part of Bihar which
        has affinity with Bengal will form a zone for the Bengali
        Hindus.
 (ii)   *Orissa* comprising all Oriya-speaking people.
 (iii) *West Bihar and UP* up to the line of the Lucknow–Delhi
        Block extending from the Himalayas down to the Vindhyas
        and including some of the Central Indian States. This will
        be Hindustan proper with a rejuvenated Hindi probably
        supplying a fresh inspiration.
 (iv)   *The Rajput States* of Rajputana.
 (v)   *Gujarat* with the Hindu Kathiawar principalities where
        Gujarati culture may pursue its own life.

(vi)   Marathas.

The Dravidian group of cultures:

(vii)   The Canarese,
(viii) The Andhra,
(ix)   The Tamilian, and
(x)   The Malayali, will have their separate existence.
(xi)   *A Hindu–Sikh Block* including a portion of Kashmir in
        the north-west Muslim Block. The districts of Kashmir
        with predominant Muslim population may by mutual
        agreement be transferred to the Punjab proper and in
        return a portion of the north-east of the present Punjab
        comprising the Kangra Valley be added to the jurisdiction
        of the Maharaja. The Hindus of Sind may be assigned to
        the adjoining Hindu zones of Gujarat and Rajputana. The
        Hindu–Sikh zone will be composed of all the non-Muslim
        states at present under the Punjab States Agency and part
        of the Hindu State of Kashmir.

The demarcation indicated in the book is merely suggestive in
character and may be properly determined by a Royal Commission
appointed for the purpose.

   The scheme contemplates that the Hindus and Muslims living
in Muslim and Hindu zones respectively should be transferred
to the nearest Hindu or Muslim zones and thus comparatively
homogeneous zones should be created. Harijans should be left
to choose the Hindu or Muslim zones and form their permanent
homelands. The transference and exchange of populations should
be carried out gradually in the course of some years and may start
on a voluntary basis as an experimental measure.

The Constitution should have the following provisions:
(i)   *Public Law of Indian Nations:* Individuals belonging to
       one or other of the several nationalities may for special
       purpose live in zones to which they do not culturally belong.
       They should be afforded security of person and rights of
       citizenship.
(ii)   *Religious shrines, etc.:* Religious shrines, monuments,
       graveyards should be preserved and looked after by
       each federal state under the supervision of the central
       government.

(iii)   *Christians, Buddhists, Parsis, etc.:* The smaller nationalities will be afforded by each State all the necessary religious and cultural safeguards which might be needed to preserve their individuality. They will have the right at the same time to ask for cantonal life, if they so desire at any time.

(iv)   *Harijans:* They should be given perfect liberty to choose the Hindu or Muslim zones to form their permanent homelands where they will enjoy the fullest rights of citizenship.

The author has prepared a Constitution which may replace the Act of 1935.

It gives to every provincial federal unit as full autonomy as possible and safeguards the right of the Indian States and their rulers by reducing the federal list of subjects to a bare minimum.

It provides for zonal or regional boards for contiguous federal units possessing common affinities to evolve common policies in respect of subjects of cultural and economic importance common to them, leaving the individual units to legislate in the light of the policies so evolved.

It gives to every provincial unit and the Centre a composite, stable executive with an agreed policy instead of a parliamentary executive in the English sense.

It also provides a machinery whereby cultural and economic security may be afforded to the Muslim and other minorities at the Centre as well as in the federal units.

It is a scheme for a federation of India composed of units with as much autonomy as possible except in matters which are absolutely common to all, such as defence, foreign affairs, commerce, communications and the like, and provides that residuary powers should rest in the units.

Several cultures subsist in India and each should have freedom to develop and grow. Each should have the necessary sense of security so as to make it a willing and contented unit of the federation. A contingency in which legislation bearing on a cultural subject has to be passed by the Centre should be avoided.

With full autonomy conceded to federal units and elimination in consequence of the concurrent list, the need of a co-ordinating agency will be felt in the zones; and the zonal boards are suggested to enable such groups to evolve common policies on common problems, leaving the individual federal units, whether Indian

States or provinces, to legislate in the light of the common policies so evolved. The formation of such boards will dispense with the need of constituting such groups into sub-federations, which will simply multiply administrative and legislative paraphernalia.

As a safeguard against possible tyranny of a communal majority, the proposal provides for a stable, though composite, executive, comprising members from all groups and parties. Its policy would be the result of a compromise between different points of view arrived at by mutual agreement at a conference of representatives of political organizations of the different communities on an all-India basis. Yet the executive will not constitute a 'coalition' government which is always unstable, but a composite stable government such as exists in America. It is suggested as a basis for discussion that the Prime Minister in each province should be elected by the entire legislature to function during the lifetime of the legislature. He should be free to select his own colleagues on the executive in terms of the ratio to be fixed on an all-India basis by agreement between the communities concerned. The executive so selected by the elected Premier will not be removable by an adverse vote of the legislature.

The following safeguards for Muslims should be incorporated in the Constitution:

A. *Representation in Legislature:*

(i)   Separate electorates as well as existing proportion of Muslims in several provinces should be maintained.

(ii)   The Indian States should return to the Central Legislature a sufficient quota of Muslims, at least one-third of the seats at the Centre.

(iii)   Muslims should be allowed adequate and effective representation on the zonal or regional boards commensurate with their total strength in the Legislatures of the units composing the zone.

B.   *Legislation:* All subjects touching their religion, personal law and culture will be the concern of the Muslim members of the Legislature concerned, constituted into a special committee for the purpose, and strengthened by the co-option of, not more than a third of their number, representative Muslims learned in Muslim law and religion. The decision of this committee should be accepted by the

Legislature. Should such decision affect the interests of other communities, they might be reviewed by the Legislature as a whole, but no amendments affecting their basis should be permissible.

C. *Executive:* The Executive should be a composite Executive representing Hindus and Muslims with an agreed policy acceptable to both and not liable to be turned out by the Legislature, but independent of it as in the USA and to remain in office during the life of the legislature, the Prime Minister being elected by the entire Legislature instead of by the people as in America. He will choose his colleagues or ministers from the members of all groups in the Legislature, an equitable number of whom should be Muslims enjoying the confidence of the Muslim) members of the Legislature and should be selected from a panel suggested by them. For portfolios regarding law and order and education, a minister and an assistant minister should be appointed, one of whom should be a Muslim.

D. *Public Service Commission:* One at least of the members of the Commission in provinces where Muslims are in a minority should be a Muslim, part of whose duty shall be to see that the ratio fixed for the Muslims in public services is properly adhered to.

E. *Judiciary:* The personal law of the Muslims should be administered by Muslim judges.

F. *Muslim Board of Education and Economic Uplift:* It should be provided to control and supervise the cultural side of education of Muslims and their technical and industrial training and to devise measures of economic and social uplift.

G. *Special Taxation:* If for any special object Muslims are willing to tax themselves, the necessary legislation should be passed.

During the transitional period, migrations should be on a voluntary basis. For this legislation should be passed for each region and a Royal Commission should be appointed to lay down a suitable programme of gradual exchange of populations. The transitional Constitution should be such as to fit into the conception of the ultimate federation outlined. This will necessitate creation of certain new provinces on cultural and linguistic lines without involving immediate exchange of population. The new provinces may be constituted even piecemeal but one should be immediately carved out of the present UP which will be the permanent home for all Muslims living at present in the UP and Bihar. This newly created province should have a Muslim Prime Minister to direct its policy to become a Muslim zone.

The Latif scheme suffers from two very serious defects. It requires very extensive exchange of populations, sometimes covering long distances, and not only as between one province and another of British India but also as between provinces of British India and Indian States. The very tremendousness of the expenditure and effort involved in such exchange makes it impracticable, even though it may be spread over a number of years. Uprooting of large sections of populations from their locality and surroundings—topographical, physical and climatic—in which they have lived for generations and planting them in unknown and strange localities will cause incalculable suffering to the people concerned. Migration is intended to be voluntary in the beginning but at a later stage it will have to be made compulsory. If it is voluntary, it is not likely to be resorted to by any considerable number of either Hindus or Muslims who are both equally attached to their lands. If it is compulsory, the suffering involved will be simply unbearable. It will affect, as has been pointed out by 'A Punjabi' in *Confederacy of India,* nearly two-thirds of the total population of India. Exchange of population on such a large scale involving hundreds of millions of people and covering hundreds of thousands of square miles of territory has never been heard of or attempted in history.

Secondly, the scheme contemplates the perpetuation of the States more or less in their present condition as also of a federation under the British. It may be that the author has left the political question of relation between the ruler and the ruled open to be settled by the people as a whole, whether in British India or in the States. But in framing such a Constitution it is not possible to leave such a fundamental question open and to concentrate on the communal aspect of it alone. All political parties in India have by their resolutions expressed their agreement about independence being their goal, except perhaps the liberals who consider dominion status as equivalent to independence. So also is it impossible to allow the autocratic form of government that subsists in the Indian

States to continue and it must be replaced by a democratic form in which the utmost that the Princes can expect for themselves will be limited constitutional monarchy like that of England, power being transferred to representatives of the people.

The author has said that the demarcation made by him is only suggestive and may have to be settled by a Royal Commission or other agreed agency. Any criticism, therefore, of the scheme will also be equally provisional. It may, however, be pointed out that the proposed Deccan Block comprising Hyderabad, Berar and a strip of territory restored in the south running through the districts of Kurnool, Cuddappah, Chittoor and North Arcot and Chingleput down to the city of Madras seems to have no foundation, as the Muslim population in the whole of this area, even after its augmentation by the transfer of the entire Muslim population of the CP, the Bombay and Madras Presidencies, and Mysore, Cochin and Travancore, will have an area allotted to it out of all proportion to its numbers as compared with other areas allotted to the non-Muslim population. It will not be a linguistic province but will have Marathi, Telugu, Canarese and also to some extent Tamil within it. If there is to be a redistribution, there is no reason why the portions speaking these languages in Hyderabad should not be taken to the portions of India where they are spoken by larger numbers of people. This involves a break up of the Hyderabad State. If that has to be avoided it may be done without further complicating the problem by bringing in other areas from British India under it. It is a question not free from doubt whether the Muslims in that area with all the addition to their population that is contemplated by transfer from other parts will still have a majority.

The introduction of zonal boards seems to be a superfluity. The units are either autonomous or not. It does not improve matters if an additional authority in between them and the central federation is introduced. Any subject of common interest between two or more units may be dealt with by *ad hoc* arrangement if the Centre is not trusted to deal with such matters even at the request of the units concerned. It is unnecessary to discuss here in detail the other provisions regarding the Constitution, as many of these provisions have to be worked out in detail. The USA or the Swiss Constitution may furnish us with models on which to base a Constitution for India with necessary changes and modifications to suit Indian conditions, if that satisfies the Muslims. But that is a subject which may not be dealt with here and, may be, its mixing up with territorial re-distribution and exchange of vast populations will complicate its discussion on its merits.

~

TWENTY-ONE

SIR SIKANDAR HAYAT KHAN'S SCHEME

Another scheme is that proposed by the late Sir Sikandar Hayat
Khan in his pamphlet *Outlines of a Scheme of Indian Federation*
in which not only the British Indian provinces but also the Indian
States join.

(1)   For the purpose of establishing this All-India Federation
      on a regional basis the country shall be demarcated into
      seven zones:

   (i)   *Assam and Bengal* (minus one or two western districts
         to reduce the size of the zone); *Bengal States* and
         Sikkim.

   (ii) *Bihar* and *Orissa* plus the area transferred from Bengal
         to Orissa.

   (iii) *United Provinces* and *UP States.*

   (iv) *Madras* and *Travancore, Madras States* and *Coorg.*

   (v)   *Bombay* and *Hyderabad; Western India States* and
         Bombay States; Mysore and *CP States.*

   (vi) *Rajputana States* (minus Bikaner and Jaisalmer); *Gwalior
         and Central India States; Bihar and Orissa States; CP
         and Berar.*

   (vii) *Punjab, and Sind; NWFP and Kashmir; Punjab States
         and Baluchistan; Bikaner and Jaisalmer.*

The demarcation here suggested is only tentative and may be
altered, if necessary.

(2)   There shall be a Regional Legislature for each zone
      consisting of representatives of both British India and
      Indian States units included in that zone. Every unit will
      send representatives in accordance with the share allotted
      to it in the schemes embodied in the Government of India
      Act, 1935, for representation in the Federal Assembly.

(3)   The representatives in the various Regional Legislatures shall collectively constitute the Central Federal Assembly which will consist of 375 members (250 from British India and 125 from the Indian States) subject to what is stated below in paragraph 21.

(4)   One-third of the total number of representatives in the Federal Assembly shall be Muslims.

(5)   The other minorities shall be allotted the share apportioned to them in the Federal Assembly by the Government of India Act, 1935.

(6)   The Regional Legislature shall deal only with subjects included in the Regional list but may, at the request of two or more units included in the zone, legislate with regard to subjects falling in the provincial list. Such enactments would, for application in any unit within the region, require confirmation by the government of the unit concerned and shall thereafter supersede any provincial or state legislation on the subject.

(7)   In the Regional Legislature no Bill or measure on a subject in the Regional list shall be considered to have been passed unless two-thirds of the representatives vote in its favour to give additional security to smaller units.

(8)   The Regional Legislatures may by resolution authorize the Federal Legislature to undertake legislation regarding subjects in the regional or provincial list. But such authorization shall not be effective unless at least four out of the seven zones ask for such action. And unless such authorization is endorsed by all the seven Regional Legislatures the enactment so passed shall have force only in the zones which ask for such legislation.

(9)   Any law enacted by the Federal Legislature at the request of the zones and by the Regional Legislatures at the request of the units shall be repealed if in the case of the Federal Legislature at least three zones, and in the case of Regional Legislatures at least half the number of units in that zone ask for its repeal.

(10)   The Federal Executive shall consist of the Viceroy representing the King-Emperor and a Council of Ministers not less than seven and not more than eleven in number, including the Federal Prime Minister.

(11) The Federal Prime Minister shall be appointed by the Viceroy from among the members of the Federal Legislature and the remaining ministers also from among the members of the Legislature in consultation with the Federal Prime Minister but subject to the following:

(i) That each zone shall have at least one representative in the Cabinet.

(ii) That at least one-third of the ministers shall be Muslims.

(iii) That at least two if the number of ministers does not exceed nine, and at least three if it exceeds nine, shall be chosen from amongst the representatives of Indian States.

There will be no objection to (ii) and (iii) overlapping. Every attempt shall be made to provide adequate representation to other important minorities also.

(iv) That during the first twenty (or fifteen) years from the inauguration of the Federal Scheme the Viceroy may nominate two of his ministers with the portfolios of 'defence' and 'external affairs', either from amongst the members of the Legislature or from outside. Thereafter all the ministers shall be selected from amongst the members of the Legislature.

The following tentative allocation of portfolios and designation of members is suggested:

(1) Federal Prime Minister.
(2) Minister of Defence.
(3) Minister of External Affairs; also to deal with Indian States.
(4) Federal Finance Minister.
(5) Minister of Interior (Home).
(6) Minister of Communications.
(7) Minister to look after Minority Interests.
(8) Minister of Co-ordination to keep in touch with Regions and arrange co-ordination and uniformity in matters of common concern.
(9) Minister of Commerce and Industries.

(12) (i)   The normal term of office of ministers shall be the same as the life of the Federal Legislature (i.e. five years),

(ii)   The ministers will retain office at the pleasure of the Viceroy.

(iii)   A minister representing a particular zone shall be removed if he loses the confidence of a majority of his Regional Legislature.

(iv)   The ministry as a whole except the ministers referred to in paragraph 11 (iv) shall resign if a vote of no-confidence against the ministry is carried in the Federal Legislature.

(13)   The representatives of the Regional Legislature shall be chosen in the following manner:

(i)   In the case of British Indian units by the Provincial Legislature in accordance with the procedure laid down in the Government of India Act, 1935, for the election of representatives to the Federal Assembly.

(ii)   In the case of Indian States as nearly as may be possible in accordance with the procedure outlined hereunder:

(a)   During the first ten years from the date of inauguration of the Regional and Federal Legislatures three-fourths to be nominated by the Ruler and one-fourth to be selected by him out of a panel to be elected by the State Assembly or other similar institution which shall be set up for this purpose.

(b)   During the next five years two-thirds to be nominated by the Ruler and one-third to be elected as in (a).

(c)   After fifteen years one-half to be nominated and one-half to be elected as in (a) above.

(d)   After twenty years and thereafter one-third to be nominated and two-thirds to be elected as in (a) above. If the number of seats allotted to a State or group of States is less than two, then the Ruler shall nominate for the first fifteen years and thereafter the State's representatives shall be elected as in (a) above.

(14)   There shall be a Committee of Defence to advise in matters relating to defence, with the Viceroy as President, and consisting of—the Federal Prime Minister; the ministers for Defence, External Affairs, Finance and Communications;

the Commander-in-Chief; the Chief of the General Staff; a senior naval officer; a senior air force officer; seven regional representatives—one from each zone; five official experts to be nominated by the Viceroy; two non-officials to be nominated by the Viceroy; and the Secretary of the Defence Department.

(15) A Committee shall be constituted to advise on matters connected with External Affairs consisting of the Viceroy as President, and the Federal Prime Minister, the Minister for External Affairs, seven regional representatives (one from each zone) to be selected by the President from amongst the members of Regional Legislatures, two officials and two non-officials to be nominated by the Viceroy, and the Secretary for External Affairs, as members.

If in any of these committees the number of State representatives falls short of 3, the difference shall be made up by the appointment of additional members selected by the President from a panel proposed by the Chamber of Princes.

(16) The Federal railway authority shall be so constituted as to include at least one representative from each of the seven regional zones.

(17) Effective Safeguards shall be provided in the Constitution:

(i) for the protection of the legitimate interests of the minorities;

(ii) to prevent racial discrimination against British-born subjects;

(iii) against violation of treaty and other contract rights of the Indian States;

(iv) to preserve the integrity and autonomy of both British Indian and Indian States units against interference by the Federal Executive or Federal or Regional Legislature;

(v) to ensure the safety of India against foreign aggression and the peace and tranquillity of the units as also of the country as a whole;

(vi) to prevent subversive activities by the citizens of a unit or a zone against another unit or zone;

(vii) to protect the culture and religious rights of the minorities.

(18)   The composition of the Indian Army (as on 1 January 1937) shall not be altered. In the event of reduction or increase in its peace-time strength, the proportion of the various communities as on 1 January 1937 shall not be disturbed. This may be relaxed in the event of war or other grave emergency which may arise on account of a threat to the safety of the country.

(19)   Only those subjects, the retention of which is essential in the interests of the country as a whole and for its proper administration, shall be allocated to the Centre, for example, defence, external affairs, communications, customs, coinage and currency, etc. The remaining subjects at present included in the Federal List shall belong to the units or zones. Residuary powers in regard to subjects which are not specifically included in the Federal List shall vest in the units and in the case of subjects allocated to zones, in the Regional Legislatures.

(20)   In case of doubt whether a subject is federal, concurrent, regional, or provincial (or State), the decision of the Viceroy in his discretion shall be final.

(21)   The Federal Legislature shall be unicameral, provided that additional seats distributed equally among the seven zones may be given to the Federal Assembly to enable special interests which are now given representation in the Upper House (the Council of State) to be represented in it.

(22)   Adequate and effective machinery shall be set up both at the Centre and in the provinces to look after and protect the interests of the minorities.

It is claimed for the scheme that instead of bringing British Indian provinces and Indian States into the federation as two distinct components, it provides for their entrance on a regional basis which will be conducive, to the solidarity of the country and stability of the central government. It will for the same reason encourage collaboration between contiguous units whose geographical proximity, common language, and affinity of economic interest form natural ties and thus facilitate reciprocal arrangement among various units of a zone about a common line of action pertaining to law and order, establishment of institutes of industrial and agricultural research, experimental agricultural farms, etc. It will permit British and States' units to enter the federation without doubts and misgivings both *inter se* and as regards interference by the Centre in the internal affairs, as the federal jurisdiction will be limited. It will, while giving minorities a greater sense of security, effectively safeguard the integrity and autonomy of the units.

On the other hand, it may be pointed out that the scheme is avowedly only a scheme of amendment of the Government of India Act, 1935, and does not aim at the independence of India. It does not contemplate democratic election in the Indian States at any time even in the future and seeks to join in the federal as also in the Regional Legislatures two classes of men as members—those coming from British India being elected representatives of the people, and those coming from the States being nominees, pure and simple, of the Princes or in some cases nominated out of elected panels. It provides for outsiders who are not elected representatives being appointed by the Viceroy as members of the Cabinet in charge of the two important portfolios of defence and foreign affairs. It destroys joint responsibility of the Cabinet by making the individual ministers responsible to their respective Regional Legislatures and by maintaining the outside members in office in spite of a vote of no-confidence of the Federal Legislature. It unduly limits the field for the choice of ministers by requiring from them communal, regional and States qualifications, which it may be difficult to reconcile with ability and efficiency and which will also involve divided allegiance. Its great merit is that it does not seek to divide the country on communal lines either for political or cultural purposes, and regards India as one single country.

~

TWENTY-TWO

SIR ABDULLAH HAROON COMMITTEE'S SCHEME

In February 1940, the Foreign Committee of the All-India Muslim League had issued invitations to the authors of the various schemes of constitutional reform of India to meet together under its auspices jointly to examine the various schemes and see whether (i) consolidated scheme could not be framed. The invitees met and constituted themselves into a committee and prepared a scheme at its subsequent meetings on the basis of the resolution of the All-India Muslim League at its Lahore Session which had been framed in the light of an outline placed by Sir Abdullah Haroon, the Secretary of the Foreign Committee, in the hands of Mr M.A. Jinnah, the President. The Committee, however, drew up a plan to cover the Muslims in non-British India as well, and it is thus fuller than the one revealed in the Pakistan resolution.

The Committee recommended that

(1)   One Muslim State can be formed in the north-west in which the percentage of Muslims will be in the vicinity of 63 and

(2)   The other in the north-east with a Muslim population of 54 per cent.

TABLE III

(I) North-Western State or Zone (1931 Census)

		Total population	Muslim population
Punjab		2,35,80,852	1,33,32,460
Sind		38,87,070	28,30,800
NWF (Settled)		24,25,076	22,27,303
NWF Tribal area administered by British		13,67,231	13,17,231
British Baluchistan		4,63,508	4,05,309
Delhi Province		6,36,246	2,06,960
	Total	3,23,60,063(?)	2,03,20,063 or 62.79 per cent

(II) The North-Eastern Zone should comprise Assam, Bengal (excluding Bankura and Midnapore districts) and Purnea from Bihar.

Total Population	..	5,70,10,946
Muslims	..	3,08,76,421—i.e. 54 per cent
Non-Muslims	..	2,61,34,523—i.e. 46 per cent

Among the non-Muslims roughly about 85,00,000, i.e. 32 per cent are member of the Scheduled Castes, about 15,00,000, i.e. 6 per cent are tribals, about 4 lakh Christians and the rest, caste Hindus.

(III) 'The Committee deems it a duty to point out that even in their own interests as of the rest of the Muslims, it would be desirable to ensure and perpetuate the Muslim influence wherever it predominates in any form in non-British India. Hence it is that all Native States, large or small, ruled by Muslim Princes, should be regarded for purposes of the Muslim constitutional plan as *sovereign Muslim States*. This must be made a basic demand . . . it would be appropriate that the League should concentrate its aim on the independence and integrity of an expanded dominion of the Nizam with an opening to the sea, as it will be a source of infinite strength to the Muslims in India outside the dominion. Who knows that in the fullness of time the Muslims of India might find it to their advantage to make Hyderabad their rallying point and the centre of their growing strength.'[1] Thus this will be the third wide sphere of Muslim influence.

The Committee also examined the possibilities of the Native States adjacent to the Muslim States federating with the latter for some common purposes. Should such arrangement be made, the position would be as follows:

The Committee took pains to analyse the figures of the various communities constituting the minorities in the north-west zone and found that in the British Indian provinces of the north-west the Scheduled Castes came to 14,13,532 or 4.36 per cent, the Sikhs to 31,39,964 or 9.70 per cent and the caste Hindus to 70,19,278 or 21.69 per cent. Similar figures for the Indian States are also mentioned, the caste Hindus being 24,94,093 or 22.33 per cent and the Sikhs 10,58,142 or 10.42 per cent. (N.B. The percentage

---

[1] *The Pakistan Issue*, pp. 79–80.

250 INDIA DIVIDED

TABLE IV
Population of Native States Adjacent to Muslim States
Northern Muslim Zone

Name	Total population	Muslim population
British Indian Provinces as shown above	3,23,60,063	2,03,20,063
Frontier States		
Dir, Swat and Chitral	9,02,075	8,52,000
Baluchistan States		
Kalat	3,42,101	3,31,234
Las Bela	63,008	61,550
Sind States		
Khairpur Mirs	2,27,183	1,86,577
Punjab States		
Bahawalpur	9,84,612	7,99,176
Kapurthala	3,16,757	1,79,251
Patiala	16,25,520	3,63,920
Nabha	2,87,574	57,393
Faridkot	1,64,364	49,912
Jind	3,24,676	46,002
Malerkotla	83,072	31,417
Loharu	23,338	3,119
Pataudi	18,873	3,168
Dujana	28,216	5,863
Chamba	1,46,870	10,839
Mandi	2,70,465	6,351
Suket	58,408	733
Kalsia	59,848	21,797
Simla Hill States	3,30,850	10,017
Sirmur	1,48,568	7,020
Bilaspur	1,00,994	1,458
Kashmir	36,46,243	28,17,636
If Bikaner and Jaisalmer join then add		
Bikaner	9,36,218	1,41,578
Jaisalmer	76,255	22,116
Total	4,35,26,151	2,63,30,190 (or 69.49 p.c)
Excluding Bikaner and Jaisalmer	4,25,13,678	2,61,66,526 (or 61.54 p.c.)

of caste Hindus in the States appears to be an arithmetical error and should be 24.56 and not 22.33.)

In the case of the eastern Muslim zone the following adjoining States can be persuaded to federate:

TABLE V

Population of Eastern Muslim Zone

	Total population	Muslim population
Bengal States		
Cooch Bihar and Tripura	9,73,316	3,12,476
Assam States		
Manipur and Khasi Hills	6,25,606	24,600
British Provinces	5,70,10,946	3,08,76,421
Total	5,86,09,868	3,12,13,497 or 53.15 per cent

The percentage of the communities constituting the minorities of the total population is as follows:

TABLE VI

Area	Caste Hindus	Scheduled Castes	Tribal	Christians
British Bengal	29.9	13.7	1.5	–
Bengal States	64.9	3.0	–	–
British Assam	36.6	21.0	8.2	2.5
Assam States	43.7	–	44.9	7.4

The areas that will fall within the two zones will be as follows:

	British India in sq. miles	States in sq. miles	Total in sq. miles
Eastern zone	225,352	213,370	438,722
North-western zone	129,637	17,754	147,391
Total of the two zones	354,989	231,124	586,113

Looked at from the point of the whole of India the position is as follows:

Total population of whole India ..	..	35,05,29,557
Muslim population ..	..	..	7,76,78,245
Muslim population within the western and eastern zones (States included)	..	5,75,42,787 or 74.07 per cent

Thus the Committee gives protection to about 74.07 per cent of the Muslims by its proposals.

'The Lahore Resolution of the League does not look forward to the proposed regional states assuming immediately, as they are formed, powers of defence, external affairs, customs, etc. This argues that there should be a transitional stage during which these powers would be exercised by some agency common to them all. Such a common co-ordinating agency would be necessary even independently of the above consideration; for under the third principle of the Resolution, it will be impossible to implement effectively the provision of safeguards for minorities without some organic relationship subsisting between the States under Muslim influence and the States under Hindu influence. A federation is not to the taste of the Muslims, because they fear that the Hindus will, on the strength of their majority, dominate the Musalmans. But since some common arrangement is essential to the fulfillment of the provisions of the Resolution, an agreed formula has to be devised whereby the Muslims shall share the control at the Centre on terms of perfect equality with the non-Muslims.'[2]

It was accordingly proposed by the Committee that all the proposed States designated 'sovereign' shall enter into a joint pact to have a common agency to look after, in the name of the component States, the subjects of:

(a)   External Relations,
(b)   Defence,
(c)   Communications,
(d)   Customs,
(e)   Safeguards for minorities and voluntary intermigration, etc., subject to certain provisos:
(a)   *Defence*—Each component state shall maintain an army at its own expense, its strength being dependent on the importance of its strategic position, the Centre sharing the military expenditure according to the strength of the army maintained. In normal times the State will control its army but in times of war full control will be assumed by the central agency;
(b)   *The navy* will be entirely under the control of the Centre. Except for the delegated subjects, the States shall administer

[2] *The Pakistan Issue*, pp. 87–88.

all other subjects and residuary powers shall vest in the individual States. Both on the executive and other bodies of the common agency the Muslims shall have half the seats.

The Committee which prepared the above scheme consisted of nine members. It was in circulation among them when it found a premature publication in the *Statesman*. Professor Afzal Husain Qadri, one of the members and author of a scheme discussed above, thought that it went beyond the Lahore Resolution in including the states within it and in suggesting the constitution of interrelation between Muslim States and the rest of India. He was opposed to anything like a 'Central Machinery' or 'Centre' creeping into Muslim demands either in letter or spirit as it would savour of All-India Federation or Hindu Raj. Dr Syed Abdul Latif, author of another scheme described above, was dissatisfied with the demarcation of the north-west and north-east blocks as suggested in the report. The demarcation had been made by the Punjab, Sind and UP members to whom it had been left. 'The Lahore Resolution,' wrote Dr Latif to Sir Abdullah Haroon, 'aims at homogeneous and compact blocks or states with an overwhelming Muslim majority. But the Punjab and Aligarh members of your Committee through their imperialistic designs over essentially non-Muslim areas would like to have a larger Punjab extending even to Aligarh covering all the non-Muslim States from Kashmir to Jaisalmir, which reduces the Muslim percentage to 55. In like manner they would include in the north-east block, the whole of Bengal, Assam and a district from Bihar, which brings the percentage of Musalmans down to 54. In my humble opinion this kind of demarcation is against the spirit and aim of the Lahore Resolution; because with 46 per cent non-Muslims in the north-east block and 42 per cent in the north-west block you cannot call your states as Muslim states in any sense of the term nor style them as Muslim zones.'[3]

Mr Jinnah refused to recognize the Committee or its suggestions and proposals except as suggestions from individuals or groups.

There are some other schemes—one given by Sir Feroz Khan Noon in a speech at Aligarh in 1942 and another by Mr Rizwanullah, but I have not seen them and they are not given here.

---

[3] *The Pakistan Issue*, pp. 98–99.

~

TWENTY-THREE

THE BIRTH OF THE IDEA OF PARTITION

All these schemes have been worked out and published since 1939—some before the Lahore session of the Muslim League, others thereafter. It is generally said that it was the late Sir Muhammad Iqbal who first put forward the demand for a separate and independent Muslim State in his presidential address at the Allahabad session of the All-India Muslim League in December 1930. It is therefore desirable to quote some passages from it: 'The religious ideal of Islam, therefore, is organically related to the social order which it has created. The rejection of the one will eventually involve the rejection of the other. Therefore the construction of a polity on national lines, if it means a displacement of the Islamic principle of solidarity, is simply unthinkable to a Muslim . . . The unity of an Indian Nation, therefore, must be sought, not in the negation, but in the mutual harmony and cooperation of the many . . . And it is on the discovery of unity in this direction that the fate of India as well as Asia really depends . . .

'It is, however, painful to observe that our attempts to discover such a principle of internal harmony have so far failed. Why have they failed? Perhaps, we suspect each other's intentions and inwardly aim at dominating each other. Perhaps, in the higher interests of mutual cooperation we cannot afford to part with the monopolies which circumstances have placed in our hands, and conceal our egoism under the cloak of nationalism, outwardly immolating a large-hearted patriotism, but inwardly as narrow-minded as a caste or tribe. Perhaps, we are unwilling to recognize each group has a right to free development according to its own cultural traditions. But whatever may be the cause of our failure, I still feel hopeful. Events seem to be tending in the direction of some sort of internal harmony. And as far as I have been able to read the Muslim mind, I have no hesitation in declaring that, if the principle that the Indian Muslim is entitled to full and free development on the lines of his own culture and tradition in his own homelands is recognized as the basis of a permanent communal settlement, he will be ready to stake his all for the freedom of India. The principle that each group is entitled to free development on its own lines is not inspired by any feeling of narrow communalism . . . I entertain the highest respect for the customs, laws, religious and social institutions of other communities. Nay, it is my duty, according to the teaching of the Quran, even to defend their places of worship if need be . . .

'The units of Indian society are not territorial as in European countries . . . The principle of European democracy cannot be applied to India without recognizing the fact of communal groups. The Muslim demand for the creation of a Muslim India within India is, therefore, perfectly justified . . . I would like to see the Punjab, north-west Frontier Province, Sind and Baluchistan amalgamated into a single state . . . The exclusion of Ambala Division and perhaps of some districts where non-Muslims predominate will make it less extensive and more Muslim in population . . . Thus, possessing full opportunity of development within the body politic of India the north-west Indian Muslims will prove the best defenders of India against a foreign invasion, be that invasion one of ideas or of bayonets . . . To my mind a unitary form of Government is simply unthinkable in self-governing India. What are called residuary powers must be left entirely, to self-governing states, the Central Federal State exercising only those powers which are expressly vested in it by the free consent of federal states.'[1]

Thus in the scheme adumbrated by Sir Muhammad Iqbal there is no independent Muslim State without a Central Indian authority of any kind contemplated. He evidently wants a federation in which the units will be autonomous and suggests a new demarcation of boundaries of the provinces in the north-west so as to create a unit in which the proportion of Muslims will be greater and the area more manageable. His sentiment regarding the defence of India is in keeping with his views expressed previously in 1926 to a representative of the *Nation* wherein he had said: 'There are some timid Hindus who suspect that Muslims will play .false to their country in case of Afghan invasion. If the people of India are united and trust one another, all will defend their country against

[1] Reproduced in F.K. Khan Durrani, *The Meaning of Pakistan*, pp. 205–13.

any invader, Muslim or non-Muslim. I will certainly defend my
home against any political adventurer, who aimed at the destruction
of my home and liberty. There is no fear of *jehad*, for *jehads* are
nearly always a screen for political ambition. The solution of all
our difficulties is growth of collective consciousness. A national
pact concluded in the spirit of give and take will I think accelerate
the process of this healthy growth.'[2]

Till after the Round Table Conferences, the Muslims of India
were content to demand safeguards for the protection of their rights
as a minority. How the idea of separation has grown is described
by Dr Shaukatullah Ansari in his book *Pakistan—The Problem of
India,* and I cannot do better than quote him at length:

'In 1930–31 the Reforms were on the anvil and at the First and
Second Round Table Conference the Muslims appeared committed
to the establishment of an Indian Federation. J. Coatman, C.I.E.,
writing in 1932 at the time of the Third Round Table Conference,
said: "The creation of a strong, united India, including the whole
of British India and Indian States and the borderland in the
north-west, whose inclusion in India is one of the first and most
fundamental conditions of her nationhood, is day by day, being
made impossible, and in its place it seems that there may be
brought into being a powerful Muhammedan state in the north
and west, with its eyes definitely turned away from India, towards
the rest of the Moslem world of which it forms the fringe, whilst
away to the south and east there will be—what? A Hindu India,
homogeneous and united? Perhaps! or a vast area divided between
warring Princes and the fighting races of old Hindustan as it has
been in the past, and may easily be so again in the future? Very
likely . . ."

'The seed found a fertile soil in the minds of some young
Muslims who were opposed to the All-India Federation and
believed that the safeguards which were being provided in the
Constitution were useless, and "our brave but voiceless nation is
being crucified on the altar of Hindu nationalism." In 1933 for
the first time the Muslims, hitherto called a minority community,
were called "a nation" by a Punjabi Muslim, Chaudhry Rahmat
Ali (an undergraduate of Cambridge) who gave the movement a
shape and a form. He propounded the idea that the Punjab, NWFP

[2] *The Searchlight*, 30 April 1926.

(Afghan Province), Kashmir, Sind and Baluchistan should be formed into a separate Muslim state called Pakistan. This proposal was different from that of Dr Iqbal in that while Dr Iqbal proposed the amalgamation of those provinces into a single state forming a unit of the All-India Federation, Chaudhry Rahmat Ali proposed that these provinces should have an independent federation of their own. Leaflets advocating Pakistan were distributed by Chaudhry Rahmat Ali to the Members of Parliament and the members of the Round Table Conference, but no Indian, Hindu or Muslim, took any interest in them. Muslim witnesses described the Pakistan scheme in August 1933, to the Joint Parliamentary Select Committee as follows:

A. Yusuf Ali: "As far as I know it is only a student scheme; no responsible people have put it forward."

Ch. Zafrullah Khan: "So far as we have considered it, we have considered it chimerical and impracticable."

Dr Khalifa Suja-ud-Din: "Perhaps it will be enough to say that no such scheme has been considered by any representative gentleman or association so far."

'It is significant that questions about Pakistan were asked at this Conference. It is still more significant that the initiative came from the British—they seem, from the record, to have pressed their questions while the Indian (Muslim) delegates seem uninterested and anxious to pass on to the next point.. .. Although in India no one had heard of or talked of Pakistan and the Muslim Delegation showed no interest in it, yet the Diehard Press and the Churchill-Lloyd group of the Conservative Party waxed eloquent over it and saw in it a suggestion of the gravest import with the result that questions were asked in the Houses of Parliament on several occasions.'[3]

Whatever the origin and whatever the auspices under which the idea of separation has grown, there is no doubt that, in the words of Dr Ansari, the seed has found a fertile soil and has forced attention to be bestowed on it.

[3] Shaukatullah Ansari, *Pakistan—The Problem of India*, pp. 4–7.

PART IV

THE ALL-INDIA MUSLIM LEAGUE
RESOLUTION ON PAKISTAN

TWENTY-FOUR

INDEFINITENESS AND IMPLICATIONS

The All-India Muslim League at its Lahore session in March 1940 passed the following resolution:

(1) While approving and endorsing the action taken by the Council and the Working Committee of the All-India Muslim League, as indicated in their resolutions dated 7 of August, I7 and 18 September and 22 October, 1939, and 3 February 1940 on the constitutional issue, this session of the All-India Muslim League emphatically reiterates that the scheme of federation embodied in the Government of India Act, 1935, is totally unsuited to, and unworkable in the peculiar conditions of this country and is altogether unacceptable to Muslim India.

(2) It further records its emphatic view that while the declaration dated 18 October 1939, made by the Viceroy on behalf of His Majesty's Government is reassuring insofar as it declares that the policy and plan on which the Government of India Act, 1935, is based will be reconsidered in consultation with the various parties, interests and communities in India, Muslim India will not be satisfied unless the whole constitutional plan is reconsidered *de novo* and that no revised plan would be acceptable to the Muslims unless it is framed with their approval and consent.

(3) Resolved that it is the considered view of this session of the All-India Muslim League that no constitutional plan would be workable in this country or acceptable to Muslims unless it is designed on the following basic principle—that geographically contiguous units are demarcated into regions which should be so constituted, with such territorial readjustments as may be necessary, that the areas in which the Muslims are numerically in a majority as in the north-

western and eastern zones of India should be grouped to
constitute 'Independent States' in which the constituent
units shall be autonomous and sovereign.

(4)   That adequate, effective and mandatory safeguards should
be specifically provided in the Constitution for minorities
in these units and in these regions for the protection of
their religious, cultural, economic, political, administrative
and other rights and interests in consultation with them:
and in other parts of India where the Musalmans are in
a minority, adequate, effective and mandatory safeguards
shall be specially[1] provided in the Constitution for them
and other minorities for the protection of their religious,
cultural, economic, political, administrative and other rights
and interests in consultation with them.

This Session further authorizes the Working Committee to frame a
scheme of Constitution in accordance with these basic principles,
providing for the assumption finally by the respective regions
of all powers such as defence, external affairs, communications,
customs, and such other matters as may be necessary.

It appears from the resolution that it deals with the scheme of
federation embodied in the Government of India Act, 1935, which
it considers totally unsuited to, and unworkable in the peculiar
conditions of this country and hence altogether unacceptable to
Muslim India. After recording its emphatic view that the Muslims
of India will not be satisfied unless the whole constitutional
plan is reconsidered *de novo* and that no revised plan would be
acceptable to the Muslims unless it is framed with their approval
and consent, it proceeds to lay down the basic principle on which
any plan to be workable and acceptable to the Muslims should
be based. That basic principle is that geographically contiguous
units are demarcated into regions which should be so constituted
with such territorial readjustments as may be necessary, that the
areas in which the Muslims are numerically in a majority as in
the north-western and eastern zones of India should be grouped
to constitute 'Independent States' in which the constituent units

---

[1] 'Specially' is taken from the resolution as published in *India's Problem
of Her Future Constitution*, p. 17. In *Muslim India* by Mr M. Noman
the word used is 'specifically', p. 404, as also in Dr Ambedkar's
Pakistan or the Partition of India, p. 4.

shall be autonomous and sovereign. The resolution then proceeds to lay down that adequate, effective and mandatory safeguards should be specifically provided in the Constitution for minorities in the regions for the protection of their religious, cultural, economic, political, administrative and other rights and interests in consultation with them and similar safeguards are to be provided for the protection of Musalmans and other minorities in other parts of India where the Musalmans are in a minority. The League authorized its Working Committee to frame a scheme of Constitution in accordance with these principles providing for the assumption finally by the respective regions of all powers such as defence, external affairs, communications, customs, and such other matters as may be necessary.

No scheme prepared by the Working Committee of the League and authorized by the Resolution has yet been published, even if it has been framed. Mr M.A. Jinnah, the President of the Muslim League, declared at Madras as follows:

'Let me tell you as clearly as I can possibly do so that the goal of the All-India Muslim League is that we want to establish a completely independent state in the north-west and eastern zones of India with full control finally of defence, currency, exchange, etc. We do not want under any circumstances a constitution of an all-India character with one government at the Centre.'

When invited to elaborate the scheme and furnish details as regards the territories to be included in the regions and other matters he has refused to do so, insisting that the principle should be first accepted and then and only then will he be prepared to work out or disclose details.

So late as the last week of April 1944, during the course of discussions that were taking place between Mr Jinnah and Malik Khizir Hayat Khan, Premier of the Punjab, regarding Mr Jinnah's proposal to establish a Muslim League or Muslim League-Coalition ministry instead of the Unionist Party ministry in the Punjab, the non-Muslim ministers desired that 'in order to enable all concerned to judge the merits of the scheme its precise political and constitutional implications [should be] fully explained, and the geographical boundaries of the Punjab under the scheme of Pakistan a well as the principles to be adopted for the fixation of such boundaries [should be] indicated as clearly as possible'—on which the comment of Mr Jinnah was that it was 'an all-India question and irrelevant for the present purpose of forming the proposed coalition.'[2]

It is difficult to understand this reluctance on the part of the President of the League to disclose the scheme in its entirety, if there is a scheme ready. It would be unreasonable to suppose that a responsible body claiming to represent the Muslim Community of India would propound a theory and propose a scheme for the partition of the country without fully working out the implications of the former and the details of the latter. On the other hand one would naturally expect that if the League desires its scheme to be considered and adopted on its merits, it should be willing, if not anxious, to furnish such elucidation as may be desired by others for its discussion and acceptance with intelligence and understanding. Nor are the information and elaboration demanded by others in respect of mere details but are of a fundamental nature whose knowledge is essential for a fair consideration of it.

For example, it is necessary to know which areas, according to the Resolution, will fall in Pakistan, and which areas will constitute the Hindustan of the League conception. Similarly it is essential;. to know what the size of the non-Muslim minority in Pakistan and of the Muslim minority in Hindustan will be and what the safeguards and guarantees are that the League considers sufficient for the protection of the non-Muslim minorities in Pakistan and what safeguards and guarantees it would insist upon for Muslim minorities in Hindustan. It is not enough for the League to say that it will vouchsafe the same safeguards to non-Muslim minorities that Hindustan will guarantee to the Muslim minorities. No other group has put forward any scheme of Partition and claimed or proposed to guarantee minority rights from or to others. It is, therefore, up, to the League to formulate its own proposals for the consideration of others no less than of Muslims themselves.

Again, any scheme of reciprocity may prove unworkable on account of the size of the minority in the one part or the other. For example, if the minority happens to be something between 40 and 50 per cent of the total population in one part and only about 10 per cent or so in the other part, it is obvious that a large minority of 40 to 45 per cent will be in a very much better position than a minority of say 10 per cent or thereabouts to enforce and implement the guarantee by its own inherent strength. It may also be that reciprocity may not be acceptable when what one may offer may prove of so little value to the other that it is no inducement.

The matter may be put in a concrete form. Suppose the Hindus of the north-western and eastern zones, and particularly of the Punjab and Bengal, say that although they are in a minority in their provinces they do not want any concession or weightage in representation in the Legislature or in public services for themselves, that they are content if they get representation according to their proportion in the population and that such weightage as may be demanded by or conceded to other minorities like the Christians should be given by the majority community out of its own share; suppose further that they say that because they do not demand any concession or weightage for themselves, no concession or weightage should be given to the Muslims in the provinces where they are in a minority and that the Hindu majority in those provinces should give such concession or weightage as may be required to other minorities like the Christians. The matter might be put in another way by the Hindus of provinces in which they are in a majority. Suppose they say that they are not prepared to concede any weightage to the Muslim minority in their provinces and that the Muslims of the provinces in which they are in a majority need not give any weightage to the Hindu minority in their provinces. Let us also suppose that in both the above cases the Hindus all over the country whether they are in a minority or majority adopted this attitude, the position would be on a basis of perfect and complete reciprocity and no objection could be taken to it on that ground. There is no reason why the Hindus may not adopt this attitude. In Bengal the Hindus would stand to gain. In place of 3.2 per cent of the seats in the Legislature as given by the Act of 1935, they will get 44 per cent. In the Punjab also their position will improve to a small extent. In services instead of 50 per cent given to them, they would get about 44 per cent in Bengal and their position in the Punjab will remain more or less unaffected. The Hindus of the North-West Frontier Province, Sind and Baluchistan will stand to lose to an appreciable extent but their total population is only 14.50 lakhs and the total number of seats in the Legislatures and posts in services that they will lose will be negligible. Let us see what the Muslims of a single province like Bihar will stand to lose as against this. Their representation in the Legislature and in services will have to be reduced from 25 per cent to 12 per cent and the number of seats and posts they will lose in one province will be considerable —more than all the seats and posts that the Hindus will lose in both the Muslim zones put together. The number of Muslims affected by this cut in one single province will be 47 lakhs against 14.50 lakhs of Hindus affected in the north-western zone. The position of Muslims in regard to the rest of the Hindu zone can easily be imagined. Reciprocity thus will have no attraction for the Hindus and will not induce them to offer any concession or weightage to the Muslims.

Again, each party should be made clearly to understand what sanction will be constituted to enforce the guarantee. I have indicated only some of the points amongst many with which the whole scheme bristles that require elucidation and elaboration, for a fair and reasonable discussion and understanding acceptance of it.

The two nations theory also has its implications, which have to be understood. It appears that the protagonists of Pakistan base themselves on the religion of Islam and the social and political system which may be derived from it, for treating the Muslims as a separate nation. Other attributes which are generally supposed to attach to a nation do not apply to Muslims alone as such, and are shared in common by Muslims and non-Muslims of particular areas of India. Thus in the matter of language the Punjabi Hindu, the Punjabi Muslim and the Punjabi Sikh speak the same language irrespective of their religions. So do all the Pathans, whether Muslims or Hindus, of the NWFP speak Pushto alike. And so do all Bengalis—whether Hindu or Muslim—speak the same language, Bengali. In all these areas they occupy the same land. In all these places they have lived under the same government with the rest of British India during the British period for over one hundred years at least—even if we leave out the long period of Muslim rule.

Religion being put forward as practically the sole criterion, it is well worth remembering that people agreeing with one another in many if not most other things that matter but differing in religion, inhabit this country from one end to the other. It is reported .that commenting on this aspect of the question Mr Edward Thompson put it to Mr Jinnah that it would imply two nations confronting each other in every village and in every street and that it was a terrible prospect to contemplate. Mr Jinnah is said to have replied that it was a terrible prospect but there was no alternative.[3] Mr Jinnah has recently in a press statement contradicted that he ever gave a press interview to Mr Thompson or that he said the words attributed to him. But whether he said what is attributed to him to Mr Thompson in a press interview or otherwise or at all is beside the point and cannot alter the fact that the only result that can follow from a two nations theory on the basis of religion is the emergence and establishment of two nations in every village and every street of India. If a Muslim in any part of India by reason of his religion alone belongs to a nation comprising all Muslims in any and every other corner of India and separate from all non-Muslims including those adjacent to him, then the question naturally arises—to what State does the Muslim owe allegiance? To the State within which he lives and moves and which may not be a Muslim State—not falling within Pakistan—or to a distant Muslim State with which he may have no connection except that a majority of people living in it follow the same religion as he does? The same question will arise in regard to a non-Muslim living in a Muslim State, unless it is postulated that whereas the Muslims can and do constitute a nation, all others are formless conglomerates without the essential attribute of a nation—a single religion. Or will such a Muslim or non-Muslim have a double personality and divided allegiance? How will such divided allegiance work in an emergency like a war?

Another set of questions arises in regard to the status of such a member of a separate nation. Ordinarily, a man living within the territory of a particular State, whatever his previous nationality may have been, becomes on fulfilling certain conditions a citizen of that State. That gives him a status, confers certain rights, and imposes certain responsibilities. If the Muslim in India is a member of the Muslim nation by reason of his religion, irrespective of the fact whether the state in which he resides is a Muslim or non-Muslim State, then can he claim and can he in justice and fairness be given the status of a citizen of that State when it does

[3] The conversation is reproduced in Mr Edward Thompson's *Enlist India for Freedom*, p. 52.

not happen to be a Muslim State? Is he not more in the nature of an alien there, looking for protection and other advantages that citizenship confers, to his Muslim State which will be his national State? He can claim the rights and privileges, if any, of an alien. There is a difference which cannot be slurred over or ignored between aliens working and carrying on business within the territory of the state of another nation, and members of the same nation working and carrying on business within their own territory but being in a minority as compared with other groups of the same nation. The minority consists of members of the same nation and has rights which are well recognized. Aliens cannot have the same rights as a minority in a nation. So Muslims in provinces and States where non-Muslims will be in a majority will not be able to claim the rights of a minority, if at the same time they claim to be members of another nation. This will be true of non-Muslims also in Muslim States, if they claim to be members of another nation.

If the Muslim League wants Muslim States in the north-west and east of India for the purpose of running them according to the Muslim conception of a State, the question arises—what will be the status of non-Muslims in those States? Are they to be treated as equal citizens of the State or are they to have an inferior status?

The Muslim public law recognizes a distinction between Muslims and *Zimmis*. Are non-Muslims to get the status of *Zimmis* or of equal citizens as in a modern democratic State? Mr A. S. Tritton of the Muslim University, Aligarh, has written a book, *The Caliphs and their Non-Muslim Subjects,* in which he has discussed at great length the position of non-Muslims in the Muslim States under the Caliphs. It is not possible to summarize the book here and I content myself with quoting a few sentences from the concluding chapter of the book. Mr Tritton says: 'The rule of Islam was often burdensome, the revolt in Egypt proved it, Umar II might order a governor to distribute the surplus cash in his treasury among the Dhimmis after the needs of the Muslims had been satisfied, but as a rule they had to provide the money which the state wanted and got nothing for it. Probably, at first, the subjects did not pay heavier taxes than they had paid to the previous Governments, but in one way and another the burden grew steadily heavier. There can be no doubt that, at the end of the first century, the reign of

Umar II saw the beginning of definite disabilities for the Dhimmis. Restrictions were placed on their dress, and the attempt to oust them from official posts began . . . during the second century the Muslim spirit hardened . . . the laws about dress were made more stringent, and the idea took shape that churches might not be built . . . It is only fair to say that the conduct of the rulers was often better than the law demanded . . . On paper, many things were forbidden them [Dhimmis], the public celebration of weddings and funerals, feasts, and church ceremonies. It was a punishable offence to tread intentionally on the skirt of a Muslim's garment and they had to leave the centre of the road to the Muslims . . .

'Mutasim bought the monastery of Samarra that stood where he wanted to build a palace. Other Caliphs destroyed churches to obtain materials for their buildings, and the mob was always ready to pillage churches and monasteries. They, Dhimmis, might enjoy great prosperity, yet always they lived on sufferance, exposed to the caprice of the ruler and the passions of the mob. The episode of Al Hakim must be regarded as the freak of a madman, and not typical of Islam. But in later times the position of the Dhimmis did change for the worse. They were much liable to suffer from the violence of the crowd, and the popular fanaticism was accompanied by an increasing strictness among the educated. The spiritual isolation of Islam was accomplished. The world was divided into two classes, Muslims and others, and only Islam counted. There were brilliant exceptions, but the general statement is true. If a Muslim gave any help to the religion of a Dhimmi, he was summoned thrice to repentance, and then, if obdurate, he was to be put to death. Indeed, the general feeling was that the leavings of the Muslims were good enough for the Dhimmis.'[4]

It has been expressly stated by some writers who have written in support of Pakistan that the state contemplated by them will be a Muslim state. They think that means justice to all. In view of what has been quoted above, non-Muslims may not accept that opinion and it is necessary to have a clear and well-defined scheme to enable a correct judgement to be formed on it. It is thus clear that the demand for elucidation and elaboration of the bald Lahore Resolution is clearly justified. The League, before it propounded the theory of two nations and put forward the

[4] A.S. Tritton, *The Caliphs and their Non-Muslim Subjects*, pp. 230–33.

scheme of Partition, must have considered these and many other questions of a similar nature, and if it wants others who are not within it—whether they are Muslims or non-Muslims—to accept its programme, it must be prepared to share with them its solutions of these and similar knotty problems that arise, unless it wants them to vote for Partition blind-folded.

It would be uncharitable to suggest that the League wants others to commit themselves to a vague general theory and to an undefined scheme; and then gradually to unfold the implications and details, to force them to accept the implications and details so unfolded, and in case of their inability to subscribe to the latter in spite of their acceptance of the former, to charge them with bad faith and with having gone back on their previous acceptance.

But the way in which the matter is being exposed to public view lends support to this uncharitable suggestion. At first the League President insisted that the principle of Partition should be accepted first and cited the instance of a joint Hindu family in which when a Partition has to take place the principle has first to be accepted and then the details of Partition are worked but. This position has since been changed. When Mr C. Rajagopalachari, with the consent and approval of Gandhiji, put forward a concrete scheme which, he claimed, fulfilled the terms of the Lahore Resolution of the League, Mr Jinnah denounced it in unmeasured terms. It may be pointed out how the position has shifted. When Mr Jinnah announced his decision to receive Mahatma Gandhi at his Bombay house, he after denouncing the C.R. formula stated: 'Mr Gandhi has, at any rate in his personal capacity, accepted the principle of partition or division of India. What remains now is the question of how and when this has got to be carried out.'[5] After this declaration one would have thought that the principle of partition or division—on which such emphasis was laid before the details could be released or worked out—having been accepted, the next step would be to tackle the details and Mr Jinnah would put forward his scheme and show how and wherein it differed from the 'maimed, mutilated and moth-eaten Pakistan' of Mr Rajagopalachari. But in the prolonged discussions which followed and the results of which are embodied in the letters exchanged

[5] Statement before the Council of the All-India Muslim League at Lahore on 30 July 1944.

between Gandhiji and Mr Jinnah, fresh demands are made for acceptance of the two nations theory and of the Lahore Resolution in its entirety before any further progress can be made with the elaboration of the details of the scheme. Once again the insistence is on acceptance of a bald general principle and bald general proposal for Partition as distinguished from the mere principle of Partition which in Mr Jinnah's own words had been already accepted by Gandhiji. The acceptance of the proposition that the principle of Partition should be accepted before details can be discussed has led not to the discussion of the details, but to a further demand for the acceptance of the theory of two nations which is said to underlie the whole idea of Partition and of the Lahore Resolution. One wonders what further demands will be made if these two are also accepted. This is a natural result of insistence on a piece-meal consideration of the scheme of Partition and the principle underlying it.

TWENTY-FIVE

DISADVANTAGE OF INDEFINITENESS

The question as to what areas are to be included within Pakistan has also a history which may not be generally known. As shown elsewhere, there were several schemes by individuals for the division of India into Muslim and non-Muslim zones. Some of them wanted these zones for cultural purposes and for giving Muslims a better position in regard to the governance not only of the regions falling within the Muslim zone, but also of the country as a whole. Others were frankly for the establishment of independent Muslim States. It appears, as mentioned elsewhere, that in February 1940, shortly before the Lahore session of the All-India Muslim League which adopted the Pakistan Resolution in the last week of the following March, the Foreign Committee of the League issued invitations 'to the authors of the various schemes of constitutional reform for India, to meet together under the auspices of the said committee in order to examine jointly each such scheme and see whether a consolidated scheme cannot be finally framed.'[1] Sir Abdullah Haroon, the Chairman of the Foreign Sub-committee of the All-India Muslim League, placed a memorandum in the hands of the President Mr Jinnah, and as he says in the letter just quoted, 'obviously this Resolution [the Lahore Resolution of the League] had been framed by the Working Committee in the light of the outline placed in your [Mr Jinnah's] hands by me in the shape of a small memorandum in February last.'[2] This memorandum has not been published and it is impossible to say what it contained.

In the schemes mentioned above whose authors met at the invitation of the Foreign Sub-committee, there were two wholly

---

[1] Letter of Sir Abdullah Haroon, Chairman, Foreign Sub-Committee, All-India Muslim League, dated 13 December 1940, published in *The Pakistan Issue*, pp. 73–74.

[2] Ibid., p. 75.

different and conflicting ideas. One idea was that the Muslim zone should be a compact one and should have as large a proportion of Muslims in its population as possible by excluding all those areas from it where the Muslims were in a minority, so that a large Muslim majority with a small non-Muslim minority could manage the affairs of the zone much as the Muslims desired. This would become difficult if the Muslim majority was small and hence precarious, and thus the very object of having separate Muslim zones would be jeopardized, if not defeated. The other school was in favour of taking as large a portion of India as was possible within the Muslim zone, if only a Muslim majority, no matter if it was a small majority, could be secured. The object of the Committee appointed by the Foreign Sub-committee must have been among other things to reconcile these conflicting ideas. By the time of the annual session of the League the labours of the Committee were not finished and only an *ad interim* memorandum was submitted to the President of the League by Sir Abdullah Haroon. The Lahore Resolution, which according to Sir Abdullah Haroon was framed in the light of the outline contained in the memorandum was, it seems, framed in general and vague terms—'that geographically contiguous units are demarcated into regions which should be so constituted with such territorial readjustments as may be necessary that the areas in which the Muslims are numerically in a majority as in the north-western and eastern zones of India should be grouped to constitute "independent States" in which the constituent units shall be autonomous and sovereign.' Now, the words used to denote the extent of the territory to be included in the Muslim State or States are 'units', 'regions', 'areas' and 'zones'. None of these words is to be found in the present constitutional or administrative documents of the country. The words generally used are 'districts', 'tahsils', 'taluqas', 'provinces', etc., and nothing could have been easier than to use these well-known and well-understood expressions, if clarity, intelligibility and definiteness were intended rather than obscurity, vagueness and ambiguity. Can it be that at that time it was considered inexpedient to be definite and clear and thus expose and intensify the differences between the two schools of thought within the League itself mentioned above? Be that as it may, we have to consider what meaning these words were intended to bear.

In spite of the vagueness and indefiniteness, the words are definite enough, even as they are, and have by implication and in an indirect

This works out at 62 per cent for the Muslim population. Similarly, if we take the figures according to the census of 1931 the total population of the provinces of the Punjab, Sind, NWFP and British Baluchistan is 3,03,50,506 of whom 1,87,95,872 or 61.9 per cent are Muslims.

In making his statement to Mr Chapman, Mr Jinnah could not therefore have possibly included the whole of the Punjab in the north-western Muslim zone but only that part of it in which Muslims are in a majority.

There is another document which points to the same conclusion. Mr M.R.T. has written much in the *Eastern Times* on the subject of separation of Muslim zones from the rest of India. After the Lahore session of the League in March 1940, a book named *India's Problem of her Future Constitution* was published by Mr M.H. Saiyid, Mount Pleasant Road, Malabar Hill, Bombay, evidently on behalf of Mr M.A. Jinnah, to which he himself contributed a Preface. In the Preface Mr Jinnah says: 'To those who really wish to examine the problems of India's future Constitution, this collection may help. It is with this object in view that I have selected a few of the well-considered views in a convenient form of a booklet.' Further, 'I hope that this booklet will make a considerable contribution towards the clarification of the Lahore Resolution of the All-India Muslim League which raises a fundamental issue, and I trust every well-wisher of this vast subcontinent will approach the subject free from prejudice, bias and sentiments.' Among the views included in this book which were selected by Mr Jinnah himself is an article by Mr M. R. T. published in the *Eastern Times* of 5 January 1940—before the League session. In this article, while discussing the question of Protection versus Separation, Mr M.R.T. says: 'They [Muslims] number 28 millions in the north-west out of a total population of 42 millions in the five adjoining areas of the Punjab, Kashmir, Sind, the Frontier Province and Baluchistan. The proportion of Muslim population can further be raised by a readjustment of eastern frontier of the Punjab. If Ambala Division and Eastern Hindu and Sikh states are excluded from the Punjab, its population will be reduced from $28^{1}/_{2}$ millions at present to 21 millions, but the Muslim percentage will be raised from 55 at present to 70. This Muslim percentage will further be raised if the entire Muslim north-west is taken together as a whole. With the eastern frontier

modified as proposed, the north-west will have a total population
of 35 millions of which Muslims will number 27 millions and
non-Muslims 8 millions. The Muslim proportion of 77 per cent
will be strong enough to ensure a permanent stable government,
and this result will be achieved without having recourse to any
scheme of exchange of population.'[4] Thus this scheme which is
published with Mr Jinnah's authority as 'making a considerable
contribution towards the clarification of the Lahore Resolution'
favours the exclusion of that portion of the Punjab in which
according to him Muslims are not in a majority.

There is another matter which also indirectly supports the same
viewpoint. I have mentioned above the Committee appointed by
the Foreign Committee of the League under the chairmanship of
Sir Abdullah Haroon. It continued its labours after the Lahore
session of the League and actually prepared a scheme, with
details of the territories to be included in the north-western zone
worked out. In this scheme the Committee included the whole
of the Punjab, the Indian States of the Punjab and Kashmir, a
portion of British India beyond the eastern boundary of the Delhi
province, and a part of the district of Aligarh so as to bring
Aligarh within the zone and the Indian States of Bikaner and
Jaisalmer of Rajputana. This scheme got an unauthorized and
premature publication in the *Statesman* (Delhi) of 18 February
1941, and the Delhi correspondents of provincial papers forthwith
telegraphed a summary to their respective centres saying that the
Foreign Committee of the League had published the Report on 17
February. Dr Syed Abdul Latif was asked by Sir Abdullah Haroon
to go through the scheme and send his comments thereon which
he did on 8 March 1941, and forwarded a copy of his note to
Mr Jinnah. This seems to have annoyed Mr Jinnah who on 15
March wrote to Dr Latif making it 'clear to you and publicly,
that the Muslim League has appointed no such Committee as
you keep harping upon, and neither the Muslim League nor I can
recognize any of these suggestions or proposals of these so-called
schemes except as I have said any suggestion from individuals or
groups will receive due consideration. Please therefore let me make
it clear once for all that neither Sir Abdullah Haroon nor you
should go on talking of this Committee or that Committee and

[4] *India's Problem of her Future Constitution*, pp. 33–34.

involving the Muslim League or its authority behind the proposals that may be formulated by individuals or groups.'[5]

The position reduces itself to this. We have the President of the League declaring to the correspondent of an International News Agency that the population of Muslims in the north-western zone will be 75 per cent of the total population—a result which can be obtained only if the eastern districts of the Punjab where non-Muslims are in majority are excluded from the zone. He selects a number of views and publishes them as making 'a considerable contribution towards the clarification of the Lahore Resolution'. In this collection of views he includes the scheme of Mr M.R.T. who proposes the exclusion of the eastern districts of the Punjab, and excludes the views of others who had worked out schemes and published them in which they had included the whole of the Punjab and some other parts of British India besides some of the Indian States. When the Committee appointed by the Foreign Committee of the League under the chairmanship of a prominent member of the League, Sir Abdullah Haroon, prepares a scheme in which it includes the whole of the Punjab and some portion of British India down to Aligarh and some Indian States, Mr Jinnah repudiates the action of the Committee and the Committee itself. The conclusion seems to be irresistible that the President of the League was inclined in favour of a scheme excluding the eastern districts of the Punjab from the north-western zone and was not in favour of including the whole of the Punjab in it. In view of all these things it was essential that the President or the League should authoritatively tell the Muslims and non-Muslims of India in clear and precise language what districts and provinces of British India were intended to be included in the north-western zone. But as stated above he refused to do so and persisted in his refusal till April 1944 when the non-Muslim ministers of the Punjab wanted the details to be made known for a consideration of the scheme. It was only after Mr C. Rajagopalachari had given a concrete form in terms which are used in constitutional and administrative documents and are thus easily understood and clearly definable, and in the course of talks with Mahatma Gandhi and at a press interview, that Mr Jinnah was induced to declare for the first time that the units to be included in the Muslim zones

[5] *The Pakistan Issue*, p. 100.

contemplated in the Lahore Resolution were provinces as they stand today and not districts, which means that the whole of the Punjab was to be included in the north-western zone and the whole of Bengal and Assam in the eastern zone. We have seen how the idea of including the whole of the Punjab is contradicted by the President's own acts.

We shall refer to the case of the eastern zone now. The population of Bengal is 6,03,06,525 out of which 3,30,05,434 or 54.73 per cent are Muslims. The population of Assam is 1,02,04,733 of whom 34,42,479 or 33.73 per cent are Muslims. If both the provinces in their entirety are to be included in the eastern Muslim zone, as is now claimed to have been intended by the Lahore Resolution, the position will be that out of a total population of 7,05,11,258 of the two provinces taken together the Muslims will be 3,64,47,913 or 51.69 per cent. Mr Jinnah's statement to Mr Chapman quoted above that the Muslim population would be about 75 per cent is certainly very wide of the mark. Even if we exclude the portions of Bengal and Assam in which there is an overwhelming non-Muslim majority and include only the districts with Muslim majority in the eastern zone, the Muslim population in it will not exceed 68 or 69 per cent. Mr M.R.T. in the article reproduced in *India's Problem of her Future Constitution* says on page 34 with regard to this eastern zone as follows: 'In Bengal, too, like the Punjab, a readjustment of frontiers will raise the Muslim proportion in population to 80 per cent or more. At present the Muslims form an overwhelming majority of 75 per cent in Eastern Bengal and the Goalpara and Sylhet districts of Western Bengal which are contiguous to Eastern Bengal. If this Muslim population is formed together so as to come under a new province of Eastern Bengal and Assam, the Muslims will be placed in a permanent majority of 80 per cent in a total population of 40 millions.' The figures given by Mr M.R.T. are incorrect as will be seen later, but we are here concerned with only pointing out that in his contemplation the whole of Bengal and the whole of Assam were not to be combined to create the eastern Muslim zone but only such portions of them as had a majority of Muslims in their population. The Haroon Committee's recommendation was that the north-eastern zone 'should include the present provinces of Assam and Bengal (excluding Bankura and Midnapore districts) and the district of Purnea from Bihar whose

population is racially and culturally akin to that of Bengal.' Even
this Committee excluded some districts of Bengal. So what has
been said about the north-western zone in regard to the shifting of
the League's demand about the 'territories to be included applies
with equal force to the eastern zone also.

~

TWENTY-SIX

THE RESOLUTION ANALYSED

We have seen how the vague and ambiguous words used in the Lahore Resolution can be interpreted to bear different meanings in regard to the territories sought to be included in the eastern and north-western Muslim zones. A clear-cut, detailed and well-defined scheme is necessary for a fair and intelligent consideration of it by Muslims and non-Muslims alike. But the League has refused to give such details. We have nevertheless to consider the terms of the Lahore Resolution giving to its words the ordinary and natural meaning that they bear and make out what was intended and aimed at by the League when it passed the Lahore Resolution. Let us then analyse the resolution.

It consists of three parts. The first part reiterates that the scheme of federation embodied in the Government of India Act, 1935, is totally unsuited to and unworkable in the peculiar conditions of this country and is altogether unacceptable to Muslim India. The second part records its emphatic view that while the declaration dated 18 October 1939 made by the Viceroy on behalf of His Majesty's Government is reassuring insofar as it declares that the policy and plan on which the Government of India Act, 1935, is based will be reconsidered in consultation with the various parties, interests and communities in India, Muslim India will not be satisfied unless the whole constitutional plan is reconsidered *de novo* and that no revised plan would be acceptable to the Muslims unless it is framed with their approval and consent. Thus these two parts are addressed to the British government and declare the views of the League in regard to any constitutional proposals which they might be contemplating, and they are of importance in the context of our present discussion only to the extent they furnish a background for the third part which deals with the question of creation of independent Muslim States in the north-western and eastern zones of India.

The first paragraph of the third part expresses the considered view of the League 'that no constitutional plan would be workable in this country or acceptable to Muslims unless it is designed on the following basic principle, viz. that geographically contiguous units are demarcated into regions which should be constituted with such territorial readjustments as may be necessary, that the areas in which the Muslims are numerically in a majority as in the north-western and eastern zones of India should be grouped to constitute independent states in which the constituent units shall be autonomous and sovereign.'

The second paragraph lays down that adequate, effective and mandatory safeguards should be specifically provided in the Constitution for minorities for the protection of their religious, cultural, economic, political, administrative and other rights and interests in consultation with them both in the Muslim and non-Muslim zones.

The third paragraph authorizes the Working Committee of the League to frame a scheme of Constitution in accordance with these basic principles, providing for the assumption finally by the respective regions of all powers such as defence, external affairs, communications, customs, and such other matters as may be necessary.

The questions that arise are:

(a) Who is to frame the Constitution?

(b) What is to be the nature of the Constitution contemplated—theocratic, democratic, oligarchic, totalitarian, or any other?

(c) What is the relation of these 'independent States' going to be with the British empire and the non-Muslim zones?

(d) In case of breach of any of the mandatory safeguards for the protection of the minorities, how, by whom, and under what sanction are these safeguards to be enforced?

(e) What are the territories to be included in the Muslim State or States?

(f) What will be their resources and position?

(g) What is the authority that will be in charge of defence, external affairs, communications, customs and such other matters during the period intervening between the enforcement of the Constitution and final assumption by the independent States of power in regard to these matters?

Apart from the question of territories to be included in the Muslim zones, it is necessary fully to understand the implications of the Resolution in regard to such questions, inasmuch as Mr Jinnah insists on acceptance of the Lahore Resolution.

(a)　Who is to frame the Constitution? The framework of the Resolution and the context in which the proposal for a new constitutional plan is made show that it is to be framed by the British Parliament, even as the Act of 1935, which is condemned in an earlier part of the Resolution, was framed. Indians, for that matter Muslims, will have no hand in framing it, although the plan when framed should receive the approval and consent of the Muslims to make it acceptable to them. Acceptance of this part of the Resolution will take us back even beyond and behind the Cripps proposals which frankly conceded the right of the people of India to frame their own Constitution. Other statements made by British authorities have also conceded that right which the Musalmans, Hindus and others of India are expected to give up by accepting this part of the League Resolution.

(b)　What is to be the nature of the contemplated Constitution— theocratic, democratic, oligarchic, totalitarian, or any other? The resolution is silent on this point. The League considers the democratic form of government unsuitable to India and this view has been expressed on numerous occasions by the President. We may quote here some typical passages from the speeches and writings of Mr Jinnah:

'Having regard to the 35 millions of voters, the bulk of whom are totally ignorant, illiterate and untutored, living in centuries-old superstitions of the worst type, thoroughly antagonistic to each other, culturally and socially, the working of this Constitution has clearly brought out that it is impossible to work a democratic parliamentary government in India.'[1]

'Such, however, is the ignorance about Indian conditions among even the members of the British Parliament that in spite of all the experience of the past, it is even yet not realized that this form of government is totally unsuited to India. Democratic systems

[1]　Statement to the *Manchester Guardian* reproduced in *Recent Speeches and Writings of Mr Jinnah*, p. 86.

based on the concept of a homogeneous nation such as England are very definitely not applicable to heterogeneous countries such as India and this simple fact is the root cause of all of India's constitutional ills . . . Western democracy is totally unsuited for India and its imposition on India is the disease in the body politic.'[2]

It is, therefore, necessary clearly to define the nature of the state so that people might judge and decide whether the form of government envisaged is such as will be acceptable to them. It is as necessary for the minorities in the Muslim and non-Muslim zones as for the majorities to know, since Western democracy as ordinarily understood is unsuitable to India and unacceptable to the Muslim League, what other form or what modifications in the democratic conception of the West are acceptable to the League. The reason given by the protagonists of Pakistan for rejecting democracy for India is that the population is not homogeneous in India where the Muslims constitute such a large proportion of the total population. This reason will not cease to operate after partition in the Muslim zones, as the Hindus and other non-Muslims in those zones will not under any calculation be less in proportion of the total population of those areas than Muslims in India as a whole. The proportion of Muslims in British India is 26.83 per cent. The proportion of non-Muslims in the north-western zone will be 37–93 per cent if the entire province of the Punjab is included, and 24.64 per cent of the districts with non-Muslim majority are not included in the zone. Similarly, the proportion of non-Muslims in the eastern zone will be 48.31 per cent and 30.58 per cent according to whether districts with non-Muslim majorities are or are not included in it. It cannot be said with any consistency or show of reason and justice that democracy is unsuitable to India because the Muslims are in a minority, and that it becomes suitable when the position is reversed and they become the majority and non-Muslims the minority in the separated Muslim regions. It is therefore not an unwarranted inference that when the President of the League says that democracy is unsuitable to India, it is and will remain equally unsuitable to Pakistan and that therefore some other form of Constitution is contemplated. Why should not a clear picture of that Constitution be given to

[2] Article in the *Time and Tide*, dated 19 January 1940 reproduced in *Recent Speeches* . . . pp. 111–13.

all concerned to enable them to judge it on its merits and accept
it with their eyes open after full consideration?

(c)   What is the relation of these independent States going to
       be with the British empire and the non-Muslim zone? It
       is clear that they will be independent of the non-Muslim
       zone, but it is not clear that they will be independent of
       the British empire. If they are to be independent of the
       British empire, there is no sense or meaning in asking or
       expecting the British Parliament to frame a Constitution
       for them and for the rest of India. The third paragraph
       of part 3 clearly indicates that assumption of complete
       independence at the very outset is not contemplated but an
       interim period has to intervene during which powers relating
       to defence, external affairs, communications, customs, and
       such other matters will vest in some other authority. As
       the League has repudiated the idea of these powers being
       vested in any Indian body inasmuch as Hindus are bound
       to be in a majority in it, it follows that they can remain
       vested in the British government during this interval. The
       word 'Finally' in the third paragraph of part 3 of the
       Resolution makes it abundantly clear that the independence
       of these independent States will be of a limited character
       to begin with. The interval which must elapse between the
       establishment of the independent States and the assumption
       of full powers by them is not indicated and evidently will
       depend on circumstances which were considered incalculable
       at the time the Resolution was framed. The position, thus,
       of the Muslim independent States in the beginning will be
       less than that of a dominion of the British Commonwealth
       under the Statute of Westminster and it is not clear when,
       if ever, they are to be free of British control altogether.
       That the interpretation put here is not unwarranted is
       apparent from an interview which Mr Jinnah gave to the
       News Chronicle of London:[3]

Q. But surely there would be a civil war. You would be creating
an Indian Ulster which Hindus might one day attack in the name
of united India.

[3] Published in *The A. B. Patrika*, 4 March 1944.

Mr Jinnah: I do not agree but there would be under the new Constitution a transitional period for settlement and adjustment during which time British authority, so far as armed forces and foreign affairs are concerned, would remain paramount. The length of the transitional period would depend on the speed with which the two peoples and Great Britain adjusted themselves to the new Constitution.

Q. What if Britain then refused to leave India on grounds that relations between Hindustan and Pakistan were not good enough to live as neighbours?

Mr Jinnah: That might happen but it is not likely. Even so we should enjoy a degree of autonomy which we do not possess today. As a separate nation and a dominion we should at least be in a better position to deal with and possibly reach an agreement with the British government which we are not able to do during the present deadlock.'

It may be noted in passing that the use of the word 'dominion' in the last sentence quoted above is inaccurate, because as regards armed forces and foreign affairs the British authority will remain paramount in Pakistan during the interval, whereas in a British dominion British authority is not, and the dominion government is paramount even in respect of these matters. The use of the word 'independent' does not and cannot in the context mean even Dominion Status here and now, much less complete independence of British control or complete transfer of power to the people of the regions concerned. If the rest of India or any portion of it attains complete independence of British control, it will still have to deal with the British government in these regions albeit with a majority of Muslims in them. They will constitute islands of the British empire in an independent India. The independence contemplated is thus from the rest of India and not from the British empire at all, at any rate in the early stages.

I shall quote just one more passage from another statement of Mr Jinnah regarding the status of the new States to be created by Partition. In a statement to the press on 1 April 1940, immediately after the Lahore Resolution, we find the following:

In regard to the relationship of the Muslim Homeland with Great Britain Mr Jinnah referred to the Lahore Resolution and said: 'As regards other zone or zones that may be constituted in the rest of India, our relationship will be of an international

character. An example already exists in the relationship of India
with Burma and Ceylon.'[4] Evidently then not only Pakistan but
Hindustan also are contemplated as part and parcel of the British
empire and enjoying the same position which India, Burma and
Ceylon have today vis-à-vis the British government and also as
between themselves.

Again, Mr Jinnah in his interview referred only to armed
forces and foreign affairs, whereas the Resolution mentions
'communications, customs, and such other matters as may be
necessary'. The rest of India will have no kind of authority in any
matter whatsoever and the Muslim zones also in the interval will
not assume power in regard to these matters. The only conclusion
possible is that the British authority will continue to be paramount
in respect of 'communications, customs and such other matters
as may be necessary' also. These indeed would cover a large field
and it is not inconceivable that in some respects the powers of
the Muslim zones may be even less than those of a provincial
government under the Government of India Act of 1935.

It has been said that the independent Muslim zones will enter
into a treaty with the rest of India as between two independent
States. If the British authority is to be paramount in regard to
foreign affairs in the Muslim zones, how can the governments of
such zones enter into a treaty with the rest of India? The treaty,
if any, will therefore be between the rest of India and the British
authority, or at most between the rest of India and the Muslim
zones acting under the authority and instruction of the British
government in the same way as the Government of India today may
enter into a treaty with an independent state like Afghanistan,

(d)   In case of a breach of any of the mandatory safeguards
       for the protection of the minorities, how, by whom, and
       under what sanction are such safeguards to be enforced?

The Muslim League Resolution is absolutely silent on this point.
As the two States—the Muslim and the non-Muslim—are to be
independent of each other and not subject to any common central
control of any kind whatsoever, there seems to be no authority
that can enforce these mandatory provisions by any legal or
administrative process. Any breach will have to be treated on the

[4] Mr M.R.T. *India's Problem of her Future Constitution*, p. 31.

same basis as a hostile act of one State against another; and can be set right, in the absence of an amicable settlement, through diplomatic channels or international arbitration by the methods known for settling international disputes. Is it possible or at any rate easy for minorities in one State to invoke the aid of their nationals in other independent States for such disputes? The new Muslim States carved out of India will not be the only Muslim states in the world. There are other Muslim States in close proximity to India. Has it been possible for the Muslim minority in India to invoke the aid of these Muslim States against the tyranny and oppression of non-Muslims? If the story of tyranny and oppression by Congress ministries against Muslims has any truth and can at all furnish a justification for the creation of new Muslim States, it could furnish just grounds for protest through diplomatic channels, if not intervention, by the existing Muslim States—especially when Muslims no matter where they reside, irrespective of any other consideration, simply by reason of their religion, constitute one nation. Has any attempt been made by the Muslim minority of India to invoke such aid? As the independent States will have nothing in common between them, 'Hindustan' will find it very difficult if not impossible to intervene, if the non-Muslim minority is oppressed in Pakistan, and vice versa—Pakistan will find it equally difficult if not impossible to intervene in favour of the Muslim minority in Hindustan.

It is worthwhile recording here the experience of minorities in Europe whose rights were safeguarded by the Minority Treaties under the guarantee of the League of Nations. 'There have been laudable exceptions both in the new states and in the old; but generally speaking the fate of the minorities has been one of suffering. Almost every State has committed, and every minority suffered under, flagrant violations of the Minority Treaties. And these have been committed, to all intents and purposes, with impunity . . . But even with these qualifications, it is impossible honestly to deny that the League guarantee has proved but a broken reed to the minorities. The percentage of cases in which the League's intervention has been invoked with any real effect has been deplorably low and, even in those, considerations were generally at work other than the determination to obtain pure justice for the minorities.'[5]

[5] C.B. Macartney, *National States and National Minorities* (1934), p. 390.

For a fair treatment of the minorities in the independent States of Pakistan and Hindustan, it has been suggested that 'as a matter of fact the existence of minorities both in Hindu India and Muslim States will make it possible for them to adopt a common line of action and to restore confidence among the minorities which will thus be finally reconciled to their lot.'[6] 'The division of India will throw a great responsibility upon the majority in its respective zones to create a real sense of security amongst the minorities and win their complete trust and confidence.'[7] Now, separation is not necessary for creating a sense of responsibility in the majority towards the minorities and for winning their confidence. Indeed, unity provides a more favourable atmosphere for the growth of this sense of responsibility and it can be and should be cultivated whether there is division or not. What is really meant in the above extract is not so much a genuine sense of responsibility as a sense of fear in the majority in one State of the reaction of the majority in the other State. This can happen for one of two reasons. Each independent State may be apprehensive of active intervention by the other independent State and may thus be put on its behaviour. As shown above this is rarely, if at all, possible. The second way in which it may happen is that one independent State will not ill-treat its minority for fear that the other independent State may act similarly towards its minorities. In other words, the minorities will serve as hostages in the hands of their government for the good conduct of the other government. It is very doubtful if this can work in practice. The very idea of ill-treating people who have done nothing wrong and may for all practical purposes be the best of citizens in their own State, because some other independent government with which they have no concern has misbehaved, is so repugnant to our sense of natural justice that it is inconceivable that either Pakistan or Hindustan will resort to reprisal against its own subjects for the act of an independent government. If the story of Congress tyranny has any foundation in fact, the Muslim ministries in Muslim provinces could have retaliated in their own provinces, as the powers enjoyed by all ministries were the same under the Government of India Act; and under the Act if Congress ministries could oppress the Muslims, the Muslim ministries could equally exercise the self-same powers and oppress the Hindu minorities under them. They could at any rate have

---

[6] Mr M.R.T., *India's Problems* . . ., p. 41.
[7] Ibid., quoting Mr Jinnah at p. 30.

put pressure on the central government to use such powers as it possessed through the Governors to protect the Muslim minorities. But nothing appears to have been done either by way of reprisal or by invoking the special powers of the Governors by the Muslim ministries. Not that non-Muslim minorities had no grievances against the Muslim ministries. They had serious grievances which were ventilated in the Legislatures and the public press. But no one has asserted that the acts complained of were of a retaliatory nature done for protecting Muslim minorities in other provinces. All this can be explained only by the fact that the complaints about acts of oppression were not justified or at least not serious enough to induce Muslim ministries to take any action although they now form one of the major grounds for claiming a division of India. How will the position be any better if independent Muslim States are established in the north-western and eastern regions of India where Muslim ministries have functioned all along during this period of 'tyranny and oppression'? If anything, their being cut off altogether from the rest of India will act more as a handicap than help in this respect. The whole basis of the demand for separation is the apprehension that the Hindu majority will suppress and oppress the Muslim minority in India as a whole. If the Hindu majority can do that with impunity when the Muslims form such a large proportion of the population of India there is no reasonable ground for hoping that it will behave better when the Muslims come to be a much smaller community in Hindustan and consequently less capable of extorting fair treatment from an unjust majority. Intervention by the independent Muslim States being impossible, or at any rate difficult in most cases, any safeguards in the constitution of the independent states will prove effective only to the extent the majority is in a mood to respect them or the minority is in a position to enforce them. *Ex hypothesi* the Hindu majority cannot be depended upon to be just and fair. The Muslim minority in Hindustan will be weaker than it is today to enforce fair treatment. The safeguards, even though mandatory in their respective Constitutions, will always be open to revision by the independent States, if they are really independent, and, even if they are allowed to remain in the Constitution, will for the reasons given above prove illusory and afford no protection to the minority, as the experience of safeguards guaranteed even by the League of Nations shows.

~

TWENTY-SEVEN

THE RESOLUTION ANALYSED (CONTD.)—DELIMITATION OF
THE MUSLIM STATE

What are the territories to be included in the Muslim State or States?[1]

Table VIII gives details of the population by communities of the provinces of British India as given in the Census of India, 1941. A study of this Table will prove of use in understanding fully the question of delimitation.

The Resolution has not defined or delimited the territories, nor has any other authority of the League done so. But the Resolution has laid down the basic principle—that geographically contiguous units are demarcated into regions which should be so constituted, with such territorial readjustments as may be necessary, that the areas in which the Muslims are numerically in a majority as in the north-western and eastern zones of India should be grouped to constitute 'independent States' in which the constituent units shall be autonomous and sovereign. The tests that have to be applied in deciding whether any particular unit is to be included are:

(i)   Is the unit geographically contiguous to another unit which is to be included in the Muslim State?

(ii) Are the Muslims numerically in a majority in this unit?

(iii) Is the necessary territorial readjustment possible, to make the unit fulfil the first two tests? Besides, each unit within the zone will be autonomous and sovereign.

It has been authoritatively stated by the President of the Muslim League that the Lahore Resolution does not deal with Indian States. Dealing with the Indian States, Mr Jinnah said: 'The only important states which matter are not in the eastern but in the north-western zone. They are Kashmir, Bahawalpur, Patiala, etc. If these States willingly agree to come into federation of Muslim Homeland we

[1] See p. 281.

shall be glad to come to a reasonable and honourable settlement with them. We have, however, no desire to force them or coerce them in any way.'[2] Again, when Gandhiji wanted to know during his negotiations with him in September 1944, if in Pakistan Kashmir was included as in the original proposal, he said that now Pakistan refers only to the four provinces of Sind, Baluchistan, the NWFP and the Punjab. We have, therefore, in demarcating the Muslim zones to leave the Indian States out of consideration.

As regards the area to be included in the Muslim zone, the sentence is somewhat involved and the expressions used to denote what is to be included in Pakistan are many and unknown to present-day constitutional and administrative language current in British government documents. Thus the expressions used are 'units', 'regions', 'areas', and 'zones', none of which is defined by the League and none of which is used in current administrative and constitutional literature. The current words are province, district, tahsil, taluqa, thana, etc. and it was easy enough to express the meaning of the resolution by using these current words, if the meaning was clear to the authors of the resolution and if they intended to make it clear to others—Muslims and non-Muslims alike—including the British government. The use of ambiguous language and the reluctance to disclose the details of the proposal and clarify its implications have been to say the least, unfortunate. Not only have they prevented concentration of attention on the scheme and led to a crop of unauthorized interpretations thereof but have also created doubts in the minds of many people who have begun to put various questions some of which may be indicated. Why was such ambiguous language employed? Was it to leave undetermined the difference that existed among the protagonists of division, one set of whom insisted on homogeneous Muslim States in north-western and eastern India with large, if not overwhelming, Muslim majorities, and the other was satisfied with small, if not bare, Muslim majorities, provided larger slices of the country came under Muslim independent States? Or was it considered inexpedient to expose the whole scheme to public view and public criticism? Why has there been such reluctance to specify what is to be included in the Muslim States and what is to be excluded from them? Can it be that the whole thing is left

---

[2] Statement to press, dated 1 April 1940, printed in *India's Problem of her Future Constitution*, p. 30.

Table VIII

Population by Communities of Provinces of British India, with Percentages
(Figures in lakhs; percentages in brackets)

Province	Total population	Hindus excepting Scheduled Castes	Scheduled Castes	Total Hindus	Muslims	Christians	Sikhs	Tribes	Others
Madras	493.42	347.31 (70.4)	80.68 (16.3)	427.99 (86.7)	38.97 (7.9)	20.46 (4.1)	0.04 (0.0)	5.62 (1.1)	0.36
Bombay	208.50	147.00 (70.5)	18.55 (8.9)	165.55 (79.4)	19.20 (9.2)	3.75 (1.8)	0.08 (0.04)	16.14 (7.7)	3.76
Bengal	603.07	176.80 (29.3)	73.79 (12.2)	250.59 (41.5)	330.05 (54.7)	1.66 (0.28)	0.16 (0.03)	18.89 (3.1)	1.70
UP	550.21	340.95 (62.0)	117.17 (21.1)	458.12 (83.2)	84.16 (15.3)	1.60 (0.29)	2.32 (0.42)	2.89 (0.53)	1.11
Punjab	284.19	63.02 (22.1)	12.49 (4.4)	75.51 (26.5)	162.17 (57.0)	5.05 (1.7)	37.57 (13.2)	–	3.89
Bihar	363.40	221.74 (61.0)	43.40 (11.9)	265.14 (72.9)	47.16 (12.9)	0.33 (0.10)	0.13 (0.04)	50.56 (13.9)	0.06
CP and Berar	168.14	98.18 (58.8)	30.51 (18.1)	129.32 (76.9)	7.84 (4.6)	0.58 (0.35)	0.15 (0.09)	29.37 (17.4)	0.87
Assam	102.05	35.37 (34.6)	6.76 (6.6)	42.13 (41.2)	34.42 (33.7)	0.41 (0.40)	0.03 (0.03)	24.85 (24.3)	0.20
NWFP	30.38	1.80 (5.9)	–	1.80 (5.9)	27.89 (91.7)	0.11 (0.36)	0.58 (1.9)	–	0.001
Orissa	87.29	55.95 (64.1)	12.39 (14.1)	68.34 (78.2)	1.46 (1.6)	0.28 (0.32)	0.002 (0.0)	17.21 (19.7)	0.006

(contd.)

	Total								
Sind	45.35	10.38 (22.9)	1.92 (4.2)	12.30 (27.1)	32.08 (70.7)	0.20 (0.45)	0.31 (0.68)	0.37 (0.81)	0.09
Ajmer Merwara	5.83	3.76 (64.5)	—	3.76 (64.5)	0.90 (15.4)	0.06 (0.99)	0.009 (0.15)	0.91 (15.6)	0.19
Andamans and Nicobars	0.34	0.08 (24.9)	—	0.08 (24.9)	0.08 (23.7)	0.03 (7.7)	0.007 (2.2)	0.11 (32.8)	0.03
Baluchistan	5.02	0.40 (7.9)	0.05 (0.9)	0.45 (8.8)	4.39 (87.5)	0.06 (1.2)	0.12 (2.3)	—	0.001
Coorg	1.69	1.05 (62.1)	0.26 (15.3)	1.31 (77.4)	0.15 (8.7)	0.03 (2.0)	—	0.20 (11.6)	—
Delhi	9.18	4.45 (48.4)	1.23 (13.4)	5.68 (61.7)	3.05 (33.2)	0.17 (1.9)	0.16 (1.7)	—	0.12
Panth Piploda	0.052	0.037 (71.2)	0.009 (17.3)	0.05 (89.7)	0.003 (4.7)	0.002 (4.1)	—	0.00012 (0.22)	0.001
Total	2958.00	1508.90 (51.0)	399.20 (13.5)	1908.10 (64.5)	793.98 (26.8)	34.82 (1.19)	41.65 (1.41)	167.13 (5.65)	12.38 (0.42)

vague and ambiguous so that in due time what was considered best and most expedient might be put forward? Can it be that when once the non-Muslims have agreed to the principle of division, they might be asked to agree to whatever the territories the League demanded on pain of being charged with bad faith, if they raised any question at the time of demarcation of boundaries?

Whatever may have been the intention or motive for using such ambiguous language avoiding current expressions, the attempt has not been successful and on a fair construction of the language used there can be but one meaning that can be gathered from the Resolution as a whole. As pointed out above there can be no doubt that no territory in which Muslims are not numerically in a majority can be included in the Muslim State, and further, such territory has to be contiguous to other territory with similar Muslim majority.

Let us apply these tests and see what areas can be included in the north-western and eastern zones which have to be constituted into independent States. Let us take each province with its districts.

I. THE NORTH-WESTERN ZONE

Figures from Census of India, 1941, are given below (with percentages in brackets):

In the above figures, under the head 'Others' are included— Sikhs 31,011 or 0.68 per cent; Christians (other than Indian Christians) 6,977; Jains 3,687; Paris 3,838; Buddhists 11; Jews 1,082—Total 46,706—who are not shown separately district by district. (Common percentage for last three columns taken together).

'Others' in the above statement include—57,939 or 1.91 per cent Sikhs; 5,463 Christians other than Indian Christians; 25 Buddhists; 71 Jews; 1 Jain; 24 Parsis—Total 63,523.

In the above under the head 'Others' are included 11,918 or 2.38 per cent Sikhs; 3.369 Christians other than Indian Christians; 7 Jains; 75 Parsis; 43 Buddhists; 19 Jews and 14 others—Total 15,445.

A glance at the Tables will show that in none of the districts of Sind are non-Muslims in a majority. On the other hand, Muslims are in a majority in each and every district, their highest proportion being 90.47 per cent in the Upper Sind Frontier district and the lowest being 50.26 per cent in Thar Parkar district. The

TABLE IX

Population by Communities of Sind

Districts	Area (sq. miles)	Total population	Hindus	Muslims	Indian Christians	Tribes	Others
Dadu	7,370	3,89,380	58,372 (14.99)	3,29,991 (84.74)	74 (0.26)	154	789
Hyderabad	4,476	7,58,748	2,45,849 (32.40)	5,07,620 (66.90)	490 (0.69)	769	4,020
Karachi	8,357	7,13,900	2,22,597 (31.18)	4,57,035 (64.00)	11,310 (4.80)	884	22,074
Larkana	2,857	5,11,208	91,062 (17.81)	4,18,543 (81.85)	49 (0.31)	–	1,554
Nawabshah	3,908	5,84,178	1,40,428 (24.04)	4,36,414 (74.72)	212 (1.25)	1,326	5,798
Sukkur	5,550	6,92,556	1,95,458 (28.22)	4,91,634 (70.98)	277 (0.78)	51	5,136
Thar-Parkar	13,649	5,81,004	2,47,496 (42.58)	2,92,025 (50.26)	800 (7.14)	33,635	7,048
Upper Sind Frontier	1,969	3,04,034	28,664 (9.42)	2,75,063 (90.47)	20 (0.10)		287
Total	48,136	45,35,008	12,29,926 (27.12)	32,08,325 (70.75)	13,232 (2.13)	36,819	46,706

TABLE X

Population by Communities of the NWFP

Districts	Area (sq. miles)	Total population	Hindus	Muslims	Indian Christians	Others
Hazara	3,000	7,96,230	30,267 (3.80)	7,56,004 (94.94)	314 (1.25)	9,645
Mardan	1,098	5,06,539	10,677 (2.10)	4,83,575 (95.46)	376 (2.42)	11,911
Peshawar	1,547	8,51,833	51,212 (6.01)	7,69,589 (90.34)	3,397 (3.64)	27,635
Kohat	2,707	2,89,404	17,527 (6.06)	2,66,224 (91.99)	596 (1.95)	5,057
Bannu	1,695	2,95,930	31,471 (10.63)	2,57,648 (87.06)	467 (2.30)	6,344
D.I. Khan	4,216	2,98,131	39,167 (13.14)	2,55,757 (85.78)	276 (1.07)	2,931
Total	14,263	30,38,067	1,80,321 (5.94)	27,88,797 (91.79)	5,426 (2.26)	63,523

TABLE XI

Population by Communities of Baluchistan

Districts	Area (sq. miles)	Total population	Hindus	Muslims	Indian Christians	Others
Quetta Pishin	5,310	1,56,286	28,629 (18.32)	1,13,288 (72.48)	2,296	12,076 (9.19)
Loralai	7,375	83,685	3,129 (3.74)	79,273 (94.73)	118	1,165 (1.53)
Zhob	10,478	61,499	4,286 (6.97)	55,987 (91.04)	78	1,148 (1.99)
Bolan	407	6,009	950 (15.81)	4,812 (80.08)	22	225 (4.11)
Chagal	19,429	29,250	1,204 (4.12)	27,864 (95.26)	1	181 (0.62)
Sibi	11,457	1,64,899	6,425 (3.89)	1,57,706 (95.63)	118	650 (0.46)
Total	54,456	5,01,631	44,623 (8.89)	4,38,930 (87.51)	2,633	15,445 (3.60)

communal proportion in the province as a whole is: Muslims
70.75 per cent, Hindus 27.12 per cent and others including Sikhs,
Christians, Jains, Buddhists, Jews and tribes 2.13 per cent out of
which Sikhs constitute 0.68 per cent of the total population. The
province as a whole is contiguous to Baluchistan, and the NWFP
and the western Punjab.

Similarly, in each and every district of the NWFP the Muslims
are in numerical majority, their highest proportion being 95.46
per cent in Mardan district and the lowest being 85.78 per cent
in Dera Ismail Khan district. In the province as a whole the
Muslims constitute 91.79 per cent, the Hindus 5.94 per cent, the
rest 2.26 per cent, including the Sikhs who are 1.91 per cent of
the total population of the province. The province is contiguous
to Baluchistan, Sind and western Punjab.

Baluchistan likewise has a Muslim majority in each of its
districts, their highest proportion being 95.63 per cent in the
Sibi district and their lowest being 72.48 per cent in Quetta Pishin
district. In the province as a whole the Muslims constitute 87.51
per cent, the Hindus 8.89 per cent and others 3.60 per cent of
the total population. Among the 'Others' are included Sikhs who
form 2.38 per cent of the total population. This province is also
contiguous to Sind, the NWFP and the Punjab.

Thus there can be no doubt that these three British provinces
fulfil the test laid down by the Lahore Resolution of the Muslim
League for being included in the Muslim independent State in the
north-west of India.

The position of the Punjab is different, as a reference to the
Table XII will show (Census, 1941).

Before analysing the figures given in Table XI it is worth noting
that under 'Others 'are included Adidharmis, Jains, Parsis, Jews
and those who returned no specified religion or community. Of
these the most numerous are the Adidharmis, who according to
the Census Commissioner though included in Scheduled Castes
do not claim to be Hindus and are hence recorded separately
not only from the Hindus but also from the Scheduled Castes.
They number 3,43,685 or 1.21 per cent of the total population
of the Punjab. They are concentrated very largely in the Jullundar
division where their number is 2,50,267 or 4.60 per cent of the
population of that division. Their next largest concentrations are
in the Multan division and Lahore division where they number

TABLE XII

Population by Communities of the Punjab

Divisions or Districts	Area (sq. miles)	Total population	Hindus	Muslims	Christians	Sikhs	Others
Ambala Div.							
Hissar	5,213	10,06,709	6,52,676 (64.83)	2,85,208 (28.33)	1,292 (0.13)	60,731 (6.03)	6,802 (0.67)
Rohtak	2,246	9,56,399	7,80,474 (81.61)	1,66,569 (17.42)	1,043 (0.11)	1,466 (0.15)	6,847 (0.71)
Gurgaon	2,234	8,51,458	5,60,498 (65.85)	2,85,992 (33.56)	1,673 (0.20)	637 (0.07)	2,658 (0.31)
Karnal	3,126	9,94,575	6,66,036 (66.97)	3,04,346 (30.68)	1,249 (0.13)	19,887 (2.00)	3,057 (0.30)
Ambala	1,851	8,47,745	4,10,333 (48.40)	2,68,999 (31.73)	6,065 (0.71)	1,56,543 (18.46)	5,805 (0.68)
Simla	80	38,576	29,466 (76.38)	7,022 (18.20)	934 (2.42)	1,032 (2.67)	122 (0.32)
Total	14,750	46,95,462	30,99,483 (66.01)	13,18,136 (28.07)	12,256 (0.26)	2,40,296 (5.12)	25,291 (0.54)
Jullundar Div.							
Kangra	9,979	8,99,377	8,38,479 (93.23)	43,249 (4.81)	788 (0.09)	4,309 (0.53)	12,052 (1.34)
Hoshiarpur	2,195	11,70,323	4,68,225 (40.01)	3,80,759 (32.53)	6,165 (0.53)	1,98,194 (16.94)	1,16,980 (9.99)
Jullundar	1,334	11,27,190	1,98,160 (17.59)	5,09,804 (45.23)	6,233 (0.55)	2,98,741 (26.50)	1,14,252 (10.13)

TABLE XII (contd.)

Divisions or District	Area (sq. miles)	Total population	Hindus	Muslims	Christians	Sikhs	Others
Ludhiana	1,339	8,18,615	1,66,678 (20.36)	3,02,482 (36.95)	1,913 (0.23)	3,41,175 (41.68)	6,367 (0.78)
Ferozepur	4,085	14,23,076	2,79,260 (19.62)	6,41,448 (45.07)	12,607 (0.89)	4,79,486 (33.69)	10,275 (0.72)
Total	18,992	54,38,581	19,50,802 (35.87)	18,77,742 (34.53)	27,706 (0.51)	13,22,405, (24.31)	2.59.926 (4.78)
Lahore Div.							
Amritsar	1,572	14,13,876	2,16,778 (15.33)	6,57,695 (46.52)	25,973 (1.84)	5,10.845 (36.13)	2.585 (0.18)
Lahore	2,595	16,95,375	2,84,351 (16.77)	10,27.772 (60.62)	70.147 (4.14)	3,10,646 (18.32)	2,459 (0.15)
Gurdaspur	1,846	11,53,511	2,83,192 (24.55)	5,89,923 (51.14)	51,522 (4.47)	2,21,261 (19.18)	7,613 (0.66)
Sialkot	1,576	11,90,497	2,31,114 (19.41)	7,39,218 (62.09)	75.81 (6.37)	1,39,409 (11.71)	4,925 (0.41)
Gujranwalla	2,311	9,12,234	1,07,887 (11.83)	6,42,706 (70.45)	60,829 (6.67)	99,139 (10.87)	1,673 (0.18)
Sheikhupura	2,303	8,52,508	77,740 (9.12)	5,42,344 (63.62)	60,054 (7.04)	1,60,706 (18.85)	11,664 (1.37)
Total	12,203	72,18,001	12,01,062 (16.64)	41,99,658 (58.18)	3,44,356 (4.77)	14,42,006 (19.98)	30,919 (0.43)
Rawalpindi Div.							
Gujarat	2,266	11,04,952	84,643 (7.66)	9,45,609 (85.58) -	4,449 (0.40)	70.233 (6.36)	18 (0.00)
Shahpur	4,770	9,98,921	1,00,708 (10.08)	8,35,918 (83.68)	12,770 (1.28)	48,046 (4.80)	1,479 (0.15)

(contd.)

District							
Jhelum	2,774	6,29,658	40,879 (6.49)	5,63,033 (89.42)	893 (0.14)	24,680 (3.92)	173 (0.02)
Rawalpindi	2,022	7,85,231	82,463 (10.50)	6,28,193 (80.00)	9,014 (1.15)	64.127 (8.17)	1,434 (0.18)
Attock	4,148	6,75,875	43,190 (6.39)	6,11,128 (90.42)	1,392 (0.21)	20,120 (2.97)	45 (0.01)
Mianwali	5,401	5,06,321	62,787 (12.40)	4,36,260 (86.16)	358 (0.07)	6,865 (1.36)	51 (0.01)
Total	21,381	47,00,958	4,14,670 (8.82)	40,20,141 (85.52)	28,876 (0.61)	2,34,071 (4.98)	3,200 (0.07)
Multan Div.							
Montgomery	4,204	13,29,103	1,91,182 (14.38)	9,18,564 (69.11)	24,432 (1.84)	1,75,064 (13.17)	19,861 (1.49)
Lyallpur	3,522	13,96,305	1,62,295 (11.62)	8,77,518 (62.85)	51,948 (3.73)	2,62,737 (18.82)	41,807 (2.99)
Jhang	3,415	8,21,631	1,29,791 (15.80)	6,78,736 (82.61)	763 (0.09)	12,238 (1.49)	103 (0.01)
Multan	5,653	14,84,333	2,42,987 (16.37)	11,57,911 (78.01)	14,290 (0.96)	61,628 (4.15)	7.517 (0.51)
Muzaffargarh	5,605	7,12,849	90,547 (12.70)	6,16,074 (86.42)	227 (0.03)	5,882 (0.82)	119 (0.02)
Dera Ghazikhan	9,364	5,81,350	67,393 (11.59)	5,12,678 (88.19)	87 (0.01)	1,072 (0.18)	120 (0.02)
Baloch Trans Frontier Tract	–	40,246	160 (0.39)	40,084 (99.60)	–	2 (0.0)	–
Total	31,763	63,65,317	8,84,355 (13.89)	48,01.565 (75.43)	91,747 (1.44)	5,18,623 (8.15)	69,527 (1.09)
Total of the Province	99,089	2,84,18,819	75,50,372 (26.57)	1,62,17,242 (57.06)	5,04,941 (1.78)	37,57,401 (13.22)	3,88,863 (1.37)

TABLE XIII

Muslim and Non-Muslim Districts of the Punjab and their Population by Communities

Division or District	Area (sq. miles)	Total Population	Hindus	Muslims	Christians	Sikhs	Others	Total Non-Muslims
Muslim Majority Districts								
Rawalpindi division	21,381	47,00,958	4,14,670 (8.82)	40,20,141 (85.52)	28,876 (0.61)	2,34,071 (4.98)	3,200 (0.07)	6,80,817 (14.48)
Multan division	31,763	63,65,817	8,84,355 (13.89)	48,01,565 (75.43)	91,747 (1.44)	5,18,623 (8.15)	69,527 (1.09)	15,64,252 (24.57)
Lahore division ex Amritsar	10,631	58,04,125	9,84,284 (16.96)	35,41,963 (61.02)	3,18,383 (5.49)	9,31,161 (16.04)	28,334 (0.49)	22,62,162 (38.98)
Total	63,775	1,68,70,900	22,83,309 (13.53)	1,23,63,669 (73.29)	4,39,006 (2.60)	16,83,855 (9.98)	1,01,061 (0.60)	45,07,231 (26.71)
Non-Muslim Majority Districts								
Ambala division	14,750	46,95,462	30,99,483 (66.01)	13,18,136 (28.07)	12,256 (0.26)	2,40,296 (5.12)	25,291 (0.54)	33,77,326 (71.93)
Jullundar division	18,992	54,38,581	19,50,802 (35.87)	18,77,742 (34.53)	27,706 (0.51)	13,22,405 (24.31)	2,59,926 (4.78)	35,60,839 (65.47)
Amritsar division	1,572	14,13,876	2,16,778 (15.33)	6,57,695 (46.52)	25,973 (1.84)	5,10,845 (36.13)	2,585 (0.18)	7,56,181 (53.48)
Total	35,314	1,15,47,919	52,67,063 (45.61)	38,53,573 (33.35)	65,935 (0.57)	20,73,546 (17.96)	2,87,802 (2,49)	76,94,346 (66.63)

68,641 and 20,488 respectively. Their number is negligible in the Ambala and Rawalpindi divisions, being only 2,795 and 1,534 respectively. As has been pointed out in the Census Report of 1931: 'The most notable feature of the present (1931) census from the stand-point of returns of religion has been the adoption of the term Adidharmi by numerous Chamars and Chuhras and other untouchables. At previous censuses Chuhras unless they returned some recognized religion were always included among Hindus.' The 1941 Census Report also notes that all those who are recorded as Adidharmis belong to the Scheduled Castes but have not claimed to be Hindus. The last two censuses have thus succeeded in reducing the number of Hindus in the province by excluding the Adidharmis from amongst them.

Coming to a study of the census figures of the Punjab we find that unlike the other three provinces of Sind, NWFP and Baluchistan where the Muslims are in overwhelming numerical majority, being 70.75, 91.79, and 87.51 per cent respectively of the population, in the Punjab they constitute just a bare majority, being only 57.06 per cent of the population. Again unlike in those provinces they are not in a majority in every division or district of the Punjab. On the other hand there are districts and divisions in which non-Muslims are in overwhelming majority. The expression used in the Lahore Resolution of the League is simply 'numerically in a majority' without any qualifying word indicating the extent of the majority. It is therefore equally open to the interpretations that the majority should be an overwhelming majority or a bare majority. But when one considers the object and the reason for which Partition is sought one cannot but come to the conclusion that the majority contemplated must be an overwhelming and not a bare majority. The object of the separation is to give the Muslims an opportunity to develop according to their own notions. The reason for it is that they constitute a separate nation and as such differ from all others inhabiting this country in culture, social life and outlook, and religion; and they should therefore have a separate homeland in which they would be supreme. Now with a bare majority the Muslims will not be able to develop according to their own notions when there will be a very strong minority not prepared to merge itself in them and in fact ever ready to assert its own inherent right to develop according to its own notions. If by reason of a separate religion and consequent

separate culture, social life and outlook, a bare majority has a right
to a separate homeland, a minority which is only just a minority
cannot in justice and fairness be denied the same right. It should
be noted also that the Lahore Resolution recognizing that there
are differences among the four north-western provinces *inter se*
lays down that the constituent units of the independent State shall
be autonomous and sovereign. Leaving out of consideration for
the moment the question as to what extent and how a constituent
unit of a larger state can be sovereign and confining ourselves to
the question of the relationship that will subsist as between the
constituent units, there can be no doubt that each unit will have
to depend upon itself for its internal administration. In other
words, if the Constitution of the independent Muslim States is
to be of a democratic nature—by which I mean a Constitution
which gives to the citizens of the State without distinction of caste,
creed, or colour the right to choose their own rulers and enables
them thereby to run the administration according to the ideas
and wishes of those citizens—then it will in practice be found to
be most difficult, if not impossible, for a bare majority to run
the administration according to the notions of a bare numerical
majority of Muslims in the State. It can, therefore, with perfect
fairness and justice be claimed that the province of the Punjab, as
it is constituted today in which the Muslims form a bare numerical
majority of 57 per cent, does not fulfil the test laid down by the
Lahore Resolution and should not and cannot be separated to
become a constituent unit of the independent Muslim State in
the north-west. This result follows if we accept the proposition
that in deciding what areas are to be separated we must take
the whole province as a unit of which the population has to be
taken into consideration. It is, therefore, with good reason that
'A Punjabi 'in his book *Confederacy of India* and Mr M.R.T. in
an article have not taken the province of the Punjab as a whole
for making this calculation and have excluded portions from it in
which according to them the Muslims are in a minority.

'If Ambala division and eastern Hindu and Sikh States are
excluded from the Punjab, its population will be reduced from
$28^{1/2}$ millions at present to 21 millions but the Muslim percentage
will be raised from 55 per cent to 70. This Muslim percentage will
further be raised if the entire Muslim north-west is taken together
as a whole. With the eastern frontier modified as proposed, the

north-west will have a total population of 35 millions of which Muslims will number 27 millions and non-Muslims 8 millions. The Muslim proportion of 77 per cent will be strong enough to ensure a permanent stable government, and this result will be achieved without having recourse to any scheme of exchange of population.'[3]

'The question of the eastern boundary of the Punjab constitutes a matter of great importance and it is possible that Muslim opinion may, at some time, become divided over it: Some regarding the River Jumna or the Ridge separating the plain of the Indus from that of the Ganges as the natural boundary between this unit of Indusstan and Hindu India in its east, and others believing that the said boundary should be so fixed as to exclude all the eastern Hindu tracts of the Kangra district, some portions of the Hoshiarpur district and the whole of the Ambala division from the Punjab. Taking the former view first we can say that no doubt the River Jumna or the aforesaid Ridge would form a geographically natural boundary between Hindu India and the Punjab unit of Indusstan but as the underlying motives of the formation of the Indus Regions' Federation are to reduce communalism by reducing the Hindu element in it and to safeguard the agricultural, industrial and cultural interests of the Muslims, the fixation of the eastern boundary at the River Jumna or the Ridge which runs in a south-eastern direction passing from Delhi to Aravali Parbat, will not help in the achievement of these objectives, for it would bring in our territories the overwhelmingly Hindu areas of the Chief Commissioner's province of Delhi and the Ambala division, etc., leading to the increase of the Hindu percentage in our population, a thing which will be detrimental to our own interests. Such a boundary will not allow us to seek cultural isolation from Hindu India. It will also increase our difficulties on account of the natural affinity of a large Hindu population within our territories with the Hindus of the Hindu India. Their sympathies will always remain with their caste brethren of Hindu India. In view of this one weighty consideration it would be safer for us to accept the second opinion according to which no overwhelmingly Hindu tract should be included in our territories.'[4] 'The Muslims must,

---

[3] *India's Problem of her Future Constitution*, pp. 33–34.
[4] 'A Punjabi' *Confederacy of India*, pp. 243–44.

to begin with, press for the readjustment of the eastern boundary
of the Punjab and stress the great need of excluding the aforesaid
eastern Hindu tracts from it.'[5]

Taking another line of argument it cannot be seriously contended
even by the most ardent protagonists of Pakistan that any area
in which the Muslims are not numerically in a majority should
in justice and fairness be included in Pakistan. Any such demand
will be not only inconsistent with and contrary to the clear words
of the Lahore Resolution—the areas in which the Muslims are
numerically in a majority—but also unjust to the non-Muslim
majority of those areas and cannot fail to be interpreted by non-
Muslims as an attempt to force Muslim rule on non-Muslims. Dr
Syed Abdul Latif, who was the first in the field with a scheme
for division of India into cultural zones and for constitutionally
safeguarding the rights and interests of Muslims, writing about the
scheme which was prepared by Sir Abdullah Haroon's Committee
and which included in the north-western Muslim State not only
the whole of the Punjab but also the province of Delhi and a part
of Aligarh district, wrote in 1941:

'I am not satisfied with the demarcation of the north-west and
north-east blocks as suggested in the Committee's Report. The
Lahore Resolution aims at homogeneous and compact blocks or
States with an overwhelming Muslim majority. But the Punjab and
Aligarh members of your Committee through their imperialistic
designs over essentially non-Muslim areas would like to have a
larger Punjab extending even to Aligarh covering all the non-
Muslim states from Kashmir to Jaisalmir, which reduces the
Muslim percentage to 55. In like manner they would include in
the north-east block the whole of Bengal, Assam and a district
from Bihar which brings the percentage of Musalmans down to
54. In my humble opinion this kind of demarcation is against
the spirit and aim of the Lahore Resolution; because with 46
per cent non-Muslims in the north-east block and 42 per cent
in the north-west block, you cannot call your states as Muslim
States in any sense of the term, nor style them as Muslim zones.
I am not responsible for this demarcation as it was left entirely
to the Punjab, Sind and UP members. I would rather be content

[5] Ibid., p. 246.

with smaller states where I can command at least an 80 per cent majority of Muslims and call those states my own.'[6]

Although the Committee which had prepared this scheme ostensibly in accordance with the Lahore Resolution of the League had been formed by Haji Sir Abdullah Haroon, Kt., MLA, Chairman, Foreign Sub-committee, All-India Muslim League, who had acted all through as its Chairman, and had formally submitted its report on 23 December 1940, to the President of the League, the Committee and the scheme were repudiated by Mr Jinnah in a letter to Dr Latif dated 15 March 1941.

Considered either from the point of view of Muslim interests as explained by Mr M.R.T. and 'A Punjabi' in the quotations given above, or from the point of view of the non-Muslims who are in a majority in any areas sought to be included in the Muslim state, and who are bound to regard any such attempt as an imperialistic design of Muslims on essentially non-Muslim areas, the proposal for including any area with Muslims in a minority in it cannot justly and fairly be entertained or accepted, even if Partition is conceded.

Let us consider the position of the Punjab from this point of view—which is essentially the point of view of the Lahore Resolution of the League. We find that the Multan division of the Punjab which is contiguous to Sind and Baluchistan has a large Muslim majority of 75.41 per cent. The Muslims are in a majority in each district of this division, their highest percentage in the population being 88.9 in the district of Dera Ghazi Khan, if we leave out the Baluch Trans-Frontier Tract with a small total population of 40,246 of which 99.60 per cent are Muslims; and their lowest percentage in the population being 62.85 in Lyallpore district. Similarly in the Rawalpindi division, which is contiguous to the NWFP the Muslims are in overwhelming majority, their percentage in the population being 85.52. Their highest percentage in the population of any single district of the division is 90.42 in Attock district, and their lowest is 80.00 in Rawalpindi district. Thus if separation has to be effected, both these divisions in their entirety can be claimed to come within the north-western Muslim State on the basis of the Lahore Resolution.

When we come to the Lahore division, the position becomes somewhat complicated. The percentage of Muslims in the population

[6] *The Pakistan Issue*, pp. 98–99.

of the division as a whole is only 58.18 which can by no means be called overwhelming and which hardly gives the Muslims the right to call it a Muslim zone. Further, they are actually in a minority in the district of Amritsar where they constitute only 46.52 per cent of the population and are more or less evenly balanced in Gurdaspur district with a Muslim population of 51.14 per cent. Their highest population in that division is 70.45 per cent in the district of Gujranwala; and in the districts of Lahore, Sialkot and Sheikhupura, the Muslim percentage of the population is 60.62, 62.09 and 63.62 respectively. Applying the tests as discussed above, Amritsar, with a Muslim minority, can under no circumstances be regarded as a Muslim zone. Similarly, Gurdaspur can be claimed with as much justice by Muslims as by non-Muslims. If an overwhelming Muslim majority is not insisted upon then the other districts with Muslim majorities varying between 60 and 70 per cent of the total population may be claimed by the Muslim State, if numbers are the only criterion to be considered.

The position of Jullundar division is clear. Here the Muslims constitute only 34.53 per cent of the population and in none of its districts are they in a numerical majority, their highest percentage being 45.23 in the district of Jullundar, and the lowest being as low as 4.81 in the district of Kangra. As a single community the Hindus have a percentage of 35.87 as against 34.53 of the Muslims in the division as a whole, though in two districts, Jullundar and Ferozpur, out of five in the division, Muslims have the largest percentage in the population—45.23 and 45.07 respectively. But even in these districts they are in a minority. The Jullundar division does not, therefore, satisfy the test laid down by the Lahore Resolution of the League and cannot go with the districts of the Multan and Rawalpindi divisions from which they are also cut off by districts of the Lahore division coming in between.

In the Ambala division the Muslims constitute only 28.07 per cent of the population and in no district of the division more than 33.56 per cent, which is their highest percentage in the district of Gurgaon. As against this the Hindus are 66.01 per cent in the division, their highest percentage being 81.61 in the district of Rohtak and their lowest being 48.40 in the district of Ambala. It is thus clear that this Division or any of its districts cannot come within the north-western Muslim independent State, if the test laid down by the League itself is applied.

We can now take the north-western zone as a whole. The

position after excluding the areas which have to be excluded as shown above will be as given in Table XIV.

TABLE XIV

Population of Muslims in the North-West Zone from which Districts with Non-Muslim Majorities are Excluded

Province	Total Population	Muslim Population	Muslim Percentage
Sind	45,35,008	32,08,325	70.75
NWFP	30,38,067	27,88,797	91.79
Baluchistan	5,01,631	4,38,930	87.51
Punjab (excluding the Ambala and Jullundar divisions and Amritsar district of Lahore division)	1,68,70,900	1,23,63,669	73.28
Total North-Western Zone	2,49,45,606	1,87,99,721	75.36

The position without excluding the predominantly non-Muslim areas of the Punjab will be that out of a total population of 3.64,93,525 the north-western independent State, the Muslims will be 2,26,53,294 or 62.07 per cent. It is a question whether such a zone with this small Muslim majority can really be called a Muslim zone.

II. THE EASTERN ZONE

Let us now turn to the eastern zone. Let us take Bengal:

A glance at Table XV shows that in Burdwan division the Muslims are in a small minority, being no more than 13.90 per cent of the population of that division and in no single district of that division is the percentage of their population more than 27.41, their lowest percentage being as low as 4.31. All the districts of the division are bounded on all sides by predominantly non-Muslim districts of Bihar, Bengal and Orissa except the districts of Sirbhum and Burdwan, which have on one side Bengal districts with a Muslim majority while they too have predominantly non-Muslim districts on other sides. This division does not fulfil any of the conditions laid down by the Lahore Resolution and cannot in any case be claimed for the eastern Muslim zone.

TABLE XV

Population by Communities of Bengal

Division or Districts	Area (sq. miles)	Total population	Muslims	Hindus	Indian Christians	Tribes	Others
Burdwan Div.							
Burdwan	2,705	18,90,732	3,36,665 (17.81)	13,93,820 (73.72)	3,280 (0.17)	1,51,355 (8.00)	5,612 (0.30)
Birbhum	1,743	10,48,317	2,87,310 (27.41)	6,86,436 (65.48)	344 (0.03)	74,084 (7.07)	143 (0.01)
Bankura	2,646	12,89,640	55,564 (4.31)	10,78,559 (83.63)	1,216 (0.90)	1,54,246 (11.97)	55 (0.00)
Midnapur	5,274	31,90,647	2,46,559 (7.73)	26,81,963 (84.06)	3,834 (0.12)	2,53,625 (7.95)	4,666 (0.14)
Hooghly	1,206	13,77,729	2,07,077 (15.03)	10,99,544 (79.81)	543 (0.04)	69,500 (5.04)	1,065 (0.08)
Howrah	561	14,90,304	2,96,325 (19.88)	11,84,863 (79.50)	994 (0.07)	3,919 (0.26)	4,203 (0.29)
Total	14,135	1,02,87,369	14,29,500 (13.90)	81,25,185 (78.98)	10,211 (0.10)	7,06,729 (6.87)	15,744 (0.15)
Presidency Div.							
24 Parganas	3,696	35,36,386	11,48,180 (32.47)	23,09,996 (65.32)	20,823 (0.59)	51,085 (1.44)	6,302 (0.18)
Calcutta	34	21,08,891	4,97,535 (23.59)	15,31,512 (72.62)	16,431 (0.78)	1,688 (0.08)	61,725 (2.93)
Nadia	2,879	17,59,846	10,78,007 (61.26)	6,57,950 (37.38)	10,749 (0.61)	12,671 (0.72)	469 (0.03)

(contd.)

Murshidabad	2.063	16,40,530	9,27,747 (56.55)	6,84,987 (41.75)	394 (0.02)	26,138 (1.59)	1,264 (0.80)
Jessore	2,925	18,28,216	11,00,713 (60.21)	7,21,079 (39.44)	1,057 (0.06)	4,978 (0.27)	389 (0.02)
Khulna	4,805	19,43,218	9,59,172 (49.36)	9,77,693 (50.31)	3,538 (0.18)	2,675 (0.14)	140 (0.01)
Total	16,402	1,28,17,087	57,11,354 (44.56)	68,83,217 (53.70)	52,992 (0.41)	99,235 (0.77)	70,289 (0.55)
Rajshahi Div.							
Rajshahi	2,526	15,71,750	11,73,285 (74.64)	3,29,230 (20.95)	1,166 (0.07)	67,298 (4.28)	771 (0.05)
Dinajpur	3,953	19,26,833	9,67,246 (50.20)	7,74,622 (40.20)	1,448 (0.08)	1,82,892 (9.49)	625 (0.03)
Jalpaiguri	3,050	10,89,513	2,51,460 (23.08)	5,51,647 (50.63)	2,589 (0.24)	2,79,296 (25.63)	4,521 (0.41)
Darjeeling	1,192	3,76,369	9,125 (2.42)	1,78,496 (47.43)	2,599 (0.69)	1,41,301 (37.54)	44,848 (11.92)
Rangpur	3,606	28,77,847	20,55,186 (71.41)	8,02,849 (27.90)	389 (0.01)	18,200 (0.63)	1,223 (1,223)
Bogra	1,475	12,60,463	10,57,902 (83.93)	1,87,532 (14.88)	286 (0.02)	14,387 (1.14)	356 (0.04) (0.03)
Pabna	1,836	17,05,072	13,13,968 (770.6)	3,85,755 (22.51)	285 (0.02)	6,906 (0.40)	158 (0.01)
Malda	2,004	12,32,618	6,99,945 (56.78)	4,65,678 (37.78)	466 (0.04)	66,449 (5.39)	80 (0.01)
Total	19,64	1,20,40,465	75,28,117 (62.52)	36,73,809 (30.51)	9,228 (0.08)	7,76,729 (6.45)	52,582 (0.44)

(contd.)

Division or Districts	Area (sq. miles)	Total Population	Muslims	Hindus	Indian Christians	Tribes	Others
Dacca Div.							
Dacca	2,738	42,22,143	28,41,261 (67.29)	13,60,132 (32.21)	15,846 (0.38)	4,029 (0.10)	875 (0.02)
Mymensing	6,156	60,23.758	46,64,548 (77.44)	12,96,638 (21.52)	2322 (0.04)	59.722 (0.99)	528 (0.01)
Faridpur	2,821	28,88,803	18,71,336 (64.78)	10,06,238 (34.83)	9,549 (0.33)	1,363 (0.05)	317 (0.01)
Bakargunj	3,783	35,49,010	25,67,027 (72.33)	9,58.629 (27.01)	9,357 (0.26)	284 (0.01)	13,713 (0.39)
Total	15,498	1,66,83,714	1,19,44,172 (71.59)	46,21,637 (27.70)	37,074 (0.22)	65,398 (0.39)	15,433 (0.09)
Chittagong Div							
Tipparah	2,531	38,60,139	29,75,901 (77.09)	8,79,960 (22.80)	428 (0.01)	1,524 (0.04)	2,326 (0.06)
Noakhali	1,658	22,17,402	18,03,937 (81.35)	4,12,261 (18.59)	535 (0.20)	34 (0.00)	635 (0.03)
Chittagong	2,569	21,53,296	16,05,183 (74.55)	4,58,074 (21.27)	395 (0.20)	6.348 (0.29)	85,296 (3.87)
Chittagong Hill Tracts	5,007	2,47,053	7,270 (2.94)	4,881 (1.98)	60 (0.02)	2,33,392 (2.84)	87,707 (1.03)
Total	11,765	84,77,890	63,92,291 (75.40)	17,55,176 (20.70)	1,418 (0.02)	2,41,298 (2.84)	87,707 (1.03)
Total Bengal	77,442	6,03,06,525	3,30,05,434 (54.73)	2,50,59,024 (41.55)	1,10,923 (0.18)	18,89,389 (3.13)	2,41,775 (0.40)

TABLE XVI

Muslim and Non-Muslim Districts of Bengal and their Population by Communities

Division or District	Area (sq. miles)	Total Population	Muslims	Hindus	Indian Christians	Tribes	Others	Total Non-Muslim
Nadia	2,879	17,59,846	10,78,007 (61.26)	6,57,950 (37.38)	10,749 (0.61)	12,671 (0.72)	469 (0.03)	6,81,839 (38.74)
Murshidabad	2,063	16,40,530	9,27,747 (56.55)	6,84,987 (41.75)	394 (0.02)	26,138 (1.59)	1,264 (0.08)	7,12,783 (43.44)
Jessore	2,925	18,28,216	11,00,713 (60.21)	7,21,079 (39.44)	1,057 (0.60)	4,978 (0.27)	389 (0.02)	7,27,503 (39.79)
Rajshahi Div. excluding Darjeeling and Jalpaiguri	15,400	1,05,74,583	72,67,532 (68.72)	29,43,666 (27.84)	4,040 (0.40)	3,56,132 (3.37)	3,213 (0.03)	33,07,051 (31.28)
Dacca Div.	15,498	1,66,83,714	1,19,44,172 (71.59)	46,21,637 (27.70)	37,074 (0.22)	65,398 (0.39)	15,433 (0.09)	47,39,542 (28.40)
Chittagong Div.	11,765	84,77,890	63,92,291 (75.40)	17,55,176 (20.70)	1,418 (0.02)	2,41,298 (2.84)	87,707 (1.03)	20,85,599 (24.59)
Total Muslim Majority Dts.	50,530	4,09,64,779	2,87,10,462 (70.09)	1,13,84,495 (27.79)	54,732 (0.13)	7,06,615 (1.72)	1,08,475 (0.26)	1,22,54,317 (29.90)
Burdwan Div.	14,135	1,02,87,369	14,29,500 (13.90)	81,25,185 (78.98)	10,211 (0.10)	7,06,729 (6.87)	15,744 (0.15)	88,57,869 (86.10)
24-Parganas	3,696	35,36,386	11,48,180 (32.47)	23,09,996 (65.32)	20,823 (0.59)	51,085 (1.44)	6,302 (0.18)	23,88,206 (67.53)
Calcutta	34	21,08,891	4,97,535 (23.59)	15,31,512 (72.62)	16,431 (0.78)	1,683 (0.08)	61,725 (2.93)	16,11,356 (76.41)

(contd. next page)

TABLE XVI (contd.)

Division or District	Area (sq. miles)	Total Population	Muslims	Hindus	Indian Christians	Tribes	Others	Total Non-Muslim
Khulna	4,805	19,43,218	9,59,172 (49.36)	9,77,693 (50.31)	3,538 (0.18)	2,675 (0.14)	140 (0.01)	9,84,046 (50.64)
Jalpaiguri	3,050	10,89,513	2,51,460 (23.08)	5,51,647 (50.63)	2,589 (0.24)	2,79,296 (25.63)	4,521 (0.41)	8,38,053 (76.91)
Darjeeling	1,192	3,76,369	9,125 (2.42)	1,78,496 (47.43)	2,599 (0.69)	1,41,301 (37.54)	44,848 (11.92)	3,67,244 (97.58)
Total Non-Muslim Majority Dts.	26,912	1,93,41,746	42,94,972 (22,21)	1,36,74,529 (70.70)	56,191 (0.29)	11,82,774 (6.11)	1,33,280 (0.69)	1,50,46,774 (77.79)

The Presidency division including the city of Calcutta has a minority of Muslims, their percentage being only 44.56 as against 53.70 of the Hindus. But some of its districts have a Muslim majority. These are Nadia, Murshidabad and Jessore where their percentage in the population is 61.26, 56.55 and 60.21 respectively. In the other districts of 24-Parganas and Khulna their percentage is 32.47 and 49.36 as against 65.32 and 50.31 of the Hindus alone. In Calcutta the Muslims are only 23.59 per cent or less than one-fourth of the total population as against 72.62 per cent of the Hindus alone. On the score of population the division as a whole cannot belong to the Muslim zone; and if one goes by the districts even then 24-Parganas, Calcutta and Khulna cannot go to it. So far as Calcutta is concerned, it is bounded on all sides by areas which are predominantly non-Muslim and no adjustment of boundaries can convert it into a Muslim zone. All the districts of this division touch non-Muslim districts and also touch districts with Muslim majorities with the exception of Calcutta which does not touch any Muslim area on any side of it.

In the Rajshahi division, Jalpaiguri and Darjeeling districts have a small minority of Muslims, their percentage in the population being 23.08 and 2.42; while the district of Dinajpur is on the border line, having a Muslim population of 50.19 per cent only. The other districts of the division have Muslim majorities, their highest percentage in the population being 83.93 in the district of Bogra and the lowest 56.78 in the district of Malda. The districts of Jalpaiguri and Darjeeling with such small Muslim populations cannot in fairness be claimed as Muslim zones and even the district of Dinajpur with just 50 per cent of Muslims can hardly be described or claimed as a Muslim zone.

The position of Dacca division is different. Here the Muslims are 71.59 per cent of the population and in each district in this division they are in a majority, their highest percentage in the population being 77.44 in the district of Mymensingh and the lowest being 64.78 in the district of Faridpur.

Similarly, in the Chittagong division the Muslims have a majority, their percentage in the population being 75.40. They are also in a majority in the districts of the division except in the Chittagong Hill Tracts where they are only 2.94 per cent of the population. The majority in the Hill Tracts consists of tribes who constitute 94.47 per cent of the population.

If we take the province of Bengal as a whole as it is at present
constituted, consisting of the five divisions of Burdwan, Presidency,
Rajshahi, Dacca and Chittagong, the percentage of Muslims in the
population of the province is 54.73 which cannot fairly entitle
Muslims to call it a Muslim zone and claim it for a separate Muslim
State with independent status. No government of a representative
type can be stable in this state, and there is no reason why 54.73
per cent of the population should enforce their will on the rest
in such a fundamental matter as the separation of the area from
the rest of India of which it has been an integral part since as
far back as the memory of man can reach.

If we take the districts, then the districts of Burdwan division
have to be excluded from the Muslim zone and so also the districts
of 24-Parganas, Khulna and Calcutta of the Presidency Division.
The districts of Jalpaiguri and Darjeeling with large non-Muslim
majorities have also to be excluded and the district of Dinajpur
as stated above falling just on the boundary line may be claimed
with equal justice by Muslims and non-Muslims alike. The other
districts of the Rajshahi division as also the districts of Dacca
and Chittagong divisions with the exception of Chittagong Hill
Tracts which have Muslim majorities may very well be claimed as
falling within the Muslim zone according to the Muslim League
Resolution.

Assigning the doubtful district of Dinajpur and the Chittagong
Hill Tracts to the Muslim zone the position in the Muslim and
non-Muslim districts of Bengal will be as shown in Table XVI,
p. 313.

The position in both the zones will be changed to some extent
if the districts of Dinajpur and the Chittagong Hill Tracts are
excluded from the Muslim zone.

It will be noticed that in the Muslim zone as shown above the
Muslims will constitute 70.09 per cent, the Hindus 27.79 per cent,
and the tribes 1.72 per cent of the population. In the non-Muslim
zone the Hindus will be 70.70 per cent or slightly more than the
Muslims in the Muslim zone; and the Muslims 22.21 per cent
or much less than the Hindus in the Muslim zone and the tribes
constitute 6.11 per cent of the population. The total population of
the tribes in the province as a whole comes to 18,89,389 or 3.13
per cent of the total population. Their position has to be considered
separately and I shall deal with it when dealing with the figures

of Assam, as the problem arises there even more prominently than in Bengal and as the same principles govern it.

We shall now consider the position in Assam.

Looking at the tables, it is difficult to understand on what basis the province of Assam is claimed as a Muslim zone. In the province as a whole the Muslims are only 33.73 per cent as against the Hindus who are 41.29 per cent of the population. If we take the districts, then Sylhet is the only district in which the Muslims are 60.71 per cent of the population. In no other district do they constitute a majority of the population although in the districts of Cachar and Goalpara they are the most numerous as a single community, being 36.33 per cent and 46.23 per cent of the population respectively. The utmost that can be fairly claimed as a Muslim zone is the district of Sylhet, although a majority of 60.71 per cent can hardly be called an overwhelming majority. In some of the smaller districts, the tribes are in an overwhelming majority, while in others where the Hindus do not by themselves constitute a majority, the tribes and the Hindus together constitute the majority. In eight out of fourteen districts of the province, the percentage of Muslims is less than 5, in three less than 1. As the claim of the Muslim League to any area is based on Muslims being numerically in a majority in that area, it cannot stand where they are not in such majority, although they may be the most numerous as a single community in that area—the majority being formed of a combination of other communities. No other community as such has claimed separation from the rest of India and as a matter of fact, others have opposed the idea of such separation. It is therefore on the strength of the Muslim majority alone that the League can put forward such a claim.

In this connection it is necessary to consider the position of the Tribes. Table XIX above will show how the number of Hindus in the province has been brought down by adopting the tribal origin instead of the religion of a large number of persons recorded under the head of tribes as the basis for classification. We shall also see how the number of Muslims has increased in the province.

It will be noticed that the population of Hindus has dropped from 57.20 per cent in 1931 to 41.29 per cent in 1941 in British Assam and from 56.28 to 41.54 per cent in Assam as a whole including the States, while that of the tribes has increased from 8.25 per cent to 24.35 per cent in British Assam and from 10.73

TABLE XVII
Population by Communities of Assam

Division or Districts	Area (sq. miles)	Total Population	Muslims	Hindus	Christians.	Tribes	Others
Surma Valley and Hill Div.							
Cachar	3,862	6,41,181	2,32,950 (36.33)	2,25,816 (35.22)	3,979 (0.62)	1,78,264 (27.80)	172 (0.03)
Sylhet	5,478	31,16,602	18,92,117 (60.71)	11,49,514 (36.88)	3,055 (0.09)	69,907 (2.24)	2,009 (0.06)
Khasi and Jaintia Hills	2,353	1,18,665	1,555 (1.31)	12,739 (10.74)	424 (0.36)	1,03,567 (87.27)	380 (0.32)
Naga Hills	4,289	1,89,641	531 (0.28)	4,198 (2.21)	30 (0.02)	1,84,766 (97.43)	116 (0.06)
Lushai Hills	8,142	1,52,786	101 (0.06)	2,447 (1.60)	51 (0.03)	1,47,042 (96.24)	3,145 (2.06)
Total	24,124	42,18,875	21,27,254 (50.42)	13,94,714 (33.06)	7,539 (0.18)	6,83,546 (16.20)	5,822 (0.14)
Assam Valley Div.							
Goalpara	3,969	10,14,285	4,68,924 (46.33)	3,06,323 (30.19)	285 (0.03)	2,37,993 (23.46)	860 (0.08)
Kamrup	3,840	12,64,200	3,67,522 (29.07)	6,96,549 (55.09)	1,168 (0.09)	1,97,926 (15.65)	1,035 (0.08)
Darrang	2,804	7,36,791	1,20,995 (16.42)	3,47,758 (47.19)	6,643 (0.90)	2,60,748 (35.38)	647 (0.09)
Nowgong	3,898	7,10,800	2,50,113 (35.18)	2,88,351 (40.56)	4,147 (0.58)	1,66,525 (23.42)	1,664 (0.23)

(contd.)

	Area (sq. miles)	Total population	Muslims	Hindus	Christians	Tribes	Others Non-Muslims
Sibsagar	5,128	10,74,741	51,769 (4.81)	6,43,191 (59.84)	15,707 (1.46)	3,60,768 (33.56)	3,306 (0.31)
Lakhimpur	4,156	8,94,842	44,579 (4.98)	5,01,036 (55.98)	4,745 (0.53)	3,35,230 (37.46)	9,252 (1.03)
Garo Hills	3,152	2,23,569	10,398 (4.65)	14,307 (6.39)	29 (0.01)	1,98,474 (88.77)	361 (0.16)
Total	26,947	59,19,228	13,14,300 (22.12)	27,97,415 (47.26)	32,724 (0.55)	17,57,664 (29.74)	17,125 (0.29)
Sadiya Frontier Tracts	3,309	60,118	864 (1.43)	18,506 (30.78)	516 (0.86)	39,974 (66.49)	258 (0.43)
Balipara Frontier Tracts	571	6,512	61 (0.94)	2,588 (39.74)	31 (0.48)	3,812 (58.53)	20 (0.31)
Total Assam	54,951	1,02,04,733	34,42,479 (33.73)	42,13,233 (41.29)	40,810 (0.40)	24,84,996 (24.35)	23,225 (0.23)

TABLE XVIII

Muslim and Non-Muslim Districts of Assam and their Population by Communities

Division or Districts	Area (sq. miles)	Total population	Muslims	Hindus	Christians	Tribes	Others Non-Muslims	Total
Muslim-majority districts								
Sylhet	5,478	31,16,602	18,92,117 (60.71)	11,49,514 (36.88)	3,055 (0.09)	69,907 (2.24)	2,009 (0.06)	12,24,485 (39.27)
Non-Muslim-majority districts								
Whole Assam excluding Sylhet	49,473	70,88,131	15,50,362 (21.87)	30,63,709 (43.22)	37,755 (0.53)	24,15,089 (34.07)	21,216 (0.30)	55,37,769 (78.13)

TABLE XIX

Distribution of Main Communities in Assam at the Censuses of 1901, 1911, 1921, 1931 and 1941

Province	Total Population 1941	Number per 10,000 of the Population														
		Hindu					Muslims					Tribes				
		1941	1931	1921	1911	1901	1941	1931	1921	1911	1901	1941	1931	1921	1911	1901
British Assam	1,02,04,733	4129	5720	5433	5418	5578	3373	3196	2896	2810	2689	2435	825	1479	1652	1652
Assam States	7,25,655	4516	4362	5994	5816	5996	436	393	455	419	365	4674	4491	3433	3758	3632
Total Assam	1,09,30,388	4154	5628	5461	5438	5598	3178	3007	2778	2693	2531	2584	1073	1573	1755	1744

per cent to 25.84 per cent in Assam as a whole between the 1931 and 1941 censuses. This sudden and large discrepancy is explained by Mr K.W.P. Marar, ICS, Superintendent of Census Operations in Assam in 1941, as follows:

'The essential point is that the table shows the community origin, not the religious attribution. Had time and finances permitted, other details could have been given to link up fully with 1931 but in this truncated census this was not possible. Community and religion may seem to many as one and the same and inseparable, and are in fact so in most cases. But where there are tribes, community and religion need not always be the same and in the present census they have all been classified on the basis of community and not of religion. Thus a Khasi returning himself as a Hindu, Christian, Muslim, or Animist at the last census would have been classified under any of those headings of religion according to the faith he professed or attributed to him, but this time he has been classified as a Khasi. This is the main reason for the great apparent fall in the proportion, in the whole population of Christians and to a less extent of Hindus and Buddhists. At the same time there is more than a corresponding increase in the proportion of the tribal people . . . If the figures be examined in the light of what is stated above they will be found to disclose no "alarming" tendencies. All the communities have shown natural increase in varying degrees and in no district have the pre-existing communal proportions been disturbed to any appreciable extent except by migration.

'There is no question of removal of Hindus or of Christians. A separate note on Christians follows and Hindus are present in the same proportions as before; in the absence of caste or religion sorting the 1931 practice would have meant that no record of the number of persons of tribal origin, which is so important a matter in Assam and represents one of the reasons for the extensive reserved areas in that province, would have been forthcoming.'[7]

One need not quarrel with the idea of recording persons of tribal origin in a separate column, if at the same time their religion was also recorded. As the Census Superintendent says, 'the Hindus are present in the same proportions as before', but a glance at the Tables showing their numbers and proportions gives an entirely wrong and misleading picture of the position. The Census

[7] *Census of India*, 1941, Volume IX, 'Assam,' Tables, pp. 21–22.

Superintendent after giving the above explanation regarding the great fall in the number of Christians and Hindus has taken pains to ascertain, as far as he could even in the truncated census of 1941, the number of Christians. He gives the estimated number of Christians in Assam as a whole—British and States—to be 3,86,000, although the number recorded as Christians is no more than 67,184, the remaining 3,19,000 being only an estimate of tribal Christians prepared on the basis of the 1931 figures. Thus while a more or less accurate picture of the number of Christians in the province is given in the Report, the reader is left to be content, with regard to the number of Hindus, with the vague proposition stated in a note that they 'are present in the same proportions as before.'

Mr M.W.M. Yeatts, CIE, ICS, Census Commissioner for India in 1941, after explaining the necessity for the change introduced in the Census of 1941 of recording the tribal origin of persons as distinguished from the religion which they professed, goes on: 'The fact is of course that while between Islam or Christianity and other religions there exists as it were a definite wall or fence over which or through which the convert must go, there is nothing between what is usually though vaguely described as animism and the equally vague and embracing concept of Hinduism but a very wide no man's land; and the process by which a Tribesman is assimilated to a Hindu is not that of conversion or the acceptance of a particular creed or joining in a definitely marked out section of the population, but a more or less gradual traversing of this no man's land. The traverse may and generally does occupy more than one generation and it would take an expert to say at what period and in which generation more than half the no man's land had been crossed so that one could say that the assimilation was more than half completed. . . . It is in this light therefore that the community tables and the subsidiaries which give ratios should be examined. Viewed thus, the position emerges that in British India 64 per cent of the population are Hindus, 27 Muslims, 1 Indian Christian. Persons of tribal origin represent 5 per cent. Of this 5 per cent approximately one-twentieth fall within the Christians on a religion basis. The remainder can be regarded as in greater or less degree of assimilation towards the Hindu majority. At one end there is in continued existence a tribal way of life. At the other there is more or less complete assimilation. In between there is every degree in the continuous process represented by the transition. The degree differs for each province and state and as I have stressed is a matter for local estimation.'[8]

Again: 'Allowing for the tribal classification question therefore one could say that the Hindu–Muslim proportions in Bengal are practically unaltered from 1931 . . . The Bihar, Central Provinces and Assam figures of course bring in the tribal classification and assimilation question in a fairly marked degree, but if the religion allocations of 1931 were repeated as a basis for community classification the effect would be of a fractional drop in the percentage of Hindus.'[9]

That the tribes have more in common with Hindus than with any other religious group is the opinion of competent authorities, and the process of assimilation has been going on from time immemorial. Assimilation of tribes to Hinduism has been achieved on a colossal scale in the centuries and millennia that have elapsed and that without any apparent or violent breach with their past. It is therefore only just that their number should be counted with the Hindus, at any rate, in the case of those who declare themselves as Hindus as used to be done in the censuses previous to 1941.

Mr Verrier Elwin, MA (Oxon), FRAI, FNI, who has been living among the tribes in the Central Province for years and studying them and their culture, was the President of the section of Anthropology and Archaeology at the thirty-first session of the Indian Science Congress which was held at Delhi in January 1944. He chose 'Truth in Anthropology' as the subject of his presidential address and laid stress on the very great need of a high standard of truth in all our field work in order that the science of Anthropology may be established in India. He says: 'It is necessary to stress this, for Anthropology is regarded with some suspicion in India. There are several reasons for this. The attempt of certain scholars and politicians to divide the aboriginal tribes from the Hindu community at the time of census created the impression that science could be diverted to political and communal ends. In earlier years the census authorities tried to distinguish animism and Hinduism. Later the expression "Followers of Tribal Religions" was used. The test proposed was to ask a

[8]   *Census of India*, 1941, Vol. I 'India', pp. 28–29.
[9]   Ibid., p. 30.

person whether he worshipped Hindu or tribal gods. This test was meaningless. The religion of the aboriginals in Peninsular India at least is obviously of the Hindu family, Hinduism itself having many elements which a theologian would call animistic. In the religious columns, therefore, the aboriginals should have been returned from the beginning as Hindus. Any other classification was worse than useless. It is very difficult even for a trained theologian to decide the exact description of the religion of the various tribes. It is obviously impossible for an illiterate and ignorant enumerator to do so. What we want to know is how many aboriginals there are in India so that we can insist that they have a square deal in the counsels of the country. But now we know accurately neither the religious nor racial situation, and the unfortunate fact that a number of anthropologists interested themselves in the complicated business of deciding the exact way in which aboriginals should be distinguished from the Hindu religion has done our science harm in public estimation.'[10]

The effect of all this mishandling by the census authorities has been, as admitted by them in the quotations given above, to reduce considerably the number of Hindus and their proportion in the population of some of the provinces and States and of India as a whole. As pointed out by Mr Yeatts, the Census Commissioner of India: 'The Muslim figure can be regarded as practically unaffected by the tribal origin question and here we have the record of gradual increase which previous decades had already presented and for which the reasons have been discussed at some length in the reports of these years. The Bengal component is practically unaltered and the Punjab one increased by about $\frac{1}{2}$ or 1 per cent. The most noticeable rise is in Assam and once again represents migration from Mymensingh and East Bengal generally.'[11]

Table XIX on p. 320 shows the proportions of the important elements in the population of Assam. The sudden decrease in the number of Hindus has been explained above. It will be noticed that the proportion of Muslims has gone on steadily increasing. In 1901 they formed only 26.89 per cent of the population of British Assam while by 1941 their percentage had increased to 33.73. The increase is due to a large extent to immigration of Muslims

[10] Proceedings of the Thirty-first Indian Science Congress, Delhi, 1944, p. 91.
[11] Census of India, 1941, Vol. I 'India', Tables, p. 29.

from East Bengal, particularly from the district of Mymensingh to the districts of Assam. The Census Report of 1931 has devoted 'a whole chapter to the discussion of the question of immigration and has pointed out that there are three main currents of migration into Assam:

(i)   immigration to Assam tea gardens;
(ii)   immigration of Eastern Bengal colonists;
(iii) immigration of Nepalis. Mr C. S. Mullan, MA, ICS, the Census Superintendent for Assam, 1931, points out that 'at the present census however there has been a considerable change. From Bengal immigrants have continued to pour into Assam as in the previous decade but in the case of the cooly recruiting provinces the stream has not flowed at the old rate.'[12] It is necessary to give here a pretty long quotation from the Census Report of Assam regarding the immigration of Eastern Bengal colonists into Assam.

'Probably the most important event in the province during the last twenty-five years—an event, moreover, which seems likely to alter permanently the whole future of Assam and to destroy more surely than did the Burmese invaders of 1820 the whole structure of Assamese culture and civilization—has been the invasion of a vast horde of land-hungry Bengali immigrants, mostly Muslims, from the districts of Eastern Bengal and in particular from Mymensingh. This invasion began some time before 1911, and the Census Report of that year is the first report which makes mention of the advancing host. But, as we now know, the Bengali immigrants censused for the first time on the *chur* lands of Goalpara in 1911 were merely the advance guard—or rather the scouts—of a huge army following closely at their heels. By 1921 the first army corps had passed into Assam and had practically conquered the district of Goalpara. The course of events between 1911 and 1921 has been described in the 1921 Census Report as follows:

'"In 1911 few cultivators from Eastern Bengal had gone beyond Goalpara, those censused in the other districts of Assam Valley numbering only a few thousands and being mostly clerks, traders and professional men. In the last decade (1911–21) the movement has extended far up the Valley and the colonists now

[12] *Census of India*, 1931, Vol. III, 'Assam Report,' Part I, p. 44.

form an appreciable element in the population of all the four lower
and central districts, the two upper districts (that is, Sibsagar and
Lakhimpur) are scarcely touched as yet. In Goalpara nearly 20
per cent of the population is made up of those settlers. The next
favourite district is Nowgong where they form about 14 per cent of
the whole population. In Kamrup waste lands are being taken up
rapidly/specially in the Barpeta sub-division. In Darrang exploration
and settlement by the colonists are in an earlier stage, they have
not yet penetrated far from the banks of the Brahmaputra . . .
Almost every train and steamer brings parties of those settlers and
it seems likely that their march will extend further up the Valley
and away from the river before long."

'Let us now examine the progress of the invasion since 1921.
It must in the first place be remembered that the children of the
settlers born after their arrival in Assam have been recorded as
Assam-born and hence do not appear in the figures and that
the table below shows the total number of the people born in
Bengal and not the number of settlers only; still the figures give
us a very good idea of what has been taking place during the
last ten years:

In Table XX the figures for Mymensingh district have been given
in brackets as that district is the one which is chiefly responsible
for the flood of immigrant settlers.

'These are startling figures and illustrate the wonderful rapidity
with which the lower districts of the Assam Valley are becoming
colonies of Mymensingh . . . I have already remarked that by 1921
the first army corps of the invaders had conquered Goalpara. The
second army corps which followed them in years 1921–31 has
consolidated their position in that district and has also completed
the conquest of Nowgong. The Barpeta sub-division of Kamrup has
also fallen to their attack and Darrang is being invaded, Sibsagar
has so far escaped completely but the few thousand My-mensinghias
in North Lakhimpur are an outpost which may, during the next
decade, prove to be a valuable basis of major operations . . .

'The exact number of these Eastern Bengal settlers (including
their children born in Assam), who are at present living in the
Assam Valley is a difficult matter to estimate. Mr Lloyd in 1921
estimated that including children, born after their arrival in this
province, the total number of settlers was at least 300,000 in that
year. As far as I can judge the number at present must be over

TABLE XX

Number of Persons Born in Bengal in Each District of the Assam
Valley in 1911, 1921 and 1931

(MS=Mymensingh District; 000s omitted)

Year	Goalpara	Kamrup	Darrang	Nowgong	Sibsagar	Lakhimpur
1911	77 (MS 34)	4 (MS 1)	7 (MS 1)	4 (MS 1)	14 (MS Nil)	14 (MS Nil)
1921	151 (MS 78)	44 (MS 30)	20 (MS 12)	58 (MS 52)	14 (MS Nil)	14 (MS Nil)
1931	170 (MS 80)	134 (MS 90)	41 (MS 30)	120 (MS 108)	12 (MS Nil)	19 (MS 2)

half a million. The number of new immigrants from Mymensingh, alone, has been 140,000 and old settlers have undoubtedly been' increasing and multiplying. As pointed out in the Census Report for 1921, the colonists have settled by families and not singly. This can be seen from the fact that out of the total of 338,000 persons born in Mymensingh and censused in Assam over 152,000 are women. What of the future? As far as can be foreseen the invasion is by no means complete; there are still large areas of waste land in Assam—particularly in the North Lakhimpur sub-division—and Kamrup, in spite of the large number of immigrants, which it has absorbed during the last ten years, is capable of holding many more. The Mangladai sub-division is also capable of further development. Now that most of the waste lands of Goalpara and Nowgong have been taken up, the trend of immigration should, therefore, be more and more towards Kamrup, Mangladai and North Lakhimpur. The latter sub-division should prove a veritable "El-Dorado", if news of its empty spaces awaiting the hoe and plough of the colonists reaches the ears of the main body of trekkers.

'It is sad but by no means improbable that in another 30 years Sibsagar district will be the only part of Assam in which an Assamese will find himself at home."[13]

The Census Report of 1941 completes the story with a short but significant sentence quoted above—'The most noticeable rise [in the Muslim population] is in Assam and once again represents migration from Mymensingh and East Bengal generally.'[14]

This policy of colonization of Assam by the Muslims of Bengal was continued under the joint auspices of the Muslim League ministries of Sir Saadullah in Assam and Sir Nazimuddin in Bengal, as the following Bengal government communiqué published in the press, in the last week of October 1944, shows:

'The Government of Assam in their resolution dated 21 June 1940 prohibited settlement of land with persons coming from outside the province after 1 January 1938. This decision affected the border districts like Mymensingh from where large numbers of agriculturists go to Assam in search of agricultural land on account of heavy pressure on such lands in this province. During the last session of the Bengal Legislative Council a motion

[13] Census of India, 1931, Vol. III, *Assam Report*, Part I, pp. 49–52.
[14] *Census of India*, 1941, Vol. I '*India*', Tables, p. 29.

was carried for presenting an address to His Excellency requesting him to urge upon the Government of India to take immediate steps so that all existing restrictions imposed by the Government of Assam on cultivators from their province in getting settlement of land in the Assam Valley might be removed. Accordingly, the Government of Bengal requested the Government of Assam to withdraw or suspend the restrictions imposed by the said Resolution in the interest of inter-provincial amity and as a measure of relief to the distressed people of Bengal.

'The Government of Assam have stated in reply that the policy regarding settlement of lands with immigrants has since been liberalized and that they are trying their level best to accelerate the process by de-reserving surplus lands in the professional grazing reserves in certain districts. The Government of Assam are, however, unable to abolish the restrictive measures wholly, particularly in areas where the tribal people are numerous, as these people are apprehensive of the near approach of immigrants as a result of which many of them suffered in the past, but that Government have given an assurance that they will continue the process of gradual abolition of the restrictions and to open up fresh areas for immigrant settlement as far as is consistent with the necessity for reservation of lands for indigenous people and protection of the tribal classes.'

It is only necessary to make it clear that in doing so the Saadullah ministry went back on the decision of the late Governor of Assam, Sir Robert Reid, who after reviewing the land settlement policy had withdrawn a Development Scheme of Sir Saadullah's previous ministry. Sir Robert Reid says in a recent article: 'The indigenous Assam tribes who originally populated the area [Assam Valley] have been largely reinforced, not to say overrun, by a stream of vigorous Muhammadan immigrants from Mymensingh in Bengal. This gives satisfaction to the Muslim, but not the Hindu community, for the more Muhammadans you have in Assam, the stronger the case for Pakistan.'[15] The attack now is not only on the land falling out of the line in the system popularly known as the Line System whereby immigrants were confined to areas where they would not disturb the interests of the established population

[15] Quoted in an article—'The Background of Immigration into Assam', published in, the *Hindustan Standard,* 19 December 1944.

but also on what are known as the professional grazing reserves whose sanctity has remained inviolate until recently ever since the beginning of the British rule, by de-reserving portions of such Reserves. It is in regard to these Reserves that the communiqué says that the Assam government has given an assurance that they will continue the process of gradual abolition of restrictions and to open up fresh areas for immigrant settlement.

There is thus a pincer movement against the Hindus of Assam —the significance of which cannot be lost on the Hindus and tribes alike—one encouraging Muslims from Eastern Bengal, particularly Mymensingh district, to migrate into Assam and to take possession of land which the inhabitants of the areas concerned need for their own expansion and can ill-afford to lose; and the other separating the tribes from the Hindus so as to reduce the number of the latter and thus convert them in course of time to a minority or at least to present a picture in which no single community can be said to constitute a majority in the province as a whole. The irony of the situation is that the enumeration of tribes separately is justified by Mr Yeatts, the Census Commissioner of 1941, on the ground that it was necessary to obtain full figures of persons of tribal origin for whose benefit Sections 91 and 92 of the Government of India Act were enacted, and reserved or partially reserved areas, for which Governors had special responsibilities, were created.[16] How these special responsibilities are being given effect to in regard to lands in Assam is apparent from the following quotation from a Report of Mr S.P. Desai, an experienced ICS Officer of Assam: 'The Assam Land and Revenue Regulation is, so far as the immigrant encroachers are concerned, virtually non-existent. The immigrants openly claim to have short-circuited the local staff and officers. Every day new bamboo sheds and temporary huts are springing up in the reserves. I found that the immigrants absolutely ignored the local officers (from the Sub-divisional Officers downwards) so much so that they did not even answer questions put to them. The few Nepali graziers and Assamese Pamuas finding no protection from anywhere give "dohai" in the name of the King-Emperor. To this some of the thoughtless among the immigrants are said to have replied that the immigrants themselves are the King. Verily the cup of humiliation for the Assamese is full. They feel that

[16] *Census of India*, 1941, Vol I, '*India*', Tables, p. 28.

the law is meant for them and not for the immigrants, that the Government which is the custodian and trustee of their interests has failed them. All sections of the local population are greatly perturbed and their talk exhibits deep-seated bitterness.'[17]

Encouraged by the policy of the Muslim League ministry and assisted by the immigrant members of the Legislative Assembly, these invading hordes of immigrants began to indulge in various acts, of lawlessness and oppression such as maiming of cattle and buffaloes, riotous assaults on the grazers, accompanied sometimes even by murder. This naturally raised resentment and indignation throughout the country. In the session of the Legislative Assembly held in November 1944, the government was severely criticized by the Opposition party which appeared in the Legislature as a body for the first time after two and a half years with other coalitionists. A suggestion was thrown out to Sir Muhammad Saadullah to convene a conference where the whole question of land settlement might be considered and action might be taken by the government in order to remove the grave discontent among the people. The Governor himself addressed the Assembly on this subject, wishing peace and amity between the communities. Sir Muhammad accepted the offer of the Opposition; and accordingly a conference was held in December 1944. In the conference the whole question of land settlement was examined in reference to two main points:

(i)   the adoption of a policy of planned settlement of waste lands with landless people of the soil along with the immigrants, who were unduly favoured hitherto, and of protection to the tribal people in belts to be specially reserved for them; and

(ii)   to maintain the integrity of the grazing reserves by eviction of trespassers therefrom.

But the resolution which was adopted by the government in January 1945 after the conference did not include the safeguards agreed upon in the conference and in some particulars went against the fundamentals of the decisions of the conference itself. For example, the decision of the conference was that the claim to waste land

---

[17] Quoted in 'The Background of Immigration into Assam' published in the *Hindustan Standard*, 19 December 1944.

would be confined only to immigrants who came to Assam before 1938; but in the government resolution exceptions were made in case of certain kinds of encroachers into the grazing reserves who came even after 1938, and wide discretion was given to the local officers 'to keep in possession encroachers who had been in occupation of and cultivating land in the grazing reserves over three years.' As regards settlement of waste land, any person having five bighas of land was not considered entitled to any settlement; and as most of the indigenous cultivators had such quantity of land but not enough for an economic holding, this clause operated as a serious disqualification to their getting settlement. Similarly the area which was to have been reserved for the tribal people was not defined, leaving room for much uncertainty and confusion. The matter was again taken up by the Assembly in its Budget session in March 1945. By this time the Opposition had gained some strength and Sir Muhammad Saadullah, evidently afraid of a defeat and resignation, entered into an agreement with the Opposition. He agreed to remove his old Muslim League Revenue Minister, and actually took a nominee from the Opposition in his place. After the prorogation of the Assembly, however, Sir Saadullah instead of implementing the agreement as early as possible took as much as three months' time merely to frame and publish the new resolution. The report now is that he and other Muslim League ministers of his cabinet are putting all manner of obstruction in the execution of the policy agreed to by him. It is also being reported that the Muslim League leader Mr Mohammad Ali Jinnah is issuing for adoption by the Cabinet instructions which go against the basic policy of the agreement. In the meantime the dissolution of the Assembly is in sight, and there is no knowing how the whole situation will shape hereafter.'[18]

In spite of all this, however, the Hindus are still in larger numbers in the province as a whole than the Muslims. If the tribes are added to the Hindus, then, so combined they constitute a larger majority. It may be noted that the League Resolution lays down that the constituent units of the two zones shall be autonomous and sovereign. It is unintelligible how Assam with a non-Muslim majority and with only 33.73 per cent Muslims in its population can be an 'autonomous and sovereign' Muslim State. If anything

[18] It should be noted that this was written in the latter half of 1945.

it will be an autonomous and sovereign non-Muslim State in the eastern zone. But if the Sylhet district with a Muslim majority is excluded the other districts of the province and the district of Sylhet will stand as shown in Table XVIII on p. 318.

But the ingenuity of the protagonists of Pakistan is inexhaustible and Assam is claimed on various grounds. They are:

(1) Because Assam is within the zone where Muslims are in a majority.

(2) Because the majority of the non-Muslims in Assam are tribal people.

(3) Because the Muslims are in a majority in the province. This conclusion is reached in the following manner. The province of Assam has a population of one crore nine lakhs, of whom only forty-five lakhs or 41.5 per cent are Hindus. The Hindus thus form a minority of the total population. Twenty-nine lakhs or 26.7 per cent of the total population are tribal people who are unfit to live a civilized state life and in all constitutional discussion they have to be omitted. Constitutional rights, of minority, should belong to the civilized section of the population who are either Hindus or Muslims numbering eighty lakhs. In the tea gardens and oil mines of Assam a huge number of labour populations are engaged; but they are non-domiciled and migratory. This non-domiciled alien population should necessarily be omitted from constitutional consideration. Their total number is 15.2 lakhs. This number being deducted from the total, political rights are restricted to 65 lakhs of people only. Hence the Muslims numbering 34.75 lakhs constitute the majority in the province.

(4) Agriculturists from bordering districts of Bengal are migrating and settling down in the uncultivated parts of Upper Assam. These agriculturists are mainly Muslims. To finance and cater for their needs middle class members, who are Hindus, are also settling among them as shopkeepers, traders, mahajans, doctors, etc. In one word Eastern Bengal districts are literally expanding to Assam.

(5) 'Not only in the province as a whole but also division by division the Muslims are in a majority. In the Surma Valley division, Muslims constitute 51 per cent of the total

population. Minus the tribal people, Muslims are clear over 65 per cent of the people entitled to political rights. In the Assam Valley districts Hindus constitute 47 per cent of the total population and are thus clearly in a minority. As the migratory labour populations are almost all working in the Assam Valley and as they are all Hindus, the *bona fide* normal Hindu residents number only 12.98 lakhs. Here also Muslims form a majority of the total population who are entitled to political rights.'[19]

(6) Because Eastern Pakistan must have sufficient land for its huge population and Assam will give it scope for expansion.

(7) Because Assam has abundant forest and mineral resources, coal, petroleum, etc. and Eastern Pakistan must include Assam in order to be financially and economically strong.

(8) Because in Assam the majority of the people are Bengali-speaking.

Now let us consider these grounds—

No. 1—One would have thought that a Muslim zone is that in which Muslims are in a majority. But it seems a Muslim zone is something different and includes also a province in which they are in a minority which has to be included in Pakistan because it falls within the Muslim zone.

No. 2—Majority of non-Muslims in Assam are not the tribal people but Hindus, assuming for the sake of argument but not by any means conceding, that the tribal people are not Hindus.

Nos. 3 and 5—Taking the figures given by Mr Mujibur Rahman, we see how the tribal population numbering 29 lakhs is not only separated from the Hindus but declared unfit for 'civilized state life 'so that the 'civilized section 'of the population may be reduced from 109 lakhs to 80 lakhs. Even then the Hindus who are forty-five lakhs constitute an absolute majority and are certainly more numerous than the Musalmans who are only 34.75 lakhs. The Hindus who work in tea gardens and oil mines numbering

[19] Mujibur Rahman, 'Eastern Pakistan: Its Population, Delimitation and Economics', quoted by H. N. Barua in *Reflections on Assam-cum-Pakistan*, pp. 82–83.

15.2 lakhs must further be deducted from the total, so that the Musalmans may be declared to constitute a majority. Assam is thus a province with a Muslim majority! A more glaring jugglery of figures is difficult to imagine.

The only fault in this reasoning is that if the same or a similar process of cutting down the number of Hindus is employed, the Hindus may be reduced to a minority in India as a whole, and thus the whole of India becomes Pakistan and no case is left for separating the north-western and north-eastern zones from the rest of India and confining them to Pakistan.

Nos. 4, 6 and 7—Assam has land and Musalmans need land. Assam has forests, mines, petroleum, coal and other natural resources and Pakistan needs them. Is not that enough? Why should not Assam be included in Pakistan to satisfy the needs of Pakistan? No Imperialist and colonial power has claimed domination over other countries on any other ground. Why should Pakistan? We know further that India has not only to consent to a division but also to find and supply the wherewithal for the maintenance of Pakistan.

If as is now claimed the whole of the two British provinces of Bengal and Assam are combined, the communal position in the eastern Muslim zone will be as follows:

If we take only the districts with Muslim majorities in the two provinces, the communal position in the eastern Muslim zone will be as follows:

The result thus of taking the two provinces of Bengal and Assam in their entirety is to reduce the already bare Muslim majority of 54.73 per cent in Bengal into a nominal majority of 51.69 per cent while if the areas with non-Muslim majorities are separated, then the Muslim majority in Assam and Bengal, with each district having a Muslim majority, comes to 69.42. There is thus no Muslim zone in the east properly so called if the two provinces in their entirety are taken together, and in any case 69.42 per cent of Muslims in the eastern zone is much nearer the figure of 75 per cent mentioned by Mr Jinnah to Mr Chapman in the interview quoted above than 51.69 per cent, which will be their percentage in the population if the two provinces are taken in their entirety without excluding the portions with non-Muslim majorities.

TABLE XXI
Population by Communities of the Eastern Muslim Zone Including Districts with Non-Muslim Majorities

Province	Total population	Muslims	Hindus	Christians	Tribes	Others	Total Non-Muslims
Bengal	6,03,06,525	3,30,05,43 (54.72)	2,50,59,024 (41.55)	1,66,509 (0.28)	18,89,389 (3.13)	1,86,169 (0.31)	2,73,01,091 (45.27)
Assam	1,02,04,733	34,42,479 (33.73)	42,13,223 (41.29)	40,810 (0.40)	24,84,996 (24.35)	23,225 (0.23)	67,62,254 (66.27)
Total	7,05,11,258	3,64,47,913 (51.69)	2,92,72,247 (41.51)	2,07,319 (0.29)	43,74,385 (6.20)	2,09,394 (0.30)	3,40,63,345 (48.30)

TABLE XXII
Population by Communities in the Eastern Muslim Zone Excluding Districts with Non-Muslim Majorities

Zone	Total Population	Muslims	Hindus	Indian Christians	Tribes	Others	Total Non-Muslims
Bengal minus Districts with Non-Muslim Majorities	4,09,64,779	2,87,10,462 (70.09)	1,13,84,495 (27.79)	54,732 (0.13)	7,06,615 (1.72)	1,08,475 (0.26)	1,22,54,317 (29.90)
Assam minus Districts with Non-Muslim Majorities (District of Sylhet)	31,16,602	18,92,117 (60.71)	11,49,514 (36.88)	3,055 (0.09)	69,907 (2.24)	2,009 (0.06)	12,24,485 (39.27)
Total of Eastern Zone with Muslim Majority in each District	4,40,81,381	3,06,02,579 (69.42)	1,25,34,009 (28.43)	57,787 (0.13)	7,76,522 (1.76)	1,10,484 (0.25)	1,34,78,802 (30.57)

To sum up the position disclosed by the census figures we find the following:

(1)   In the provinces of Sind, NWF, and Baluchistan the Muslims are in a numerical majority in each province and in each district of every province.

(2)   In the Punjab they are numerically in a majority in each district of the Rawalpindi and Multan divisions and also consequently in each of the two divisions which comprise 12 districts and if we count the Baluch Frontier tract also as a district, then in thirteen districts.

(3)   In the Lahore division they are numerically in a majority but they are in minority in the district of Amritsar, their population being 46.52 per cent, and only in nominal majority in the district of Gurdaspur.

(4)   In the Jullundar division they are in a minority, being only 34.53 per cent of the population as against 35.87 per cent Hindus and 24.31 per cent Sikhs. The position of the Hindus will be improved considerably if the Adidharmis who belong to the Scheduled Castes are counted with them.

(5)   In the Ambala division the Muslims are numerically in a minority, being only 28.07 per cent as against the Hindus who are 66.01 per cent.

(6)   If we take the north western region to comprise the four provinces of Sind, NWFP, Baluchistan and the Punjab in their entirety, then the Muslim percentage will be 62.07.

(7)   If the Ambala and Jullundar divisions and the Amritsar district of the Lahore division are excluded and the north-western zone comprises only the three provinces of Sind, NWFP, Baluchistan and only that portion of the Punjab in which Muslims are in a majority—the Rawalpindi and Multan divisions and the Lahore Division minus the district of Amritsar, then the percentage of Muslims will be 75.36.

(8)   In the eastern zone the Muslims are in a numerical minority in the province of Assam, their percentage being only 33.73 as against 41.29 of the Hindus and 24.35 of the tribes, the percentage of the Hindus going much above 50, if even that portion of the tribes who are completely assimilated with and declare themselves to be Hindus is added. In the

single district of Sylhet the Muslim percentage is 60.71; in every other district they are in a minority.

(9)   In Bengal as a whole the Muslim percentage is 54.73.

(10) In the divisions of Chittagong and Dacca the Muslims are in a majority and so also in each of the districts of those divisions except the Chittagong Hill Tracts.

(11) In the Rajshahi division as a whole they are in a majority but in the Jalpaiguri and Darjeeling districts of that division they are in a minority, their percentage being 23.08 and 2.42 respectively in those districts. In the district of Dinajpur they are on the border-line, being only 50.20 per cent.

(12) In the Presidency division as a whole including Calcutta they are in a minority, being only 44.56 per cent as against 53.70 per cent Hindus; but in the districts of Nadia, Murshidabad and Jessore they constitute a majority of the population, and are just less than half, being 49.36 per cent, in the district of Khulna.

(13) If the Muslim zone in Bengal consists of only those districts in which the Muslims are in a majority, their percentage will be 70.09.

(14) The percentage of Muslims in the districts in which they are in a minority will be 22.21.

(15) If the two provinces of Assam and Bengal in their entirety are combined to constitute the eastern zone, the Muslims will be 51.69 per cent of the population.

(16) If the districts in which the Muslims are in a numerical minority are excluded from the eastern zone, then the percentage of Muslims in it will be 69.42.

Separation is claimed on the ground that Muslims constitute a majority of the population in some regions of India. If India were to be taken as a whole—as nature appears to have intended and history so far as known appears to have endorsed—the population of Muslims in India as a whole, including the States, is 23.8 per cent and that of non-Muslims 76.2 per cent while in British India, excluding the States, the percentage of Muslims in the population is 26.8 and that of non-Muslims 73.2. If the non-Muslims who constitute 38 or 25 per cent of the population in the north-western region and 48 or 32 per cent in the eastern region, according as the Muslim minority districts are included or excluded can be asked to submit to separation of their respective regions from the rest of India, why cannot the Muslims who are only 23.8 per cent in India as a whole and 26.8 in British India be asked to remain within India as they have done so long? If the Muslims who constitute 75 per cent or even less of the population in some regions can justly and fairly demand and enforce separation from India of the regions where they predominate, why cannot the non-Muslims who are 76.2 per cent in India as a whole and 73.2 per cent in British India with equal justice and fairness refuse to submit to separation, particularly in view of long historical association in administration, if in nothing else?

In the foregoing pages I have tried to delimit the areas which will fall in the north-western and eastern Muslim zones in accordance with the terms laid down by the Lahore Resolution of the League in March 1940. I should not be understood as laying down any boundary lines of my own conception. This can be done only if the residents of the areas sought to be separated agree to separation; and by residents must be understood not only the Muslims but also the non-Muslims of those areas. For the sake of argument I have assumed that a majority of the Muslims of those areas both in the north-west and east favour Partition, and hence I have taken the Provinces of Sind, NWFP, and Baluchistan in their entirety and only the western districts of the Punjab, and the eastern and some northern districts of Bengal and the district of Sylhet in Assam as constituting the Muslim zones. But unless their desire is expressed in favour of Partition in an unequivocal and unquestionable manner by some device, it may be argued not without some reason and force that even a majority of the Musalmans of those areas may not favour partition. But leaving Musalmans apart, there are others who insist that they cannot be ignored.

TWENTY-EIGHT

~

PARTITION OF SIKHS AND BENGALIS

Let us take Sikhs who are concentrated in the British Punjab and the Punjab States. They have expressed their opposition to any scheme of separation of any portion of the Punjab from the rest of India and proclaimed their determination to resist it at all costs. But in case Partition and separation are forced by the Muslims, they insist that the areas in which their population resides and in which their religious shrines exist and with which they have religious and historical associations should be created into a separate State. This area, they claim, will spread to the River Chenab on the west and to the Jumna on the east, to the borders of Rajputana in the south and to the State of Kashmir and the mountain regions on the north. Mr V.S. Bhatti in a pamphlet named *Khalistan* regards this state which falls between Pakistan on the west and Hindustan on the east as a buffer State between the two and lays down its boundary. 'The proposed Sikh State would be bounded—North by Kashmir, north-west and West and South-West by the river Chenab and the Punjab behind Multan, South by Rajputana and the gulf of Cutch, and East by the Jumna; and in the north-east embrace the Simla Hill States and Kulu. As this Sikh State will be the abode of the Khalsa it would not be inappropriate to call it Khalistan. It should consist roughly of the Sikh States, Patiala, Nabha, Jhind, Faridkot, Kapurthala, Kalsia, Malerkotla, the Simla Hill States, and the Districts or Divisions of Ludhiana, Jullundar, Kulu, Ambala, Ferozpur, Lahore, Amritsar, Lyallpur, Gujranwala, Sheikhupura, Montgomery, Hissar, Rohtak, Karnal, Multan and Delhi. And a corridor consisting of thin strips of Sind, Bahawalpur, and Rajputana enabling the Sikhs to have an outlet to the gulf of Cutch, for without a seaport they will be bottled up and depend on others for their trade.'[1]

[1] V.S. Bhatti, *Khalistan*, p. 4.

Mr Saint Nihal Singh in an article in the *Hindustan Review*—'A project for partitioning the Punjab'—points out that the Sikhs insist that if there is to be Pakistan, then the Sikhs must have their Azad Punjab which according to its propounders would include 3,500,000 Sikhs of British India and more than 1,250,000 Sikhs residing in the States or nearly 4,800,000 Sikhs out of their total population of 5.10 millions according to the census of 1941. The boundaries of the Azad Punjab according to this scheme, although worked out in detail are still left fluid. 'The delimitation, it is proposed, should be entrusted to a commission composed of persons who can be expected to bring an impartial mind to bear upon the highly controversial issues with which they will have to deal. In announcing this decision on 5 June 1943, the sponsors of the scheme—the Shiromani Akali Dal—stipulated that in determining the limits, population, property, land revenue, cultural traditions and historical associations, must be duly pondered.' The scheme as propounded will comprise four commissionerships—namely Multan (only a part), Lahore, Jullundar and Ambala. The districts affected are:

Multan division—Multan (portion only), Montgomery, Lyallpur, Jhang and Muzaffargarh.

Lahore division—Lahore, Sheikhupura, Gujranwala, Amritsar, Gurdaspur and Sialkot.

Jullundar division—Ambala, Karnal, Hissar, Rohtak, Gurgaon and Ferozpur.

Ambala division—Ambala, Karnal, Hissar, Rohtak, Gurgaon and Simla.

The 2,00,00,000 persons (in round figures) living in Azad Punjab exclusive of the portion of the Multan district lying alongside the Montgomery district, would comprise:

Sikhs	34,42,508
Muslims	91,91,608
All other non-Muslims (mostly Hindus)	72,45,336
Total	1,98,79,452

As Mr Sant Nihal Singh has said: 'Mistrust of the Hindus poisoned the Muslim mind. "Pakistan" was projected.

'Mistrust of the Muslims poisoned the Sikh mind. A scheme for partitioning the Punjab is being pushed. The men behind it are as determined as they are possessed of political drive and organizing ability.'

If therefore Pakistan is insisted upon, the Sikhs refuse to be ignored and insist on a partition on their own terms.

It will be recalled that in 1905 Lord Curzon partitioned Bengal and established two provincial governments—one comprising Assam and the eastern and northern districts of Bengal proper, and the other the remaining districts of Bengal, and Bihar and Orissa. This partition was intensely resented by the Hindus of Bengal generally and some influential Musalmans as well and led to the great anti-partition agitation of the first decade of the present century which had far-reaching consequences in rousing national consciousness throughout the country and the inauguration of the movement of boycott of British goods and adoption of Swadeshi. The British government ultimately cancelled the partition, although it had declared it to be a settled fact. This created discontent among the Musalmans for whose benefit the partition, at one stage of the agitation against it, had been declared to have been made. The point that is sought to be made out here is that in the foregoing discussion on the basis of the Muslim League Resolution of March 1940, the area of Bengal which may be separated from the rest of it will correspond more or less to that of Eastern Bengal of the partition of 1905. The Bengali Hindus who had that partition annulled in 1911 by the intensity of their agitation are not likely to acquiesce in it now. Much less are they likely to acquiesce in Bengal being cut off altogether from India and in this they will have the support of the Hindus from other parts of India. I have therefore contented myself with pointing out the implications of the Lahore Resolution of the League.

PART V

RESOURCES OF THE MUSLIM STATES

TWENTY-NINE

AGRICULTURE

We must now consider the resources of the Muslim States. India is an agricultural country and by far the largest proportion of the population whether in the Muslim or in the non-Muslim zone depends upon agriculture for its support and sustenance. It is therefore necessary to take the agricultural resources of the two zones into consideration.

I. EASTERN ZONE

We shall take up the eastern zone first. This zone is fertile but very thickly populated, the population being 787 per sq. mile, and in spite of the richness of the soil it cannot produce enough food for its large population, as will be shown below.

The total population of Bengal in 1941 was just over 6 crores and 3 lakhs and the total area in 1936–37 available for cultivation, after deducting forests and other non-cultivable area, was 3,51,07,049 acres. Out of this, 2,44,66,300 acres constituted the net cropped area, leaving a balance of 1,06,40,749 acres which could be brought under the plough, if every bit of land which can bear cultivation is cultivated. The cropped area per head of the population would be 0.40 acre and the additional land which could be cultivated would come to 0.17 acre per head of the population. Thus even when all the available land is cultivated, it cannot give more than 0.57 acre per head of the population according to the census of 1941. If we took the figures separately for the Muslim zone and non-Muslim zone as determined above, the position would be as follows:

It thus appears that in the Muslim zone and the non-Muslim zone the area of cultivable land per head of the population is almost the same but that a greater proportion of the cultivable land is already cultivated in the Muslim zone leaving only a smaller

TABLE XXIII

Population and Land in Muslim and Non-Muslim Districts of Bengal

	Total Area Available for Cultivation	Per head (Acres)	Net Cropped Area (In Acres)	Per head (Acres)	Balance of Cultivable But Not Cultivated Area (In Acres)	Per head (Acres)	Percentage of Cultivated land	Percentage of Cultivable land
Muslim zone	2,39,48,462	0.58	1,78,33,600	0.43	61,14,862	0.14	74.4	25.6
Non-Muslim zone	1,11,58,587	0.57	66,32,700	0.34	45,25,887	0.23	59.4	40.6

proportion awaiting cultivation whereas in the non-Muslim zone a somewhat larger area is still uncultivated. This is the position when we take the Chittagong Hill Tracts, which are sparsely populated and that almost entirely by tribes and have a larger surplus, comparatively speaking, of cultivable but uncultivated land, that is, 14,22,017 acres with a population of 2,47,053, giving additional 5.75 acres per head of the population of the district as against 0.14 acre available in the Muslim zone. If this land is reserved for the tribes, as is likely, the additional land per hea4 of the population would be less than what is shown in the above statement.

It must be borne in mind that the population has been itineraries and the largest increase has been in the eastern or the Muslim zone of the province. In districts most thickly populated like Dacca (1,542 per sq. mile), Mymensingh (979 per sq. mile), Faridpur (1,024 per sq. mile), Tipperah (1,525 per sq. mile), Noakhali (1,337 per sq. mile), the land already under crop in 1936–37 constituted 95.6 per cent, 84 per cent, 99 per cent. 93 per cent and 92 per cent respectively of the total cultivable land there. The increase in the population of the Dacca and Chittagong divisions, which fall, entirely within the Muslim zone, between 1881 and 1931, was by 60 per cent and 88 per cent respectively; and that between 1931 and 1941 was 19.9 per cent and 25.2 per cent respectively. A similar increase in the Rajshahi division—which with the exception of two of its districts also falls within the Muslim Zone— was between 1881 and 1931 was 26 per cent and that between 1931 and 1941 only 12.8 per cent. A similar increase in the Presidency division leaving out Calcutta and 24-Parganas between 1931 and 1941 was 15.6 per cent.

It is thus clear that in Bengal, additional area available for cultivation is very limited, and that in the Muslim zone is still more limited—almost negligible—and therefore expansion of agriculture cannot keep pace with natural increase of population. Leaving the future increase of population out of consideration for the moment, let us see if the province can support its present population with the food grown on its own soil. It has been shown below that Bengal is a deficit province in respect of its food and this fact was brought home in a most painful manner by the famine of 1943. There were undoubtedly other causes of that tragedy but this cause cannot be ignored and should not be underestimated.

As Sir Azizul Haque has pointed out in *The Man behind the Plough*: 'Rice is the main diet of the people of the province and for the cultivator, his chief food is rice and dal with very little of other dishes like vegetables, fish, or meat. He takes rice for his breakfast, for his lunch and/or his dinner. For the province the production of rice is therefore a matter of national health and safety and yet Bengal does not produce enough rice needed for her own domestic consumption.'[1]

On the basis of the Census of 1931 he has calculated that out of a total population of 5,18,73,436, over 4 crores will require full meals, if we deduct from the total the non-rice-eating community and reduce the numbers of those like children requiring less than full meals to the level of those requiring full meals. 'Taking the daily requirement of rice at 14 chataks per day per adult, the total requirement comes to 319 million maunds of rice per annum.[2] Even if the ration is taken at 12 chataks, the standard jail ration, the aggregate quantity needed is, just a little over 273 million maunds of rice. Converted to paddy the figures on the 14 chatak basis come to 479 million maunds and on the 12 chatak basis to 410 million maunds of paddy.'[3] Add to this 2.2 crore maunds required for seed at the rate of i maund per acre for 2.2 crore acres sown in 1936–37. The total requirement of paddy will be 50.1 or 43.2 crore maunds according as we take 14 chataks or 12 chataks of rice as the daily requirement of each rice-eating adult in the province. Taking the figures of production for ten

---

[1] Sir Azizul Haque, *The Man behind the Plough*, p. 51.

[2] One ounce of rice gives 108 to 114 calories of heat (R.N. Chopra *Tropical Therapeutics*, p. 1632). Taking an average of 111 calories for each ounce and 2:2 ounces to be equal to 1 chatak, we get 244 calories for one chatak of rice. From 14 chataks we can get 3416 calories and from 12 chataks 2928 calories, provided every little bit is converted into heat—which does not happen in actual practice. According to Col. R.N. Chopra, 'As a rule it is approximate to assume that a man or woman who leads a quiet life at home with little exercise requires about 2500 calories, that if he is engaged in a sedentary occupation 3000 calories are required, that if he engages in a moderate amount of exercise or is a labourer doing light work, he can get along on 3500 calories and that if he does hard work 4000 calories or even more are necessary.' (Ibid., p. 153)

[3] Haque, *The Man behind the Plough*, p. 52.

years from 1927–28 to 1936–37 Sir Azizul Haque concludes that
there has been an annual average deficit of 16. 1 crore maunds
or 9.3 crore maunds on the basis of 14 chataks or 12 chataks
respectively. Bengal is thus in annual deficit of her normal food
requirements. If to the produce of the province is added the net
average available import of rice after deducting the re-exports, we
get an additional 2 lakh tons of rice equivalent to 3–4 lakh tons
of paddy, which is equivalent roughly to I crore maunds of paddy.
'Against an average deficit of 161 million maunds, this addition
of 1 million maunds does not substantially alter the position that
the production of rice is much below the minimum requirements
of the Province.'[4]

Mr Kalicharan Ghosh in his *Famines in Bengal, 1770–1943*,
has calculated that Bengal needs 25.7 crore maunds or 93.70
lakh tons of rice, calculating 5.5 maunds as consumption per
head of the population. In making this calculation he has taken
into consideration and given deduction for children, widows and
others requiring less than two full rice meals a day. Against this
requirement there is the average available supply of 85 lakh tons,
thus leaving a clear deficit of 13.46 lakh tons or about 3.67 crore
maunds annually.[5] This is very much less than 16.1 or even 9.3
crore maunds calculated by Sir Azizul Haque. This is due to the
very much smaller quantity allotted to each adult per day—Sir
Azizul Haque calculating at 14 chataks or 12 chataks, Mr Ghosh's
calculation being at less than two chataks a day.

We have seen that increase in cultivation of fresh land does not
and cannot keep pace with the increase of population in Bengal,
particularly in the Muslim zone of it. The only hope of making
Bengal better supplied with food grown within its own boundaries
lies not in increased or extensive cultivation but in intensive
cultivation. As things stand there is no facility for irrigation in
the Muslim zone by canal or otherwise, the two canals in the
province being in the districts of Burdwan and Midnapur of the
Burdwan division, and the Muslim zone has to depend entirely on
weather and rains for its crop. It is also doubtful if any artificial
irrigation in the eastern Muslim zone is at all possible, and if

[4] Ibid., pp. 55–56. There is an evident misprint here. We should read
   10 million mounds instead of 1 million maunds.
[5] K.C. Ghosh, *Famines in Bengal, 1770–1943*, Appendix, pp. 193–94.

such irrigation is likely to lead to any considerable improvement in the productive capacity of the land, which for the most part is ordinarily moist and subject more to flood and cyclone than to drought. It may be hoped, however, that it may not be beyond the resources of science to harness the big rivers and make them yield more food instead of the disaster which they periodically cause by floods to the people inhabiting those regions.

Intensive cultivation also is not free from difficulty on account of the size of the holdings, and the constant sub-division even among the small existing holdings that is going on. Sir Azizul Haque has calculated that the size of a standard holding of an agriculturist family of five persons is 7 acres, of which 5.3 acres are cultivated and 1.7 acres fallow; and taking into consideration the fact that a portion of the holding may have double crops, he roughly puts the gross area under cultivation per family to be 6.5 acres of which 5 acres may be taken to be sown with paddy, $^{1}/_{2}$ acre with jute and 1 acre with other crops.[6] It is also worth noting that even though the holding of an agriculturist may consist of 7 acres, it may have many plots of tiny size, each separated from others by plots belonging to other agriculturists. Except for manuring it is difficult to see how the productive capacity of these small bits of land can be increased to any considerable extent. With its heavy rainfall washing away manure, and much of the land remaining for long periods under water, the scope for artificial manuring is also limited. Large-scale farming, assuming that it can give better results than intensive cultivation of small plots by agriculturists who but for the more or less fixed rent which they have to pay to the zamindar, are more or less in the position of peasant proprietors, is possible only if some sort of collective farming is introduced. This is by no means an easy matter, as the Indian peasant, whether Hindu or Muslim, is attached to his little plots of land and will not be easily persuaded or coerced to agree to their being merged with those of others.

It is enough just to refer to the position of other crops, like sugar-cane, pulses or oil-seeds, none of which is produced in sufficiently large quantities to supply the needs of the province, which has to depend upon imports of these articles or their products from elsewhere.

[6] Haque, *The Man behind the Plough*, pp. 93–94.

Sugar is a very important item in the diet of the people and there was a time when Bengal used to produce large quantities of sugar. But the position is very much changed now. 'Of the total sugar manufactured and imported into India, Bengal consumes about 13 per cent. But her production is only 2.8 per cent of India's total output. In 1935–36 there was an import into this province of 20,79,494 maunds of *gur* and 29,43,311 maunds of white sugar. In 1936–37 Bengal produced 6,25,175 maunds but she consumed 35,39,250 maunds of white sugar.'[7]

Oil is another item which is equally necessary for a balanced diet. Sir Azizul Haque says that 'Bengal still consumes the largest quantity of mustard oil. Yet the normal acreage in 1914-15 was 14,59,100 acres and it came down to 7,23,800 acres in 1934–35, being reduced by more than half in 20 years.'[8] No wonder that in 1939–40 the total quantity of oil-seeds (linseed, sesamum, rape and mustard) produced in Bengal, according to the *Statistical Abstract of India*,[9] was only 2,05,000 tons or 55,96,500 maunds which converted into oil at the rate of 33.3 per cent gave only 18,65,500 maunds of oil or $1^{1}/_{4}$ seers per head of the population per year, thus leaving a deficit of at least 10 seers per head of the population, if we calculate the consumption of oil per head even at $^{1}/_{2}$ chatak a day, which is less than the ration allowed in jails. In other words, Bengal produces only about 11 per cent of her oil requirements and has to import eight times as much edible oil as it produces.

A rough calculation of the pulses will give a deficit of about 80 per cent of the requirements, and this has to be imported.

If the famine of 1943 was instrumental in showing the precarious food position of Bengal, it also showed how India as a whole came to the help of Bengal, as it had clone for Bihar at the time of the great earthquake ten years earlier in 1934. Only, the horrors of the Bengal famine with men and women and children dying in lakhs like flies in the streets and bylanes of Calcutta and the lanes and fields of mufassil Bengal for months, were infinitely more indescribable and unbearable than those of the earthquake which finished its work of destruction within a few short minutes,

[7] Haque, *The Man behind the Plough*, p. 91.
[8] Ibid., p. 39.
[9] *Statistical Abstract of India*, 1930–31 to 1939–40, p. 556.

although its effects lasted for a long time. Bengal has not yet recovered from the effects of this disaster which has a lesson of its own which we can ignore only at our peril. I do not know if there are instances of aid being rushed to an independent country even by its immediate neighbours, not to speak of aid from countries situated a thousand or more miles away, in case of an emergency like this—the sort of aid given to Bengal by provincial and central governments and non-official relief organizations.

In reply to questions in the Bengal Legislative Council, the Hon'ble Mr Suhrawardy, minister, stated on 24 July 1944 that between January and December 1943, the total quantity of rice and paddy imported into Bengal from all provinces and places was 54,33,437 maunds and 5,27,934 maunds respectively. Of this amount no less than 26,18,009 maunds of rice and 3,38,532 maunds of paddy came from the provinces of Bihar and Orissa. The value of food materials like rice, wheat, wheat products, jowar, bajra, maize,-gram, pulses and barley imported into Bengal between April and December, 1943, came to Rs 21.18,74.165.[10]

The Food Member, Sir J.P. Srivastava, informed Mr A.N. Chattopadhyaya in the Central Assembly on 28 February 1945, that the total quantity of rice purchased by the Bengal government during 1944 was over a million tons and that the Government of India had arranged the supply of 2,35.470 tons of rice between 2 November 1943 and 2 November 1944, and 4,69,127 tons of wheat between 1 April 1943, and 30 April 1944.[11]

Being a part of India and having a central government have proved of some value to Bengal at least in an emergency and may well do so in future.

Bengal is however rich in respect of one crop—jute, which is a money crop. Out of a total of 21,54,800 acres under jute in Bengal in 1936–37 no less than 20,11,800 acres were cultivated in the eastern and northern districts which fall within the Muslim zone. The total quantity of jute produced in 1936–37 was 104 lakh bales of 400 Ibs each; 59 lakh bales were consumed by Indian mills and 49 lakh bales were exported to foreign countries from Bengal. The average annual production during fifteen years ending 1936–37 was nearly 95 lakh bales and the consumption by mills

[10] *Hindustan Standard*, 26 July 1944.
[11] Ibid, 2 March 1945.

and export to 'foreign, countries was very nearly the same, but the price of jute within the same period varied between Rs 18–13–0 per maund which was the highest, in 1925–26, and Rs 3-8-0 which was the prevailing-price in 1932–33, 1933–34, 1934–35.[12] Being the money crop which supplies the cultivator with the wherewithal to pay his rent for the land, to purchase his cloth and to meet his other cash requirements, it plays a very important part in the village economy. Its price, however, is liable to wide fluctuations not so much on account of the fluctuations in demand and supply of the article as on account of trade manipulation. The mills in India and the foreign consumers are both in a position to dictate their own terms to the cultivator who is unable to hold his stock for higher prices and is compelled by his economic helplessness to sell it at whatever price the consumers decide to pay for it. It has thus become a most unsteady and uncertain source of supply of cash to the cultivators and cannot, at any rate in the existing circumstances, be depended upon to help the agriculturist to make up the deficiency in food to which he is subject as shown above. The consumers of jute—the mills both Indian and foreign—being outside the independent Muslim State in the eastern zone, it will be a question how far that State will be able to regulate its price and help the agriculturists even after its establishment on an autonomous and sovereign basis.

Besides, jute is liable to be ousted on account of the sheer necessity, of having to produce more food crops, unless the price it fetches is high enough to enable food to be purchased in larger quantities than what would be produced on the same land. Sir Azizul Haque has calculated that 'jute is an unremunerative produce if the average harvest price [of jute] is less than Rs 5 per maund under the present market conditions 1936–7;[13] and he has shown that between 1928–29 and 1934–35 the agriculturist on the whole was a great loser.

Sylhet is the only district of Assam that falls within the eastern Muslim zone as shown above. It has an area of 5,478 sq. miles with a population of 31,16,602 or 569 per sq. mile, according to the Census of 1941, the population per sq. mile in 1931 being 497—an increase of 14.4 per cent in ten years. The population of

[12] Haque, *The Man behind the Plough*, pp. 66–68.
[13] Haque, *The Man behind the Plough*, p. 62.

no other district in the province exceeds 329 per sq. mile and its
density for the province as a whole is 186 per sq. mile. It is thus
clear that Sylhet like Bengal is a most densely populated area. The
total area in the province of Assam under food crops including
rice, pulses and other foodgrains in 1936–37 was 56,83,774 acres
or 1.8 acres per head. The area under food crops in the district
of Sylhet in 1936–37 was 19,82,566 acres which works out at
0.63 acre per head of the population. If the produce is taken at
the rate of 896 lbs per acre which is the quinquennial average
for 1936–37 for winter rice per acre, the rice per head will come
to 564 lbs per wear, or just a little over 1.5 lbs a day. It should
be noted that we have taken all the land as being cultivated with
paddy. Even this somewhat exaggerated figure is hardly sufficient
to support a man in a healthy condition. It is not necessary to
give any other detailed figures, except mentioning that this district
unlike Muslim Bengal districts has a very small area under jute.
This district along is not likely to give any appreciable help in
relieving the food shortage of Bengal. We have seen in an earlier
chapter how emigration has been going on for the last forty years
or so, on an extensive scale from Eastern Bengal to Assam. But
this emigration, while it has added to the Muslim population of
Assam, has not at all affected the food situation in Bengal; and it
could not be expected to do so when we consider that in Bengal
during the same period the population has increased by more than
181 lakhs and during the last decade (1931–41) by nearly 102
lakhs which is very nearly the entire population of Assam.[14]

Tea is an important commodity produced in Bengal and Assam.
But the position of the Muslim districts of Bengal in this respect
is not at all satisfactory. Out of a total area of 2,03,100 acres
under tea in Bengal in 1936–37 only 7,700 acres fall in the
Muslim zone, and the remaining 1,95,400 acres fall within the
non-Muslim zone being confined to the districts of Jalpaiguri
and Darjeeling. The position in Assam is better. Out of a total
of 4,38,925 acres in the province as a whole in 1936–37, 88,957
acres were in the district of Sylhet which may fall within the
Muslim zone. Of the balance the most important districts for
growing tea are Sibsagar, Lakhimpur, Darrang and Cachar—all
outside the Muslim zone.

[14] *Census of India*, Vol. I, Tables, p. 62.

II. NORTH-WESTERN ZONE

Turning to the north-western Muslim zone we find a better picture so far as agriculture and food crops are concerned.

The population of the districts of the Punjab falling in the Muslim zone is 1,68,900 and the area 63,775 sq. miles, or 264 per sq. mile. In the NWFP the density of population is 213 per sq. mile, and that in Sind and Baluchistan is 94 and 9 per sq. mile respectively. The density for the whole zone including parts of the Punjab, and the whole of the NWFP, Sind and Baluchistan is 138 per sq. mile as against 810 per sq. mile of the Muslim zone of Bengal and 569 of the district of Sylhet.

The area actually sown in the north-western zone excluding Baluchistan is shown in Table XXIV. It may be noted that in this Table we have taken the figures of the whole of the Punjab and not only of the districts falling within the zone which I will do a little later. The figures are for 1939–40.

The position regarding the area per head of the population in the Muslim and non-Muslim zones of the Punjab according to the figures for 1937–38 given in *Agricultural Statistics of India* is given in Table XXV on p. 357.

It will thus be seen that in the Punjab, Sind and NWFP not only is the area sown per head of the population larger than in Bengal but also the area available for expansion of agriculture is larger than that in Bengal. This is on account of the extensive irrigation works in the Punjab and Sind.

I have not been able to get all the figures for Baluchistan such as I have secured for other provinces. It appears that in 1933–34 the total area sown was 4,49,094 acres and the total area harvested was 2,73,872 acres, which works out at 1.1 acres sown and 0.7 acre harvested per head of the population as recorded in the Census of 1931, and at 0.81 acre sown and 0.54 acre harvested per head according to the Census of 1941.

The Punjab and Sind are fortunate in having a very extensive system of irrigation by canals and it may be hoped that there is much room not only for further extending agriculture but also for intensive cultivation of the area already cultivated.

The following Tables show the position of areas cropped and irrigated in 1939–40.

TABLE XXIV

Area Sown and Food Produce in the Punjab, NWFP and Sind in 1939–40

Province	Net Area — Actually sown in Acres	Rice — Area in Acres	Rice — Produce in Tones	Wheat — Area in Acres	Wheat — Produce in Tons	Other Foodgrains — Area in Acres	Other Foodgrains — Produce in Tons	Total under Foodgrains — Area in Acres	Total under Foodgrains — Produce in Tons	Cotton — Area in Acres	Cotton — Produce in Tons
Punjab	2,57,44,129	9,76,552	2,87,000	95,65,976	37,60,000	93,55,869	14,72,000	1,98,98,397	55,19,000 (15,06,68,700) mds	26,41,105	10,17,000
Per Head of Population	0.9							0.7	5.3 mds	0.09	
NWFP	20,00,617	36,423	-	9,31,373	2,60,000	9,77,235	3,23000	19,45,031	5,83,000 (1,59,15,900) mds	17,351	3,000
Per Head of Population	0.66							0.65		5.2 mds	
Sind	49,45,843	13,28,713	4,43,000	12,70,563	3,26,000	16,45,010	1,90,000	42,44,286	9,59,000 (2,61,80,700) mds	8,54,390	3,09,000
Per Head of Population	1.1							0.93	5.8 mds	0.18	
Total for Three Provinces	3,26,90,589	23,41,688	7,30,000	1,17,67,912	43,46,000	1,19,78,114	19,85,000	2,60,87,714	70,61,000 (19,27,65,300) mds	35,12,846	13,29,000
Per Head of Population	0.90							0.70	5.4 mds	0.10	

TABLE XXV

Area Per Head and Under Different Crops in the Punjab, Sind and NWFP in 1937–38

	Total Area in Acres	Area not Available for Cultivation in Acres	Net Area Available for Cultivation in Acres	Area Cultivation but Not Cultivated in Acres	Net Sown in Acres	Area under Foodgrains in Acres
Non-Muslim Districts of the Punjab	2,18,92,338	67,39,576	1,51,52,762	37,68,649	1,13,84,113	97,78,981
Muslim Districts of the Punjab	3,82,62,386	82,57,553	3,00,04,833	1,40,92,069	1,59,12,764	1,16,32,107
Sind	3,01,79,486	1,42,66,347	1,59,13,139	58,99,512	48,73,248	42,96,211
NWFP	84,37,582	30,39,984	53,97,598	28,51,700	21,09,029	21,12,929

TABLE XXV (contd.)

	Area under Oil Seeds in Acres	Area under Sugar in Acres	Area under Cotton in Acres	Population	Net Area Sown Per Head of Population in Acres	Area available for Further Cultivation Per Head of Population in Acres	Area under Foodgrains Per Head of Population in Acres
Non-Muslim Districts of the Punjab	4,12,771	2,56,550	7,79,779	1,15,47,919	0.98	0.32	0.84
Muslim Districts of the Punjab	4,88,783	2,53,464	23,55,752	1,68,70,900	0.94	0.83	0.69
Sind	2,13,512	7,420	9,70,174	45,35,008	1.08	1.30	0.94
NWFP	91,739	70,084	22,195	30,38,067	0.69	0.93	0.69

TABLE XXVI

Area Cropped and Irrigated in the NW Zone

	Area Sown in Acres	Area Irrigated in Acres	Percentage of Areas Irrigated to Area Sown	Total Miles of Canals, Branches and Distributaries	Total Capital Outlay (Direct and Indirect) to end of 1939–40 Rs
Punjab	2,57,44,129	1,35,21,889	62.5	20.193	39,26,90,268
Sind	49,45,843	42,43,949	85.8	9.620	30,00,88,760
NWFP	20,00,617	4,75,413	23.5	979	3,15,21,444
Baluchistan	4,49,094	1,45,402	32.3	252	1,45,11,276
Total for NW Zone	3,31,39,683	1,83,86,653	55.4	31,044	73,88,11,748
Total for British India	20,99,59,786	2,82,92,938	13.4	74.911	1,53,89,42,433
Percentage of NW Zone to British India	15.6	61.4		41.4	47.9

(contd.)

	Gross Receipts (Direct and Indirect) Rs	Working Expenses (Direct and Indirect) Rs	Net Revenue Rs	Percentage on Total Capital Outlay	Total Value of Crops Irrigated Rs	Value of Crops Irrigated Per Head of Population Rs
Punjab	7,10,90,148	1,53,98,222	5,56,91,926	14.19	50,74,57,696	17-3-0
Sind	1,68,61,293	68,85,554	99,75,739	3.32	11,02,12,677	24-5-0
NWFP	23,22,557	9,80,071	13,42,486	0.42	2,66,82,912	8-12-0
Baluchistan	3,94,540	2,55,955	1,38,585	0.95	4,48,398	0-14-0
Total for NW zone	9,60,68,538	2,35,19,802	6,71,48,736	9.08	64,48,01,683	17-10-0
British India	14,60,42,127	4,56,93,471	10,03,48,656	6.52	1,36,29,08,373	3-8-0
Percentage of NW zone to British India	62.4	51.4	66.9		47.3	

If we compare the area in the Muslim zone of the Punjab with that in the non-Muslim zone irrigated by government canals as distinguished from other private sources of irrigation like wells tanks, etc., we find the following:

	Total area irrigated by govt canals	Percentage of govt canals irrigated area to total similarly irrigated in the province
Muslim zone of the Punjab ..	87,08,089 acres	78 per cent
Non-Muslim zone of the Punjab ..	24,95,199 acres	22 per cent
Total Punjab	1,12,03,288 acres	

The Muslim zone of the Punjab has thus the bulk of the area benefited by government canals. It is thus clear that the north-western zone is in a very favourable situation so far as irrigation is concerned as compared with the whole of British India. The area sown in the north-western zone is only 15.6 per cent of that sown in British India. But the area irrigated is no less than 61.4 per cent of the total area irrigated in British India. Out of a total mileage of 74,911 of canals, their branches and tributaries in the whole of British India, no less than 31,044 or 41.4 per cent falls within the north-western zone; and of the total outlay of capital of 153.89 crores no less than 73.88 crores or 47.9 per cent are invested in irrigation works in the north-western zone alone. Of the total net revenue of 10.03 crores obtained from irrigation from the whole of British India no less than 6.71 crores or 66.9 per cent are raised in the north-western zone; and the value of crops irrigated in the north-western zone is 64.48 crores as against 136.29 crores or 47.3 per cent. Whereas the value of irrigated crop in the north-western zone is Rs 17–10 per head of the population, it is no more than Rs 3–8 for British India. It may be noted that the revenue received from irrigation in the Punjab is no less than 42 per cent of the total ordinary revenue of the province; 13.4 for Sind and 7.5 for the NWFP If we take the figures for Sind and the Punjab alone, they reveal a still more advantageous position for those provinces. No less than 85.8 per cent of the total area sown in Sind is irrigated by canals and similarly no less than 62.5 per cent of the total sown in the Punjab is irrigated by canals.

The area irrigated by canals in the north-western zone is no less than 55.4 per cent of the total area sown as compared to only 13.4 per cent in the whole of British India, including the north-western zone. If we compare the figures of north-western zone with those of British India excluding the north-western zone, the result will be still more favourable to the north-western zone—for British India excluding the north-western zone the area irrigated by canals comes to only 5–5 per cent of the area sown.

With all this advantage, however, even the north-western zone cannot be said to be a province which produces more food than it requires. Whatever small surplus of any particular grain there may be is consumed in the neighbouring area. At the Crop Planning Conference held at Simla in June 1934, the position of rice and wheat was described province by province by the Imperial Council of Agricultural Research. It was pointed out that the Punjab was not a producer or consumer of rice in considerable quantities. As regards wheat it was said that its production could not be termed excessive. Whatever surplus there was, was easily exported to the adjoining provinces and Calcutta and that a real over-production might ensue, when the maximum limit of 20 lakh acres under wheat was reached in Sind.[15] From the figures quoted above it will appear that the figure had not been reached in Sind till 1939–40.

In January 1945 Sardar Baldev Singh, Development Minister of the Punjab, stated in Calcutta that although three years previously the Punjab was a deficit province in respect of rice, it had a surplus of rice in 1944–5 of 30 lakh tons. So both the Punjab and Sind have been expanding agriculture at a quick pace and may very well be able soon to give a large surplus to other provinces of India. This sudden increase has undoubtedly been greatly stimulated by the war.

Calculating the consumption of foodgrains at the rate of 14 chataks or 12 chataks a day by each adult in the Punjab, Sind and NWFP, and taking 75 per cent of the entire population as equivalent to the population requiring adult diet, we get the following results:

In the north-western zone also population has been increasing and at a higher rate than in any other province. The increase

---

[15] Proceedings of the Crop Planning Conference (Delhi, 1934), pp. 7–10, quoted by Professor Benoy Kumar Sarkar in *The Sociology of Population*, pp. 38–39.

TABLE XXVII
Food Position in the North-Western Zone

Province	Population	75% of Population (taking adult diet)	Production per year (In mds)	Consumption @14 chataks per day per adult of the year (In mds)	Deficit (mds)	Consumption @12 chataks per day per adult for the year (In mds)	Surplus (mds)
Punjab	2,84,18,819	2,13,14,114	15,06,68,700	17,01,79,790	1,95,11,090 (11.42%)	14,58,68,235	48,00,465 (3.29%)
Sind	45,35,008	34,01,256	2,61,80,700	2,71,56,730	9,76,030 (3.59%)	2,32,77,510	29,03,190 (12.47%)
NWFP	30,38,067	22,78,550	1,59,15,900	1,81,92,695	22,76,795 (12.51%)	1,55,93,895	3,22,005 (2.06%)

TABLE XXVIII
Increase in Population in the North-Western Zone

Province	Population in 1941	Population in 1891	Difference between 1941 and 1891 No.	%	Population in 1931	Difference between 1941 and 1931 No.	%
Punjab	2,84,18,819	1,86,52,614	97,66,205	52.3	2,35,80,864	48,37,955	20.5
Sind	45,35,008	28,75,100	16,59,908	57.0	38,87,070	6,47,938	16.7
NWFP	30,38,067	18,57,519	11,80,548	63.5	24,25,076	6,12,991	25.2
Baluchistan	5,01,631	3,82,106	1,19,525	31.2	4,63,508	38,123	8.2
British Indian Provinces	29,58,08,722	21,29,70,616	8,28,38,106	38.8	25,67,57,818	3,90,50,904	15.2

during the fifty years between 1891 and 1941 and during 1931–41 is shown in Table XXVIII.

With the extensive canal system, the production of foodgrains has increased and will expand still further. But it seems the expansion in agriculture cannot keep pace with that in the population which in the course of fifty years has risen by more than 52 per cent in the Punjab, by 57 per cent in Sind and by more than 63 per cent in the NWFP This, however, is a problem which this area has to solve along with the rest of the country and in solving which it is perhaps better situated than any other province at present.

Apart from food crops the north-western zone, particularly the Punjab and Sind, have cotton cultivation on an extensive scale. In 1939–40 the Punjab produced 10,17,000 bales (400 Ibs each) of cotton, Sind 3,09,000 bales and the NWFP ,3,000 bales. The area under cotton in the three provinces was 26,41,105, 8,54,390 and 17,351 acres respectively.[16] The importance of this crop, which is a money crop, will become apparent when it is remembered that out of a total 33,81,000 bales produced in British India no less than 13,29,000 bales or 39.3 per cent are produced in the north-western zone and that the area under cultivation of cotton, particularly of superior quality, is increasing year by year in the Sukkur Barrage area of Sind—it has increased from 3,42,860 acres in the pre-Barrage period of 1932–33 to 8,55,277 acres in 1939–40 as the result of assured perennial irrigation. Moreover, the increased cultivation has been entirely under American cotton for which a better price is obtained.[17] Similar, though not to the same extent, is the case with the Punjab where also the area under improved varieties is increasing year by year.

The money value calculated at the average price of cotton prevailing in 1939 at Rs 105 per bale of 400 Ibs comes, for the Punjab, to nearly Rs 9 crores and for Sind to Rs 3.25 crores as against Rs 35.50 crores for the whole country.

The bulk of this cotton is exported either to other provinces or to foreign countries, as the number of cotton textile mills in these provinces is almost negligible, and hand-spinning, although popular in the Punjab, cannot consume any appreciable quantity of it. Of 380 cotton textile mills with over ten lakh spindles and

[16] *Statistical Abstract for British India*, 1930–31 to 1939–40, p. 554.
[17] Annual Report of the Department of Agriculture of Sind, 1939–40, pp. 7–8.

over two lakh looms that were in existence in India in 1938–39 no more than seven mills with about 72,000 sidles and less than 2,000 loams were in the Punjab and Sind, there being none in the NWFP and Baluchistan.[18]

In the above discussion the north-western zone means the three provinces of the Punjab, including the districts with non-Muslim majorities, Sind and the NWFP where non-Muslim districts of the Punjab are not specifically excluded.

[18] M.P. Gandhi, *Indian Textile Cotton Industry* (1939 Annual), p. 62 and Appendix I

Charles H. Behre, Professor of Geology, Columbia University, USA, writing in *Foreign Affairs* says: 'India, exclusive of Burma, now is or promises soon to be important in world trade as a source of coal and petroleum, iron ore, manganese ore, chrome ore, gold, bauxite, salt, magnesite, mica, gypsum, various gemstones, monazite and certain refractory materials.

'Industrial power in the modern world is based on the trinity of coal, iron and oil. Together coal and iron are the foundations for industrialization in our present age. They are to the development of the machine what oxygen and hydrogen are to the growth of the human body; they must be present in combination. Oil, though also valuable, is far less essential; in time of peace, a state rich in coal can do entirely without oil deposits, if exchange in mineral commodities is free. Even if it has no oil, it may convert its coal to liquid-fuel as Germany does. Oil is of little direct value in the making of steel, and cannot as yet be substituted for coal in the steel industry. Coal remains essential.

'Our first conclusion is apparent: India is not abundantly supplied, with oil but she possesses large reserves of most important industrial minerals—Coal, iron, several of the ferro-alloys which "make" good steel, and the subsidiary minerals in ample quantity to make her a powerful and reasonably self-sufficient industrial nation. The per capita supply is relatively low in comparison with that of most of the great industrial-nations, but per capita consumption could be materially raised without seriously endangering reserves of the more essential minerals in the reasonably near future.'

Let us now see how these minerals are distributed over the country and what share of these valuable materials falls within the Muslim zones in the north-western and eastern regions as compared with that in the rest of the country.

In Table XXIX I have not included some minerals like salt (64,674 tons) produced entirely in the western Punjab, bauxite

TABLE XXIX
Mineral Production in the Muslim Zones, 1938

Mineral	Muslim Bengal		Punjab		Sind		NWFP		Baluchistan	
	Quantity	Value	Quantity	Value (Rs)	Quantity	Value	Quantity	Value	Quantity	Value (Rs)
Coal (tons)	—	—	1,84,028	10,20,856	—	—	—	—	14,388	91,842
Petroleum (gallons)	—	—	2,11,13,420	52,78,355	—	—	—	—	—	—
Chromite (tons)	—	—	—	—	—	—	—	—	21,892	3,26,014
Copper Ore and Matte (tons)	—	—	—	—	—	—	—	—	—	—
Iron Ore (tons)	—	—	—	—	—	—	—	—	—	—
Manganese Ore (tons)	—	—	—	—	—	—	—	—	—	—
Magnesite (tons)	—	—	—	—	—	—	—	—	—	—
Mica (cwt.)	—	—	—	—	—	—	—	—	—	—

TABLE XXX

Mineral Production in British India and Muslim and Non-Muslim Zones

Mineral	Total Muslim Zone Quantity	Value (Rs)	British India Quantity	Value (Rs)	British India Excluding Muslim Zone Quantity	Value (Rs)
Coal (tons)	1,98,416	11,12,668	2,52,78,218	9,46,30,718	2,50,79,802	9,35,18,050
Petroleum (gallons)	2,11,13,420	52,78,355	8,70,82,371	1,65,43,142	6,59,68,951	1,12,64,787
Chromite (tons)	21,892	3,26,014	27,086	4,25,942	5,194	99,928
Copper Ore and Matte (tons)	–	–	2,88,076	32,40,640	2,88,076	32,40,640
Iron Ore (tons)	–	–	14,21,701	26,91,829	14,21,701	26,91,829
Manganese Ore (tons)	–	–	7,66,341	3,20,93,709	7,66,341	3,20,93,709
Magnesite (tons)	–	–	23,052	1,34,876	23,052	1,34,876
Mica (cwt.)	–	–	1,08,834	40,89,488	1,08,834	40,89,488
Total		67,17,037		15,38,50,344		14,71,33,307

(10,134 tons) produced entirely in the non-Muslim zone and some other less important minerals.

Coal is easily and undoubtedly the most valuable mineral. The whole of it falls outside the Muslim zone with the exception of a small quantity that is raised in the Punjab and Baluchistan. The coal-fields of Bengal are all situated in the district of Burdwan, which with a Muslim population of less than 18 per cent, naturally falls outside the Muslim zone. The oil-fields of Assam also fall outside the Muslim zone.

Mineral oil is to be found to some extent in the Punjab, NWFP and Baluchistan. Dr J. Coggin Brown, Superintendent of the Geological Survey of India, in his book *India's Mineral Wealth* has given figures of average annual production of petroleum in India from 1900 to 1933 when Burma was included in India. The proportion in the period 1929–32 was: from Burma 81.4 per cent, from Assam 15.5 per cent and from the Punjab 3.1 per cent. He quotes Sir Edwin Pascoe: 'In many parts of the Punjab, however, and in the Baluchistan area the rock fields have been too deeply truncated by agents of denudation or have been dislocated by earth movements and much of the original stores of oil have disappeared; oil seepages are common enough, but most of them appear to be mere "shows", not connected with reservoirs that can be tapped by artificial means.'[1] Some test drillings have proved unsuccessful, but the producing oil-field at Khaur is working successfully. The total value of mineral products of the whole of British India in 1938 was Rs 15,38,50,000 out of which minerals worth only Rs 76,17,000 or 4.3 per cent came from the north-western zone, the eastern zone contributing nothing. The position will be worse for the Muslim regions, if we take the figures of the Indian States along with those of British India. No wonder that Professor Behre has come to the conclusion that 'India's minerals are so distributed between the parts of India in which Hindu and Muslim people preponderate that if India were divided on the basis of religious population the Hindu State would be rich and the Muslim State would be conspicuously poor. This disproportion is sufficiently great so that, speaking generally, it does not even seem to be cancelled out by differences in population density. Not only is this fact of Hindustan's relatively greater mineral wealth true for

[1] J.C. Brown, *India's Mineral Wealth*, p. 60.

the present, as judged from a comparison of the minerals now produced, it will doubtless be an even more striking fact of the future, as the industrialization of India advances. The significant conclusion as to the question of Pakistan and Hindustan is corollary to this fact. Hindustan has great reserves of coal and iron; it has excellent reserves of the more important ferro-alloy metals (though these must be supplemented by the import of others) and of the non-metallic minerals and gold; it has considerable reserves of bauxite and some copper. Pakistan has a small amount of coal and iron; few-ferro-alloys; and little bauxite. But Pakistan has as much of the ferro-alloys, other than manganese and chromium, as has Hindustan; it has adequate reserves of the other subsidiary minerals, except magnesite; and it has most of the oil.

'Our second conclusion, in short, is that the Hindu and Muslim areas of India are interdependent. Not only would Hindustan need some of the resources of Pakistan; for industrial life Pakistan would desperately need great quantities of the resources of Hindustan.' And Professor Behre concludes his survey with the following significant words:

'This report does not pretend to assess the responsibility for the delay in the settlement between India and Great Britain, any more than it wishes to belittle the importance to the peoples of India of their religious values. It notes merely that from the point of view of mineral resources the Hindu and Muslim areas of India intimately intergrown are also interdependent economically. It urges that political interdependence is a wise solution where economic interdependence is so intimate and so essential. It implies that the Muslim sections of India would have more to lose than the Hindu sections if a separation by states on religious lines were carried out. And it suggests finally that the economy of India as a whole is interdependent with that of other parts of Asia.'

A similar conclusion is reached by Sir Homi Mody and Dr Matthai who write:

'India satisfies the requirements of an optimum unit for economic development in terms of area, population and resources more than any other single country in the world except the United States of America and Soviet Russia . . . Division of India would weaken both Pakistan and Hindustan but the former would suffer more than the latter . . . in respect of mineral resources, lacking coal and iron and ferro-alloys, the position of Pakistan in respect of

Forests are regarded as a great asset by all countries. In India they have not been fully developed and the revenue derived from them is on the whole inconsiderable. It is therefore not necessary to go into great detail here but the general position may be briefly stated.

In the eastern zone (that is, Bengal) the Forest Department has divided the forests into two circles, the northern and the southern circles. The forests comprised in the northern circle fall entirely within the non-Muslim portion of Bengal and of those in the southern circle roughly two-thirds fall within the Muslim and one-third within the non-Muslim portion of Bengal. The net revenue in 1939–40 for the whole province was Rs 6,58,033 and taking the figures for the two portions separately on the basis of the division of the forests in the two parts the non-Muslim portion's share will be roughly Rs 4.50 lakhs and that of the Muslim portion over Rs 2 lakhs.[1]

In the Punjab, out of a total area of 5,184 sq. miles of forest for the whole province, the eastern circle which falls outside the Muslim zone has 3,877 sq. miles and the western circle which falls within the Muslim zone has 1,307 sq. miles. The total revenue for both the circles in 1937–38 was Rs 23,60,192 and the expenditure was Rs 22,85,007 leaving a negligible surplus of only Rs 75,185 for the whole province.[2]

Sind in this respect is better situated. It has 1,134 sq. miles of forest with a revenue of Rs 7,76,348 and expenditure of Rs 3,62,741, leaving a surplus of Rs 4,13,606 in 1939–40.[3]

---

[1] Based on the Report of the Forest Dept. of Bengal, 1939–40,
[2] Based on the Report of the Forest Dept. Punjab, 1937–38.
[3] Based on the Report of the Forest Dept. of Sind, 1939–40.

Let us see the position of industries now.

In Table XXXI, the figures for Bengal and the Punjab are for the whole provinces and not only for the portions falling within the Muslim zone. They are therefore misleading and particularly so in the case of Bengal as the industries in that province are concentrated in and around Calcutta which falls outside the Muslim zone. Jute is undoubtedly produced in the Muslim zone but the jute mills are almost all within a few miles of Calcutta on the banks of the Hooghly. Of some thirty cotton textile mills in Bengal not more than seven fall within the Muslim zone, the rest being all in western Bengal outside the Muslim zone. These have about 1,12,000 spindles and over 2,600 looms as against 10 lakh spindles and over 2 lakh looms in India. It is the jute mills which singly give employment to the largest number of men. Iron and steel works are all within the western non-Muslim districts. Similarly, all important industries are in and near about Calcutta, with the exception of rice mills and jute presses which are spread over the whole province. Among the government and local fund factories the most important are the ordnance factories, railway workshops, dockyards and printing presses. These also are concentrated in Calcutta and its suburbs. It may thus safely be asserted that in spite of the fact that the figures for Bengal make a satisfactory show, so far as industries are concerned, they relate more by far to the non-Muslim zone than to the Muslim zone.

Professor Coupland has put the position succinctly as follows: 'Bengal as it is now, with 20 per cent of the population of British India, possesses (on the basis of the average number of workers, employed in factories) 33 per cent of its industry. In Eastern Bengal without Calcutta, the percentage of British Indian industry falls to 2.7.'[1]

[1] R. Coupland, *The Future of India*, p. 96.

TABLE XXXI

Resources of Muslim States' Industries, 1939

I Government and Local Fund Factories

Industry PERENNIAL	Bengal A	B	Punjab A	B	Sind A	B	NWFP A	B	British Baluchistan A	B	British India A	B
Clothing	–	–	1	109	–	–	–	–	–	–	2	2,157
Breweries and Distilleries	–	–	–	–	1	34	–	–	–	–	2	175
Carpentery	–	–	–	–	–	–	–	–	–	–	3	549
Cotton Mills	1	19	1	195	–	–	–	–	–	–	5	1,701
Dockyards	4	2,048	–	–	–	–	–	–	–	–	8	4,943
Electrical Engineering	9	1,115	9	1,009	1	43	5	148	–	–	34	3,592
Engineering (General)	10	1,912	5	920	3	581	–	–	1	48	52	7,745
Forage Presses	–	–	–	–	–	–	–	–	1	43	1	43
Mints	1	933	–	–	–	–	–	–	–	–	2	1,836
Ordnance Factories	3	9,275	6	6,556	1	535	5	270	1	1,075	25	30,709
Printing Presses	11	3,521	6	1,480	1	175	1	105	–	–	45	12,555
Railway Workshops	16	15,173	7	11,402	5	1,736	–	–	–	–	74	55,784
Saw Mills	1	25	1	8	1	–	–	–	–	–	6	245
Tanneries	1	32	–	–	–	–	–	–	–	–	1	32
Telegraphs	1	1,118	–	–	–	–	–	–	–	–	2	1,331
Water Pumping Stations	5	770	1	65	2	62	1	22	–	–	26	2,101
Woollen Mills	1	161	–	–	–	–	–	–	–	–	3	626
Miscellaneous	4	567	6	526	2	97	–	–	5	423	54	4,942
Total Perennial	68	36,669	43	22,270	17	3,263	12	545	8	1,589	345	1,31,066

A = Number of Factories   B = Average Daily Number of Workers Employed

(contd. on next page)

TABLE XXXI (contd.)

Industry PERENNIAL	Bengal A	Bengal B	Punjab A	Punjab B	Sind A	Sind B	NWFP A	NWFP B	British Baluchistan A	British Baluchistan B	British India A	British India B
SEASONAL												
Forage Press	–	–	4	108	–	–	6	225	–	–	19	1,048
Miscellaneous	–	–	1	24	–	–	–	–	–	–	10	332
Total Seasonal	–	–	5	132	–	–	6	225	–	–	29	1,380
Total Government and Local Fund Factories	68	36,669	48	22,402	17	3,263	18	770	8	1,589	374	1,32,446
All other Factories												
Textile												
Cotton (Spinning)												
Weaving and others	33	31,859	14	9,211	–	–	–	–	–	–	836	4,86,853
Jute Mills	97	2,81,229	–	–	–	–	–	–	–	–	106	2,98,967
Hosiery	41	1,945	62	1,863	1	30	–	–	–	–	152	7,708
Silk Mills	6	1,886	4	563	2	70	–	–	–	–	107	6,251
Woollen Mills	–	–	6	2,661	–	–	–	–	–	–	13	6,807
Miscellaneous	6	991	25	1,936	–	–	–	–	–	–	89	10,491
Total	183	3,17,910	111	16,234	3	100	–	–	–	–	1,303	8,17,077
II Engineering	259	65,247	55	3,116	29	2,228	2	94	4	265	1,001	1,48,424
III Minerals and Metals												
Foundries	–	–	46	1,554	2	64	–	–	–	–	110	6,066
Iron and Steel Smelting and Steel Rolling Mills	6	16,914	–	–	–	–	–	–	–	–	90	40,790
Lead Smelting and Lead Rolling Mills	1	262	–	–	–	–	–	–	–	–	1	262
Petroleum Refining	–	–	2	803	–	–	–	–	–	–	4	2,981
Miscellaneous	6	457	23	1,108	–	–	–	–	–	–	53	5,024
Total	13	17,633	71	3,465	2	64	–	–	–	–	187	55,123

(contd.)

II All other Factories (contd.)

IV Food, Drink and Tobacco												
Flour Mills	11	1,181	18	1,178	13	789	–	–	–	–	80	5,794
Rice Mills	400	18,742	43	1,056	–	–	–	–	–	–	1,158	45,409
Tobacco	4	1,339	1	50	1	77	–	–	–	–	165	19,839
Others including Miscellaneous	27	2,924	26	595	9	301	4	96	–	–	477	26,365
Total	442	24,186	88	3,279	23	1,167	4	96	–	–	1,880	97,407
V Chemicals, Dyes etc.	118	17,212	32	1,554	9	1,642	–	–	–	–	588	55,945
VI Paper and Printing												
Paper and Pulp Mills	4	6,268	1	995	–	–	–	–	–	–	14	11,553
Printing and Book-binding	96	6,575	44	2,019	16	509	5	109	–	–	655	30,942
Miscellaneous	17	1,096	2	56	–	–	–	–	–	–	40	1,882
Total	117	13,939	47	3,070	16	509	5	109	–	–	709	44,377
VII Processes relating to Wood, Stone, Glass etc.												
Brick, Tiles, Carpentry and Cabinet-making	15	1,357	7	1,017	6	325	–	–	–	–	186	20,553
Cement, Lime and Potteries	13	3,514	5	835	2	524	–	–	–	–	46	13,088
Glass	12	2,280	3	204	–	–	–	–	–	–	74	8,934
Saw Mills, Stone Dressing and Miscellaneous	18	1,137	4	151	1	41	–	–	2	109	159	9,715
Total	58	8,288	19	2,207	9	890	–	–	2	109	465	52,290

(contd. on next page)

TABLE XXXI (contd.)

Industry PERENNIAL	Bengal		Punjab		Sind		NWFP		British Baluchistan		British India	
	A	B	A	B	A	B	A	B	A	B	A	B
VIII Skins and Hides Processes	5	4,017	2	155	1	16	–	–	–	–	66	12,906
IX Gins and Presses	33	19,155	–	–	–	–	–	–	1	60	181	25,987
X Miscellaneous												
Rope Works, etc.	58	9,665	2	187	6	232	–	–	–	–	218	19,712
Total Perennial	1,286	4,97,252	427	33,267	98	6,848	11	299	7	434	6,598	13,29,248
SEASONAL												
Food, Drink and Tobacco												
Rice Mills	–	–	–	–	102	2,037	–	–	–	–	102	2,037
Sugar	13	3,558	4	1,303	1	177	–	–	–	–	254	74,872
Tea	288	18,828	10	215	–	–	–	–	–	–	1,055	67,303
Coffee, Tobacco, Ice, Aerated Water and Miscellaneous												
Miscellaneous	–	–	–	–	–	–	–	–	–	–	97	9,836
Total	301	22,386	14	1,518	103	2,214	–	–	–	–	1,508	1,50,048
Chemicals and Dyes	–	–	–	–	–	–	–	–	–	–	22	1,989
Cotton, Gins and Baling	8	2,263	311	21,115	103	12,565	7	199	–	–	1,879	1,23,879
Jute Process & Miscellaneous	62	12,869	–	–	3	105	–	–	–	–	85	13,527
Total Seasonal	371	37,618	325	22,633	209	14,884	7	199	–	–	3,494	2,89,445
Total–All other factories	1,657	5,34,870	752	55,900	307	21,732	18	498	7	434	10,092	16,18,691
Grand Total	1,725	5,71,539	800	78,302	324	24,995	36	1,268	15	2,023	10,466	17,51,137

A = Number of Factories   B = Average Daily Number of Workers Employed

The position of the Punjab is somewhat different. Lahore falls within the Muslim zone and the industries that are working there fall within that zone. The figures of the Punjab may therefore be taken roughly as showing with some exaggeration the position of the Muslim zone. If, therefore, we leave the Bengal figures out of consideration and take those for the whole of the Punjab along with those of the NWFP, Sind and Baluchistan, we shall get a more or less correct appreciation of the industrial position of the Muslim zones of India. The total number of factories in the Punjab, the NWFP, Sind and Baluchistan including factories and workshops belonging to the government and local funds and those owned by others is 1,175; and they give employment to 1,06,588 persons. The size of the individual factories is small as compared with that of British India as a whole. The total number of factories in British India is 10,466 and they employ 17,51,137, persons. Thus while the number of factories in the north-western provinces comes to 11.23 per cent of the factories in British India, the numbers employed by them come only to 6.1 per cent of the numbers employed by all the factories in British India. In other words, the average number of employees in a factory in the north-western provinces is ninety while that in British India is 167 per factory. Of these factories and workshops those owned and run by the government and local funds in the north-western provinces bear a large proportion to the total. Their number is ninety-one and they employ 28,024 persons, which shows that while the number of factories is only 7.7 per cent the number of employees is 26.3 per cent; or in other words the larger factories are government or local fund factories. Among the larger government factories are the ordnance factories and railway workshops. Among industries owned and run by private parties there is no single industry which gives employment to as many persons as the railway workshops or ordnance factories except cotton ginning and baling which are the biggest single industry in the Punjab and Sind.

It is thus apparent that the north-western zone is not an industrially developed area, even as industrial development has taken place in British India, and the largest factories and workshops belong to the State.

If for the reasons stated above we exclude the Bengal industries from our calculation as falling mostly outside the Muslim zone of Bengal the industrial position of the north-western and eastern zones as compared with British India as a whole appears to be still more unsatisfactory. The population of the Muslim zones of Bengal and the Punjab, and of the NWFP, Sind and Baluchistan constitutes 26.7 per cent of the total population of British India, but the number of industrial establishments—government, local funds, and others—is only 13.9 per cent and the number employed by them is only 7.36 per cent of that of British India, and as stated above the larger ones are ordnance factories and railway workshops.

Among industries which absorb the bulk of the capital invested in India are cotton mills, jute mills and sugar mills. While cotton is produced largely in the Punjab and Sind and jute in Eastern Bengal, the mills which spin and weave them are mostly outside Muslim zones in the north-western and in the east. In 1939–40 joint stock companies registered in India owning cotton mills had a paid up capital of Rs 33.93 crores. To this must be added £271,778 being paid up capital of companies registered in foreign countries and owning cotton mills in India in 1938–39. Similarly, the paid up Indian capital of jute mills was Rs 20.46 crores and £3,295,587. Sugar mills absorbed Rs 10.97 crores and £306,656. The Muslim zones have but a small share in these industries. So also the mining and quarrying companies have a paid up Indian capital of Rs 19.98 crores and foreign capital of £111,056,444. The Muslim zones have no share at all in this enterprise as they have no mines of coal, iron, copper, etc., and have only a share in petroleum.

The passage quoted earlier from the Report of Professor Charles H. Behre in *Foreign Affairs* is borne out by a study of these figures. It may be noted, however, in passing that Professor Behre's conclusions are based on the assumption that the whole of Bengal and Assam, including the petroleum area which exists in the extreme north-east of Assam, will be included in the eastern zone, which as we have shown earlier is not derivable from the League Resolution on the subject. Similarly, he also includes the whole of the Punjab in the north-western region. His conclusions would have been even more emphatic against the proposal for a division of India on the basis of religion in the interest of the Muslim zones themselves, if he had excluded from his consideration the western portion of Bengal where all the coal and most of the industrial establishments are concentrated, excluded the whole of Assam including the oil-fields minus the district of Sylhet, and also the eastern districts of the Punjab in some of which certain industries are concentrated.

The position of Indian manufacturing industries is nicely summarized by Dr A.M. Lorenzo in his *Atlas of India* (Oxford Pamphlets on Indian Affairs):

'The proper view of industrial evolution and progress in India is physico-environmental. The principal industries of India tend to segregate in certain well-defined regions. The iron and steel industry is localized in Bengal and Bihar near the coal and iron mines, the centres of production being Jamshedpur, Kulti, Burnpur, and Manoharpur; the cotton industry is centred in the province of Bombay because of climatic (humidity) factors and the proximity to raw materials, the centres of production being Bombay, Sholapur, Hubli and Ahmedabad; jute mills cluster around Calcutta in Bengal; sugar mills are dotted along the railway track among cane-producing regions in the UP and Bihar; cement is manufactured in the Central and Southern tableland near the sources of raw materials, e.g. limestone, gypsum and clays; paper mills are mainly in Bengal, Bombay and the UP; leather in the UP and Madras; glass in the Central and Upper Ganges plain.'[2]

One need only add to make the position further clear that none of the provinces falling within the north-western zone is even once mentioned, and the references to Bengal are practically all in respect of factories situated outside the Muslim zone.

What should be borne in mind is that the present conditions are likely to be further accentuated in the future. The physico-environmental conditions which have to a great extent determined the concentration of industries in particular regions will not change, nor will the distribution of the mineral and other resources, by any political adjustment of boundaries or creation of separate independent states.

Table XXXII gives the figures of the inland trade in certain principal articles between the provinces which will constitute the north-western and north-eastern Muslim zones on the one hand and the rest of India on the other for the year 1939–40 in thousands of maunds. Excess of imports over exports is represented by a minus sign.

Both the zones have an excess of imports in respect of coal and coke, cotton piece goods, iron and steel and sugar; and excess of

[2] A.M. Lorenzo, *Atlas of India*, sec. 8.

TABLE XXXII
Inland Trade in Certain Principal Articles between the Muslim Zones and the Rest of India

Province	Coal and Coke			Raw Cotton			Cotton Piece Goods			Grain, Pulse and Flour and Rice Not in the Husk			Wheat		
	A	B	C	A	B	C	A	B	C	A	B	C	A	B	C
Assam	70	3,345		123	2		2	266		207	1,180		..	73	
Bengal	1,47,043	63,487		143	207		129	957		7,291	7,652		29	230	
Calcutta	3,963	1,53,611		62	429		1,737	1,563		8,504	3,002		187	3,464	
Total Eastern Province	1,51,076	2,20,443	−69,367	328	638	−310	1,868	2,786	−918	16,002	11,834	4,168	207	3,767	−3,560
Punjab	706	44,866		6,637	12		176	1,358		1,483	1,310		13,542	79	
NWFP	1	2,539		133	1		4	300		29	174		18	278	
Sind and Baluchistan	25	8,943		2,163	41		42	467		5,508	48		6,473	43	
Karachi	889	1,586		2	6,271		654	55		1	2,952		1	8,335	
Total North-west Province	1,621	57,934	−56,313	8,935	6,325	2,610	876	2,180	−1,304	7,021	4,484	2,537	20,034	8,735	11,299

TABLE XXXII (contd.)

Province	Iron and Steel			Oil Seeds			Salt			Sugar			Raw Jute		
	A	B	C	A	B	C	A	B	C	A	B	C	A	B	C
Assam	112	1,266		473	20		2	1,290		4	475		2,851	2	
Bengal	4,040	6,409		374	1,823		594	5,822		378	1,540		26,052	137	
Calcutta	7,279	7,963		417	7,216		10,607	110		804	1,056		209	30,687	
Total Eastern Province	11,431	15,638	-4,207	1,264	9,239	-7,975	11,203	7,222	3,981	1,186	3,071	-1,885	29,112	30,826	-1,714
Punjab	392	3,010		2,252	462		1,946	313		64	3,624		6	2	
NWFP.	12	260		43	56		..	334		53	322		..	.75	
Sind and Baluchistan	187	946		2,922	121		11	280		13	322		..	1	
Karachi	1,446	177		38	2,480		232	12		1,056	904		..	4	
Total North-West Province	2,047	4,393	-2,336	5,255	3,119	2,136	2,189	939	1,250	1,186	5,172	-3,986	6	82	-76

exports in respect of salt and grains including rice but excluding
wheat in the eastern zone. In raw cotton, wheat, and oil-seeds the
north-western zone has an excess of exports over imports. These
figures relate to the provinces as a whole. If the districts with
non-Muslim majorities are excluded then the position in respect
of both coal and coke and iron and steel will become very much
worse for the eastern zone, as the eastern and northern districts of
Bengal with Muslim majorities will show practically no export of
these articles and the western districts with non-Muslim majorities
will practically show no imports of them and the net balance of
imports against the Muslim zone will be very much enhanced. On
the same basis, the position of the eastern Muslim zone will show
an improvement in respect of jute. The excess of import of jute
implies that it is imported for export to foreign countries. This
is because coal and coke and iron and steel are produced in the
western non-Muslim districts and jute is produced very largely in
the eastern Muslim districts. As regards wheat, which is one of
the principal exports from the Punjab, it may be pointed out that
non-Muslim India will not have to be dependent on the Punjab
for wheat in the way the Muslim zones will have to be dependent
on the non-Muslim zones for coal and iron and steel, inasmuch as
non-Muslim India produces almost as much wheat as it consumes
at present. Punjab wheat has also to face heavy competition with
Australian wheat whose import into India increased from 13,000
tons in 1935–36 to 150,000 tons in 1938–39.

When confronted with these problems on which depends the
future well-being of the people inhabiting the regions proposed to
be separated from the rest of India, Mr M.A. Jinnah is reported
to have told Mr Herbert L. Mathews, in an interview appearing
in the *New York Times* of 21 September 1942: 'Afghanistan is a
poor country but it goes along; so does Iraq and that has only a
small fraction of the 70 million inhabitants we would have. If we
are willing to live sensibly and poorly so long as we have freedom,
why should the Hindus object? . . . The economy will take care
of itself.' This may furnish a good debating point but is hardly
the way to deal with a question affecting the well-being of 70
million Musalmans and uprooting and demolishing in a cruel and
unceremonious manner what has taken centuries to build up.

~

THIRTY-THREE

REVENUE AND EXPENDITURE

We have next to consider how the two Muslim zones will stand regarding their public revenue and expenditure. The League Resolution contemplates 'Independent States' in the north-western and eastern zones of India with full control finally of defence, foreign affairs, communications, customs, currency and exchange, etc. The word 'States 'is used in the plural in the Resolution of the League as also by Mr Jinnah in his presidential address at the Madras session of the League (194]) and it would seem that the two States are to be independent not only of the rest of India but also of each other. It is also contemplated that the constituent units will be 'autonomous and sovereign'. It is not quite clear that there will be a federation of autonomous and sovereign units. The omission to use the word federation and the use of the word sovereign in regard to the units would indicate the contrary. But let us assume that a federation of the units in each of the north-western and eastern zones is contemplated. Each federation will have to maintain a federal administration with all the departments and paraphernalia of an independent federal state. The units will have, further, to maintain their own administrative machinery. We shall have something corresponding to the central government of India in each federation and within each federation there, will be units corresponding to the provinces of British India. We shall have accordingly two sets of budgets of revenue and expenditure—the federal or central budget of each zone and the budget of each unit or the provincial budget. We know that each provincial government has its own revenues derived from various sources such as land revenue, provincial excise, etc., and has to maintain the provincial administrative machinery as also what are called social services or nation-building departments, such as education, public health, etc. The central government has its own sources of revenue such as customs, and has to maintain its own administrative machinery to deal with the federal subjects among which the most important are defence and foreign affairs. It may be assumed that the units as also the federal States will have machinery more or less similar to that of the provincial governments and the central government of British India. The sources of revenue and items of expenditure will also be therefore similar and we can form some idea of their finances by considering the financial position of the provinces which will fall within the zones and the proportion of the central revenues and expenditure which will fall to the share of the separated zones. There are two difficulties, however, in this connection which have to be borne in mind. While it is easy to get the budget of each province as a whole, we cannot get the figures district by district, so that if an entire province does not fall within a Muslim zone but only some districts of it, others remaining outside the Muslim zone, it becomes very difficult if not impossible to get accurate figures of revenue and expenditure relating to that portion of a province which falls within a Muslim zone. In the second place, so far as the federal or central figures are concerned the difficulty of allotting the revenue and expenditure to the separated zones is even greater than in the case of provincial figures. It may also be noted that any conclusion or discussion regarding the finances of the units or the federations can at best be only provisional. The war has created conditions and is going to bring into prominence problems which make any calculations based on past budgetary position extremely tentative. With these cautions in mind it will nevertheless be helpful to proceed on data of current revenue and expenditure. I would accordingly deal with the provincial budgets and the federal budgets of the north-western and eastern Muslim zones separately.

I will first take the provincial budgets. The years 1938–39 and 1939–40 are the latest normal years before the Second World War and may be taken as furnishing safe data.

A reference to Tables XXXIV and XXXV shows that the revenue and expenditure of each province are balanced and if they are maintained at the same level after these provinces are separated they will continue to balance each other. It may be noted, however, that Assam, NWFP and Sind are able to balance their budgets with the subventions of 30 lakhs, 1 crore, and 1 crore 5 lakhs respectively from the Government of India. Their own provincial

revenues were unable to meet their expenditure and but for this
grant-in-aid they would have considerable deficits.[1] In the case
of the province of Assam the expenditure on social services was
71.41 lakhs and 73.86 lakhs in 1938–39 and 1939–40 respectively,
and it is clear that but for this subvention the province would be
unable to meet nearly half the amount spent on social services.
The position of the NWFP would become precarious without this

'TABLE XXXIII

**Subventions and Other Payments Made by the Centre to the Provinces under
the Government of India (Distribution of Revenues) Order as Amended**
(In lakhs of rupees)

	Income Tax		Jute Duty		Subventions	
Paid to	1938–39 Accounts	1945–46 Budget	1938–39 Accounts	1945–46 Budget	1938–39 Accounts	1945–46 Budget
Bengal	30.00	465.80	221.27	121.22	..	..
Bombay	30.00	465.80	..	..	..	..
Madras	22.50	349.35	..	..	..	..
UP	22.50	349.35	..	..	25.00	..
Punjab	12.00	186.32	..	..	..	..
CP	7.50	116.45	..	..	..	..
Bihar	15.00	232.90	17.12	7.80	..	..
Assam	3.00	46.58	11.69	10.08	30.00	30.00
Orissa	3.00	46.58	0.92	0.90	43.00	40.00
NWFP	1.50	23.29	..	..	100.00	100.00
Sind	3.00	46.58	..	..	105.00	..

It is not clear, from the text of the Lahore Resolution of 1940, whether
the new States, formed out of the northern and western provinces, and
those on the east, with Muslim majorities, would federate amongst
themselves, or remain each an independent sovereign State by itself.
The actual wording of the Resolution suggests the latter course. In
that event, the incidence of the budgetary burdens would be much
more heavy on the more backward or poorer provinces of Pakistan;
and there will be no central government of theirs to grant subventions
such as are given to some of these units under the present Government
of India.

It may be noted, however, that Sind, having paid off its debt, needs no
subvention, which has accordingly been discontinued since 1943–44.

TABLE XXXIV
Provincial Revenues
(In lakhs of rupees)

	Bengal		Assam		Punjab		NWFP		Sind	
	'38–39	'39–40	'38–39	'39–40	'38–39	'39–40	'38–39	'39–40	'38–39	'39–40
Custom	221.27	221.97	11.69	13.39	–	–	–	–	–	–
Income-tax	30.00	55.80	3.00	6.41	12.00	22.32	1 .50	2.79	3.00	5.58
Salt	12	–	2	–	–	–	–	–	–	–
Land Revenue	324.10	386.10	112.64	136.90	263.53	234.20	18.41	18.59	36.04	36.85
Provincial Excise	159.35	165.28	35.33	33.96	101.59	104.98	8.76	8.87	37.46	36.33
Stamps	257.77	256.44	18.12	17.63	78.12	74.55	7.40	7.06	16.89	17.16
Forest	22.41	23.98	16.69	17.46	23.03	25.39	5.97	5.22	8.65	7.76
Registration	24.12	27.32	1.77	2.01	8.36	8.50	67	69	2.00	2.07
Receipts under Motor Vehicles Act	21.90	21.31	3.71	4.09	12.83	13 .49	2.08	2.38	2.10	2.68
Other taxes and duties	38.94	46.61	6	2.37	2.81	11.44	59	1.13	3.64	6.66
Total	1099.98	1204.81	203.03	234.22	502.27	494.87	45.38	46.73	109.78	115.09
Railways and Subsidized Railway Companies	14	14	–	–	–	–	–	–	–	–
Total Irrigation Works	–	–	–	–						
Civil	4.65	–	–	1	451.17	508.70	12.47	13.81	72.39	88.71
Administration	90.93	93.68	13.35	13.37	80.79	90.32	8.34	8.07	10.56	14.76
Civil Works, etc.	29.09	35.50	10.33	10.91	43.47	39.65	11.20	10.13	10.60	9.96
Miscellaneous Receipts	21.09	25.77	1.62	4.52	31.24	28.31	2.86	3.23	1.63	2.91

(contd.)

	Bengal '38–39	Bengal '39–40	Assam '38–39	Assam '39–40	Punjab '38–39	Punjab '39–40	NWFP '38–39	NWFP '39–40	Sind '38–39	Sind '39–40
Debt Services and Interest	29.35	29.62	12	26	4.61	3.76	58	63	4.73	7.31
Total	175.25	184.71	25.42	29.07	611.28	670.74	35.45	35.87	99.91	123.65
Contributions etc.	30	30	30.03	30.04	3.07	3.85	100.01	100.01	105.04	105.12
Extraordinary Receipts	1.08	41.85	–	–	19.24	41.63	–	–	55.56	85.11
Grand Total	1276.61	1431.67	258.48	293.33	1135.86	1211.09	180.84	182.61	370.29	428.87

TABLE XXXV
Provincial Expenditure
(In lakhs of rupees)

	Bengal		Assam		Punjab		NWFP		Sind	
	'38–39	'39–40	'38–39	'39–40	'38–39	'39–40	'38–39	'39–40	'38–39	'39–40
Direct Demands on Revenue	97.64	104.65	35.92	48.58	86.46	85.06	8.53	8.51	26.03	28.26
Irrigation	38.92	38.97	69	59	149.82	158.26	4.77	4.58	127.98	170.67
Debt Services	15.73	17.15	33.90	4.12	–21.02	–17.46	2.40	1.82	1.67	5.17
Civil Administration :										
(a) General	519.71	534.71	79.86	82.11	329.58	328.74	72.12	78.16	83.00	85.00
(b) Social Services	308.09	324.88	71.41	73.86	323.84	325.88	36.68	38.25	52.52	55.85
Civil Works	128.69	142.32	43.83	47.84	140.37	92.34	39.54	37.51	23.99	30.34
Miscellaneous	154.64	194.77	33.87	35.23	152.23	195.47	12.63	15.29	28.62	27.60
Miscellaneous Capital Account, within the Revenue Account	13.20	10.82	–	–	–	–	1.63	74	1.99	2.19
Electricity Scheme	–	–	–	–	–	27.32	–	2.09	–	–
Interest on Capital	–	2.97	–	–	–	–	–	–	–	–
Extraordinary Items										
Total	1276.62	1371.24	299.48	292.33	1161.28	1195.61	178.30	186.95	345.80	405.08

TABLE XXXVI

Social Services: Details of Expenditure
(In lakhs of rupees)

Item	Bengal		Assam		Punjab		NWFP		Sind	
	'38–39	'39–40	'38–39	'39–40	'38–39	'39–40	'38–39	'39–40	'38–39	'39–40
Scientific Departments	29	30	4	5	36	29	5	5	–	–
Education	155.18	162.60	36.05	38.67	161.35	163.51	22.25	23.38	30.61	31.31
Medical	55.96	56.33	14.54	14.40	52.58	50.60	6.75	7.76	7.88	8.54
Public Health	40.60	39.39	8.86	8.21	20.37	18.01	1.77	1.59	2.57	2.66
Agriculture	14.03	21.64	5.78	6.30	35.50	36.62	2.37	2.41	7.72	9.67
Veterinary	5.30	5.83	1.58	1.63	17.60	18.49	1.60	1.53	1.19	1.23
Cooperation	13.38	14.49	96	92	14.92	17.81	1.21	1.21	1.28	1.23
Industries	18.32	20.22	2.73	2.78	19.36	18.80	62	25	85	91
Aviation	–	–	–	–	–	–	–	–	–	–
Broadcasting	–	–	–	–	–	–	4	–	–	–
Miscellaneous	5.03	4.08	87	90	1.80	1.75	6	3	42	30
Total	308.09	324.88	71.41	73.86	323.84	325.88	36.68	38.25	52.52	55.85

subvention. It is unable to meet even the cost of its administration and in each of the two years there would have been a heavy deficit of over 22.25 lakhs and 28.50 lakhs respectively in the cost of administration alone. The amount spent on social services and civil works would have to be entirely cut down and these departments altogether shut up. Similarly in the case of Sind there would be a deficit, though somewhat smaller than in the case of NWFP, in the cost of administration; and the social services and civil works would have to be stopped altogether if aid were not available from the central funds. Baluchistan is a responsibility of the central government. Its revenues in 1932–33 came to 20.54 lakhs and the expenditure to 91.56 lakhs, thus leaving a heavy deficit of over 71 lakhs to be met by the central government. We thus see that if Assam, NWFP, Sind and Baluchistan are separated, the federal governments of the two zones will have to continue this subsidy—30 lakhs in the case of the eastern Muslim zone and 2.76 crores in the case of north-western Muslim zone to enable the units to carry on their administration at the level of 1938–39, 1939–40.

It may be pointed out, however, that it would be impossible to maintain the expenditure on social services at that level for the simple reason that they were at a very low level, as the following Table will show:

Any increase of expenditure under these heads must necessarily mean addition to the revenue either by fresh taxation within the province or a larger subvention from the federal government. It is difficult to contemplate any curtailment in the expenses

TABLE XXVII

Expenditure on Social Services

	Average expenditure on social services 1938–39 and 1939–40 (in lakhs of Rs)	Average expenditure per head of the population		
		Rs	As	Ps
Bengal	.. 316.48	0	8	5
Assam	.. 72.63	0	11	3
Punjab	.. 324.86	1	2	3
NWFP	.. 37.46	1	3	8
Sind	.. 54.18	1	3	1

of administration. These provinces have given no indication so far except for a short time in the NWFP that they consider the overhead charges excessive and as such requiring curtailment. It is generally said that the scale of salaries of the higher posts is out of all proportion to the national income of the people of India and it was in the hope of emphasizing this fact, if not of actually bringing down the administrative expenses, that the Congress fixed the emoluments of ministers at a low figure. The Muslim League and its ministers have not accepted that position and thus given no indication of any intention of economizing expenditure under that head. In the absence of such economy in the case of the heads of the administration it would be futile to expect, if it is not wrong, to cut down the salaries of the lower paid staff. It is therefore not unreasonable to infer that economy in administrative expenditure to any considerable extent cannot be expected. So any increase in expenditure on social services can only be either by fresh taxation within the province or further grant from the federal government.

There is another point with regard to the provincial budget which needs to be stated. In the given Tables as also in the discussion, the provinces of Bengal, Assam and the Punjab have been taken in their entirety as falling within the Muslim zones. In another chapter we have shown that only portions of these provinces will fall within the Muslim zones. In that case the revenue as well as expenditure of these Provinces will be reduced, but to what extent it is difficult, if not impossible, to say accurately. The figures are not available district by district. At any rate it will involve a very complicated and prolonged investigation to get accurate figures district by district. A rough and ready method may be adopted—the method of distributing the revenue and expenditure of the province between its Muslim and non-Muslim districts in proportion to the imputation of each. While this method may give a more or less correct idea of the revenue side, it will give a wrong picture of the expenditure side. A province or federal unit which is autonomous and sovereign has to maintain the various departments and the Head of the State with his staff for administrative purposes even though the unit be a small one. For example, if Bengal is split up into Muslim Bengal and non-Muslim Bengal, there will have to be two Heads of State with their respective staffs instead of one, two provincial secretariats instead of one, and so on. The cost of district administration may continue as before but the cost of maintaining the provincial heads and secretariats will be very nearly doubled when the province is divided into two units, one Muslim and the other non-Muslim. It is difficult to calculate what the actual expenditure will be, but it may be safely asserted that the Provincial administration will cost considerably more than what would be represented by a proportionate distribution of the present expenses on population basis as falling to the share of the Muslim districts of an existing province. In taking therefore the expenditure of the provinces of Bengal and the Punjab particularly we must be prepared for a heavier expenditure on the provincial head with his staff and the provincial secretariat than a mere proportionate share in the present expenditure on the population basis. The province of Assam will not present the same difficulty as only one district of it—Sylhet falls within the Muslim zone and it will have to be tacked to Bengal and will not have to maintain a separate provincial administration. In other words, the budgets of the Punjab and Bengal which are shown as balanced budgets in Tables XXXIV and XXXV will cease to be balanced budgets on the present basis of revenue when the non-Muslim districts are separated from them. The extent of the deficit cannot be calculated but that there will be a deficit which will not be inconsiderable there can be ho doubt. This is borne out by the experience of provinces which have been carved out of other provinces. We have the recent examples of Sind and Orissa. Each of them after its separation has been unable to balance its budget and the Government of India has had to make heavy grants-in-aid to them. We have seen that Sind gets 1 crore 5 lakhs a year and Orissa got 43 lakhs both in 1938–39 and in 1939–40. It is necessary to emphasize this aspect of the provincial finances, since Professor Coupland in his otherwise careful analysis of the finances of Pakistan has assumed that' provincial finance would operate more or less as it has done in undivided India,'[2] and has not therefore thought it necessary to go into it at all. Sir Homi Mody and Dr Matthai in their memorandum to the Sapru Committee have also omitted to mention this.

It is unnecessary to give the figures of revenues and expenditures of the Muslim districts of Bengal, Assam and the Punjab calculated

[2] R. Coupland, *The Future of India*, p. 91.

separately on the basis of their population. It may only be stated that the population of the Muslim districts of these provinces will be: Bengal 67.9 per cent, Assam 30.5 per cent and the Punjab 59.4 per cent of their total respective populations.

It now remains to consider what proportion of the revenue and expenditure of the central government of India would be allotted to the north-western and the eastern Muslim federations. As stated above the difficulty in obtaining exact figures is more or less insurmountable. Professor Coupland in *The Future of India* and Sir Homi Mody and Dr Matthai have after complicated calculations arrived at certain figures which I shall adopt for my present purposes except where otherwise indicated. Professor Coupland gives the figures for 1938–39. Sir Homi Mody and Dr Matthai, who have adopted the same method as Professor Coupland with some modifications, have calculated the figures for 1939–40. We have thus got the figures for the same two years as in the case of the provinces and these are given in Tables XXXVIII and XXXIX opposite.

From these Tables it will be noticed that the revenue from railways shows a great difference as calculated by Professor Coupland and Sir Homi Mody and Dr Matthai. Professor Coupland has pointed out that 'the Railways in Pakistan territory worked in 1938–39 at a net profit of 128 lakhs on the commercial lines and a net loss of 182 lakhs on the strategic lines.' He does not take into account the loss on the strategic lines as these are considered separately in connection with defence. Even so the figure 150 lakhs would not be reached but he takes that figure on the basis of expected increase in the earnings by reason of enhancement of passenger freights. It is obvious that this method unjustifiably increases the revenue, which on Professor Coupland's own figures ought to be (128–182)=-54 lakhs and the total revenue for the north-west zone for 1938–39 would be 732.05 lakhs instead of 936.05 lakhs.

In calculating the expenditure Professor Coupland has not taken into consideration several items which he has mentioned and it is feared generally that the expenditure of maintaining the paraphernalia of an independent sovereign State would be very much higher than is estimated, inasmuch as in the case of an independent federal administration the same considerations will arise as have been indicated above in the case of a new provincial administration. But accepting the figures as they are we find that there will be a surplus of 93.02 lakhs in the north-west zone on the basis of the figures of 1938–9 and of 238.5 lakhs on those of 1939–40. The cost of defence has not been included in the above statements and it has to be considered whether this small surplus will be able to meet the cost of defence in the north-west independent Muslim State. Professor Coupland, whose sympathy for the Muslim League point of view is apparent throughout his book, comes to the clear conclusion that it is impossible for the north-western zone to meet the cost of defence. His conclusion may be stated in his own words:

TABLE XXXVIII[3]

Proportion of the Revenue of the Central Government of India Received from North-Western and Eastern Zones

(In lakhs of Rs)

Item	Central	1938–39 North-Western Zone	1939–40 North-Western Zone	Eastern Zone
Customs	4050.53	448.06	582.9	1236.3
Excise	865.73	100.92	78.0	121.1
Corporation Tax	203.72	15.28	17.1	73.5
Other Income-taxes	1374.44	121.10	150.4	297.5
Salt	812.04	76.65	119.1	207.6
Opium	50.89	–	–	–
Railway	137.32	150.00	–111.8	–140.8
Posts and Telegraphs				
Currency and Mint	11.40	5.17	21.3	36.0
Other heads	103.20	18.87	19.8	1.6
Total	7639.27	936.05	876.8	1832.8

* R. Coupland, *The Future of India*, p. 92.
* Sir Homi Mody and Dr Matthai, *A Memorandum on the Economic and Financial Aspects of Pakistan*, p. 7.

[3] The figures in the text are those of 1938–9 and 1939–40. Table XL gives them more up to date, being taken from the Explanatory Memorandum accompanying the budget of the Government of India for 1945–46. The figures for the provinces are for all provinces put together, and not for each province separately. But the general trend remains unaffected by the war which has brought a temporary prosperity to the Punjab and Sind; while the deficit in Bengal has been very much increased. Sind has paid off its debt and needs no subvention, which is discontinued as from 1943–44. The subvention position remains unchanged in the NWFP and Assam. (Table XXXIII, p. 385)

INDIA DIVIDED

TABLE XXXIX

Proportion of Expenditure of the Central Government of India Allotted to
the North-Western and Eastern Muslim Federation
(In lakhs of rupees)

| | 1938–39 | | | 1939–40 | |
Item	Central	North-Western Zone	Item	North-Western Zone	Eastern Zone
Direct Demands on Revenue	423.60	51.49	Civil Administration	145.8	203.1
Irrigation	9.24	7.02	Debt Services	216.4	441.7
			Superannuation		
Debt Services	1338.54	186.00	Allowances	40.7	65.5
Civil Administration	984.69	145.56	Grants-in-aid		
Civil Works	219.58	10.83	to Provinces	205.0	30.0
Miscellaneous	204.32	33.13	Other items	30.4	47.6
Defence	4618.00	–			
Contributions and Adjustments	306.32	205.00			
Total	8104.29	639.03	Total	638.3	787.9

'It appears then that the greatest difficulty of Pakistan and its
gravest risk lie in Defence. If the probabilities discussed above are
really probable, it would have to face the prospect of defending the
north-western Frontier without the help of Hindu India; and to do
that on anything like the same scale as it was done before the war,
even without considering the increased cost of modern armament,
would be far beyond its powers. Even to raise a substantial fraction
of the money needed would require such extra taxation on the one
hand and such drastic cutting down of administrative cost and social
services on the other as would greatly lower the general standard of
living and not only render the backward masses of the people still
more backward but doom them to that state for years to come. And
that might not be all. Might there not be some anxiety as to the
safety of Pakistan's Eastern Frontier too? In the earlier part of this
chapter an attempt was made to state the advantages of partition
as objectively as possible, and the examination of its disadvantages
must be no less objective. What, then, is the conclusion to which
the facts or the reasonable probabilities point in this crucial matter
of defence? Is it not clear beyond dispute that Pakistan would not
be able to maintain the security it has hitherto enjoyed as part of

TABLE XL

(Footnote 3 on p. 392)

India's Public Revenue, Expenditure and Debt since 1938

(In lakhs of rupees)

	1938–39	1939–40	1944–5 (Revised)	Total 1939–40 to 1944–45	1945–46 (Budget)
I Central Government Budget					
1 Revenue	84.52	94.57	356.88	1,122,61	362.34
2 Expenditure	85.15	94.57	512.65	1,599.55	517.63
3 Surplus (+) or Deficit (-)	–0.63	..	–155.77	–476.94	–155.29
4 Percentage of (1) to (2)	99.3	100.0	69.7	70.2	70.0
II Total Government Outlays					
A On India's Account	85.15	94.57	572.06	1,478.93	535.39
1 Civil Expenditure	38.97	45.03	115.42	132.22	123.40
2 Defence Expenditure	46.18	49.54	456.64	1,346.71	411.99
(a) On Capital Account	..	..	59.41	149.38	17.76
(b) On Revenue Account	46.18	49.54	397.23	1,197.33	394.23
(i) Basic normal budget	38.07	36.77	36.77	220.62	36.77
(ii) Rise in prices	..	1.19	16.92	47.48	19.76
(iii) War measures (net)	..	3.52	334.22	878.46	328.51
(iv) Non-effective charges (net)	8.11	8.07*	9.32	50.80	9.19
3 Percentage of Defence Expenditure (revenue account) to expenditure	54.2	52.4	77.5	74.9	76.2
B Recoverable War Expenditure	..	4.00	439.53	1,393.88	488.80
III Central Government Debt at end of year—Total interest-bearing obligations (including unfunded debt and deposits)	1,205.76	1,203.86	1,819.02	..	2,180.57
IV Provinces					
1 Revenue	84.74	90.83	200.78	784.12	188.17
2 Expenditure	85.76	89.22	208.05	767.96	191.74
3 Surplus (+) or Deficit* (-)	–1.02	+1.61	–7.27	+16.16	–3.57
4 Debt position (Gross Total Debts)*	163.20	167.61	215.49	52.29	..

*Including new taxation.

*Includes (1) Permanent debt, (2) Floating debt, (3) Unfunded debt, and (4) Loans from central government.

India? Even the minimum necessities of defence would strain its resources to the utmost and hold up the social advancement of its people. For the rest it would have to take the risk.'[4] In support of his views he has also quoted from a speech of Sir Sikandar Hayat Khan in the Punjab Legislative Assembly.

Professor Coupland has not dealt with the eastern zone nor has he dealt with the Muslim zones excluding the non-Muslim districts. Sir Homi Mody and Dr Matthai have dealt with both. In the above statement, the figures for the eastern zone, taking the two entire provinces of Bengal and Assam, are given. Table XLI gives the net revenue and expenditure of the eastern and north-western zones district-wise, excluding the non-Muslim districts:

TABLE XLI*

Revenue and Expenditure of Muslim Zones District-wise, 1939–40
(In lakhs of rupees)

Net Revenue			Net Expenditure		
Item	Eastern Zone	North-Western Zone	Item	Eastern Zone	North-West Zone
Customs	775.0	402.2	Civil		
Central Excise	75.5	53.8	Administration	126.8	100.6
Corporation Tax	46.0	12.0	Debt Services	276.7	149.5
Other Income-taxes	186.5	103.7	Superannuation		
Salt	130.0	82.2	Allowances	41.0	28.0
Posts and Telegraphs			Grant-in-aid		
Currency and Mint	22.0	14.7	to Province	18.8	141.4
Railway Net Loss	−88.5	−77.2	Other Items		
Miscellaneous	1.0	13.6			
Total	1147.5	605.0	Total	493.3	440.5

It will appear that the surpluses will be reduced but not so the needs of defence which may be considered from another point of view. It will not be a correct approach to the problems of Defence to allot the expenditure on it on the basis of the population in the two zones. Both of them are on the frontier and they will have naturally to bear the burden of defending the

---

[4] Coupland, *The Future of India*, pp. 95–96.

* Modi and Matthai, *A Memorandum*, p. 9.

frontiers against foreign invasion by land. The liability of the north-western frontier to such invasion has long been the accepted policy of rulers of India not only during the British period but also during the Muslim period ever since the early days of the Sultanate. The liability of the eastern frontier has become apparent in the course of the Second World War and can not be ignored in the future. It is true that the coastline falling within the two Muslim zones will not be very extensive but they will have none the less to maintain adequate naval defence also. Taking the cost of defence as it was before the war and dividing it on the basis of population, unsatisfactory and even misleading as that basis is, we get results as embodied in Table XLII showing a heavy deficit on account of defence even though it does not take into account any increased expenditure on account of mechanized armaments which will be necessary in future.

There is another aspect of the question of defence which cannot be ignored. When we have a separate independent Muslim State, it will have to maintain its own defence forces drawn from among its own nationals and pay for them. The rest of India will have to maintain its own defence services composed of its nationals and pay for them. The financial implications of this separation, so far as the defence services are concerned, will be highly disadvantageous to the north-west Muslim State: Dr Ambedkar has pointed out that the Indian Army as it was constituted in 1930 comprised 58.5 per cent of its personnel from among the inhabitants of the regions which fall within the north-western zone.[5] The proportion of Musalmans in the Indian Army has been separately calculated and Dr Ambedkar points out that they constitute 36 per cent of the Indian infantry and 30 per cent of the Indian cavalry and they come almost exclusively from the Punjab and the NWFP.[6] With the separation of this zone from the rest of India and its establishment as an independent state, the rest of India or Hindustan will naturally recruit its defence forces from among its own nationals and all those belonging to the north-western zone will be thrown out of the defence forces unless they are employed by the north-western independent state. The learned doctor calculates that the Pakistan

[5] Dr B.R. Ambedkar, *Thoughts on Pakistan*, p. 70.
[6] Ibid, pp. 76–77.

TABLE XLII

Deficit on Account of Defence Expenditure in Muslim Zones

Eastern Zone (In lakhs of rupees)

Year	On Provincial Basis			On District Basis		
	Balance of revenue available for defence	Expenditure on defence	Deficit	Balance of revenue available for defence	Expenditure on defence	Debit
1939–40	1044.9	1197.8	152.9	654.6	748.9	94.7
	Western Zone (In lakhs of Rs)					
1938–39	93.02	642.01	548.99			
1939–40	238.5	619.76	381.26	164.5	423.73	259.23

area which is the main recruiting ground of the present Indian Army contributes very little to the central exchequer as will be seen from the following figures:

TABLE XLIII

Contributions of the NW Zone and the Provinces of Hindustan to the Central Exchange

Contributions to the Central Exchequer:	
Punjab	Rs 1,18,01,385
NWFP	,, 9,28,294
Sind	,, 5,86,46,915
Baluchistan ..	Nil
Total	Rs 7,13,76,594

'Against this the provinces of Hindustan contribute as follows:-

Madras	Rs 9,53,26,745	
Bombay	,, 22,53,44,247	
Bengal	,, 12,00,00,000–	(only half revenue)
UP	,, 4,05,53,00	is shown because
Bihar	,, 1,54,37,742	nearly half population
CP and Berar	,, 31,42,682	is Hindu.)
Assam	,, 1,87,55,967	
Orissa	,, 5,67,346	
Total	Rs 51,91,27,729	

'The Pakistan Provinces, it will be seen, contribute very little. The main contribution comes from the Provinces of Hindustan.

In fact it is the money contributed by the Provinces of Hindustan which enables the Government of India to carry out its activities in the Pakistan Provinces. The Pakistan Provinces are a drain on the Provinces of Hindustan. Not only do they contribute very little to the Central Government but they receive a great deal from the Central Government. The revenue of the Central Government amounts to Rs 126 crores. Of this about Rs 52 crores are annually spent on the Army. In what area is this amount spent? Who pays the bulk of this amount of Rs 52 crores? The bulk of this amount of Rs 52 crores which is spent on the Army is spent over the Muslim Army drawn from the Pakistan area. Now the bulk of this amount of Rs 52 crores is contributed by the Hindu Provinces and is spent on an Army which for the most part consists of non-Hindus.'[7]

It is thus clear that the north-western region will not only lose the benefit of the huge amount that the central government of India collects from the rest of India and spends within the north-western region but will have to find money for supporting its forces. There will be loss of income which the people of that region derive through their employment in the Army and on top of that they will have to be taxed for maintaining their own army. Mr K.T. Shah points out that this 'invisible tribute' comes to a very tidy sum. He says: 'Because the Indian Army used to be recruited in a very large proportion from the Punjab, the pay, pensions and all allowances of these officers and men, including camp followers as well as profits of contractors amount to a very tidy sum. At the lowest this would amount to an invisible tribute to the Punjab of over 10 crores per annum from the rest of India on the basis of pre-War expenditure on this head. The War, needless to add, has increased it beyond recognition. In the post-War world it cannot fall much short of 25 crores per annum.'[8]

This anticipated loss to the province must have been one of the reasons why Sir Sikandar Hayat Khan insisted that in case of any revision of boundaries or establishment of regional governments as contemplated in his scheme, the proportion of Muslims in the army should not be less than what it was on 1 January 1937. During the Second World War also, the north-western zone has

[7] Ambedkar, *Thoughts on Pakistan*, pp. 86–87.
[8] K.T. Shah, *Why Pakistan? Why Not?*, p. 164.

furnished a large proportion of combatants to the Indian Army and thus derived the benefits mentioned by Mr K.T. Shah. It was stated by the War Secretary in the Central Assembly in March 1945 in reply to a question that of the total enrolment of combatants of the Indian Army, the Punjab furnished 29.9 per cent, NWFP 4 per cent and Sind 0.4 per cent, a total of 34.3 per cent in all.

PUBLIC DEBT (1939–40)

The public debt of the central and provincial governments in India stood as follows at the close of 1939–40:

TABLE XLIV
Public Debt in 1939–40

Central Government:		
In India	Rs	5,05,51,10,816
In England	£	329,328,394
Total	Rs	9,44,61,55,399 (on the basis of Rs 13⅓ per £)
Provinces:		
Bengal	Rs	30,00,000
Assam	,,	50,00,00
Punjab	,,	34,05,50,515
NWFP	,,	57,24,900 } Total Rs 63,19,52,167
Sind	,,	23,56,76,752
Coorg	,,	3,62,582
Madras	,,	11,96,92,319
Bombay	,,	31,18,72,720
UP	,,	31,13,92,886
Bihar		Nil
CP and Berar	,,	4,88,40,863
Orissa		Nil
Total	Rs	1,43,21,12,937

Out of the total public debt of 143 crores which the provinces owe, the governments of the Punjab, Sind, and NWFP owe over Rs 63 crores. Most of it, however, is invested in irrigation works which are a paying concern in the Punjab and bid fair to become so in Sind also. The eastern zone has no public debts worth the name.[9]

[9] The following Table brings up to date the debt position in the provinces collectively.

TABLE XLV

Debt Position of Provinces since 1936–37

(In crores of rupees)

		At the end of 1938–39	At the end of 1944–45
I	Public Debt		
	(a) Permanent Debt	15.07	50.92
	(b) Floating Debt	1.50	68.23
	(c) Loans from Central Government	123.24	66.57
II	Unfunded Debt	23.39	29.77
III	Gross Total Debt (Total of I and II)	163.20	215.49
IV	Net Debt (Deducting outstanding loans and advances made by provincial governments)	102.48	185.79

It will, however, be a very complicated kind of accounting when the public debt of India has to be distributed between Muslim and non-Muslim zones in case of separation. But there can be no doubt the north-west and eastern zones will have to bear their burden which will not be a light one.

Besides, the public debt of the central government has increased enormously during the war. Any calculation based on the figures of 1939–40 will be thoroughly misleading. It will be nearly 2,000 crores in place of $944^{1}/_{2}$ crores in 1939–40; and even on the basis of a *pro rata* distribution according to the population of the Muslim districts in the two zones, their share together with their own debts will come to something like 500 crores, the interest on which at 3 per cent will come to something like 15 crores a year—which is nearly double of what the two zones will have in hand after meeting the administrative expenses alone, exclusive of the cost of defence. But as stated above, the allotment of liabilities will not be so simple but a most taxing and complicated affair. Sir Ardeshir Dalal has pointed out: 'The economic and financial difficulties of splitting up this unit [British India] into a number of fragments are so great as to be well-nigh insuperable. The Railways, Posts and Telegraphs, Irrigation and Water Works have to be cut up. Adequate adjustments with regard to the national debt incurred on all these projects will have to be broken up and created anew. The Army will similarly have to be broken up and past liabilities and future expenditure adjusted. A large sum of money has been spent out of the revenues of India on projects, such as the Sukkur Barrage in Sind. Payment will have to be made by Pakistan for this as well as for similar expenditure incurred by the Government of India for capital works inside Pakistan and counterbalanced against the Pakistan share of capital expenditure incurred by the Government of India in Hindustan. When all these complicated, difficult and heart-breaking processes have been gone through, if they can be gone through without innumerable bickering and trouble, Pakistan will emerge out of it a comparatively poor, resourceless State. With innumerable problems immediately to be handled and a burden of debt difficult to repay, it will cut itself off from the great economic and industrial future which a self-governing India may look forward to.'[10]

[10] Interest-bearing Obligations and Interest-yielding Assets of the Government of India
(Explanatory Memorandum)
Table XLVI brings up to date the debt position in detail. In considering this Table, it must be borne in mind that even if the estimate of the debt outstanding on 31 March 1946 is not reached, as given in the Budget for 1945–46, because of the war coming to an end earlier than anticipated, the actual debt has very substantially increased, it would be substantially over Rs 2,000 crores, and the provincial share would be in proportion.
(a) The outstandings at the end of each year are shown in the statement (b) Sterling obligations have been converted into rupees at Is. 6d. per rupee. Provinces have already their own debt, not all of it covered by productive assets. The share of the Government of India debt, which on partition will fall to their lot, would be so much additional burden; and there is a much greater proportion of unproductive debt in the central government than in the provincial account.
The assets listed, as against the debt, are, in several cases, of doubtful productive character, e.g. sterling securities, or the Burma debt. If any of these are unrealizable, or do not bear interest to support their own burden, the incidence will be *pro rata* greater on the provinces individually. A close scrutiny of every asset would be necessary before final allocation is made.
Non-effective charges of pensions etc. are not yet settled, as regards the war expenditure directly chargeable to India's account, under the agreement of October, 1939.

TABLE XLVI

Railways (1939–40) (In thousands of rupees)

Railways System	Total Capital at charge	Gross Earning	Working Expenses	Net Earnings	Percentage of working expenses to gross earnings	Percentage of net earnings on total capital at charge
Assam Bengal	2,64,874	21,335	16,826	4,506	78.86	1.70
Bengal and NW	22,84,94	36,290	18,482	17,808	50.93	7.79
Bengal Nagput	7,84,597	1,10,446	74,344	36,102	67.31	4.60
BB and CI	7,75,020	1,28,703	74,100	54,603	57.57	7.05
Eastern Bengal	5,30,646	63,659	55,320	8,339	66.90	1.57
East Indian	14,99,417	2,15,546	1,31,084	84,462	60.82	5.63
GIP	11,77,970	1,42,298	91,101	51,197	64.02	4.35
MSM	5,63,460	80,171	48,926	31,245	61.00	5.55
North-western (total)	15,32,602	168,979	1,19,645	49,334	70.80	3.22
Rohilkhand and Kumaon	47,591	7,693	3,719	3,974	48.34	8.35
South Indian	4,86,853	55,126	38,688	16,438	70.18	3.38
North-western (Commercial)	11,94,431	1,55,043	1,00,700	54,343	64.95	4.55
North-western (Military)	3,38,171	13,936	18,945	-5,009	135.95	-1.48

TABLE XLVII

Explanatory Memorandum Budget 1945–46 Government of India
Interest-bearing Obligations and Interest-yielding Assets of Government of India
(In crores of rupees)

In India	1938–39 (Pre-War year)	1945–46 (Budget Estimate)
Public Debt		
Loans	437.87	1,484.43
Treasury Bills and Ways and Means	46.30	86.61
Advances	484.17	1,571.40
Unfunded Debt		
Service Funds	1.03	.74
Post Office Savings Bank including Defence Savings Bank	81.88	110.20
Post Office Cash and Defence Savings	59.57	43.90
State Provident Funds	72.40	97.20
National Savings Certificates	..	51.65
Other Items	10.25	13.08
Total Unfunded Debt	225.13	316.77
Deposits		
Depreciation and Reserve Funds	27.34	125.89
Other Deposits	..	129.28
In England		
Public Debt		
Loans	396.50	13.42
War Contribution	**20.62**	**20.62**
Capital portion of annuities created in purchase of Railways	47.82	26.01
	464.94	60.05
Unfunded Debt		
Service Funds	4.18	3.55
Total obligations in England	469.12	63.60
Total interest-bearing obligations	1,205.76	2,206.58
Interest-yielding Assets		
Capital advanced to Railways	725.24	797.38
Capital advanced to other Commercial Department	27.42	42.10
Capital advanced to Provinces	123.28	76.97
Capital advanced to Indian States and other interest-bearing loans	20.71	18.65
Debt due from Burma	49.73	48.15
Deposits with HMG for redemption of Railway liabilities	..	26.01
	946.38	1,009.26
Cash securities held on treasury account	30.30	547.02
Balance of total interest-bearing obligations not covered by above assets	229.08	650.30

Of these principal railways in British India, the Eastern Bengal Railway falls almost entirely and the Assam Bengal partially within the eastern zone. The total capital investment on them comes to Rs 79–55 crores and their net earnings to Rs 1 crore 28.45 lakhs or at 1.6 per cent. The NW Railway which falls almost entirely within the north western zone has a total investment of Rs 153.26 crores and earns a net profit of Rs 4 crores 93.34 lakhs, which works out at 3.22 per cent on the investment. It will be seen that the net earnings of the railways falling within the two zones are lower than those of any other principal railway in British India, and in this respect also the Muslim zones are in a worse position than the other parts of British India. This aspect of railway finance has assumed larger importance now, inasmuch as most, if not all, of the principal railways are now State railways and any profits that they can earn will go to the revenues of the various States, or else any loss on account of interest payable on the investment which they may incur will have to be borne out of the revenues of the State to which they will belong.

~

THIRTY-FOUR

THE PROPOSAL FOR PARTITION EXAMINED

I. ARGUMENTS FOR PARTITION

We have discussed at length the fundamental basis of a claim for the division of India into Muslim and non-Muslim States, namely, that the Hindus and the Musalmans constitute two separate and independent nations. We have considered various schemes of division of India for cultural and political purposes and seen to what extent each of them conforms to or differs from the fundamental basis laid down by the Resolution of the All-India Muslim League for creating independent Muslim zones in the north-west and east of India. The League has not given any detailed plan of partition and has contented itself with laying down in general terms the basis for division. We have had, therefore, to consider what areas in the light of the principles laid down by the League Resolution can be constituted into such separate zones and what the resources of such independent Muslim zones are and are likely to be. We are now in a position to consider the proposal for Partition in a general way from the point of view of the separate Muslim zones and the non-Muslim zone and in the setting of international and world conditions as they are developing today.

Professor Reginald Coupland has summarized the argument for Partition in a very cogent and forceful manner and I may not do better than quote him at length:

(1) In the first place the prospect of Partition goes far to resolve that complex of pride and fear which has been the chief cause of the recent deepening of the Hindu–Muslim schism. For more than half the Indian Muslims it eliminates the fear of a Hindu Raj and all it might mean for them immediately and ultimately, by cutting them clear out of its ambit. And Partition ministers to their pride by converting them from a minority in one great State into a majority

in two smaller ones and by recognizing that they are not merely a community in a composite Indian Nation but a nation by themselves, entitled to its national independence in its national homelands. Moreover it broadens their footing in the world . . . Their States would stand side by side with the Muslim States of the Middle East. They would be more fully conscious than they can be today that they belong to a great brotherhood whose homelands stretch far beyond the bounds of India. If, on the other hand, they turn their backs on the outer world, if they acquiesce in a permanent subjection to the Hindu majority in an isolated India, they doom themselves to something like the fate of the minorities in Europe . . .

(2) Secondly, Pakistan, it is claimed, will solve the minority problem throughout India as nothing else can. It adopts the balance theory in a form in which alone it can be valid. Muslim States are balanced against one or more Hindu States, to which, whatever their size, they are equal in national status. There will still be minorities in them all . . . But, though communal homogeneity is an impracticable ideal, though there will be millions of Muslims in the Hindu States, not to mention other minorities, they will no longer constitute a serious problem, for the simple reason that the inter-communal struggle for power, precipitated by the mere approach of India's final liberation from neutral British control, will cease to exist in the Partition States. Coalition Governments and other statutory safeguards for minorities are part of the League's programme for the Muslim States; but it will be recognized they are essentially Muslim States in which Muslim policy and culture will predominate, just as the Hindu States will be essentially Hindu. Nor will their respective minorities be encouraged any longer to keep up their quarrel with the majorities . . . to ensure a communal ascendancy at the all-India centre. There will be no such centre . . . And the majorities, it is argued, are more likely to discharge this responsibility—and the minorities similarly to become reconciled to their position—because it will be understood on both sides that in the last resort the "hostage" principle can be brought into play more effectively between independent States than between Federated Provinces.

(3) Thirdly, it is claimed that Partition will ease the problem of defence for all India . . . The north-west Frontier will lose all importance once a Muslim state is established in the north-west. The tribesmen and the people beyond the frontier are all Muslims. They will lose all religious and political fervour for *jehad* against non-Muslims once they find that they have to reckon with their brothers in Islam . . . The position could be stabilized, moreover, by non-aggression treaties of full-scale alliances between Pakistan and her Muslim neighbours. Why should she not make a fifth subscriber to the Pact of Saadabad which bound together Turkey, Iraq, Persia and Afghanistan for mutual security in 1937?

(4) Fourthly, in an undivided India, when military organization is in Indian and mainly Hindu hands, the proportion of Muslims in the Indian Army is bound to be reduced . . . In the event the proportion of Muslim soldiers, which in 1939 was more than one-third and is now 30.8 per cent, would fall to less than one quarter. This would not only affect the standard of living in the Punjab, which, as has often been pointed out, owes so much to the pay and pensions of Punjabi troops. It would give Hindu Raj the ultimate guarantee of Military Power.

(5) Fifthly, by Partition and only by Partition, it is said, can Indian Muslims acquire the power of economic self-determination. Hindu–Muslim antagonism has always had its economic side, and one of the chief reasons why the Muslims dread the prospect of a Hindu Raj is the power it would give the Hindus to confirm and strengthen their economic domination in all parts of India . . . The virtual monopoly possessed by the Hindu shop-keepers and money-lenders in retail trade and marketing even in an overwhelmingly Muslim countryside, the Hindu preponderance in the growth of urban life, in the new professional and commercial middle class, even in the Punjab or Sind—all that was bad enough, but the rise of industrialism made matters worse . . . The North-West Muslim homeland is overwhelmingly agrarian. Its population amounts to 12.3 per cent of the population of British India, but so far as can be estimated, the proportion of its industries is only 5.1 per cent of those of British India

and that of its mineral development only 5.4 per cent. Bengal as a whole is much more highly industrialized. It has 20 per cent of the population of British India, and, to reckon by the number of workers employed in factories, 33 per cent of its industry. But the industrial area is mainly that of predominantly Hindu Calcutta and its neighbourhood; apart from Calcutta the North-East Muslim homeland is even more dominantly agricultural than the north-west. Indian industry, in fact, is located mainly in Hindu areas; it is financed and owned mainly by Hindu capitalists; it provides livelihood mainly for Hindu labour . . . Pakistan at least could control its own economy. In the north-west, at any rate, it could establish and protect its own industries. Instead of sending its raw cotton to the mills of Bombay, it could build more mills of its own and protect their products with a tariff. And later on if capital were available, it could apply its great reserves of water-power to further industrial development. Karachi, too, might be developed till it eclipsed Bombay as the port of entry for all north-west India . . .'[1]

II. ARGUMENTS FOR PARTITION ANSWERED

Let us consider each of the points mentioned above.

1   It may be noted how difficult, if not impossible, it becomes to give cool and dispassionate consideration to such important matters when prejudice and passion have been worked up to a high pitch. Ordinarily, the complex of pride ought to be an antidote to the complex of fear but if Professor Coupland's analysis is right, they both co-exist. What, after all, is the complex of fear due to? Ever since the British acquired political power and took charge of the governance of India, it is they who have been governing and ruling the country. If Muslims have lost their position of advantage and superiority it is not on account of Hindus or other non-Muslims of India abusing their political power—of which they were deprived just as the Muslims had been. It is a historical fact that in the earlier days of British rule,

[1] R.Coupland, *The Future of India*, pp. 75–79.

the Muslims were more suspect than the Hindus and it is also undeniable that for some years they were oppressed and suppressed more than the Hindus. But it is equally undeniable that when it was discovered that the Hindus were beginning to challenge the authority of the British, they decided that the time had arrived when the policy of patting the Hindus on the back should be changed and the Muslims given their due turn of receiving a patting. The result of this change in British policy has undoubtedly been the creation of suspicion and distrust among the Hindus and Muslims of each other, leaving the third party in the unmolested and undisturbed possession of power for the time being. A dispassionate study of events and an unprejudiced consideration of the situation should have created distrust of the third party's motives and activities but unfortunately, a curious twist has been given. The backwardness of the Muslims cannot be attributed to anything that the Hindus were primarily responsible for, but to the policy of the British government in whose hands all power has remained concentrated for more than 150 years. Such power as has been ostensibly transferred to Indian hands has been under the Acts of 1919 and 1935 for the enactment of which also the entire responsibility rests with the British. Under the Act of 1935 the Muslims have been ruling in all the Provinces where they are in a majority—and also in Assam where they are in a minority. Particularly in the two largest Provinces, the Punjab and Bengal, as also in Sind, Muslim rule has been uninterrupted since the inauguration of the Act in April 1937. The central government has all along remained British. Except for the brief period of 27 months the Hindu majority has had no chance of administering even the provinces where the Muslims are in a minority. If the Muslims have remained backward, how can the Hindu majority be blamed for it? It has never had a chance in the Centre and but a short spell of a chance in the Hindu majority provinces. What have the Muslim ministers done during the last eight years in the north-western and eastern zones to overcome the obstacles in the way of progress of Muslims? If it be assumed that they were unable to effect any radical reforms because of the opposition of the

Hindu minority in those provinces—a proposition which cannot be sustained by any evidence—then may it not be legitimately asked how the position will improve by an outright separation, if the minorities continue as they are today unless it be intended that they shall be deprived of all political rights and otherwise so suppressed and depressed as to be unable to offer even constitutional resistance to the majority? It would be a different matter if the minorities were to be eliminated by some means or other from each of the autonomous units of the independent Muslim States in the north-west and the east of India, and particularly from the Punjab and Bengal. But that is not seriously suggested and it is clear, if what is stated in the League Resolution is accepted, that minorities will continue; and adequate, effective and mandatory safeguards shall be specifically provided in the Constitutions for the protection of their religious, cultural, economic, political, administrative, and other rights and interests in consultation with them on a basis of reciprocity with the non-Muslim State. As we have seen they will not be a small minority in the Punjab where the Muslims will be only 57 per cent, nor even in the north-western zone where the Muslims will be only 62 per cent, if the whole of the Punjab is included in it; and not more than 75 per cent if the predominantly non-Muslim areas are excluded from the zone. Similarly, in the eastern zone if the whole of Bengal and Assam are included in it the Muslim proportion will be something between 51 and 52 per cent of the population, and in no case more than 69 per cent if the predominantly non-Muslim areas are excluded. It is therefore difficult to see how these zones can be said to constitute Muslim States which necessarily implies and requires an overwhelming population of Muslims in them. Of course the Muslims will have the satisfaction of being in a majority in two smaller States instead of being a minority in one big State. The point which the Muslims have to consider is whether it is worthwhile cultivating and satisfying this sense of pride in view of the sacrifices involved in it.

As regards broadening their footing in the world, that too depends to a large extent on their being Muslim States. There is no country

INDIA DIVIDED

in the world which is being ruled by the Muslims today where non-Muslims form such a big minority as they will do in the north-western and eastern zones of India. For the rest, there is nothing to prevent Muslims of India having their sympathies with Muslims of other countries. Indeed, Hindus have never stood in their way, although they have naturally expected that the Muslims will pull their full weight in the trials and tribulations of India also. Not long ago the non-Muslims rose like one man with the Muslims in defence of the rights of Muslims in other parts of the world in the days of the Khilafat agitation and suffered and sacrificed with them as much for the protection of the rights of the Khalifa of the Muslims as for redressing the grievances of Indians—Hindus, Muslims and Sikhs alike—in the Punjab. The Hindus have done nothing against any Muslim country, and there is no reason to think why India should not join and be a signatory to a pact with the Muslim countries of the Middle East for mutual advantage. But after all is said and done, it must be admitted that it is for the Muslims to decide whether they will insist on a satisfaction of this pride in preference to their long historical association and present and future advantages, which a strong, united India can enjoy as compared to a small State which is bound to be weaker than India as a whole and equally bound to weaken the rest of India. This cannot and ought not of course to deprive the non-Muslims of the areas concerned of their say in a matter of such vital importance to them, particularly when the proposed division cuts right across the history of eight centuries . . .

That the non-Muslims of the areas concerned as also of the rest of India should look askance at the proposal of Partition is perfectly understandable in view of the effect that such a proposal will have on them, as also in view of the declared—though long-range—intentions of the protagonists Partition. It cannot be denied that a divided India will be weaker and will not be able to command the same hearing in international counsels that a strong united India will have. It will not be able to secure the same terms from other countries in the matter of trade facilities, its own industrial development, and in a hundred other ways. This will be so especially in the case of the Muslim zones which will be admittedly smaller than the rest of India. But the latter, too, will suffer and suffer grievously on account of this Partition.

But more than this, there is a genuine fear generated by the declarations of the protagonists of Partition. I will quote here some extracts which will show that the fear of an attempt to re-establish Muslim rule in the wake of separation is not-unfounded. Mr F.K. Khan Durrani introduces his book *The Meaning of Pakistan* with a Preface written so late as 12 November 1943, in which the following passage occurs: 'There is not an inch of the soil of India which our fathers did not once purchase with their bipod. 'We cannot be false to the blood of our fathers. India, the whole of it, is therefore our heritage and it must be reconquered for Islam. Expansion in the spiritual sense is an inherent necessity of our faith and implies no hatred or enmity towards the Hindus. Rather the reverse. Our ultimate ideal should be the unification of India, spiritually as well as politically, under the banner of Islam; The final political salvation of India is not otherwise possible.'[2]

'It is necessary,' says 'A Punjabi', 'to make it clear that the separation of our regions from Hindu India is not an end in itself but only a means for the achievement of an ideal Islamic state. The proposed separation will undoubtedly lead to our emancipation from the economic slavery of the Hindus. But as our objective is the establishment of an ideal Islamic State, it also denotes, complete independence. After independence has been achieved, it would be impossible for us to maintain for long, in an unIslamic world, our ideal of an Islamic State. As such, we shall have to advocate a world revolution on Islamic lines. Consequently, our ultimate ideal is a world revolution on purely Islamic lines. Separation, emancipation from economic slavery of the Hindus, and freedom from the constitutional slavery of the British are only some of the means for the achievement of our ultimate ideal of a world revolution on completely Islamic lines.'[3]

'Muslim minorities have lived in the past in various parts of the world on the best of terms with the members of other religions. But they have never accepted the role of a minority whenever, in view of their numbers or physical strength, they felt themselves strong enough to form an independent Muslim State . . . This movement for independent Muslim States in India will give a tremendous encouragement to similar movements in China and Russia, where Muslims have so far been assigned the status of minorities.

[2] F.K. Khan Durrani, *The Meaning of Pakistan*, p. x.
[3] 'A Punjabi', *Confederacy of India*, pp. 269–70.

'In Central Asia, Muslims are a majority of 95 per cent out of a population of 80 millions and yet at present they are kept under subjection by the Chinese and Soviet Governments.

'Islamic political problems are everywhere of an allied nature. Liberation of one Muslim country will directly affect another. The fate of Muslims in India will have direct repercussions in other parts of the world, particularly in the Western Provinces of China and Southern and Eastern parts of Russia where Muslims are in a majority. Acceptance of minority status within the sub-continent of India will besides sealing once for all the fate of 90 million Muslims in India, lead to permanent enslavement of 30 millions of Muslims in Soviet Russia and 50 millions in China.

'It is quite natural to suppose that if India achieves independence as a united country under the aegis of the Congress, it will enter in future into permanent alliance with China and Russia so as to keep the Muslims in the latter three countries under permanent domination. The creation of an independent Muslim State in Central Asia will always be viewed with suspicion by the future Congress Government in India as this will lead to a movement for separation among the Muslims in India as well.'[4]

'The desire of the Indian Muslims to have Muslim States of their own is a part of a movement for the unification of the Muslim World (Silsila-i-Jamia-Vahdat-Umam-Islam) started in Turkey during the lifetime and at the instance of the late Ataturk under the patronage of the late Syed Jalil Ahmad Sinyusi.' One of its aims is to create more Muslim republics in all those parts of the world which are predominantly Muslim, in addition to the Muslim States already functioning. Among the ten newly proposed republics one is to consist of Muslim Bengal, another is to be constituted by the Muslim north-west India and the third by the Hyderabad State.'[5]

In view of these declarations no one can blame non-Muslims if they look upon the proposal for Partition as the thin end of the wedge which in course of time is intended to complete its work by reconquering India for Islam, by freeing the Muslims of Central Asia from the yoke of China and Russia and ultimately by bringing

[4] Mr M.R.T. in *India's Problem of her Future Constitution*, pp. 60–67.

[5] Ansari, *Pakistan—the Problem of India*, p. 47.

about a world revolution on Islamic lines. The ambition of those who see these visions has to be admired, even though they may have been seen in the background of suspicion and distrust of Hindus, Chinese and Russians, who are considered as having no other business than that of suppressing the Muslims—for which there is no foundation.

It may also be noted that this objective of the conquest of India and of the world for Islam belies the fear that the Hindu majority will oppress this virile Muslim minority with such high aspirations.

(2)   It is difficult to understand how the creation of two new Muslim States out of India will solve the minorities problem in India and in the new States. There is no country in the world which has a completely homogeneous population. In the very nature of things there are bound to be minorities in each country and India is no exception, and neither will the Muslim and non-Muslim zones of India after Partition be exceptions. The expedient of doing away with the Muslim minority by exchange of population between the Muslim and non-Muslim zones has been rightly ruled out as impracticable both on financial and human grounds. We have seen the size of minorities in the Muslim zones. The non-Muslims in the north-west zone will be 25 or 38 per cent of the population according as the predominantly non-Muslim districts of the Punjab are excluded from or included in the Muslim zone. Similarly in the eastern zone the non-Muslims will constitute 31 or 48 per cent of the population according as the non-Muslim districts of Bengal and Assam are excluded from or included in the eastern zone. If we take the north-western and eastern zones together, the Muslim population will be 71.56 or 55.23 per cent according as we exclude or include the non-Muslim districts of the Punjab, Assam and Bengal. The Muslims left behind in the non-Muslim zone of British India will be only 10.75 per cent of its total population if we exclude the whole of the Punjab and the whole of Assam and Bengal from the non-Muslim zone and 13.22 per cent if the non-Muslim districts are included in the non-Muslim zone and excluded from the Muslim zone.

Out of a total population of 793.95 lakh Muslims in British India no less than 202.95 lakh (i.e. 25.59 per cent), or 299.94 lakh (i.e. 37.77 per cent) Muslims will be left in the non-Muslim zone, according as non-Muslim districts in Assam, Bengal and the Punjab are included in or excluded from the Muslim zones; Their percentage from province to province will vary between 1.68 in Orissa and 15.30 in the UP and will be 33.22 in the small province of Delhi.

TABLE XLVIII

Muslim Population in Non-Muslim Provinces
(a) If the whole of the Punjab and Bengal and Assam are included in Muslim Zones

Province	Total Population in lakhs	Muslims in lakhs	Percentage of Muslims of total
Madras	493.42	38.96	7.90
Bombay	208.50	19.20	9.21
UP	550.21	84.16	15.30
Bihar	363.40	47.16	12.98
CP and Berar	168.14	7.84	4.66
Orissa	87.29	1.46	1.68
Ajmer Merwara	5.84	0.90	15.40
Andamans and Nicobar	0.34	0.08	23.70
Coorg	1.69	0.14	8.78
Delhi	9.18	3.05	33.22
Total	1888.01	202.95	10.75

TABLE XLIX

Muslim Population in Non-Muslim Provinces
(b) If non-Muslim Districts of the Punjab, Bengal and Assam are excluded from Muslim Zones

Province	Total Population	Muslims	Percentage
Bengal	193.42	42.95	22.21
Assam	70.89	15.50	21.89
Punjab	115.49	38.54	33.37
Total	379.80	96.99	25.27
Other Non-Muslim Provinces	1888.01	202.95	10.75
Grand Total	2267.81	299.94	13.22

TABLE L

Muslim Population in Muslim Provinces

	If Non-Muslim Districts are Excluded			If Non-Muslim Districts are Included		
Provinces	Total Population	Muslims	Per cent	Total Population	Muslims	Per cent
Bengal	409.65	287.10	70.08	603.36	330.05	54.73
Assam	31.16	18.92	60.71	102.05	34.42	33.73
Punjab	168.70	123.63	73.25	284.19	162.17	57.07
NWFP	30.38	27.89	91.79	30.38	27.89	91.79
Sind	45.35	32.08	70.75	45.35	32.08	70.75
Baluchistan	5.02	4.39	87.50	5.02	4.39	87.50
Total	690.26	494.01	71.56	1070.05	591.00	55.23

On the other hand the number of non-Muslims in the north-western zone will be 138.40 lakhs or 61.46 lakhs and in the eastern zone 340.64 lakhs or 134.79 lakhs according as the non-Muslim districts are included in or excluded from the Muslim zones. In other words, there will be no less than 479.04 lakhs or 196.25 lakhs of non-Muslims if the two Muslim zones are taken together according as non-Muslim districts are included in or excluded from them. Thus the total population of minorities—Muslim and non-Muslim—in the non-Muslim and Muslim zones will be no less than 681.99 or 496.19 lakhs according as non-Muslim districts are included or not in the Muslim zones.

There will thus be formidable minorities, if numbers are considered, in the Hindu and Muslim zones. The non-Muslim minorities will be much greater than the Muslim minorities, being no less than 25 or 38 per cent in the north-western zone and 31 or 48 per cent in the eastern zone as against 13.22 per cent or 10.75 per cent of Muslims in the non-Muslim zones according as the predominantly non-Muslim districts are excluded from or included in the Muslim zones.

Thus while the Muslim minority in the non-Muslim zone or zones will be spread over a tremendously large area from the Himalayas to Cape Comorin and from Bengal to the Punjab, and so ineffective in any particular area, the non-Muslim minorities will be concentrated in the two Muslim zones in a compact area and will be, therefore, quite effective as minorities in asserting their rights and demanding their privileges.

Elimination of minorities would be possible only if there is an exchange of population on a vast scale. Exchange of population can be on a voluntary basis or compulsory. Voluntary migration of so many millions of Muslims and non-Muslims from the non-Muslim and Muslim zones is inconceivable. The experience of voluntary migration for exchange of population in the Balkans was most disappointing for the simple reason that the people would not move of their own accord out of their old surroundings. In India the attachment to land of both Hindus and Muslims is so great that it can be safely asserted that neither would care to leave the locality where they had been settled simply to become members of another State. Nor is the experience which the Muslims had at the time of the Khilafat movement of *hijrat* likely to encourage any large-scale movement of populations. Besides the distance, the difference in the environments, languages, climatic conditions, mode and methods of living of the population among which the emigrants will have to settle down will be such as not only to discourage any such enterprise but altogether to rule it out. Then the cost of moving such large populations, uprooting them from where they have remained settled for generations and settling them in altogether new surroundings, and the loss of property. involved in the process, even though compensation may be provided for, will impose a burden which neither the Muslim nor the non-Muslim States will be able to bear. The suffering will be immense and the scheme financially and administratively impossible of accomplishment. In case of compulsory exchange all these difficulties will be increased a hundred-fold, and to all the other difficulties will be added the difficulty of shifting the population under police and military guard—which is unthinkable. Those who speak about the exchange of a few hundred thousands between Greece and Turkey ignore that in India it will involve 68 or at least 50 millions and the distances to be covered will be immense and the costs will be so tremendous that even if the states are able to bear them, they will be crippled for a long time on account of this heavy burden which it will impose on them.

The League Resolution suggests that adequate, effective and mandatory safeguards should be specifically provided for the protection of their religious, cultural, economic, political, administrative and other rights and interests in consultation with the minorities in the Muslim and non-Muslim zones.

Now, if there are to be Muslim and non-Muslim independent States and if they have to frame their own Constitutions, how

THE PROPOSAL FOR PARTITION EXAMINED

can any of such independent states be bound to provide such safeguards? Supposing the independent states after their coming into existence refuse to make such provision in their respective Constitutions, how is any of them to be forced to do it? Assuming that such safeguards are provided to begin with, but are altered to the disadvantage of the minorities or abrogated altogether, what is to be done to enforce the safeguards? Assuming they are allowed to remain a part of the Constitution but are not given effect to or otherwise curtailed in their application, how is an independent State to enforce them in the other independent state? It is of course presumed that the States will be independent and one will have no authority over the other nor will there be any central authority above both which may be charged with the duty of enforcing the provisions in the Constitutions. The use of the words mandatory and statutory will not improve matters, as there will be no authority to enforce the mandate and the States will be free to alter their statutes.

The experience of the League of Nations where enforcement of minorities clauses of treaties was guaranteed by the League of Nations does not encourage the hope that any outside authority can be easily invoked to enforce their observance in spite of such guarantee. The hostages theory cannot work in practice. One wrong cannot justify another. Even the old law of an eye for an eye and a tooth for a tooth did not provide for one man's eye or one man's tooth for the sin of another, nor did it justify the sin of one man being visited on another man; much less can anyone justify on any human or moral principle the rule that one set of persons should be victimized or oppressed or tyrannized over for the fault of another set of men whom they do not know and to whose acts of commission or omission they were not parties in even a remote manner and with whom they had nothing in common except that they both worshipped God in a particular way. To use the words of an eminent Musalman, 'the hostage principle will not work, and if it does it will shift the basis of politics from civilization to barbarism.'[6] And despite what the protagonists of Pakistan may say, I refuse to believe that the better mind of the Muslims or non-Muslims will ever consent to revert to this barbarism.

[6] Sir Sultan Ahmad, *A Treaty between India and the United Kingdom*, p. 84.

The existence of separate and independent States makes it infinitely more difficult for one state to enforce fair treatment of any group of its own citizens by another than if both were members of a federated State. There is only one peaceful method open to each independent State in any such emergency—diplomatic representation. That failing, war is the only sanction left. It may be only economic war or it may take the shape of war with arms. It is not easy to have a war for even serious complaints unless the people on both sides are brought to a stage when no other alternative is left. It is certainly not possible for pin-pricks. No State will embark on the hazards of a war unless it is seriously hit and the chances are that when it comes to deciding in favour of it or against it, the interests of the people of the State will weigh very heavily as against the interests of their co-religionist minority in a remote and distant corner of the country.

Nor is it all a theoretical discussion. There are Muslim States in existence next door to India. They have never in history so far gone to war with India because the Muslims there were ill-treated. Not a ripple was noticed on the placid waters of these Muslim States when the so-called atrocities were perpetrated on Muslims in India either by the British during their long rule or by the Congress governments during their short administration of twenty-seven months. Not even did the Muslim League ministries in the Punjab or Bengal or Sind raise their little finger when the Congress ministries are said to have misbehaved. It is all moonshine to imagine that the creation of two new Muslim States will alter the position to such an extent as to ensure and enforce fair treatment of Muslims in the non-Muslim zones or vice versa. Minorities have in all cases to depend on the fundamentals of human nature, and those universal moral and human rules which govern the conduct of all civilized persons, whatever their religion. It is no good insisting that the non-Muslims are incapable of having any other objective than that of oppressing and tyrannizing over the Muslims and that the non-Muslims at the same time must accept that the Muslims are incapable of doing an unjust or unfair thing towards non-Muslims. There is a certain naiveté in the assertion openly made or the assumption tacitly made that the Muslims cannot trust the non-Muslims and cannot therefore submit to a central government in any form or shape, however attenuated its powers and however circumscribed its functions may be, and

THE PROPOSAL FOR PARTITION EXAMINED   421

that at the same time the non-Muslims must trust the Muslims and accept their assurance that they will give them a fair deal. If trust begets trust, distrust equally begets distrust, and if you distrust the non-Muslims and question their bona fides at every step you have no right to expect that the latter will not return the compliment. The creation of independent States does not solve the minority problem. It makes it more difficult of solution. It leaves the minorities, whether Muslim or non-Muslim, in the independent States more helpless, less capable of taking care of themselves, and worse situated in regard to the invocation of any outside authority for enforcing their rights.

(3) and (4) Nor will Pakistan ease the problem of the defence of India either on the north-western or eastern frontier of India. It is said that the tribesmen and people beyond the north-western frontier are all Muslims, and once a Muslim state is established there, they will lose all religious and political fervour for *jehad* against non-Muslims. This hope has no basis in fact and no warrant in history. It will not be for the first time in Indian history that there will be a Muslim State in India. Indeed, right from the time when Qutbuddin Aibak made himself the Sultan of Delhi down to the time when the Sikhs established themselves as rulers in the north-western corner of India, there has always been a Muslim State. All the invasions of India from that corner during this long period of more than 600 years were by Muslims against Muslim rulers and not against Hindu rulers as there was no Hindu ruler then. Since as early as the days of Allauddin Khilji, the Muslim Sultans of Delhi have had to combat the danger of ever recurring raids from the north-west. Allauddin had effectively to garrison the frontier outposts of the kingdom, but Muslim raiders and invaders came again and again. And this remained the policy all through the period of Muslim rule. To mention only the most well known of the invasions it will suffice to say that the invasions of Timur, Babar, Nadir Shah and Ahmad Shah Abdali were all led by Muslims against Muslim kings of India and there is no warrant in history for the very facile and complacent assumption that once a

Muslim State is established in the north-west all danger
of invasion will on that account cease to operate. An
invasion in these days may not be easy, but it will be
for other reasons and not because there is a Muslim
State on the north-western Frontier that an invasion
will not occur.

It is not only against the Muslim rulers of India that other Muslims
have led expeditions or vice versa. Musalmans have fought amongst
themselves for power, for throne, and for kingdom. Islam, in spite of
its teaching that all differences of race and country should disappear
the moment people adopt it, has not succeeded in preventing these
wars between Muslim and Muslim any more than Christianity has
succeeded in outlawing war even among Christians. Not to go very
far into past history, we know that the Arabs did not hesitate to
fight the Turks during the First World War. When the Muslims of
Hindustan were doing their best to help the Sultan of Turkey to
maintain his power and prestige as Khalifa of the Musalmans, the
Arabs were revolting against him. In Persia, Raza Shah Pahlavi,
who is justly regarded as the maker of modern Persia, has had to
vacate his throne and spend his last days in exile on account of the
intrigues and machinations of European powers helped and supported
by Muslims of his own country. Between the First Great War and
the Second, Afghanistan has seen at least two revolutions—King
Amanullah being replaced by Bachchasakka and Bachchasakka being
replaced by Nadir Shah—all Muslims undoubtedly. Even today an
attempt is being made to bring nearer to each other the various Arab
States leaving alone the Turks, the Persians and the Afghans. Islam
has thus not been able to knit together all Muslims of different races
and nationalities or even of the same country and while one hopes
that not only Muslims but all nations will have the good sense and
intelligence to learn to live together without war and bloodshed, it
is no use pretending that Muslim States are not capable of entering
upon an adventure of war against one another.

This is so far as invasion from the north-west is concerned. There
is not even this excuse available as regards the eastern frontier
which is now no less exposed than the north-western frontier. The
only effect of the creation of an independent Muslim State on the
east will be to deprive non-Muslim India of its natural defence
without any corresponding gain to the Muslim state of the sort
pleaded in favour of the north-western Muslim zone.

The argument, such as it is, is applicable only to the north-western Muslim zone. The very reason that it is put forward as an argument in favour of easing the problem of defence makes the question of defence of the non-Muslim zone more difficult. If there is religious and political fervour for *jehad* against a non-Muslim State of India, the same will become intensified by the creation of a Muslim State within the natural boundaries of India, when the strong natural defence offered by the mountains on the north-west of India is given up by non-Muslim India and it is left to defend its territory as best it can without the aid of such natural barriers. If there is any basis for this argument in favour of Pakistan, the non-Muslims will be perfectly justified in apprehending, particularly after the declarations of the long-range objectives of the establishment of Pakistan mentioned earlier, that the proposal to deprive them of the natural defence of the country has a sinister motive behind it, and this may induce them not to agree to a partition in any case.

There may, however, be much to be said in favour of Dr Ambedkar's thesis that 'a safe army is better than safe border.'[7]

The question of defence has to be considered in the light of the latest developments in the nature and form of armaments and the technique of strategy rendered necessary thereby. But even in view of the old technique there will be a considerable sea-coast left to be defended by the Muslim State both in the north-west and in the eastern zone, apart from the enormous sea-coast left to be defended by the rest of India. All this at once raises the question of the resources of the Muslim and non-Muslim States for purposes of defence. They will both have to provide not only for defence against aggressors from outside India but also as between the Muslim and non-Muslim States within the present boundaries of India. It does not require any elaborate calculation to show that in case of Partition while the resources of both the Muslim and non-Muslim States will be considerably reduced, their defence requirements will enormously increase and it may well be that each by itself will find itself so crippled as to render effective defence beyond the means of any without unbearable hardship to the people at large inhabiting each zone. We have seen in the chapters on finance and industrial resources the position of the

---

[7] Dr B.R. Ambedkar, *Thoughts on Pakistan*, p. 95.

Muslim and non-Muslim States, and it can be safely asserted that both in respect of finance and industrial resources, while considerably crippled by separation, the non-Muslim zone will be in a better and stronger position as compared with the Muslim States. The Muslim States will have neither the finance nor the material resources to equip themselves for defence. In any case 'it is a matter of vital importance to all inhabitants of India that her defences do not become disorganized and many-sided, too elaborate to be effective and too expensive to be maintained; her position in the international world must be fully assured.'[8]

There is another aspect of the question of defence to which reference is made by Professor Coupland which has to be further considered particularly by the protagonists of Pakistan. If independent Muslim and non-Muslim States are established, each will undoubtedly maintain its own army, navy and air-force, which will be composed naturally of its own nationals. This will have the effect of considerably changing the composition of the personnel of the army. Dr Ambedkar has pointed out that in 1856 just before the Mutiny, the Indian infantry comprised not less than 90 per cent of its men from north-east India, UP and Bihar and less than 10 per cent from the north-western zone. In 1858 just after, the Mutiny and as the result of change of policy due to it, the position was completely altered and the army consisted of 47 per cent from the north-western zone, 6 per cent from Nepal, Garhwal and Kumaon, and 47 per cent from north-east India, UP and Bihar. 'The distinction between martial and non-martial classes which was put forth for the first time in 1879 as a matter of principle and which was later on insisted upon as a matter of serious consideration by Lord Roberts and recognized by Lord Kitchener as a principle governing recruitment of the Indian Army had nothing to do with the origin of this preponderance of the men of the north-west in the Indian Army.' It had resulted by 1930 in increasing the percentage of men from the north-western zone to 58.5, from Nepal, Garhwal and Kumaon to 22, and reducing that of men from the north-east, UP and Bihar to n, the remaining being contributed by south India, 5.5 per cent and by Burma, 3 per cent.[9]

[8] Sultan Ahmad, *The Treaty* . . ., p. 87.
[9] Ambedkar, *Thoughts on Pakistan*, p. 70.

Table LI below taken from Dr Ambedkar's book shows in an unmistakable manner the fact that the communal composition of the Indian Army has been undergoing a profound change.

'The figures show a phenomenal rise in the strength of the Punjabi Musalman and the Pathan. They also show a substantial reduction of the Sikhs from the first to the third place; by the degradation of the Rajputs to the fourth place and by the closing of the ranks to the UP Brahmins, the Madrasi Musalmans and the Tamilians.'[10]

Analysing the figures relating to the communal composition of the Indian Army in 1930, Dr Ambedkar comes to the conclusion that the Musalmans were 36 per cent of the infantry, if we exclude the Gurkhas from the total, or 30 per cent if we include them, and they were 30 per cent of the Indian cavalry. With the exception of a negligible proportion of per cent of the infantry that came from the neighbourhood of Delhi, all the remaining Musalmans

TABLE LI

Changes in the Communal Composition of the Indian Army

Area and Communities	Percentage in 1914	Percentage in 1918	Percentage in 1919	Percentage in 1930
I The Punjab and				
NWFP and Kashmir	47.0	46.5	46.0	58.6
1 Sikhs	19.2	17.4	15.4	13.58
2 Punjabi Muslims	11.1	11.3	12.4	22.6
3 Pathans	6.2	5.42	4.54	6.35
II Nepal, Kumaon				
Garhwal	15.0	16.6	12.2	16.4
Gurkhas	13.1	16.6	12.2	16.4
III Upper India	22.0	22.7	25.5	11.0
1 UP Rajputs	6.4	6.8	7.7	2.55
2 Hindustani Musalmans	4.1	3.42	4.45	Nil
3 Brahmins	1.8	1.86	2.5	Nil
IV South India	16.0	11.9	12.0	5.5
1 Marathas	4.9	3.85	3.7	5.33
2 Madrasi Musalmans	3.5	2.71	2.13	Nil
3 Tamils	2.5	2.0	1.67	Nil
V Burmans	Nil	Negligible	1.7	3.0

[10] Ibid., p. 75.

in the infantry and over 19 per cent of the entire cavalry came from the Punjab and NWFP.[11] The figures for subsequent years were not disclosed by the Government in spite of several attempts made by the members of the Central Assembly to get them in answer to questions. It was therefore with good reason that Sir Sikandar Hayat Khan as a Punjabi Musalman in the outlines of a scheme of Indian federation insisted that the composition of the Indian Army as on January 1937, shall not be altered and in case of reduction, the communal proportion shall be maintained subject to relaxation only in case of war or other emergency. Besides the Musalmans, the Sikhs who constituted 13.58 per cent of the army in 1930 also came from the Punjab. One immediate and inevitable result of separation will be the demobilization of this large percentage of the personnel of the Indian Army from the army of the non-Muslim zone, leaving the Muslim State to absorb them, if it can, in its own army. It is true that in view of the insistent demand from all parts of India to do away with the artificial distinction between the martial and non-martial classes, which as we have seen was based on expediency—more as a reward to the Punjab and a punishment to the UP and Bihar for the part played by the residents of those areas in the Mutiny than on any real or historical grounds, no national government will be able to maintain the proportions mentioned above and will have to ensure a fairer distribution as between the provinces, even if no division takes place. Even so the break will not be so sudden or extensive as in the case of Partition and the establishment of independent states. Professor Coupland has said that even a reduction of the Muslim proportion in the army which in 1939 was more than one-third and is now 30.8 per cent, to less than 25 per cent would affect the standard of living in the Punjab which owes so much to the pay and pensions of Punjabi troops.[12] How much worse the situation will be when this avenue of employment in the Hindustan army is entirely closed on account of separation can well be imagined.

It may be argued that those who are now employed in the Indian Army will be employed in the army of the separated Muslim State. This may happen, although it is difficult, if not impossible, for the small Muslim State to maintain an army on a scale big

[11] Ibid., p. 76.
[12] Coupland, *The Future of India*, p. 77.

enough to employ the whole demobilized personnel. But even if it does employ them all, the entire cost will have to be raised by the Muslim State from among its own people without any contribution from the rest of India. The non-Muslim zone will stand to gain what the Muslim zone will lose, as the amount—whatever it may be—that will be spent by the former on its army will be spent among the people who will contribute the revenue.

(5) By Partition and only by Partition, it is said, can Indian Muslims acquire the power of economic self-determination. There are two aspects of the economic question. One relates to the loaves and fishes of office. The Muslim zones, if converted into independent States, can hardly improve the position of the Musalmans in this respect in those areas. The percentage of public employment is already fixed for the various communities, and if it is considered inequitable or unjust in any particular it can be revised. But unless it is intended that non-Muslims shall be practically excluded from State employment or reduced to a position of inferiority on account merely of their religion, it is difficult to understand how their proportion could be much altered. Besides, it should be remembered that it is in respect of employment by the State that any reciprocity between Muslims and non-Muslims in their respective states can best be given effect to without raising serious international complications. With their larger proportion in the population in the Muslim States, the non-Muslims will always be in a stronger position than the Muslims in non-Muslim States. It will be difficult, if not impossible, for Muslims in non-Muslim States, 'with a population of 1 to 13 per cent of Muslims, to claim the same proportion or weightage in services as the non-Muslims in the Muslim States with their population ranging between 25 and 48 per cent. The result is bound to be a reduction in the percentage of Muslim employees in the non-Muslim States without a corresponding reduction in the number of non-Muslim employees in the Muslim States on the basis of fairness and reciprocity. Any agreement as regards weightage will be open to revision in case of separation, for the simple reason that such agreement did not contemplate separation, and what may be conceded to members of the same State

cannot and need not be conceded in case of out and out
separation. The Muslims in Hindustan thus stand to lose
in respect of State employment without any corresponding
gain to Muslims in the Muslim States, even if it be assumed
that larger employment to Muslims in the Muslim States
will be any consolation or economic advantage to Muslims
in Hindustan in the face of the loss of employment.

The second aspect relates to economic improvement by industrial
expansion. Now it cannot be asserted that the dominant position,
which non-Muslims are said to occupy in industry in India is due to
any political advantage that they have enjoyed. Whatever political
power there is or has been in the country has been enjoyed neither
by Hindus nor by Muslims but by the British, and if Hindus have
attained a stronger position than Muslims, it is not due to their
political dominance, which they have never enjoyed, but to their
enterprise. If economic superiority were due to political dominance
determined by their proportion in their population, the Parsis
would be nowhere in the picture, as they form an infinitesimal
percentage of the population of India. Yet they hold and occupy
a position which is inferior to none, if not superior even to that
of the Hindus. No one grudges them their prosperity and they
have never complained of being suppressed by the vast ocean of
humanity of India which is not Parsi. There is therefore no point
in saying that Hindus hold a dominant position. They can be
reduced or degraded from that position only if the Muslim state
uses its political power communally and not justly and fairly as
among its nationals. In other words they cannot lose their position
unless they are discriminated against in the Muslim state. If that
is the intention of the protagonists of Pakistan—and there can
be no other if what is claimed in favour of Partition is to be
accepted as giving the shape of things to come—they should not
expect non-Muslims to accept that situation. The position would
be different, of course, if Hindus had political power and had used
it to their own advantage and to the detriment of Muslims. But as
stated above they have never enjoyed any power in the Centre and
whatever power they enjoyed in the provinces for a short period
of twenty-seven months has been enjoyed by the Muslims in the
Pakistan provinces for at least eight years, without interruption
and with the best of goodwill on the part of the British. It is

also worth remembering in this connection that some Hindus and Sikhs of the Punjab have established their industrial concerns even outside the Punjab by sheer dint of their ability and enterprise. The Hindus of Rajputana, of Kathiawar and Gujarat and of Chettinad, like the Memons and Khojas among Musalmans, constitute the great commercial and industrial community in India. They have not attained their position by reason of any political dominance. Other Musalmans are not likely to improve their position unless they intend to suppress all others and this will hardly be fair to their non-Muslim nationals in the Muslim independent States.

III ARGUMENTS AGAINST PARTITION

The grounds on which separation is claimed are thus either unsubstantial or such as are not likely to be accepted as a just and fair basis for separation. On the other hand, there are very substantial reasons against separation.

We may shortly indicate some of them here.

(1)   The days of small independent States are numbered if not gone already. Recent experience has shown that no small state can preserve its independence. Even large States are hard put to it to preserve it. The natural tendency is in favour of combinations of States. Something in the nature of a Super-State even above the bigger States is not beyond the range of practical politics today. It would therefore be flying in the face of world forces to reduce the size and strength of India and establish in its stead a number of small States. It may well be that the spirit of separation may not end with the Partition of the Muslim zones and once it begins to operate it may lead to a situation in which India may have to be cut up not only into Muslim and non-Muslim States but even the Muslim and non-Muslim States may be cut up into several smaller States apart from the States of the Princes. This will make India, if it ever attains independence after being thus cut up into numerous small principalities, a house divided against itself and exposed to intrigues by foreign powers. As a result, all its component independent States will be weak, unable to protect themselves against foreign aggression, and liable to be played against one another.

(2)   The national resources of the country as a whole can be much better utilized to the benefit of all, if there is mutual accommodation and agreed joint action, which will become impossible in case of independent States. The mere fact that two States are independent puts up a barrier against such mutual accommodation and joint action between them. Planning on a large scale becomes impossible in case of small states, all of which are not equally well endowed by nature and most of which have to be dependent on others for some very important article or other absolutely necessary for the welfare and protection of a modern state. The larger the area, the greater the variety, the wider the distribution of natural resources—agricultural, mineral and power-producing—the better the chances of a planned economy. India will have lost this advantage as a result of division, and in this respect the Muslim States on the north-west and east will be the worst sufferers, as has been indicated elsewhere in this book. We have seen how the Muslim states will not have the resources to run the administration and meet the cost of defence.

(3)   The crying need of India today is that the State should spend more and more on the nation-building departments. India has suffered immeasurably in the past under the British government which has regarded itself more as a police state than anything else, neglecting and starving the nation-building departments. The whole country has a great lee-way to make up and the Muslim States will be no exception to this. Division of the country will inevitably lead to reduction of resources and make it difficult for each of the Muslim and non-Muslim zones to meet this growing demand.

(4)   The modern tendency even in Muslim countries is to base politics and economics more and more on other considerations than religion. Whatever the Muslim League and the protagonists of Pakistan may say, there is no doubt that the Muslim States of the world today are becoming—if they have not become already—secular States, just like the Christian countries of Europe. The question is whether Indian Muslims will be able to turn the tide of events and establish and maintain the state on any other basis in India.

(5) It is well known that the proposal for Partition has aroused strong opposition from all non-Muslims and also from Muslims. It is not for me to say whether the Muslim League or those other groups like the Jamiat-ul-Ulema, the Jamiat-ul-Mominin, the Ahrars, the Nationalist Muslim organizations, the All-India Shia Conference and others represent the majority of Muslims. The fact remains that these latter have expressed their opposition to separation. Whatever the position may be so far as Muslims are concerned, the Hindus and the Sikhs have declared their unequivocal determination to resist Partition. This is bound to become more pronounced and more bitter with the persistence with which the proposal for division is pressed. It is difficult to forecast what shape this conflict may take in the future. One thing is certain: Partition is not likely to be attained with the goodwill of those most concerned, and this ill will is bound to persist on both sides, even if the proposal succeeds, even after the separation is effected. Distrust which is the basis of the proposal is bound to grow and any hope that after separation things will settle down and the independent States will soon become friendly will have been built on sand. The chances are that bitterness and distrust will make mutual accommodation more difficult and necessitate the maintenance of protection forces on both sides. Economic warfare is not beyond the range of possibility, even if nothing worse happens.

(6) All this is bound to make the position of minorities in the independent States infinitely worse. As a result of this conflict between the majorities in the Muslim and non-Muslim zones they will have lost what sympathy and goodwill they should have and their position will have become far worse than what is it today. For the minorities it will veritably be a case of jumping from the frying pan into the fire. The non-Muslim minorities will have the situation forced upon them, if the proposal succeeds. But the Muslim minority will have chosen it, worked for it and extorted it from the non-Muslims and could not blame any one else for it.

Further, as explained elsewhere, the minorities in the Muslim States will be better able, on account of their numbers and

PART VI

ALTERNATIVES TO PAKISTAN

THIRTY-FIVE

THE CRIPPS PROPOSAL

Since the Muslim League passed the Pakistan Resolution at its Lahore session in March 1940, various schemes have been put forward with a view to meeting the legitimate desires of the Muslims of India. These may be treated as alternatives to Pakistan.

The first and foremost place should be given to the Draft Declaration of the British War Cabinet which has become popularly known as the Cripps proposal on account of its being first made known to India by Sir Stafford Cripps. We are concerned here only with that part of it which deals with the nature of the Indian Union and the agency for drawing up a Constitution for it, and not with the *ad interim* arrangement proposed in it nor with the negotiations which Sir Stafford Cripps carried on and the ultimate outcome thereof. The Draft Declaration was intended 'to lay down in precise and clear terms the steps which they [His Majesty's Government] propose shall be taken for the earliest possible realization of Self-Government in India. The object is the creation of a new Indian Union which shall constitute a Dominion, associated with the United Kingdom and the other Dominions by a common allegiance to the Crown, but equal to them in every respect, in no way subordinate in any respect of its domestic or external affairs.' 'Immediately upon the cessation of hostilities steps shall be taken to set up in India, in the manner described hereafter, an elected body charged with the task of framing a new Constitution for India,' with provision 'for the participation of the Indian States in the Constitution Making Body', and 'His Majesty's Government undertake to accept and implement forthwith the Constitution so framed subject only to:

(i)   the right of any Province of British India that is not prepared to accept the new Constitution to retain its present constitutional position, provision being made for its subsequent accession if it so decides. With such non-acceding

      Provinces, should they so desire, His Majesty's Government will be prepared to agree upon a new Constitution, giving them the same full status as the Indian Union, and arrived at by a procedure analogous to that here laid down.

(ii)   the signing of a Treaty which shall be negotiated between His Majesty's Government and the Constitution-making body covering all necessary matters arising out of the complete transfer of responsibility from British to Indian hands and for the protection of racial and religious minorities; but will not impose any restriction on the power of the Indian Union to decide in the future its relation to the other Member States of the British Commonwealth. The Constitution-making body shall be composed as follows unless the leaders of Indian opinion in the principal communities agree upon some other form before the end of hostilities.

'Immediately upon the result being known of the provincial elections which will be necessary at the end of hostilities, the entire membership of the Lower Houses of the Provincial Legislatures shall, as a single electoral college, proceed to the election of the Constitution-making body by the system of proportional representation. This new body shall be in number about one-tenth of the number of the electoral college. Indian States shall be invited to appoint representatives in the same proportion to their total population as in the case of the representatives of British India as a whole, and with the same powers as the British Indian members.'

It will appear from the summary given above that the British government proposed that steps should be taken on the cessation of hostilities to create a new Indian Union, which would have the full status of a dominion with the power to secede, if it so chose, from the British Commonwealth. The new Constitution was to be framed by a Constitution-making body which was to be elected by the method of proportional representation by an electoral college consisting of all the members of the Lower Houses of the Provincial Legislatures for which fresh elections would have been held. It would also have representatives appointed by the Indian States who would bear the same proportion to the provincial representation as their population bears to the population of the provinces. The Constitution framed by the Constitution-making body would be

accepted and implemented by the British Government subject
to the proviso that any province which was not prepared to
accept the new Constitution would be free not to accede to the
Union and would be entitled to frame a Constitution of its own
and to have the same status as the Indian Union. There would
be a treaty negotiated between the British government and the
Constitution-making body covering all matters arising out of a
transfer of responsibility and the protection of racial and religious
minorities. It did not start with separate independent states but
with an Indian Union, leaving it to any province which did not
accept the Constitution not to accede to the Union and to have the
same status vis-à-vis the British Government as the Indian Union.
In the words of Professor Coupland, 'the British Government
had clearly stated its objective as a new Indian Union to form a
Dominion under a new constitution for India. No one can read
the Draft Declaration without recognizing that the non-adherence
provisions are intended only as a means of preventing in the
last resort a break-down of the whole scheme for setting India
free.'[1] It was principally for this reason that the Muslim League
rejected the Draft Declaration in that it did not contain a definite
pronouncement in favour of Partition, and while it recognized
Pakistan by implication, it relegated the creation of more than
one Union to the realm of remote possibility.

In his Presidential address at the Allahabad Session of the All-
India Muslim League on 4 April 1942, and in a statement at a
Press Conference on 13 April 1942, Mr Jinnah was quite clear
and rejected the scheme on the grounds:

(i)   that its main objective was the creation of a new Indian
        Union; the alleged power of the minority in the matter of
        secession suggested in the document was illusory;
(ii)   that the Constitution-making body would be a sovereign
        body, elected from amongst the members of the eleven
        Assemblies meeting together as one college by means
        of proportional representation, not separate electorates.
        Musalmans even by separate representation would not be
        more than 25 per cent in it but by the system of proportional
        representation they might be less in number; its decisions

[1] R. Coupland, *Indian Politics*. 1936–42, p. 276.

would be taken by a bare majority and so it was a dead certainty that from it would emerge a Constitution for an All-India Union;

(iii) that the most vital point was as to how a province or provinces would exercise their right not to accede— that if a province in the Legislative Assembly of the province was in favour of accession by 60 per cent votes, then that would be the end of it; but if they got 59 per cent and the minority happened to be 41 per cent, then there would be a plebiscite of the people of the province. Thus the entity and integrity of the Muslim nation had not been recognized; territorial entity of the provinces which are mere accidents of British policy was overemphasized and the right of national self-determination of Muslims as distinguished from that of the two nations put together was not unequivocally recognized. In the Legislative Assemblies of the Punjab and Bengal—the two largest Muslim majority provinces, the Muslims were not in a majority and the Muslims would be at the mercy of the Hindu minority; and in the NWFP and Sind the weightage given to non-Muslims would make it extremely difficult for Muslims to realize their goal.

The scheme was thus not acceptable because Pakistan was not conceded unequivocally and the right of Muslim self-determination was denied, although the recognition given to the principle of Partition was much appreciated.[2]

[2] *Some Recent Speeches and Writings of Mr Jinnah*, pp. 350–64.

THIRTY-SIX

PROFESSOR COUPLAND'S REGIONAL SCHEME

Professor Reginald Coupland in *The Future of India* has put forward a scheme based on what he calls Regionalism. He takes the idea of Regionalism from the scheme of Indian Federation by Sir Sikandar Hayat Khan and adopts the scheme of regional delimitation conceived by Mr M.W.M. Yeatts, Census Commissioner of India, and advocated in his Introduction to the Census of India, 1941, for a fifty-year plan for the development of India's water-power resources. According to this scheme, northern India should be delimited into three river basins:

(i)   the Indus basin stretching from Kashmir to Karachi (corresponding in political terms to Pakistan),

(ii) the basins of the Ganges and the Jamuna between the Punjab and Bengal (corresponding to Hindustan), and

(iii) the basin of the Ganges and the Brahmaputra between Bihar and the eastern frontier (corresponding to north-east India). The bisection of the Ganges basin accords with the physical facts. Soon after the Ganges bends southwards on the eastern border of Bihar to meet the Brahmaputra some 150 miles away, the country begins to change its character. It is no longer the country of the northern plain; it is the country of the Great Delta.'[1]

(iv) The fourth region corresponds roughly to the Great Peninsula. According to Professor Coupland, regional division by river basins corresponds with economic needs. The possibilities of economic welfare largely depend on the proper use of its vast water-power. Hydroelectric installations and full utilization of the rivers demand a long-range plan which cannot be carried out within separate areas or with separate resources of provinces, and needs super-provincial

[1] R. Coupland, *The Future of India*, p. 120.

TABLE LII

Population by Communities in Professor Coupland's Regions

(In millions)

Name of Region of British India	Provinces of British India	Indian States	Area — Including Indian States in 1000 sq. miles	Area — Excluding Indian States in 1000 sq. miles	Population including Indian States — Hindus	Muslims	Tribes	Total	Population excluding Indian States — Hindus	Muslims	Tribes	Total	Proportion of Population including Indian States — Hindus	Muslims	Others	Proportion of Population excluding Indian States — Hindus	Muslims	Others
Indus	NWFP	Kashmir	569.73	...	...	...	...	...	9.38	...	...	...	34.8	...	...	25.2	...	...
	Punjab	NW Frontier Agencies and States	...	218.35	21.34	...	...	...	...	22.75	...	...	...	52.0	...	...	61.3	...
	British Baluchistan	Punjab States and Hill States	...	...	...	31.90	...	...	...	...	0.13	37.08	...	...	13.2	...	...	13.5
	Sind	Baluchistan States	...	...	...	...	1.22	61.25	...	...	...	...	...	...	...	...	...	...
	Ajmer Merwara	Rajputana except Gwalior	...	...	...	...	...	...	...	...	...	...	...	...	...	...	...	...
	United Provinces	UP States, Gwalior	311.80	...	...	...	...	...	...	...	...	...	...	...	...	...	...	...
Ganges	Orissa	Orissa States	208.20	208.20	91.89	...	...	...	79.15	13.29	...	...	78.7	12.0	...	79.0	13.8	...
	Bihar	Central India States East of Gwalior	...	...	...	14.03	...	...	...	...	7.07	100.09	...	...	9.3	...	...	7.8
	Orissa	Chhattisgarh States except (a) below	...	...	...	...	9.81	116.55	...	...	...	...	...	...	...	...	...	...

(contd.)

	States from Rajputana, (a) Bharatpur, Byridi, Dholpur, Karanli, Ketah													
Delta	Bengal	Bengal States 156.96	132.39	...	...	...	29.97	36.45	...	...	41.7	50.1	41.5	51.6	...
	Assam	Assam States	30.66	...	...	...	...	...	...	...	...	50.1	...	51.6	...
	Sikkim		...	36.85	5.59	73.50	...	4.37	70.51	...	...	8.2	...	...	6.9
Deccan	Madras Bombay CP and Berar	Western India 539.25 States, Central India	302.79	...	...	...	72.42	6.61	...	...	80.5	...	83.0	...	...
	Coorg	States West and South of Gwalior, Gujarat	110.44	11.22	...	...	...	...	5.13	87.18	...	11.3	...	7.5	9.5
	Panth Piploda	States, Baroda States from Rajputana (b) Banewara, Danta Dungarpur, Palanpur States from Chhattisgarh (c) Bastar Chikhidan, Kanker, Kawardha, Khairagarh, Nandgaon	...	...	8.77	136.82	...	...	...	...	...	8.2	...	...	...

co-ordination and co-operation, and involves cost and
control which can be produced only on a regional basis.
India might be divided on this basis into four regions as
shown in Table LII.

In calculating the proportion the learned Professor has made a
small arithmetical error and I have put down the correct figure
in this Table arrived at on the basis of the figures of population
given by him, which are quoted in the two Population columns.

Regionalism differs, according to the Professor, on the one hand
from Partition and on the other from Federation. It preserves the
unity of India and assumes the establishment of an inter-regional
Centre, but a Centre of a new kind which would possess only
those minimum powers which it must possess if the unity of India
is to be preserved at all and it would exercise those powers not
on the direct authority of an all-India electorate but as the joint
instrument or agent of regions.

The minimum powers which any Indian Centre must possess
would be those which reflect the unity of India as seen from
abroad, as follows.

(i)   Foreign affairs and defence,
(ii)   External trade or tariff policy, and
(iii) Currency. Defence means the maintenance and control of
       only those armed forces including the air force and navy
       which are required for the defence of India against aggression
       from without.

The control of emigration and immigration as also naturalization
are linked with foreign affairs and must be central subjects, but
that would not preclude a region, if it so desired, from establishing
a second nationality of its own.

The cost of staffing the Centre, of a diplomatic service, of
collecting customs and so forth would not be great. The only
heavy item of expenditure would be defence, and the cost of
Indian defence before the present war was more or less evenly
balanced by the yield of customs revenue. It would be a matter
for consideration whether the Centre should be authorized to levy
direct taxation to meet a deficit or whether it should be met by
contributions from the regions on a basis fixed in the Constitution.
Similar constitutional provision might be made for the distribution
of a potential surplus among the regions.

To these necessary minimum central subjects, it might be more convenient and economical to add communications including railways, air services, coastal sea traffic, wireless, telephone, telegraph and possibly postal services; but in normal times they are not a positive necessity for the inter-regional Centre and the assumption of their control by the Centre in war time might be provided for in an emergency clause in the Constitution. Some other subjects also might more conveniently and economically be under Central control, such as census, scientific survey; also industrial development, regulation of mines and oil-fields, control of major ports and navigation, fire-arms, explosives, etc.; but these lend themselves to regional decentralization. There may be a provision for central legislation by request in regard to matters which require uniformity, which means that such central legislation will only be by permission of the regions.

An inter-regional Union might be described as a loose federation but it must be borne in mind that Regionalism introduces a new idea or new logical sequence. It first divides India into a number of great States which could be wholly independent but they decide to share their power for certain common purposes. All existing federations are so devised as to combine the principle of national unity with the principle of local autonomy. But there is no such dual principle in Regionalism. The Centre is a purely inter-regional institution. It would be regarded as an agency: the members of its executive and legislature would act as agents of their Regions. It will differ, however, from a Confederacy which is only a league, only a kind of alliance, which possesses no power or authority of its own, and whose decisions on which the units are agreed must be executed by the units at their expense. The inter-regional Centre on the other hand would be a government, give its own orders to its own soldiers and officials and pay its own way. In fact it would occupy a middle position—it would be more than a Confederacy but less than a normal federation.

The legislature of the inter-regional Centre unlike the federal Legislature contemplated by the Act of 1935 will not reflect the strength and aspiration of Indian nationalism for the simple reason that the regional idea recognizes that the ideal of a single Indian nationhood has not been attained. It would reflect the separate nationalisms of the regions represented in it. The number of its members should therefore be the same from each region and should not exceed the minimum required to give adequate representation to its component units. This should be so regardless of the size of the regions and regardless of their population. The members should derive their authority from and be responsible to their regions and they might be elected by the regional legislatures and on a system devised to secure that the provinces and States were fairly represented. In case all or some of the provinces and States comprised in the Ganges Basin and Deccan regions do not agree to join regions, and desire to continue as provinces and States, then it would be necessary so to devise their representation at the inter-regional Centre that the number of their representatives should be the same as if the non-regional provinces had in fact combined in regions. In other words, the two Muslim regions—the Indus Basin and the Delta regions will have the same number of representatives in the inter-regional central legislature as the Ganges Basin and Deccan regions, irrespective of the fact whether the latter have or have not formed themselves into regions.

The scope of the Centre being limited to the minimal three subjects and in view of the narrow field of business, four departmental ministers with one or two without portfolio would form the Cabinet. There should be a statutory coalition government and up to a point the precedent of the Swiss Constitution would seem applicable. The Prime Minister and his colleagues might be elected by the Legislative Council to hold office for the same term of years as the Council. They would have to depend, like the Swiss Executive, on securing a majority in the Council to carry a legislation but not be responsible to the Council for their administration from day to day. On the Swiss model there should be an even distribution of executive posts among the regions—at least one post and not more than two to be allotted to each region. The provinces not constituting regions should be grouped as regions for this purpose also. The Prime Minister should be alternately a Hindu and a Muslim.

The powers of a Supreme Court would be similar to those of the existing Federal Court to interpret the law of the Constitution. It should be composed of one Judge from each region, non-regional provinces being grouped as a region for this purpose also.

How would this new system affect the communal problem? Professor Coupland thinks that the answer depends on the kind of communal balance established at the Centre. Under the regional system there would be no national element in the process of the election of the inter-regional legislature. The members would represent the regions and the regions only. They would in fact be delegates or agents of the regions under mandate from their governments and Legislatures and would have to vote accordingly. Thus the communal balance in the Central Legislature would not be a balance between the opinions of individual members or parties but a balance between the policies of the regions. This would give an opportunity to the representatives of the two major communities of working together day by day in the common service of India, and a time might come when Hindus and Muslims, while keeping their different characteristics as different Swiss or Canadian nationalities keep theirs, might become conscious of an Indian nationhood as real as that of Switzerland or Canada. He would therefore advise Hindus to accept a Union on any terms now so that it might become ultimately possible. His appeal to the Muslims is that although his scheme does not concede full independence to the Muslim States it meets their claim on every other point and should therefore be accepted by them. It accepts the two-nations principle. It establishes the Indian Muslim nation in a national State or States. It recognizes that those States, whatever their size or population, are equal in status with the Hindu States, or groups of provinces. It does not violate their independence, but it enables them, by means of their own chosen agents, to share their powers in a minimal field with other States.

I have outlined Professor Coupland's regional scheme in his own words as far as possible. There can be no doubt, as has been stated by the learned author himself, that it proceeds on the basis that there are two nations in India and that an Indian nation does not exist. He proceeds on this assumption to meet the Muslim League's claim for Partition as far as he can go. And in doing this he has pressed into service Regionalism founded on geographical and economic unity to make out a case for autonomous Muslim States based on distribution of religious and communal population. In the words of Dr Radha Kamal Mukerjee, 'it is a grievous error in agricultural geography that underlies Professor Coupland's identification of regional division on economic principles with political demarcation of the Muslim homeland.'[2]

[2] Dr Radha Kamal Mukerjee, *An Economist Looks at Pakistan*, p. 12.

The scheme is further open to the very serious objection that it does not consistently and logically follow even Regionalism. He admits that a considerable portion of the Punjab falls really within the Ganges Basin but he has nevertheless included it in the Indus Basin. There is no geographical reason which can justify the tacking to this region of nearly three-fourths of Rajputana, which, in the words of the Professor, 'has a marked physical and ethical character of its own.' And if for any reason this territory is to be joined to the Indus River Basin, there appears to be no reason why the four southern States which have no affinities with Gujarat should be joined with Gujarat in one Region and why Gujarat itself or at any rate its northern half, which is watered in a great part by rivers arising in the Aravalli Hills and the heavy rains there, should not be allotted to this region and should be relegated to the Deccan. Coming to the Ganges Basin we find that it is proposed to be formed equally arbitrarily out of territories cut out or tacked on in complete disregard of geographical and physical considerations. It is well known that many of the rivers which rise in the Himalayas have their source and catchment areas outside British territories and considerable difficulty is experienced in British provinces in dealing with them. The River Kosi which is responsible for so much havoc in north Bihar is one such and among others may be mentioned the Bagmati and the other rivers which sometimes cause floods and havoc in the districts of Muzaffarpur and Darbhanga. The Sone and the Narbada have their source in the Amarkantak hills but they flow in opposite directions from the watershed. Heavy rains in the Amarkantak cause devastating floods in regions so far apart from one another as the districts of Shahabad and Patna and sometimes also Saran in Bihar and the districts of Jabalpur, Hoshangabad and further down in the CP, and also in parts of Gujarat.

Professor Coupland has mentioned at great length the Tennessee Valley Authority scheme of the USA and has suggested his river basins on its analogy. He has, however, ignored one factor which is essential for the success of any such scheme. You cannot cut up rivers arbitrarily and take them in parts for any scheme of development of the areas washed by their waters. The entire length of the river comprising its source, catchment and downward course right to the point where it joins either some other river or the sea has to be taken together. The Professor arbitrarily cuts the Ganges at a point where it takes a southward bend. If the appearance of the country and the nature of its soil are considered there is nothing to distinguish the northern portion of Bihar—the north-western and northern portion of Champaran and the northern portion of the districts of Muzaffarpur, Darbhanga, Monghyr, Bhagalpur and Purnea—from the northern districts of Bengal and practically the whole of the Assam Valley. Even if we cut the Ganges into two at the point suggested by the Professor, we have one branch of the Ganges known as Bhagirathi and later as the Hoogly which may be taken as washing the western districts of Bengal which go more with the districts of Bihar than with the land washed by the Meghna and the Padma in the east. Besides, there is the Damodar flowing from Chhota Nagpur through the districts of western Bengal where it causes such serious devastation on account of its floods. While these lines are being written a Conference is meeting under a member of the Government of India where representatives of the governments of Bihar and Bengal are considering what should be done to stop the devastation. The Regionalism of Professor Coupland and the consequent division would require some *ad hoc* arrangement between the Ganges Basin and the Delta to deal with this problem and will not by itself be able to solve it. The fact is that the division which the Professor suggests is wholly arbitrary and is in fact a travesty of Regionalism, which if applied in a reasonable and natural manner, will constitute altogether different divisions and will not be able to match two Muslim zones against the rest of India on a footing of equality, which appears to be the sole object of the Professor in dividing the country into four regions.

This becomes still more apparent when we consider the fourth region which covers the whole of the country minus the territories comprised in the three regions of the north. If this vast tract of country about 1000 miles in length and about half of that in breadth can be made into one region, there is no reason why the country as a whole should not be treated as one region except that division into four Regions and no more or no less is required to serve the objective of matching two Muslim zones, which can under no circumstances be more than two, against two non-Muslim zones. Professor Coupland knows that there is no excuse of even a river basin for the demarcation of the Deccan region which is frankly and obviously a conglomeration of the provinces and States which are left out after creating the other three regions.

The learned Professor has not taken into consideration any other matter in creating his regions. Professor Radha Kamal Mukerjee has pointed out that 'the notion of Regionalism in Regional Sociology stands for the unity and solidarity that a region's way of living, occupation, language, folk tradition and culture represent.' 'It is a travesty of the idea of Regionalism to discard linguistic and cultural facts.'[3] If India is not a nation because of these linguistic and cultural differences as prevalent in different parts of it, then each of the regions will be an India in miniature with all these differences, and if the regions with all their internal differences are expected to be able to carry on, there is no reason why India as a whole should not be able to carry on. In fact Professor Coupland recognizes that his division into regions not being based on any intelligible principle, the units within a region may not agree to join that region. He expects that the units of the Indus and Delta regions will have no difficulty in coalescing into regions but he anticipates difficulty in the Ganges Basin and the Deccan region. Once this difficulty appears, the matching of two Muslim against two non-Muslim regions becomes impossible. But nothing daunted, the Professor proposes that the units of the latter two regions should be treated as constituting the two regions, for the purpose of their representation in the inter-regional Centre irrespective of the fact whether they constitute such regions or not.

In constituting the four regions he has also not taken into consideration either the extent of territory or the population. As Table LII given on p. 440 shows, the Indus region with an area of 569.73 or 218.35 thousand sq. miles and the Delta with an area of only 156.96 or 132.39 thousand sq. miles according as Indian States are included in them or not are matched against 311.80 and 539.25 or 208.20 and 302.79 thousand sq. miles according as the Indian States are included or not in the Ganges Basin and the Deccan. The difference in the population is even more marked. As against a population of 612.50 or 370.80 lakhs in the Indus region and 735.0 or 705.10 in the Delta region according as States are included or not, we have 1165.50 lakhs or 1000.90 lakhs in the Ganges Basin and 1368.20 or 871.80 lakhs in the Deccan according as States are included in them or not. If we take the proportion of Muslim and non-Muslim populations in the

[3] Mukerjee, *An Economist* . . ., p. 13.

four regions the position is no less remarkable. If we take British India and States, the Muslims will be in the nominal majority of 52.0 and 50.1 per cent in the Indus and Delta regions as against 48.0 and 49.9 per cent of non-Muslims in those regions. If we take British India alone, the Muslims will have a majority of 61.3 and 51.6 per cent in the Indus and Delta regions as against 38.7 and 48.4 per cent of non-Muslims in them. As against this nominal majority of Muslims in the Muslim regions, we have overwhelming non-Muslim majorities of 88.0 and 91.8 per cent against 12.0 and 8.2 per cent of Muslims in the Ganges and Deccan regions comprising British India and States and 86.8 and 92.5 per cent in British India as against 13.2 and 7.5 per cent of Muslims in the aforesaid two regions.

All this anomaly, discrepancy and irregularity has to be quietly swallowed because two Muslim regions have to be matched against two non-Muslim regions. If that is the sole objective, it is much better, more straightforward and more honest to say that there should be equality of status and power, though not of responsibility and burden between the Muslim and non-Muslim provinces and States irrespective of any other consideration. The camouflage of Regionalism and economic convenience wears too thin to deceive anyone, whether Muslim or non-Muslim.

When we consider the constitution that is proposed by Professor Coupland the position becomes amply clear. The inter-regional Centre will have a Legislative Council whose members will have no independent status but will act only as delegates of their respective regions under their mandates. Not only the members of the Legislature but the executive also will be under similar obligation. It does not strike the Professor that if any Constitution can be framed which will lend itself most blatantly to deadlocks, it will be the Constitution which he proposes. All other Constitutions anticipate such deadlocks as may possibly arise in their working" and provide against them. Professor Coupland's Constitution not only opens the door wide for deadlocks but almost makes their non-occurrence an impossibility and yet suggests no means for dissolving them.

The hope that the experience of working together at the Centre will make the idea of unity possible is entirely unfounded, when care is taken to make it clear that those who are expected to work together have not to work and act according to what they consider best and right and just after consultation and discussion amongst themselves but according to what others, thousands of miles away from one another, having no opportunities of exchanging views and discussing matters as they arise, decide to be best and right and just. There is no meaning in working together, when those who are together do not work but act as automatons, and those who really work do not meet but act through their automatons from a great distance. Moreover, what hope can there be for any kind of unity emerging when all possible obstacles are put in its way by making the units feel and act as Muslim and non-Muslim units, and nationalism is not allowed at any stage and in any corner to have so much as even a look in?

It is unnecessary to notice any other aspect of the Constitution beyond pointing out that it is intended to ensure equality of status and power to the Muslim regions with the non-Muslim regions. It is nowhere suggested—in fact the contrary is assumed—that this equality in status and power should also imply an equality in the burdens to be borne by the four regions. It is said that the maintenance of the inter-regional Centre, apart from the department of defence, will not be a very costly affair. The cost of Defence was more or less balanced by the revenue derived from customs before the Second World War and if that continues to be the position after the war, the question of ways and means, it is supposed, is easily solved. The learned Professor has not thought it worth-while to point out in this connection what the contribution of the four regions to this revenue has been in the past and is expected to be in the future. He thinks it enough to lay down the rule that the Muslim regions will enjoy equality of power with the other regions in spending the revenue and the non-Muslim regions will enjoy the sole privilege of having to contribute the bulk of it without having to share such a valuable privilege with the Muslim regions. Unity is good but unity on any terms may be purchased at too high a price.

~

THIRTY-SEVEN

SIR SULTAN AHMAD'S SCHEME

A third scheme has been proposed by Sir Sultan Ahmad in *A Treaty between India and the United Kingdom*. After considering the proposal for Pakistan he comes to the conclusion that 'if the north-west and north-east Pakistans are completely independent sovereign States, with no constitutional bond with the rest of India, they must fail as a practical proposition inasmuch as they will have no military security or economic stability, and also because they would not secure peace and justice to the Muslims in the rest of India. Other alternatives must therefore be found and considered. In doing so we must not forget that we have to satisfy the aggrieved Muslim of India who is afraid of Hindu domination in every walk of life.'[1] He puts forward his alternative scheme, which he claims has the virtue of being practical and under the peculiar conditions of India of today not unreasonable. He bases it on the Draft Declaration of the British government and calls it the Union of India, which will be composed of several units as so many sovereign federated States with a Centre. The frontiers of the units may be redrawn where necessary. The provinces in the north-west and the north-east will form two such units with altered frontiers, if desired, so that the Muslim majority might be substantially increased therein. The units will be autonomous and sovereign, with full freedom in all internal affairs. The external freedom of the units will be subject only to the powers transferred to the Union by common agreement between the units.

(i)   *Powers:* The Centre will have power and authority over the following subjects: defence, foreign relations, currency, customs, broadcasting, airways, railways, shipping, post and telegraph. Residuary powers will be vested in the units.

---

[1] Sir Sultan Ahmad, *A Treaty between India and the United Kingdom*, p. 88.

(ii)   *Composition of the Federal Assembly* will be as follows:
        Muslims 40 per cent, Hindus 40, depressed classes 10; the
        rest such as Indian Christians, Anglo-Indians, Sikhs, Parsees,
        tribes, etc. 10. This would make the majority more fluid
        and dependent on lively combination of the various groups,
        giving an equally good chance of winning a majority to
        the Hindu and to the Muslim. Also the majority will be
        so narrow as to make it dependent on the goodwill and
        support of the opposition.

(iii)   *The Constitution-making Body* should be formed as follows:
        80 seats have been suggested above for the Muslims and the
        Hindus. These 80 seats should be filled up by 40 double
        constituencies, each constituency returning a Muslim and
        a Hindu member. Each of these constituencies should be
        divided into 500 circles. In each circle separate registers
        should be prepared of adult Muslims and adult Hindus
        who might be literate or own a house or pay any tax.
        In each circle such Muslims and Hindus should elect
        separately a Muslim and a Hindu representative. Thus in
        each constituency there would be 500 Muslims and 500
        Hindus elected by separate electorates. These 1000 persons
        would form a joint electorate and would elect one Muslim
        and one Hindu member. A similar suitable method could be
        adopted for the depressed classes as well as for the others.
        Ten per cent or even 5 per cent of the Lower Houses so
        constituted might form the Constitution-making Body.

(iv)   *The Executive:* (a) The Cabinet will reflect the same
        communal ratio as the Assembly, (b) The Executive will
        be responsible to the Legislature, (c) The Prime Minister
        will be alternately a Muslim and a non-Muslim, (d) The
        Deputy Prime Minister will be a Hindu when the Prime
        Minister is a Muslim and a Muslim when the Prime Minister
        is a Hindu. (e) The Defence Minister will be a Muslim if
        the Commander-in-Chief is a non-Muslim and vice versa,
        (f) Collective responsibility will be a matter of convention.
        This will act, apart from principle, also as a safeguard
        against any decision affecting a certain community without
        ascertaining its will; for the ministers of the community
        concerned resigning, the Cabinet would break up.

(v)   *Civil Services:* As far as possible and .subject to efficiency the same ratio will be reflected in the appointments for the civil services. Promotions would generally depend on efficiency and seniority.

(vi)   *Public Bodies:* In all organizations of local self-government, corporations, municipal councils, various similar Boards and Commissions, the same ratio as above shall be reflected.

(vii)   *Army Services:* The composition of the Indian fighting forces will be Muslims 50 per cent, non-Muslims 50 per cent.

(viii)   *Clauses of the Safeguards:* In this connection reference may be made to the Declaration of Fundamental Rights and Minority Rights issued by the Congress and Mr Jinnah's Fourteen Points which demanded safeguards—(a) religious, social and cultural, and (6) political and administrative. As regards (a) the Bandemataram song as now rid of its objectionable passages and Iqbal's song should be officially put together. Muslim insignia should be given a place on the Congress flag. Cow sacrifice should be tolerated but performed without demonstration. Azan should present no difficulty and a lull in the music before a mosque should ensure that Hindu processions would not be disturbed. To avoid controversy, the English language and the Roman script should be the language and script of the Centre. In the provinces, the use of local vernaculars might be permitted (b) These relate to territorial redistribution affecting the Muslim majority in a province; a statutory guarantee of the personal law and culture of the Muslims; a statutory enactment of the communal ratio in services under the State and local bodies. The first would not arise if Pakistan were dropped. The others should be admitted. Other grievances which may have appeared in the meanwhile should be settled.

(ix)   *Guarantee of Safeguards:* The Draft Declaration favoured the arrangement of retaining Britain's obligation in respect of minorities. India may not accept this position or any other foreign guarantee only if she has that respect for the sovereignty of the Union of India that faith in her full dominion status, which can effectively replace the guarantee vested in an outside authority. If such be the case we shall place our trust in the law of our land and seek redress of our grievances by appeal to the Courts of the units or the Supreme Court of the Union or finally to the International Court.

(x) *Cultural Safeguards* relating to freedom of faith, and religious, educational, and charitable institutions might be given on the lines of the Estonian Cultural Autonomy Law; cultural councils might well be set up in the units for the protection and administration of the religious, social and educational rights and institutions of the minorities.

(xi) *Political Safeguards:* No Bill may be proceeded with if it is considered by a community to affect it adversely, unless three-fourths of the members of that community agree to it.

(xii) Resolutions affecting the Sikh community may be moved only in the Punjab Assembly and they would be subject to the safeguard in para (xi).

(xiii) Resolutions affecting the Parsi community may be moved only in the Bombay Assembly and they would be subject to the safeguard in para (xi).

THE UNITS

As regards representation in the Assemblies and the Executive and public services of the federated States the following suggestions may be considered:

(a) The minorities might retain separate electorates but should follow the method of representation suggested under the head 'Constitution-making body' for the Centre.

(b) The minorities might retain their present weightage, except that in Bengal the weightage to the Europeans should be substantially reduced.

(c) The boundaries of the units might, if necessary, be altered, but not in a manner which would convert a majority into a minority.

(d) As far as possible and subject to efficiency the same communal proportion shall be reflected in the Executive and public services of the units as in the Assemblies.

(e) Provisions suggested in paragraphs (iv), (v), (vi), (viii), (ix), (x), (xi) and (xii) above would also apply, whenever relevant, to the Units, specially the minority safeguards.

Another alternative is suggested. Equality in the Centre may be managed by giving alternating absolute majority of 51 per cent to the Hindu and the Muslim. This would do away with vote-catching manoeuvres and would create an atmosphere increasingly congenial for understanding and joint action. The knowledge that the other party would before long have its turn at the helm of power and might pay back in the same coin would serve to maintain a salutary control over any perverse tendencies of either side. Its drawback is that it reduces to nonentity the other minorities, which under the 40:40 per cent plan would hold the balance of power.

The scheme of Sir Sultan Ahmad outlined above has the merit of being straightforward and forthright. It says what it wants and makes no attempt to camouflage its real intention and objective under the cover of Regionalism or any other -ism. It therefore requires to be carefully considered on its merits. No one in British India who is not committed to the view of the Muslim League is opposed to federation. The League is the only organization in the country which has declared itself against federation in any form, however attenuated, and under all circumstances. Nor will there be any insuperable difficulty in arriving at an agreement regarding the subjects which will be within the powers and authority of the Centre. The list given by Sir Sultan is fairly exhaustive and leaves out only one important subject about which a difference of opinion is likely and that is large-scale planning—but it is not likely to be insuperable and unadjustable. No Congressman can raise any objection to the residuary powers being vested in the provinces after the resolution of the All-India Congress Committee passed in August 1942, which has come in for such bitter criticism at the hands of the Government and the President of the All-India Muslim League.

The rest of the scheme is based on certain assumptions. The fundamental assumption is that the Hindus, who constitute a majority of the population, have been, are and will ever, in future be acting in unison, with the object of oppressing the Muslims. It is therefore necessary to devise a constitutional scheme which

will make any such action on their part impossible. The attack
on the Hindus has been from three sides for which, of course, Sir
Sultan Ahmad is not responsible. The first attempt is to disrupt the
community by treating the Scheduled Castes separately from Hindus,
thus reducing the proportion of the Hindus in the population. The
second attack is by cutting away the tribes from the Hindus who
according to the best anthropological opinion as shown elsewhere
ought to be counted with the Hindus, thus further reducing their
proportion. The last attempt is to deprive the Hindus still further
of their legitimate representation even on this reduced basis in
the Legislature and Executive and the services of the government
by the Constitution. Sir Sultan Ahmad proposes that the Hindus,
reduced as they will be in proportion to the whole population to
51 per cent by cutting out the Scheduled Castes who constitute
13.5 per cent and the tribes who are 5.65 per cent from them,
should have 40 per cent representation at the Centre as against
40 per cent representation of the Muslims who constitute only
26.83 per cent of the population. Even the Scheduled Castes for
whom the League professes so much concern have to get their
representation reduced to 10 per cent. In this connection it is worth
while recalling a bit of not very ancient history. The Lucknow Pact
between the Indian National Congress and the All-India Muslim
League provided for considerable weightage for Muslims in the
provinces where they were in a minority. Thus in the United
Provinces and the Madras Presidency they got 30 and 15 per cent
representation when their population was only 14 and 6.15 per
cent respectively. In Bihar and Orissa, they got a representation
of 25 per cent for a population between 10 and 11 per cent. But
in the two provinces of Bengal and the Punjab where they were
in a majority of 52.3 and 51 per cent they got a representation
of 50 and 40 per cent respectively. This pact was accepted by
the British government and representation as agreed was given
to the communities in the Constitution of 1920. The Musalmans,
however, got dissatisfied with it and repudiated it. They contended
that it was unjust because it reduced the proportion of Musalman
representation in the provinces where they were in a majority and
they demanded that in no case should the representation be such
as to reduce a majority to a minority or even to an equality. The
tables are now completely turned and schemes reducing the large
Hindu majority to the position of a helpless minority are being

seriously put forward by those who sympathize with the Muslim League point of view. Rule by a majority is bad and condemnable where the Hindus, as in the whole of India, are in a majority, but it is quite right where the Muslims, as in the north-western and eastern zones, are in a majority. Sir Sultan Ahmad's distribution of representation in the Centre is based on these considerations. The Hindu majority is reduced to 40 per cent to be on a basis of equality with the Muslim representation which is raised to 40 per cent. Sir Sultan claims it as a merit of his scheme that the balance of power as between the Hindus and the Muslims will be in the hands of the minorities. '

Nor does this balancing end with the Legislature. It goes right through the entire scheme of the appointment of the Executive and the services. In some respects it goes even further. It provides that the Prime Minister shall be alternately a Muslim and a non-Muslim. Non-Muslims include Christians, Sikhs, Parsis, tribes, Scheduled Castes and all others who are not Muslims. It includes also the Hindus. The scheme ensures by a constitutional provision that the Muslims will have one of themselves as Prime Minister after a certain interval but the Hindus are left entirely in the lurch and, if the minorities, including the Muslims, combine, will never get the chance of having a Prime Minister. It may be said that it is unfair to assume that the minorities will combine to keep out the Hindu from the Prime Ministership. Is it any more unfair to assume this than to assume the contrary—that the Hindus and other non-Muslims will combine to keep out the Muslim from the Prime Ministership? There is as much chance or likelihood, if not more, of Muslims and other minorities combining to keep the Hindu out as of the Hindus and other non-Muslims combining to keep the Muslim out. It is well that Sir Sultan has not reserved the Prime Ministership for Hindus and Muslims alternately, keeping all others out. Similarly the Defence Minister will be a Muslim if the Commander-in-Chief is a non-Muslim and vice versa. The Hindu is excluded here also altogether from these two posts if only the Muslims and others combine. All this looks more like penalizing and depressing and suppressing the Hindu majority than safeguarding and protecting the interests of the Muslim minority by constitutional devices.

The provision regarding public bodies as embodied in paragraph (vi) of Sir Sultan's scheme is unintelligible. Is it intended that the same proportion of 40 and 40 per cent as between Hindus and Muslims will be applicable to all corporations, municipal councils, local Boards, etc., irrespective of their proportion in the population and in all the provinces? The proposition would seem to be unstateable in any serious discussion of the question and I think Sir Sultan Ahmad has fallen into an error in putting it without considering its implications. It is inconceivable that he should seriously suggest that Muslims should have a representation of 40 per cent in a municipality or local board of Orissa where their population is not more than 1 or 1.5 per cent.

The composition of the fighting forces of India will be Muslims 50 and non-Muslims 50 per cent—which again may mean that it will not be unconstitutional or illegal under the Constitution if not a single Hindu is included in them. They may consist entirely, say, of Sikhs and Christians, besides Muslims. It may be said that this cannot obviously be what Sir Sultan Ahmad means. But I am only interpreting the language used by him and one is entitled to expect precise language from a person of the position of Sir Sultan, particularly when his words do not suffer from any ambiguity where rights of Muslims are concerned.

It is not necessary to go in detail into religious, social and cultural safeguards except to point out that under the scheme, while cow sacrifice and azan should not be interfered with, Hindu processions should purchase immunity from disturbance by observing a lull in their music before a mosque.

He cuts the Gordian knot of controversy about language and script by adopting the English language and the Roman script for the Centre, leaving the provinces to use the local languages.

In pointing out what appear to be one-sided provisions in the scheme and unfairness and injustice they involve to the Hindus, I should not be understood as holding that there are no elements in it which may form the basis for discussion or that it is not capable of improvement, if the points raised are discussed in a calm atmosphere and free from prejudice and preconceived notions.

~

THIRTY-EIGHT

SIR ARDESHIR DALAL'S SCHEME

In some articles which were published in the press in May 1943, under the caption of 'An Alternative to Pakistan', Sir Ardeshir Dalal pointed out: 'India is not only a very well-defined geographical unit with natural frontiers formed by the mountains and the sea, it has been from time immemorial a cultural and spiritual unit. That unity has been forged through countless ages by the culture, traditions and usages of the successive generations of men who have migrated or conquered, settled down and been absorbed through the predominant qualities of tolerance and adaptability which are the characteristics of Indian civilization. Pakistan involves disruption of this unity,' and can be considered only if no other alternative is possible. After briefly considering the implications he comes to the conclusion that 'the consequences of Pakistan will be more disastrous to Muslims themselves than to others and that 'the economic and financial difficulties of splitting up this unit of India into a number of fragments are so great as to be well-nigh insuperable.' 'So long as political parties continue to be based on religious rather than political and economic issues, the Muslims feel that under the British parliamentary form of government which is offered to them they would remain in a state of continued subjection and will never have the opportunity to govern as political parties do elsewhere. That is at the root of their objection to any Central Government under a united India. It is for the Hindus as the major political party in the country to offer to make all reasonable sacrifices in order to win confidence of the minorities which has been impaired.' It is in this light that he has presented his alternative to Pakistan and it is as follows.

The future Constitution of India shall be of a federal and rigid type with a parliamentary executive and a judiciary, as in common law states, subject to the rule of law with a Supreme Federal Court. Only the essential minimum of subjects shall be

left to the Centre, all other subjects and all residuary powers to
the federating units.

The Central Subjects shall be defence; foreign relations; currency;
credit; customs; federal taxes on income; immigration, emigration
and naturalization; railways; post and telegraph; waterways; and
development of industries. There should be no objection to a re-
arrangement of boundaries for the federating states so as to allow
Muslims in areas in which they form the majority to constitute
themselves into semi-autonomous units.

There would be a *Charter of Fundamental Rights* guaranteeing
the personal, civil, and religious liberties of every individual on
the following lines:

All citizens of the Federation of India shall be equal before
the law.

Freedom of speech, of the press, and of association shall
be guaranteed. No person shall be tried or punished save by
a competent court according to law. Every dwelling shall be
inviolable.

No person shall suffer any disability on account of his religion
or faith or belonging to any particular race, caste, class, or creed.
Liberty of religion and conscience shall be guaranteed, including
liberty of belief, worship, observance, propaganda, association and
education. All religions shall be equal before the law.

The State will give full protection to minorities with regard to
those interests which they regard as fundamental to their separate
existence as minorities with special reference to education, language,
religion and personal law. All minorities shall have equal right to
establish, manage and control at their own expense charitable and
religious institutions and schools and establishments for instruction
and education with a right to use their own language and to
exercise their own religion therein.

In every village in which persons legally responsible for the
education of at least fifty children of a minority community
demanded it, a minority primary school shall be set up by the
authorities concerned for instruction in its own language.

All schools, colleges, and technical and other institutions
established by the minorities, if complying with codes and
regulations, shall be entitled to the same assistance from state and
local funds and be subject to the same control, if any, as similar
institutions for the general public or the majority community.

The Electoral Franchise will have to be widened but communal electorates will have to be retained. The device of multiple-member constituencies with reserved seats for minorities other than Muslims or even for Muslims, if they so desire, may be extended. In the case of local self-governing bodies, the principle of multiple-member constituencies with reservation of seats may be adopted.

The freightage assigned to the Muslims and Scheduled Castes in the different provincial legislatures under the Constitution of 1935 shall be retained with the exception that for Bengal a modification of the Poona Pact may be made by mutual arrangement, if possible. If boundaries of units are altered, the allocation of seats will of course have to be altered. In those reconstituted units if Muslims are in a minority, the same weightage will be given as at present; but in the units in which Hindus form a minority, they will also have to be given weightage. In units with a preponderating Muslim population it would not be unfair if the general seats are assigned to the Muslim majorities. In no unit or State should the allocation of seats to minority communities be such as to reduce the majority to a minority.

The Executive Government in the Federating States shall be formed by ministers chosen from among the elected representatives in the Legislature but they shall be coalition governments formed on the following basis: All minorities which constitute more than a minimum percentage of the population (to be fixed) shall have a right to be represented in the Cabinet, approximately in the same proportion as their total population bears to the total population of the State or province. An alternative would be for the minorities to be represented in the Cabinet in the same proportion as in the Legislature.

The exact number of ministers will have to be laid down by a commission appointed for the purpose. The ministers representing each minority community should be selected by the representatives of the community in the legislature by a system of proportional representation. Nothing in the above shall prevent the Prime Minister or other authority forming a cabinet from selecting a member of a minority community to be a member of the executive government over and above the statutory minima assigned to minorities.

The number of seats allocated to Muslims in the Central Legislature shall be one-third of the total number of seats, but the number of seats assigned to all the minority communities as distinguished from those assigned to women, or special interests such as labour, landholders, commerce, etc. shall not exceed half of the total number of seats.

The executive government at the Centre shall be a coalition Government with not less than one-third Muslim personnel. The Muslim members of the executive government shall be elected by the Muslim representatives in the Legislature by the P.R. system. One representative of the Sikhs and one representative of the Scheduled Castes shall be elected in a similar manner by their elected representatives in the Legislature. The ministers representing the minority communities should not exceed 50 per cent of the total number of the Cabinet. Nothing in the above shall prevent the Prime Minister from appointing a member of a minority community to the Cabinet over and above the fixed statutory minima.

The government shall be *responsible to the Legislature* which may vote a resolution of lack of confidence. Such a resolution shall not be carried save by an absolute majority of the votes of the members of the legislature at a meeting at which not less than two-thirds of the members shall be present.

No *Bill or Resolution or any part thereof* shall be passed in any Legislature if it is opposed by three-fourths of the members of any community in that particular body on the ground that it will seriously damage the religious and cultural interests of that community or is against the personal laws by which they have hitherto been governed. No community shall possess this right unless the number of its members on that legislature is at least 15 per cent of the total. *In the event of a dispute* as to whether any such Bill or resolution falls or does not fall within the provisions of this clause, the matter shall be referred to the Federal Court.

The Federal Court shall be composed of five Judges, of whom two shall be Muslims.

The percentage of Muslims in the army shall in no case be less than that existing in 1938.

The existing provisions regarding *communal representation in the services* as laid down in Government of India Resolution No. F 14|17-B 33 of 4 July 1934, shall be embodied by Statute in the Constitution with such minor modifications as may be necessary.

No *change* shall be made *in the Constitution* without a two-thirds majority of the Central Legislature sitting as one body for the purpose and the consent by a bare majority of each of the Legislatures of the federating units also sitting as one body, if the Legislatures consist of a lower and upper House.

The constitutionality of all measures will be subject to the final decision of the Federal Court.

No suggestions have been made in the above proposals about the constitution of second chambers, concurrent and separate jurisdiction and a number of other points which will arise in considering a Constitution for India. These must be left to the bodies framing the Constitution. They do not affect the main issue, which is that of the provision of adequate safeguards for the minorities.

The Indian States had better be left out for the present.

It is not claimed that the Constitution sketched out above is ideal. 'I regard the constitution of coalition governments as the very essence of these proposals.' The main features which ensure the safeguards for the minorities are that it is a written Constitution only capable of being revised by a procedure which will ensure an adequate voice for the minorities, that it protects the religious and cultural autonomy of the minorities and ensures for them a fair share in the services of the State including the army. It provides for representation in the Legislatures with weightage to the minorities as well as a representation in the executive government both in the States as well as the Centre. It leaves the federating units as autonomous as it is possible for any federation to do. Finally it provides a Federal Court with a final right to intervene if any of the provisions of the Constitution are infringed.

The safeguards are not mere paper safeguards. They cannot be violated without completely breaking the Constitution and perhaps provoking a civil war. On the worst assumption it will only be an experiment for a period of ten years after which the Muslim minority, if it so chooses, will be free to seek and work out its own way.

Besides, it must not be forgotten that at the end of the war an international body is bound to come into existence which will be more powerful than the League of Nations and will be bound and able to afford a very real and genuine measure of protection to the minorities.

Sir Ardeshir Dalai is a Parsi and has thus the advantage of being neither a Hindu nor a Muslim between whom the conflict for power largely arises. His scheme therefore may be treated as one proceeding from an impartial and unprejudiced person who may not be even unconsciously biased in favour of one or the other, of the two principal communities. He insists on coalition governments both at the Centre and in the provinces and fixes the proportion of Muslims in the legislature and in the Cabinet in excess of what their population would entitle them to, the only limit being that the representatives of the minorities will not exceed 50 per cent of the total number. The representatives of minorities in the Cabinet will be elected by the members representing them* in the Legislature by the method of proportional representation. It will be open to the Prime Minister to appoint a member of a minority community to the Cabinet in excess of the number fixed for that community. It thus becomes possible for the minorities to have even more than 50 per cent of seats in the Cabinet if they enjoy the confidence of the Prime Minister to such extent.

~

THIRTY-NINE

DR RADHA KUMUD MUKHERJI'S NEW APPROACH TO THE COMMUNAL PROBLEM

Dr Radha Kumud Mukherji, in a pamphlet named *A New Approach to the Communal Problem,* basing himself on the experience of the Minorities Treaties entered into by various countries of Europe after the First World War under the auspices and guarantee of the League of Nations and on the Constitution of the Soviet Republics of Russia and its development, has come to certain conclusions which are embodied in it and which are summarized below.

The communal problem is a universal problem, as it has been a physical impossibility that political and national frontiers should also coincide with racial, religious and social frontiers. Every State has to accommodate different elements and communities in its composition, and there is no State which has been able to eliminate a minority. It therefore becomes necessary to devise methods for dealing with them. Before the first Great War, the Treaty of Paris of 30 March 1856, which followed the Crimean War, laid down that in any country a class of subjects should not be recognized as inferior to other classes for either religious or racial reasons. After the first Great War a scheme was devised which was given legal value in the form of Minorities Guarantee Treaties as international stipulations, which were binding on the different member-States forming the League of Nations—which at one time comprised as many as fifty-two States of the world as its members.

The differences between communities living under a common State may be brought under one or other of three categories:

(i) Language,
(ii) Race,
(iii) Religion.

A minority, to claim special treatment, must be numerically large enough to form, as is stated in the Turkish Constitution, 'a

466   INDIA DIVIDED

considerable proportion of the population' and this was agreed
to be fixed at 20 per cent of the total population of the state,
for special treatment was not economically and administratively
feasible for a smaller minority.

The protection that was guaranteed to minorities was limited
to differences of race, religion and language. Historic and cultural
characteristics arising out of these alone were considered worthy
of all respect and recognition so that the community might be
enabled to progress along its own lines of evolution to make
its contribution to the general culture, of mankind. Therefore a
community was held entitled to the cultivation of its own language
and mother-tongue. Its children should be taught in and through
the medium of their mother-tongue and in its own script in the
primary schools, and the State must establish minority schools
on the basis of a minimum of pupils seeking such education, the
number being fixed at forty children within the same school district.
Further, minorities should receive a share, proportionate to the
number of their pupils, of the funds allowed for the budgets of
the school districts for the maintenance of elementary schools apart
from the general administration expenses and grants-in-aid.

Racial protection was assured by declaring every community to
be entitled to the preservation and expression of its racial integrity
and individuality as reflected in its particular manners, customs,
personal laws, the laws of marriage or inheritance, which are its
sole concern. Similarly religious protection of a community has
been long established in every civilized country. The provisions
of the Turkish Constitution may be taken as a basis which laid
down that all inhabitants shall be entitled to the free exercise,
whether in public or in private, of any creed, religion, or belief,
the observance of which shall not be incompatible with public
order and good morals. Turkish nationals belonging to non-
Muslim minorities shall enjoy the same treatment and security
in law, and in fact, as other Turkish nationals. In particular they
shall have an equal right to establish, manage and control at their
own expense any charitable, religious, and social institutions, any
schools and other establishments for instruction and education,
with the right to use their own language and to exercise their
own religion therein.

As regards the place of minorities in administration the Turkish
Constitution lays down: 'Differences of religion, creed, or confession

shall not prejudice any Turkish national in matters relating to the enjoyment of civil or political rights, as for instance, admission to public employments, functions, and honours, or the exercise of professions and industries. Turkish nationals belonging to non-Muslim minorities shall enjoy the same civil and political rights as Muslims. All the inhabitants of Turkey, without distinction of religion, shall be equal before the law. All nationals shall be treated on a footing of equality as regards admission to public employments, functions, and honours, including military ranks, and to public establishments and as regards the granting of degrees, distinctions, etc.'

Thus the scheme offers positive protection to the minorities in certain matters and interests which are vital to their self-expression and gives them complete autonomy and, independence in these respects. But there is a limit to minority protection, and that limit is the integrity of the State which all its communities must be equally concerned to defend at all costs and which no community can be allowed to weaken in pursuit of its exaggerated and extravagant ideas tending towards disintegration of the State itself.

The USSR is carrying on with communal problems at their worst. The Union comprises:

(i)   A population of 17 crores,
(ii)   180 different nationalities,
(iii)   151 different languages
(iv)   11 National Republics, and
(v)   22 Autonomous Republics.

The communal problem was bequeathed to it by the Tsarist regime and was bristling with difficulties of the first magnitude. The Tsarist regime was not interested in the unification of the various peoples inhabiting the vast territories and preferred them living on terms of great hostility with one another. The empire was governed in the interests of the Great Russians to whom all other nationalities and peoples were held as inferior and subordinate, and a deliberate policy of ruthless Russification of all non-Russian nationalities dictated by an aggressive and militant Russian nationalism was followed. This led to a reaction in the various nationalities and disintegrating tendencies were in full swing on all sides and received added strength and emphasis from the slogan of self-determination. When the Bolsheviks came into power they reversed the Tsarist policy, and to counteract and check the disruptive tendencies they declared to the various communities like Muhammedans, Tatars, Turks, and Tartars that their beliefs and customs, their national institutions and culture were thereafter free and inviolable and were under the powerful protection of the Revolution, thus assuring self-determination to all the peoples inhabiting the territory of the former Russian Empire. A Soviet Commonwealth was organized in the form of a free Federation of Nationalities which was known under the Constitution of 1918 as the Russian Socialist Federative Soviet Republic (RSFSR). The proclamation formed the model for the other Socialist Republics established by the Bolsheviks—Ukraine, White Russia, the Trans-Caucasian Federation and the Central Asiatic Republic. All these Soviet States were combined into a larger Federation under a new name, the Union of Socialist Soviet Republics (USSR) from which the word Russian was dropped.

The USSR is federated in several superposed degrees, many of its constitutive units have themselves a federal structure. Thus the maximum of rights is enjoyed by the eleven National or Union Republics. They are possessed of complete autonomy and have share through their representatives in the joint direction of the USSR They have also the right to 'dispose freely of themselves, even to the extent of seceding from the Union'—confirmed by Article 17 of the Constitution of 1936. The twenty-two Autonomous Republics which are next in rank are not granted the right of self-determination to the point of secession but are only independent in the management of local affairs. Lastly, there is a third category of autonomous formations whose number varies from time to time and whose autonomy is limited to local affairs and is subject to control of the particular Union Republic or Autonomous Republic ruling the territory in which their enclave is situated. The first step that the new Constitution had to take to form and stabilize itself was to reshape its physical basis by a new territorial division determined by the national principle supplemented by geographical and economic considerations, abolishing the old system under which each province was the home of several races at constant conflict with one another.

Broadly speaking, the division of powers between the Centre and its constituent units of different grades is that subjects like foreign policy, defence, transport, post and telegraph are administered by the Union government: economic, financial and labour problems are jointly administered by the Union government and the member-States; while law, public health, welfare organization and education are given over to the local control of the member-States and the Autonomous Republics and Regions. Thus these various Soviets are within these limits self-governing units enjoying complete cultural autonomy. The new order stands for the principle of equality between the different races of Russia and steps are being taken for producing this equality by raising the cultural, intellectual and economic level of the backward regions and communities through self-government. Every community imparts instruction to its children in its own language. Where there were no alphabets they developed them, so that by 1934 they were able to endow seventy-four communities with alphabets.

The local liberty and self-determination of minorities is, however, subject to limitations, so that they might not impair the strength of the Union as a whole. As is observed by the Webbs: 'The State as a whole maintains its unity unimpaired and has even, like other federal States, increased its centralization of authority. It is only in the USSR that the centralization involves no lessening of the cultural autonomy of the minorities.' In practice, the local autonomy is very much reduced by the system which is based on the overlapping of the various superposed administrative organs between whose different spheres of jurisdiction there is hardly any clear and defined living demarcation. A higher administrative body can supersede that just below it and take over its functions for which the lower body is not made exclusively responsible—the responsibility being shared by both. The fundamental fact must be borne in mind that the basis of the Constitution is its economic plan which comprehends within its all-embracing scope the entire life of the country and all its parts, and this economic plan falls exclusively within the sphere of the federal administration. Article 15, which seemingly limits federal powers, in practice only safeguards the rights of communities to cultural autonomy and especially to the use of local languages.

The right of secession is confined only to eleven National or Union Republics and not allowed as a general right to the numerous Autonomous Republics and Regions. In the words of Stalin, 'the attitude of the Communist Party towards the right of secession was determined by the concrete factors of the international situation, by the interests of the Revolution. This is why the Communists fight for the secession of the colonies from the *Entente* but they must at the same time fight against the severance of border regions from Russia.' Three years before, in 1917, Stalin stated: 'When we recognize the right of oppressed peoples to secede, the right to determine their political destiny, we do not thereby settle the question whether particular nations should secede from the Russian State at a given moment . . . Thus we are at liberty to agitate for or against the secession according to the interests of the proletariat, of the proletarian revolution.' During the Purge of 1937–38 there were several references in the press to men who were accused of plotting to bring about secession of some territory from the Union. There are three grounds for transferring an Autonomous Republic to the category of Union Republics which alone have the right of secession. These are:

(i)   The Republic in question must be a border Republic not surrounded on all sides by USSR territory so that they may have nowhere to go to if they separate,

(ii) The nationality which gives its name to the Republic must constitute a more or less compact majority within it, so that no minority can be given the right to secede on behalf of the State to which it belongs,

(iii) The Republic must not have too small a population, say, not less but more than a million at least.

The USSR had thus to form itself by giving the right to secede to its constituent Republics representing its nucleus to rope them in. Being once in the Union they have no desire to vote themselves out of it and are themselves making the Union more and more centralized. India as an integral unity is not something that is in the process of making. It has been already made and has been administered as such for over a century by the present Government of India. Instead of going back on it, efforts on the lines of the USSR should be made for dealing with the conflicting view-points of those who want independent Muslim States and those opposed to it, by evolving a scheme of cultural autonomy of communities. The Muslims fear that a Union with a Hindu majority will override the sovereignty of a Muslim State. A solution of this difficulty is quite feasible within the Union and without partitioning the parent State, in several ways:

(i)   The first is to so frame the schedules of federal and provincial subjects as to make the most of provincial autonomy and to render each Pakistan State a sovereign State for all practical purposes,

(ii) The second solution is to guarantee to each community its cultural autonomy on the lines of the USSR

(iii) A third solution may be to reconstitute the provinces as linguistic units, provided they are financially self-supporting.

The objection to any such scheme in the words of Mr Jinnah is that 'the safeguards, constitutional or otherwise, will be of no use; so long as there is a communal Hindu majority at the Centre the safeguards will remain on paper.' The reply is that the rights of minorities under the scheme of cultural autonomy of communities will be protected by law and the Constitution. The Constitution may set up a separate legal machinery to deal with and enforce the safeguards granted to the minorities, like the Supreme Court to which an aggrieved community will be at liberty to take its grievances. The composition of such a Supreme Court need not be communal. The Indian Union having been created by an agreement between the parties concerned, it cannot cancel or abrogate the safeguards provided in the Constitution of the Union and the Supreme Court which will be non-communal will be able to enforce the safeguards.

~

FORTY

THE COMMUNIST PARTY'S SUPPORT TO PAKISTAN

It ought not to surprise anyone if the leaders of the Communist Party in India should seek to find justification for their support to the Pakistan demand of the All-India Muslim League in the Constitution of the USSR and the writings of M. Stalin. But it is really surprising that Dr Radha Kumud Mukherji, the President of the Akhand Hindustan Conference, should also find inspiration in the same sources and base his suggestions on the same model. It is therefore necessary to consider in some detail the view-point of M. Stalin which has been endorsed by the Communist Party and embodied in the Constitution of the USSR as it has developed since the October Revolution of 1917.

M. Stalin defines: 'A nation is a historically evolved stable community of language, territory, economic life and psychological make-up manifested in a community of culture.'[1] Like every other historical phenomenon it is 'subject to the law of change, has its history, its beginning and end. It must be emphasized that none of the above characteristics is by itself sufficient to define a nation. On the other hand it is sufficient for a single one of these characteristics to be absent and the nation ceases to be a nation.'[2] 'Modern nations are a product of a definite epoch—the epoch of rising capitalism. The process of the abolition of feudalism and the development of capitalism was also the process of formation of people into nations. The British, French, Germans, and Italians formed into nations during the victorious march of capitalism and its triumph over feudal disunity.

'Where the formation of nations on the whole coincided in time with the formation of centralized states, the nations naturally became invested in a state integument and developed into

[1] M. Stalin, *Marxism and the National and Colonial Question*, p. 8.
[2] Ibid., p. 8.

independent *bourgeois* national states. Such was the case with Great Britain (without Ireland), France and Italy. In Eastern Europe, on the other hand, the formation of centralized states, accelerated by the exigencies of self-defence (against the invasions of the Turks, Mongols and others), took place prior to the break-up of feudalism and therefore prior to the formation of nations. Here, as a result, the nations did not, and could not, develop into national states, but formed into several mixed, multinational, *bourgeois* states, consisting of one powerful, dominant nation and several weak, subject-nations. Such are Austria, Hungary and Russia.

'National states, such as France and Italy, depending mainly on their own national forces, were generally speaking unacquainted with national oppression. In contradistinction, the multinational states, based as they are on the domination of one nation—or rather of its ruling class—over the other nations, were the original home and the chief scene of national oppression and national movements. The contradictions between the interests of the ruling nations and the interests of the subject nations are such that unless they are solved the stable existence of multinational states becomes impossible. The tragedy of the multinational *bourgeois* state is that it is unable to overcome these contradictions and that every attempt it makes to "level" the nations and "protect" the national minorities while preserving private property and class inequality usually ends in a new failure and a further intensification of national hostilities.

'The subsequent growth of capitalism in Europe, the need for new markets, the search for raw materials and fuel, and finally, the development of imperialism, the export of capital, and the necessity of protecting the great sea and rail routes have led, on the one hand, to the seizure of new territories by the old national states and the conversion of the latter into multinational (colonial) states with the national oppression and national conflicts characteristic of multinational states (Great Britain, France, Germany, Italy), and on the other hand, have intensified the strivings of the dominant nations in the old multinational states not merely to preserve the old state boundaries but to extend them and to subjugate new (weak) nationalities at the expense of neighbouring states. In this way the national problem was enlarged and finally, in the very course of events, became merged with the general problem of the colonies; while national oppression was transformed from an internal question into an inter-state question, into a question of conflict (and war) between the "Great" imperialist Powers for the subjugation of weak and non-sovereign nationalities.'[3]

The imperialist war (1914–18) led to an extreme aggravation of national conflicts within the victorious colonial states (Great Britain, France, Italy), to the complete disintegration of the defeated former multinational states (Austria, Hungary, Russia in 1917), and finally to the formation of new *bourgeois* national states (Poland, Czecho-Slovakia, Yugoslavia, Finland, Georgia, Armenia, etc.), each with its own national minorities. The new national States based as they are on private property and class inequality cannot exist

(i) without oppressing their own national minorities (Poland, which oppresses the White Russians, Jews, Lithuanians and Ukrainians; Georgia which oppresses the Ossets, Abkhasians and Armenians; Yugoslavia which oppresses the Croats and Bosnians and others);

(ii) without extending their territories at the expense of their neighbours which leads to conflict and war; and

(iii) without becoming subject financially, economically and militarily to the 'Great' imperialist Powers.

This was inevitable as private property and capital inevitably disunite people, inflame national unity and intensify national oppression; and collective property and labour just as inevitably bring people closer, undermine national dissension and destroy national oppression. The existence of capitalism without national oppression is just as inconceivable as the existence of socialism without the emancipation of oppressed nations, without national freedom. Hence the triumph of the Soviet and the establishment of the dictatorship of the proletariat is a basic condition for the abolition of national oppression, the institution of national equality and the guarantee of the rights of national minorities. The establishment of a Soviet system in Russia and the declaration of the right of nations to political secession have brought about a complete change in the relations between the toiling masses

[3] Resolution adopted by the Tenth Congress of the Russian Communist Party, March 1921, reproduced in *Marxism and the National and Colonial Question*, pp. 270–71.

of the nationalities of Russia. In isolation the existence of the various Soviet Republics was uncertain and unstable because of the menace to their existence offered by the capitalist states. Their joint interests: in the matter of defence, a restoration of their productive forces shattered during the war, and the fact that those Soviet Republics which are rich in food must come to the aid of those which are poor in food, all imperatively dictated the political union of the various Republics as the only means of escaping imperialist bondage and national oppression.[4]

The above extract authoritatively lays down the principles as conceived by the Communist Party of Russia; these principles have been explained at length by M. Stalin and others in 'their speeches and writings extending over a period from long before the Revolution of 1917 down to the present day. Let us consider in the light of the above principles, as so explained, the claim of the Muslim League that the Musalmans of India constitute a nation separate from the other nation or nations of India and as such are entitled not only to the right of secession but also to actual separation—here and now—from India, of the areas in which they are numerically in a majority.

If we apply the tests whereby it is to be judged whether a community constitutes a nation or not according to the principles of the Communists, the Musalmans of India as a whole cannot be said to constitute a nation. They do not all speak one and the same language, which is different for different provinces and territories. In fact the Muslims of a particular province speak the language of the province to which they belong and which language is also spoken by the non-Muslim communities of that province and which differs from the language of other provinces. This is true not only of the distant provinces but also of contiguous provinces in the north-western region where Baluchi, Sindhi, Pushto and Punjabi are spoken by the residents of the four provinces. These differ from one another as much as they differ from say Hindi or Hindustani or Bengali and Gujarati.

They cannot be said to inhabit the same territory unless we take India as a whole constituting one territory. The territories in the north-western and eastern regions of India where Musalmans predominate in population are separated from one another by

[4] Adapted from the same resolution, reproduced in *Marxism . . .*, pp. 273–74.

nearly a thousand miles. Nor can it be said that the Musalmans as such have a separate economic life which distinguishes them from non-Muslims. Their economic life is the same as that of the non-Muslims in the area which they inhabit and is separate from that of Muslims and non-Muslims alike in other regions which differ.

It is noticeable that M. Stalin does not mention religion at all as a basis for the foundation of a separate nation. In fact in several places in his writings he ridicules the idea that the Jews on the basis of their religion alone can be said to constitute a separate nation. But we may assume that what he calls psychological make-up manifested in a community of culture 'does include the influence of religion which undoubtedly plays an important part in the cultural development of a community. Despite what Islam may have taught, there is no doubt that Islamic culture in India as a whole is not uniform. It has indeed varied in its content and manifestation in different parts and Musalmans present as variegated a kaleidoscope as any other community in this respect. The difference between Shias and Sunnis is practically as old as Islam itself. Then we have many groups of Musalmans who observe the Hindu law of succession and still maintain many of the customs of the Hindu community to which they originally belonged. We have also the recent sect of Qadianis. Many of these differences are about religious tenets and principles but they also pervade and permeate the social life of the Musalmans. It must be admitted, however, that despite these differences there is an overall Muslim culture which is common to all Musalmans. In that sense there is an overall Indian culture also which is common to Muslims and non-Muslims of India in spite of many differences among them. It thus follows that according to the Communist definition, the Musalmans of India as a whole do not constitute a separate nation. The Indian Communists also recognize this. 'Gandhiji has the greatest objection to accepting religion as basis of nationhood. He is right in the sense that religion alone does not make a nation. It will be a digression here to discuss what part religion does play in influencing the psychological make-up of a people and in moulding their national culture, both of which are among the attributes of a nation. It is enough for us to state that the Indian Muslims cannot be regarded as a nation on the basis of their common religion. But to say this alone is to state only half the truth.'[5] The other half of the truth, according to Mr Joshi, is that India constitutes a family of nationalities.

The second point which requires consideration is the historical one—of the growth of the question of nationalities. M. Stalin divides this into three periods. 'The first period is the period which saw the break-up of feudalism in the West and the triumph of capitalism. The formation of people into nations occurred during this period'[6]—in Great Britain (without Ireland), France and Italy. 'In Eastern Europe, on the contrary, the process of formation of nationalities and the elimination of feudal disunity did not coincide in time with the process of formation of centralized States . . . Mixed States arose, each made up of several nationalities which had not yet formed themselves into nations but which were already united in a common State . . . These multinational States of the East were the birth-place of that national oppression which gave rise to national conflicts, national movements, the national problem and the various methods of solving that problem.'[7] Russia in the Tsarist Regime was one of these Eastern States of Europe where the question arose on account of the oppression of the border regions by the Great Russians.

'The second period in Eastern Europe is marked by the awakening and invigoration of subject nations (Czechs, Poles, Ukrainians) which, as a result of the imperialist War, led to the dissolution of the old *bourgeois* multinational States and the formation of new national States enthralled to what are known as the Great Powers.

'The third period is the Soviet period, the period of the destruction of capitalism and the abolition of national oppression.'[8]

Now in India we have not had the same kind of development. We have undoubtedly one centralized State covering the whole of British India and exercising an overriding power over the Indian States. But in this centralized State, Indians of no community or province have had any power. Whatever oppression nationalities have had to suffer has not been at the hands of any Indian group or community exercising power in this Central State as was the

---

[5] P.C. Joshi, *They must meet again*, p. 7.
[6] Stalin, *Marxism* . . ., p. 99.
[7] Stalin, *Marxism*, pp. 99–100.
[8] Ibid., pp. 100–01.

case in Eastern Europe—in Russia in particular. All nationalities
of India have been subject to the same Central power which is a
foreign power. The problem that arises here is not of safeguarding
the rights of nationalities *inter se* but against the common Central
power which equally dominates each and all of such nationalities.
The case of India therefore falls in the category not of European
nationalities but of the colonial countries. Logically, therefore,
the question which ought to demand and receive precedence is of
attaining freedom from the imperialist domination of Great Britain
and not separation of the oppressed nationalities from one another.
This is exactly what the Congress has been insisting upon.

It may be said, however, that the nationalities which constitute
a minority should be assured that when freedom from imperialist
domination and oppression is attained, they should not be exposed
to the risk of similar domination by the majority which will come
into power on the elimination of the imperialist power. This
assurance can be given by recognizing the right of self-determination
or secession subject to certain self-evident and essential limitations
similar to those which the USSR Constitution imposes. 'The question
of the right of nations freely to secede must not be confused with
the question that a nation must *necessarily* secede at any given
moment . . . When we recognize the right of oppressed peoples
to secede, the right to determine their political destiny, we do not
thereby settle the question whether particular nations *should* secede
from the Russian State at the given moment. I may recognize the
right of a nation to secede, but that does not mean that I compel
it to secede. A people has a right to secede, but it may or may
not exercise that right, according to circumstances. Thus we are
at liberty to agitate for or against secession, according to the
interests of the proletariat; of the proletarian revolution. Hence
the question of secession must be determined in each particular
case independently, in accordance with existing circumstances,
and for this reason the question of the recognition of the right to
secession must not be confused with the expediency of secession
in any given circumstances.'[9] What is demanded in India is not
merely the recognition of the right to secession but an actual
secession here and now and before the country has been able to
get rid of the dominant imperial power.

[9] Stalin, *Marxism* . . ., p. 64.

It is thus apparent that M. Stalin and the Russian Communist Party do not insist on one uniform pattern of action to be adopted in all countries irrespective of their peculiar conditions. M. Stalin in particular emphasizes the differentiation between revolution in imperialist countries, countries that oppress other peoples, and revolution in colonial and dependent countries, countries that suffer from the imperialist oppression of other States;[10] and he quotes as authoritative the statement from a thesis of the Communist International that in countries like China and India 'foreign domination perpetually hinders the development of social life,' and that 'therefore the first step of a revolution in the colonies must be to overthrow foreign capitalism.'[11] Is it not in keeping with this that in India the first step must be the ending of the foreign domination and not a division of the country?

It must also be noted that while the Communist Party adopted as its policy the right of nations to self-determination, the right of peoples to lead an independent political existence, it also holds equally strongly that oppressed nationalities cannot achieve their emancipation without the abolition of private property and capital, without the establishment of collective property and labour, and without the establishment of the dictatorship of the proletariat. It is therefore on the twin principles of the recognition of the right to secession of nationalities and of the establishment of a Soviet state and of the dictatorship of the proletariat that the fraternal collaboration of peoples within a single confederate State can be built up. It will not do to take up one aspect—the right of secession and leave out the other—the establishment of the dictatorship of the proletariat. It is evident that a consistent adoption of both the aspects will create many difficulties, and those who support Pakistan as demanded by the Muslim League know this and are consequently vocal about the one but silent about the other in this context. It is not without reason also that Mr Jinnah and the Muslim League generally are cold, if not positively hostile, towards the support which the Communist Party of India is offering so effusively to the League proposal.

[10] Ibid., p. 232.
[11] Ibid., p. 236.

~

FORTY-ONE

SAPRU COMMITTEE'S PROPOSALS

Some time ago a Committee consisting of persons who have held prominent positions in the public life and service of British India and Indian States was formed under the presidentship of Sir Tej Bahadur Sapru. It was claimed on behalf of the Committee that its members were not prominently associated with any communal group in the country and had not identified themselves with any proposal for the solution of the constitutional and communal problem in India; and it could therefore be expected to make suggestions which would not be partisan. The Committee has published its conclusions in two incitements—the first dealing with an interim arrangement for the establishment of a national government at the Centre and the second with the future Constitution of India. I shall deal here only with this second set of proposals.

The Committee's published proposals do not contain any specific recommendation on the question of the independence of India and its proposals are expected to be implemented by the British Parliament. The proposals, however, apart from the implementing authority of the British Parliament, are consistent both with a Dominion Constitution and a Constitution for an independent India.

The Constitution-making Body shall be constituted in the manner prescribed in clause D of the Draft Declaration brought by Sir Stafford Cripps, subject to the following modifications—(i) The total strength of the Body shall be 160 distributed as follows: Special interests—commerce and industry, landholders, universities, labour and women 16; Hindus excluding Scheduled Castes 51; Muslims 51; Scheduled Castes 20; Indian Christians; Sikhs 8; backward areas and tribes 3; Anglo-Indians 2; Europeans 1; Others 1. The Committee fixes the number at 160 whereas the Cripps Proposals had stated it to be one-tenth of the number in the legislative assemblies, which also would work out at about the same figure. Its proposal in this respect differs from the Cripps Proposals in that it fixes the number of seats allotted to each interest or community and in so doing has put the Muslims and Hindus other than those belonging to the Scheduled Castes on a basis of equality, whereas the Cripps Proposals had provided for election according to the method of proportional representation, which would have enabled the different groups in the Legislatures to return only as many as and no more than their number justified, and thus the Muslim representation would be considerably less and the Hindu representation considerably more than what is proposed by the Committee. This modification the Committee has recommended in the interests of communal unity.

No decision of the Constitution-making body will be valid unless it is supported by three-fourths of the members present and voting. His Majesty's Government shall enact the Constitution on the basis of the valid decisions of the Constitution-making body supplemented whenever necessary by its own awards on matters in which the requisite majority for decision was not forthcoming.

Division of India: The Committee is opposed to any division of India into two or more' separate independent sovereign States as endangering the peace and orderly progress of the whole country without any compensating advantage to any community.

Indian States: Provision should be made for their accession as units of the Union on agreed terms but the establishment of the Union should not be contingent on the accession of all or some or any of them.

Non-accession and Secession: No province of British India may elect not to accede to the Union nor may any unit—whether a province or a State—which has acceded be entitled to secede therefrom.

The Committee considers it undesirable to delay the new Constitution on account of any realignment of provincial boundaries on linguistic or cultural basis which should be left over for subsequent treatment.

The Committee makes certain recommendations for the Constitution Making Body.

There shall be a *Head of the State* (that is, Union in India) who shall be the repository of (a) all such powers and duties as may be conferred or imposed on him by or under the Constitution, and of (b) such other powers as are now vested in His Majesty the

King of England including powers connected with the exercise of the functions of the Crown in its relation with Indian States.

The Head of the State shall hold office for five years and ordinarily not for more than one term.

The Head of the State:

(i)   should be elected by an Electoral College composed of the members of the two Houses of the Union Legislature either without any restriction as to their choice or subject to their choice being confined to the Rulers of Indian States having a minimum population or revenue or both; or

(ii)   shall be elected by the Rulers of the Indian States referred to above from amongst themselves; or

(iii) shall be appointed by the King of England on the advice of the Union Cabinet either without any restriction or subject to the choice being confined to the Rulers of the Indian States referred to above. Even if the third alternative is adopted and the link with the British Crown is maintained the post of Secretary of State for India and all control that he or the British Cabinet exercises over the Indian administration should be abolished.

The Head of a Unit other than an Indian State shall be appointed by the Head of the State on advice of the Union Cabinet.

The Union Legislature shall consist of the Head of the State and two Chambers—the Union Assembly and the Council of State. The strength of the Union Assembly shall be so fixed that there shall be on the average one member for every million of the population. Ten per cent of the total strength shall be reserved for the representatives of special interests—landholders, commerce and industry, labour, women. The remaining seats shall be distributed among the following communities: Hindus other than Scheduled Castes; Muslims; Scheduled Castes; Sikhs; Indian Christians; Anglo-Indians; Other communities. In case the Muslim community agrees to the substitution throughout of joint electorates with reservation of seats for separate communal electorates, and in that case only, the Committee would recommend that in the interests of promoting communal harmony, the Hindu community should agree that in the strength of the Union Assembly, excluding the seats allotted to special interests, Muslim representation from British India shall be on a par with the representation given to the Hindus (other than

Scheduled Castes) in spite of the great disparity in their respective population strength.

Should this recommendation be not implemented in its entirety, the Hindu community should be at liberty not merely not to agree to parity of representation but also to ask for a revision of the Communal Award.

The representation given to the Sikhs and Scheduled Castes in the Government of India Act being inadequate and unjust should be increased, the quantum being left to the Constitution Making Body to fix.

For the Union Assembly there shall be adult franchise for seats other than those reserved for special interests.

Distribution of Power: The detailed drawing of lists shall be done by the Constitution-making body. The Committee recommend the following principles for guiding that body: The powers and functions assigned to the Centre should be as small in number as possible provided that they shall include.

(i) matters of common interest to India as a whole, such as foreign affairs, defence, relations with Indian States, inter-unit communications, commerce, customs, posts and telegraphs;

(ii) Settlement of inter-unit disputes;

(iii) Co-ordination where necessary of the legislation and administration of different units; and

(iv) Such other matters or action as may be required for ensuring the safety and tranquillity of India or any part thereof or for the maintenance of the political integrity and economic unity of India or for dealing with emergencies.

The Residuary Powers: Those not included in either of the two lists relating to the Union and the units, shall vest in the units.

All customs barriers between one unit and another shall be abolished provided that units prejudicially affected shall be entitled to compensation from the revenues of the Union.

Union Executive: The Executive of the Union shall be a composite Cabinet in the sense that the following communities shall be represented on it:

(i) Hindus, other than Scheduled Castes;

(ii) Muslims;

(iii)   Scheduled castes;
(iv)   Sikhs;
(v)   Indian Christians; and
(vi)   Anglo-Indians.

The representation of these communities shall be as far as possible, a reflection of their strength in the Legislature.

The Cabinet shall be deemed to be duly constituted notwithstanding the absence of the representative of any community on account of the refusal of the community to join it.

The Cabinet shall be collectively responsible to the Legislature, and shall be led and held together by a Prime Minister who shall ordinarily be the leader of a party which by itself or in combination with other parties is able to command a stable majority in the Legislature. By convention, the offices of Prime Minister and Deputy Prime Minister should not be monopolized by any one community.

The other ministers shall be appointed on the advice of the Prime Minister; one of these ministers shall be designated Deputy Prime Minister. By a standing rule the Deputy Prime Minister shall not belong to the same community as the Prime Minister.

An alternative to the above is suggested. The Cabinet whose composition shall be the same as above shall be elected by the Central Legislature in a joint session by the system of the single transferable vote; the ministers shall hold office for the duration of the Legislature. The Legislature shall elect from among the ministers a President and a Deputy President who shall not both belong to the same community.

Minister for Indian States: There shall be a minister in charge of the functions in relation to Indian States and with him shall be associated a body of persons not fewer than three and not more than five in number who shall be called Indian States Advisers, and who shall be chosen in the manner agreed upon with the Indian States. The minister shall consult the Indian States Advisers on all important matters and obtain their concurrence in certain matters specified in the Constitution Act.

Judiciary: There shall be a Supreme Court for the Union and a High Court in each of the units. The numbers and salary of the Judges shall initially be fixed by the Constitution Act and shall not be liable to modification except on the recommendation of the High Court, the government concerned and the Supreme Court and with the sanction of the Head of the State, provided that the salary of no Judge shall be varied to his disadvantage during his term of office.

The Chief Justice of India shall be appointed by the Head of the State and the other Judges of the Supreme Court by him in consultation with the Chief Justice of India. The Chief Justice of a High Court shall be appointed by the Head of the State in consultation with the Head of the Unit and the Chief Justice of India. Other Judges of a High Court shall be appointed by the Head of the State in consultation with the Head of the Unit, the Chief Justice of the High Court concerned and the Chief Justice of India. A Judge of the High Court or the Supreme Court shall be appointed for life subject to an age limit prescribed by the Constitution Act.

A Judge of the High Court may be removed from office by the Head of the State on the ground of misbehaviour or infirmity of mind or body if on reference being made to it by the Head of the State, the Supreme Court reports that the Judge ought on any such grounds to be removed. A Judge of the Supreme Court may be removed from office by the Head of the State on the same grounds if on reference being made to it a Special Tribunal appointed for the purpose by him reports that the Judge ought to be removed.

Defence: There shall be a portfolio of defence which should be held by a minister responsible to the Legislature but the actual control and discipline of the army should be placed in the hands of a Commander-in-Chief.

A national army shall be created and developed as rapidly as possible. For the creation of such an army the Committee recommends as follows:

(a) Such British units as may temporarily be required for the efficient defence of India and such officers as may be needed for officering the national army until an adequate number of Indian officers becomes available, shall be obtained by a treaty or agreement between the Union Government and His Majesty's Government,

(b) As soon as the war is over all recruitment of British officers to the Indian forces should cease. British officers not belonging to the Indian Army and not required for specific appointments should be reverted to the British army establishment. An institution should be established for the training in sufficient numbers of officers of all the three arms—air, land and sea. Defects in the present educational system should be removed. The University Officers Training Corps should be established where not existing, and expanded.

Representation in Public Services: The orders now in force at the Centre regarding the representation of communities in public services may continue till the new Constitution comes into operation. The Committee, however, recommend that the $8^1/_3$ per cent now allotted to the Sikhs, Indian Christians, Anglo-Indians and Parsis may be split up as follows: Sikhs $3^1/_2$ per cent, Indian Christians 3 per cent, Anglo-Indians and Parsis $1^5/_6$ per cent: but the special provisions relating to Anglo-Indians in certain services under Section 242, of the Government of India Act, 1935, are not affected by this recommendation.

The Chairman and members of the Public Services Commission of the Union and units shall be appointed by the Head of the State or the Head of the Unit in consultation with the Prime Minister of the Union or Unit concerned.

Fundamental Rights: A comprehensive Declaration of Fundamental Rights should be incorporated in the Constitution assuring the following:

(a) liberties of the individual,
(b) freedom of press and association,
(c) equality of rights of citizenship of all nationals,
(d) full religious toleration,
(e) protection to language and culture of all communities and abolishing all disabilities imposed by tradition or custom on Scheduled Castes and safeguarding special religious customs like wearing of kirpans by Sikhs.

Minorities Commission: There shall be an independent Minorities Commission at the Centre and in the provinces composed of representatives of each community (but not necessarily a member of that community) represented in the legislature elected by members of the legislature belonging to that community. No member of the legislature shall be eligible for election and the term of office of the members of the Commission shall synchronize with that of the legislature. The function of the Commission shall be to keep a constant watch over the interests of minority communities, to call for such information as the Commission consider necessary; to review periodically the policy pursued in regard to the implementation of non-justiciable fundamental rights and to submit reports to the Prime Minister. The recommendations of the Commission shall be considered by the Cabinet and the Prime Minister shall place the report of the Commission with a full statement of action taken thereon before the legislature which shall have facilities provided for a discussion thereon.

Minorities in the Punjab: The Committee recommends the case of the Sikhs, Hindus and Indian Christians relating to their representation in the Punjab Legislature for careful examination and consideration by the Constitution Making Body.

Amendment of the Constitution: A motion for amendment of the Constitution shall not be moved in the Union Legislature before six months have expired from the publication thereof and shall not be deemed to have been approved unless it has secured the support in each of the two Chambers of a majority of not less than two-thirds of its sanctioned strength. Further, such amendments shall not have effect unless approved by the Legislatures of not less than two-thirds of the units.

No amendment in respect of vital matters which shall be scheduled in the Constitution shall be made at all for five years from the coming into force of the new Constitution.

This scheme has been criticized by different persons from different points of view. What is considered to be a defect by one group of critics is regarded as a merit by another group and so many of the criticisms cancel one another. The fact that it does not adopt the extreme view-point of any particular group may be an argument in its favour. While it rejects the Muslim League's proposal for a division of India, it gives to Muslims parity with the caste Hindus in the Constitution-making body as also in the Central Legislative Assembly and in the Union Cabinet. If it gives equality of votes to the Muslims with the caste Hindus in the Constitution-making body, the Central Assembly and in the Central Cabinet, it makes such parity contingent on Muslims giving up separate electorates. It does not rule out independence but leaves

the door for a Dominion Constitution equally open. It makes the
office of the Head of the State elective but restricts the choice of
the electors to the order of Princes. It places relations with the
Princes in the hands of the Cabinet of the Union but makes the
Princes exclusively eligible for election to the office of the Head of
the State. It limits the term of office of the Head of the State to
five years but makes it possible for the office to go round in the
group of the larger States. It makes the Cabinet responsible to the
Legislature but it makes the Cabinet also composite, comprising
representatives of all groups in the Legislature. It divides the
Assembly into communal groups but makes the electorate joint,
thus allowing all communities to influence the election of members
of other groups. It aims at providing checks and balances so that
no one communal group may dominate either the Constitution-
making body or the Union Assembly and Cabinet. The details of
the Constitution are left to be worked out by the Constitution-
making body.

Apart from any other criticism, there seems to be no reason for
limiting the choice of the Head of the State from amongst some
Princes and at the same time making no provision for transferring
their power in their own States to the people. The Princes as a
body have given no proof of their ability or willingness to function
in a democratic Constitution and it is incongruous that instead of
being asked to transfer their power in their own States to their
people they should be promoted to a position of monopoly of the
office of the Head of the State of not only their own respective
States but of the whole country.

~

FORTY-TWO

DR AMBEDKAR'S SCHEME

Dr Ambedkar has recently put forward a new solution of the communal problem which he claims to be better than Pakistan. His solution is based mainly on the principle that a majority community may be conceded a relative majority of representation but it can never claim an absolute majority. This principle is applied both to provinces in which Hindus are in a majority and to provinces in which Muslims are in a majority. In either case the representation given to the majority does not exceed 40 per cent. Dr Ambedkar is emphatically opposed to the proposal of a Constituent Assembly which he considers superfluous inasmuch as so much of the Constitution of India has been written out in the Government of India Act, 1935, that it is an act of supererogation to appoint a Constituent Assembly to do the thing over again, when all that is necessary is to delete those sections of the Act which are inconsistent with Dominion Status.

Dividing the communal problem into the three categories of representation in the Legislature, in the Executive and in the services, Dr. Ambedkar lays down the principles which should govern each. As regards the services all that is necessary is to convert present administrative practice into statutory obligation. As regards representation in the Executive, the representation of the Hindus, the Muslims and the Scheduled Castes should be equal to the quantum of their representation in the Legislature. As regards other minorities a seat or two should be reserved for their representation and a convention established that they would get a fair portion of representation in the corps of parliamentary secretaries that would have to be raised.

The Executive should cease to be a Committee of the majority party in the Legislature but should be so constituted that it would have its mandate not only from the majority but also from the minorities in the Legislature. It should be non-parliamentary in

the sense that it shall not be removable before the term of the
Legislature and it should be parliamentary in the sense that the
members of the Executive shall be chosen from the members of
the Legislature and shall have the right to sit in the House, speak,
vote and answer questions.

The Prime Minister as the Executive Head of the government
should have the confidence of the whole House; the person
representing a particular minority in the Cabinet should have the
confidence of the members of the community in the Legislature. A
member of the Cabinet shall not be liable to be removed except
on impeachment by the House on the ground of corruption or
treason. Following these principles, the Prime Minister and the
members of the Cabinet from the majority community should be
elected by the whole House by the single transferable vote and
the representatives of the different minorities in the Cabinet shall
be elected by the single transferable vote of the members of each
minority community in the Legislature.

The following representation is proposed for the various
communities:

TABLE LIII

Communal Representation Proposed by Dr Ambedkar

In the Central Assembly—Hindus who form 54.68% of the population should get 40% representation					
Muslims	„	„	28.5%	„	32%
Scheduled Castes	„	„	14.3%	„	20%
Indian Christians	„	„	1.6%	„	3%
Sikhs	„	„	1.49%	„	4%
Anglo-Indians	„	„	0.5%		
(Percentage of population is taken after deducting the number of aboriginal tribes from the census figures)					
In Bombay	Hindu	„	„	76.42%	„	40%
	Muslims	„	„	9.98%	„	28%
	Scheduled Castes	„	„	9.64%	„	28%
	Indian Christians	„	„	1.75%	„	2%
	Anglo-Indians	„	„	0.07%	„	1%
	Parsis	„	„	0.44%	„	1%
In the Punjab	Muslims	„	„	57.06%	„	40%
	Hindus	„	„	22.17%	„	28%
	Sikhs	„	„	13.22%	„	21%
	Scheduled Castes	„	„	4.39%	„	9%
	Indian Christians	„	„	1.71%	„	2%

The distribution is said to be made on the following principles:

(1) The majority rule is untenable in theory and unjustifiable in practice.
(2) The relative majority of representation given to a majority community in the Legislature should not be so large as to enable the majority to establish its rule with the help of the smallest of minorities.
(3) The distribution of seats should be so made that a combination of the majority and one of the major minorities should not give the combine such a majority as to make them impervious to the interests of the minorities.
(4) The distribution should be so made that if all the minorities combine they could without depending on the majority form a government of their own.
(5) The weightage taken from the majority should be distributed among the minorities in inverse proportion to their social standing, economic position and educational conditions so that a minority which is large and which has a better social, educational and economic standing gets a lesser amount of weightage than a minority whose numbers are less and whose educational, economic and social position is inferior to that of the others.

Dr Ambedkar claims that his scheme is better than Pakistan for Musalmans because in it

(1) the danger of a communal majority which is the basis of Pakistan is removed;
(2) the weightage at present enjoyed by the Muslims is not disturbed;
(3) the position of Muslims in the non-Pakistan provinces is greatly strengthened by an increase in their representation which they may not get if Pakistan comes.

Dr Ambedkar asks the Hindus to give up their insistence on the rule of majority which is responsible for much of the difficulty over the communal question and to be satisfied with relative majority and satisfactory safeguards to the minorities as outlined by him.

A little consideration of the principles enunciated by Dr Ambedkar shows that he proceeds on the assumption that Hindus and Muslims shall, or rather should, never combine—which is justified neither in theory nor by fact. It further shows that while he considers majority rule as also a rule by the majority in combination with what he calls the smallest minorities untenable in theory and unjustifiable in practice, he does not see any such difficulty in allowing a minority in combination with another minority to rule not only the majority by itself but also the majority combined with all the other minorities. From the figures given by him it appears that the representation that he is prepared to give to a majority, whatever its size, is only 40 per cent, the rest being divided among the minorities. It is, therefore, always possible for the minorities to exclude the majority altogether from ever getting a chance of forming a ministry. He has not applied the third principle enunciated by him to the Centre or the two provinces whose figures he has worked out. It is possible on those figures not only for the majority and one of the major minorities in combination to command a fairly comfortable majority but even for two of the major minorities in the Centre and Bombay to do so.

His fifth principle is a novel one. But it seems it is intended to apply only to the Scheduled Castes and not to others. The tribes are admittedly among the most backward people in the country educationally, economically and socially. But in the whole scheme there is no mention of them except for pointing out that in calculating the percentages of population of various communities, their number has been deducted from the census figures. In the total population of British India they constitute no less than 5.65 as against 13.50 per cent Scheduled Castes, 26.83 Muslims, 1.18 Christians and 1.41 Sikhs, all of whom get extra representation whereas the tribes are ignored altogether. In some provinces they are more than the Scheduled Castes in numbers, for example in Assam they are 24.35 as against 6.63 per cent Scheduled Castes; in Bihar they are 13.91 as against 11.94 per cent Scheduled Castes; and in Orissa they are 19.72 as against 14.19 per cent Scheduled Castes; in CP and Berar they are almost equal to the Scheduled Castes, being 17.47 against 18.14 per cent Scheduled Castes, and in Bombay 7.74 as against 8.89 per cent Scheduled Castes. They are more than the Musalmans in the population of the provinces of Bihar, CP and Berar, and Orissa in which the Musalmans are only 12.98, 4.66, and 1.68 per cent respectively of the population. There seems to be very good reason for excluding the tribes—because their proportion in the population of India and of the provinces as shown above would place them above the Scheduled Castes in many provinces and above the Muslims in some. If the fifth principle of Dr Ambedkar is applied they would be entitled to higher representation even than the Scheduled Castes on account of their backwardness and the whole scheme of dividing up power between the Scheduled Castes and the Musalmans would be upset.

Apart from the principles which the learned Doctor has enunciated there are some others which are implicit in his proposals. In the election of the ministers, the minorities are entitled to have their representatives in the cabinet elected by themselves exclusively, while the representatives of the majority in the cabinet have to be elected by the whole House by the single transferable vote. This will result in the number of representatives of the majority community in the Cabinet elected exclusively with the votes of the members of that community in the legislature being reduced to 40 per cent of 40 per cent, that is, 16 per cent of the total, the rest, or a majority of them, being elected by the votes more or less exclusively of the minorities. The minorities will thus have not only their own representatives in the Cabinet whose number shall bear the same proportion to the total number of ministers as their numbers in the legislature bear to its total number, but they can also, by combination, have their own nominees elected to a majority of places intended for the representatives of the majority community in the Cabinet.

Again, unless the Hindus and the Muslims combine they cannot form a government without the help of the Scheduled Castes but if any one of them combines with the Scheduled Castes it can establish its rule regardless of the other and of other minorities.

Dr Ambedkar has worked out the figures for the Centre, Bombay and the Punjab only and not for the other provinces in the scheme as published in newspapers. If the figures for all the provinces are worked out it will be found that it is not possible to apply the principles laid down by him without exposing their absurdity. As, for example, it is difficult to say how he would distribute 60 per cent of the seats among small minorities comprising in the aggregate only 8.21 per cent of the population in the NWFP or amongst the Scheduled Castes (14.19 per cent), Muslims (1.68) and Christians (0.32) who in the aggregate constitute only 16.19 per cent in Orissa, apart from the tribes who have been excluded from calculation.

~

FORTY-THREE

MR M.N. ROY'S DRAFT CONSTITUTION

Mr M.N. Roy has published a Draft Constitution of India. It 'deals with fundamental questions and controversial issues leaving details to be filled in at a later stage.' 'The fundamental questions are about

(i)   the procedure of the transfer of power,
(ii) the structure of the State, and
(iii) the source of authority.

The position of other communities such as the depressed classes has also been a matter of controversy. The draft seeks to answer the fundamental questions and meet the controversial issues.' 'The basic assumption of this draft is that a democratic Constitution presupposes transfer of power to the Indian people as a whole.' A Constituent Assembly being impracticable in the absence of a revolution, the transfer of power must take place on the initiative of the British Parliament which must in the first instance transfer power formally and legally to the Indian people, and in the second place, create a constitutional authority in India to enable the people to exercise the right of sovereignty in practice. 'A Provisional Government is an indispensable necessity of the procedure of replacing one Constitution by another on the basis of a transfer of sovereignty.' This Provisional Government will be appointed by the British Parliament just as executors are appointed by a testator. There will thus be a Bill of Succession which will transfer power to the Indian people in respect of all territories in British India and in the Indian States, abrogate all treaties with the latter according to a previously concluded bilateral agreement, endorse the appended Constitution believing that it will establish democratic freedom, appoint the Governor-General who will appoint the Provisional Government. The Provisional Government, which will derive its authority from the Act and not be responsible to any elected body, will fix the territorial extent and population basis of People's Committees, delimit the areas of Indian provinces on the basis of linguistic and cultural homogeneity and according to administrative convenience, conduct the elections of Provincial People's Councils and Provincial Governors and constitute Provincial Governments, ascertain from the newly formed Provincial Governments whether any Province desires to remain out of the Federal Union of India, conduct the election of Governor-General and of the Deputies to the Federal Assembly and the nomination of the members of the Council of State and thus constitute the Supreme People's Council of the Federal Union of India and take similar measures in provinces which may not join the Federal Union of India. It shall resign upon the formation of the Provincial and Federal Executive Governments.

The difficulty presented by the position of Princes is sought to be solved by asking the British government to come to an understanding with them leading to the liquidation of their rights of governance over Indian territory and fixing some monetary allowances to enable them to live with dignity.

The Constitution provides for a declaration of fundamental rights and fundamental principles among which there will be one to the effect that 'the rights of minorities shall be protected by proportional representation through separate electorates on all elected public bodies.' In laying down the form and structure of the Federal Union, the Constitution provides that 'no Province which desires to remain outside the Federal Union shall be a constituent unit thereof.'

Before the Federal Union of India is constituted, the Provincial People's Councils elected under the Constitution shall have the right to entertain a proposal that the province concerned may keep out of the Federal Union. If the proposal is passed by a majority, it shall be submitted to a referendum of the adult population of the province. The proposal must be supported by a majority of voters in the province in order to be effective. Provinces keeping out of the federation shall be governed by the provisions of the Constitution in so far as they do not relate exclusively to the federal structure and may constitute themselves into another federation. The Federal Union of India will conclude a treaty of co-operation and mutual assistance with them on matters of mutual interest including customs, currency and railway administration. The Federal

Union of India will be a member of the larger federation known
as the British Commonwealth on terms and conditions stipulated
in a treaty. After the Federal Union of India is constituted, the
constituent units of the federation shall retain the inherent right
to secede from the Union. The proposal of secession must be
submitted to a referendum by the Provincial Government and
shall be effective if it receives the sanction of a majority of all
the voters in the province.

I have not summarized the other parts of the Constitution dealing
with the Federal Assembly, the Council of State, the Supreme
People's Council, the Governor-General, the Organs of Legislative
Power, the Organs of Executive Power, the Provinces, the Economic
Organization of Society, the Judiciary, and Local Self-Government,
as they deal with matters not germane to our present discussion
which is concerned only with the communal problem and its
suggested solution by the establishment of Pakistan. It would not
be fair to deal with those important aspects as a side issue in this
context, particularly when there is no special provision in them
impinging on the communal problem as such.

For his suggestion dealing with the communal problem
summarized above, Mr Roy claims that 'the Muslim League point of
view has been fully met. The demand for the separation of certain
regions before the transfer of power to the people of India as she
is at present constituted, runs up against the problem of procedure.
The draft eliminates that problem. Transfer of power takes place
on the basis of treating India as a constitutional unit. Thereafter,
provinces delimited by the Provincial Government, which will not
be responsible to any Indian elected body, will be at liberty not to
join the Federation. On the other hand, having made provision for
separation of provinces desiring to separate, the draft provides for
a Federal structure which leaves no room for fissiparous tendencies.
Federalism and Centralism are reconciled.'

All that I need state here in this connection is that the Muslim
League does not seem prepared to leave the decision of the
question of secession to the realm of futurity and to the hazards
of a referendum of all the adults in the province, nor is it likely
to agree to a redrawing of provincial boundaries on the basis of
linguistic and cultural homogeneity which may not coincide with
boundaries drawn on religious and communal basis, and that by
an authority about whose constitution nothing definite is known

except that it will be appointed by the Governor-General who in his turn will have been appointed by Parliament. Nor is the provision for the protection of the rights of minorities by means of proportional representation through separate electorates on all elected public bodies likely to satisfy it.

In the preceding pages I have given the various schemes which have been proposed as alternatives to the proposal of the Muslim League for the establishment of independent Muslim States in the north-west and east of India, to enable the reader to consider them and form his own opinion on them. It is not necessary for me to give any concrete suggestions of my own. So far as I am aware, there is no communal group or organization other than the Muslim League which has put forward a proposal for the Partition of India into Muslim and non-Muslim independent States. Even amongst Musalmans there are other organizations which have opposed the proposal. It is not for me to determine whether these other groups are entitled to speak for a majority of the Muslims or what proportion of them. Nor is it necessary to determine it, as we shall see hereafter, for my present purpose. Non-Muslim organizations have, I believe, without any exception, expressed their opposition to it. Those who are thus opposed to any scheme of Partition can take up any of these schemes as basis for discussion and hammer out something which will be fair and just to all and will satisfy all parties. I do believe it is possible at a round table conference to evolve such a scheme and it will serve no useful purpose at any such conference to have one more scheme added to those detailed above and others which I have not seen or discussed. So far as the Muslim League is concerned, it has expressed its decision through its president and other leaders that it is not prepared to discuss any scheme which does not start with accepting the Lahore Resolution of the League. That must be accepted as a preliminary, as a condition precedent, to any further talk. It will not therefore require or discuss any scheme which does not proceed on that basis. Not only that, it is not prepared to discuss any scheme which does not accept its own interpretation of that Resolution and at the same time it refuses to interpret it in concrete terms which may make the picture clear and intelligible. The formula which C. Rajagopalachari put forward is claimed by him to fulfil the Lahore Resolution of the League. It purports to put down in concrete form what the Resolution has laid down as a principle and in general terms. But the League President was not prepared even to discuss it and during the prolonged talks with Mahatma Gandhi, he tried only to 'instruct' him in the principles and policies underlying that Resolution without coming to any details. Thus, no concrete scheme is required by the Muslim League. I have therefore after some deliberation decided not to add to such schemes. Any scheme, however, must fulfil two fundamental conditions. It must be fair and just to all communities. It must be more. It must also rise above the din and dust of present-day controversy and visualize for this country and for its millions something of which all may be proud and for which they can live, work and die. A man is member of a community; but he is also *a man*—perhaps a man more than member of a community. No scheme, however elaborate, which satisfies all communal claims most meticulously but leaves man as man uncured and unprovided for, will be worth the paper it will be written on. That scheme alone will be worthy of the people of this great country which enables its humblest citizen to live a happier and nobler life than it has been his lot to live in the past.

It is really a question offering two alternatives before the people of India to make their choice. The choice has to be made between two alternative schemes—one involving a division of the country and its people into separate zones and nationalities; the other maintaining the unity of the country and providing for the fullest possible development—moral, intellectual and material—of all groups, including the smallest, which inhabit it and removing all barriers—social, political, or economic—tending to bar or fetter that development. The choice has to be made by the Muslims as much as by the Hindus and others who inhabit this country. The choice has to be made by them with their eyes open, their minds informed and alert, after studying and considering all the pros and cons. There should be and can be no question of coercion or force. Nor should there be any question of overreaching the other party. It cannot be denied that the issues involved are of tremendous significance not only to this country but in the context of world affairs to millions living outside it also. We must be prepared to judge each question as it arises in cold reason and above all with intellectual integrity and with a determination to be just and fair to all. Given this determination to be just and fair, it is not impossible to find a solution acceptable to all. It is no use saying that attempts to reach a settlement have failed in the past. That would only indicate our weakness, prove our want of faith in ourselves.

But for a discussion to be fruitful or even possible, we should give up issuing ultimatums, we should cease laying down conditions precedent to any discussion, we must stop laying down that as the minimum of our demand to be accepted prior to the opening of any discussion, which will be the maximum that can be claimed or conceded. Discussion, persuasion, give and take are the only methods open to us. What is more, they are the only civilized methods. We dare not think of any other method, even though the world may be witnessing its use on a gigantic scale by the civilized nations today.

El Hamza has tried to show in his book by visual representation that Pakistan will be bigger in area and population than some of the smallest and smaller countries and nations of Europe. Why should we be content to be bigger than the smallest or the smaller ones of Europe? Why should we not aim at an India that will be bigger than the biggest of Europe, bigger than the biggest of America, very nearly as big as the biggest of Asia? Is not that an ambition worth living and dying for? Not that we want to be big to be able to suppress and oppress others who may be smaller and weaker. The long history of India mentions no instance of aggression by her on any neighbouring or distant country. We want to be big to serve ourselves and serve others—to serve the smallest among ourselves and the smallest among others. Remove all obstacles and hindrances in the way of this service by all means. Cut down ruthlessly all temptations and all encouragements to using the power that bigness confers for oppression or suppression by all means. But let us not give way to despair and seek a solution of despondency.

There can be no doubt that Partition is a solution of despair. It cannot solve the problem of minorities, even if it does not aggravate it. My apprehension is that it will aggravate it. It is bound to leave behind a bitter legacy. Its enforcement is bound to be followed by ebullient, joyous exuberance on one side and sullen, smouldering resentment on the other. It is of such stuff that fratricidal feuds and world-wide wars are made. We shall be wise not to underestimate them. We shall be wise also not to underestimate the fund of good will and fellow feeling that a thousand years of joint life and joint endeavour have given us, which may yet lead to a satisfactory settlement.

But—and there is a but which cannot be ignored—if all this has no appeal and Partition there must be, we should be prepared for the aftermath and not hug the delusion that thereafter all will be plain sailing. It is at least as easy to visualize the disastrous consequences as it has been to paint the pleasant picture of it. In any case we should be prepared to be fair, honest and just, and if all of us are actually that in our life and our dealings, something may yet be done to mitigate the disaster and reduce the resultant bitterness. I do not wish to end this book with a note of despair. I am not without hopes in the justice, fairness and commonsense of our people—Hindus, Muslims, Sikhs, Christians, Parsis and others—and feel that they will be able to evolve something that will be worthy and worthwhile, something that our successors will be proud of, something that will place before a distracted world an ideal worthy of emulation. That can be achieved only if we march with truth as our light and non-violence as our support.

We have seen within our own generation two devastating world wars. The experiment made after the First World War of solving the problem of nationalities by establishing national states has failed and resulted directly in a second and more widespread and more devastating World War. It may be that Europe has not profited by two such disasters and will still insist on maintaining peace in the world by standing guard on nationalities waiting for the chance to fight one another. Can we not make our own contribution by setting up within our land a State which, despite all differences—and even bitter memories, if you please—is able not only to protect but also to fulfil the highest aspirations of all its people? It does not mean denial of self-determination but the fulfilment of it. Only all have to choose it and work it with good will and integrity.

I carried the story of the attempts to solve the Hindu–Muslim problem up to the Simla Conference in July 1945. Since then some other developments have taken place which may be noted here to bring it up to date. We have seen that in the course of the discussions which Mahatma Gandhi had with Mr Jinnah in 1944, it emerged more or less clearly for the first time that in demarcating the areas which were to be included in the Muslim zones, the units for considering whether they had a majority of Muslims in them were to be the provinces and not districts or any other smaller areas. The League and its leaders had persistently refused to give any indication of their mind on this point till his C. Rajagopalachari put forward his formula providing that 'a commission shall be appointed for demarcating contiguous districts in the north-west and east of India, wherein the Muslim population is in absolute majority' and practically forced Mr Jinnah to state to the representative of the *News Chronicle* of London on 4 October 1944, that India should be divided into two sovereign parts of Pakistan and Hindustan 'by the recognition of the whole of the north-west Frontier Province, Baluchistan, Sind, Punjab, Bengal and Assam as sovereign Muslim territories as they now stand'.[1] In another interview to the representative of the *Daily Worker* of London on 5 October 1944, he said: 'To understand the Pakistan demand in its full significance, it is to be borne in mind that the six Provinces, viz. the NWFP, Baluchistan, Sind, and the Punjab In the north-west, and Bengal and Assam in the north-east of this sub-continent, have a population of 70 million Muslims and the total population of Muslims would not be less than 70 per cent.'[2] At a press conference which he gave

[1] *Jinnah–Gandhi Talks*, p. 75.
[2] Ibid., p. 79.

after the termination of the Gandhi–Jinnah talks 'Mr Jinnah
referred a questioner to the Lahore Resolution which stated that
the division should be on the basis of the present boundaries of
the six provinces, i.e. the NWFP, the Punjab, Sind, Bengal, Assam
and Baluchistan, subject to territorial adjustments that might be
necessary. He emphasized the words "subject to" and explained
that territorial adjustments did not apply to one side only but
to both sides, Hindustan and Pakistan,' making it clear that 'the
question of demarcating or defining the boundaries can be taken
up later in the same way as the question of boundaries arising
between two nations is solved.'[3]. It is thus made clear that the
units are to be the provinces and not any smaller areas like the
commissionerships or districts, taluks or sub-divisions. One point
was still left vague, that is, the question of territorial adjustments.
We shall see later how that is being interpreted now.

We may notice here Mr Jinnah's statement to the representative
of the *Daily Worker* that Pakistan so defined as to comprise the six
provinces mentioned above will have a population of 70 million
Muslims and the total population of Muslims would not be less
than 79 per cent. Mr Jinnah evidently does not believe in figures
and seems to think that arithmetic no less than geography and
the history of a thousand years can be controlled and altered by
mere assertion of a palpably untenable proposition. The Tables of
population given in another part of this book will show that the
total population of the north-western zone comprising the four
provinces of the NWFP, Baluchistan, Sind and the Punjab would
be 3,64,93,525, out of which the number of Muslims would be
2,26,53,294, or 62.07 per cent. Similarly, the total population of
the eastern zone comprising the provinces of Assam and Bengal
in their entirety will be 7,05,11,258, out of which the Muslims
would be only 3,64,47,913, or 51.69 per cent. If the two zones are
taken together, their total population will come to 10,70,04,783
of which the Muslims would be 5,91,01,207 or 55.23 per cent.
We see that the population of the Muslims in the two zones
taken together is only 59 millions and not 70 millions as stated
by Mr Jinnah and that its proportion to the total population
of the two zones is only 55.23 per cent and not 70 per cent as
claimed by him.

[3] Ibid., p. 72.

Some clarification is now available of the 'territorial adjustments' referred to above. In an interview to Mr Donald Edwards of the BBC, Mr Jinnah was asked about the difficulty of forming a Pakistan State out of the two areas, one in the north-east of India, one in the north-west, nearly a thousand miles apart, with a Hindu corridor dividing them. Mr Jinnah replied: 'When you travel from Britain to the other parts of the British Commonwealth, you pass through foreign territory—Suez Canal, for instance. It is all done by amicable arrangement. We travel from Muslim areas of the north-east to the Muslim areas of the north-west across this so-called Hindu corridor without any difficulty today. Why should that arrangement not continue? The Hindus must not be allowed to put difficulties in the way of a State that wants to be their neighbour in a friendly way. They must not be allowed to close the doors of communication between the Muslims of north-west India and the Muslims of north-east. This must be one of the terms of the treaty.'[4]

This statement, by the way, makes the two zones in the north-east and north-west of India into one single Muslim State. It would be recalled that the Lahore Resolution of the League passed in March 1940 said that the areas in which the Muslims are in a majority in the north-western and eastern zones of India should be grouped to constitute 'Independent States' and not one single State. Mr Jinnah now claims that not only should the two zones constitute one single State but that the Hindu State must also provide a corridor of nearly a thousand miles between the two Muslim zones. He mentions that there is free passage between the eastern and the western zones today and asks—why should that arrangement not continue? The simple answer to that question is that the two zones and the intervening territory are today included in one single State and as such they have not only a free passage as between them but are under one central government with its headquarters at Delhi. After separation, the two States of Pakistan and Hindustan will be independent sovereign States and there can be no question of one independent State allowing passage through its territory to another independent State to enable the latter to have a land route to one of its outlying parts.

In the same interview, Mr Jinnah was questioned as to why Assam with its huge Hindu population should be part of Pakistan.

[4] *The Dawn*, 2 April 1946,

He replied: 'There is no other way of fitting Assam anywhere
except in Pakistan.' Evidently Mr Jinnah thinks that if Bengal is
included in Pakistan, Assam is cut off from the rest of India and
it must therefore be included in the eastern zone of Pakistan.
Now, Assam will be cut off from Hindustan only if the districts
of Jalpaiguri and Darjeeling with a Muslim population of 23 per
cent and 2.4 per cent respectively and the Hindu State of Cooch
Behar with 62 per cent Hindus in its population are included
in the Muslim zone. Logic and fairplay have no place when the
question to be considered is which areas are to be included within
the sovereign Pakistan State. Districts with overwhelming Hindu
population both in the Punjab and in Bengal and Assam must be
included within Pakistan because today they happen to be parts
of provinces which are claimed to be Muslim zones. Hindus must
not be allowed to stand in the way of a corridor being provided
between the two Muslim zones. Assam should be included in the
eastern zone because it is cut off from Hindustan. It must be cut
off from Hindustan because no corridor can be allowed by the
Muslim State to join Assam with Hindustan through the districts
which are overwhelmingly Hindu in population. Evidently it is a
case of heads we win, tails you lose.

Another point has come out recently. Mr Suhrawardy, the
prime minister of the League ministry of Bengal, claims that not
only the whole of Bengal and Assam but also the districts of
Singhbhum, Manbhum, Santhal Parganas and Purnea of Bihar
should be included within Pakistan. They will, of course, form
part of the eastern zone. Pakistan will then be in a position to
say that most of the iron and copper ore, most of the coal and
all the oil and many of the other metals that are to be found in
India are within Pakistan. People have been at pains to point out
that Pakistan will be lacking in most of these essential commodities
which cannot be dispensed with in any independent State. Mr
Suhrawardy answers by claiming that the areas which possess
these commodities must be included within Pakistan. They will
thus be made self-sufficient in this respect It, of course, does not
matter that they are not included within the provinces claimed
for Pakistan and the Muslim population in them is very small,
only 18.12 per cent of the total population.

It may also be pointed out in passing that in the population
of the eastern zone, as it will be when these districts are included
within it, the Muslims will be actually in a minority of 48.34 per

TABLE LIV

Muslim and Non-Muslim Population in the North-Western and Eastern Zones with Four Districts of Bihar Added

	Total population	Muslim population	Percentage of Muslim population	Non-Muslim population	Percentage of non-Muslim population
North-Western Zone	3,64,93,525	2,26,53,294	62.07	1,38,40,231	37.92
Bengal and Assam	7,05,11,258	3,64,47,913	51.69	3,40,63,345	48.30
Total of NW Zone and Bengal and Assam	10,70,04,783	5,91,01,207	55.23	4,79,03,576	48.30
Bihar Districts					
Purnea	23,90,105	9,76,048	40.84	14,14,057	59.16
Santhal Pargana	22,34,497	2,62,836	11.76	19,71,661	88.24
Manbhum	20,32,146	1,32,234	6.51	18,99,912	93.49
Singhbhum	11,44,717	43,233	3.77	11,01,484	96.23
Total of Bihar Districts	78,01,465	14,14,351	18.12	63,87,114	81.87
Grand Total of NW Zone, Bengal, Assam and four Districts of Bihar	11,48,06,248	6,05,15,558	52.71	5,42,90,690	47.28

cent, and whatever justification there is for claiming a separate independent State of Muslims on the basis of their being in a majority in the population of an area ceases to exist after this territorial adjustment. Even if we take the total population of the two zones together, the proportion of the Muslim population will be reduced from a small majority of 55.23 per cent to a nominal majority of 52.71 per cent. Thus we now know what is meant by territorial adjustment, which according to Mr Jinnah must be on both sides. Hindustan must give and Pakistan must take.

Another question has been engaging public attention ever since the two nations theory was propounded. All Muslims being one nation by reason of their religion alone, irrespective of any other considerations like the territory they inhabit, the language they speak, etc., the question naturally arises: what would be the position and status of the Muslims who will be left in Hindustan, which according to the League proposal will be a Hindu State. Mr Jinnah, on being asked what he proposed for those areas where the Muslims are in a minority replied in the course of the interview referred to above: 'Those areas, like Madras for instance, will have a Hindu Government and the Muslim minority there will have three courses open to them: they may accept citizenship of the State in which they are: they can remain there as foreigners; or they can come to Pakistan. I will welcome them. There is plenty of room. But it is for them to decide.' Mr Jinnah accepts the position that the Muslims who are citizens of India today will, after Partition, cease to be citizens of Hindustan and therefore they will have three alternatives to choose from. Let us examine these three alternatives.

The first alternative is that they may accept citizenship in the State in which they are. It may be pointed out that citizenship can be acquired by a foreigner in a State only under rules made for that purpose by the State concerned. It is open to any State which is independent to regulate and control its own population and to lay down restrictions on foreigners acquiring citizenship and even to prohibit it altogether. The history of the British Dominions like South Africa, Canada and Australia, which are all members of the British Commonwealth and Empire, to which India also belongs, and which owe allegiance to the same King-Emperor to whom Indians are in law required to owe allegiance, shows how they have successfully and effectively prevented Indians from acquiring the rights of citizenship. The United States of America also regulates immigration and does not permit any and every foreigner to acquire the right of citizenship simply because the foreigner wishes to have that right. So if Hindustan is to be really a free and sovereign State, it will have the same right to regulate its citizenship and to lay down rules for and even to prohibit acquisition of the rights of citizenship by foreigners. It will not lie with the Muslims left in Hindustan to become its citizens unless Hindustan permits it. Mr Jinnah, of course, assumes that Hindus must not be allowed to put difficulties in their way.

The second alternative is that they can remain there as foreigners. Here again he makes the same assumption. Hindustan, like any other independent State, will not be bound to allow foreigners to remain on its territory, particularly when they happen to be in such large numbers as the Muslims will be. It is also worth remembering that an independent State may regulate and even prohibit the acquisition of property, particularly immovable property, by foreigners within its territory. We have the illustration once again of South Africa before our eyes.

The third alternative is that the Musalmans who will be left in Hindustan can go to Pakistan. This, of course, is legally possible. Every foreigner is entitled to leave the foreign State and to go to his own State unless he is accused of a crime for which he is triable in the foreign State. The Musalmans of Hindustan can leave Hindustan if they so desire but they cannot carry away with them their lands and houses, even if they are allowed and are in a position to take away their movables like cash, jewellery, cattle and furniture. Hindustan will not be bound to give any compensation for what they leave behind. They will have migrated out of Hindustan of their own free will by reason of their having adopted a foreign nationality. It is difficult to believe that the Muslims of Hindustan will choose this alternative of emigration from Hindustan. Their attachment to their lands and homes will make any such break most difficult, if not impracticable. The distance which they will, in many cases, have to travel before they can reach Pakistan will be immense and the consequent suffering will be unbearable. Last, though not least, the complete dislocation of their finances and economy, which emigration will involve, will effectively prohibit any such enterprise. They will have, therefore, only the first two alternatives to choose from and there they will not be free to do so as the foreign State of Hindustan will have an effective and determining voice in the matter.

All these considerations which arise out of the two nations theory do not appear to trouble the protagonists of Pakistan. Mr Jinnah now evidently accepts the position, which indeed cannot be questioned, that the Muslims in Hindustan will have the status of foreigners or aliens and will, therefore, be subject to the same disabilities that a foreigner suffers from. The same consideration might not apply to Hindus and non-Muslims who will be left in Pakistan, as they do not claim to be members of another nation and as such citizens of another State. But in any case, even if they are treated as foreigners, or aliens, the difference in their position will be that foreign citizenship will have been forced upon them against their will, while in the case of Muslims it will have been chosen by them of their own free will with their eyes open and indeed against the wishes and in face of the opposition of the Hindus and other non-Muslims.

This addendum will not be complete without reference to general elections to the Assemblies both Central and Provincial. The Muslim League attained phenomenal success in the elections to the Central Assembly and secured all the seats reserved for Musalmans. It may, however, be pointed out that the Nationalist Muslims secured nearly one-fourth of the total votes polled as against the League. In Sind they secured 32 per cent and in the Punjab 30 per cent of the total Muslim votes cast. The NWFP sends only one representative to the Central Assembly who is returned by a joint electorate of Muslims and non-Muslims. So also does Delhi send one representative elected by a joint electorate. Both these places were captured by Muslim candidates who had been set up on behalf of the Congress.

At the provincial elections the Muslim League had set up candidates for seats reserved for Musalmans and there was contest in many of them between the League candidates on the one hand and other Muslim candidates set up by Jamait-ul-Ulema, the Momins, the Ahrars and other nationalist Muslim organizations and some Independents on the other. The League secured the seats mentioned below in the provinces claimed by the League for Pakistan and in which elections have been held. Baluchistan has no assembly at present and hence no elections.

TABLE LV

Analysis of Muslim Voting for Provincial Elections

Provinces	Seats Secured by League	Seats Secured by Non-League Muslims	Votes for the League	Percentage of votes for League	Votes Secured by Non-League Muslims	Percentage of Votes for Non-League Muslims
NWFP	17	21	1,47,880	41.4	2,08,896	58.5
Sind	26	8	1,99,651	56.8	1,52,235	43.2
The Punjab	73	13	6,79,796	65.1	3,58,235	34.3
Assam	31	3	1,88,071	69.0	84,453	31.0

The Muslim League was unable to form ministries in the NWFP, the Punjab and Assam. In the NWFP and Assam, the Congress had an absolute majority in the Assembly and as such the Congress Party alone was in a position to form ministries and it was asked by the Governor to do so and it did. It may also be mentioned that in the NWFP not only had the Congress an absolute majority in the Provincial Assembly but it had also a majority from among the Muslim members in it. In the Sind Assembly, the Congress along with non-League Muslims had twenty-nine members; the League had twenty-eight. There were three Europeans, who declared themselves to be neutral in the matter of formation of the ministry. The Governor, however, chose to invite the League to form the ministry, which it did, and the ministry is able to function with the help of the three European members. The only other province where the League has been able to form a ministry is Bengal.

The leaders of the League have, however, declared that they did not fight the elections with a view to forming ministries but for the larger and higher purpose of establishing Pakistan and they claim that the elections have shown that Musalmans are overwhelmingly in favour of Pakistan. The figures given above, however, show that in the north-west Frontier Province, a majority of Musalmans is opposed to the Pakistan idea. In Sind, no less than 43 per cent and in the Punjab, 34 per cent of Muslim voters are opposed to the League and Pakistan. In Assam, which is overwhelmingly non-Muslim, 31 per cent even of the Muslims are opposed to it. The figures for Bengal are not given because they were not available at the time of writing this. It is unnecessary to go into the figures of the other provinces which are not claimed by the League for Pakistan and the opinion of Musalmans there can have significance only as being a vote in favour of the Musalmans of those provinces being regarded as foreigners there. It may also be pointed out that it would be most unfair not to recognize the right of non-Muslims of the areas sought to be separated to express themselves on the question of separation. If their votes at the elections are counted along with those of the Musalmans who are opposed to Pakistan, it will be clear that the provinces as a whole are opposed to Pakistan and the results of the Assembly elections, far from being in favour of Pakistan, are opposed to it.

While elections for the Provincial Legislatures were going on, Lord Pethick-Lawrence, then Secretary of State for India, made an announcement in the House of Commons on 19 February 1946, in which he said that the British government had, with the approval of His Majesty the King, decided to send out to India a special mission of Cabinet Ministers, namely, Lord Pethick-Lawrence, Sir Stafford Cripps and Mr Albert V. Alexander, to act in association with the Viceroy and to hold preparatory discussions with elected representatives of British India and with the Indian States in order to secure the widest measure of agreement on

(1) the method of framing a Constitution,
(2) the setting up of a constitution-making body and
(3) the bringing into being of an Executive Council having the support of the main Indian parties.

On 15 March 1946, on the eve of the departure of the Cabinet Mission, Mr Attlee, the Prime Minister, made another statement in the House of Commons, in which he made it clear that the Cabinet Mission was going out to India with the intention of using its utmost endeavours to help her to attain freedom. He said, 'India herself must choose as to what will be her future situation and her position in the world. Unity may come through the United Nations or through the Commonwealth, but no great nation can stand alone by herself without sharing what is happening in the world. I hope that India will elect to remain within the British Commonwealth. I am certain that she will find great advantage in doing so; but if she does, she must do it of her own free will, for the British Commonwealth and Empire is not bound together by chains of external compulsion. It is a free association of free peoples. If, on the other hand, she elects for independence—and in our view she has a right to do so—it will be for us to help make the transition as smooth and easy as possible.' Referring to the minorities, he said, 'We are mindful of the rights of the minorities, and the minorities should be able to live free from fear. On the other hand, we cannot allow a minority to place their veto on the advance of a majority.' Regarding the Indian States, he said, 'I am hoping that the statesmen of Britain and of Princely India will be able to work out a solution of the problem of bringing together in one great polity the various constituent parts, and there again we must see that the Indian States find their due place.'

The Mission arrived in India towards the end of March, and set about its work in conjunction with Lord Wavell in right earnest. It interviewed leaders of different groups, parties and communities, with a view to ascertaining their view points and, after some time, was able to arrange a conference between the representatives of the Congress and the All-India Muslim League on the one hand and themselves on the other. This conference met in Simla for several days and, although no agreement could be reached, the view points of both the parties became clear. The Cabinet Mission and the Viceroy issued another statement on 16 May 1946, with the full approval of His Majesty's Government in the United Kingdom. It said: 'Since no agreement has been reached, we feel that it is our duty to put forward what we consider are the best arrangements possible to ensure a speedy setting up of the new Constitution . . . We have accordingly decided that immediate arrangements should be made whereby Indians may decide the future Constitution of India and an Interim Government may be set up at once to carry on the administration of British India until such time as a new Constitution can be brought into being.' The statement, after examining the question of a separate and fully independent sovereign State of Pakistan as claimed by the Muslim League, came to the conclusion that 'the setting up of a separate sovereign State of Pakistan on the lines claimed by the Muslim League would not solve the communal minority problem; nor can we see any justification for including within a sovereign Pakistan those districts of the Punjab and Bengal and Assam in which the population is predominantly non-Muslim.' They considered, further, whether a smaller sovereign Pakistan, confined to the Muslim majority areas alone, might be a possible basis of compromise, but they felt 'forced to the conclusion that neither a larger nor a smaller sovereign state of Pakistan would provide an acceptable solution for the communal problem.' 'Apart from the great force of the foregoing arguments,' they declared, 'there are weighty administrative, economic and military considerations.' In the result they said: 'We are, therefore, unable to advise the British Government that the power which at present resides in British hands should be handed over to two entirely separate sovereign States.' They put forward their own proposals in paragraph 15 of the Statement, which is as follows:

'We recommend that the Constitution should take the following basic form:

(1) There should be a Union of India, embracing both British India and the States, which should deal with the following subjects:

Foreign affairs; defence; and communications; and should have the powers necessary to raise the finances required for the above subjects.

(2) The Union should have an Executive and a Legislature constituted from British Indian and States' representatives. Any questions raising a major communal issue in the Legislature should require for its decision a majority of the representatives present and voting of each of the two major communities as well as a majority of all the members present and voting.

(3) All subjects other than Union subjects and all residuary powers should vest in the provinces.

(4) The States will retain all subjects and powers other than those ceded to the Union.

(5) Provinces should be free to form Groups with executives and legislatures, and each Group could determine the provincial subjects to be taken in common.

(6) The Constitutions of the Union and of the Groups should contain a provision whereby any province could, by a majority vote of its Legislative Assembly, call for a reconsideration of the terms of the Constitution after an initial period of 10 years and at 10-yearly intervals thereafter.'

With a view to obtaining as broad-based and accurate a representation of the whole population as was possible in the Constitution-making Assembly, they thought that an election base on adult franchise would obviously be the most satisfactory procedure, but that that would lead to a wholly unacceptable delay in the formulation of the new Constitution, and as a practicable alternative, they proposed that the recently elected Provincial Legislative Assemblies should be utilized as the bodies to elect the Constitution-making Assembly. Inasmuch as the numerical strengths of the Provincial Legislative Assemblies did not bear the same proportion to the total population in each province, it was decided that the fairest and most practicable plan would be:

(a) to allot to each province a total number of seats proportional to its population, roughly in the ratio of one to a million, as the nearest substitute for representation by adult suffrage.

(b)   to divide this provincial allocation of seats between the main communities in each province in proportion to their population.

(c)   to provide that the representatives allotted to each community in a province shall be elected by the members of that community in its Legislative Assembly.

For these purposes, they recognized only three main communities in India, namely, General, Muslim and Sikh, the general community including all persons who are not Muslim or Sikh. As the small minorities would, on population basis, have little or no representation, an arrangement was made to give them full representation, so that their special interests might be looked after, and that was to provide for an Advisory Committee on the rights of citizens, minorities and tribal and excluded areas, which should contain full representation of the interests affected. Its function would be to report to the Union Constituent Assembly upon the list of fundamental rights, clauses for the protection of minorities and a scheme for the administration of tribal and excluded areas, and to advise whether these rights should be incorporated in the Provincial, Group or Union Constitution.

As regards the general Constituent Assembly, it was proposed in paragraph 19 that each Provincial Legislative Assembly should elect a certain number of members as representatives (General, Muslim or Sikh) to the Constituent Assembly by the method of proportional representation with the single transferable vote. The numbers were fixed on the basis of one member for one million of the population in the province. The provinces were divided into three sections, A, B and C. Section A comprised Madras, Bombay, the United Provinces, Bihar, the Central Provinces and Orissa, in each of which non-Muslims are in a majority and the Muslims in a minority. The total number of seats in the Constituent Assembly from these provinces was to be 187, of which 167 were General and twenty Muslim. Section B comprised the Punjab, the NWFP and Sind, with a total of thirty-five members, of whom nine were General, twenty-two Muslim and four Sikh. Section C comprised Bengal and Assam, with seventy members, of whom thirty-four were General and thirty-six Muslim. Thus British India would have a total of 292 seats, of which 210 were to be General, seventy-eight Muslim and four Sikh.

In order to represent the Chief Commissioners' Provinces, there would be added to Section A the member representing Delhi in the Central Legislative Assembly, the member representing Ajmer-Merwara in the Central Legislative Assembly, and a representative elected by the Coorg Legislative Council. To Section B would be added a representative of British Baluchistan. The States were to be given ninety-three seats in the Constituent Assembly, based on the same calculation of one member for every million of the population. The method of selection was to be determined by consultation.

Paragraph 19 of the statement proceeded to lay down that:

(iii)   The representatives thus chosen shall meet at New Delhi as soon as possible.

(iv)   A preliminary meeting will be held at which the general order of business will be decided, a Chairman and other officers elected, and an Advisory Committee on the rights of citizens, minorities, and tribal and excluded areas set up. Thereafter, the Provincial representatives will divide up into the three sections shown under A, B and C.

(v)   These sections shall proceed to settle the Provincial Constitutions for the Provinces included in each section, and shall also decide whether any Group Constitution shall be set up for those Provinces and, if so, with what Provincial subjects the Group should deal. 'Provinces shall have the power to opt out of the Groups in accordance with the provisions of sub-clause (viii) below.

(vi)   The representatives of the Sections and the Indian States shall reassemble for the purpose of settling the Union Constitution.

(vii)   In the Union Constituent Assembly, resolutions varying the provisions of paragraph 15 above or raising any major communal issue shall require a majority of the representatives present and voting of each of the two major communities. The Chairman of the Assembly shall decide which (if any) of the resolutions raise major communal issues and shall, if so requested by a majority of the representatives of either of the major communities, consult the Federal Court before giving his decision,

(viii) As soon as the new constitutional arrangements have come into operation, it shall be open to any province to elect to come out of any Group in which it has been placed.

Such a decision shall be taken by the new legislature of
the province after the first general election under the new
Constitution.'

The Viceroy was forthwith to request the Provincial Legislatures
to proceed with the election of their representatives, and the States
to set up a Negotiating Committee. A Treaty, was to be negotiated
between the Union Constituent Assembly and the United Kingdom
to provide for certain matters arising out of the transfer of power.
While the Constitution-making was proceeding, the administration
of India had to be carried on. It was, therefore, necessary to set up
at once an Interim Government having the support of the major
political parties. The Viceroy, accordingly, started discussions with
a view to the formation of an Interim Government in which all
the portfolios, including that of War Member, would be held by
Indian leaders who had the full confidence of the people. The
British government 'recognizing the significance of the changes
in the Government of India, will give the fullest measure of co-
operation to the government so formed in the accomplishment
of its tasks of administration and in bringing about as rapid and
smooth a transition as possible.'

The Statement closed with an appeal and a profound hope that
the proposals would be accepted and operated by the people of
India in the spirit of accommodation and goodwill in which they
were offered.

The Statement was subjected to close scrutiny by all the parties
concerned. The President of the Muslim League, in his statement
of 22 May 1946 expressed regret that the Mission should have
negatived the Muslim demand for the establishment, of a complete
sovereign State of Pakistan, and dealt with some of the important
points of the operative parts of the Statement in detail. The Congress
Working Committee passed a resolution on 24 May 1946, which,
after mentioning certain points which required elucidation and
amendment, laid emphasis on one point in. particular. It said: 'The
Statement of the Cabinet Delegation affirms the basic principle of
provincial autonomy and residuary powers vesting in the provinces.
It is further said that the provinces should be free to form
groups. Subsequently, however, it is recommended that provincial
representatives will divide up into sections, which shall proceed to
settle the provincial Constitutions for the Provinces in each section

and shall also decide whether any group Constitution shall be set up for those provinces. There is a marked discrepancy in these two separate provisions, and it would appear that a measure of compulsion is introduced which clearly infringes the basic principle of provincial autonomy. In order to retain the recommendatory character of the Statement, and in order to make the clauses consistent with each other, the Committee read paragraph 15 to mean that, in the first instance, the respective provinces will make their choice whether or not to belong to the section in which they are placed. Thus the Constituent Assembly must be considered as a sovereign body, with final authority for the purpose of drawing up a Constitution and giving effect to it.'

With regard to the Indian States, the Working Committee pointed out that 'the Constituent Assembly cannot be formed of entirely disparate elements, and the manner of appointing State representatives for the Constituent Assembly must approximate, in so far as is possible, to the method adopted in the Provinces.' It insisted that the status, powers and composition of the Provisional Government should be fully defined. The Cabinet Mission issued another Statement on 25 May with a view to meeting the points raised by the various parties. It laid down that when the Constituent Assembly had completed its labours, His Majesty's Government would recommend to Parliament such action as might be necessary for the cession of sovereignty to the Indian people, subject only to two matters mentioned in the Statement, namely, adequate provision for the protection of the minorities and willingness to conclude a treaty with His Majesty's Government to cover matters arising out of the transfer of power.

With regard to the interpretation put by the Congress, the Cabinet Mission said that it did not accord with the Delegation's intentions. The reasons for the grouping of the provinces were well known, and this was an essential feature of the scheme and could only be modified by agreement between the parties. The problem of how the States' representatives should be appointed was to be discussed with the States. As regards the Congress demand for a clarification of the position of the Interim Government, the Statement said the present Constitution must continue during the interim period and the Interim Government could not, therefore, be made legally responsible to the Central Legislature. There was, however, nothing to prevent the members of the government, individually or by common consent, from resigning if they failed to pass an important measure through the Legislature, or if a vote of no-confidence was passed against them. The Congress had demanded the withdrawal of British troops from India, and the Statement of 25 May declared that there was no intention of retaining British troops in India against the wishes of an independent India under the new Constitution; but that during the interim period, which it was hoped would be short, the British Parliament had, under the present Constitution, ultimate responsibility for the security of India, and it was necessary, therefore, that the British troops should remain. The Statement made it clear that the scheme stood as a whole and could only succeed if it was accepted and worked in a spirit of co-operation.

On 6 June 1946 the Council of the All-India Muslim League passed a resolution reiterating that 'the attainment of the goal of complete sovereign Pakistan still remains an unalterable objective of the Musalmans in India, for the achievement of which they would, if necessary, employ every means in their power and consider no sacrifice or suffering too great.' But having regard to the grave issues involved, and 'inasmuch as the basis and the foundation of Pakistan are inherent in the Mission's plan by virtue of the compulsory grouping of the six Muslim provinces in Sections B and C', the League expressed its willingness to co-operate with the Constitution-making machinery, in the hope that it would ultimately result in the establishment of complete sovereign Pakistan. The resolution said: 'It is for these reasons that the Muslim League is accepting the scheme and will join the Constitution-making body, and it will keep in view the opportunity and the right of secession of provinces or groups from the Union which have been provided in the Mission's plan by implication. The ultimate attitude of the Muslim League will depend on the final outcome of the labours of the Constitution-making body, and on the final shape of the Constitutions which may emerge from the deliberations of that body jointly and separately in its three sections. The Muslim League also reserves the right to modify and revise the policy and attitude set forth in this resolution at any time during the progress of the deliberations of the Constitution-making body, or the Constituent Assembly, or thereafter, if the course of events so requires.' With regard to the arrangement for the proposed Interim Government at the Centre, the Council authorized the President to negotiate with the Viceroy and to take such decisions and actions as he deemed fit and proper.

While these discussions on the implications and interpretations of the Statement of 16 May were proceeding with the Mission as a whole, the Viceroy was negotiating with representatives of the Congress and the Muslim League on the number of members and the personnel of the Interim Government. As these negotiations did not result in an agreement between the parties, the Cabinet Delegation and the Viceroy issued another statement on 16 June 1946. After pointing out that the efforts to arrive at an agreement had failed and that it was urgent and necessary that a strong and representative Interim Government should be set up, this statement announced that the Viceroy was issuing invitations to certain persons, who were named, to serve as members of the Interim Government on the basis that the Constitution-making might proceed in accordance with the Statement of 16 May. Among the persons invited were six Hindus, all members of the Congress, including one member of the depressed classes, five Muslims, representatives of the Muslim League, one Sikh, one Christian and one Parsi, the last of whom at the time held an official position under the Government of India. It was stated that the distribution of portfolios would be in consultation with the leaders of the two major parties, and that the above composition of the Interim Government was in no way to be taken as a precedent for the solution of any other communal question. The Statement fixed June 26 as the date for inaugurating the new government. Paragraph 8 of this statement said: 'In the event of the two major parties or either of them proving unwilling to join in the setting up of a Coalition Government on the above lines, it is the intention of the Viceroy to proceed with the formation of an Interim Government which will be as representative as possible of those willing to accept the Statement of 16 May.' The Governors of the provinces were directed to summon the Provincial Legislative Assemblies forthwith to proceed with the elections necessary for setting up the Constitution-making machinery as laid down in the statement of 16 May.

This statement was again considered by the parties with great care, and ultimately, on 26 June 1946, the Working Committee of the Congress passed a resolution, in which it reviewed at length

the Cabinet Mission's Statements of 16 May and 16 June and
the correspondence that had passed in the meantime between the
Congress President and the Members of the Cabinet Delegation
and the Viceroy, and stated that, while these proposals fell short
of the Congress objectives, the Committee had considered them
earnestly to find some way for the peaceful settlement of India's
problem. It pointed out that limitation of the Central authority
weakened the whole structure and was unfair to some provinces
and some of the minorities, notably the Sikhs, but said that, taking
the proposals as a whole, they felt there was sufficient scope for
enlarging and strengthening the Central authority and for fully
ensuring the right of a province to act according to its choice
in regard to grouping and to give protection to such minorities
as might otherwise be placed at a disadvantage. The Working
Committee decided, therefore, that the Congress should join the
proposed Constituent Assembly. But as regards the Provisional
Government, it was pointed out that it must have power and
authority and responsibility and should function, in fact, if not
in law, as a *de facto* independent government, leading to the
full independence to come. The members of such a government
could only hold themselves responsible to the people and not
to any external authority. In the formation of a provisional or
other government, Congressmen could never give up the national
character of the Congress or accept an artificial and unjust parity,
or agree to the veto of a communal group. The Committee were,
therefore, unable to accept the proposals for the formation of an
Interim Government as contained in the Statement of 16 June.

In the course of discussion the Muslim League had claimed that
the Muslim members of the Interim Government should be its own
nominees and none other, and that there should be parity between
the Congress and the League in the Interim Government. While
the latter point had in a way been rejected by the Statement of
16 June by the inclusion of six Congressmen against five Muslim
League members, the Congress claim to nominate for the Interim
Government a Muslim from its own quota of six members had
been rejected by the inclusion of only nominees of the League
as the Muslim members. The Congress, therefore, had no option
but to reject the Statement of 16 June unless it was prepared to
treat itself as a purely Hindu organization and to concede that
the Muslim League alone was entitled to put forward names of

Muslim members for the Interim Government. After the Congress Working Committee resolution had been passed, the Muslim League Working Committee passed a resolution agreeing to join the Interim Government on the basis of the statement of the Cabinet Delegation dated 16 June and the clarifications and assurances given by the Viceroy after consultation with the Cabinet Delegation. It is unnecessary to go into the details of the negotiations that took place; it would suffice to quote the Viceroy's letter to Mr Jinnah, dated 25 June stating the position as it stood on that date. It said: 'We [the Cabinet Mission and the Viceroy] informed you that the Congress had accepted the Statement of 16 May while refusing to take part in the Interim Government proposed in the Statement of 16 June. This has produced a situation in which paragraph 8 of the Statement of 16 June takes effect. This paragraph said that if either of the two major parties was unwilling to join in the setting up of a Coalition Government on the lines laid down in the Statement, the Viceroy would proceed with the formation of an Interim Government which will be as representative as possible of those willing to accept the Statement of 16 May. Since the Congress and the Muslim League have now both accepted the Statement of 16 May, it is the intention to form a Coalition Government including both those parties as soon as possible. In view, however, of the long negotiations which have, already taken place, and since we all have other work to do we feel that it will be better to have a short interval before proceeding with further negotiations for the formation of an Interim Government. The Cabinet Mission thereafter adjourned further negotiations for an Interim Government for a short interval, while the elections to the Constituent Assembly were being held. In the meantime, they advised the Viceroy to appoint a caretaker government, composed of officials, to take charge of the administration till such period as an Interim Government was formed. The Mission left India at the end of June 1946.

The Muslim League felt very much cut up by the decision of the Cabinet Mission and the Viceroy not to form an Interim Government consisting exclusively of members of the League, and leaving out the Congress representatives.

A meeting of the All-India Congress held on 7 July ratified the decision of the Working Committee accepting the Statement of 16 May but rejecting that of 16 June.

The Council of the All-India Muslim League met towards the end of July and passed a resolution withdrawing its acceptance of the Cabinet Mission's proposals, which had been communicated to the Secretary of State for India by the President of the League on 6 June 1946. By another resolution, the Council resolved that 'now the time has come for the Muslim nation to resort to direct action to achieve Pakistan, to assert their just rights, to vindicate their honour and to get rid of the present British slavery and the contemplated future caste Hindu domination.' It directed the Working Committee to prepare forthwith a programme of direct action to carry out this policy and to organize the Muslims for the struggle to be launched as and when necessary. As a protest against, and in token of their deep resentment of, the attitude of the British, the Council called upon the Musalmans to renounce forthwith the titles conferred upon them by the British government.

Meetings of the Provincial Legislative Assemblies were held in July and members were elected to the Constituent Assembly, in accordance with the terms of the Statement of 16 May. The Sikhs did not at first elect their representatives, but did so at a later stage after certain points had been cleared and assurances given to them. Negotiations for the formation of Interim Government were started again, and since the Muslim League had withdrawn its acceptance of the Statement of 16 May the Congress was left alone in the field. The Congress tried to negotiate with the League to form a Coalition Government, but failed, and ultimately the Viceroy invited Pandit Jawaharlal Nehru to constitute an Interim Government, which he did. It consisted of six Hindus, including one depressed class member, three Muslims, of whom two belonged neither to the Congress nor to the League, one Sikh, one Christian and one Parsi. The members took office on 2 September 1946.

In pursuance of its resolution passed on 29 July the Muslim League fixed 16 August as 'Direct Action Day', to be observed by Muslims all over the country. The demonstration was organized on a large scale, and in Bengal that day was declared a public holiday by the League ministry, in spite of protests from all classes outside the League. The day opened in Calcutta with rioting, looting, murder and arson, which lasted for several days, causing immense loss of life and property. Communal rioting broke out in several other places also, and has, as a matter of fact, been going on in different parts of the country more or less continuously since then. The riots in Calcutta were followed shortly afterwards by a very serious outbreak in East Bengal, in the district of Noakhali, which spread to the adjoining districts of Comilla, Chittagong, Dacca, etc. Hindus suffered terribly. The news of the atrocities committed in Calcutta and in Noakhali reached Bihar from where large numbers go to Bengal for employment and there was very serious rioting in Bihar, starting in Saran district and spreading to the districts of Patna, Gaya, Monghyr, etc. In these places the Muslims suffered terribly. Some time later riots started in the north-west Frontier Province and the Punjab, where they are still continuing and where the Hindus and Sikhs have been subjected to tremendous loss of life and property.

Soon after the Interim Government was formed, the Viceroy started negotiations with the Muslim League with a view to bringing in its representatives and inducing them to join it. It was pointed out on behalf of the Congress that the reason why League members had not been included in the Interim Government when it was formed was that it had withdrawn its acceptance of the Statement of 16 May and thereby refused to enter the Constituent Assembly and participate in the work of Constitution-making as contemplated therein. It was, therefore, necessary that they should be required to accept the Statement of 16 May and thereby indicate their readiness to join the Constituent Assembly before they could be admitted into the Interim Government.

Lord Wavell, it would appear, however, did not get a clear decision from the League on that point, and contented himself with a statement in a letter which he wrote to Mr Jinnah on 4 October that 'since the basis for participation in the Cabinet is, of course, acceptance of the Statement of 16 May, I assume that the League Council will meet at a very early date and reconsider its Bombay resolution.' Mr Jinnah, in his letter dated 13 October stated that they had decided to nominate five members on behalf of the Muslim League in terms, amongst others, of the Viceroy's letter dated 4 October. Lord Wavell assumed that Mr Jinnah had accepted the stipulation regarding acceptance of the Statement of 16 May and invited him to nominate five persons to the Interim Government. Among Mr Jinnah's nominees was a member of the depressed classes. They joined the Interim Government in the last week of October and have remained there since then.

Before the members of the League joined the Interim Government, the other members had acted as a team and a Cabinet. The Viceroy, too, had recognized the Interim Government as a Cabinet, and in all the papers the word 'Cabinet' had officially begun to be used, presumably under the instructions of the Viceroy. In our deliberations also we acted like a Cabinet. The League members, however, were not prepared to accept the Interim Government as a Cabinet, but only as an Executive Council under the Government of India Act, in which each member was more or less the head of a department and had no responsibility to any one except the Viceroy. It must be said, however, that only on a few occasions have differences arisen between the League members and others in the Cabinet. That is only natural because most problems that come up are of a nature which does not admit of differences on communal lines, and the whole agitation based on the theory of two nations has really no foundation in the experience of actual administration. But that position was theoretically maintained, with the result that in some cases questions would be considered, not on their merits, but from the angle whether the decision would, in any way, impinge on the theory of two nations and thereby possibly affect the demand for Pakistan based on that theory. The position became more and more difficult, and a demand was made on behalf of the Congress that the Muslim League Members should accept the Statement of 16 May and decide to join the Constituent Assembly and recognize the basis of working the Interim Government, or go out of the Interim Government. This became necessary in view of the meeting of the Constituent Assembly which had been called for 9 December. As the time for the opening session of the Assembly approached, the urgency of settling this problem was realized. The British government invited representatives from the two groups in the Cabinet to visit London for discussions. After some preliminary correspondence, Pandit Jawaharlal Nehru, Sardar Baldev Singh, Mr Jinnah and Mr Liaqat Ali Khan went to London with Lord Wavell in the last week of November. It was stipulated, however, that in no circumstances would the session of the Constituent Assembly be postponed and that Pandit Nehru should return before that date. They had discussions in London which, as was not unexpected, failed to bring about an agreed settlement. His Majesty's Government, thereupon, came out with another statement on 6 December. It was said the object of the conversations had been to obtain the participation and co-operation of all parties in the Constituent Assembly, and the main difficulty had been over the interpretation of paragraphs 19(v) and (viii) of the Cabinet Mission's Statement of 16 May relating to meeting in sections. The Statement said: 'The Cabinet Mission have throughout maintained the view that decisions of sections should, in the absence of agreement to the contrary, be taken by a simple majority vote of representatives in the sections. This view has been accepted by the Muslim League, but the Congress have put forward a different view. They have asserted that the true meaning of the Statement read as a whole is that provinces have a right to decide both as to grouping and as to their own Constitution. His Majesty's Government has had legal advice which confirms that the Statement of 16 May means what the Cabinet Mission have always stated was their intention. This part of the Statement, with this interpretation, must, therefore, be considered as an essential part of the scheme of 16 May and should therefore be accepted by all parties in the Constituent Assembly. It urged the Congress to accept the view of the Cabinet Mission in order that way may be made for Muslim League to reconsider their attitude. But if in spite of this reaffirmation of the Cabinet Mission, that Constituent Assembly desires that this fundamental point should be referred for decision to the Federal Court, such a reference should be made at an early date.' One important point on which the Statement laid stress was that there was no prospect of success in the Constituent Assembly except upon the basis of an agreed procedure. Should a Constitution come to be framed by a Constituent Assembly in which a large section of the Indian population had not been represented, His Majesty's Government could not contemplate, as the Congress have stated they could not contemplate, forcing a Constitution upon any unwilling part of the country. The effect of this statement was to reject finally the interpretation which the Congress had put upon the Statement of 16 May by which a province was entitled to decide at the earliest stage whether it should or should not join the Section to which it was assigned, and was not required compulsorily to join the Section and to have the question whether it would be a member of the Group or not decided not by a vote of the members of that province but by a majority vote of the Section as a whole. The question had assumed great practical importance because of the peculiar position of Assam. It is a province in which the Muslim population is only 33.7 per cent and yet it had been assigned to Group C, along with Bengal, with the result that in that Section, Assam was in a very small minority as against Bengal, and even if Assam by a majority was not willing to join that Section, it could not make its own will effective if the question was to be decided by a majority vote of the Section as a whole and not of the Assam representatives alone. The Cabinet Mission plan had been vitiated by the undue and unjust tilting of the balance against Assam and forcing it by the Bengal representatives' vote to join Section C. It was also feared that as the power to frame the Constitution of the provinces within the Section was given to the Section as a whole, Bengal representatives, particularly the Muslim representatives, who formed a majority in the Section, would frame a Constitution which would make it impossible for the Assam Assembly under the new Constitution to decide against joining Group C, thus nullifying the right of opting out of the Group given to province by the Cabinet Mission Statement of 16 May. The Congress held that an interpretation which led to such an unfair situation was not correct, that it was not borne out by the words of the Statement and that it created conflicts between its different parts. But all this carried no weight with His Majesty's Government and the statement of 6 December made it clear that their intention was correctly represented by their interpretation. In other words, the intention of the Cabinet Mission had, from the very beginning, been to give this kind of unfair treatment to Assam. The question before the Congress, therefore, was whether or not to accept this interpretation and whether or not to scrap the whole of the Statement of 16 May. The Congress Working Committee and the All-India Congress Committee, relying on the strength of the people of Assam to assert themselves if any attempt was made to deal with them unjustly and to impose upon them a Constitution which would deprive them of the right of opting out ultimately, decided to accept the interpretation put by H.M.G. and to proceed with the Constituent Assembly on the basis of that interpretation. It was hoped that this would bring the Muslim League into the Constituent Assembly, but the League still refused to come in, and the situation remained what it had been before Lord Wavell left for London accompanied by three of his colleagues of the Interim Government and Mr Jinnah. This was evidently a situation which could not last.

The Constituent Assembly met in Delhi according to schedule, on 6 December 1946. Members representing all groups, sections and communities in the country except the nominees of the Muslim League attended. There were two Muslim representatives from the north-west Frontier Province, one from the United Provinces and one from the province of Delhi. All members representing the Scheduled Castes, every one of them belonging to that community, attended the first session. So did the representatives of Christians, Anglo-Indians, Sikhs and Parsis. Congressmen, Hindu Mahasabhaites, members of the Liberal Federation and persons belonging to no party also attended without exception. The only members who stayed away were the nominees of the Muslim League. The Constituent Assembly proceeded cautiously and did not take any decision of consequence, in order that the Muslim League members might have an opportunity of considering the position and joining it at a later date without having to face any clear-cut decisions. The discussion on a resolution defining the objectives of the Constituent Assembly was also left incomplete, to be taken up at a subsequent session. The Constituent Assembly framed certain rules of procedure for itself, but even in framing these, it took care to see that any rules which might raise controversy were left open for further consideration.

But the League would not enter, and its refusal to act in accordance with the Statement of 6 December 1946, was followed by an orgy of riots. The position was intolerable. The situation in the country was becoming more and more difficult every day. Administration by the Government of India was also becoming increasingly complicated on account of there being two separate groups within the Cabinet. Something had to be done. The pressure of events was such that the British government could not very well wait and watch and let matters drift, and they came out with another Statement of policy on 20 February 1947, which was placed before the Houses of Parliament and published in India simultaneously. This Statement, after outlining the previous history of the negotiations proceeds:

'(6)   It is with great regret that His Majesty's Government find that there are still differences among Indian parties which are preventing the Constituent Assembly from functioning as it was intended that it should. It is of the essence of the plan that the Assembly should be fully representative.

(7) His Majesty's Government desire to hand over their responsibility to authorities established by a Constitution approved by all parties in India in accordance with the Cabinet Mission's plan, but unfortunately there is at present no clear prospect that such a Constitution and such authorities will emerge. The present state of uncertainty is fraught with danger and cannot be indefinitely prolonged. His Majesty's Government wish to make it clear that it is their definite intention to take the necessary steps to effect the transference of power into responsible Indian hands by a date not later than June, 1948.

(9) His Majesty's Government are anxious to hand over their responsibilities to a government which, resting on the sure foundation of the support of the people, is capable of maintaining peace and administering India with justice and efficiency. It is, therefore, essential that all parties should sink their differences in order that they may be ready to shoulder the great responsibilities which will come upon them next year.

(10) After months of hard work by the Cabinet Mission, a great measure of agreement was obtained as to the method by which a Constitution should be worked out. This was embodied in their statements of May last. His Majesty's Government thereupon agreed to recommend to Parliament a Constitution worked out, in accordance with the proposals made therein, by a fully representative Constituent Assembly. But if it should appear that such a Constitution will not have been worked out by a fully representative Assembly before the time mentioned in paragraph 7, His Majesty's Government will have to consider to whom the powers of the Central Government in British India should be handed over, on the same date, whether as a whole to some form of Central Government for British India, or in some areas to the existing Provincial Governments, or in such other way as may seem most reasonable and in the best interests of the Indian people.

(11) Although the final transfer of authority may not take place

until June 1948, preparatory measures must be put in hand in advance. It is important that the efficiency of the Civil Administration should be maintained and that the defence of India should be fully provided for. But inevitably, as the process of transfer proceeds, it will become progressively more difficult to carry out to the letter all the provisions of the Government of India Act, 1935. Legislation will be introduced in due course to give effect to the final transfer of power.'

In regard to the Indian States, His Majesty's Government declared that they did not intend to hand over their powers and obligations under paramountcy to any government of British India. They further expressed the intention to negotiate agreements in regard to matters arising out of the transfer of power with representatives of those to whom they proposed to transfer power.

This Statement fixed a date by which power was to be transferred. It made it clear that unless a government was established with the authority and consent of all, His Majesty's Government might have to decide to whom power could be transferred; and in case of difficulty, they might have to transfer it to more than one authority in the country. It also made it clear that so far as the Princes were concerned, paramountcy was to end and not to be transferred to the government in British India. This statement thus made it necessary for all parties in India to establish an authority to which power could be transferred.

Another statement made at the same time announced the recall of Lord Wavell and the appointment of Lord Mountbatten of Burma as the Viceroy of India. Lord Mountbatten arrived in India on 23 March 1947, and took charge. The new Viceroy found India, particularly the north-western part of it and Bengal, in the grip of serious communal riots in which the sufferings were mostly on one side, namely on the side of the Hindus and Sikhs. The statement of 20 February had contemplated transfer of power to more than one authority in the country, and the Muslim League seemed to be concentrating its attempts on capturing the provinces where it was not in power. In Bengal, there was a Muslim League ministry functioning. Assam, which was also claimed by the Muslim League, although it happened to be a non-Muslim majority province in which the Hindus constituted by far the largest majority, was being run by a Congress ministry. In the Punjab there was a Unionist ministry, which had amongst its members Muslims, Sikhs and Hindus, but from which the Muslim League as a party had kept itself aloof. In the north-west Frontier Province, the Congress had, at the general election in 1946, won not only a majority of the seats, but also a majority of the Muslim seats, and there was, in consequence, a Congress ministry in office there. In Sind, the general election in 1946 had returned a majority opposed to the Muslim League. There were two European members who played a very important part, but they were unable to give the League Party a clear majority. The Governor, however, ignored the majority party and asked the leader of the League to form the ministry with the help of the two Europeans, which he did. After some months a fresh election was manoeuvred and the Muslim League managed to secure a majority, so that the Muslim League has now a ministry in Sind. It would thus appear that there are only two provinces—Bengal and Sind—in which the Muslim League has a majority in the Legislative Assembly and has, therefore, formed its own ministry. Its attempts, after the declaration of 20 February have been directed towards capturing by some means or other the ministries in the other provinces claimed by the League for Pakistan, so that when the time for transfer of power actually comes, the League may claim that it is in possession of those provinces, that League ministries are functioning there and that power should, therefore, be transferred to them. A serious mass agitation, accompanied by violence, rioting, arson, loot and murder on an extensive scale, was accordingly launched in the Punjab and the north-west Frontier Province. Sir Khizr Hayat Khan Tiwana, the Unionist Prime Minister of the Punjab, resigned, and as it was not possible to form a Muslim League ministry for want of support in the Assembly, the administration of the province was taken over by the Governor under Section 93 of the Government of India Act, and the province has ever since been governed in that way. In the north-west Frontier Province, the ministry has stuck to its position and declared that it has the support of the majority in the Assembly and has no reason to submit to coercion by the League, with the result that a serious state of disturbance continues in that province. Lord Mountbatten had envisaged this situation when he was appointed Viceroy and had to find a solution for it. He brought with him as Advisers a number of experienced officers. He held consultations with party leaders and others and formulated certain proposals of his own. It became clear that the League would not be content with anything less than a division of the country into Muslim and non-Muslim regions, and that the disturbances would continue until a settlement one way or the other was reached. No one outside the League is in favour of a division of India. Not only the Hindus and Sikhs and Congressmen, but also Christians, Parsis and Muslims outside the League are all bitterly opposed to any division. At the same time, the Congress has always held that it cannot force any portion of the country to remain with it if it chose otherwise. The statement of 6 December referred to this principle of the Congress when it declared that it could not contemplate forcing a Constitution upon any unwilling part of the country. The question, therefore, was whether any portion of the country which decided in favour of secession should be forced to remain with India, and it was felt that it could not be done. It followed as a corollary from this that neither could the League force any portion of a province to go with it if it did not choose to. There are large tracts in the central and eastern portions of the Punjab and in the western and northern portions of Bengal the majority of the population of which is non-Muslim. These portions cannot be forced to go with the League's Pakistan if they do not want to and, therefore, the proposition emerged that if the Muslim League insisted upon secession of certain portions of India on the ground that their population, the majority of which was Muslim, wanted such secession, equally could others who did not wish to go with them keep out. Therefore, if Pakistan was to be established, the Punjab and Bengal had to be divided.

Lord Mountbatten had first sent some of his Advisers under Lord Ismay to consult His Majesty's Government, and subsequently he himself flew to London. He returned to India with a statement on behalf of His Majesty's Government, and the authority to take such steps as were necessary to effect transfer of power. The statement was published simultaneously in India and London on 3 June 1947. It lays down the method for ascertaining the wishes of those provinces and parts of the country which are supposed to be in favour of secession, and in case division is decided upon, the procedure to effect that division. The Legislative Assemblies of the Punjab, Sind and Bengal have to decide whether or not they

wish to join the Indian Union. In case they do not wish to join
the Indian Union, then the members of the Legislative Assemblies
of Bengal and the Punjab have each to be divided into two blocs.
In one bloc will sit separately members of the western districts
of the Punjab which have a Muslim majority, and in the other
representatives of the districts which have a non-Muslim majority,
to decide whether or not they want a division of the province.
Similarly the members of the Muslim majority districts of Bengal
and the members of the non-Muslim majority districts will sit
separately and take decision on the same question. If the decision
by any of them is in favour of a division of the province, the
province will be divided and the boundaries will be settled by
a Boundary Commission which will take into consideration all
factors, and not only the population of a district, in determining
the boundaries. The statement announced that legislation would
be introduced in Parliament conferring Dominion Status on India
almost immediately, and that if division was decided upon in
India, then there would be two dominions, otherwise only one.
Paramountcy would cease simultaneously with the establishment of
Dominion Status. It is expected that legislation will be completed
and power transferred by the middle of August at the latest, thus
anticipating the dead-line originally fixed for transfer of power by
ten months or so.

The North-West Frontier Province has been asked to decide the
question by a referendum, and in British Baluchistan some method
is going to be adopted for ascertaining the wishes of the people.
As regards Assam, there is only one district, Sylhet, which has
a Muslim majority, and in case it is decided that Bengal should
be partitioned, a referendum will be held in Sylhet district to
decide whether it should continue to form part of Assam or be
amalgamated with the province of Eastern Bengal. This statement
of policy was accepted by the Working Committee of the Congress,
and its acceptance has since been endorsed by the AICC. The
Council of the All-India Muslim League accepted the plan at a
meeting held on 9 June 1947, with certain reservations.

Events are moving at a tremendous pace. The Provincial
Assemblies of the Punjab and Bengal are to decide before the
end of June whether the provinces are to join the Union of India,
and if not, whether the provinces are to be divided. The chances
are that they will decide in favour of division of the provinces

and against joining the Union of India. In anticipation of this decision, the terms of reference of a Boundary Commission and the personnel of the Boundary Commission are already under consideration. Arrangements for effecting division, if it is decided upon, are already under way, and will be put into action as soon as decisions have been taken. Steps have already been taken for organizing the referendum in the north-west Frontier Province, and as soon as Bengal decides to divide, similar arrangements will be made for a referendum in Sylhet. As soon as the British Parliament passes the Act, Dominion Status will be established in India. It is hoped that legislation in Parliament will be undertaken in July and completed before the Houses of Parliament go into recess early in August, and that the actual establishment of Dominion Status and the transfer of power to the dominions in India will be effected by the middle of August 1947.

As the question of division of the provinces of Bengal and the Punjab has assumed overwhelming importance, it may not be out of place here to indicate the basis on which the partition should be effected. In the Punjab, the Sikhs occupy a peculiar position. Nearly 95 per cent of the entire Sikh population is concentrated in the Punjab. Most of their religious shrines and places of importance in their great history are within the Punjab. They are a sturdy and industrious people and have acquired a name not only for their valour on various battle-fields all over the world but also as great agriculturists and colonizers. They have, since the opening up of a large tract of what used to be dry desert land in the Punjab, by the excavation of various canal systems brought under cultivation large tracts of land of which they are in possession. They have also shown great enterprise in industry and own many industrial concerns not only in the Punjab but also in places outside the province. If the Punjab is divided strictly on population basis, by assigning districts with Muslim and non-Muslim majorities to the two parts, as has been done for grouping the members of the Legislative Assembly into two section for deciding the question of Partition, then various complications will arise There is the district of Gurdaspur where Muslims and non-Muslims are more or less equally divided, the Muslims being 51.14 per cent and the non-Muslims 48.86 per cent. The non-Muslims claim that although they may be in a minority of 43 per cent in the province of the Punjab as a whole and the Muslims in a majority of 57 per cent, they have been paying the bulk of the taxes, and also have a larger proportion amongst the voters for the Provincial Assembly. The following figures may be of interest:

	Population according to 1941	Votes of Assembly	Land Revenue	Income Tax	Other Taxes	Average economic share
Non-Muslims	43%	56%	56%	90%	70%	70%
Muslims	57%	44%	44%	10%	30%	30%

It is claimed on their behalf that it would not be fair to divide the Punjab and its assets simply on the basis of population when they have contributed such a high proportion and its building up in the past. This question arises also with regard to irrigation. The Punjab has the biggest irrigation system in the country and, as has been already stated, several districts have been developed within recent years with the help of these canals. It is one of the important points which need to be considered that no division should take place which upsets the canal system and renders it ineffective. For example, it is no use dividing a canal system and placing one part irrigated by it in the Muslim zone and another in the non-Muslim zone. Such a division is bound to create bickerings and lead to conflicts in the operation of the canals, and the distribution of their waters. The Sikhs particularly possess large areas in certain districts which fall within the Muslim zone. They have brought all this land under cultivation through their own enterprise. Similarly, there are Musalmans who have developed such lands. The assignment of plots to individuals is more or less on a geometrical pattern of squares, and climatic conditions, quality of soil and irrigation facilities being more or less similar; one square can easily and without much trouble or complication be exchanged for another. The wisest course might therefore be to bring about an exchange of populations and squares between Muslims and non-Muslims, all the Muslims going over, to the districts which may be assigned to the Muslim zone, all non-Muslims from those districts being transferred to a district assigned to the non-Muslim zone. If ever an exchange of population and landed property can be effected without much harassment and suffering and without much cost and trouble, it can be done in the colonies of the Punjab, and if a measure like this is adopted, it will be possible to transfer the larger part of the Sikh population from what are now Muslim majority districts to what will be the non-Muslim zone. If the division is effected on a strict population basis, district-wise, the Sikh population in the British Punjab will be hopelessly divided. Out of their total population of 37,57,401 in the British Punjab, there will on this basis, be 20,73,546 or 55 per cent in the non-Muslim zone and 16,83,855 or 45 per cent in the Muslim zone.

It has also to be remembered that when two independent sovereign states are to be established, it is natural and desirable to have some sort of natural boundary, which may be easily recognized and which may also serve as a sort of hedge between the two States. Such a natural boundary is furnished by the River Ravi, the area to the east of it forming the non-Muslim zone and that to the west of it forming the Muslim zone. The upper portion of this area is irrigated by the canals under the Upper Bari Doab Circle and the lower portion by the Lower Bari Doab Circle. The head of the former system of canals falls within the Pathankot tehsil, in the district of Gurdaspur, which has a large non-Muslim majority. Within this area will fall the district of Montgomery, which is a colony. To the west of it are other colony districts and exchange of population and exchange of land can very easily be effected, and will serve to reduce considerably the number of Sikhs in the Muslim zone and correspondingly increase their number in the non-Muslim zone. It has been calculated that if a division on this basis takes place, more than 70 per cent of the Sikhs will be in the eastern Punjab instead of only about 55 per cent. Many of their shrines and places of worship will also fall within their zone.

Similarly, in Bengal too there are areas within a Muslim majority district which are predominantly non-Muslim. For example, there are areas adjoining Hindu areas in the Muslim-majority district of Faridpur which are inhabited predominantly by members of the Scheduled Castes, and the great Hindu saint and reformer, Shri Gauranga Mahaprabhu, lived and flourished in a district which will fall within the Muslim zone, although it is contiguous to Hindu-majority districts and is itself a predominantly Hindu area. The question of a natural boundary has to be taken into consideration in the case of Bengal too. It will be for the Boundary Commission to go into these matters and to draw a line which shall be just and fair and also a practical line of demarcation between two sovereign States.

So a division of India will take place if the provinces with Muslim majorities so decide. But if division is decided upon, then Bengal and the Punjab have also to be divided. Division will undoubtedly raise a host of problems relating to administration and division of assets. The country has been run by one single administration for a long time. We have common railways, common telephone and telegraph lines, common roads and a host of common institutions which serve not only one province but several provinces and the country as a whole. These will have to be divided in one way or another. We have immovable properties, buildings, etc. belonging to the Government of India spread over the provinces which are to be divided. Then there are canals which will run through the divided parts. Some kind of division of assets of this kind must necessarily follow. There is India's heavy national debt—something in the neighbourhood of 2,200 crores. If the assets are to be divided, the liabilities too will have to be divided, and so also the sterling balances. Then there is the personnel of various grades of what may compendiously be called the civil services, as distinguished from military personnel. Something will have to be done about a division of this kind of human assets of the government. Last, but not least, are the defence forces and their stores and equipment and the immense movable and immovable properties in possession and under the control of the defence department. These too may have to be divided. It will be a stupendous task to carry out a division of all these, and above all, the question yet remains unsettled as to the basis on which this division is to be effected. It may well be that when the actual division has been accomplished, the result may turn out to be a veritable Dead Sea Apple or a *Delhi ka Laddu,* which the man who gets it regrets as much as the man who does not.

MAPS

AND

GRAPHS

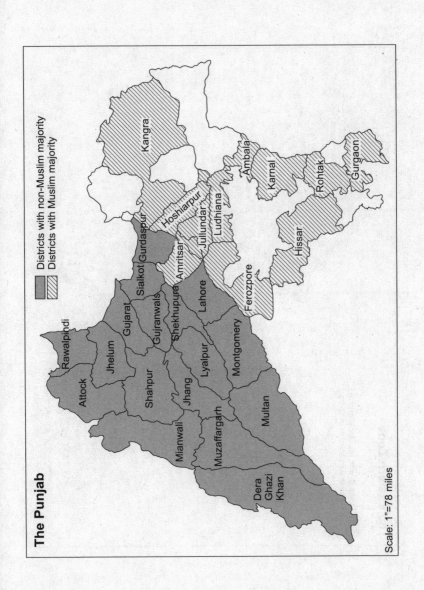

The Punjab

Districts with non-Muslim majority

Districts with Muslim majority

Kangra

Ambala

Karnal

Rohtak

Gurgaon

Hissar

Hoshiarpur

Jullundar

Ludhiana

Gurdaspur

Sialkot

Amritsar

Ferozpore

Rawalpindi

Gujarat

Gujranwala

Shekhupura

Lahore

Montgomery

Attock

Jhelum

Shahpur

Jhang

Lyalpur

Mianwali

Muzaffargarh

Multan

Dera Ghazi Khan

Scale: 1"=78 miles

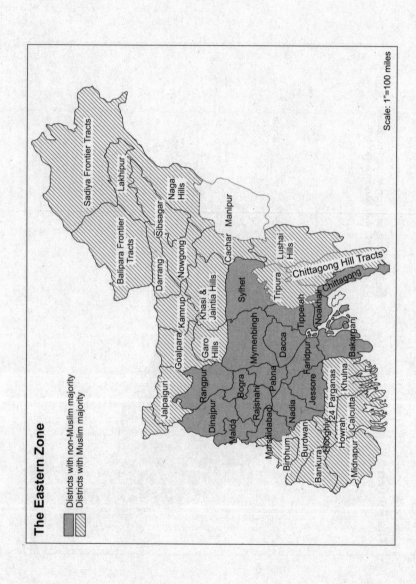

The Eastern Zone

- Districts with non-Muslim majority
- Districts with Muslim majority

Scale: 1"=100 miles

Sadiya Frontier Tracts

Lakhipur

Balipara Frontier Tracts

Naga Hills

Darrang — Sibsagar

Nowgong

Cachar   Manipur

Goalpara   Kamrup

Khasi & Jaintia Hills

Lushai Hills

Sylhet

Tripura

Chittagong Hill Tracts

Chittagong

Garo Hills

Mymenbingh

Jalpaiguri

Dacca

Tipperah

Noakhali

Rangpur

Bogra

Pabna

Faridpur

Bakarganj

Dinajpur

Rajshahi

Jessore

Malda

Nadia   Khulna   24 Parganas

Murshidabad

Burdwan

Birbhum   Hooghly   Calcutta

Bankura   Howrah

Midnapur

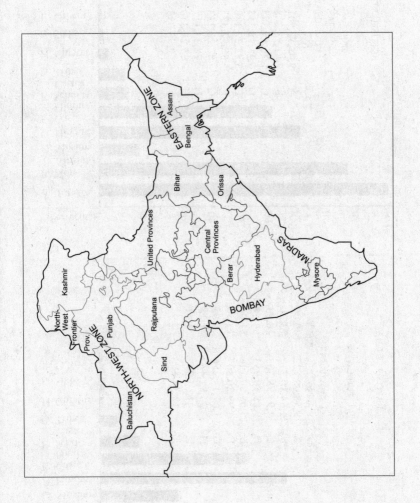

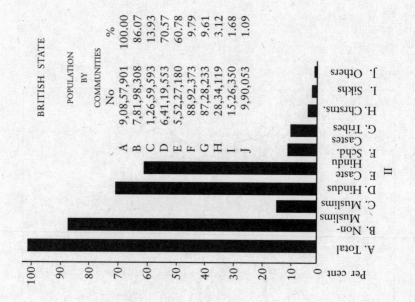

BRITISH STATE

POPULATION BY COMMUNITIES

	No	%
A	9,08,57,901	100.00
B	7,81,98,308	86.07
C	1,26,59,593	13.93
D	6,41,19,553	70.57
E	5,52,27,180	60.78
F	88,92,373	9.79
G	87,28,233	9.61
H	28,34,119	3.12
I	15,26,350	1.68
J	9,90,053	1.09

II

A. Total
B. Non-Muslims
C. Muslims
D. Hindus
E. Caste Hindu
F. Schd. Castes
G. Tribes
H. Chrstns.
I. Sikhs
J. Others

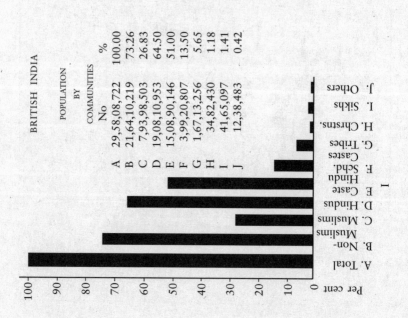

BRITISH INDIA

POPULATION BY COMMUNITIES

	No	%
A	29,58,08,722	100.00
B	21,64,10,219	73.26
C	7,93,98,503	26.83
D	19,08,10,953	64.50
E	15,08,90,146	51.00
F	3,99,20,807	13.50
G	1,67,13,256	5.65
H	34,82,430	1.18
I	41,65,097	1.41
J	12,38,483	0.42

I

A. Total
B. Non-Muslims
C. Muslims
D. Hindus
E. Caste Hindu
F. Schd. Castes
G. Tribes
H. Chrstns.
I. Sikhs
J. Others

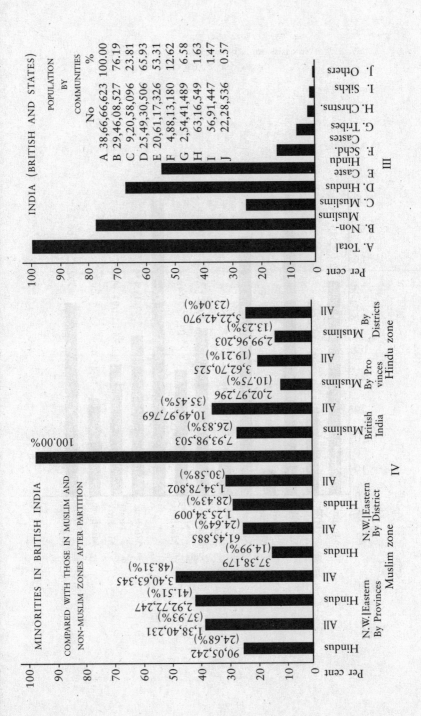

MUSLIMS AND NON-MUSLIMS IN THE PROVINCES
OF NW AND EASTERN ZONES

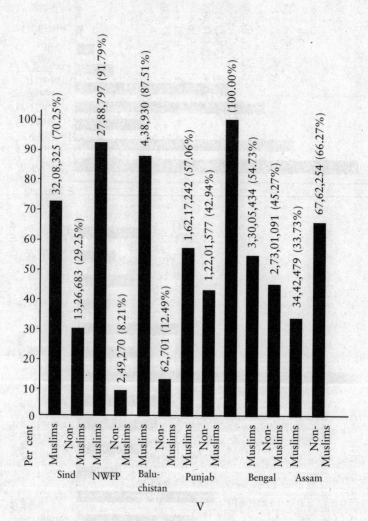

V

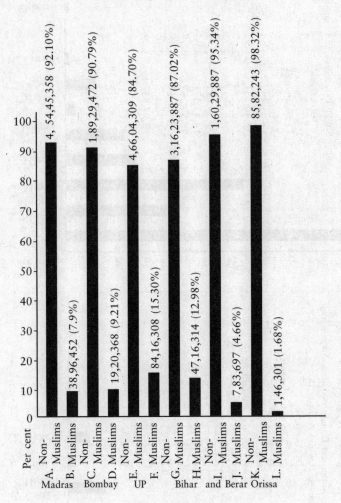

HINDU-MAJORITY PROVINCES

VI

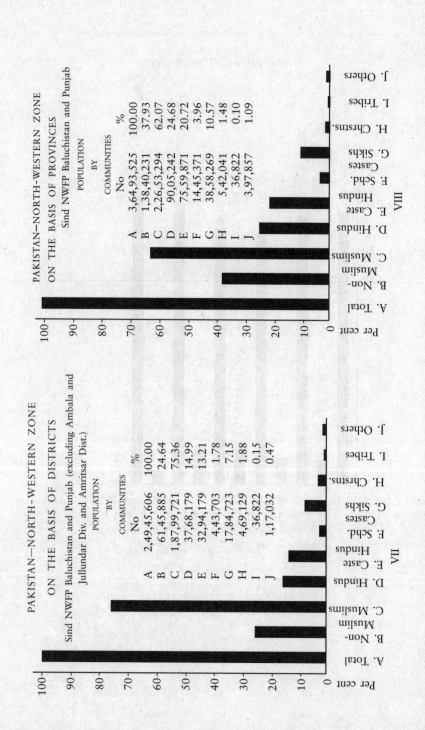

PAKISTAN—NORTH-WESTERN ZONE ON THE BASIS OF PROVINCES — Sind NWFP Baluchistan and Punjab — POPULATION BY COMMUNITIES — VIII

PAKISTAN—NORTH-WESTERN ZONE ON THE BASIS OF DISTRICTS — Sind NWFP Baluchistan and Punjab (excluding Ambala and Jullundar Div. and Amritsar Dist.) — POPULATION BY COMMUNITIES — VII

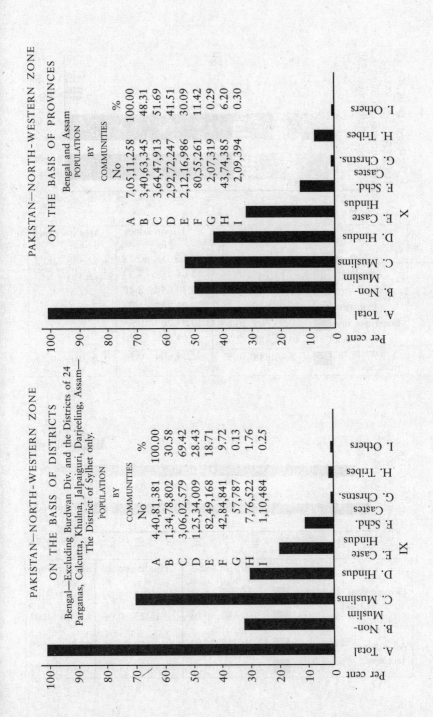

PAKISTAN—NORTH-WESTERN ZONE

ON THE BASIS OF DISTRICTS

Bengal—Excluding Burdwan Div. and the Districts of 24 Parganas, Calcutta, Khulna, Jalpaiguri, Darjeeling, Assam—The District of Sylhet only.

POPULATION BY COMMUNITIES

	No	%
A	4,40,81,381	100.00
B	1,34,78,802	30.58
C	3,06,02,579	69.42
D	1,25,34,009	28.43
E	82,49,168	18.71
F	42,84,841	9.72
G	57,787	0.13
H	7,76,522	1.76
I	1,10,484	0.25

XI

Per cent

A. Total, B. Non-Muslim, C. Muslims, D. Hindus, E. Caste Hindus, F. Schd. Castes, G. Chrstns., H. Tribes, I. Others

PAKISTAN—NORTH-WESTERN ZONE

ON THE BASIS OF PROVINCES

Bengal and Assam

POPULATION BY COMMUNITIES

	No	%
A	7,05,11,258	100.00
B	3,40,63,345	48.31
C	3,64,47,913	51.69
D	2,92,72,247	41.51
E	2,12,16,986	30.09
F	80,55,261	11.42
G	2,07,319	0.29
H	43,74,385	6.20
I	2,09,394	0.30

X

Per cent

A. Total, B. Non-Muslim, C. Muslims, D. Hindus, E. Caste Hindus, F. Schd. Castes, G. Chrstns., H. Tribes, I. Others

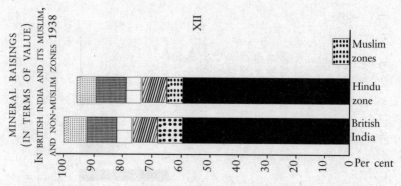

MINERAL RAISINGS
(IN TERMS OF VALUE)
In BRITISH INDIA AND ITS MUSLIM, AND NON-MUSLIM ZONES 1938

XII

	British India		Hindu zones		Muslim zones	
	No.	%	No.	%	No.	%
Coal	9,46,30,718	61.50	9,35,18,050	60.78	11,12,668	0.72
Petroleum	1,65,43,142	10.76	1,12,64,787	7.33	52,78,355	3.43
Copper ore	32,40,640	2.10	32,40,640	2.10	...	...
Iron ore	26,91,829	1.75	26,91,829	1.75	...	...
Manganese ore	3,20,93,709	20.86	3,20,93,709	20.86	...	...
Mica	40,89,488	2.70	40,89,488	2.70	...	...
Chromite or magnesite	5,60,818	0.37	2,34,804	0.16	3,26,014	0.21

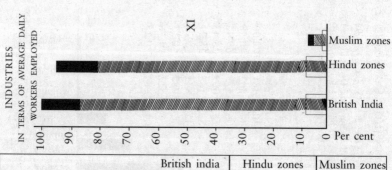

INDUSTRIES
IN TERMS OF AVERAGE DAILY WORKERS EMPLOYED

XI

		British india		Hindu zones		Muslim zones	
		No.	%	No.	%	No.	%
Government and local fund factories	Perennial	1,31,066	7.48	1,03,123	5.90	27,943	1.60
	Seasonal	1,380	0.08	1,023	0.06	357	0.02
All other factories	Perennial	13,29,248	75.91	12,59,358	71.91	69,890	3.99
	Seasonal	2,89,448	16.50	2,58,796	14.78	30,647	1.75

INDEX

Abbasids, 21, 42, 107

Abdali, Ahmad Shah, 87, 421

Abri Said Ibn Abulkhair, 43

Acton, Lord, 39

Adab-e-Alamgiri, 52

Adil Shah I, Ibrahim, 97

Adil Shahi dynasty, 47

adult franchise, 206

Afghanistan, 27, 42, 95, 114, 286, 382, 408, 422

Afghans, 87, 91, 92, 422

agriculture: in Assam, 354; in Bengal, 345, 347–54; in Eastern Muslim Zone, 345–54; in North-Western Muslim Zone, 355–64

Ahmad Shah Bahadur Ghazi, 48

Ahmadnagar, 92, 93

Ahrars, 431, 509

Aibak, Qutbuddin, 88, 96, 421

Ain-i-Akbari, 77, 101

Ajanta, 75, 76, 77

Ajmer Shareef, 50

Akbar, 47, 48, 77, 80, 88, 90–93, 97, 101; policy of *Sulh-i-Kul* (religious tolerance), 91

Alamgiri Hukumat, 48

Alexander, Albert V., 511

Ali Brothers, 28, 148, 150

Ali Imam, 63

Ali, A. Yusuf, 257

Ali, Maulana Zafar, 63

Ali, Maulvi Enayat, 116

Ali, Maulvi Mazhar, 114

Ali, Mir Syyid, 77

Ali, Moulana Mohammad, 153, 155

Aligarh College. *See* Muhammadan Anglo-Oriental College

Aligarh Education Scheme, 119

Aligarh politics, 119, 124*ff*

All-India Federation, 232, 241, 253, 256–57

All India Shia Conference, 431

All Parties Conference, Lucknow, 162, 207

All Parties Convention, Calcutta, 162, 206

Allies, 147, 149, 150

Amanullah, King of Afghanistan, 422

Ambala: in Partition schemes, 217, 220, 226, 255; in League resolution of Pakistan, 275, 303–05, 308, 337, 340–41

Ambedkar, B.R., 6, 13, 26, 35–36, 120, 262, 397, 423–45; scheme, 489–93

Amery, Leo S., 108, 196

Anglo-Indian Defence Association, 130

Anglo-Indians, 170

Anjuman-i-Himayat Urdu, 145

Ansari, M.A., 146, 149, 150, 168

Ansari, Shaukatullah, 256, 257

Arabia, 84, 149

Arabic, 71, 72

Archbold, Mr, 140, 204

Arjun Dev, Guru, 47

Khem Karan, 77
Khilafat movement, 183, 184,
    205, 412, 418; and after,
    149ff; Hindu support, 150;
    Khilafat Committee, 158, 161;
    Khilafat Conference, 167
Khilji, Allauddin, 89, 106, 421
Khodabaksh, Salahuddin, 66–67
Khojas, 142
Khorasan, 42
Khudai-Khidmatgars, 190
Khulastul-Tawarikh, 47
Khusro, Amir, 68
Khusru (son of Jahangir), 92
Al-Kindi, 42
kingship, doctrine of, 106
Kirtibas, 70
Kishen Prasad, Maharaja, 97
Kitabal-Bud, 42
Kitchener, Lord, 424
Krishak Praja Party, 190
Kutub Shahi, 47

Lahore, 3, 33, 36, 89, 98, 133,
    160, 162, 163, 166, 194, 209,
    215; in partition schemes,
    222, 248, 254, 261, 272; in
    League's resolution of Pakistan,
    275, 276, 298, 307–08, 337,
    340, 341, 377; in Cripps
    proposal, 435
Lajpat Rai, Lala, 29, 151
Lal Gir, Mahant, 47
Land Settlement, 331
language issue, 23–24; Hindu–
    Muslim commonality,
    68–72. *See also* Hindi–Urdu
    controversy
Latif, S.A., 36; scheme for
    partition, 232–40, 253, 276,
    306, 307
Lawrence, John, 120, 139
League of Nations, 16, 34, 287,
    289, 419, 463, 465

learning, promotion of, 49
Legislative Councils, 99, 125,
    126, 144, 148, 158, 164;
    Muslim representation, 204,
    209
Line System, 329
Linlithgow, Lord, 32, 193
Lloyd, George, 205, 257, 326
local autonomy principle, 443
Local Self-Government Bill, 122
Lodi, Ibrahim, 87, 89
Lodi, Khan Jahan, 93
Lodi, Sultan Mahomud, 88
Lodi, Sikandar, 88
Lorenzo, A.M., 379
Low, Sydney, 139
Lucknow Pact (1919), 25, 28,
    144ff, 191, 205, 456
Lyall, Alfred, 52

Macartney, C.A., 14, 16, 17, 18,
    35–37, 39
Macaulay, Lord Thomas
    Babington, 111
Macdonald, Ramsay, 144, 165,
    169
Macdonell, Anthony, 135, 137, 145
Macklin, A.S.R., 188
Madho, 77
Mahabat Khan, 92
Mahabharata, 70, 71, 76
Maham Ankah, 90
Mahapattar, 81
Mahes, 77
Maheshwar Nath, 49
Mahmud of Ghazni, 96
Mahomedan Anglo-Oriental
    Defence Association of Upper
    India, 130 (spl Mahomedan or
    Mohamedan)
Mahor, 48
Mahratta Empire, Mahrattas; rise
    and decline, 109–10, 112, 113,
    170

Sukkur Barrage, 363, 402
Sulaiman Khan (of Bihar), 42, 91
Suleman Range, 11
Sultan Ahmad, 99; scheme,
    451–58; units, powers, 451;
    units, 454–55
Sultanate, 88
Sunnis, 41, 51, 93, 476. *See also*
    Shias
superstitions and formalism, 46
Supreme Federal Court, 459
Sur, Ibrahim, 90
Sur, Sikandar, 90
Suraj, 77
Surdas, 77
Surjan, 77
Swaraj Party, 158, 160–61
Swaraj, 27–28
Swiss Constitution, 444
Syed Mahmud, 47, 51
Sylhet, 218, 220, 224, 278, 317,
    336, 338, 339, 353–55, 378,
    391, 532–33

Tabligh movement, 154
Taj Mahal, 73
Taluqdar Association of Oudh, 129
Tansen, 80
Tanzim movement, 154
Tara, 77
Tarachand, Dr, 66
Tartars, 87
taxation; for Muslims, 237
taxes, non payment, 166
Taylor, B.G., 187
Tennessee Valley Authority
    scheme, 446
territorial: adjustments, 503–04;
    nationalism, 26; redistribution,
    453
theocracy, 21, 33
Thompson, Edward, 168, 266–67
Tilak, a Hindu commander of
    Mahmud of Ghazni, 96

Tilak, Bal Gangadhar, 24, 148
Timur, 51, 87, 421
Timurids, 75, 76, 77
Tippoo Sultan, 109, 112
Tiwana, Malik Khizr Hayat
    Khan, 263, 530
Todarmal, 91, 97
topographical diversity, 6
Trans-Caucasian Federation, 468
tribal classification and
    assimilation question, 321–24
Tripathi, Ramnaresh, 69
Tripoli war, 146
Tritton, A.S., 268
Tufail Ahmad, Maulvi, 135, 140,
    143, 152
Tughlak, Muhammad, 97
Tulsidas, 69, 77
Turbati, Muzaffar Khan, 91
Turkey, 147; defeat in World
    War I, 149, 150; nationalist
    movement, 146; Sultan of, 422
Turkish Constitution, 465–67
Turks, 87, 422, 468, 473
Tutlamaee temple, 49
two nations theory, 3, 215, 228,
    266–67, 269, 508
Tyabji, Badruddin, 127, 128

Udham Singh, Sirdar, 47
Ukraine, 468
Ulema, interference in the state
    affairs, 106
Umar II, 268–69
Umayyads, 42
union executive, 483–84
Union of India, Draft Declaration,
    451, 453 (check this entry)
Union of Soviet Socialist
    Republics (USSR), communal
    issue, 467–71; Constitution,
    465, 468–69, 471, 472, 478;
    establishment of Soviet system,
    474–75